A Guide to Federal Contracting

A Guide to Federal Contracting

Principles and Practices

Dan Lindner

 Bernan Press

Lanham • Boulder • New York • London

Published by Bernan Press
An imprint of The Rowman & Littlefield Publishing Group, Inc.
4501 Forbes Boulevard, Suite 200, Lanham, Maryland 20706

www.rowman.com
800-865-3457; info@bernan.com

Unit A, Whitacre Mews, 26-34 Stannary Street, London SE11 4AB

ISBN:978-1-59888-965-9
E-ISBN:978-1-59888-966-6

∞™ The paper used in this publication meets the minimum requirements of American National Standard for Information Sciences—Permanence of Paper for Printed Library Materials, ANSI/NISO Z39.48-1992.

Printed in the United States of America

Contents

Introduction

The Federal Government is the largest buyer of goods and services in the world, spending hundreds of billions of dollars per year, employing hundreds of thousands of people as civil servants or contractors. Yet no textbook is commercially available to discuss how it is done. Current treatments of the subject are often written by lawyers and rely on case law to support policies, which is excellent for legal counsel but often obtuse and detached from the practitioner's point of view. Other books delve in depth into certain facets of acquisition, but do not cover a number of other issues and may be too detailed for the classroom student or on-the-job practitioner. This publication is intended to fill this void – to demystify the volumes of regulations and policies, and provide in one volume a succinct yet thorough treatment of Federal contracting requirements and regulations.

My approach is based on what I call the "five P's" of Federal contracting. We begin by reviewing basic contracting legal Principles which apply in both the public and private sectors. This is critical to understand the theory of contracting, and how a private firm's dealings with the Federal Government will differ from those with commercial concerns. Next come the Planning needs of Federal acquisition, demonstrating the extensive scope and variety of considerations that go into setting up a procurement action, as well as the impact of Federal legislation and initiatives. Third is the Placement of awards, concerning the processes used to solicit and evaluate offers, and the variety of methods that the parties use to come to an agreement. A discussion on Pricing follows, which addresses the methods used to develop the contractor's proposal and record contract costs. It also covers the Government's analysis of cost and price, and considerations in the negotiation process. The fifth chapter discusses the plethora of Post-Award actions that occur during contract performance, reflecting the scope and complexity of Federal contracts.

The book is organized using a sequential numbering scheme with each level of subdivision separated by a period, since this is the method used in the FAR and its departmental supplements. Each section of text begins with a title and any applicable Unified Commercial Code or Federal Acquisition Regulation (FAR) reference, before discussing the concept. Many sections end with a list of appropriate FAR provisions or clauses and any prescriptive language. Although many Federal agencies have their own supplemental guidance (especially the Department of Defense), this book tries to be general in approach and refrains whenever possible from delving into department specifics.

This book grew out of a course I taught to prepare professionals to take the Certified Professional Contract Managers examination for a certification issued by the National Contract Management Association, the professional society for contracting personnel (both Government and contractors). Terms of art are identified in italics in the section of the book where they are most important, not necessarily the first time they are used. This is consistent with the concept of a reference book, since most readers will turn to a specific area of interest rather than read the book from front to back. In many sections, regulatory citations headline a thorough discussion of the topic. Acronyms are kept to a minimum, including only those frequently used in the profession, and spelled out at the point of first major usage (not necessarily where first used). References to a personal position, such as (s)he, are used to avoid any bias. The term (sub)contractor is used whenever a concept applies equally to both prime and subcontractor.

Many people have contributed to my success through my years of experience as a Federal contracting officer and project manager. Within the Federal contracting profession, I have been blessed to work with countless professionals who provided their guidance and wisdom, especially Marie Flynn, Dave Brickley, John Dunegan, Graham Wright, Frank Ford, Grey Cammack, and Elliott Branch of the Department of the Navy. Similarly, I am grateful to Hugh Hosford, Ed Traccarella, Paul Robert, and Norm Brown for their legal counsel, B. J. Koehler for knowledge of socioeconomic programs, Bob Lynch for accounting insight, and Bob Long for contract administration experience – all first-rate civil servants. Within the contractor community, I am especially pleased to have known and worked with Jim Sharpe at Northrop Grumman and Norm Steeves at Raytheon, plus a number of consultants – Chuck Schefer, Todd Coen, and Christine and Mark Podracky. The experiences I obtained with the National Contract Management Association and Defense Acquisition Regulatory Council were invaluable in learning much and meeting many. On a personal note, my greatest thanks go to my wife, Jennie, for tolerating the countless hours I spent working on this tome, and our sons, Eric and Alex, for their support.

Chapter 1

Contract Principles

1.1 CONTRACTS AND THE LAW

Our legal system is based on two separate paths of thought.[1] *Civil Law* is based on legislative codes and statutes, drawn on the Greek and Roman systems and current legal principles. To put it simply, civil laws may change but legal principles do not. Judges apply legal principles to the facts without creating law.

By contrast, *Common Law* (also known as *case law*, or *law by decision*) was developed in England as a body of law common to the entire population. Because this was an environment without a standing legislature, judges made law by hearing the facts in the case. These decisions become a precedent or original rule of law. This concept is also known as *stare decisis*–to stand by decided cases unless their basis of fact has changed. Its deep roots in England led to common law being a forerunner for the legal system in our Colonial Era.

A major difference between these schools of thought involves the treatment of equity. The common-law judge had limited authority to grant relief – only the King could grant monetary damages or property restoration. As a result, separate courts of equity arose over time due to requests for relief (e.g., forfeiture, injunction, rescission, and specific performance).[2] In contrast, civil law is adjudicated by standing courts authorized to decide such cases based on statutes, and to grant relief to petitioners.

Because of this sea of confusion, the *Statute of Frauds* was adopted in England in 1677, and after our independence was instituted in American law.[3] It requires that certain contracts be in writing, that they identify the parties, set forth applicable terms and conditions, and be signed by the obligated party.

These precautions preclude any argument during an action for breach that the agreement never existed.

As our national economy expanded after World War II, the plethora of rules that varied among different states demanded a code of rules to foster consistency throughout the nation. Hence, the American Law Institute worked in conjunction with the National Conference of Commissions of Uniform State Laws to develop the *Uniform Commercial Code (UCC)*.[4] Formally adopted by 1972 for each state (except Louisiana, which uses the Napoleonic Code due to its French roots), it is also used in Washington, D.C., and Puerto Rico. The UCC clarifies and simplifies laws for commercial transactions and unifies state laws. The UCC also applies to personal property transactions, but has little effect on real property. The UCC consists of ten sections or articles:[5]

- Sales;
- Leases;
- Negotiable Instruments;
- Bank Deposits and Collections;
- Funds Transfers;
- Letters of Credit;
- Bulk Sales;
- Documents of Title;[6]
- Investment Securities; and
- Secured Transactions.

The UCC does not address intangible goods or licenses. To fill this gap, the Uniform Computer Information Transactions Act (UCITA) was created to cover software licensing and online transactions. Drafted by the National Conference of Commissioners on Uniform State Laws, the UCITA addresses warranties for data accuracy and non-infringement. The intent is to protect the validity of licenses as long as consumers have the right of return if they object to the license's terms. However, the UCITA has raised objections from consumer groups and state attorneys general out of concern that it weakens consumer protection and provides terms which are favorable to software producers. As such, the American Law Institute has withdrawn support for the UCITA, and only two states have adopted it.[7]

Federal contracts are not subject to the UCC, but rather are governed by a separate set of regulations to be discussed throughout this book. However, the legal underpinnings of Federal contract law are based on the legal principles covered by the UCC.

1.2 COMMERCIAL CONTRACTING

1.2.1 Terms

A *contract* formally defines an agreement between parties to perform an act or fulfill a promise. The basic elements of a contract are:

- two or more competent parties;
- consent;
- consideration;
- proper subject matter; and
- mutual obligation.

The terms listed above need to be defined. Multiple parties are necessary because one cannot make a legal contract with oneself (New Year's resolutions are not legally enforceable!). But the parties must be considered to be *competent*, meaning they are capable of understanding what they are agreeing to. This is why children and mental patients are not deemed competent to enter into contracts.

Consent is demonstrated through offer and acceptance, which we will discuss at length in the next section. *Consideration* is something of value which induces the contract. Inevitably, this is either a benefit or a loss to either or both parties. The concept of *proper subject matter* is all about legality – the contract cannot require illegal activity such as price fixing, unlicensed labor or a noncompetitive agreement. Finally, the contract must impose *mutual obligation* on all parties, whereby one commits to a specific promise or act in exchange for the other party agreeing to a specific promise or act.

There are several different types of contracts based on the circumstances creating them:

- *express contract* – terms are oral or written;
- *implied in fact* – existence and terms are manifested by conduct of the parties rather than by any written formal agreement;
- *implied in law* – an obligation is imposed on a party by law or court decree to prevent *unjust enrichment*, where one party benefits at the expense of another;[8]
- *quasi-contract* – a contract that should have been formed but was not, again invoked by the court to avoid unjust enrichment;
- *unilateral* – promise for an act (or failure to act). This often is reflected in *performance*, an act of consideration in exchange for the promise to pay or otherwise benefit;[9] and

- *bilateral* – promise for a promise, where each promise constitutes consideration for the other promise.

Other than small purchases, the Federal Government insists on express, bilateral agreements, either by accepting a signed proposal or by both parties signing a document. Normally, this means the Government will pay a set amount once the contractor performs a service or delivers a product. Of course, there are a number of variations in how and when payment is actually derived, but this is the general notion.

A contract cannot be implied if it leads to harm or inequity to either or both parties, but can be implied if doubt prevails in the minds of the parties and the court.[10] Moreover, if a contract expires and the parties continue to behave according to its terms, then a new contract is inferred with the same provisions as the prior one. Here again, the Federal Government insists on express, bilateral agreements to avoid such confusion.

Contracts are considered to be either formal or informal in nature. *Formal contracts* are written and either under seal or on record. When recording the rights and obligations of the parties, including the terms of agreement, the parties have created an express contract. Federal contracts are express and formal in nature. In contrast, *informal contracts* (also known as *parol* or *simple contracts*) are neither under seal nor of record. They may be written or oral. It can be hard to prove the existence of parol contracts because dissatisfaction or misunderstanding (or even fraud) may be present. Moreover, witnesses may disagree on the terms of the agreement, since memory is not as reliable as written evidence. Hence, we have more justification for reducing agreements to writing.

We can also categorize contracts in another way. At least six adjectival descriptions of contracts are observed in the legal profession. Some are easily understood. A contract is *executed* when the object of the contract is fully performed. A contract is *executory* if not yet fully executed by either or both parties. But other descriptions are more complicated.

An *unenforceable* contract cannot be legally enforced, such as not being put into writing when required, or if a statute of limitations has expired. Again, Federal contracts are written and signed to avoid this problem.

A *void* contract cannot be enforced by either party, often due to fraud. *Fraud* is any form of unethical conduct in the creation of the contract, such as a lack of apparent authority, capacity, fair dealing, honesty, legality, or promise. In effect, a void contract is a noncontract.

A *voidable* contract is either void or valid at one party's option. A voidable contract is legally enforceable but may be considered to be nonbinding if one party bears a legal disability or was a victim of fraud at the time of execution. This would occur to a party who is a minor, mentally incapacitated or intoxicated at the time of contract formation. The contract is void only if the disadvantaged party chooses to treat it as void, probably by refusing any enforcement. Such a contract may be ratified by the same disadvantaged party, either as an express or implied contract. Even with ratification however, there must still be intent and complete knowledge of all material facts and circumstances.

Finally, an *unconscionable* contract contains unreasonable terms favoring one party, leaving no meaningful choice for the other party, such as one-sided warranties or "take-it-or-take-it" situations. No reasonable person or government would enter into such a bargain, however a desperate, poor or uneducated consumer might. Hence the court needs to step in and ensure the integrity of the free enterprise system. The Federal Government should not experience any of these last three situations.

Any party to a contract is expected to behave as a reasonable party. Each must exercise *due diligence* by providing useful information to the other party to assist in their assessment of the product or service as well as contract terms and pricing. Each must also deal in *good faith* of honesty and observe both care and reasonable commercial standards of fair dealing. These obligations may not be negated by agreement. However, the parties may agree on any reasonable standards to measure the performance of these obligations. This is why the Federal Government has an elaborate process for conducting procurements fairly and impartially.

Commercial contracts for the sale of goods are governed by Article 2 of the UCC, which is rather liberal in its treatment of contract enforcement. As long as the parties can show agreement and acceptance of goods tendered, the course of performance demonstrates that a contract is in force. In the event of a conflict between the UCC and a state law, the law governs.[11] Any party needing remedy must be put into as good a position as if the other party had fully performed. However, any damages must be specifically provided in the UCC or by rule of law. We shall see that Federal contracts are governed by laws and regulations which are much stricter than the UCC.

1.2.2 Offer and Acceptance

A valid contract requires intent by both parties to be bound by the terms of the contract. *Intent* reflects planning and commitment to carry out a future act. Proving intent requires an objective test to determine mutual assent. To do this, one must examine the parties' acts and words. Moreover, there must be an apparent meeting of the minds.

Such a meeting is usually manifested by an *offer and acceptance*. An offer is usually in the form of a proposal to enter into a contract. It is made by an *offeror* to an *offeree*, and can be in the form of words or action. A mere price quotation or estimate is not a binding proposal. Rather, a proposal must define performance by describing subject matter, place and time. Price is usually but not always included.

Duration of the offer is a function of the parties' behavior. An offer is valid until rejected or counter-offered by the offeree. An offer will lapse if not accepted within its prescribed time period (commercially, this is three months and in the Federal Government it is normally two months, unless specified otherwise in the solicitation). An offer is automatically revoked if the subject matter becomes impossible to perform (e.g., death, illegality or insanity), however an offer accepted before the incapacity of either party is still binding.

An offer may be revoked by the offeror at any time before acceptance, except for an option or after substantial partial performance has occurred. This is because an option is a right obtained by one party to retain for a specified time under specified price and terms. So to avoid unjust enrichment by either party, the option has become binding and cannot subsequently be revoked.

Acceptance is communicated by the offeree's words or actions to accept the terms of the offer. Hence, the offeree/acceptor must know of the offer. Signing a contract indicates knowledge and acceptance to all terms, which is why the Government always signs its formal contracts. Even if the offeree states additional contract terms, the acceptance is still valid as of the transmittal date. Acceptance by silence does not occur in bilateral contracts unless the offeree accepts or uses the shipment or promise to ship, completes performance, or is bound to act by previous dealings between the parties.

The offeree must show acceptance by the method that is requested or authorized by the offeror. Often the offeror will require acceptance in writing. Under the *postal rule*, a written acceptance is binding as soon as the acceptor places it in the mailbox. The post office becomes in effect an agent of the offeree, and the offeror bears the risk of loss or late acceptance. Since the acceptance of a unilateral contract requires an act rather than a promise, notice of intended performance is unnecessary unless requested by the offeror. If the offeror feels uncomfortable with this arrangement, (s)he can always require written acceptance before beginning performance (an email usually suffices). Because of this technological advance, written acceptance does not often become an issue today.

Alternatively, for a bilateral contract where both parties must sign the agreement, the offer is effective only when the offeree receives it. Acceptance of a bilateral contract must be properly addressed and postage prepaid. Negotiated Federal contracts are always bilateral, whereas unilateral awards based on formal offers are accompanied by formal notice to the successful offeror (often with a congratulatory phone call or email!).

An offer may be accepted only by the offeree or his/her authorized agent. However, acceptance of an option may be assigned or transferred without consent of the offeror. Silence by itself is generally insufficient to constitute acceptance; so is an illegal act such as coercion.

Rejection of the offer or revocation of conditional acceptance is a more restrictive situation. Here, rejection is effective only upon receipt by the other party. The postal rule does not come into play for a rejection. Also, a late or defective acceptance is considered a counteroffer, which must then be accepted by the offeror to become effective. If an offer is rejected, the offeror is no longer liable for it, and the offeree may not later accept it.

We have already seen that consideration is something of value to induce the contract that either benefits one party or is a loss to the other. Consideration can be an act, forbearance from conducting an act, a promise, or a change in a legal relationship. An illusory offer ("all you want for a certain price") is neither binding nor enforceable. In fact, consideration must be mutually binding (known as *mutuality of obligation*), such as a promise or act in exchange for another promise or act.

There is no legal or UCC guidance to determine what is deemed *adequate* consideration – that is normally a matter for the parties to agree to without judicial review. The parties usually agree on adequacy of the consideration in terms of equivalent goods, services or money. However, adequacy cannot be a past consideration or something a party is legally bound to do. A moral obligation usually cannot be consideration unless it is based on a pre-existing legal duty or benefits due to the offeror. Ultimately, adequacy means that both parties benefit to some degree, hopefully in an equivalent amount.

Needless to say, courts frequently must step in when the parties are unable to agree on what they think they agreed to (or not agreed to). To overcome this confusion, the court will use the concept of *promissory estoppel* to enforce a promise (by word or conduct) that could be expected to induce action or forbearance by the other party. This concept assumes that the promissee relied on the promise and suffered as a result. In such a case, promissory estoppel provides a legal substitute for consideration. The Federal Government rarely falls into this trap, but does have a method to deal with it, as we shall see.

Courts may need to decide if a mistake by either or both parties truly resulted in a binding contract. Subjective intent is what the court will investigate to answer this dilemma, and whether such intent significantly changed the subject matter of the contract. The court may then decide to void the contract. Acceptable grounds for voiding include:

- blackmail or duress, where one party acts or threatens the other party to perform an involuntary act, such as signing an undesirable contract or

bringing suit on an unrelated matter. There is no meeting of the minds and therefore no binding contract;
- fraud, because it involves deceit and precludes a meeting of the minds;
- substitution of another contract for that bargained for, although the court may instead insist on rewriting the contract;
- undue influence, where one party controls the other to substitute its will and preclude free choice, usually due to psychological weakness or financial power; or
- willful misrepresentation or concealment of a material fact, once again because there is no real meeting of the minds.

Courts tend to be wary when both parties ask to void a contract. Some other common scenarios that courts may reject as grounds for avoiding a contract include:

- a party misinterpreting the law;
- failure to read a contract before signature;
- illiteracy, since the party can always ask for an interpretation; and
- unilateral mistake, which is most likely to occur in an erroneous bid.[12]

The Federal Government adheres to the concept of offer and acceptance by soliciting for binding offers which the offerors sign. The Government then accepts the offer of its choice by signature. Consideration is accomplished by payment of a specified sum(s) of money in exchange for performance, a mutually binding arrangement.

1.2.3 Performance

The duty of performance is often conditional upon the occurrence of a specified act or promise (but not merely a lapse of time). A *condition* is a qualification placed upon a promise or duty, which keeps it from being absolute. Conditions are ever-present in contracts:

- a condition precedent exists before the promisor incurs any liability, such as a disaster under an insurance contract;
- a condition concurrent exists when both parties must perform simultaneously, often a payment for sale of goods or land; and
- a condition subsequent ends the obligation for performance or payment, such as a final payment.

Unfortunately, conditions are not always specified in the contract, or even obvious to both parties. To address this concern, the concept of an *implied condition* is introduced, to include a contract provision which the parties should have reasonably expected to be in the contract. Hence, even if only one party strictly complied with the contract terms, the other party might still recover in court if it also substantially performed its obligation. This doctrine ensures fairness and prevents needless forfeit of investment. Nevertheless, recovery may be offset by any damages caused by failure to render complete performance. So if the deviation from the contract was merely accidental or trivial, the plaintiff will receive only nominal damages.

Although contractual duties are normally discharged by act of the parties in fulfillment of the contract terms, other outcomes are possible. A *novation* substitutes a new obligation or party to extinguish the old contract or discharge an original party. This process happens in Government contracts when a contractor merges with another firm or goes bankrupt. Alternatively, a new contract may be created with the new party using the same terms as the original. Or, the parties may agree to voluntarily discharge contract duties.

Impossibility of performance can also discharge the duty, either subjectively or objectively. *Subjective impossibility* results from an extreme event such as natural disaster or war which makes performance abnormally expensive. Similarly, *impracticability* results from unreasonable difficulty or expense, or a major loss which renders performance impossible. The event must occur after contract formation and the parties did not expect it to occur. By contrast, *objective impossibility* means that nobody can perform, such as destruction of subject matter, events occurring after the contract formation which preclude performance (such as destruction of the work site), or the promisor's inability to perform (such as illness or death). So for example, if a popular singer cancels a live concert due to suffering from the flu, it is a case of subjective impossibility, but if the concert must be cancelled because the arena burns down, we have encountered objective impossibility. The Federal Government can accommodate all such scenarios through contract termination.

1.2.4 Contract Interpretation

Disputes over contract terms and requirements do occur often, unfortunately. Contract interpretation then comes into play to determine what the parties actually agreed to. The contractor performing the services has the responsibility to seek clarification from the other party before going to court.

Once in judicial review, the court will read and interpret the contract as a whole and in light of all circumstances to determine the intent of the parties. Any ambiguous language is interpreted with its everyday meaning and construed most strictly against the author, a concept known as *contra preferentum*. If there are multiple possible interpretations, then the court will give meaning to the words that work against the author of the disputed language. So, the writing party has the burden of proof as to intent of the words (except for *patent ambiguities*, which are apparent within the terms of the contract itself). Express or specific terms within the contract take priority over general terms, though the court will supply a missing term if the intent is evident or otherwise provided by law.

The Government writes a detailed solicitation of offers so that, following the concept of contra preferentum, most if not all of the document will be construed against the Government in court. However, any terms written by the contractor and accepted by the Government will be construed against the offeror. Similarly, any special provisions written into the contract take precedence over standard clauses.

Resolving such disagreements is not easy. Acts of parties after contract execution but before the controversy may reveal their real intent. The court will also follow the *parol evidence rule*, which permits the court to hear evidence other than the written contract such as all prior oral and written agreements, and any contemporaneous oral agreements. The effect is to integrate this evidence into the contract, though it may not modify the terms of an ambiguous contract. If the parties agree to the meaning of the ambiguity, then a contract has been formed, otherwise there is no meeting of the minds. If only one party knew of the ambiguity, then whatever meaning is given by the other party will govern. However, there are numerous approaches that courts can explore before implementing this rule, both in common law and under the UCC, including:

- ambiguity;
- consideration not received by either party;
- course of performance between parties;
- condition precedent that did not occur to make the contract valid;[13]
- customary usage of trade;
- important terms missing from contract;
- mistake or illegal act;
- oral changes or additions to an executed contract; or
- prior course of dealing between parties.

UCC § 1-303

Several patterns of behavior listed above must be discussed a bit further. A *course of performance* is a sequence of conduct between the parties after the contract is executed. For example, one party repeats its previous performance, and the other party either accepts the performance or declines to formally object. A *prior course of dealing* is a bit different – a sequence of previous behaviors before the agreement is signed. These behaviors then create a common basis of understanding between the parties. So, a party can demonstrate that a clause that was not enforced in the past should not be enforced in the current contract. The court can then use the course of performance or dealing to interpret the parties' conduct and any ambiguous language. In contrast, a *usage of trade* is a regular practice or method of multiple firms dealing in a specific trade or location. This regularity is not restricted to the parties of the current contract, but does lead one to expect that it will be observed for the given transaction.

Terms of an agreement are construed by the court to be consistent with each other. If such an approach is unreasonable, then the court follows this priority of interpretation:

- express terms;
- course of performance;
- course of dealing; then
- usage of trade.

UCC § 2-209

A party that has waived a portion of a contract may later retract the waiver. (S)he merely needs to notify the other party that strict performance will again be required. However, care must be taken to ensure that no material change of position occurred if one party relied on the waiver. If so, the retraction may be ruled to be unjust, or may require some compensation to the other party. This is why it is usually a dangerous idea to retract a waiver.

UCC § 2-302

A court which finds the contract or any of its terms to have been unconscionable at the time it was made may refuse to enforce the contract. On the other hand, the court could limit application of a term to avoid creating an unconscionable result, or else choose to enforce the rest of the contract without the unconscionable term.

Ironically, the parties may conclude a contract even if the price is not settled. In such a case, the price should be that in effect at the time for delivery, or else will be fixed either at a market standard or by a third person or agency, such as an arbitrator or court. Of course, this problem won't arise if the price is established upfront, or by an agreed-to formula, as the Government does.

1.2.5 Bailment

A *bailment* is a transfer of personal (as opposed to real) property for a specific purpose without transfer of title.[14] The *bailor* delivers the property to the *bailee*, who accepts it for a temporary period of time for a specific purpose. Ultimate possession of the property reverts to the bailor, who may then keep it or transfer it to another party. The bailment terminates upon:

- completion of contract performance;
- destruction by a third party or act of God;
- subsequent agreement of the parties; or
- when the property becomes unfit for use.

The contract or local custom will dictate the amount of care and liability by the bailee toward the property. Generally, the bailee does not gain the right to use the property. Hence, renting an apartment is not a bailment, even though the rentor stays for a time and returns the apartment to the landlord upon moving. This is also why self-parking garages often print on their ticket that they have not entered into a bailment to protect your car from damage (and why they post "Park at Your Own Risk" signs), because the garage has assumed no right to possess your car. However, leaving your car with a valet in a parking garage does constitute a bailment, since you give the valet the right to drive your car to and from a parking space.

A prime example of a bailment in Federal contracting is special tooling or test equipment furnished to a contractor to perform a contract. The Government retains title to the equipment but loans it to the contractor. Another example is a deliverable item sitting in a warehouse or delivery truck.

1.2.6 Agency

Agency is a fiduciary relationship in which a person or firm handles a principal's affairs (especially money and property) to deal with a third party. The principal expressly authorizes the agent to act on the principal's behalf. This decision binds the principal to a relationship with this third party. An agent can be an employee or another contractor. The Federal Government uses specially trained employees known as *contracting officers* (who will be discussed in depth later in this book) to perform this mission.

Agency can be created by:

- agreement;
- apparent (but not implied) authority;
- operation of law due to the principal's neglect or act of God; or
- ratification of actions by the principal.

The issue of authority can be confusing when dealing with an agent. *Authority* means the principal is responsible for the agent's actions. The principal is also *estopped* (prevented by law) from denying the agent's authority in court; this is a legal doctrine designed to avoid unjust enrichment. There are several different variants of authority, which adds to the confusion. Authority can be *express* (oral or written), *implied* (inferred from the principal's words or conduct), or *apparent* (the principal allows a third party to believe the agent has the authority to act).

The principal may ratify the agent's actions if and only if the principal could have acted for him/herself at the time of the action. As long as the agency is disclosed to the third party, the agent is not liable for his/her actions to that party. However, if the agency is merely apparent, the agent may be liable to the principal for damages or loss. Again, this confusion can be avoided through written express authority and verifying the other party's apparent authority.

An agent's duties include:

- act only as authorized;
- care and diligence;
- good conduct;
- loyalty and candor to principal without any conflict of interest;
- maintain money and property accounts; and
- obey directions of principal.

Duties of a principal include:

- compensate the agent for services;
- indemnify the agent for any loss or damage that is not his/her fault;
- inform the agent of risks of harm or loss;
- not to interfere with the agent's work; and
- perform in accordance with the contract.

Agency can be terminated by:

- bankruptcy;
- change in business conditions;
- death or insanity;
- impossibility of performance;
- mutual agreement;
- option of either party;
- renunciation by agent;
- revocation of authority by expiration date; or
- war.

Once again, the common way to avoid any confusion is a written document of authority. Government contracting officers have warrants that list any restrictions on their authority. Contractors who have agents or authorized employees should do the same.

1.2.7 Warranty and Liability

UCC § 2-312 through 317

A *warranty* is a promise by the seller as to quality, quantity or title. It provides assurance to the other party that specific facts that have been promised are in fact true or will occur. Legal remedy is available if the promise is not true or is not complied with.

The warranty may be either express or implied. An *express warranty* is either written into the contract or manifested by the seller's conduct. Any statement of fact or promise about the goods (including a description or model) which is set forth in the contract creates an express warranty that the goods shall conform to that fact or promise. Similarly, any promise of remediation or repair made by the seller creates an obligation to fulfill that promise. The Federal Government prefers express warranties in its supply contracts, either its own clause or the contractor's standard commercial warranty.

In contrast, an *implied warranty* occurs by operation of law, and any disclaimers or exclusions are construed against the seller. Implied warranties include merchantability and fitness for purpose. *Merchantability* provides that an item is reasonably fit for its intended purposes of use (i.e., at least average quality compared to items that will sell without objection in the trade or market). An implied warranty of merchantability applies to any regular merchant of the goods. Merchantable goods must be:

- adequately contained, packaged and labeled;
- conform to any promises or statements of fact made on the container or label;
- fit for purpose;
- of consistent kind, quality and quantity within each unit; and
- within specifications for the trade or contract.

An implied warranty of fitness for purpose arises where the buyer relies on the seller's skill or judgment to select or furnish suitable goods. *Fitness for purpose* addresses the need for which the customer will use the items, as long as this is consistent with the intended purpose of the manufacturer or service provider. This is the only instance where an implied warranty can displace an express warranty.

Implied warranties cannot include expressions like "as is" that would alert the buyer to the lack of an express warranty. An implied warranty may also be excluded or modified by course of dealing or performance, or by usage of trade.

Once failure to comply with a warranty is demonstrated, liability comes into play. *Liability* extends the warranty to users other than the buyer. Liability addresses negligence in preparation or manufacture, misrepresentation of character or quality of goods, or providing contaminated products. For instance, this concept requires dangerous products to bear a warning label. In addition, a manufacturer is responsible for injury caused by subcontracted parts. Further, *pecuniary liability* arises when one firm or individual is responsible to another for loss or improper application of funds or property. Government contracts include standard clauses addressing warranties and subsequent liability.

1.2.8 Assignment

An *assignment of contract* transfers the rights of performance from one party to another. The assignment must be written, can be total or partial, and does not require consideration (e.g., it can be a gift). The assignee takes on all rights and obligations of the assignor.[15]

Common law may not have allowed assignment in its early days, but today most contracts are assignable and the practice is becoming more common as firms increasingly undergo merger and acquisition. Federal contracting does so by using a novation technique.

Nevertheless, assignments are not always permitted, such as contracts for personal services or which expressly forbid assignment (although they can still assign money due, including judgments). Transfer of title is prohibited if it would materially impact the other party (e.g., change a contractual duty, increase risk or impair the chance of return performance).

UCC § 2-210

Either party may assign any or all rights without materially changing the duty, burden or risk of the other party. Likewise, either party may perform its duties through a delegate unless prohibited in the contract, or if the other party has a substantial interest in requiring the original party to continue to perform or control performance (such as a recording artist). An assignee who accepts a delegation creates a promise to perform those duties, which is enforceable by either party.

1.2.9 Delivery

UCC § 2-308

The place for delivery is normally stated in the contract; if not, it is by default the seller's place of business. Unless otherwise agreed, specifications of assortment of goods are at the buyer's option, and shipment arrangements are at the seller's option.[16] *Tender* (formal presentation) of goods entitles the seller to both acceptance and payment.

UCC § 2-501 through 508

The seller holds goods at the buyer's instructions and gives the buyer notification to take delivery. The contract dictates the manner, time and place for their tender.[17] The seller retains an interest in the goods so long as it retains title. Upon delivery, the buyer obtains an insurable and property interest in the goods, even if they are nonconforming and even if (s)he has an option to return or reject them. This interest can be identified at any time and in any manner agreed to by the parties.

If shipment is required to a destination, the seller must provide the goods to a carrier, promptly notify the buyer of the shipment, and furnish any document for the buyer to obtain possession of the goods.

If tender or delivery is rejected as nonconforming and the time for performance has not yet expired, the seller may notify the buyer of intention to cure the problem and then make a conforming delivery. Also, the buyer may provide the seller with more time to tender conforming goods.

UCC § 2-311

Either party may be excused for delay in performance if it is materially affected by a specification or a delay in the other party's cooperation. The affected party may continue to perform, or treat the failure as a breach and refuse to deliver or accept the goods. We shall see that the Government has remedies available to it should a contractor delay performance, and likewise can provide day-for-day extensions should it be responsible for contractor delay.

There are so many different ways in which goods may be shipped that the Government has developed clauses of many flavors to specify what is to be done. This subject will need to be covered in much more depth later in this book.

1.2.10 Risk of Loss

UCC § 2-503 through 510

The seller retains risk of loss (and risk of any failure by a bailee to properly perform or issue a proper title) until the buyer has had a reasonable time to review the document or directions. If tender or delivery fails to conform to the contract, the risk of loss remains on the seller until cure or acceptance occurs. On the other hand, if the buyer repudiates or is in breach, (s)he bears the risk of loss.

The risk of loss passes to the lessee when the goods are delivered to the carrier. However, if the seller must ship the goods to a destination specified in the contract, risk of loss passes once the goods are delivered to the final destination. If the goods are held by a bailee for delivery without being moved (known as *shipment in place*), risk of loss passes to the buyer upon receipt of:

- acknowledgment by the bailee of the buyer's right to possession of the goods;
- possession or control of a correct document of title or other written direction;
- the goods themselves (if sold by a merchant); or
- tender of delivery if none of the above.

1.2.11 Inspection

UCC § 2-511 through 515

Either party may notify the other that it chooses to inspect, test and sample the goods. The parties may agree to a third-party inspection or survey to determine the conformity or condition of the goods, and may agree that the findings will be binding upon them in any subsequent litigation or adjustment. The buyer bears the cost of inspection, but (s)he may recover from the seller if the goods do not conform and are rejected. Since it is best to spell out these issues upfront, the Federal Government always includes an Inspection clause in its contracts.

1.2.12 Documents of Title

A *document of title* is written proof that its owner is entitled to receive, hold and dispose of both the written instrument itself and the goods that it covers. Common examples are a bill of lading or warehouse receipt. The document is deemed *negotiable* if it requires that the goods be delivered to the bearer or upon order of a specifically named person.

1.2.12.1 Warehouse Receipts

UCC § 7-202 through 210

A warehouse receipt must provide for each of the following to avoid liability for damages due to omission:

- date of issue of the receipt;
- description of the goods or the packages containing them;
- identification code of the receipt;
- identity of the party to whom the goods will be delivered;
- location of the warehouse facility where the goods are stored;
- note that the receipt is issued for goods that the warehouse owns;
- payment amounts made and/or liabilities incurred for which the warehouse claims a lien or security interest;[18]
- rate of storage and handling charges; and
- signature of the warehouse or its agent.

A warehouse segregates goods covered by each receipt to permit their identification and delivery. Different lots of goods may be commingled, but the warehouse is liable to each owner for his/her share of loss or damage to goods if it fails to take due care.

A storage facility has very specific and significant rights. The warehouse has a lien against the bailor on the goods covered by a warehouse receipt or storage agreement, or on the proceeds thereof. It can recover damages from the issuer due to nonreceipt or incorrect description, unless stated otherwise. However, the warehouse loses its lien on any goods that it voluntarily delivers without authority or unjustifiably refuses to deliver.

The warehouse may notify the owner of the goods or the party who claims an interest in them to require payment of charges and removal of the goods once the agreed-to storage period expires, or else at least 30 days after giving notice. If the goods are not removed by that date, the warehouse may sell them. The warehouse may specify in the notice a shorter time period to remove any perishable goods, or else sell them at public sale at least one week thereafter.

1.2.12.2 Bills of Lading

UCC § 7-301 through 308

A *bill of lading* is a document issued by a carrier to acknowledge that the listed goods have in fact been received for transport to the specified place and consignee. The document serves as a formal contract of carriage, and may set forth all terms of agreement or refer to an existing contract. The carrier signs it to confirm that the goods match the contract description and are in good condition at time of receipt. A bill of lading contains at a minimum the following:

- description of goods;
- freight rate;

- gross, net or tare weight;
- name of the shipping company; and
- nationality of the carrier.

Carriers can be distinguished by their terms of hire. *Common carriers* such as airlines, rail lines and truckers are regulated entities available for any firm, and provide their services to the general public. They usually follow preestablished delivery schedules, routes and rate tables. In contrast, *contract carriers* work ad hoc by contract to a select clientele, and a *private carrier* ships its own goods only.

The carrier is responsible for any loss during shipment because it guaranteed the accuracy of the information furnished to the issuer at the time of shipment. The carrier will indemnify the issuer against damage caused by any inaccuracies. This obligation is discharged by delivery. The only instances where a common carrier is not liable for the goods are by act of an enemy or God, inherent defect of goods, or shipper fault or fraud.

If permitted by the bill of lading and so directed by the holder of a negotiable bill (or the consignor on a nonnegotiable bill), a carrier may deliver the goods to a person or destination other than that stated in the bill, or may otherwise dispose of the goods. The consigner may not recover for misdelivery in these circumstances.

Just like the warehouse with stored items, a carrier has a lien on the goods or on the proceeds for charges after their date of receipt. The lien may be enforced by public or private sale of the goods at a reasonable time, place or terms, after notifying all persons known to claim an interest in the goods. Before the sale, any claimant may pay the amount necessary to satisfy the lien and any associated expenses. And again as with a warehouse, the carrier loses its lien on any goods that it voluntarily delivers or unjustifiably refuses to deliver.

1.2.13 Termination

Contracts can be legally terminated by:

- acts of parties;
- impossibility of performance;
- operation of law; or
- performance.

Termination by Acts of Parties results from either or both parties performing a specific event, such as:

- accord and satisfaction, where the parties agree that performance was acceptable and to discharge the obligation;
- account stated: a new agreement between the parties as to final balance due, in order to discharge obligations under the prior contract;
- mutual release by returning property or money paid;
- novation; or
- one party waives or prevents the other from performing.

Termination by Impossibility of Performance occurs if the parties did not know of the impossibility, or due to death or disability of a key contract performer.[19] Acts of God, nature or an enemy do not excuse performance unless they make it impossible, or if the contract so permits. Strikes and accidents do not normally excuse performance. In all these cases however, if the party seeking relief is guilty of contributory fault, it cannot collect damages.

Termination by Operation of Law results from a law or court decree that serves to forbid performance, such as expiration of the statute of limitations covering the period of time in which to file charges or a lawsuit. Bankruptcy does not preclude the obligation to fulfill the contract. Insolvency can terminate a contract, but the buyer can still recover goods from an insolvent seller if (s)he paid all or part of the purchase price.

Termination by Performance indicates that final payment has been made or the period of performance has expired. This means contract completion as originally intended by the parties. It is the only type of termination that does not require one party to furnish written notification to the other party.

Of course, the Government anticipates all of these scenarios by including prescribed clauses into its contracts, as we shall see later.

1.2.14 Breach

An unjustifiable failure to perform all contractual duties results in *breach* of contract. If one party hinders or prevents the performance of the other party, breach is the result. Breach also occurs if the goods did not conform to the contract requirements once leaving the seller's control. A variant of breach is *anticipatory repudiation*, where the promisor tells the promisee that (s)he cannot or will not perform the contractual duties.

UCC § 2-601 through 615

If the goods fail in any way to conform to the contract, the buyer may accept all or some of the shipment, or reject it entirely. Rejection must be within a reasonable time after their delivery or tender, and requires the buyer to notify the seller. Upon rejection, the buyer forfeits the right to ownership of the goods. If the buyer takes physical possession of the goods before rejecting them, such as a drop shipment, (s)he must hold them until the seller removes them.

Acceptance occurs when the buyer notifies the seller that the goods are conformant, or else will take or retain them in spite of their nonconformity. If the buyer does not make a rejection within a reasonable time or as specified in the contract, acceptance is assumed and cannot later be revoked. Acceptance of any part of any indivisible commercial unit (such as a machine) is deemed to be acceptance of that entire unit. However, if the buyer fails to notify the seller of a defect which could be found by inspection, then the buyer cannot rely on the defect to claim rejection or breach. In any event, upon rejection the seller may request a final written statement of all defects.

There are circumstances where the buyer may revoke acceptance of a lot or commercial unit if its nonconformity substantially impairs its value. The buyer may have assumed that its nonconformity would be cured, but cure has yet to occur. Perhaps the buyer had not discovered the nonconformity due to difficulty of discovery before acceptance (such as a latent defect), or due to seller assurances. In any event, acceptance must be revoked within a reasonable time after discovery of the nonconformity and before any substantial change in condition of the goods. Revocation is not effective until the buyer notifies the seller.

A buyer may not use the goods after rejection or revocation of acceptance, unless the seller concurs. The buyer may be obligated to pay the seller for the value of such usage.

Either party may demand in writing adequate assurance of due performance, and may suspend any related performance until its receipt. Failure to provide such assurance within 30 days is grounds for repudiation of the contract.

When delivery is made in separate lots to be separately inspected (known as an *installment contract*), the buyer may reject any installment if the nonconformity substantially impairs the lot's value and cannot be cured, or if associated documentation is defective. This rejection may cause breach of the entire contract if the defect impairs future performance. However, if the buyer accepts a nonconforming installment without notifying the seller of cancellation, then performance is deemed acceptable. On the other hand, if the seller gives adequate assurance that it will cure the defect(s), the buyer must accept that installment, but may still demand proper performance as to future installments.

Delay in delivery or nondelivery in whole or in part may not be a breach of contract if performance has become impracticable due to an unforeseen contingency or by good faith compliance with a government regulation or order. The seller must notify the buyer that there will be delay or nondelivery, and has the right to withhold or stop delivery unless the buyer provides a resolution.

Clearly, breach is a very complicated contractual situation which shows that things have not gone according to plan. This situation is mitigated greatly in Federal contracting by clearly spelling out the parties' responsibilities in delivery and inspection contract clauses.

1.2.15 Remedies

1.2.15.1 Equitable Relief

There are several means to obtain equitable relief by an injured party. Common forms of remedy include damages, reformation, rescission, restitution, and specific performance. Some are available only to one party, while others are available to both parties.

Damages are money that is paid for injury caused by breach. If a party fails to perform, the amount of damages is whatever is necessary to compensate the injured party to return to the position (s)he would have occupied if performance had been completed.[20] Damages due to failure which is already known to occur in the future (anticipatory repudiation) are assessed as of the scheduled performance dates.

Similarly, if one party has only provided partial performance, then damages will cover only the expense of completion. This amount may or may not cover the balance of the contract price, but no more, to prevent unjust enrichment. However, the value of materials lost through breach can be recovered.

Damages for defective performance reflect the difference in value between what is actually tendered and what is required. If a defect can be remedied by repairs, then the damages reflect the price of the repairs performed. However, there are several other types of damages that a court can award:

- *compensatory damages* place the plaintiff in as good a position as if the defendant had performed the contract. The compensation covers losses that are a direct, immediate and natural result of the act. The injured party cannot recover attorney's fees;
- *consequential damages* include any loss of which the buyer, at the time of contracting, had reason to know but could not be prevented. This includes injury to person or property resulting from breach of warranty;
- *construction contract damages* are the reasonable cost[21] of reconstruction and completion per contract terms. At the least, this is the difference in value between full and defective performance. The injured party may recover rental cost during delayed performance (usually per a liquidated

damages clause) and loss of profit. Interest can be charged as of date of breach;

- *foreseeable damages* are injuries contemplated by the parties at the time the contract was made;
- *incidental damages* include commissions and expenses incurred by the seller to stop delivery and to transport and care for the goods. These expenses include inspection, receipt, transportation, and care and custody of goods which were rightfully rejected;
- *liquidated damages* are payments in lieu of default where the amount cannot be easily calculated. The injured party has a duty to mitigate damages; and
- *punitive damages* are charges to punish the party for reasons beyond mere breach of contract and to discourage others from similar behavior in the future.

Monetary damages are not the sole remedy available to the courts. *Reformation* is a technique to rewrite the contract if it does not reflect the bargain struck by the parties. This is usually due to either fraud or mutual mistake in drafting the contract. Relief for the reasonable value of services rendered is possible in this situation. On the other hand, *rescission* will terminate the contract and restore the parties to their original state as if they never entered into the contract. Usually, the party seeking rescission surrenders all benefits received under the contract.

Another remedy known as *restitution* allows the court to order payment or return of property and money paid.[22] The injured party has a *reliance interest* to be compensated for its detriment suffered or expenses incurred by relying on the other party. However, unlike rescission the contract might not be vacated by the court.

The remedy known as *specific performance* requires one party to perform as promised because monetary damages cannot compensate for the breach (e.g., a sale of land). The court will also enforce a negative covenant which prohibits a key person from working for anyone else during the contract term. However, a personal-services contract is not usually enforced for a variety of reasons (impaired performance, fear of continuing an already strained relationship, and even a sense of slavery, which is prohibited by the 13th Amendment to the Constitution. Nonetheless, contractual prohibition of an act may be enforced.

Under the Equal Access to Justice Act (28 USC 2412), small businesses and individuals are entitled to recover legal fees if they prevail in certain actions against the Government. These expenses are usually used to cover fees of attorneys and expert witnesses.

UCC § 2-725

Action for breach of a warranty accrues when the seller has made delivery or completed installation or assembly of the goods, or when the aggrieved party discovers or should have discovered the breach. For breach of a remedial promise, a right of action accrues as soon as the promise is not performed when due. An action for breach of sale must be filed either within four years after the right of action has accrued or one year after the breach was or should have been discovered, whichever is later.

1.2.15.2 Seller Remedies

UCC § 2-703 through 710

Breach of contract by the buyer includes a wrongful rejection, attempt to revoke acceptance of goods, or failure to perform on time. The seller has numerous courses of action to choose from:

- cancel the contract;
- obtain specific performance;
- reclaim the goods;
- recover damages for non-acceptance or repudiation (including liquidated damages);
- recover the price;
- require payment directly from the buyer;
- resell the goods; or
- stop delivery of the goods.

If the seller resells the goods due to breach, (s)he may also recover the difference between the resale price and contract price, together with any incidental damages. However the seller must subtract expenses saved due to the breach. The net proceeds of any resale must be credited to the buyer and any goods not resold are titled to the buyer. The seller might be entitled to consequential or incidental damages.

1.2.15.3 Buyer Remedies

UCC § 2-711 through 717

A breach of contract by the seller includes wrongful failure to deliver or perform a contractual obligation, making a nonconforming delivery or performance, and repudiation. Again, the buyer may choose from a number of options:

- cancel the contract;
- cover damages to all affected goods whether or not identified to the contract;[23]
- deduct or recover damages for accepted goods or a remedial promise, including nondelivery or repudiation;
- obtain specific performance;
- obtain the goods by court order (known as replevin); or
- recover the amount paid or liquidated damages.

Upon rightful rejection or revocation of acceptance, a buyer has a security interest in any goods in his/her possession or control to the extent of any payments made for their receipt, inspection, custody, and transportation. The buyer may hold such goods and resell them.

If the seller fails to deliver or repudiates performance, or the buyer rightfully rejects or revokes acceptance, then the buyer may purchase substitute goods. Here again, the buyer may then recover from the seller the difference between the cost of repurchase and the contract price, together with any consequential or incidental damages, but must deduct expenses saved in consequence of the seller's breach.

A buyer who accepted nonconforming goods and properly notified the seller may recover the loss caused by the seller's breach. The measure of damages for breach of warranty is the difference at the time and place of acceptance between the value of the goods accepted and the value they would have had if conformant.

Any incidental and consequential damages may also be recovered. Incidental damages resulting from the seller's breach are the same as for buyer's breach. Consequential damages are also the same as for buyer's breach, plus injury to person or property resulting from any breach of warranty.

1.2.16 Illegal Contracts

UCC § 2-201

Four circumstances are recognized to bar consent:

- mistake;
- fraud;
- duress; or
- undue influence.

A *mistake* relates to a material fact or identity, often because the subject matter or something essential to performance ceases to exist before the agreement is consummated. However, unilateral mistake is not a basis for contract rescission, nor is a mutual mistake a basis for price adjustment.[24]

Fraud is a false representation of a material fact made with knowledge of its falsity or ignorance of the truth. The deceiving party intended some action by the party deceived, which relied and acted upon this false representation, and as a result was injured. Fraud is very difficult to prove because intent must be demonstrated. Within Federal contracting, fraud means acts or attempts to defraud the Government or to corrupt its agents, create a cause for debarment or suspension, or violate the False Claims Act (31 U.S.C. 3729) or Anti-Kickback Act (42 U.S.C. 1320).

This definition of fraud includes hidden defects and half-truths. A *defect* is a condition where something is missing or the product is incomplete or has a structural weakness. The defect is deemed *patent* if it is easily discovered or one party otherwise knew about it. If the seller is aware of a defect and tries to conceal the defect and misleads the buyer, the latter has recourse to pursue fraud. Regardless, the old commandment of "caveat emptor" ("let the buyer beware") is still good advice.

The defect is *latent* if it existed at the time of acceptance but was not readily discoverable. This occasionally happens in construction where the ground is different than expected (e.g., buried skeletons, caves, higher or lower water tables, etc.). If the wronged party cannot show foreknowledge or willful ignorance, any claim will not be sustained in court. This is why Government contracts include defect and warranty clauses.

Duress means creating fear in the other party through a crime or tort to compel assent. The affected party loses freedom of choice and believes that it had no alternative but to perform in such a manner to avoid harm. To constitute duress, the victim must suffer irreparable loss without recovery from the wrongdoer, and the other party must have no right to perform the act. Such a contract is thereby void.

Undue influence means illegally controlling another person's will or judgment. It differs from duress by not including any physical threat or extortion. Instead, undue influence includes deception, flattery, insinuations, and misrepresentation. Courts are naturally suspicious when a party makes this claim, out of concern that the motivation might be solely to avoid unfavorable contract terms. Nevertheless, when a court does intervene in this instance, it is often to order restitution rather than rescinding the contract.

There are several bases for *illegal contracts*:

- acts against public interest (e.g., corruption);
- discrimination;

- failure to obtain a license to practice a trade;
- relieving a party of negligence;
- unreasonable and excessive restrictions on the seller to avoid future competition; or
- violations of law.

The most famous example of illegal contracts results from Federal law. *Antitrust* actions frustrate the normal competitive forces of the marketplace and restrain trade, leading to reduced economic growth, individual initiative and market values. Public objections to such actions in America date back to the 19th century.

Antitrust practices can manifest in several ways. A *reciprocal purchase agreement* requires a supplier to buy from its customer, which impacts competition and economic efficiency. It could be ethical if it is not coercive and covers actual needs; however, it could lead to restraint of trade due to forced purchase or reduced competition. A variation of this practice is a *tying agreement* which requires a customer to buy another product in order to purchase the originally desired product.

Retail-price maintenance has also come into question for propriety. This involves a manufacturer and a wholesaler or retailer agreeing to fix the consumer price in all outlets, known as a *vertical price agreement.* The consumer benefits to some extent because competition shifts from price to quality, even though price competition is not present. The manufacturer bears the burden of enforcement.

Additionally, contracts can be found to be illegal for violating any of several Federal restraint-of-trade laws. The *Sherman Anti-Trust Act* (15 U.S.C. 1) prohibits contracts and activities that unreasonably restrain trade and commerce. It forbids *price fixing*, or conspiring to set prices among competing firms, even without a formal agreement. The Supreme Court responded to challenges of this Act by introducing the *rule of reason*, saying that only unreasonable restraints of trade were within scope of the act and therefore illegal.[25] Market control alone does not show the presence of monopoly.

The *Clayton Anti-Trust Act* (15 U.S.C. 12) prohibits price discrimination and restrictions on future contracts. This includes mergers, interlocked corporate management and compulsory contracting with a firm to obtain its business. The Clayton Act excludes organized labor as a commodity, so a labor union can organize anywhere without fear of any allegation of monopolizing the labor supply.

The *Robinson-Patman Act* (15 U.S.C. 13) expanded the Clayton Act by prohibiting price discrimination to buyers or customers with the intent to injure, or to prevent competition with anyone who grants or receives discrimination.

If the Federal Trade Commission brings an antitrust suit against a potential contractor, a contracting officer would be interested in the:

- affected product lines and division;
- impact of nondelivery;
- nature of complaints;
- possible impact on prices and deliveries;
- search for an alternate supplier; and
- timing.

Unusual payments (e.g., bribes and kickbacks) to corporate officials from foreign sources are illegal under the Foreign Corrupt Practices Act (15 U.S.C. 78), even though the practice might be widely recognized and accepted overseas. Contactors must therefore have an effective system of internal accounting controls and maintain financial accounts, books and records that are accurate, current and complete in all respects.

1.3 LEASES

UCC § 1-203

Leases are similar to contracts yet different, and therefore require separate discussion. A *lease* is a contract which grants one party the sole right to take possession of someone else's property.[26] The owner of the property is the *lessor* and the user is the *lessee*. When the lease concerns a building, the terminology is unique: the owner is the *landlord*, the user is a *tenant*, the contract is a *tenancy*, the right to possession by the tenant is a *leasehold interest*, and the payment in consideration for the lease is *rent*. A lease for land permits the tenant to rent and use the land, but the lessor owns the buildings and other permanent objects upon it.

A lease is not the same as a license because it does not entitle a licensee to use property subject to termination at the property owner's will. Instead, a lease creates a security interest in personal property or fixtures by securing payment or performing an obligation. Common elements of a lease include:

- conditions for renewal or nonrenewal;
- identification of the property or item leased;
- names of the parties;
- provisions for a security deposit and its return;
- specific consideration (usually a lump sum or periodic payments) for granting use;

- starting date and duration; and
- unique conditions and remedies (e.g., insurance, usage restrictions, maintenance).

The formal requirements for a real property lease are determined by the law and custom of the jurisdiction where the real property is located. However, for personal property, formal requirements are dictated by where the rental agreement is made.

Regardless of geography, any tenancy that covers more than one year must be in writing. A shorter-term lease does not have to be written, but should be. In either case, a *periodic tenancy* exists for a period of time determined by the terms of the rent payment (e.g., weekly, monthly or annually). It may be renewed automatically without further action by either party, or may be terminated at any time by giving notice to the other party. The notice must state the effective date of termination, which often is the last day of the last payment period.

1.3.1 Formation

UCC § 2A-201 through 221

Creating a lease is quite similar to that for a contract. A written offer by a merchant to lease goods cannot be revoked for lack of consideration during the time it is valid (three months unless otherwise stated). Acceptance can be made in any reasonable manner. However, an agreement modifying a lease needs no additional consideration to be binding.

As with a contract, any written fact or promise or any description of goods, sample or model made by the lessor to the lessee creates an express warranty of conformance. Further, the lease warrants that nobody else holds a claim to or interest in the goods due to any act or omission by the lessor which interferes with the lessee's performance. These warranties give the lessee confidence that no legal issues will impede performance. In the spirit of contra preferentum, if the lessee furnishes specifications to a lessor or supplier, the lessor is absolved against any claim for infringement arising out of its compliance.

Leases normally contain no implied warranty with regard to patent defects. The recipient is responsible for inspection for any defects. However, any exclusion or modification of a warranty against interference or infringement must be in writing.

All warranties must be consistent with each other; if not, the intention of the parties determines which warranty is dominant. Preference is always given to exact or technical specifications, a sample from an existing bulk quantity, any express warranty, or else any implied warranty of fitness for purpose.

As with contracts, risk of loss is retained by the lessor until shipment. The risk of loss passes to the lessee when the goods are delivered to the carrier. However, if the destination is specified in the lease, then risk of loss passes to the lessee only after final delivery.

If the goods are damaged without fault of either party, the lease is terminated if the loss is total. If the loss is partial however, the lessee may demand inspection and has the option to accept the goods with no further right against the lessor.

1.3.2 Performance

UCC § 2A-401 through 407

As in contracts, a lease imposes an obligation on each party not to impair the other party's expectation of receiving due performance. Either party may demand in writing some assurance of due performance from the other party. Until a response arrives, the insecure party may suspend its performance. If the response does not arrive within 30 days after receipt of the written demand, the lease is repudiated. Moreover, acceptance of any nonconforming delivery or payment does not prevent the insecure party's right to demand adequate assurance of future performance.

Another similarity with contracts involves delivery. Delay in delivery or nondelivery by a lessor or supplier is not considered a default if performance has become impracticable by an unexpected contingency. Nor does compliance in good faith with a government regulation or order constitute default.

The lessee may notify the lessor in writing to terminate the lease, or to modify it by accepting a different number of deliverable items than expected, with adjustment for payable rent. If the lessee fails to modify the lease within 30 days, then the lease lapses with respect to those deliveries.

1.3.3 Default

UCC § 2A-108

If the court finds a lease or clause unconscionable at the time it was made, it may:

• award reasonable attorney's fees to the lessee;
• grant appropriate relief;
• limit the application of the unconscionable clause;

- recognize the remainder of the lease contract without the unconscionable clause; and/or
- refuse to enforce the lease contract.

UCC § 2A-502 through 506

Either party can bring an action for indemnity or default when the act or omission is, or should have been, discovered. Such a cause for action can also occur if the actual default occurs later.

No party in default under a lease is entitled to notice of default. Nevertheless, the agreement may include specific rights and remedies for default, and may limit or alter the measure of damages recoverable. An action for default, including breach of warranty or indemnity, must be initiated within four years after the cause of action. However, the parties may agree in the lease to reduce the period of limitation to as little as one year.

Damages for default, act or omission, as well as indemnity for loss or anticipated benefits, may be liquidated by any reasonable formula. Typically, the lessee is entitled to restitution of any payments exceeding 20% of the remaining balance of the lease.

1.3.3.1 Default by Lessor

UCC § 2A-508 through 522

The burden is on the lessee to establish a default by the lessor. Lessee remedies include cancellation, recovery of paid rent and security, or damages for all goods affected or undelivered. If a lessor fails to deliver conformant goods or repudiates the lease, the lessee may also recover (replevin) the goods and either hold them or dispose of them in good faith.

If the goods or their delivery fail in any respect to conform to the lease, the lessee may reject or accept all, some or none of the goods. Rejection of goods requires the lessee to notify the lessor within a reasonable time after tender. The lessee must hold and care for any rejected, nonperishable goods in its care for disposition by the lessor or supplier.

Should nonconformity or default regarding deliveries substantially impair the value of an installment lease as a whole, then the entire lease is in default. But the aggrieved party can reinstate the lease by accepting a nonconforming delivery. If a delivery is rejected and the time for performance has not yet expired, the lessor or supplier may notify the lessee of its intent to cure and then make a conforming and timely delivery. Otherwise, a lessee's failure to state a defect precludes default, rejection or remedy.

Acceptance occurs after the lessee has a reasonable opportunity to inspect the goods. This signifies to the lessor or supplier that the goods are conforming or else will be retained in spite of their nonconformity. A lessee may revoke acceptance within a reasonable time if the default or nonconformity substantially impairs the value of the deliverable(s), or an expected cure has not occurred. The lessee can also collect damages due to the default.

1.3.3.2 Default by Lessee

UCC § 2A-523 through 532

If a lessee wrongfully rejects or revokes acceptance, fails to make a payment when due, or repudiates with respect to a part or the whole, then the value of the whole lease is substantially impaired. Therefore, the lessee is in default of the lease and the lessor may:

- cancel the lease;
- proceed regarding goods not covered by the lease;
- recover the loss and any incidental damages, less expenses saved due to the default;
- stop delivery of the goods by any bailee; or
- withhold delivery and take possession of any goods previously delivered.

A lessor may stop delivery of goods in the possession of a carrier or other bailee if (s)he discovers the lessee to be insolvent. The lessor could also repudiate delivery or refuse to make a payment due before delivery. After the lessee defaults, the lessor may take possession of the goods and dispose of them and any undelivered balance by lease or sale. The lessor may also recover any accrued and unpaid rent, the present value of the rent for the remaining term of the lease, and any incidental damages, less expenses saved due to the default.

A subsequent party who buys or leases from the lessor through the disposition of goods takes the goods free of the original lease and of any rights of the original lessee. The lessor need not pay the lessee for any profit made on any disposition.

If a third party causes injury to a party to the lease, the lessor has a right of action against the third party. By contrast, the lessee has a right of action against the third party only if it has a security or insurable interest in the goods or bears the risk of loss.

1.4 FEDERAL CONTRACTING ENVIRONMENT

1.4.1 Background

A Federal *contractor* is any individual or legal entity that directly (or indirectly through an affiliate) submits offers or receives awards for a Government contract or a subcontract under a Government contract. It includes any entity that conducts business with the Government as agent or representative of another contractor.

Federal Government contracts include many features that differ from those described above for commercial contracts:

- administrative disputes and claims process rather than binding arbitration, followed by direct appeal to court;
- Congressional notification of awards;
- Government liability somewhat limited because it is a sovereign, but equitable estoppel may sometimes be invoked;
- irrevocable sealed bids used in a rigid bidding process;[27]
- no recognition of apparent authority. Express authority is required of the parties' representatives to bind their employer. The Government is not usually held responsible for unauthorized acts of its employees, but may ratify these actions if in the Government's best interest;
- pre-printed boilerplate provisions not subject to negotiations;[28]
- protests over award;
- socioeconomic objectives prescribed by law; and
- unilateral change authority over contractor performance without requiring contractor concurrence.

Acceptance is also a different concept for Federal contractors. Government acceptance is performed to specification and is final, whereas commercial firms accept by act of ownership. Government express warranties preserve remedies after acceptance, whereas the UCC protects only for merchantability and fitness for purpose. It is true, however, that patent defects do permit recovery of damages in both commercial and Government sectors.

There are several levels of meaning given to the documentation used to operate Federal acquisition. Though people often use these terms interchangeably, they are in fact of different levels of impact and applicability. *Laws* are mandates enacted by Congress and must be complied with, unless they allow for a waiver or deviation. *Executive orders* are issued by the President, but have the same force and effect as laws. *Regulations* are developed by various bodies throughout the Executive Branch of the Federal Government, and also have the same force and effect as laws. *Standards* include mandatory actions, rules or regulations which the Government is bound to follow, as well as best practices of the industry, which are not always mandatory on the Federal Government.[29] *Policies* are high-level requirements set by the President or the department or agency head. Policies set the tone for operations, but do not drive a particular solution or technology. *Guidelines* are general statements which implement specified operations. *Procedures* are step-by-step specifics of implementing guidelines and standards.

1.4.2 Federal Statutes

Article I, Section 8, Paragraph 18 of the Constitution gives Congress the authority to enact laws to implement Federal powers, which includes acquisition from the private sector when necessary. These *open-market* purchases of supplies or services from private commercial sources can be used if no mandatory sources exist for the requirement, or if the open market can fulfill the requirement at reduced expense to the Government.

There are numerous Federal statutes that impact procurement in some fashion. They are introduced and discussed throughout the text with their respective subject areas.

Executive Orders issued by the Office of the President provide operational direction to agencies. Their authority rests in Article II, Section 3, Clause 4, which requires the President to "take care that the laws are faithfully executed." They are similarly introduced and discussed in their subject areas.

Other Federal sources of information that apply to procurement include:

- 4 CFR Part 21 GAO Bid Protest Regulations of Government Contracts (Government Accountability Office [GAO]);
- Contract Pricing Desk Guide (General Services Administration [GSA]);
- Federal Acquisition Jumpstation (National Aeronautics and Space Administration [NASA]);
- Federal Acquisition Regulation and Circulars;
- ProcNet, http://procnet.pica.army.mil;
- Modular Contracting Guide (GSA);
- North American Industry Classification System (NAICS) (Census Bureau, Department of Commerce);
- Procurement Reference Library (NASA);
- Procurement Technical Assistance Program (George Mason University/ Defense Logistics Agency);
- SHARE A-76!, a DOD Cost Comparison Knowledge Base;[30]
- The Multiagency/GWAC Program Managers Compact: A Consensus on Principles Applicable to the Acquisition of Services under Multiagency Contracts and Governmentwide Acquisitions, September 9, 1997 (ARNet);
- www.abanet.org/contract/home.html Public Contract Section (American Bar Association);
- www.abilityone.gov/index.html Javits-Wagner-O'Day Government site;
- www.acquisition.gov Federal Acquisition Virtual Library;
- www.acquisition.gov/comp/caac/index.html Civilian Agency Acquisition Council;
- www.arnet.gov Office of Federal Procurement Policy (OFPP) Policy Letters (Office of Management and Budget [OMB]);

- www.dau.mil Defense Acquisition University;
- www.dol.gov/esa National Pre-Award Registry (Office of Federal Contract Compliance Programs, Department of Labor [DOL]);
- www.dol.gov/oasam Audit Requirements for Grants, Contracts, and other Agreements, Part 96 (DOL);
- www.epls.gov List of Parties Excluded from Federal Procurement and Nonprocurement Programs;
- www.fai.gov Federal Acquisition Institute (GSA). The institute develops acquisition workforce standards through training, education and research. It identifies education needs, evaluates agency procurement education programs, monitors career development programs, and maintains a reference library;
- www.fbo.gov Electronic Posting System (EPS) for vendors (GSA);
- www.fms.treas.gov/c570/index.html Companies holding certificates of authority as acceptable sureties on Federal bonds, and acceptable reinsuring companies (Financial Management Service, Department of the Treasury);
- www.fpdsng.com/fpdsng_cms Federal Procurement Data System;
- www.gpo.gov/davisbacon/ Davis Bacon Wage Determination Database;
- www.gsbca2.gsa.gov GSA Board of Contract Appeals Rules of Procedure and Cases: Appeals, Travel Cases, Rate Cases, Relocation Cases, October 1992 to present;
- www.jwod.com Javits-Wagner-O'Day commercial site;
- www.nib.org National Industries for the Blind;
- www.unicor.gov UNICOR;
- http://www.dol.gov/whd/contracts/sca.htm Service Contract Act Wage Determination Database; and
- www.whitehouse.gov/omb/memoranda_default/OFPP Administrative Memoranda (OFPP).

1.4.3 Federal Regulations

FAR 1.1 thru 1.5

Regulations are the result of the Executive Branch implementing a statue or executive order or policy. They are considered quasi-legislative in nature by Federal courts, which gives them similar respect without substituting their judgment as to content.[31]

Authorized by the Federal Property and Administrative Services Act of 1949 (41 U.S.C. 251, et seq.), the *Federal Acquisition Regulations System* writes and maintains standard acquisition policies and procedures for all executive departments and agencies. An *agency* is any department, military service or entity of the Executive Branch.[32] This system comprises the *Federal Acquisition Regulation* (FAR) and any supplementary agency acquisition regulations. FAR is issued under the authority of the Office of Federal Procurement Policy Act of 1974 (31 U.S.C. 1352), as amended at 41 U.S.C. 410. It is maintained under the statutory authorities of GSA, DoD and NASA.[33]

The FAR is updated periodically as regulations are approved for inclusion. Updates are made through Federal Acquisition Circulars (FACs). They are numbered sequentially after identifying the year of the current FAR edition. This book is current through FAC 05-93, through the end of 2016.

The Federal Acquisition System strives to obtain the best value product or service for the Government, maintain public trust, and fulfill public policy goals. The system envisions such objectives as:

- achieving public policy goals;
- acquisition team members working together with authority to make decisions within their area of responsibility;
- competition whenever practicable;
- contractors with a proven record of success;
- cost reductions;
- fair and open business dealing to maintain public integrity;
- maximum use of commercial off-the-shelf (COTS) products and services; and
- satisfied customers.

The FAR uses the same numbering system as this book. Discussion is broken down into part, subpart, section, and subsection. These are divided by periods except for use of a hyphen between subpart and section. Subdivisions at a lower level are designated by parenthetical letters and numbers, logically distinguished by alternating capital and small letters with Arabic or Roman numerals. Hence the most complicated citation would look something like: 1.2-3.4(E)(6)(g)(viii).

The *Office of Federal Procurement Policy* (OFPP) is an office within the Office of Management and Budget (OMB) to assist in FAR development and develop overarching acquisition policy for the entire Federal Government.[34] OFPP has issued reports about best procurement practices, workforce development and contracting out governmental functions. However, OFPP may not always practice a proactive approach, to carefully avoid organizational battles with executive agencies and departments with their own defined jurisdictions and their own tried-and-true methods. For example, the Department of Labor exercises sole authority to issue labor policies, not OFPP. As a result, OFPP has achieved few policy accomplishments of note.

The FAR is managed by the FAR Secretariat within the GSA and consists of two councils. The Civilian Agency Acquisition Council (CAAC) reports to the administrator of GSA. The CAAC members are full-time representatives of the:

- GSA (chair);
- each department except Defense, Justice, and Housing and Urban Development;[35]
- Environmental Protection Agency;
- Social Security Administration; and
- Small Business Administration.

Because a large amount of contract dollars are spent by the Department of Defense (DoD), it draws special interest from Congress, along with numerous statutory requirements unique to itself. Hence, DoD has created the Defense Acquisition Regulations Council (DAR Council), reporting to the Secretary of Defense. Members of the DAR Council represent the:

- Undersecretary of Defense (chair);
- Army;
- Navy (including Marine Corps);
- Air Force;
- Defense Contract Management Agency;
- Defense Logistics Agency; and
- National Aeronautics and Space Administration.[36]

Although they are politically separate, both councils must:

- agree on any FAR revisions;
- submit to the FAR Secretariat all proposed actions for publication;
- consider all comments received;
- arrange public meetings;
- prepare a final revision; and then
- submit final rules to the FAR Secretariat for publication.

Individual agencies are free to develop and implement their own regulations to supplement FAR. Prominent among these supplements are the DoD FAR Supplement (DFARS) and NASA's Procurement Regulation. DoD's supplement is in fact even larger than the FAR due to the myriad of defense-unique legislation and peculiar requirements of military weaponry.[37] Agency regulations are not run through the FAR Secretariat for review and comment, but rather are managed by the department or agency itself. However, they must still go through public comment if they impact contractors in terms of cost or administrative burden, and are therefore submitted through the FAR Council for publication in the *Federal Register*. Public comment periods are normally 60 days (30 for urgency). Due consideration is given to all responses, and the proposed rule may be altered to enter a final state. Final rules are also submitted to the FAR Council for publication in the *Federal Register*.

All proposed regulations are also subject to two specific statutes. The Paperwork Reduction Act (44 U.S.C. 3501, et seq.) mandates that any regulation requiring the public (including a contractor) to provide information or complete a form must explain to an office within OMB why it needs the information and how much time and money the public will spend in its completion and submission. Secondly, the Regulatory Flexibility Act (5 U.S.C. 601, et seq.) requires the agency to examine the impact of its proposed regulation and information collection on small businesses and consider flexible alternatives to mitigate this burden.

The FAR Council adjusts all statutory acquisition-related dollar thresholds in the FAR for inflation every five years (the next revision is anticipated in 2020) based on the Consumer Price Index.

A department or agency may seek a *deviation* to use (or not use) a policy or provision as required in FAR, including modifications thereto, or to change a prescribed financial limitation. This may be perfectly acceptable to recognize a unique agency circumstance, or as an improved method of doing business. The agency head can approve any individual deviation that pertains to only one contract action, but a deviation applying to a class of contract actions must be reviewed by the FAR Secretariat, DAR Council or NASA Assistant Administrator for Procurement, before agency head approval. Deviations to comply with a treaty or executive agreement are automatically granted if they are not inconsistent with statute-based FAR coverage.

1.5 FEDERAL CONTRACT FORMATION

1.5.1 Acquisition Organization

The acquisition office is the focal point for the acquisition team to handle each procurement action. This office hosts the contracting officer, negotiator, legal counsel, and small business specialist. The requiring activity or program will provide the program manager and technical representative, and its cognizant finance office will furnish the comptroller both to certify availability of funds and to provide the accounting data against which the contractor will be paid. Other specialists such as logisticians and security specialists are furnished by agencies as required. Each acquisition team member uses personal initiative and sound business judgment to provide best value service to meet customer needs. Teamwork is the key to success of the acquisition.

Among the goals of a purchasing organization, both Government and corporate, are to:

* develop reliable multiple sources of supply to ensure uninterrupted flow of materials;
* integrate with other organization functions;
* maintain good vendor relations; and
* minimize inventory investment.

Written purchasing policies and a procedures manual are necessary to communicate and clarify goals of the contracting office. Policies can be furnished to both employees and vendors to illustrate organizational responsibility and authority, facilitate consistent buying practices, set any limits and prohibitions, and disseminate procedural changes.

Some organizations use a centralized purchasing office to perform all operations. This arrangement permits:

* economic ordering;
* formal and on-the-job training;
* long-range planning;
* negotiating strength;
* operating multi-site operations; and
* procurement research.

However, centralized procurement can challenge local vendor selection or responsiveness to local customer concerns, and could result in longer lead times. Hence, many agencies also use decentralized field contracting offices to support a local facility in a wide range of requirements. Examples of such local facilities include a military base or station, national park or veterans' hospital. Local buying has several advantages:

* buy smaller quantities of materials and simple specialized items;
* obtain services from local operators, thereby improving community relations;
* reduce transportation costs; and
* shorten lead times.

Purchasing and production departments/program offices have a common goal of efficient and productive operations. Their philosophies differ however – production wants all they need of the best materials, while procurement wants a reasonable quantity of acceptable quality. Yet these departments must effectively communicate with each other regarding requirements and priorities, such as urgent need versus lead time. They must also cooperate in developing standards and specifications.

Corporate decisions may have ramifications for the corporate procurement office which places subcontracts. A firm may undergo vertical integration to gain control of additional shares of production and marketing, which means the purchasing department may need to expand. Or a firm can horizontally expand to buy a competitor, which promotes opportunities to buy in larger quantities. Finally, a firm that diversifies introduces the opportunities to buy into other product lines. Consolidations or mergers also have implications for the corporate procurement office. Issues to deal with include establishing a common purchasing policy, consolidating orders to achieve economies of scale, and buying exclusively from other divisions.

Many contracting offices use a checklist to review incoming purchase requests to ensure that all necessary documents are present, and to help the contract specialist notify the requestor what else is needed. These checklists will then serve as a to-do list for the contract specialist as a visual cue of what remains to be done, and a record of dates when individual steps in the procurement process have been accomplished.

Contracting offices may be subject to *contract management review* to assess their interpretation and application of contracting policies, general performance, use of good business sense, and operational issues such as staffing talent and shortages. They may also participate in a *fast-track program*, an acquisition with tight time constraints which compresses or overlaps design, development, production, testing, and other support processes.

The performance of a contracting office must be measured to validate its success as an organizational asset. Performance measurement criteria include management effort and profitability, as well as purchasing effectiveness, efficiency and proficiency. A common metric is *procurement administrative lead time*, the period between receipt of a valid purchase request and award (some firms extend this time to include receipt of goods ordered). Also, review and approval by upper management is required for a number of contracting actions. These normally include acquisition plans, negotiated deals (to ensure consistency with pre-negotiation position and good business sense), and legal actions. The firm or agency may have an average length of time for the given transaction type to use as a barometer for performance. Similarly, standards assess each procurement employee to measure quality by number of errors and timeliness for completing each action.

The procurement request must be workable before this lead time may commence, since the contract specialist cannot begin procurement work until the package is adequate. Lead time is thus a valid metric to assess the effectiveness of the contracting office. Typically, each specialist will need to submit an exception report explaining why actions have been on hand for an excessive period of time, as defined by office management. As a rule of thumb, excessive time could be 30 days for simplified actions and six months for major acquisitions. Factors which impact lead time include:

- advanced planning;
- completion of procurement package;
- level of competition;
- procurement complexity; and
- requirements definition.

1.5.2 Contracting Officer

FAR 1.6

The *contracting officer* is a Federal employee who is authorized to award and administer contracts on behalf of the United States. This official receives a warrant (suitable for framing) from the agency head which sets forth any limitations on authority, such as dollar threshold of obligation. (S)he bears great latitude to exercise business judgment and maintain fairness and integrity of the acquisition process, and has the authority to determine the application of rules, regulations and policies to a specific contract. Contracting officers are selected based on their experience in Government or commercial contracting and administration, education (e.g., accounting, business administration, law, or engineering), and training in acquisition courses. Some military personnel also hold warrants as part of their work duties. Warrants are terminated for departure or reassignment, or for unsatisfactory performance, but cannot be terminated retroactively.

Contracting officers often have assistants (often called *procurement analysts* or similar nomenclature) who develop documentation and solicitations, analyze cost and pricing data, assist in negotiations and source selection activities, and handle a myriad of other tasks. These are usually civil servants or contract employees, and provide an environment to develop future contracting officers.

FAR Part 4

Only contracting officers sign contracts on behalf of the United States, normally after signature by the contractor, ensuring that the signer(s) have authority to bind the contractor. Contracting offices distribute copies of contracts or modifications within 10 working days after final signature to the contractor, procuring contracting officer, paying office, administrative contracting officer, and accounting office(s). Electronic commerce and transmission of documents is encouraged for all parties. Contractors who must submit any paper documents are encouraged to print double-sided on recycled paper, although there is no penalty for not doing so.

Contracting officers work closely with legal counsel to select appropriate solicitation provisions and contract clauses. *Provisions* are used in solicitations, while *clauses* are included in contracts, though many citations are used for both purposes. Provisions and clauses are listed in their topical section throughout this book, including their FAR citation.

The authority to make decisions and be accountable for same is delegated to the lowest level within the agency that is permitted by law or regulation. Agencies can also issue a *delegation of procurement authority* to another agency to take advantage of a contracting vehicle already in place, or to consolidate requirements for greater purchasing power.

The contracting officer is part of an interdisciplinary *integrated project team* created from multiple stakeholders to successfully execute an acquisition. Government team members must be empowered to make acquisition decisions within their areas of responsibility, including selection, negotiation and administration of contracts and determining the application of rules, regulations and policies on a specific contract. The contracting officer uses the warrant to commit the Government, leads the negotiation team, and serves as business manager for the acquisition.

All acquisition officials, especially contracting officers, must meet education and training standards established by the department or agency.[38] Undergoing extensive training for the position, the contracting officer must have the personality and experience to work with technical personnel, yet reports along a separate chain of command. Key traits for the contracting officer are:

- ability to perceive and exploit power;
- analytical capability of contractor:
  - accounting systems,
  - costs and prices,
  - decision-making process, and
  - purchasing system;
- communicating effectively as Government spokesperson;
- knowledge of acquisition laws and regulations;
- knowledge of economic and market conditions, and the industry and product/service;
- mathematical analytic techniques (e.g., learning curves, regression and correlation);
- performance measurability;
- planning ability; and
- sound judgment and common sense.

1.5.3 Central Contractor Registration

FAR 4.11

Prospective contractors must register in the System for Award Management (SAM), which consolidates a number of previous databases, such as the Central Contractor Registry and the Online Representations and Certifications Application database, in order to receive a contract or agreement. The only awards allowed for unregistered contractors are:

- classified contracts;
- contracts under $30,000 with foreign firms;
- deployed or contingency contracting;
- micropurchases (currently limited to $3,500) paid on a Government purchase card; and
- public urgency.

The contracting officer twice verifies the contractor's enrollment in SAM: once when establishing a competitive range, and again before issuing an award. If not listed, the contractor is provided a specified number of days to enroll or else lose the award. Once enrolled in SAM, a prospective contractor receives a Commercial and Government Entity (CAGE) code unique to its location, and its basic identification information is stored in the database. A firm with multiple locations will have multiple CAGE codes. CAGE codes are assigned by the Defense Logistics Agency for firms operating within the United States and its possessions, or by a NATO agency or member nation if outside this geographic area.[39]

The contractor should also have a Data Universal Numbering System (DUNS) number for database entry. This is a unique nine-digit number assigned by Dun & Bradstreet to register the firm to obtain solicitations, submit offers and issue shipping notices and invoices. A unique number is assigned to each division, location and subsidiary of the firm. It is a necessity to conduct electronic commerce as a trading partner, which serves to expedite the procurement process and expedite cross-industry and international transactions. Issuing unique numbers eliminates any confusion that might result when multiple firms have similar names, and its electronic nature permits cross-reference to delivery and performance information and other members of the same corporate family.

The firm must complete a questionnaire of several pages affirming compliance with Federal laws, then submit these *representations and certifications* to SAM (https://www.acquisition.gov) for use across all Federal contracting offices, rather than completing them for each solicitation and every contracting office. The contractor should update SAM data entries annually to ensure currency and accuracy, especially if its size status changes for different categories of supply or service.

Contract Clauses

FAR 52.204-6, Unique Entity Identifier, or 52.204-7, System for Award Management.
FAR 52.204-13, System for Award Management Maintenance.
FAR 52.209-9, Updates of Publicly Available Information regarding Responsibility Matters.
FAR 52.212-1, Instructions to Offerors—Commercial Items.

1.5.4 Contract Reporting

FAR 4.6

The Federal Procurement Data System (FPDS) is a web-based means for agencies to report contracts, orders and modifications. Data is reported to Congress, GAO and OMB to assess the effectiveness of socioeconomic programs and public policy initiatives, and to publicize Federal award data. The contracting officer submits a *contract action report* for each procurement action, and must confirm its content for accuracy before award. FPDS also runs an *ezSearch* function on its website www.fpds.gov for users to locate Federal contracts and procurement data. All actions are reported to FPDS except:

- any non-appropriated fund obligations, even if mixed with appropriated funding;
- contract actions in which the required data would constitute classified information;
- grants and entitlement actions;
- interagency agreements;
- lease and supplemental lease agreements for real property;
- letters of obligation used for A-76 studies;
- orders from GSA stock and the GSA Global Supply Program;
- resale activity (e.g., commissaries, exchanges or GSA or AbilityOne service stores);
- revenue–generating arrangements (e.g., concessions);
- training expenditures not issued as contracts or orders; and
- transactions at or below the micro-purchase threshold, including imprest fund and Government purchase card charges.

1.5.5 Government Contract Files

FAR 4.8

Contracting offices maintain complete contract files for each solicitation and each award. Contracts generally result in three different files – contracting office, contract administration office and paying office. The contracting office file (sometimes called a *jacket*) includes many documents, which should be tabbed for easy location upon file review. These documents should be stored in roughly the following order, as applicable:

* purchase request;
* acquisition planning information;
* Justifications and Approvals;
* Determinations and Findings (e.g., contract type and deviations from regulations);
* documentation of availability of funds;
* synopsis of proposed solicitation;
* list of sources solicited;
* list of sources denied with reasons;
* set-aside decision;
* Government cost estimate;
* solicitation and all amendments thereto;
* security requirements and evidence of required clearances;
* complete copy of each offer or quotation;
* abstract of bids or proposals;
* determinations of late offers or quotations (unsuccessful offers may be stored separately with a cross-reference in the contract folder);
* contractor's representations and certifications;
* preaward survey reports;
* source selection documentation;
* determination of contractor responsibility;
* Small Business Administration Certificate of Competency;
* records of contractor compliance with labor and equal employment opportunity policies;
* Certificates of Current Cost or Pricing Data;
* packaging and transportation data;
* cost or price analysis;
* audit reports or reasons for waiver;
* record of negotiation;
* required approvals of award and legal review;
* notice of award;

- original signed contract and modifications;
- synopsis of award;
- notice to unsuccessful offerors and record of debriefing;
- acquisition management reports;
- bond documents and notices to sureties;
- report of postaward conference;
- notice to proceed;
- stop-work orders;
- overtime premium approvals granted at the time of award;
- documents requesting and authorizing modification of contract administration functions and responsibility;
- (dis)approvals of requests for waivers or deviations from contract requirements;
- rejected engineering change proposals;
- royalty, invention and copyright reports;
- contract completion documents;
- documentation of termination actions;
- cross-references to pertinent documents that are filed elsewhere;
- documents that reflect other pertinent contracting office actions; and
- chronological list identifying and dating the awarding and successor contracting officers.

The contract administration office file includes:

- copy of the contract and all modifications;
- authorized modification of contract administration functions and responsibility;
- security requirements;
- cost or pricing data and certificates of currency;
- cost or price analysis;
- preaward surveys;
- purchasing system information;
- consent to subcontract or purchase;
- bonds and surety information;
- postaward conference records;
- delivery and task orders;
- notice to proceed and stop-work orders;
- insurance policies or certificates;
- advance or progress payments documentation;
- expediting and production surveillance records;
- quality assurance records;

- property administration records;
- termination actions;
- cross-references to pertinent documents filed elsewhere;
- administrative actions; and
- contract completion documents.

The paying office contract file contains:

- the contract and any modifications;
- invoices, vouchers and supporting documents; and
- record of payments or receipts.

A contract or agreement is considered to be physically complete and no longer active when delivery or services are complete and accepted, all options have expired, or termination has been issued by the contracting officer. Agreements for rental or storage are physically complete upon termination or when the contract period expires.

All contract files are closed out to minimize storage needs once the contracting officer completes the following actions:

- receive notification of physical completion;
- resolve remaining administrative issues:
  - appeals, litigations or terminations,
  - classified material disposition,
  - final patent and royalty reports,
  - plant or property clearance reports, and
  - value engineering change proposals;
- finalize price:
  - contract audit,
  - interim or disallowed costs,
  - prior year indirect cost rates, and
  - subcontract settlements;
- ensure the contractor completes a closing statement and final invoice;
- deobligate any excess funds;
- issue a contract completion statement; and
- issue a final invoice.

The paying office closes its contract files when issuing the final payment voucher. Files for simplified acquisitions are generally closed upon receipt of property and final payment. Files for higher-value firm-fixed-price contracts are due for closeout within six months after the contracting officer receives evidence of physical completion. Files for other contract types requiring settlement of indirect cost rates are closed within 36 months of when the contracting officer receives evidence of physical completion, or longer if rates remain unsettled. Any other contract is normally closed within 20 months of physical completion.

FAR 4.7

Closed-out contracts are sent to off-site storage and retained for possible litigation or inquiry. Various contract-related documents have differing retention periods, as follows:

Table 1.1

DOCUMENT	*RETENTION PERIOD*
Simplified acquisition files (non-construction)	3 years after final payment
Contract files exceeding the simplified acquisition threshold (non-construction)	6 years and 3 months after final payment
Construction contracts: $2,000 or less	3 years after final payment
Construction contracts: Over $2,000	6 years and 3 months after final payment
Construction contractor's payrolls and related data	3 years after contract completion
Unsuccessful offers within the simplified acquisition threshold	1 year after date of award or until final payment, whichever is later
Unsuccessful offers above the simplified acquisition threshold	Same as contract file (if filed separately, until contract completion)
Data submitted to FPDS	5 years after submittal
Files for canceled solicitations	5 years after cancellation
Records pertaining to Contract Disputes Act actions	1 year after final action or decision
Investigations, protests or cases pending or in litigation	Until final clearance or settlement, or specified retention period, whichever is later
Contractor and subcontractor records of contract negotiation and administration	3 years after final payment
Financial and payment records	4 years after final payment
Timesheets and payroll disbursements	2 years
Supply and service requisitions	2 years
Maintenance and property records, purchase orders, and quality and inspection records	4 years after final payment
Contractor paper copies of key records	1 year to validate accuracy of the imaging system

Solicitation Provisions

FAR 52.204-5, Women-Owned Business (Other Than Small Business), unless a small business set-aside below the simplified acquisition threshold and performed outside the United States.

FAR 52.204-6, Data Universal Numbering System (DUNS) Number, if expecting to notify FPDS.

FAR 52.204-7, Central Contractor Registration, in which case do not include the following representations and certifications:

- 52.203-2, Certificate of Independent Price Determination.
- 52.203-11, Certification and Disclosure Regarding Payments to Influence Certain Federal Transactions.
- 52.204-3, Taxpayer Identification.
- 52.204-5, Women-Owned Business (Other Than Small Business).
- 52.209-5, Certification Regarding Responsibility Matters.
- 52.209-2, Prohibition on Contracting with Inverted Domestic Corporations–Representation.
- 52.214-14, Place of Performance—Sealed Bidding.
- 52.215-6, Place of Performance.
- 52.219-1, Small Business Program Representations (Basic & Alternate I).
- 52.219-2, Equal Low Bids.
- 52.219-19, Small Business Concern Representation for the Small Business Competitiveness Demonstration Program.
- 52.219-21, Small Business Size Representation for Targeted Industry Categories Under the Small Business Competiveness Demonstration Program.
- 52.219-22, Small Disadvantaged Business Status (Basic & Alternate I).
- 52.222-18, Certification Regarding Knowledge of Child Labor for Listed End Products.
- 52.222-22, Previous Contracts and Compliance Reports.
- 52.222-25, Affirmative Action Compliance.
- 52.222-38, Compliance with Veterans' Employment Reporting Requirements.
- 52.222-48, Exemption from Application of the Service Contract Act to Contracts for Maintenance, Calibration, or Repair of Certain Equipment Certification.
- 52.222-52, Exemption from Application of the Service Contract Act to Contracts for Certain Services—Certification.
- 52.223-1, Biobased Product Certification.
- 52.223-4, Recovered Material Certification.
- 52.223-9, Estimate of Percentage of Recovered Material Content for EPA-Designated Items (Alternate I only).

- 52.223-13, Certification of Toxic Chemical Release Reporting.
- 52.225-2, Buy American Act Certificate.
- 52.225-4, Buy American Act—Free Trade Agreements—Israeli Trade Act Certificate (Basic, Alternate I & II).
- 52.225-6, Trade Agreements Certificate.
- 52.225-20, Prohibition on Conducting Restricted Business Operations in Sudan—Certification.
- 52.225-23, Required Use of American Iron, Steel, and Manufactured Goods—Buy American Act—Construction Materials Under Trade Agreements.
- 52.226-2, Historically Black College or University and Minority Institution Representation.
- 52.227-6, Royalty Information (Basic & Alternate I).
- 52.227-15, Representation of Limited Rights Data and Restricted Computer Software.

FAR 52.204-8, Annual Representations and Certifications, except for commercial item solicitations.

Contract Clauses

FAR 52.204-1, Approval of Contract.

FAR 52.204-4, Printed or Copied Double-Sided on Recycled Paper, if over the simplified acquisition threshold.

FAR 52.204-2, Security Requirements, if classified work is involved. Use Alternate I for an educational institution and Alternate II for construction or architect-engineering contracts.

FAR 52.204-9, Personal Identity Verification of Contractor Personnel.

1.6 STANDARDS OF CONDUCT

1.6.1 Ethics

Ethics address professional actions in terms of behavior, character, conduct, and morality. Executive Order 12674, "Principles of ethical conduct for Government officers and employees," April 12, 1989, as modified by Executive Order 12731 (same title), October 17, 1990, requires all public servants to:

- act without preferential treatment to any private organization or individual;
- avoid any actions creating the appearance of violating the law or ethical standards;[40]

- avoid financial transactions using Government information for private interest;
- comply with all laws and regulations that provide equal opportunity for all Americans;
- disclose waste, fraud, abuse, and corruption to appropriate authorities;
- make no unauthorized commitments alleging to bind the Government;
- place loyalty to the Constitution, law and ethics above private gain;
- protect and conserve Federal property;
- refrain from any financial interests or outside employment or activities that conflict with duty; and
- solicit or accept no gift or item of monetary value from any contractor or its employee.

Each agency head develops annual agency ethics-training plans which include mandatory annual briefings on ethics and standards of conduct for all designated employees, including contracting officers and procurement officials. Members of the Senior Executive Service and military flag officers must file financial reports annually and face limits on outside income. All Federal employees have current and post-employment restrictions on their financial interests and activities, which are subject to civil sanctions.

Military officers also face ethics rules. Per 18 U.S.C. 281, retired regular military officers cannot ever sell anything to their former department, or else they will face a $10,000 fine and two years in prison. 37 U.S.C. 801 prohibits the same officers from selling to anybody in DoD for the first three years of retirement. Since avoiding even the appearance of a conflict of interest is paramount, retired officers must complete a DD Form 1357 annually to address their activities. There is no criminal penalty for failure to furnish, however it does contain an acknowledgement of the Privacy Act to avoid privacy concerns. Since this requirement is stated for all officers before they sign on, it is not considered to be discriminatory or a conflict of interest. This restriction does not apply to reserve officers in order to avoid concern over civilian job instability and insecurity, nor to active or reserve enlisted personnel.

Contractor employees undergo training each year to ensure that neither they nor their immediate family members have any financial interest or simultaneous employment with a subcontractor. Nor can they have any offer of prospective employment with another firm who might benefit from the knowledge they obtain during contract performance. Some contractors will go so far as to forbid their employees any financial benefit gained from any firm which does business with the Federal Government.

1.6.2 Conflict of Interest

FAR 3.11 and 9.5

A *conflict of interest* occurs if a person or entity has a personal or financial interest that conflicts or appears to conflict with his or her official responsibility. An *organizational conflict of interest* arises when the nature of the work to be performed on a contract creates an actual or potential conflict of interest for the entity on the current or a future contract. This would more likely occur when providing consulting or management support services, engineering effort with follow-on development or production, or technical evaluations of other contractor proposals. Such services could lead to an unfair competitive advantage or impair objectivity or unbiased judgment in contract performance. There are statutes on both the Federal and state levels to address these conflicts, and most firms impose similar restrictions on their employees to ensure corporate responsibility. There are several scenarios which could lead to such conflicts, each of which will need to be fully discussed below.

No company may use proprietary or sole source information obtained from a Government official for personal gain – namely, obtaining a contract.[41] The contracting officer alerts the company in writing of the issue and why it is a perceived conflict, and requests a response. Then the Government decides whether to establish a conflict on record, withdraw the concern, or pursue a waiver. The agency head or designee may waive any conflict of interest upon written determination that enforcing the rule would not be in the Government's interest.

To avoid making decisions favoring its own capabilities, any contractor that provides systems engineering or technical direction cannot become responsible for follow-up development or production effort, and must agree not to receive a supply (sub)contract for the system. This restriction requires some explanation. A *system* organizes hardware, software, data, facilities, material, personnel, and services to perform a specific operational function with desired results. *Systems engineering* applies scientific and engineering efforts to convert this operational need into a description in terms of system design, written specifications, test requirements and data evaluation, and interfaces resolution. The goals of systems engineering are to:

- achieve technical parameters;
- assure compatibility of program interfaces;
- integrate with other disciplines and specialties; and
- optimize total system definition and design.

Key to success of systems engineering is the *technical direction* from the Government program office needed to write work statements and performance parameters, direct other contractors' performance, and address technical controversies.

Another scenario concerns a *nondevelopmental item*, either a commercial product or one that was developed under a previous contract. These items require no research, development, test, or evaluation (with or without minor modification) to make the product suitable for Government needs. They may or may not already be in Government inventory. However, any contractor who develops specifications for a nondevelopmental item which will be competitively acquired cannot furnish the item as either a prime or subcontractor for a reasonable period of time (at least for the initial production contract). Again, this prevents the contractor from biasing specifications to favor its own product or production capabilities. Of course, this is not a problem if the contractor is the sole source of supply, or one of several contractors involved in developing the statement of work. Moreover, this rule does not apply where the contractor furnishes information for a product it already supplies, or serves as an industry representative to help the Government develop specifications while under Government supervision. Of course, such a contractor has often done an extensive amount of development in the field and can apply its knowledge to the Government's advantage. If so, the Government would not be wise to impose a conflict resolution, even if competition suffers.

A contractor who evaluates products or services from another vendor cannot evaluate its own products or services. It must perform under Government-imposed safeguards to ensure objectivity.

Any contractor who obtains proprietary information from other firms during contract performance could gain an unfair competitive advantage in future work. The contractor must therefore sign a *nondisclosure agreement* with these other firms to protect their information from unauthorized use or disclosure and promise not to use it for any purpose other than that for which it was furnished. Similarly, any marketing consultant engaged by the contractor must sign such an agreement, since the consultant might have access to proprietary information which could give the contractor an unfair advantage in future competition. The contracting officer retains signed copies of all of these agreements.

Where contractor employees perform acquisition functions close to inherently Government functions, they may gain access to nonpublic information. To protect its interests, the Government can obtain from each such employee a disclosure of financial interests of the employee and family and household members. This disclosure must be updated by the employee whenever a financial circumstance changes, rather than merely updating on an annual basis. The employee must also sign a nondisclosure agreement. Any conflicts must be reported by the contractor to the contracting officer for review and resolution. This issue does not apply to a self-employed individual contracting with the Government.

Under any of these scenarios, should the contracting officer decide that an acquisition presents a potential organizational conflict of interest, (s)he must submit to the chief of the contracting office before solicitation an analysis and recommendation of action, with a proposed solicitation provision and contract clause. The provision alerts potential offerors to the nature of the potential conflict, proposed restraint on their future activities, and whether these terms are subject to negotiation. The head of the agency can waive the requirement if determining this is in the Government's best interest.

Solicitation Provision and Contract Clause

FAR 52.203-16, Preventing Personal Conflicts of Interest, if over the simplified acquisition threshold and for acquisition functions which are similar to inherently Government functions.

1.6.3 Procurement Integrity

FAR 3.104

Restrictions on individual behavior ensure integrity of the procurement process. Some restrictions are absolute in nature. Bribes and gratuities are strictly forbidden. Procurement-sensitive information and contractor-specific information cannot be released outside appropriate channels. An employee cannot use nonpublic information to advance one's own interest or a financial transaction. Also, no proposal or source-selection information may be disclosed before award by a Government official (past or present) or advisor who had access to such information. Similarly, anybody who receives such information and does not report it is subject to criminal sanctions.

In accordance with the Procurement Integrity Act (41 USC 423), Government employees cannot seek employment with potential offerors or contractors on a task where they are personally and substantially involved. The term *participating personally and substantially* means to:

- develop or approve a solicitation, specification or statement of work;
- evaluate offers;
- negotiate price or terms and conditions;
- recommend, review or approve an award; or
- supervise an employee who performs any of these duties.

This definition excludes:

* certain general advisors;
* clerical support;
* members of boards or advisory committees who evaluate and recommend technologies or methods to achieve agency objectives; or
* participation in A-76 management studies.

Any Government official engaged in a procurement action above the simplified acquisition threshold who is contacted by an offeror regarding possible employment must report the contact to a supervisor. The official must either reject the possibility of employment or else be disqualified from further involvement in the procurement action.

A one-year compensation ban applies to certain Federal officials if the award value exceeded $10 million. These officials include:

* contracting officer;
* evaluator for either source selection or for financial or technical reasons;
* payment approver;
* program manager;
* rate determination official; or
* source selection authority.

However, this prohibition applies only to the division of the contractor performing under the given contract – the official is free to accept employment from the same corporation in a separate division or affiliate unrelated to this contract. Any violation of these laws could result in contract termination and contractor suspension or debarment. If the contract is with DoD, damages are also possible.

All evaluators of proposals must be free of conflict of interest and *bias*, the intent and act of favoring or disfavoring a particular offeror. The Government takes great care in educating its evaluators and protecting against conflicts and biases. Unless it can prove that the agency maliciously intended and in fact did cause it injury, an offeror will have great difficulty gaining relief from the courts or GAO.

1.6.4 Other Improper Practices

FAR 3.103

Any firm fixed-priced offeror above the simplified acquisition threshold certifies that it has not engaged in price *collusion*, or any agreement or understanding with another offeror. This includes any effort to induce another party not to submit an offer, as well as disclosing an offer price before public announcement of award. This restriction does not apply for two-step bids or utility services where prices are regulated. The contracting officer rejects any offer that is improperly certified, unless the offeror encloses a signed statement describing why he disclosed prices, in which case the contracting officer investigates whether collusion has in fact occurred. The contracting officer reports any positive findings to the Attorney General for investigation and prosecution.

FAR 3.3 through 3.10

Potential antitrust violations are reported to the Attorney General because they could indicate agreements between competitors to restrict open-market behavior. Examples of possible antitrust behavior include:

- an industry price list used by multiple companies;
- bidding low on some geographical areas or products and high on others;
- comments by employees (past or present) or competitors that such an agreement exists;
- identical calculation or spelling errors in two or more offers;
- joint bids without proper agreements of a teaming or pool arrangement;
- rotation of offers to allow competitors to take turns as low bidder; or
- simultaneous price increases.

Although contractors often have standing arrangements to pay contingent fees or commissions to marketing firms or consultants to solicit or obtain contracts, the potential of improper influence is evident. Therefore, a provision is included in all negotiated contracts above the simplified acquisition threshold (except for commercial items) to prohibit contingency fees other than standing arrangements with commercial agencies, at the risk of contract denial or price reduction by the amount of fee paid.

The Government policy of paying fair and reasonable prices means that an offer below anticipated costs is suspicious because the contractor could be planning to increase the contract price later through change orders, or else establish a noncompetitive future where prices will be greatly increased to recover initial losses. The Government can try to avoid these problems through multiyear contracting by pricing out the entire quantity to ensure the same unit pricing each year, or by using fixed-price options to avoid future unexpected price adjustments.[42]

The Anti-Kickback Act of 1986 (41 U.S.C. 51–58) specifically bars subcontractors from paying prime contractors to improperly obtain or reward favorable treatment regarding a contract award, or including the amount of a kickback in the contract price. Criminal and civil penalties may be imposed.

The GAO and the Inspector General of the contracting agency have the right to inspect the contractor's facilities and books, and the contracting officer can withhold the dollar amount of the kickback from payment. This restriction does not apply below the simplified acquisition threshold or for commercial items.

To avoid any conflict of interest or appearance of favoritism, no contractor owned or controlled by a Government employee may receive an award. This does not apply to special Government employees (as defined in 18 U.S.C. 202) who serve as consultants or on advisory committees. However, the contract cannot arise directly out of the individual's activity as a special Government employee, nor can award be influenced by the special employee.

Where a contractor or its official has been convicted (or pled guilty) and sentenced for the crimes listed below, or fails to disclose violation of same, the agency head or designee may rescind contracts and recover payments and property, and can begin suspension or debarment action:

- antitrust violations;
- bribery;
- embezzlement;
- falsification or destruction of records;
- forgery;
- fraud;
- making false statements, such as using a "Made in America" label on a foreign-made item;
- receiving stolen property;
- tax evasion;
- theft; or
- violating Federal criminal tax laws.

Every contractor must certify that neither it nor any employee has influenced a member or employee of Congress. Contractors may participate in general business discussions with agency personnel concerning their product or service offerings in conjunction with agency needs, and may engage in technical discussions regarding an unsolicited proposal submitted on its own initiative without a formal Government solicitation. Contractors are also free to hire employees or consultants to assist in bid and proposal preparation.

Any contractor employee can file a complaint with the Inspector General of the agency that awarded the contract claiming illegal demotion, discrimination or dismissal. The head of the agency can order the contractor to take affirmative action or reinstate the employee with backpay and compensation for legal fees. Failure of the contractor to comply with this order will result in referral to the Attorney General for injunctive relief and compensatory and exemplary damages. Similarly, the contractor cannot fire, demote or discriminate against an employee who discloses to a Government authority any information concerning abuse of authority, danger to public health or welfare, mismanagement of contract funds, or violation of any law or regulation.

A contractor who fails to disclose a violation of Federal law involving fraud, conflict of interest, bribery, or gratuity faces up to three years of suspension and debarment. A *gratuity* is any item of monetary value given to an individual in expectation of receiving preferential treatment, and a *bribe* is a gratuity of money. Similarly, failure to refund an overpayment could lead to suspension or debarment.

Several other similar restrictions are also in force. Unless a contractor furnishes only commercial items or performs entirely outside the United States, it must display a poster provided by the Government identifying the Inspector General's Fraud Hotline existence and telephone number in accordance with agency direction. Both DoD and NASA have the authority to reduce or suspend contract payments for up to six months based on evidence of fraud without any formal conviction. DoD also has a Voluntary Disclosure Program for contractors to disclose their potential civil or criminal fraud violations and conduct their own internal investigation, which freezes any Government administrative action until the investigation is verified. Finally, insider trading of securities or property or assets is illegal if based on non-public information obtained from a consultancy.

A pilot program applies to most civilian agencies[43] to prohibit any reprisal for an employee who discloses mismanagement, waste or abuse under a Federal contract or subcontract to the Inspector General of the agency. Based on the findings of the Inspector General, the contracting officer may direct the contractor to resolve the problem, reinstate the employee, and/or compensate the employee for legal fees and damages.

Contract Clauses

FAR 52.203-2, Certificate of Independent Price Determination.

FAR 52.203-5, Remedies to the Government for Contingent Fees.

FAR 52.203-7, Anti-Kickback Procedures.

FAR 52.203-11, Certification and Disclosure Regarding Payments to Influence Certain Federal Transactions.

FAR 52.203-12, Limitation on Payments to Influence Certain Federal Transactions.

FAR 52.203-13, Contractor Code of Business Ethics and Conduct, for solicitations and contracts expected to exceed $5.5 million and a performance period of at least 120 days.

FAR 52.203-14, Display of Hotline Poster(s).

FAR 52.203-15, Whistleblower Protections Under the American Recovery and Reinvestment Act of 2009 (Public Law 111-5), in contracts funded by the Act.

FAR 52.203-17, Contractor Employee Whistleblower Rights and Requirement to Inform Employees of Whistleblower Rights.

1.7 LEGAL CONSIDERATIONS

1.7.1 Inherently Governmental Functions

FAR 7.503

Contractors cannot perform *inherently governmental functions*. Agencies decide what tasks are entailed in this term, subject to OMB approval. Examples of these functions include effort to:

- administer public trusts;
- approve agency responses to Freedom of Information Act requests;
- approve contractual documents;
- approve Federal licenses and inspections;
- ascertain agency or foreign policy and application of regulations;
- award and administer contracts;
- collect, control and disburse public funds (unless authorized by statute);[44]
- command military forces;
- conduct administrative hearings to determine eligibility for a security clearance or participation in Government programs;
- conduct criminal investigations;
- control Treasury accounts;
- decide budget policy, guidance and strategy;
- decide Government property disposition;
- decide whether contract costs are reasonable, allocable and allowable;
- determine Federal program priorities for budget requests;
- determine what supplies or services are to be acquired by the Government;
- direct and control Federal employees;
- direct intelligence and counterintelligence operations;
- draft testimony and correspondence responses to Congress or a Federal auditor;
- interview and select individuals for Federal Government employment;
- perform prosecutions and adjudications;

- ratify position descriptions and performance standards for Federal employees;
- terminate contracts; and
- vote on any source selection boards or performance evaluation boards.

Examples of functions that are not generally considered to be inherently governmental functions, but which might come close to crossing the line, include:

- acquisition planning;
- arbitration or providing alternative methods of dispute resolution;
- budget preparation;
- construction secured from electronic eavesdropping;
- developing regulations or statements of work;
- evaluating another contractor's performance;
- feasibility studies and strategy options to develop policy;
- gaining access to confidential business information;
- inspection services;
- legal advice and interpretations of regulations and statutes;
- policy interpretation (e.g., attending conferences on an agency's behalf or conducting agency training courses or community relations campaigns);
- preparing responses to Freedom of Information Act requests;
- prisoner detention or transport and national security details;
- reorganization and planning activities; and
- technical evaluation of contract proposals and advising a source selection board.

Several precautions are in place to address these gray areas. A designated agency official provides with the statement of work a written determination that no functions to be performed are inherently governmental. This assessment includes discretionary authority, decision-making responsibility, and accountability of Government officials using contractor services or work products. Also, consulting services should be temporary or intermittent in duration and cannot be used to bypass personnel ceilings or pay limitations. Finally, preference for award cannot be given to former Government personnel.

1.7.2 Federal Budget

A *budget* lists all planned expenses and revenues for a firm or a given program. A budget can be thought of as a model of how the firm or program might perform financially if certain plans are fully implemented. Management will then measure financial performance against the budgeted forecast to assess performance. Budgets usually cover an entire twelve-month period, known as a *fiscal year*, which may or may not coincide with the calendar year (the Federal Government's fiscal year begins October 1 and expires September 30). All governments at all levels prepare budgets. Nearly all states are required to have balanced budgets, where revenues equal expenditures, but the Federal Government is allowed to run deficits.[45]

The budgeting process in the Federal Government is unique and follows a series of individually named steps which are followed one at a time. First, the annual United States Government budget is prepared by the Office of Management and Budget, which conducts data calls through all Federal departments and agencies, and compiles the results. The budget includes a spending plan that shows the state of the Treasury at three different points of time:

- end of last fiscal year (September 30);
- end of current fiscal year; and
- end of upcoming fiscal year.

The President then signs the budget and submits it to Congress by the first Monday of February. Related documents such as the Economic Report of the President are included, along with a description of proposed spending priorities and justifications. This submission is necessary because Federal budget authority to enter into financial obligations derives from the Constitution, which says, "No money shall be drawn from the Treasury, but in Consequence of Appropriations made by Law."[46] At this point, Congress enters the budgeting process.

Both the House of Representatives and the Senate have Committees on the Budget which draft budget resolutions, usually before the Easter break. These resolutions are then submitted to their respective chambers for consideration and adoption. The two chambers then select members to serve on a conference committee to resolve differences between the two versions, after which the chambers will vote on the conference version. This resolution may bind Congress, but not the nation, so it does not require presidential approval. Rather, it is a blueprint for the upcoming appropriation process.

Next, congressional committees and staff members hold public hearings and mark-up sessions, and inevitably make numerous substantial changes. Some changes result from legitimate disagreements with the administration over spending priorities and program needs, while others are congressional initiatives resulting from political desires to spend Federal dollars on a specific project or initiative.[47] The end result will be a process to authorize and appropriate funds to operate the Federal Government.

Unfortunately, these are two separate processes with two separate sets of players. *Authorization* by Congress permits agencies to run programs, but funding is not included. This is because funding for Federal programs must first be authorized by an oversight committee for the department or agency concerned. Their deliberations lead to an Authorization Act for the department. These committees have the authority to decide what programs and policies to allow. This also means that the authorization phase comes before the appropriation phase.

Appropriation is the process by which Congress approves funds for specifically authorized programs. Appropriations are set aside by Congress for specific purposes, such as operations and maintenance, procurement, and research and development. However, the Appropriations Committee for both the House and Senate are responsible for "seeing the big picture" of Federal operations and is free to make changes to the Authorization Committee decisions. So despite the directions set down in the various authorization acts, the Appropriations Committee of each chamber sets the funding levels, which may not be consistent with the authorization bill. All appropriations must go only to authorized programs, but not all authorized programs may be funded. To add to the confusion, authorizations for some programs may lapse yet still be funded, while other authorized programs may receive no funds at all. Appropriation bills may also contain policy direction, which may or may not coincide with the Authorization Committee's wishes.

There are currently 12 appropriation bills enacted each fiscal year, corresponding to the jurisdiction of the respective House and Senate appropriation subcommittees:

- Agriculture;
- Commerce, Justice and Science;
- Defense;
- Energy and Water;
- Financial Services;
- Homeland Security;
- Interior and Environment;
- Labor, Health and Education;
- Legislative Branch;
- Military Construction and Veterans Affairs;
- State and Foreign Operations; and
- Transportation, Housing and Urban Development.

Once both chambers of Congress agree on an appropriations bill, it must be signed by the President to become law. The President is free to veto the bill within ten days of arrival, outlining in writing his reasons for veto. Congress may override the veto by a 2–3 margin in each chamber, in which case the bill automatically becomes law without further action. Otherwise, Congress must act to revise the bill to meet the President's objections, propose an alternate approach, and then resubmit the bill to the President.

If Congress cannot enact a bill by the end of the fiscal year, a *continuing resolution* may be adopted to continue Government operations at the same spending rate as the prior year. If such a resolution is not adopted and signed by the President, the Government is theoretically out of business and Federal agencies must shut down. This is because the *Anti-Deficiency Act* (31 U.S.C. 1341) prevents the contracting officer from making any commitments without sufficient appropriated funding. Contractors must cease performing against their contracts or else face the prospect of not being reimbursed for their effort.[48] The department then spends the funds provided by the continuing resolution at the same pace as in the prior year, or in compliance with additional congressional direction.

As if more bewilderment were necessary, some appropriations bills may be enacted, but not others. It is therefore conceivable that come October 1, some departments may be fully funded and operating as usual, while others are either under a continuing resolution or else shut down (or maybe partly closed and partly open). The legislative process is truly a series of multiple power centers, repetitive processes and endless compromises.

Each budget item can be classified as either discretionary or direct spending. *Discretionary spending* is an appropriation for a fixed period of time, usually concurrent with the fiscal year. Since these funds must be obligated by September 30, Federal contracting offices are under pressure to obligate them by the end of the fiscal year before they expire (hence the term *expiring funds*).

In an alternative vein, *multi-year funding* is specifically granted by Congress for programs they designate. Congress will make multi-year appropriations for purposes of housing, research and development, and some military systems. This approach reduces administrative burden, broadens the competitive base through higher quantities, lowers costs, and permits continuity of performance or phase-out costs. Alternatively, *no-year funds* assure timely liquidation for acquisition and availability of adequate funds at time of award, but are not required to be funded in any specific year.

By contrast to discretionary spending, *direct spending* is enacted by law but not dependent on an annual appropriation bill. This includes most entitlement programs such as Food Stamps, Medicare, Medicaid, and Social Security. It is not normally used to fund Federal contracts.

Once money has been fully appropriated, the executive agencies proceed through several steps to ensure the money goes where intended. *Apportionment* is how OMB provides appropriated funds to the departments and agencies. *Allotment* is how a department divides apportioned funds among its operating divisions. Each division then follows their department guidance to provide funds to the individual program office.

Once funds have been provided to the appropriate office, they must go through yet another lengthy process to get on contract. *Commitment* is the administrative reservation of funds against a future contract, and is done before the procurement package reaches the contracting officer. *Obligations* are funds reserved for payment by an agency's authorized administrative component (e.g., comptroller or accounting authority). *Expenditures* or *outlays* are funds actually disbursed to a contractor for work completed. This will not match the budget authority for the fiscal year because some of the funds can be disbursed in future years, just so they are obligated in the current fiscal year. The program office and contracting officer must take care to ensure that funds are used only for their intended purpose (known colloquially as the *color of money*) to ensure that the directions of Congress are correctly implemented.

The biggest difference between public and private sector accounting is fiscal accountability. A Government agency must demonstrate compliance with law and budgetary directives for managing resources. By contrast, the private sector uses budgeting as a planning tool, not as a compliance (and sometimes not even as a management) tool. Another difference is that the Government recognizes revenue when the money is available, not when earned to liquidate liabilities. Similarly, the Government records expenses when charged to revenue rather than when incurred.

1.7.3 International Trade

FAR 25.4

The Federal Government has entered into a variety of free trade agreements and the World Trade Organization Government Procurement Agreement which identify certain supplies and services that are exempted from the restrictions of the Buy American Act. Offers from these nations bear the same consideration as domestic offers and do not incur a price differential for evaluation purposes.

The following regulations govern the export of commercial and defense articles:

- The International Traffic in Arms Regulations (22 CFR 120–130),[49] issued by the Department of State, control the export of defense-related articles, services and technical data, ensuring compliance with the Arms Export Control Act. The U.S. Munitions List identifies these items.

- The Export Administration Regulations (15 CFR 730–774), issued by the Department of Commerce, control the export of dual-use commodities, software, and technology. These items are commercial in nature, but may have military applications as well. They are listed by Export Control Classification Number on the Commerce Control List.
- National Security Decision Directive 189, National Policy on the Transfer of Scientific, Technical and Engineering Information,[50] directs that the products of fundamental research be unrestricted as much as possible. Contracts for unclassified fundamental research generally do not involve any export-controlled items, information or technology.

Trafficking persons for involuntary servitude and debt bondage is forbidden to DoD contractors, with penalties imposed by agency regulation. If the contracting officer receives information of such an event, (s)he must immediately notify the Combatant Commander responsible for the geographical area in which the incident has occurred. No comparable policy applies to civilian agencies.

The contracting officer may direct the contractor to litigate the applicability of a foreign tax if the contract is a cost-reimbursement type, or a fixed-price type with a tax – escalation clause. Some international treaties may exempt the United States from paying specific taxes. The Department of State publishes a list of treaties on its website at www.state.gov.

1.7.4 Delegation of Authority

Authority to make decisions within the acquisition community is generally delegated to the lowest level, consistent with law. The contracting officer has the authority to determine the application of rules, regulations and policies on a given contract.

FAR 1-602.3 and 50.103-2

As prescribed by Public Law 85-804 (15 U.S.C. 1431), under rare circumstances the Government can amend a contract without consideration to ensure fairness and the national interest, such as when a loss under one contract will impair the contractor's ability to perform on a separate, essential contract. The loss must be more than just lost profit – it must go to the heart of the contractor's ability to perform. If the Government caused the action which led to the contractor's distress, fairness would dictate such an adjustment.

Mistakes can be corrected as well by the contracting officer, such as ambiguity in contract wording as to the meaning of the parties, obvious mistakes that the parties did not see during contract formation, or mutual mistake of a material fact.

Unauthorized (or informal) commitments occur when a firm responds to a Government official's written or oral instructions and delivers supplies or services in anticipation of compensation without a formal contract. The official must have the apparent authority to issue the instruction, but lack real authority (which should be a rare occurrence, since somebody has overstepped their authority to create the situation). Again, fairness would dictate the contractor be paid a reasonable amount for expended effort. Only the head of the contracting activity can ratify an unauthorized commitment. However, if the value of the action exceeds $70,000, ratification must be furnished by the Secretary of the Department. The resulting contract must still fulfill all requirements for properness, including a fair and reasonable price and available funding at the time of the occurrence. The firm must submit its request for payment within six months of the incident which gave rise to the informal commitment.

Contract Clause

FAR 52.250-1, Indemnification Under Public Law 85-804, for indemnification aginst hazardous or nuclear risks. Add Alternate I for cost-reimbursement contracts.

1.7.5 Personal Identity Verification

FAR 4.13

If a contractor will have routine physical access to a federally controlled facility and/or information system during performance, the contract will contain provisions to comply with Federal Information Processing Standards Publication (FIPS PUB) Number 201, "Personal Identity Verification of Federal Employees and Contractors," and Office of Management and Budget (OMB) Guidance M-05-24, "Implementation of Homeland Security Presidential Directive (HSPD) 12-Policy for a Common Identification Standard for Federal Employees and Contractors."[51,52] Agency procedures require that the contractor account for all Government personal identity cards or badges issued to its employees, and return them upon contract completion or employee departure. If the contractor fails to do so, final payment may be withheld.

Contract Clause

FAR 52.204-9, Personal Identity Verification of Contractor Personnel.

1.7.6 Recovery and Reinvestment

FAR 4-15

The American Recovery and Reinvestment Act of 2009 (Public Law 1115), commonly known as the Recovery Act,[53] was designed to combat a serious economic recession by creating jobs promoting advances in health and science, and investing in national infrastructure needs such as public works and energy efficiency. The contracting officer tries to establish separate contract line items to ease reporting requirements and avoid commingling recovery funds with other sources. The contractor must report:

- completion status of the work;
- delivered supplies and rendered services;
- estimated number of jobs created and retained as a result of the Act funds;
- invoice amounts;
- names and total compensation of the five highest-compensated officers for the calendar year of contract award; and
- similar information on first-tier subcontractors.

Contract Clause

FAR 52.204-11, American Recovery and Reinvestment Act—Reporting Requirements, except for classified contracts.

1.7.7 Protection of Individual Privacy

FAR 24.1

The Privacy Act of 1974 (5 U.S.C. 552a) mandates agencies follow certain procedures and safeguards to collect, store and disseminate *personally identifiable information* which permits one to infer an individual's identity (e.g., name, home address, or office phone list). Protecting such information is essential to engender public trust in data collection and prevent identity theft. Agencies prescribe their own procedures for protecting such information, such as applying protective markings, encrypting internal e-mail, keeping data off Internet pages or share drives, and locking up hardcopy. These procedures will warn the individual against unauthorized information loss or sharing, browsing without authority, or leaving a workstation without protection. Any Government employee who willfully discloses or obtains such information could be fined up to $5,000, and any contractor could be responsible for paying costs for replacement, theft protection and possibly attorney's fees.

Within the context of privacy, a *record* is any item or collection of information about an individual that is maintained by an agency (e.g., criminal or employment history, education, financial transactions, and medical history). A record contains the individual's name and identifying number or symbol (including a fingerprint, photograph or voiceprint). When an agency contracts to design, develop, maintain, or operate a *system of records* (a group of records from which information is retrieved by the individual's name or identifying number or symbol) on individuals on behalf of the agency, then the contractors and their employees are considered employees of the agency in terms of Privacy Act criminal penalties. The system of records is deemed to be maintained (or collected, used or disseminated) by the agency and is subject to the Privacy Act. Agencies which fail to require that such contractor operations conform to the act may be civilly liable to individuals who claim injury under the act. The contract work statement specifically identifies the system of records on individuals and the design, development or operational work to be performed. The solicitation will also make available any agency rules and regulations implementing the act.

Contract Clauses

FAR 52.224-1, Privacy Act Notification.

FAR 52.224-2, Privacy Act.

1.7.8 Freedom of Information Act

FAR 24.2

A proposal submitted in response to a competitive solicitation is not provided to any person under the Freedom of Information Act (5 U.S.C. 552), unless incorporated by reference in a contract. Agencies do not disclose any information that is exempt from disclosure by the Freedom of Information Act due to:

- agency personnel practices;
- classified information;
- confidential commercial or financial information;
- interagency or intra-agency memoranda;
- law enforcement;
- personal and medical information pertaining to an individual; and
- trade secrets.

Releasable information is provided through the Federal Register, a requestor visit to the archives with copy privileges, or mailing a copy to the requestor.

1.8 INTELLECTUAL PROPERTY

Intellectual property pertains to creations resulting from mental labor and original thought. These creations are intended to improve competitiveness, employment, productivity, public services, or standard of living. They give rise to intangible yet legal monopoly rights for the creator or owner, which are then codified in paper or software. For example, someone who buys this book owns the physical or electronic copy purchased, however the author retains the intellectual rights to the content (through a copyright).

1.8.1 Patents

FAR 27.2

A *patent* is a set of rights granted by a government to an inventor which lasts for a predetermined number of years (usually 20), in exchange for the inventor publicly disclosing details of the invention. One can patent a product, process or composition, including an improvement thereto, but not an abstract idea or a law of nature or physics. Patent rights originated in common law.

A patent prevents another party from making, using or selling the item or process without the inventor's permission. However, it does not in and of itself grant the inventor the right of use or practice, but rather just a property right. An employer owns the patent for an invention developed by its employee; in all other instances, the individual owns the patent rights.

The Government encourages practical commercial use of any inventions made under its contracts.[54] Permitting the contractor to retain patent rights (with licensing to the Government for contract performance only) not only motivates commercial development of inventions and promotes competition, but it also minimizes the costs and rights of Government usage. General rules for U.S. patents with its contractors are:

- the Government may authorize and consent to the use of inventions to perform contracts, even if covered by existing U.S. patents;
- contractors providing commercial items indemnify the Government against liability for patent infringement. But if the product is specifically manufactured for the Government, the contractor will usually be indemnified by the Government for patent infringement;

- the Government recognizes rights in data developed at private expense and therefore restricts its demands for data delivery and rights to only what it needs for its purposes;
- contractors must obtain permission from copyright owners before including their copyrighted works in data deliveries;[55]
- the only remedy for patent or copyright infringement in Government contracting is for monetary damages in the Court of Federal Claims (injunctive relief will not be granted);[56]
- a third party can neither enjoin the Government nor sue a contractor for infringement; and
- the Government requires notice and assistance from its contractors regarding any claims for patent or copyright infringement.

Section 6 of Executive Order 12889, "Implementation of the North American Free Trade Act," of December 27, 1993, waives the need for a Federal contractor to obtain advance authorization to use or manufacture an invention. However, the patent owner must be notified in advance (or in cases of urgency, as soon as possible) whenever the agency or its contractor knows or should know that a patented invention is or will be used or manufactured without a license. This notification does not constitute admission of patent infringement.

Solicitation Provisions and Contract Clauses

FAR 52.227-1, Authorization and Consent, whenever patents are involved. This clause is optional in simplified acquisitions and prohibited when complete performance and delivery are outside the United States. Use the clause with its Alternate I for research and development, but not for standard construction and architect-engineer effort. Use the clause with its Alternate II for communication services with a common carrier which are not regulated by a tariff schedule approved by a regulatory agency.

FAR 52.227-2, Notice and Assistance Regarding Patent and Copyright Infringement, if using the Authorization and Consent clause.

FAR 52.227-3, Patent Indemnity, for delivery of commercial items. Do not use this clause for simplified acquisition procedures, performance and delivery outside the United States, or when inconsistent with commercial practice. Use the clause with either its Alternate I (to identify excluded items) or II (to identify included items) if performance also requires delivery of noncommercial items. Use the clause with its Alternate III for a common carrier whose communication services and facilities are not regulated by a tariff schedule from a regulatory body.

FAR 52.227-4, Patent Indemnity Construction Contracts, for construction or fixed-price contracts to dismantle, demolish or remove improvements. Do not use for architect-engineer services. Use the clause and Alternate I for patent indemnification to use nonstandard or noncommercial structures, products, processes, or methods.

FAR 52.227-5, Waiver of Indemnity, in addition to the appropriate patent indemnity clause.

FAR 52.227-10, Filing of Patent Applications Classified Subject Matter, where the classified nature of the work might result in a patent application containing classified subject matter.

1.8.2 Inventions

FAR 27.3

An *invention* is a discovery that is or may be patentable.[57] Recall that the Government uses the patent system to promote the use of inventions arising from federally supported research or development to boost free enterprise and commercialization. This approach ensures that the Government obtains sufficient rights in federally supported inventions to meet its needs and protect the public against their nonuse or unreasonable use.

The contractor must notify the Government of an invention created or made under contract performance (known as a *subject invention*) within two months after notification by the inventor. *Made* means the invention's conception or first actual reduction to practice. Generally, each contractor may, after required disclosure to the Government, elect to retain title to any subject invention.

The contractor will then issue a license to cover its technical data, knowledge or related assistance. The license can be exclusive, partially exclusive or nonexclusive. The license is *exclusive* if it allows production or sales within a given territory without competition.

The Government reserves a license to practice, or have practiced for it, any subject invention with the following five rights, at a minimum:

- irrevocable – cannot be terminated by the licensor during the contract period of performance (the only remedy is for monetary damages);
- nonexclusive – more than one party has the right to practice, which reflects the Government's desire to promote use of the invention;
- nontransferable – ownership of the invention remains with the original owner and is not transferred to either the Government or a third party;
- paid-up – all royalties are included within the contract price; and

- worldwide – no restriction on the geographic territory for the right to practice.

Regardless of the type of license, the Government reserves the rights to:

- continue prosecution of a patent application;
- receive and retain title to an invention in which the contractor has failed to disclose or file a patent application in time;
- require periodic reporting on how any subject invention is being used by the contractor or its licensees or assignees;[58] or
- retain additional rights to comply with treaties or other international agreements.

A special problem results for inventions which are not created as part of contract performance. A *background invention* was created before contract award or at private expense, and is licensed or owned by the contractor. Any background inventions used during contract performance will be subject to negotiated rights and restrictions between the parties. Generally, a commercial item or one developed without Government financial support (either internally or with support of an external, non-Government entity) will yield only the contractor's standard commercial license.

The Government has the right to revoke or modify the contractor's license. However, the contracting officer must first furnish the contractor with a written notice of intention to do so, and allow the contractor 30 days to show cause as to why the license should not be revoked or modified. The contractor has the right to appeal the contracting officer's decision.

The contracting officer (dis)approves, in writing, any contractor request to transfer its licenses to an outside party. If the Government wishes a third party be licensed for performance but the patent holder does not concur, the Government has avenues open to it.

Agencies have *march-in rights* that require the contractor (or its assignee or licensee) to grant a license to responsible applicants for any invention conceived or first reduced to practice under a Government contract. This must be a functional and workable invention (rather than one which is simulated or contemplated but still nonexistent). A contractor may not be happy about this if it has invested in technological research or simulation. As a result, some commercial firms may refuse to participate in Federal research and development contracts, and private lenders may consider this right to be too risky for investment. On the other hand, the Government may object to paying a royalty for an item not yet workable. Here the parties must negotiate a contract clause to protect their respective rights. March-in rights are rarely invoked but are available if the contractor fails to grant a license when required.[59] The Government can also exercise march-in rights if the contractor or assignee has not satisfied health or public-use requirements.

Even if the contractor refuses to grant such a license, the agency can grant the license itself if it shows that the contractor is not achieving practical application of the subject invention. *Practical application* means to manufacture a composition or product, practice a method or process, or operate a machine or system. Before a license is granted, however, the contractor or assignee has an opportunity to establish that the invention is being utilized and that its benefits are available to the public on reasonable terms.

No contractor or assignee titled to any invention may grant anybody the exclusive right to use or sell the invention in the United States unless that person or entity also manufactures domestically any products which include the subject invention. This is a manifestation of the Buy American preference endemic to Government contracting. However, the agency can waive this requirement if the contractor or assignee has tried without success to grant licenses to potential domestic manufacturers, or if domestic manufacture is not commercially feasible.

If the contractor elects not to retain title to an invention, the Government may grant the inventor retention of rights. However, if a Government employee is a co-inventor under a contract with a small business or nonprofit organization, the employee's agency may license or assign its rights in the invention from its employee to the contractor.

Alternatively, the Government may choose to acquire title to a subject invention. In this case, the contractor is normally granted a worldwide, revocable, nonexclusive, paid-up license which extends throughout the corporate structure to all divisions and subsidiaries. Such a license includes the right to grant sublicenses if legally required.

Other special situations may lead to Government titling. The Government may require a foreign contractor to assign to it the title to an invention. It may also restrict or eliminate the contractor's right to retain title in an invention in order to promote Federal patent policy or national security, or in accordance with agency regulations. This mostly applies to managing naval nuclear propulsion or weapons facilities. However, even when the Government has the right to acquire title, the contractor may still request greater rights to a subject invention. These additional rights are subject to negotiation.

A small business or nonprofit contractor may assign title to the Government for national security. Such a contractor may also elect to own an unclassified invention with unlimited dissemination within six months of its report to the agency.

When the Government acquires the entire right, title and interest in an invention by contract, the chain of title from the inventor to the Government is clearly established by an assignment. The path of assignment is either from the inventor through the contractor to the Government, or from the inventor directly to the Government with the consent of the contractor.

A contract with a small business or nonprofit firm precludes the Government from requiring a license of any contractor-owned invention to third parties. However, the agency head may approve a written justification that use by others is necessary to achieve practical application of subject invention. The contractor may appeal this determination within 60 days after the notification.

Contracting activities establish appropriate procedures to detect and correct failures by the contractor to comply with its obligations under the patent rights clauses. These efforts focus on research and development, high dollar value projects, and any firm who may not be complying with its contractual obligation. The agency will use means such as:

- checking the Official Gazette of the United States Patent and Trademark Office for other patents issued to the contractor;
- inspecting contractor laboratory notebooks and technical reports;
- interviewing agency and contractor technical personnel; and
- observing the work on-site.

The contracting officer must carefully choose a proper patent rights clause from the selection below. Often, (s)he will consult a patent attorney who specializes in patent law. If one Government agency requests another to award a contract on its behalf, the request either specifies the patent rights clause to be used or else directs the awarding agency to use its own clause. In any case, there is no patent rights clause required for construction work or architect-engineer services that use only previously developed equipment, methods and processes. Variations in aesthetics or artistry alone are insufficient grounds to include a patent rights clause.

Contract Clauses

FAR 52.227-11, Patent Rights Ownership by the Contractor. The contracting officer may modify to require contractor invention listings and filing information, and furnish the Government an irrevocable power to inspect and copy the patent application file if a Government employee is a co-inventor. Use alternate versions as follows:

- Alternate I to grant a foreign government a sublicense per treaty or executive agreement;
- Alternate II to allow for impact of future treaties or agreements;
- Alternate III for a nonprofit organization to operate a Government-owned facility;

- Alternate IV to operate a Government-owned facility; and/or
- Alternate V to reserve the right to inspect data at the contractor's facility.

FAR 52.227-13, Patent Rights Ownership by the Government, if:

- the contractor is not located in the United States or is subject to the control of a foreign government;
- the agency head determines that restriction or elimination of the right to retain title to any subject invention will better promote the Government's policy and objectives;
- a Government authority in foreign intelligence or counterintelligence activities determines that restriction or elimination of the right to retain any subject invention is necessary to protect national security; or
- the contract includes the operation of a Government-owned, contractor-operated facility of the Department of Energy primarily dedicated to naval nuclear propulsion or weapons-related programs.

The contracting officer may supplement the clause to require the contractor to:

- furnish a copy of each subcontract containing a patent rights clause;
- provide the filing and issue dates, serial and patent numbers, and title for any patent application filed on any subject invention in any country;
- submit interim and final invention reports and notification of all subcontracts awarded for experimental, developmental or research work; and
- submit periodic reports on the utilization of a subject invention.

Use the clause with its Alternate I if the Government must grant a foreign government a sublicense in subject inventions pursuant to a treaty or executive agreement, or the agency head determines at time of award that it would be in the national interest to sublicense foreign governments or international organizations pursuant to any existing or future treaty or agreement. Use the clause with its Alternate II to reference such a treaty or agreement.

1.8.3 Rights in Data

FAR 27.4

This section does not apply to the Department of Defense (DoD) – it has its own methodology to determine rights in data. This process is discussed in DFARS Part 227. All other federal departments and agencies follow the policies outlined in this section.

Data is recorded information, regardless of form or the media on which it may be recorded. Within the context of data rights, the term includes technical data and computer software. It does not include administrative, cost or pricing, financial, or management information.

Across the Federal Government, agencies require data to obtain competition and ensure logistics support. They disseminate and publish the results of their activities, and release technical information to promote subsequent technological developments. Because contractors may have proprietary interests in their data, agencies protect proprietary data from unauthorized use and disclosure, and encourage contractors to participate in and apply innovative concepts to Government programs.

The Government acquires data with *unlimited rights* when it is first produced in the performance of a contract, which permits the Government to:

- disclose;
- distribute copies to the public;
- perform and display publicly;
- prepare derivative works;
- reproduce;
- use; and
- to have or permit others to do the above in any manner for any purpose.

These rights pertain to *form, fit and function data* that provide a technical description of the product, which will enable physical and functional interchangeability of items or processes. This approach covers such product features as configuration, functional characteristics, and performance capabilities and requirements. The Government will use this data to competitively procure comparable items, which is why it will usually require unlimited rights. The definition excludes algorithms, computer software, formulas, flow charts, processes, and source code. However, this definition does apply to manuals or training material to install, operate and maintain items or processes.

Generally, a contract contains only one data rights clause. However, where more than one is needed, the contract distinguishes the portion of contract performance to which each clause pertains.

The contractor can protect its data and restricted computer software by insisting on limited rights for the Government to its form, fit and function data. *Limited rights* restrict the Government to those rights set forth in a Limited Rights Notice provided by the contractor. Limited rights data also embody *trade secrets*, information of a secret process or procedure used by the firm to gain a competitive advantage. A trade secret is a process or design that is confidential in nature pertaining to items or components developed at private expense, including minor modifications thereto.

Examples include drawings, formulas, processes, and techniques. Again, this definition excludes computer software. Trade secrets never expire so long as the information is kept secret.

Firms protect their trade secrets through state law (implementing the Uniform Trade Secrets Act[60]) rather than any Federal protection. Agencies cannot disclose limited rights data outside the Government without contractor permission. Any permitted Government disclosure is subject to prohibition against further use and disclosure by the recipient. This protection is manifested through use of nondisclosure agreements which specify sensitive information that the parties will share but agree not to disclose to third parties, or through *noncompete clauses* (where one party agrees not to compete against the other party). Either both parties to these agreements are firms or agencies, or else one party is an employee of the firm or agency.[61] Situations where these restrictions could occur include:

- emergency repair or overhaul work;
- evaluation outside the Government;
- release to a foreign government when in the Government's best interest;[62] and
- use by support – service contractors on the same program.

The Government can require delivery of *restricted computer software* developed at private expense with limited rights. The contracting officer identifies and specifies the deliverable computer software, either in the contract or else during contract performance. Restricted computer software cannot be reproduced by the Government or disclosed outside the Government. However, it may be used or copied for use with the computers for which it was acquired or for a backup computer. The software can be modified or combined with other software subject to the same restricted rights, and could be disclosed or reproduced for use by support-service (sub)contractors. Many companies consider the source code and the software design and specificatons to be trade secrets and copyright the balance of the software. The license then protects it from forbidden practices such as reverse engineering.

The contracting officer may specify different rights in the contract, consistent with the purposes and needs for which the software is to be acquired (e.g., networking, remote terminals, etc.). These restricted rights may differ from the program documentation and databases. Any additions or limitations to restricted rights are expressly stated in the contract or collateral agreement incorporated in the contract.

There is a way for an employer to use his/her employee's invention. A *shop right* is a common-law right of an employer to use an invention patented by one or more employees without liability for infringement. The employer receives a royalty-free license to use a patented invention of the employee(s) developed on the employer's time or facilities.

Solicitation Provision

FAR 52.227-15, Representation of Limited Rights Data and Restricted Computer Software, when also containing the Rights in Data—General clause, if the contracting officer desires to have an offeror state whether limited rights data or restricted computer software are likely to be used to meet the data delivery requirements set forth in the solicitation.

Solicitation Provisions and Contract Clauses

FAR 52.227-14, Rights in Data–General, in solicitations and contracts where data will be produced or acquired, except for the following:

- architect-engineer services or construction;
- co-sponsored research and development in which a clause providing for less than unlimited rights has been authorized;
- existing data or commercial software;
- construction, design, management, or operation of a Government-owned facility to perform research, development or production work;
- performance outside the United States;
- production of special works; or
- small business innovation research.

Use the clause with its Alternate I if an agency determines to adopt the alternate definition of "Limited Rights Data." Use the clause with its Alternate II if a contracting officer determines to obtain limited rights data, and specify any purposes for which limited rights data are to be disclosed outside the Government. Use the clause with its Alternate III if a contracting officer determines it is necessary to obtain restricted computer software and specifies any greater or lesser rights regarding the use, reproduction or disclosure of restricted computer software than those set forth in the Restricted Rights Notice. Use the clause with its Alternate IV in contracts for basic or applied research (other than to manage or operate Government facilities or on-site programs, or where international agreements require otherwise) to be performed solely by universities and colleges (the contract may exclude items or categories of data from the permission granted). Use the clause with its Alternate V if the Government invokes the right to inspect certain data at a contractor's facility.

FAR <u>52.227-19</u>, Commercial Computer Software License, in solicitations and contracts (other than from GSA's Multiple Award Schedule contracts) for commercial computer software.

1.8.4 Copyrights

FAR 27.404-3

A *copyright* protects an author from another party copying or using his/her creative works without permission. This prohibition includes modifying content into a derivative work, or distributing copies of the work without permission. A copyright is valid for the life of the author plus 70 years.

The contractor must usually obtain contracting officer permission before asserting rights in any copyrighted work containing data which was first produced during contract performance. In its request, the contractor identifies or provides the data involved and the intended publication or dissemination media. The contracting officer usually grants the contractor's request for a copyright unless the data is intended primarily for internal use by the Government, or merely the official views of the agency. The request could also be denied if the Government determines that it should be disseminated without restriction (e.g., in the national interest or normally distributed to the public). However, contractors do not need prior approval of the contracting officer to assert a copyright in technical or scientific articles published in academic, professional or technical journals, or symposia proceedings.

For copyrighted data first produced during contract performance, the contractor grants the Government a paid-up, nonexclusive, irrevocable, worldwide license. This license grants the right to reproduce the data, prepare derivative works, and display publicly by or on behalf of the Government. Unlike other data, however, the Government does not have the right to distribute copyrighted material to the general public. Agencies may revise the license to better disseminate the data or comply with international agreements.

The contractor must affix copyright notices and acknowledge Government sponsorship to data when it asserts copyrights, often on the first page, or else risk the data being treated as if with unlimited rights.

If a contractor delivers any data not first produced under the contract, it must acquire or grant to the Government a copyright license for the data, or otherwise obtain contracting officer permission.

Agencies do not place any restrictions on the conduct of, or reporting on the results of, unclassified basic or applied research by educational institutions. However, they may restrict the release or disclosure of computer software intended for practical application or agency distribution programs. The agency may also restrict an educational institution from exercising data rights, including assigning copyrights to the Government or other party, though this is not common for basic or applied research.

1.8.5 Markings

FAR 27.404-5

The Government has the right to return data containing unauthorized markings, or to cancel or ignore the markings. For example, marking adjustments could be necessary to comply with the Freedom of Information Act. The Government must notify the contractor in writing and allow 60 days to respond substantiating the validity of the markings. If the final decision is negative, the markings will be cancelled or ignored and the data released from disclosure prohibitions, unless the contractor files suit within 90 days.

Data delivered without a limited rights or restricted rights notice or copyright notice is presumed to have been delivered with unlimited rights as to disclosure, reproduction or use. However, within six months the contractor may request permission to place the omitted notice on qualifying data at its own expense. The contracting officer may permit adding a notice if the contractor:

* acknowledges that the Government is not liable for disclosure or use to date;
* identifies the data;
* proves that its omission was inadvertent; and
* shows that use of the proposed notice is authorized.

The contracting officer may permit correction, at the contractor's expense, of incorrect notices.

Contracting officers may obtain the right to inspect data at the contractor's facility to verify a contractor's assertion regarding the limited rights or restricted rights status of the data, or for evaluating work performance under the contract. This right may be exercised up to three years after acceptance of all items to be delivered under the contract.

1.8.6 Special Works

FAR 27.405-1

The contract may specify the purposes and conditions (including time limitations) under which data for special works may be used, released or reproduced for noncontract performance. *Special works* include:

* agency histories;
* data whose release could prejudice follow-on acquisitions or agency enforcement or regulatory activities;

- development of computer software programs that may give a commercial advantage or are agency-mission sensitive;
- investigatory reports;
- motion pictures or television recordings and scripts;
- musical compositions and sound tracks;
- personally identifiable information whose disclosure would violate the right of privacy;
- reports and books not involving research, development or experimental work;
- surveys of Government establishments; and
- works instructing Government officers and employees about their official duties.

As a rule, the contractor must indemnify the Government against any liability incurred as the result of any violation of copyrights, libel, right of privacy or publicity, or trade secrets due to any data production or compilation performed for Government use. However, this position is subject to negotiation or modification. For instance, the contracting officer may delete Government copyright assignment of data that was produced under the contract. When special works are produced for a public purpose rather than Government use, agencies may modify the clause with other data rights provisions that meet mission needs yet still protect freedom of speech and expression, and the creator's artistic license.

Commercial computer software and documentation is acquired under licenses customarily provided to the public consistent with Federal law and needs. However, a vendor's standard commercial lease, license or purchase agreement may be directed to commercial sales and therefore may not be appropriate for Government contracts. Hence, the contract terms take precedence over the vendor's standard commercial agreement.

No clause is required in contracts solely to acquire books and periodicals (unless reproduction rights are to be acquired), existing data (other than limited rights data) without disclosure prohibitions, or on-line database services available to the general public.

Solicitation Provisions and Contract Clauses

FAR 52.227-17, Rights in Data Special Works, if primarily to produce or compile data (other than limited rights data or restricted computer software) for the Government's internal use, when there is a specific need to limit data distribution and use, or to obtain indemnity for liabilities that may arise out of the data content, disclosure or performance. Use the clause if existing works are to be edited, modified or translated. The contract may specify the purposes and conditions (including time limitations) under which the data may be used, released or reproduced by the contractor for other than contract performance. Contracts for production of audiovisual works and sound recordings may include limitations in talent releases and music licenses.

FAR 52.227-18, Rights in Data Existing Works, if exclusively for existing audiovisual and similar works without any modification. The contract may need to address any reproduction rights to be acquired.

1.8.7 Data Acquisition

FAR 27.406

Data deliverables may include drawings, manuals and reports. Data activities such as cataloging, maintenance and updating, preparation, reformatting, and storage are expensive for both the Government and the contractor. Hence, contract data requirements must be minimized, and may even be assessed by a data requirements review board prior to solicitation to ensure their necessity and propriety. The contract must specify the data to be delivered because data rights clauses address only the respective rights of the Government and contractor regarding the data use, disclosure or reproduction. To accomplish this, the contracting officer specifies in separate contract line items all known data requirements, including the place and time for delivery and any restrictions for data handling. These items are spelled out in a *contract data requirements list* that is attached to the contract, and includes specifications for writing the data and delivery instructions.[63] The contract may identify and specify which data is to be delivered with unrestricted rights and which with limited rights. As a rule, listed data may be ordered any time up to three years after final acceptance. The contractor is entitled to reimbursement for converting data into the prescribed format.

Form, fit and function data may be solicited with unlimited rights (instead of the usual limited or restricted rights) for the offeror to price out. To minimize storage costs for data retention, the contracting officer may relieve the contractor of retention requirements. The contracting officer may also permit the contractor to identify any data which is not necessary to meet the Government's requirements and therefore should not be ordered.

If the Government wishes to acquire unlimited rights to technical data contained in a winning proposal, the offeror may specifically identify proposal pages containing technical data to be excluded from the grant of unlimited rights. Any excluded commercial, financial or technical information in the proposal will be used for evaluation purposes only.

The contracting officer reviews any delivered technical data included on a contract data requirements list, and the contractor's declaration that the data are complete, accurate and compliant with contract requirements. If (s)he finds to the contrary, the contracting officer requests the contractor to correct the deficiencies, and may withhold payment until the data delivery requirements have been met.

Some contracts involve co-sponsored research and development where the contractor contributes funds (by cost-sharing or repayment of nonrecurring costs), but cannot segregate Government contributions to any item or process developed or produced under the contract. In such cases, the contracting officer may limit the acquisition of, or acquire limited rights to, any data developed and delivered under the contract. These lesser rights must still assure that the data is used for agreed-to governmental purposes (and perhaps also reprocurement rights), and must address any disclosure limitations or restrictions imposed on the data. The contractor could be required to directly license others to meet the contract objectives. On the other hand, if the contractor's contributions are identified in the contract and can be segregated by performance requirements and contract funding, then any resulting data may be treated as limited rights data or restricted computer software.

Solicitation Provisions and Contract Clauses

FAR 52.227-16, Additional Data Requirements, for experimental, developmental, research, or demonstration work. Do not use for basic or applied research to be performed solely by a university or college. The contract amount must be $500,000 or less, unless all the requirements for data are believed to be known at the time of contracting and specified in the contract.

FAR 52.227-23, Rights to Proposal Data (Technical), if a contracting officer desires to acquire unlimited rights in technical data contained in a successful proposal upon which a contract award is based.

Contract Clauses

FAR 52.227-20, Rights in Data SBIR Program, in all Phase I, II and III contracts awarded under the Small Business Innovation Research Program.

FAR 52.227-21, Technical Data Declaration, Revision, and Withholding of Payment Major Systems, for major systems acquisitions or their support. This includes detailed design, development or production of a major system or any individual component, part, (sub)assembly,[64] subsystem, or spare part integral to the major system. The subject technical data is specified in the contract.

FAR 52.227-22, Major System Minimum Rights, in contracts to procure major systems or in support of major systems for civilian agencies other than NASA and the Coast Guard.

1.8.8 Royalties

FAR 27.202

A *royalty* is a right delegated to an individual or corporation by the Government (hence the name, since it is a sovereign entity) to share in the profit or product reserved by the grantor. A royalty is a payment to the holder of a copyright, patent or trademark for its use under a Federal contract.[65] This would include payments made to an author or composer for a sold work or to an inventor for each sold patented item.

If the proposal includes a charge for royalties, the contracting officer forwards the information to the cognizant patent office for advice. The contracting officer must take care to avoid paying royalties to which the Government has a royalty-free license, or at a rate greater than which the Government is licensed, or if they are improperly charged. Hence, the contracting officer may request a copy of the license, and the contractor may need to redact any confidential information before furnishing a copy.

When the Government is obligated to pay a royalty on a patent because of an existing license agreement and the contracting officer believes that the licensed patent applies to a prospective contract, the solicitation includes notice of the license, patent number and royalty rate cited in the license. The solicitation requires an offeror to state if it is the patent owner or licensee. The Government may either evaluate an offeror's price by adding an amount equal to the royalty, or negotiate a price reduction with an offeror who is licensed under the same patent at a lower royalty rate.

Agencies provide necessary policy and procedures regarding foreign technical assistance agreements and license agreements involving intellectual property, including avoiding unnecessary royalty charges.

Solicitation Provisions

FAR 52.227-6, Royalty Information, in a negotiated solicitation for which royalty information is desired and cost or pricing data are obtained. It can be used in sealed bid solicitations only if the need for such information is approved at a level above the contracting officer to properly protect the Government's interests. Use the provision with its Alternate I if the solicitation is for communication services and facilities by a common carrier.

FAR 52.227-7, Patents–Notice of Government Licensee, if the Government is obligated to pay a royalty on a patent involved in the prospective contract. Otherwise, the contracting officer may require offerors to provide information sufficient to provide this notice to the other offerors.

Solicitation Provision and Contract Clause

FAR 52.227-9, Refund of Royalties, in negotiated fixed-price solicitations and contracts when royalties may be paid. The clause may be used in cost-reimbursement contracts with agency approval of royalties to protect the Government's interests.

1.9 State and Local Taxes

FAR 29.4

The Federal Government is not exempt from Federal excise taxes imposed on purchasing:

- ammunition and firearms;
- coal;
- fishing equipment;
- heating and motor fuels; and
- motor vehicle tires.

In these cases, prices are solicited on a tax-exclusive basis, or else justified on a tax-inclusive basis. However, excise taxes are not imposed for:

- a nonprofit educational institution;
- emergency vehicles;
- export to a foreign country or distant U.S. possession within six months;
- resale or further manufacture (however, tires or inner tubes are still subject to excise tax);
- the exclusive use of a state or territory (or the District of Columbia); or
- use as fuel or stores onboard a war vessel (including aircraft and guided missiles bought on a tax-exclusive basis).

The Federal Government is exempt from a communications usage tax, and from the federal highway vehicle users tax if the vehicle is owned or leased by the Federal Government.

Federal purchases and leases are generally exempt from state or local taxes, although exemption forms may need to be filled out and filed. However, the law of agency does not apply to contractors, so subcontractors may be subject to state or local taxation. Also, because equipment rental contracts involve contractor-owned equipment, the possibility of property and usage taxes occurs.

The state of North Carolina has a unique law that authorizes local governments to be reimbursed by the state government for sales and use taxes paid on equipment and materials included in any building construction, alteration or repair. The Federal Government is entitled to such a refund, but must formally request it through a contractor-certified statement for property purchase and withdrawal.

The New Mexico Gross Receipts and Compensating Tax applies to cost-reimbursement contracts for services performed in whole or in part within the state. If the contractor acquires personal property as a direct cost and passes title to the U.S. Government, then the tax payment is an allowable cost.

Contract Clauses

FAR 52.229-1, State and Local Taxes, for leased equipment under a fixed-price indefinite-delivery contract, within the United States or its outlying areas, but unspecified at time of award.

FAR 52.229-2, North Carolina State and Local Sales and Use Tax, for construction to be performed in North Carolina. Use Alternate I for vessel repair.

FAR 52.229-3, Federal, State, and Local Taxes, for fixed-price contracts exceeding the simplified acquisition threshold and performed within the United States or its outlying areas.

FAR 52.229-4, Federal, State, and Local Taxes (State and Local Adjustments), instead of 52.229-3, for noncompetitive contracts to avoid contingency pricing for postaward changes in state or local taxes.

FAR 52.229-6, Taxes Foreign Fixed-Price Contracts, for fixed-price contracts exceeding the simplified acquisition threshold to be performed in a foreign country by. a commercial firm.

FAR 52.229-7, Taxes Fixed-Price Contracts with Foreign Governments, for fixed-price contracts that exceed the simplified acquisition threshold issued directly to a foreign government.

FAR 52.229-8, Taxes Foreign Cost-Reimbursement Contracts, for cost-reimbursement contracts to be performed in a foreign country, unless contracting directly with a foreign government.

FAR 52.229-9, Taxes Cost-Reimbursement Contracts with Foreign Governments.

FAR 52.229-10, State of New Mexico Gross Receipts and Compensating Tax.

NOTES

1. A *system* is defined in this book as a combination of elements that interact to achieve a specific purpose.

2. *Rescission* is unmaking a contract, whereas *termination* ends a contract prematurely. Rescission can be either unilateral or bilateral, based on either the need for equity or legal sufficiency, or on the presence of fraud, impossibility or mutual mistake.

3. The official name is "An Act for Prevention of Frauds and Perjuyies." It can be found at http://www.british-history.ac.uk/statutes-realm/vol5/pp839-842, Institute of Historical Research, London, United Kingdom. The original publication is Statutes of the Realm: Volume 5, 1628–80, Great Britian Record Commission, South London, United Kingdom, 1819.

4. The American Law Institute and the National Conference of Commissioners on Uniform State Laws, Uniform Commercial Code, Thomson West, Eagan, MN, 2014. A readily available location to access the UCC is https://www.law.cornell.edu/ucc.

5. References to sections in UCC will be designated by the section symbol §.

6. A *document of title* provides proof that the possessor has the right to receive, hold and dispose of the goods and document. Common examples are a bill of lading, warehouse receipt or delivery order.

7. These states are Maryland and Virginia. However, since it has no bearing on Federal contracting, UCITA will not be discussed further in this book.

8. This concept ensures fairness to the other party regardless of the amount of money involved, again despite the lack of any written formal agreement. Assent of parties is not required.

9. The offeree may or may not act as expected, but performance is nonetheless recognized by the court, because no promise was made.

10. We will address this issue later as an informal commitment.

11. UCC § 1-302 and 305.

12. Typographical or mathematical errors can be easily corrected and are not grounds for avoidance.

13. A condition precedent can also be a specific event that must occur in order for a party's right to become enforceable.

14. *Real property* is land or anything attached to it by act of man or nature, while *personal property* is any other tangible item that is movable. So your house is real property, but your furniture is personal property.

15. The assignor is still liable as a surety to the promisee, but this topic will be discussed later.

16. An *assortment of goods* defines the relationship in terms of features (e.g., type, model, measure, color).

17. In a court of law, to make tender in a timely manner is said to be *seasonable*, however this term is not used in Federal contracting.

18. If the precise amount of advance payments or liabilities is unknown at the time of the issue of the receipt, then a statement that they have been incurred and their purpose suffices.

19. This is known in Federal contracting as *key personnel*, and will be discussed later.

20. This tenet is known as the *benefit of the bargain*.

21. A cost is *reasonable* if not exceeding that which a prudent person would incur in the course of competitive business.

22. This approach is stated in *Russell v. Farley*, 105 U.S. 433 (1881): "[w]here no bond or undertaking has been required . . . the court has no power to award damages sustained by either party in consequence of the litigation, except by making such a decree in reference to the costs of the suit as it may deem equitable and just." All legal citations are from Government Printing Office, United States Reports, Washington, D. C. In this particular citation, the decision was handed down in year 105 of our nation and the case begins on page 433.

23. *Covering* includes any incidental damages, including pain and suffering.

24. The concept of mutual mistake is critical to Government contractors, for it is their only recognized method to obtain relief if the facts vary from the parties' beliefs at the time of contract.

25. *Addyston Pipe and Steel Co. v. U.S.*, 175 U.S. 211 (1899).

26. The official term in the UCC is *lease contract*, however the common term will be used in this book.

27. As used in this book, *process* means a group of tasks that are sequential and logically related to provide a product or service, either to a customer or to another organization of the firm.

28. The *Christian Doctrine* requires parties to read required clauses into Federal contracts that were inadvertently omitted. This position derives from *G.L. Christian and Associates v. U.S.*, 375 U.S. 954. The Christian Doctrine says that Government regulations have the force and effect of law, and must be read into the contract as if written into it, even if the contracting officer omits any FAR-prescribed clauses. Government contractors are presumed by the courts to be familiar with FAR and therefore should know what clauses are required in the contract.

29. An *industry standard* is a uniform identification of design, performance, quality, quantity, or service.

30. DoD is shorthand for the Department of Defense.

31. *Skidmore v. Swift & Co.*, 65 S.Ct. 161, and *American Telephone and Telegraph Co. v. United States*, 57 S.Ct. 170.

32. To avoid redundancy, the term *agency* will be used throughout the book to also include a department.

33. FAR is printed in the Code of Federal Regulations, Title 48, Chapter 1, and available online at www.acquisition.gov/?q=browsefar and in print from the Government Printing Office. The current edition was published in 2005. This regulation will be cited throughout this book.

34. OMB is responsible for developing and issuing Government-wide guidance on management processes, such as procurement, and to recommend and monitor funding levels.

35. Both Justice and Housing have lower levels of contract awards than other cabinet departments, and therefore do not pursue acquisition regulatory matters as vigorously.

36. The legislation that created NASA provided it with authority to write its own procurement regulation. NASA procurement policies follow DoD regulations very closely. So when it came time for NASA to select which council to sit on, it found more in common with the DAR Council, and thereby gained a seat at its table. Nonetheless, DoD in no way controls NASA's procurement regulations or procedures.

37. To discuss the policies and processes of DoD procurement would require another volume of similar size to this one.

38. DoD has taken the lead in establishing such standards to comply with 10 UCC 87, Defense Acquisition Workforce Improvement Act (DAWIA). However, all Federal departments and agencies with procurement authority have established their own program of on-the-job professionalism.

39. Certain entities do not have CAGE codes, so they receive a unique entity identifier. These are usually foreign entities who never perform within the United States, or else are an individual student or dependent of a foreign service or military member.

40. There is no allowance for a whistleblower to obtain part of any penalty imposed by a court, as would be the case in a *qui tam* action, where the claimant sues on behalf of both the Government and self to assert a right or demand.

41. *Proprietary information* is not publicly available and may only be used with the owner's permission.

42. An *option* is a unilateral contract right for a specified time during which the Government may elect to obtain additional quantities of supplies or services, or extend the period of performance.

43. This program does not apply to DoD, NASA, the Coast Guard, or the intelligence community.

44. Exceptions are concession sales or examining vouchers and invoices, which are not considered to be inherently governmental in nature.

45. The only state that permits a budget deficit is Vermont. By contrast, only Oregon restricts a surplus, which is currently 2%.

46. Article I, section 9, clause 7.

47. This is also known as *earmarking* or, more colloquially, *pork barrel politics*. The rise of the Tea Party movement could challenge the future of this political tradition.

48. This approach is known as "working at risk."

49. National Archives and Records Administration, Code of Federal Regulations, Washington, D.C., 2007. This citation means Title (similar to chapter) 22, pages 120 through 130.

50. National Security Council, "National Security Decision Directive 189, National Policy on the Transfer of Scientific, Technical and Engineering Information," National Archives and Records Administration, Washington, D.C., 1985.

51. Federal Information Processing Standards Publication (FIPS PUB) Number 201, "Personal Identity Verification of Federal Employees and Contractors," National Institute of Standards and Technology, Gaithersburg, Md., 2013.

52. Office of Management and Budget (OMB) Guidance M-05-24, "Implementation of Homeland Security Presidential Directive (HSPD) 12–Policy for a Common Identification Standard for Federal Employees and Contractors," OMB, Washington, D.C., August 5, 2005.

53. The text of this statute can be found at Government Printing Office, United States Statutes at Large, volume 123, page 115, Government Printing Office, Washington, D.C., 2009.

54. The potential of patent infringement is not usually a bar to award.

55. A *copyright* protects an author's exclusive rights to copy and distribute original works.

56. This court has exclusive jurisdiction to hear claims for monetary damages due to Federal laws, regulations and contracts. The statute of limitations calls for filing a claim within six years from first accrual of the claim. The court is located across the street from the White House in Washington, D.C.

57. This includes any variety of plant that is or may be protectable under the Plant Variety Protection Act (7 U.S.C. 2321, et seq.). A plant variety is made when it has been reproduced with recognized characteristics. Yes, a person really can patent a plant!

58. Contractors mark their utilization report with a confidential or proprietary legend.

59. At the time of this writing, this topic is being quietly discussed in Congress for use by the National Institute of Health to control drug prices, but not yet introduced as legislation.

60. Published by the Uniform Law Commission to protect trade secrets for corporations operating throughout the country, this act is now adopted in all but three states plus Washington, D.C., Puerto Rico and the U.S. Virgin Islands. The only holdouts are Massachusetts, New York and North Carolina.

61. DoD has a unique hybrid that exists within limited and unlimited rights, known as *Government Purpose License Rights*. These give the Government rights to use the data for its own purposes, including reprocurement, while allowing the contractor to retain unlimited rights for commercial use. These rights normally transition to an unlimited status after five years unless the parties agree otherwise.

62. Release to a foreign government would normally occur only for one of the reasons listed herein.

63. Typically, this list is DD Form 1423. Specifications may be written in local format or entered on a DD Form 1664.

64. An *assembly* or *assemblage* is a collection of items designed to accomplish a general function and both identified and issued as a single item.

65. A *trademark* is a distinctive indicator, such as a design or logo, used by an individual or firm to identify its products or services to consumers, and to distinguish them from competitors. The owner of a registered trademark may sue for infringement to prevent unauthorized use, but registration is not required if it is used only in a certain geographical area. If not used over a five-year period, the owner loses his/her legal standing.

Chapter 2

Planning

2.1 MARKETING AND RESEARCH

Marketing is the process by which a firm decides what products or services are of interest and value to current and potential customers, and then induces demand to buy those products or services. Marketing identifies a customer base and its needs and wants. In this way, a firm decides what steps are necessary to satisfy and retain a prospective customer, and how to do so better than its competitors. This effort is absolutely necessary for its growth and survival.

The firm must then review the findings from its marketing efforts to develop a target customer base. It will develop a *marketing strategy* to enable it to focus resources on the most likely sales targets and obtain a competitive advantage over the marketplace. For example, creating the Department of Homeland Security led to many Federal contractors identifying it as a new market target and revenue source (especially with the downturn in Defense spending). This strategy is the basis for a *marketing plan* of specific actions and tactics to reach these goals.

Marketing strategies may differ with each firm's needs, but most firms choose from several common schemes. *Market domination* is intended to obtain a significant amount of market share. Such a firm may adopt a position as technological leader (or cost leader), challenger, follower, or product differentiator. Any of these roles provide the firm with an approach to establish a dominant position in the marketplace. Second, a firm may be an *innovator* through product development. It will exploit the cutting edge of technology, either as pioneer or follower. Alternatively, a firm with an established product or service may commit to a *growth strategy* through diversified or intensified product choice. Or it can integrate, either horizontally or vertically. *Horizontal integration* emphasizes specialized and integrated employee skills, while *vertical integration* requires the firm to broaden its product line and bring associated work in-house.

When developing its marketing strategy, a contractor must also consider its customer type.[1] Examples include consumer marketing (*Business to Consumer – B2C*), industrial marketing (*Business to Business – B2B*) and Federal marketing (*Business to Government – B2G*). B2C is a one-to-many relationship with unidentified customers in distant relationships (often through retailers and mass-marketing) for low-value items (with high-value exceptions such as houses or cars). Within Federal contracting, this marketing type is primarily involved with standard commercial items.

Both B2B and B2G marketing involve a known seller building a face-to-face relationship with prospective customers. These transactions may involve complex deals for high-valued items, requiring many meetings between trained professionals and multiple decision-makers. Integral to both B2B and B2G, the process of *solution selling* (or *technical selling*) involves making an appointment with the customer, understanding his/her needs, and then developing a solution. This can also be done in a broader sense by setting up a table at trade shows, with mobile signboards, colorful trifold brochures, and lots of business cards and free handouts!

Regardless of the method, care must be taken not to "sell the solution" before understanding the customer's requirements. The idea is to create a marketing program around the customer's requirements and the firm's proposed solution, rather than trying to sell an established product or service without modification or customer input.

As another process to use when developing a marketing strategy, *market segmentation* begins by searching for classes of buyers who differ in product interest or tendencies. This process emphasizes customer needs, wants and behavior. Segmentation can be based on demographic or geographic criteria, such as Federal Government only or East Coast only. In any event, these segments must be measurable and substantial. In this process, the firm must consider its competitors and how it differentiates its offering from theirs. A firm must also consider market demand, especially whether it is expected to be durable or merely short-term. Finally, a firm must consider costs involved in new market entry, including advertising and product refinement to adapt to market demands.

A firm performs *positioning* when it creates a brand or image in the minds of the market and potential customers. Once the firm defines the target market, it collects data from customers to learn how they perceive the product and its attributes, and to assess their level of market dominance. The firm will then assess how well the product or service fits within the target market. Common methods to conduct this assessment include customer benefits, problem solution, public perception and image, and stimulation of customer senses and cognition. Another approach is *narrowcasting*, such as word-of-mouth and targeted advertising in trade journals.

Once positioning is determined, the firm is ready to enter the desired marketplace. *Market entry* is the strategy to deliver product to the marketplace. A firm could choose to enter one market at a time, such as a specific department or agency, or several markets with similar requirements at once. This decision would entail considering such options as in-house production, importing, licensing, or teaming.

Having said all this, there are few similarities between B2B and B2G other than for standard commercial items. Government-unique products have no commercial sales base, and many other products developed for the Government have limited commercial sales opportunities. The Government sets rules on marketing based on the public interest, which do not apply in the private sector. Of course, Government source selection and pricing are restrictive procedures compared to the more flexible corporate buying processes. Finally, business decisions are made to achieve long-term Government goals, sometimes at the expense of the short term.

Moreover, the Government is not a homogeneous market. It is differentiated by the type of product purchased, contract policies and types, and geography. In contrast, a commercial firm can have a complex network of wholesalers, brokers and retailers to move products efficiently from manufacturer to distributor.[2] Hence, a firm wishing to enter the Government marketplace must consider:

- administrative burden;
- areas of possible commercial expansion;
- competitors' activities;
- performing a cost-benefit analysis;
- socioeconomic requirements; and
- unique aspects of government contracting.

Once a firm decides to market to the desired customer base, it uses the *promotion* process to transmit information about itself and its offering. Promotion includes advertising displays and prints, direct mail campaigns, and personal sales calls. More subtle and less-targeted methods of public relations, such as sponsoring a youth sports team or participating in trade shows and conventions, can also be useful means of promotion. In Federal contracting, promotion can include business development initiatives such as visiting program managers and agency decision-makers to learn about their needs and exchange general information about product or service offerings.

Should a Federal contractor decide to focus on one market, it can use *account-based marketing* as a more targeted approach to sell as many products or services to the chosen customer. This serves to expand business within existing customer accounts. Government buyers are often satisfied with this approach because their existing suppliers keep them up to date with relevant proposals, and contractors enjoy the ease of maintaining their current customer base. This also obviates the need for a shotgun approach to potential customers with an unknown level of interest. This approach is especially useful for firms that sell information technology and other consulting services.

Firms must focus on key accounts to make this approach workable. They will look at customer preferences, profitability, revenue history, and the desire for a long-term relationship with a client having similar interests. The firm may then argue that the client cannot find this kind or level of service anywhere else, in an effort to secure the sale.

To ensure that the marketing program actually reaches its objectives in a cost-effective manner, marketing managers must measure progress against predetermined objectives. These objectives are derived from the corporate mission (or more bluntly, its reason for operating), identifying customers and their needs, and technology needed to meet those needs. Typical methods include sales forecasts and incentives, customer relationship initiatives, and return on investment. The marketing manager then establishes individual evaluation criteria to indicate success or failure. Common criteria include sales, profit and return on investment. The manager uses data, comparisons and projections to derive standards and measure individual criteria performance.

By the same token, agencies conduct *market research* to collect and analyze information about the marketplace in order to develop the best strategy to acquire and support supplies and services. The procurement office will seek sources and solutions before developing new requirements documents or soliciting. Market research helps to determine:

- ability of the industrial base to produce a quality product or service. The *industrial base* reflects the national capacity and capability to produce goods sufficient to meet commercial and military needs;
- availability of items that contain recovered materials;
- commercial or nondevelopmental items (including electronic and information technology) that are available or can be modified to meet agency needs;
- competitiveness of a planned procurement, including price sensitivity;
- distribution and support capabilities of potential suppliers, including alternative arrangements and cost estimates;
- ease of entry and exit to/from the market;
- if bundling is necessary and justified;
- information for economic and technical evaluations;
- past purchasing experience and suppliers;

- potential small businesses;
- practices of firms who produce, distribute and support commercial items, e.g.:
  - buyer financing,
  - contract type,
  - discounts,
  - maintenance,
  - marking and packaging, and
  - warranty terms;
- rapid delivery capability;
- reasonableness of the requirement and specifications against industry capabilities, manufacturing processes and market demand; and
- whether the Government can fill the requirement in-house at a lower price.

Market research is performed for all acquisitions unless:[3]

- awarded using simplified acquisition procedures (but sole-source acquisitions of commercial items are subject to market research) or contracting procedures expressly authorized by statute;
- contract modifications and priced options evaluated as part of the initial competition and within the scope of an existing contract;
- orders placed under a requirements or definite-quantity contract which was awarded after market research; or
- orders placed under indefinite-quantity contracts if all responsible sources were permitted to compete for the requirements.

FAR 10.002

Contracting officers document their market research results in a manner appropriate to the size and complexity of the acquisition. The contracting officer may use market research conducted within the past 18 months, since the rule of thumb is that after 18 months, the information is too outdated to rely on. Techniques for conducting market research may include any or all of the following:

- hold presolicitation conferences to involve potential offerors early in the acquisition process;
- obtain recent market research and source lists of similar items from other contracting activities or agencies;
- participate in interactive on-line communication among acquisition, customer and industry personnel regarding market capabilities to meet requirements;

- publish formal requests for information in technical or scientific journals or business publications;
- query the Government-wide database of contracts and procurement instruments at www.contractdirectory.gov/contractdirectory; and
- review catalogs and other generally available product literature published by dealers, distributors and manufacturers.

Solicitation Provision and Contract Clause

FAR 52.21-1, Market Research, for noncommercial item contracts over $5.5 million.

2.1.1 Announcing Proposed Actions

FAR 5.2 and 10.0

Per the Small Business Act (15 U.S.C. 637(e)) and the Office of Federal Procurement Policy Act (41 U.S.C. 416), contracting officers release information on proposed contract actions to increase competition, broaden industry participation, and assist small socioeconomic concerns to obtain (sub)contracts. This process is done electronically for any proposed contract action expected to exceed $25,000. For proposed contract actions between $10,000 and $25,000 that are not orally solicited, the notice can still be done by electronic means; otherwise, it must be displayed in a public place by the solicitation date for at least 10 days until quotations have been opened. The contracting office may also notify local trade associations, issue handouts, or place announcements in newspapers or trade magazines without cost to the Government. Actions estimated below $10,000 need not be announced.

Electronic solicitation is the standard method of solicitation, especially for actions over $25,000. The contracting office sends an announcement to Federal Business Opportunities (better known as FedBizOpps, www.fedbizopps.gov). This is a *Government Point of Entry* (GPE), a public-facing website sponsored by the General Services Administration (GSA). However, the contracting officer has many commonsense exceptions to preclude submitting the notice, such as if the proposed procurement:

- accepts a proposal under the Small Business Innovation Development Act of 1982, or that demonstrates a unique and innovative concept, and publication of a notice would disclose proprietary information or originality of research or thought;
- cannot phrase the announcement without compromising national security;

- has a file size or format not on CD-ROM or electronic mail, and therefore is not cost-effective to submit through the GPE;
- is an order placed under any contract which was previously solicited, such as an indefinite-delivery contract;
- is reserved for minority firms or for the severely handicapped or blind organizations;
- is for brand name–only commercial items for authorized resale;
- is for perishable subsistence supplies;
- is for the services of an expert to support the Federal Government in any current or anticipated litigation or dispute;
- is for utility (not telecommunications) services and only one source is available;
- is so urgent that the Government cannot wait 15 days for responses;
- is subject to an international agreement or treaty which restricts solicitation to specified source(s);
- results in the senior procurement executive determining that GPE access is not in the Government's interest;
- solicits only local sources to perform services outside the United States and its outlying areas for a Defense agency; or
- will not exceed the simplified acquisition threshold and permits electronic proposals.

The notice must be published at least 15 days before issuance of a solicitation, which is usually the next business day after submission to FedBizOpps. To acquire commercial items, the contracting officer may establish a shorter period to issue a solicitation, or else combine the synopsis and solicitation.

The contracting officer provides enough response time, normally at least 30 days from the date of issuance, although (s)he can allow less time for commercial items or purchases below the simplified acquisition threshold. However, agencies will allow at least 45 days for research and development actions exceeding the simplified acquisition threshold. For acquisitions under the World Trade Organization Government Procurement Agreement or a free trade agreement, the period of time is at least 40 days, though it can be reduced to 10 days if the acquisition falls within the agreement's annual forecast.

The following entities may transmit a notice to FedBizOpps to seek competition for subcontracts or meet their plan goals, and to increase participation by qualified socioeconomic entities:

- contracting office notice of solicitation cancellation or suspension of proposed contract action;
- contracting office for a total or partial small set-aside or local area set-aside;

- contractor receiving an award exceeding $100,000 that is likely to result in the award of any subcontracts; or
- subcontractor with a $100,000 award who anticipates a subcontracting opportunity exceeding $10,000.

2.1.2 Synopses of Contract Awards

FAR 5.3

Contracting officers synopsize most awards exceeding $25,000 at www .fedbizopps.gov. The contracting officer can announce a smaller dollar-value award if it is likely to result in the award of any subcontracts. A notice is not required if the award is:

- an order under an indefinite-delivery contract (because the contract award itself was already announced);
- due to acceptance of an unsolicited research proposal that demonstrates a unique and innovative research concept (do not want to reveal that information to the competition);
- for the services of an expert to support the Federal Government in any current or anticipated litigation or dispute (to avoid prejudicing an upcoming legal action);
- for utility (not telecommunications) services and only one source is available (obvious who is getting the award);
- from a proposal submitted under the Small Business Innovation Development Act (another innovation award whose secrets must be withheld from the competition);
- made for perishable subsistence supplies (no time to wait for responses to the synopsis);
- such that disclosure of agency needs would compromise the national security (protected by national security); or
- to a foreign firm and performance is outside the United States and its outlying areas (limited number of qualified contractors).

Regardless of dollar value, unless the award is competitive fixed-price, an award notice includes the rationale for contract type and/or lack of competition.

The agency head or designee may release long-range acquisition estimates to help industry plan to meet the acquisition requirements, without indicating the existing or potential mobilization of the industry as a whole. Hopefully, unknown or unexpected companies will show interest and answer the call to submit offers, and actually broaden the marketplace.

Advance written authorization is not required to place advertisements in media other than newspapers. Orders may be placed directly with the media or through an advertising agency via basic ordering agreements. The services of advertising agencies often can be obtained at no cost to the Government (other than space cost) because many media give advertising agencies a commission or discount on the space cost that is not given to the Government. Paid advertisements are used only as a last resort and require written approval by a designated official.

2.2 COMPETITION

Competition is an environment where the buyer relies on the marketplace to encourage multiple sellers to independently contend for award. Seeking competition harnesses the motive to send the buyer's business elsewhere, and is often an ideal method to:

- enhance the industrial base for mobilization and surge capacity;
- improve delivery schedules, efficiency, quality, and reliability;
- increase the program manager's leverage over contractor activity;
- motivate contractors to suggest design changes, leading to efficient production techniques and long-term planning; and
- reduce prices.

Care must be taken to avoid fallacies in assumptions regarding the attractiveness of competition. Cost savings projections are not always accurate due to the dynamic and nonlinear nature of the corporate world. Moreover, investment costs for a new contractor must also be considered, such as drawing creation and validation, facility development and setup, technical data rights, and tooling and test equipment.

2.2.1 Full and Open Competition

FAR 6.1

10 U.S.C. 2304 and 41 U.S.C. 253 require, with certain limited exceptions, that contracting officers promote full and open competition in soliciting offers and awarding contracts. This is a broad statement which requires some clarification in regard to supplies, services and research.

The Government buys commercial off-the-shelf (COTS) supplies whenever possible. Such items are sold, leased or licensed, or offered for sale to the general public. They include items that evolved from other commercial items due to technological advances. Items that are not offered to the general public may still qualify as nondevelopmental items (and therefore treated as COTS) if developed exclusively at private expense and sold in substantial quantities competitively to multiple government agencies (state and local included). Such items are therefore Government off-the-shelf, or GOTS.

Commercial services would be those that are offered to the general public using the same workforce as on the Government contracts. Such services are sold competitively in substantial quantities commercially based on established catalog or market prices for specific tasks. Basic and applied research is bought competitively if award results from a broad agency announcement identifying areas of interest and a peer or scientific review.

The procurement is said to be *unrestricted competition* if all firms are eligible to compete regardless of any preference program. However, if a socioeconomic preference program limits the number of firms which can be considered, it creates an instance of *restricted competition*. These will be discussed in great depth later in this book.

2.2.2 Other Than Full and Open Competition

FAR 6.3

41 U.S.C. 253(c) (for civilian agencies) and 10 U.S.C. 2304(c) (for DoD, NASA and Coast Guard) each authorize, under certain conditions, contracting without providing for full and open competition. Each contract awarded without providing for full and open competition refers to the specific authority under which it was awarded. A lack of advance planning or funding by the requiring activity is not a basis for avoiding full and open competition. When not providing for full and open competition, the contracting officer still solicits offers from as many potential sources as is practicable under the circumstances. However, the contracting officer must justify in writing why (s)he is not obtaining full competition. The following seven exceptions are the only authorized conditions which allow less than full and open competition.

1 – Only One Responsible Source and No Other Supplies or Services Will Satisfy Agency Requirements

A firm may receive a contract without competition if the Government accepts its unsolicited research proposal. The firm must demonstrate a unique and innovative concept or capability not available to the Government and not resembling a pending competitive acquisition. This exception also covers a follow-on contract to continue development or production of a major system or highly specialized equipment. However, the contracting officer must explain how award to any other source would either substantially duplicate cost that will not be recovered through competition, or else would create unacceptable delays in fulfilling the requirements.

For DOD, NASA and Coast Guard only, highly specialized provisioning services may be deemed to be available only from the original source when award to any other source would result in these same concerns. Other situations which could prevent competition include:

- agency minimum needs can only be met by unique supplies or services available from only one source;
- construction of a part of a utility system and the utility company itself is the only source available to work on the system or provide the services;
- control of basic raw material;
- existence of limited rights in copyrights, data, patent rights, or secret processes; or
- the agency head determines that only specified equipment and parts meet agency needs, and only one source is available.

An acquisition using a brand name description or part number peculiar to one manufacturer does not provide for full and open competition, regardless of the number of sources solicited. Hence, the justification in these cases indicates that the use of such descriptions is essential to the Government's requirements, thereby precluding consideration of a product manufactured by another company.

Although the discussion above covers a multitude of situations, this exception is not very popular with outside reviewers because it is very broad and could be abused to cover a multitude of situations where competition might have been obtainable (such as poor planning or desire to award to a specific firm). Hence, this authority is used in preference only to exception 7-exceptions 2 through 6 always take priority over exception 1.

2 – Unusual and Compelling Urgency

This exception applies when delay in award would result in serious injury (usually financial) to the Government. Offers must still be solicited from as many potential sources as practicable.

For a simplified acquisition, the total period of performance of a contract awarded using this authority may not exceed the time necessary to meet the unusual and compelling requirements and for the agency to then enter into a competitive contract for the necessary goods and services. For an acquisition exceeding the simplified threshold, this period of time may not exceed one year unless the head of the agency determines that exceptional circumstances apply. Any time extension which would result in performance exceeding one year (options not included) will require a separate justification.

3 – Industrial Mobilization; Engineering, Developmental or Research Capability; or Expert Services

Examples of this exception include the need to:

- continue any contractors who manufacture critical items to avoid a break in production;
- create or maintain domestic capability to produce critical supplies by limiting competition to items manufactured in the United States, its outlying areas or Canada;
- develop a second source to enhance the mobilization base and foster competition, which may require technology transfer between two competitor commercial entities who suddenly need to cooperate;[4]
- divide current production requirements among multiple contractors to maintain the industrial mobilization base;
- establish or maintain an essential capability for engineering or developmental work, experiments, exploratory studies, or theoretical analyses. This includes effort at an educational or other nonprofit institution or a federally funded research and development center;
- increase or maintain competition to obtain reduced overall costs;
- limit competition for selected supplies or services approved under (or agreed to enter) the DoD Industrial Preparedness Program;
- maintain a facility, manufacturer or supplier in case of a national emergency or to achieve industrial mobilization;
- prevent the loss of a supplier's ability and employees' skills;
- provide experts (e.g., witnesses, mediators, arbitrators, fact finders, or evaluators) in a hearing, proceeding or trial (whether or not the expert is expected to testify);
- satisfy a critical need for emergency, medical or safety supplies; or
- satisfy projected needs based on a history of high demand.

4 – International Agreement

An international agreement or treaty between the United States and a foreign government or entity, or the written directions of a foreign government that reimburses the agency for the cost of supplies or services, may restrict competition to one or a limited group of sources. Place of performance can be either within the United States or the foreign country.

5 – Authorized or Required by Statute

A statute may require acquisition through another agency or from a specified source, such as:

- 8(a) Program awards;
- Federal Prison Industries (UNICOR);
- Government printing and binding;
- HUBZone awards;
- qualified nonprofit agencies for the blind or other severely disabled; or
- veterans' preference awards.

Likewise, this exception could also cover a brand name commercial item for authorized resale, such as a commissary or GSA supply store.

6 – National Security

If disclosure of the agency's needs would compromise the national security, the agency may limit the number of sources solicited. However, it is not sufficient to say that the contractor will need access to classified material to perform the contract to use this exception. A maximum number of sources must still be solicited.

7 – Public Interest

This exception is used as a last resort when no other options apply. The head of the agency or department must make such a determination and notify Congress within 30 days. This exception is not encouraged and is rarely used.

2.2.3 Justifications

FAR 6.303

A *justification and approval* (J&A) is a written document specifically supporting the need to restrict competition. It is drafted by the contracting officer and must be executed before negotiations or award unless it would unreasonably delay award, in which case it must be executed as soon as possible thereafter. The J&A provides in a prescribed format a written argument to justify the use of an exception, certifies the accuracy and completeness of the justification, and documents the approval by an authorized official. J&As may be done on a class basis or for individual acquisitions. Each justification contains facts and rationale to justify the use of the specific authority cited, describing in order:

- name of the agency and contracting activity;
- the action planned;
- the supplies or services and estimated value;
- the statutory authority permitting other than full and open competition;
- how the proposed contractor's unique qualifications (or the nature of the acquisition) requires use of the authority;
- efforts to ensure that offers are solicited from as many sources as possible, and whether a notice was/will be publicized;
- how the anticipated cost will be fair and reasonable;
- market research results or rationale why research was not done;
- why technical data packages, specifications or statements of work are not available for full and open competition;
- for exception 1, an estimate of the cost to the Government that would be duplicated if competed and how the estimate was derived;
- for exception 2, identification of data or estimated cost of harm to the Government;
- names of any sources that expressed in writing an interest in the acquisition;
- possible actions to remove barriers to competition before the acquisition; and
- contracting officer certification that the justification is accurate and complete to the best of his/her knowledge and belief.

Technical and requirements personnel certify their technical input as being accurate and complete. Legal counsel concurrence for sufficiency is also required. The J&A must be approved in writing per the following thresholds (class J&As are assessed by total value of all covered acquisitions), including option values:

- if under $700,000, the contracting officer is sufficient unless agency procedures require a higher approving level;
- between $700,000 and $13.5 million, the competition advocate for the procuring activity;
- between $13.5 and $68 million ($93 million for DoD, NASA and the Coast Guard), the head of the procuring activity, or a designated flag officer or member of the Senior Executive Service; and
- if above these amounts, the senior procurement executive of the agency.

J&As are published on a Government website and the agency website within 14 days of execution (30 days after award for exception 2). Contracting officers delete any classified, FOIA-exempted or proprietary information from the J&A before submission to the website.

Each procurement office has access to a designated employee to become a key player in developing competition plans. The *competition advocate* for the agency and each procuring activity is a senior staff aide with specialists on call to promote full and open competition, as well as acquisition of commercial items. This includes the ability to challenge restrictive statements of work, specifications or contract clauses. The advocate will identify and report to the agency senior procurement executive and the chief acquisition officer any goals and plans to increase competition for the current and upcoming fiscal year, and all actions taken to accomplish them. This official will also recommend recognition and awards to motivate program managers and contracting officers to promote competition.

There is another document sometimes written to justify contracting actions, which should not be confused with a J&A. In a variety of instances, the contracting officer needs to write a *determination and findings* (D&F) to request formal approval to take action. A D&F follows an agency-prescribed format to set forth the facts and circumstances in the form of findings to support the specific determination made. Necessary supporting documentation must first be obtained from appropriate requirements and technical personnel. Several instances which require a D&F will be mentioned throughout this book.

In terms of noncompetitive justifications, contracting officers may set aside solicitations to restrict competition to socioeconomic concerns or local firms during a major disaster or emergency without a separate justification or D&F. However, several types of awards under Exception 5 do need a D&F: Government printing, HUBZone, UNICOR, or veterans' preference. Also, when using exception 7, the D&F may take the place of a J&A.

2.3 USING GOVERNMENT SOURCES

FAR 8.002

Because there are often multiple sources to fulfill Government needs, a prioritization order for obtaining supplies must be established. This order is:

- agency inventories;
- excess from other Federal agencies;
- Federal Prison Industries, Inc.;
- supplies on the Procurement List maintained by the Committee for Purchase from People Who Are Blind or Severely Disabled;
- wholesale supply sources (e.g., stock programs of the General Services Administration [GSA], the Defense Logistics Agency, the Department of Veterans Affairs, and military inventory control points);

- mandatory Federal Supply Schedules;
- optional-use Federal Supply Schedules; and
- commercial sources (including educational and nonprofit institutions).

The priority order for obtaining services is:

- the Procurement List maintained by the Committee for Purchase from People Who Are Blind or Severely Disabled (including subcontracts);
- mandatory Federal Supply Schedules;
- optional-use Federal Supply Schedules;
- Federal Prison Industries, Inc.; and
- commercial sources (including educational and nonprofit institutions).

Information regarding the availability of excess personal property can be obtained through GSA property catalogs, bulletins and reports, as well as personal contacts and requirements submissions.

2.3.1 Federal Prison Industries, Inc.

FAR 8.6

Federal Prison Industries, Inc. (FPI), also referred to as UNICOR, is a self-supporting, wholly owned Government corporation established per 18 U.S.C. 4121-4128. It is designed to train and employ federal prisoners by providing supplies and services to Government agencies. Its supplies and services are listed in the FPI Schedule at www.unicor.gov. Examples of Unicor's range of offerings include:

- awards and plaques;
- clothing;
- data-processing services (e.g., digitizing, imaging, indexing, and optical character recognition);
- distribution and warehousing;
- electronic components (e.g., batteries, cable assemblies, circuit boards, connectors and power cords, power distribution units, surge protectors, and wire harnesses);
- eyewear and safety glasses;
- HVAC filters and steam trap systems;
- light-emitting diode and solar lighting;
- license plates;
- mattresses, linens and draperies;
- military and law enforcement training range services;

- office and dining furniture and utensils;
- printing and binding services;
- signage (both internal and external); and
- vehicle upgrades and customization.

Ordering procedures for FPI are found at the Unicor website. Before purchasing an item on the FPI Schedule, however, the contracting officer must conduct market research to determine whether the FPI item is comparable to supplies available from the public sector in terms of price, quality and time of delivery. This is because the contracting officer is still responsible for protecting public funds and must pursue the lowest price whenever possible. If the products are not comparable, the contracting officer's written determination authorizes soliciting the public sector without a waiver. Other reasons to publicly solicit rather than going to FPI include:

- acquiring services;
- estimated value below the micro-purchase threshold;
- item classified by FPI as nonmandatory;
- public exigency;
- surplus item availability; and
- use outside the United States.

FPI is treated as any other small business. Contractors are never required to use FPI as a subcontractor, but may voluntarily do so.

Needless to say, care must be taken to ensure that prisoners working on these contracts do not access classified, financial or personal data, nor any utility infrastructure or pipeline data.

2.3.2 Agencies for the Blind or Disabled

FAR 8.7

The Committee for Purchase from People Who Are Blind or Severely Disabled was established under the Javits-Wagner-O'Day Act (41 U.S.C. 46) as a Government activity that determines the supplies and services to be purchased by Government agencies from designated nonprofit agencies. The Committee establishes prices and regulations for their purchase through an entity known as *AbilityOne*. A Procurement List of available items is at www.abilityone.gov/procurement_list/index. Examples of their offerings include:

- aircraft and vehicular electrical equipment;
- clothing and textiles;

- contract closeout services;
- document destruction;
- equipment for food processing, packaging and distribution;
- furniture design and configuration;
- groundskeeping services;
- laundry and janitorial services;
- mailroom and supply center operations;
- medical and dental supplies;
- office supplies and furnishings;
- recycling services;
- switchboard operations; and
- trash removal.

AbilityOne participating nonprofit agencies employ people who are blind or have other severe disabilities approved by the Committee to furnish a commodity or a service to the Government. The Committee runs the program through two *central nonprofit agencies*: National Industries for the Blind (NIB) and National Institute for the Severely Handicapped (NISH, now known as SourceAmerica). If no direct order has been authorized by NIB or SourceAmerica, the ordering office must submit a written request for *allocation* to either agency. That agency would then designate an AbilityOne participating nonprofit agency to solicit. There are no regulatory dollar limits for individual orders.

NIB and SourceAmerica also set a delivery or performance lead time for orders. The ordering office generally grants any requests that the nonprofit agency makes to revise the delivery or completion schedule. If not, it contacts either NIB or SourceAmerica to request either reallocating the order or granting a purchase exception to allow commercial sources to fill the requirement. Similarly, if the ordering office decides to cancel an order, it notifies NIB or SourceAmerica for reallocation of the order. In these cases, the central nonprofit agency could grant a purchase exception permitting use of commercial sources, but must get Committee approval if the value of the purchase exception is $25,000 or more. Exceptions can also be granted if the quantity cannot be produced or provided economically by the participating nonprofit agencies.

The Committee sets supplies prices semiannually and services prices annually. All prices exclude delivery charges, since final destination is not predictable until actual orders arrive. The Committee has the authority to set prices without coordination with the responsible contracting office.

Sometimes an AbilityOne participating nonprofit agency produces items identical to those available through FPI. FPI may then grant a waiver to permit the Government to purchase a portion of its requirement from the

AbilityOne nonprofit agency. Otherwise, FPI takes priority for identical supplies, and defers to AbilityOne to provide services.

Contract Clause

FAR 52.208-9, Contractor Use of Mandatory Sources of Supply and Services.

2.3.3 Other Mandatory Sources of Supply

FAR 8.5

Liquid or gaseous helium must be procured from Federal helium suppliers.
The Bureau of Land Management maintains this list and posts it at www.blm
.gov/nm/st/en/fo/Amarillo_Field_Office.

FAR 8.802

The Government Printing Office normally provides all printing services for
the Federal Government. This effort can be contracted out if this office cannot provide the printing service, the agency uses its own printing service, or
if directed by statute.

FAR 8.1102-1103

When leasing a motor vehicle, the requiring activity must certify that required
leased motor vehicles are fuel efficient and small enough to meet the need
(the Government does not want to pay for a full-size car if it only needs a
compact). Any car larger than a compact must be justified by the head agency
or designee of the requiring activity.[5] Also, GSA must state that it cannot
furnish the vehicles. Current-year production models are also frowned upon
unless they are more economical than prior-year models. The contract must
specify which party is required to maintain its vehicle, including providing
gasoline, oil and antifreeze.

Contract Clause

FAR 52.208-7, Tagging of Leased Vehicles, for vehicles leased over 60 days.
   Do not use the following clauses:

- 52.211-16, Variation in Quantity;
- 52.232-1, Payments;
- 52.222-20, Contracts for Materials, Supplies, Articles, and Equipment
  Exceeding $15,000; and
- 52.246-16, Responsibility for Supplies.

2.3.4 Inverted Domestic Corporations

FAR 9.108

An *inverted domestic corporation* is a firm currently incorporated in another country, but was once incorporated in the United States. The definition includes subsidiaries and partnerships in the same situation. The concern with inverted firms is that they continue to do most of their business in the United States but have relocated overseas in a tax haven nation to mitigate or eliminate paying Federal taxes. Government agencies are prohibited from contracting with such firms unless the agency head grants a waiver. Offerors must execute a representation to the effect that they are not an inverted domestic corporation. They must also notify the contracting officer if during performance they become inverted, or if their parent becomes inverted. This is one of several issues in Federal procurement which has nothing to do with performance or pricing, but is totally a result of a political decision. Congress and the President use the power of the public purse to implement such decisions, and they represent implemented contracting policy.

Solicitation Provision

FAR <u>52.209-09</u>, Representation, Prohibition on Contracting with Inverted Domestic Corporations.

Contract Clauses

FAR <u>52.209-10</u>, Prohibition on Contracting with Inverted Domestic Corporations.

2.4 FEDERAL SUPPLY SCHEDULES

FAR 8.4

Title III of the Federal Property and Administrative Services Act (40 U.S.C. 501) established the Federal Supply Schedule program to provide Federal agencies with a simplified process to acquire commercial supplies and services and obtain volume discounts. Also called the GSA Schedules Program and the Multiple Award Schedule Program, it is run by GSA to award indefinite-delivery contracts using competitive procedures. The firms provide supplies and services at stated prices for given periods of time.

Each schedule identifies agencies that are required to use the contracts as primary sources of supply when FPI and AbilityOne cannot fulfill the requirement. These schedules exploit the price advantages of volume buying.

GSA schedule contractors publish an "Authorized Federal Supply Schedule Pricelist" of all covered supplies and services, along with pricing and the terms and conditions for each *Special Item Number,* a group of generically similar supplies or services that serve the same general purpose.

GSA delegates responsibility for certain commodities to specific agencies (e.g., the Department of Veterans Affairs to procure medical supplies). DoD manages a similar system of schedule contracting for military items, but is not a part of the Federal Supply Schedule program. Architect-engineer services are not bought under Federal Supply Schedules, due to their unique source selection process.

Schedules are stored at www.gsa.gov/elibrary. A schedule may include special ordering procedures that take precedence over normal procedures. GSA also manages an on-line shopping service named "GSA Advantage!" to electronically place orders (www.gsa.gov/fss), lists its schedules at www.gsa.gov/schedules, and provides search features (i.e., national stock number, part number and common name), delivery options, ordering, and payment using the Government-wide commercial purchase card. Moreover, GSA has a solicitation tool called "e-Buy" to post requirements, obtain quotes and issue orders electronically at www.ebuy.gsa.gov. Even contractors may publish pricelists on this site, though this is not required and is by no means comprehensive.

Orders placed against a schedule are considered to be issued using full and open competition, hence ordering activities do not seek competition out-side of the Federal Supply Schedules and do not synopsize the requirement (because award of the supply schedule itself has already been synopsized). However, the contracting officer may still need an acquisition plan and infor-mation technology acquisition strategy, must determine in writing that use of such a schedule is the best procurement approach, and may need to take steps to avoid contract bundling. Moreover, any restriction falling into one of the seven exceptions to competition still requires a J&A.

Ordering activities may place orders below the micro-purchase threshold with any Federal Supply Schedule contractor, but try to distribute orders among contractors, preferably small businesses. Above the micro-purchase threshold, however, the ordering officer surveys at least three schedule con-tractors either through GSA Advantage or else by reviewing vendor catalogs or pricelists. Of course, socioeconomic considerations are still in play, and the contracting officer is free to limit competition to small businesses only. In addition to price, nonprice evaluation factors may include:

- delivery terms;
- environmental and energy efficiency;
- maintenance availability;

- past performance;
- probable lifespan of the item selected;
- special performance features;
- trade-in considerations; and
- warranty terms.

Each schedule contract has a maximum order threshold for each item number. Schedule prices are fixed. Services are priced either at hourly rates or for an entire task (usually for installation, maintenance and repair). GSA has already determined the prices to be fair and reasonable. Although an ordering officer must still do a price evaluation, (s)he need not assess price for reasonableness, but is free to pursue additional discounts with the contractor before placing an order. The contractor is under no obligation to reduce price, however, and the ordering activity may then place an order at the contract price. Any contractor decision whether or not to reduce price presents a dilemma; on the one hand, lowering price for one customer will lead to demands to lower price for all, but on the other hand, the loss of the sale is never an attractive possibility.

For services above the micro-purchase threshold priced at hourly rates in the schedule, the ordering activity must provide a Request for Quotation (RFQ) to include the statement of work and evaluation criteria (e.g., experience and past performance), to three or more schedule contractors and any other schedule contractor who requests a copy. The activity is free to post the requirement to e-Buy. Statements of work include description, location, period of performance or deliverable schedule, performance standards, security clearances, and travel needs. The ordering activity evaluates all responses received using the evaluation criteria provided to the schedule contractors. The ordering activity documents the:

- description of the service purchased;
- evaluation methodology;
- price reasonableness determination and amount paid;
- rationale for any tradeoffs during selection;
- rationale if not using a firm-fixed-price order or performance-based order; and
- schedule contracts considered and awardee.

For proposed orders between $25,000 and the simplified acquisition threshold, any circumstances which restrict consideration must be submitted to eBuy. For proposed orders exceeding the simplified acquisition threshold, the J&A itself must be furnished. The posting requirement does not apply when disclosure would compromise national security (e.g., would reveal classified information) or create other security risks. The fact that access to classified matter may be necessary to submit a proposal or perform the contract does not, in itself, preclude use of these schedules. Also, posting is not required if the file size or format does not make it cost-effective or practicable to provide access through e-Buy, or the agency's senior procurement executive determines in writing that access through e-Buy is not in the Government's interest.

2.5 ACQUISITION PLAN

The agency's *acquisition strategy* is its business and technical management approach to achieve program objectives and fulfill requirements within resource constraints. An acquisition strategy should be tailored to program objectives and flexible enough to allow innovation and modification as the program evolves. The strategy should also try to minimize the time and cost of satisfying a need by promoting common sense, policy compliance and sound business practices. A good strategy serves as a decision aid to:

- assess situational realities such as threats, economic and political environment, relationships to other programs;
- describe the direction in which the program should head, especially mission need and targets for program changes;
- develop technological options and explore design concepts;
- document the program rules and assumptions to provide an audit trail;
- establish goals for
  - contract types,
  - cost,
  - decision criteria and weights,
  - logistics support,
  - mitigation,
  - number of sources,
  - procurement lead times,
  - risk levels and priorities,
  - software development approach,
  - schedule,
  - streamlining, and
  - testing (type, quantity and length);
- evaluate and select alternative candidate strategies based on relative (dis)advantages;
- identify opportunities and times for critical decisions;
- prioritize and integrate functional requirements;

- promote stability by minimizing technical, schedule and cost risks while considering funding, industry risk, policy, requirements, and changes in organization and personnel;
- provide a coordinated and realistic approach to economically and efficiently achieve program objectives;
- recognize resources in terms of facilities, funding, information, personnel, and time; and
- select system concepts for development which must be feasible and likely to satisfy mission requirements.

The acquisition strategy serves as an agreement between the contracting officer and program manager. The *program manager* is responsible for the design and development of the product or service and associated operations and logistics support. The contracting officer serves as business advisor to the program manager and handles procurement operations. The program manager faces a "triple constraint" of three independent factors – time, cost and performance – competing with or against each other as the program evolves. In addition, the program manager is affected by scope, risk and customer satisfaction.

Unfortunately, all interested parties have their own priorities. The program manager must recognize that the user wants a top-performing system quickly, financial officers want to lower cost, and contractors want to lower risk. Consequently, the program manager must try to consolidate these parochial interests, promote the understanding of mission priorities and requirements, and allocate resources to achieve the needed capability with acceptable risk. One way to do this, without consuming too many resources, is to analyze through "what-if" drills and identify areas of probable change or failure.

Risk management is another aspect of acquisition planning. This process identifies uncertainties that threaten cost, schedule and performance objectives, while developing and implementing actions to deal with them. Exposure to these uncertainties constitutes *acquisition risk*. Risks can originate either outside of or within the program. External risks include:

- audit recommendations;
- changing threats;
- contractor financial difficulties;
- funding cuts;
- labor strikes; and
- management directives.

Internal risks include:

- accuracy of cost and schedule estimating process and assumptions;
- achieving reliability, availability and maintainability requirements;

- contractor ability to perform;
- immature technology;
- inadequate performance standards;
- incorrect or changing requirements; and
- translating technological capabilities into reliable configurations.

The individual agencies establish criteria and thresholds to add detail in the planning process as an acquisition becomes more complex and costly. The agencies will decide when written plans are required and standard acquisition plan formats. Moreover, the department or agency must establish criteria and thresholds to use *design-to-cost* (where cost becomes a design constraint and a management concern during operations) and *life-cycle cost* (total cost to the Government to acquire, operate, support, and dispose of items acquired) techniques, as well as to ensure Government control over contract performance.

FAR 7.1

Acquisition planning begins when the agency need is identified, prior to the fiscal year in which award is required. A team is formed of contracting, fiscal, legal, logistics, and technical personnel to develop the plan. At key milestone dates (or at least annually), the planner reviews the plan and revises if necessary.

The acquisition strategy of development, production and operation is coordinated with the cognizant small business specialist if the estimated contract or order value, including options, is at least:

- $9 million for the Department of Defense;
- $6.5 million for the Department of Energy, GSA and NASA; and
- $2.5 million for all other agencies.

The written acquisition plan serves as a signed agreement between program manager and approving official that the developed approach is optimal. It identifies decision milestones and business, management and technical considerations that will control the acquisition(s). An acquisition plan can cover either one or multiple contracts. Acquisition plans for service contracts discuss strategies for performance-based acquisition methods or a rationale for not using those methods. The written plan will have two major parts: one for background and objectives, and the other for a plan of action. The acquisition background and objectives section of the plan discusses:

- *Statement of need* – acquisition alternatives, impact of prior acquisitions on each alternative, and related in-house effort;
- *Applicable conditions* – compatibility with existing or future systems or programs, and constraints on cost, schedule and capability;
- *Cost* – including life-cycle cost, design-to-cost and should-cost;
- *Capability or performance* – standards and how they are related to the need;
- *Delivery or performance-period requirements* – reasons for any urgency;
- *Trade-offs* – among the various cost, capability, performance, and schedule goals;
- *Risks* – technical, cost and schedule risks, risk-reduction efforts, consequences of failure to achieve goals, and concurrency of development and production; and
- *Acquisition streamlining* – effort that results in more efficient and effective use of resources to design and develop or produce quality systems (e.g., draft solicitation or bidders conference).

The plan-of-action section discusses:

- *Sources* – including socioeconomic firms, bundling concerns and market research;
- *Competition* – how to obtain competition (or the basis for noncompetition) at both prime and subcontract levels, component breakout plans, spare and repair parts, key logistical milestones, and technical data needs;
- *Contract type(s);*
- *Source-selection procedures* – schedule for proposal submission and evaluation, evaluation factors, and use of earned value management integrated baseline review;
- *Acquisition considerations* e.g,
  - equipment lease or purchase,
  - FAR deviations,
  - solicitation method,
  - special clauses or provisions,
  - use of multiyear contracting or options, and
  - use of performance-based acquisition or the rationale why not;
- *Use of Internet Protocol when acquiring information technology* – the requirements documents must include the USGv6 Profile (NIST Special Publication 500-267) and the corresponding declarations of conformance defined in the USGv6 Test Program.[6] Usage of Internet Protocol version 6 to agency applications, infrastructure and networks specific to individual acquisitions must comply with the agency's Enterprise Architecture.[7] The plan must also address the means to achieve capital planning and investment control;

- *Budgeting and funding* – budget estimates, basis of derivation, and funding schedule;
- *Product or service descriptions* – including performance-based acquisition descriptions;
- *Priorities, allocations and allotments*;
- *Contractor versus Government performance* – applicability of OMB Circular No. A-76;
- *Inherently governmental functions;*
- *Management information requirements* – methodology to analyze and use the earned-value data to assess and monitor contract performance (if applicable); verification for compliance with the American National Standards Institute/Electronics Industries Alliance (ANSI/EIA) Standard-748, Earned Value Management Systems; and the timing and conduct of integrated baseline reviews (whether prior to or post-award);
- *Make or buy;*
- *Test and evaluation* – of both the contractor and the Government for each phase of a major system acquisition,[8] including any concurrent testing before production release;
- *Logistics considerations* –
  - contractor or agency maintenance and service,
  - contractor data (e.g., cost, rights and usage),
  - equipment standardization for future purchases,
  - quality assurance,
  - reliability and maintainability, and
  - warranties;
- *Government-furnished property;*
- *Government-furnished information* – any added controls to monitor access and distribution;
- *Environmental and energy conservation objectives* – applicability of environmental assessment or impact statement, and proposed resolution of environmental issues;
- *Security considerations* –
  - agency requirements for personal identity verification of contractors,
  - contractor physical access to a federally controlled facility and/or information system,
  - monitoring,
  - technical requirements, and
  - security establishment and maintenance;
- *Contract administration* – e.g., inspection and acceptance;
- *Other considerations* –
  - defense production,
  - foreign sales implications,

- ∘ industrial readiness,
- ∘ performance in a designated operational area or supporting a diplomatic or consular mission,
- ∘ SAFETY Act,[9]
- ∘ standardization, and
- ∘ workplace safety;
- *Milestones for the acquisition cycle*:
  - ∘ acquisition plan approval,
  - ∘ statement of work,
  - ∘ specifications,
  - ∘ data requirements,
  - ∘ completion of acquisition package,
  - ∘ receipt of purchase request,
  - ∘ J&A and/or any D&F approval,
  - ∘ issuance of synopsis,
  - ∘ issuance of solicitation,
  - ∘ evaluation of proposals, audits and field reports,
  - ∘ start and completion of negotiations,
  - ∘ contract preparation and review, and
  - ∘ contract award; and
- *Identification of participants in acquisition plan preparation* – with contact information.

2.6 MAJOR SYSTEMS ACQUISITIONS

FAR 34

OMB Circular A-109 is the Government-wide policy on acquiring major systems.[10] The Circular defines a *major system* as a combination of elements that will function together to produce the capabilities necessary to fulfill a mission need. It sets forth management objectives and structure, as well as key decision points. A-109 also directs agencies to identify mission needs without advocating a specific approach. Congress may give input before the agency establishes objectives and commits resources. An agency can establish alternate approaches through competing development contracts, so that industry can propose a variety of technical solutions with cost trade-offs. The process includes basic research, system design, prototype demonstration, and full-scale development. A-109 also requires that mission budgeting and funding processes allow comparative analysis of agency programs and prioritized alternatives.

The process of managing major systems over their life cycle is known as *systems engineering*. This complicated process consists of many phases and steps, such as these examples:

- *Concept exploration design*:
  - needs and requirements identification and analysis,
  - feasibility analysis,
  - system design specifications, and
  - conceptual design review;
- *Demonstration design:*
  - functional analysis,
  - requirements review,
  - detailed trade-off studies,
  - development phase specifications,
  - operational support planning,
  - acquisition strategy development and documentation, and
  - preliminary design review;
- *Full-scale development:*
  - detailed product and facilities design;
  - integration of logistical, maintenance and support requirements,
  - development of engineering and prototype models,
  - product, process and material specifications,
  - funding profile,
  - critical design review, and
  - production decision;
- *Production stage:*
  - production of system components,
  - acceptance testing, and
  - system distribution;
- *Operations:*
  - system operation in user environment,
  - validated maintenance plans,
  - ensuring adequate funding and integrated logistics support,
  - change management, and
  - assessment to correct deficiencies and adapt for continued improvement;
- *Phase-out and disposal:*
  - feasibility of system phase-out versus continued maintenance, and
  - system retirement.

2.6.1 Exploration and Development Phases

Contracts performed during the concept exploration phase are for relatively short periods. These contracts hopefully refine the proposed concept and reduce technical uncertainties. The program manager must ensure that the scope of work is consistent with the Government's planned budget for this phase. Follow-on contracts for tasks in the exploration phase may be awarded as long as the concept approach remains promising, the contractor's progress is acceptable, and performance is affordable. The end result of this phase is a conceptual design review to determine if the specifications meet the need.

Contracts for the demonstration phase provide for contractors to develop and submit priced proposals for full-scale development. The contracting officer provides them with life-cycle cost factors (development, procurement, operation, maintenance, and disposal), operational test conditions, performance criteria, and selection criteria for them to prepare their proposals. These proposals may also identify items which are or will be available within the agency or Federal Supply System, or even commercially available on a competitive basis.

Full-scale development contracts provide for the contractors to submit priced proposals for production that are based on logistics, quantity and schedule requirements that will be used in making the production decision. The agency head reaffirms the mission need and program objectives, and grants approval to proceed with production.

Engineering design is critical at this stage so that high quality and low cost can be achieved. Many firms apply the *Pareto Rule* to this discipline – 80% of the manufacturing costs are incurred during the first 20% of the design process. Further, a product parameter design process can be used to find those design factors that can be adjusted to open up tolerances. These adjustments could help to achieve high quality at low cost, and improve understanding of functional and materials performance. This process can be used to choose the best idea among several alternatives.

It may be critical for a firm to ensure producibility of a given component by an outside vendor. The concept of *supplier development* may be undertaken, where a buyer tries to improve a supplier's performance and/or capabilities to meet supply needs. This may be critical where half or more of a manufactured product might consist of purchased inputs. Moreover, external suppliers will impact cost, quality, technology, and time to market, and therefore customer satisfaction and profitability. Both prime and subcontractor must commit capital, financial and personnel resources, and must agree on how to measure performance and share sensitive information in a timely manner.

Before entering production, the program office and Government may schedule a *production readiness review*. This is a formal program examination to assess design readiness and resolve production and planning issues. The review determines whether cost, performance and schedule criteria can be attained with acceptable risk. Officials must then determine if the system implements all requirements correctly and completely.

At the same time, an *Integrated Process Team* may be established of contractor and Government personnel to review all the facets of production:

- facilities;
- management of inventory and suppliers;
- manufacturing process readiness;
- personnel qualifications and certification;
- process documentation;
- quality management; and
- tooling and test equipment.

Approval at this stage leads to a production decision, either at a low-rate or else at full-rate. The program may use a risk-reduction method known as *low-rate initial production* to restrict the number of units built to reduce the Government's exposure to retrofit issues and costs. The contractor still produces enough units for final development and operational testing prior to a full production decision. Synonyms for this approach are *limited production* and *pilot production.*

2.6.2 Production Design

Once the engineering design effort is completed and a decision is made to enter production, the firm enters a new phase of management considerations. In this regard, the *production design* team tries to optimize the fabrication process. The team uses engineering and production talents to improve maintenance, plant layout, quality control, and work methods. It also strives to improve labor performance through such techniques as wage incentives and zero defects programs. The team may also use communication methods such as employee goal setting, plantwide recognition, problem identification, and suggestions.

Early in the production design process, the program manager will develop a flow chart (formally known as a *process chart*) that uses symbols to graphically depict inputs, sequential production activities and outputs to the customer. Boxes in the flow chart depict activities, and their connecting arrows show the data flow between the boxes. Managers can analyze these graphic depictions as decision aids.

A commonly used design technique to investigate design options involves tearing down a process or item to discover its underlying content. Known as *reverse engineering*, this process is designed to discover the technological principles of a product or system by analyzing its function, operations and structure. The product is usually taken apart or decomposed to analyze its workings or makeup.[11] Sometimes the intent is to reproduce the item without using any original parts, but more often it is used for design decisions. This process is especially useful for computer-aided design to create a virtual three-dimensional model of a component or system.

Software is likewise subject to detailed examination. Software may be subjected to reverse engineering to learn code or to replace unavailable documentation. After representing the system at a high level of abstraction, the computer-aided design process can trace the *source code* created by the programmer backward to its development phase without modifying it.[12] The firm can then examine the *source data* (unprocessed raw data) that was originally recorded in the media. To record data transfer between electronic systems and verify its integrity, an audit log of all transactions is maintained in most database management systems. A firm may also use black-box testing to look for software bugs or undocumented features.

Reverse engineering is legal for an item protected by trade secrets, and is not necessary for a patented item because the public disclosure provides sufficient notice. As such, a firm may reverse-engineer a competitor's product to assess whether its own patent has in fact been abridged.

2.6.3 Production Control

It is now time to move on to how the firm will manage and control the production process. *Production management* strives to produce the desired product at the desired rate at a minimum cost. The key elements of production management are performance and volume. Performance is a function of efficiency, equipment, facilities, quality, and schedule. Volume is a function of inventory level, production rate and workforce. Because these objectives are often in conflict, the firm must strive to obtain an optimal balance, given their cost and schedule constraints. This approach may require *satisficing* (selecting a course of action to meet the minimum requirements to achieve the goal) among possible outcomes. The firm must also ensure producibility within its current manufacturing labor capabilities and a reliable supply of components.

Production control is concerned with inventory control, production planning and scheduling. Serving both staff departments and line organizations, this type of control entails measuring, evaluating and adjusting system performance to meet system goals. The five phases of control are to:

• gather data from accounting statements, control charts, observation, or time cards;

- compare operating data with predetermined standards of performance. Statistical process control can monitor process variations over time to identify any nonrandom issues;
- detect causes of malfunction from customers, design engineers, output reports, and profit-and-loss statements;
- select one or more corrective actions from a set of alternatives; and
- implement the action.

There are several cautionary notes about the production control process. Care must be taken to exclude irrelevant and outdated data, and to focus on error detection and troubleshooting. The firm may need to use sequential analysis or group brainstorming to break down a problem area into component parts to discover cause-and-effect or cause-and-solution relationships. Feedback about status or output could also affect input and therefore performance, since any delay in the feedback loop could lead to system instability (e.g., stockouts). The Government usually takes a hands-off approach to avoid micromanaging the production process (after all, the contractor is paid to resolve production problems), although program office engineers may be available to provide advice to the contractor.

Production control ultimately leads to quality control. *Quality* is a function of grade and fitness for use, or perhaps consistency in characteristics. Quality tends to become more important as price becomes more competitive. *Quality control* determines how well a product is being made. Quality control may be achieved by sampling (using operating characteristics and control charts), or by variables (using upper and lower control limits). However, higher quality may require higher-priced labor, more specialized or higher-tolerance equipment, and longer production time. One can perform a series of trade-offs between quality conformance and cost, and plot them on a graph to derive an optimal point where total cost is minimized. The Government is most interested in these trade-off results to see if higher quality is worth a higher cost.

A firm may choose to either centralize or decentralize production, based on its analysis of the relative strengths and weaknesses of each approach. *Centralized production control* places all planning and control activities in one location. It allows close coordination and control with other functions such as engineering, finance, purchasing, and sales. *Decentralized production control* is common with larger firms, where individual departments handle some or all of the planning and control activities. Decentralized control tends to promote innovation, solve problems by those most familiar with them, and allow for effective monitoring.

Several programs are used to implement production control. *Manufacturing resource planning* is a method using an automated system to check capacity requirements, forecast production demands, purchase or redirect materials, and schedule production jobs. These are usually modularized computer programs that include bill of materials, control programs and scheduling for cost, design, inventory, and quality.

DoD runs a program to encourage contractors to upgrade their production equipment. The *Industrial Modernization Improvement Program* motivates contractors by awarding additional profit dollars to invest in facility improvements, including equipment, processes and software. This effort should reduce acquisition costs over the long run and improve productivity, while providing the participating contractor some insurance in case of program termination. The process includes analysis of the factory line or other production capability, validating engineering applications of new technology through a capital investment proposal, and purchase and installation of capital equipment.

Contractors may also have a formal *manufacturing technology* program to improve production equipment, processes or techniques. This program would also include effort to assure production availability, increase efficiency and reliability, and reduce lead time and costs. The program emphasizes rapid transition from development to production, best manufacturing practices, and customization through smaller production lots. DoD program managers implement this program in accordance with DoD Instruction 4200-15, Manufacturing Technology (Mantech) Program.[13]

The role of production control becomes strained compared with other aspects of the firm when things do not go according to design or plan, since it has broad influence over the production process and readiness. The production department may view the activities of designers as infringing on their responsibility, or be viewed as intrusive by other departments involved in systems or procedures. However, the production department typically has autonomy, as long as it does not affect the operating budgets of other departments. Other common problems of production control may include:

- complex assembly processes;
- delayed planning;
- equipment and worker downtime;
- inaccurate forecasts;
- inadequate capacity, materials or tooling;
- long scheduling cycles;
- repair times and priorities; and
- work-in-process backlogs.

2.6.4 Productivity

Productivity is the ratio of output to input of a production process, measured by comparing actual performance with historical figures or changes in ratios. This approach studies production processes and techniques to measure quantity of output per unit of resource (e.g., labor, money or time). By contrast, *efficiency* is a ratio of units of output to cost of input. These two concepts may or may not work together. Hence, a labor-saving approach could boost output without improving efficiency, while using lower-priced labor could improve efficiency without aiding productivity.

A special engineering discipline has grown around this subject. *Industrial engineering* provides guidance on optimal task performance. Time standards can be established for a variety of labor types. These standards assume average time for an average worker under average conditions. The standards can easily apply to manual and repetitive operations with collectible data, but are harder to develop for jobs that require thinking or planning. Use of standards may help to measure performance, but could stifle effectiveness at the expense of efficiency.

The most common tool to assess labor productivity over time is the learning curve. A *learning curve* is a mathematical analysis of efficiency or cost reduction based on the number of units produced. Using historical data, it projects efficiencies in labor, purchasing, production processes, and tools. Used for manual and repetitive tasks, it predicts the cost of future production or estimates hours to produce a unit. It assumes the amount of time to complete a task diminishes with each successive undertaking (reflected in a learning percentage). The learning percentage can be derived by arithmetic or logarithmic calculation of actual history, and can be projected into the future for same or similar products.

Nonetheless, there are some concerns about learning curves. Early pre-production units may have very high learning, distorting projections for follow-on production. Managers may use learning curves as a goal and self-fulfilling prophecy, thereby avoiding further learning opportunities. Changes in indirect labor and supervision, organizational structure and procurement methods could impact direct labor in the future by changing conditions from those incurred in the recent past. Project phaseout could lead to personnel transfers and eliminate equipment maintenance, thereby impacting performance in the latter stages of production.

Results of the productivity assessments will lead to several ramifications for the firm. Staffing decisions can be made through job design or by specifying individual or group work activities. These decisions are complicated because the worker and transformation process have inherently conflicting needs and goals, different people respond differently in a given task, and employees may question traditional work behaviors and work approaches. To minimize these differences, the firm may employ a *Best Current Practice* (BCP), a procedure proven during operations to be the most logical way to perform a function or operation. Though not a mandate or standard, it can be changed whenever the state of the art changes or a better method is devised. Jobs can also be enlarged to interest the employee, though impact on output, quality and the worker must be considered. Social group and cultural impacts are also at issue. Task boundaries must be established in terms of what, when and where, to avoid overlooking environmental factors. A particular job should have:

- a pattern that draws together a variety of tasks into a set of meaningful overall tasks;
- contribution to product utility;
- feedback of results;
- quality of production;
- reasonable length of work cycle; and
- respect in the professional and cultural community (care, skill or knowledge).

Productivity in the plant can also be increased by:

- automated factories;
- cross-training and job rotation;
- investment incentives;
- job enrichment and flexible work hours;
- material handling equipment;
- numerically controlled machine tools; and
- recovery of precious metals.

Challenges to productivity growth include:

- aging capital equipment;
- changing market conditions and structure;
- cost constraints;
- evolving technology;
- international competition; and
- reduced labor base of skilled craftsmen.

Two recent advances in office management are also becoming widely employed. *Ergonomics* is a process which analyzes user interface with equipment and furniture to enhance worker productivity and avoid physical discomfort and disability. This approach optimizes human well-being and job performance. Another approach involves accommodations for physically challenged employees to comply with the Americans with Disabilities Act (42 U.S.C. 12101), of July 26, 1990. These changes include removing architectural barriers and allowing for service animals and special telecommunications equipment.

As another technological advance to improve working conditions, a *virtual office* uses live remote communications for users to reduce office costs while preserving business professionalism. They are not the same as office business centers because they do not require a lease. They may include:

- call centers to receive telephone requests;
- conference room space on demand (perhaps including a kitchenette and waiting lobby);
- mailing address to provide 24/7 access to individual locked mailboxes;
- office equipment (e.g., conference and video calling, copier, facsimile machine, Internet, and printer);
- professional address to avoid personal security concerns of a home-based business;
- receptionist to receive and sign for incoming packages and provide document drop-off/pick-up services; and
- voicemail to store voice messages electronically.

2.6.5 Program Manager Considerations

In addition to the systems engineering life cycle already discussed, there is a *program management life cycle* which the program manager and associates follow. A typical program consists of five phases:

- Initiate:
  - compile a project charter, and
  - develop a project scope statement in a preliminary (if not final) version;
- Plan:
  - create a project management structure,
  - develop program scope,
  - develop a work breakdown structure,
  - establish communications,
  - estimate activity resources and duration:
    - define and sequence activities,
    - develop a schedule,
    - estimate and budget costs, and
    - plan quality and human resources;

- o identify and assess risk and plan responses, and[14]
- o numerate contracting needs;
- Execute:
  - o acquire and develop a project team,
  - o direct program execution,
  - o distribute information,
  - o implement quality assurance, and
  - o solicit and select contractors;
- Control:
  - o administer contracts,
  - o control cost, schedule and scope,
  - o integrate change control,
  - o maintain quality control,
  - o manage project team,
  - o manage stakeholders,
  - o monitor and control risk,
  - o monitor project work, and
  - o report performance;
- Close project and contracts.

To obtain initial program approval, the program manager estimates operational and technical characteristics, schedule, and acquisition cost. An estimating relationship is used as a factor to compute the amount and type of effort or resources necessary to acquire, develop, produce, and/or operate the system. The program manager may also use a statistical process capability analysis during both development and production phases to analyze process variability based on product specifications. Also analyzed is the procedural support data used by the contractor during the development phase for assembly, operation or maintenance tasks pertaining to production, test or inspection.

The Government will normally pay for any testing and qualification required to use or incorporate the industrial resources manufactured or developed with assistance provided under Title III of the Defense Production Act of 1950 (50 U.S.C. Appendix 2170). This program is designed to determine affordable and viable production capabilities for items which are deemed essential to the national defense. Firms receiving requests from a Title III project contractor to test and qualify a Title III industrial resource refer such requests to the contracting officer. The contracting officer evaluates the request in accordance with agency procedures to determine whether the resource is or may be used to develop or manufacture a major system or supply, and whether remaining quantities to be acquired are sufficient to justify incurring test and qualification costs. If the determination is affirmative, the contracting officer modifies the contract to require the contractor to test the Title III industrial resource for qualification.

Contract Clause

FAR 52.234-1, Industrial Resources Developed under Title III, Defense Production Act.

2.7 SOCIOECONOMIC PROGRAMS

The Federal Government has instituted a number of programs to benefit designated groups of individuals and their firms by promoting diversity and accessibility to contracts and financial support. These are collectively known as *socioeconomic programs* and result in a number of source selection preferences and additional contract-related benefits to such firms. These programs are intended to promote employment and revenue to small and minority business firms. In addition, these practices also promote multicultural diversity within a firm through equitable status for employees without regard to their ethnic, gender, physical, or religious status. Firms are encouraged to consider socioeconomic issues in choosing suppliers. However, it can be challenging to measure results of these programs on society. They certainly impose more paperwork requirements on firms and may increase procurement prices, and therefore public spending.

2.7.1 Small Business Programs

FAR Part 19

The small business policy applies only to contracts performed in the United States or its outlying areas, except as noted.

Small businesses make up roughly 99.7% of all American firms, and nearly half of all private sector employees.[15] They provide significant levels of competition and innovation. Yet they often lack the resources to handle large and complex projects, may not always be able to follow up on production issues, cannot spread costs over a wide base (and thereby may not be price competitive with large businesses), and may find it difficult to deal with the Federal Government. Hence the need for preference programs to promote awards to small businesses.

Additionally, for a firm to be considered a small business, it must be:

• a for-profit entity;
• independently owned and operated;
• located and operating primarily within the U.S.;
• not nationally dominant in its field; and
• paying taxes or using American labor, materials or products.

Implementation of socioeconomic programs requires a team of specialists to assist the contracting officer, who also plays a leading role in the program's success. The specific policies and procedures are discussed in the following sections.

2.7.1.1 Size Standards

FAR 19.102

The Department of Commerce manages the North American Industry Classification System (NAICS) (www.census.gov/eosd/www/naics) and annually determines small procurement mechanisms and size percentages by NAICS Industry Subsector and region. These percentage determinations affect all solicitations that are issued on or after its effective date. These procurement mechanisms are used as a price evaluation adjustment (sub)factor to reflect the level of participation of small concerns, and could include monetary subcontracting incentive clauses for large concerns.

The SBA establishes small business size standards by industry category of supplies and services. The industry size standards are published by the SBA at http://www.sba.gov/content/table-small-business-size-standards. The appropriate size standard is placed in the solicitation for offerors to represent their status as small or large. If multiple size standards apply to the various deliverables of a given solicitation, the standard which comprises the greatest percentage of the contract price governs.

A firm that offers to furnish an end product it did not manufacture (i.e., a *nonmanufacturer*) is considered a small business if it has no more than 500 employees and furnishes the product of another small business manufacturer or producer. A firm which buys items and packages them into a kit is considered to be a nonmanufacturer small business if it meets the size qualifications for the acquisition and if over 50% of the total value of the kit and its contents are manufactured by small business.

On the other hand, a firm which proposes a product manufactured by a large business does not qualify as a small business. Hence, a small business which is a dealer for a large business will not gain consideration as a small business. This rule does not apply, however, to a small business set-aside not over $25,000 in value if the offer is an end product that is manufactured or produced in the United States.

Some service categories are based on annual corporate income. Different categories have different income levels. For these categories, the number of employees is irrelevant when categorizing service providers.

2.7.1.2 Encouraging Small Business Participation

FAR 19.202-11

Heads of contracting activities must implement the small business programs within their activities. They have annual goals for total dollars awarded to small businesses, further broken down into the various types of socioeconomic categories. Performance of contracting office management is in part assessed on their ability to meet or exceed these goals.

To achieve program goals, contracting office management must ensure that their contracting and technical personnel maintain knowledge of small business program requirements and take all reasonable actions to increase participation in contracting. They do this through in-house training, written procedures and reviews of pending procurement actions. Moreover, each procurement office has annual socioeconomic goals to achieve, usually expressed in terms of percentage of total awards or dollars awarded to small businesses. The management techniques discussed below are designed to help achieve these goals.

Whenever more than one small business concern is capable of performing the work, the contracting officer may divide proposed acquisitions of supplies and services (except construction) into small lots (at least the size of economic production runs) to encourage more offers. Delivery schedules should be realistic enough to encourage small business participation and motivate prime contractors to subcontract with small business concerns.

The contracting office must maintain an open and professional relationship with the small business community. To any requesting small business concern, the contracting officer provides at Government expense a copy of the solicitation and specifications, contact information of a person to answer questions, and citations to applicable Federal laws or agency rules.

Each prospective contractor represents if it qualifies in one or more socioeconomic categories. Each agency measures the level of participation of these firms by total value of contracts placed during each fiscal year, and reports the data to the SBA.

SBA maintains the *Procurement Automated Source System* as a centralized inventory and referral system that contains the names and capabilities of small businesses interested in Government (sub)contracts. Purchasing offices can query the database to obtain potential sources. The database is not available to contractors or the general public.

In the event of equal low bids, awards are made first to small business labor surplus area concerns, and second to small business concerns which are not also labor surplus area concerns.

2.7.1.3 Cooperation with the SBA

FAR 19.4

Each agency with contracting authority has an Office of Small and Disadvantaged Business Utilization (known within DoD as the Office of Small Business Programs). The SBA may assign one or more *SBA procurement center representatives* to any contracting activity or contract administration office to carry out SBA policies and programs. They will review proposed acquisition packages and recommend firms for inclusion on a bidders' mailing list. They may also recommend any alternate contracting method that could increase small business prime contracting opportunities, such as newly certified firms and component breakout for separate competitive acquisitions.[16] The recommendation is due to the contracting officer within 15 days after receipt of the package. The representative will appeal to the chief of the contracting office any contracting officer's determination not to solicit any small business recommended by the SBA. On an ongoing basis, the representative will also conduct periodic reviews of the contracting activity to assess compliance with small business policies, and sponsor and participate in conferences and training to increase small business participation in the contracting office.

The SBA will also assign a *breakout procurement center representative* to any procurement office it designates as purchasing substantial amounts of noncommercial items. This representative advocates use of full and open competition and item breakout, while still maintaining the integrity of the system which uses these items. Each breakout representative is aided by at least two co-located small business technical advisors. The breakout representative is authorized to attend evaluation sessions discussing acquisition strategy and make recommendations, and to appeal any failure by the procurement center to act favorably on any recommendation. They will review any unsolicited engineering proposal, conduct a value analysis to determine any cost reduction within acquisition objectives, and forward the results to procurement center reviewers. Breakout experts will also review the validity of past competitive restrictions and technical data rights to help prepare a competitive solicitation package for a supply or service previously acquired noncompetitively. On an ongoing basis, the representative formally briefs contracting officers and other procurement office personnel about the representative's duties and objectives, and the methods designed to promote item breakout for competitive procurement, and annually reports on past and planned activities to the head of the procurement office.

The contracting officer strives to respond in writing within 30 days to any written request from a small business firm regarding a contract administration matter, or else advise when a response will be forthcoming. This policy does not apply to matters under the Disputes clause.

2.7.1.4 Set-Asides for Small Business

FAR 19.5

A *small business set-aside* is an acquisition or class of acquisitions reserved for only small business concerns to compete. A small business set-aside may be total or partial, but must still be awarded at a fair and reasonable price. The contracting officer reviews acquisitions to determine if they can be set aside for small business, and documents if and why a set-aside is inappropriate. The SBA procurement center representative may review all proposed acquisitions that are not unilaterally set aside for small business. However, the set-aside requirement does not apply to micro-purchases, acquisitions for contingency or emergency recovery valued at $20,000 or less, or purchases from NIB, SourceAmerica or Federal Supply Schedule contracts.

Each acquisition of supplies or services exceeding the micro-purchase threshold but not over the simplified acquisition threshold is automatically reserved exclusively for small business concerns. However, if the contracting officer determines there is not a reasonable expectation of obtaining competitive offers from at least two responsible small business concerns, (s)he may be able to convince the procurement center representative to forego a set-aside. If the contracting officer receives only one acceptable offer from a responsible small business under a set-aside, award can still be made to that firm. But if no acceptable offers from responsible small business concerns are received, the set-aside is withdrawn and the requirement is resolicited on an unrestricted basis.

If an action exceeding the simplified acquisition threshold does not lend itself to a total set-aside, the contracting officer may still create a *partial set-aside* of a portion of the acquisition for exclusive small business participation. This is possible if the requirement is severable into two or more economic production runs or lots.[17] The contracting officer must first be certain that one or more small business concerns have the technical competence and productive capacity to satisfy the set-aside portion at a fair market price. Both portions of the procurement must have comparable terms and delivery schedule.

Offers received from large business concerns are considered only for the non-set-aside portion. After all awards have been made on that portion, the contracting officer then addresses those small businesses who offered on both the non-set-aside and set-aside portions, in the order of priority indicated in the solicitation. Moreover, if equal low offers are received, the non-set-aside awardee has first priority to negotiate for the set-aside amount. So, a small business is at a disadvantage if it elects to only offer on the set-aside portion of the solicitation.

A contracting officer rejecting a recommendation of the SBA procurement center representative must respond in writing and permit the SBA procurement center representative to appeal the rejection to the head of the contracting activity or designee. Since this process can take up to seven weeks, the contracting officer suspends action on the acquisition, unless determining in writing that the public interest requires performance. If the head of the contracting activity agrees with the contracting officer, the SBA procurement center representative may then appeal. This requires a request to the contracting officer to continue to suspend action on the acquisition until the SBA Administrator appeals to the agency head for a final decision (this process can take up to nine more weeks). By this time, the issue has become both lengthy and political in nature. So the contracting officer must carefully consider any challenge to an SBA recommendation, and whether the procurement can be delayed for such a length of time (it often cannot). This is also our first (but not last) indication of the political power of the SBA and the small business community.

Solicitation Provisions and Contract Clauses

FAR 52.219-6, Notice of Total Small Business Set-Aside. Use the clause with Alternate I for a product in a class for which the SBA has found no small business manufacturer. Use the clause with its Alternate II when including Federal Prison Industries (FPI) in the competition.

FAR 52.219-7, Notice of Partial Small Business Set-Aside. Use the clause with its Alternate I for a product in a class for which the SBA has found no small business manufacturer. Use the clause with its Alternate II when including FPI in the competition.

FAR 52.210-13, Notice of Set-Aside of Orders, applied to an individual order under an indefinite-delivery contract.

FAR 52.219-14, Limitations on Subcontracting, in solicitations and contracts expected to exceed $100,000 if any portion of the requirement is to be set aside for small business.

2.7.1.5 Determination of Small Business Status

FAR 19.3

To be eligible for award as a small business, an offeror must represent that it meets the definition of a small business concern applicable to the solicitation, and that it has not been determined by the SBA to be other than a small business. The contracting officer accepts in good faith this representation unless another offeror or interested party (or the contracting officer him/herself) challenges the concern's representation. The offeror's representation is not binding on the SBA, however, and if challenged, the SBA will evaluate the status and issue a final determination to the contracting officer. If the finding is negative, the concern cannot become eligible for a set-aside award; if positive, the offeror is eligible for award. Since the contracting officer lacks the expertise of the SBA in the field of size determination, (s)he has no avenue of appeal.

Although a size determination is normally valid for the life of the contract, there are several exceptions. A contractor must re-represent its size status for the NAICS code in the contract within 30 days after execution of a novation agreement or associated contract modification, or after a merger or acquisition. For contracts more than five years in length, it must re-represent its size status within 120 days before the end of the fifth year of the contract or the date for exercising any option.[18]

As stated above, another offeror may challenge the size status of a firm representing itself as a small business. In order to affect a specific solicitation, however, such a protest must be timely. This means it must be received by the contracting officer by closing time of the fifth business day after bid opening (in sealed-bid acquisitions) or receipt of the contracting officer's notification that identifies the apparently successful offeror (in negotiated acquisitions). A protest may be made orally if it is confirmed in writing and postmarked or hand-delivered to the contracting officer by the next business day, or within the five-day period. On the other hand, a contracting officer's protest is always considered timely, whether filed before or after award. Any protest under a Multiple Award Schedule is timely if received by SBA prior to the expiration of the contract period.

After receiving such a protest, the contracting officer cannot award the contract until either the SBA has made a size determination or 15 business days have expired since SBA's receipt of the protest. Again, early award is permitted only to protect the public interest. The SBA Government Contracting Area Director or designee determines the small business status of the questioned firm and notifies both the contracting officer and firm of the determination. Award may be made (or denied) on the basis of that determination. If award was made before the contracting officer received notice of the appeal, the contract is considered to be valid.

Any potential offeror may appeal a contracting officer's NAICS code designation and the applicable size standard. Such an appeal must be filed within 10 calendar days after the issuance of the solicitation. Since SBA selects the standard to be used in the solicitation, they must handle the protest. SBA's Office of Hearings and Appeals (OHA) will dismiss summarily an untimely NAICS code appeal. If OHA's decision arrives to the contracting officer before the offer is due, the decision is final and (if necessary) the solicitation is amended to reflect the decision. An OHA decision received after the due date of the initial offers does not apply to the pending solicitation, but will apply to future solicitations of the same products or services.

Although other socioeconomic programs will be discussed later in their separate sections, we will include here their rules for size protests. This provides the reader with a more centralized location to access protest policies and procedures.

To be eligible for consideration on its disadvantaged status, a concern must either be certified as a small disadvantaged business (SDB) at the time of its offer or have a completed SDB application pending at the SBA or a private certifier (there are private companies who are authorized to certify a firm's socioeconomic eligibility). The contracting officer may accept an offeror's representation that it is an SDB concern for statistical purposes, and may confirm it by accessing SBA's database (PRO-Net at http://www.pro-net.sba.gov/textonly/pro-net/search.html) or by contacting the SBA's Office of Small Disadvantaged Business Certification and Eligibility.

No offeror determined to be nonresponsive, outside the competitive range, or previously found by the SBA to be ineligible for the requirement, may protest the apparently successful offeror's representation of disadvantaged status. This is because such a firm is not in line for the award even if successful in its protest, and is therefore not considered to be an interested party. Any other offeror may submit a written protest to the contracting officer after bid opening or notification of intended award. In addition, the contracting officer or the SBA may protest in writing a firm's representation of its disadvantaged status at any time after bid opening or notification of intended award, even if award has already been made. In all cases, however, SBA normally will not consider a post-award protest, unless the contracting officer agrees to terminate the contract if the protest is sustained.

When the contracting officer makes a written determination that award must be made to protect the public interest, award can occur notwithstanding the protest. Otherwise, the contracting officer will forward the protest to the SBA, and the Assistant Administrator for Small Disadvantaged Business Certification and Eligibility will notify the protestor and the contracting officer whether the protest will be processed or dismissed for lack of timeliness or specificity. Within 15 working days after receipt of a timely and specific protest, the SBA will determine the disadvantaged status of the challenged offeror and notify all parties. Failure to respond within 15 days is grounds for the contracting officer to presume that the challenged offeror is disadvantaged and award may proceed (unless the contracting officer has granted SBA an extension). Any SBA determination may be appealed by any of the three parties (awardee, protestor or contracting officer) to the SBA Administrator's designee within five working days after receipt of the determination.

The same three parties may protest an apparently successful offeror claiming HUBZone small business status. The deadlines for timely protest are the same as for SDB protests. Again, SBA determines the HUBZone status of the protested concern within 15 business days after receipt of a protest; otherwise the contracting officer may award the contract (unless the contracting officer grants SBA an extension). Here again, the contracting officer may determine in writing to award the contract if necessary to protect the public interest. Unlike the disadvantaged business, however, the SBA decision regarding HUBZone status is final and not protestable by any party.

The same protest process applies to service-disabled veteran-owned small business set-asides. SBA's Associate Administrator for Government Contracting makes the final decision in these cases, which also is not protestable.

Solicitation Provisions

FAR 52.219-1, Small Business Program Representations, if exceeding the micro-purchase threshold and the contract will be performed in the United States or its outlying areas. Use the provision with its Alternate I in solicitations issued by DoD, NASA or the Coast Guard.

FAR 52.219-22, Small Disadvantaged Business Status, when including the clause at 52.219-23, Notice of Price Evaluation Adjustment for Small Disadvantaged Business Concerns, or 52.219-25, Small Disadvantaged Business Participation Program–Disadvantaged Status and Reporting. Use the provision with its Alternate I in solicitations containing a price evaluation adjustment for small disadvantaged business concerns.

FAR 52.219-2, Equal Low Bids, in sealed-bid solicitations if performance will be in the United States or its outlying areas.

Solicitation Provisions and Contract Clauses

FAR 52.219-28, Post-Award Small Business Program Representation, if exceeding the micro-purchase threshold and the contract will be performed in the United States or its outlying areas.

2.7.1.6 Certificate of Competency

FAR 19.6

A Certificate of Competency (COC) can be issued by the SBA to affirm a small business's responsibility regarding:

- capability;
- capacity;

- competency;
- credit;
- integrity;
- perseverance and tenacity; and
- subcontracting limitations.

The COC program applies to all Government acquisitions, including those performed outside the United States (the only socioeconomic requirement that does).

If a contracting officer determines an apparent successful small business offeror to be nonresponsible, even if the next acceptable offer is also from a small business, (s)he withholds contract award and refers the matter to the cognizant SBA Government Contracting Area Office of the offeror's headquarters.[19] Contract award is withheld by the contracting officer for up to 15 business days (or longer if agreed to by the SBA and the contracting officer) after the SBA office receives all required documentation, and the small business concern applies for a COC. The SBA may elect to visit the applicant's facility with industrial and financial experts to review its responsibility. If the SBA rules against the concern, or does not issue a COC within 15 business days after receiving the referral, the contracting officer assumes that no COC will be granted and may award as intended. If the decision favors granting a COC, the contracting officer can then award the contract to the concern because a COC conclusively determines responsibility.

An offeror receiving an unfavorable decision has no avenue of appeal. The contracting agency may file an appeal and notify its agency Director of the OSDBU, within 10 business days (or a time period agreed upon by both agencies). The SBA Associate Administrator for Government Contracting will make a final written determination, which is not subject to further appeal.

2.7.1.7 Small Business Subcontracting

FAR 19.702 and .704

Any contract above the simplified acquisition threshold requires maximizing contracting opportunities for socioeconomic concerns. Therefore, each solicitation expected to exceed $750,000 ($1,500,000 for construction) with subcontracting possibilities requires the apparently successful offeror to submit a subcontracting plan covering the entire contract period (including options), with goals based on the offeror's planned subcontracting support. When a contract modification is large enough to merit its own plan, then its goals are added to those in the existing subcontracting plan. Subcontracting plans are not required from small business prime contractors, for personal services, or for contracts performed entirely outside of the United States and its outlying areas.

The plan must be acceptable to the contracting officer and is subject to negotiation. Any (sub)contractor failing to comply in good faith with the requirements of the subcontracting plan is in material breach of contract and subject to liquidated damages.

A contractor must confirm that a subcontractor representing itself as a small disadvantaged business concern is listed in SBA's database (PRO-Net) or else contact the SBA's Office of Small Disadvantaged Business Certification and Eligibility. Likewise, the contractor must confirm a HUBZone certification by accessing the Central Contractor Registration (CCR) database or by contacting the SBA. The contractor, the contracting officer or any other interested party can challenge a subcontractor's size or disadvantaged status prior to completion of performance by the intended subcontractor.

Subcontracts awarded to an Alaskan Native Corporation (ANC) or Indian tribe count towards the subcontracting goals for small business and SDB concerns, regardless of the size or SBA certification status of the ANC or Indian tribe. A contractor may rely on the written representation of status as an ANC or Indian tribe unless an interested party or the contracting officer challenges its status.

Each subcontracting plan must include:

- assurances that the offeror will:
  - cooperate in any studies or surveys,
  - submit periodic reports for the Government to determine compliance with the subcontracting plan,
  - provide its prime contract number, DUNS number and e-mail address of the Government or contractor official responsible for acknowledging or rejecting the reports, to all first-tier subcontractors with their own subcontracting plans so they can enter this information into their eSRS reports,
  - require that each subcontractor with a subcontracting plan provide the same information for its subcontracting plans,
  - for construction contracts, that it will make a good faith effort to contract with the small businesses included in its proposal or provide the contracting officer a written explanation to the contrary, and
  - not prohibit a subcontractor from discussing with the contracting officer any matter dealing with payment or utilization;
- a description of the efforts to ensure that socioeconomic concerns have an equitable opportunity to compete for subcontracts;
- a description of the procedures to comply with plan goals and requirements, including establishing source lists and efforts to locate and award to socio-economic concerns;[20]

- if the offeror included indirect costs in establishing subcontracting goals, how it determined the proportionate share of indirect costs for socioeconomic concerns;
- methods used to develop the subcontracting goals and identify potential sources;
- percentage goals for using socioeconomic concerns as subcontractors, with separate goals for each category (e.g., small, disadvantaged, etc.);
- planned subcontract amounts, both in total dollars and to socioeconomic firms;
- the name of the subcontracting program administrator and a description of duties;
- types of supplies and services to be subcontracted, both in total and to socioeconomic firms;
- whether a *master subcontracting plan* is developed on a plant or division-wide basis without goals. Master plans are effective for three years after approval, but must be maintained and updated by the contractor. Upon approval by the contracting officer, they may be incorporated into individual contract plans.

A contractor with subcontracting opportunities must submit the Individual Subcontract Report and the Summary Subcontract Report using the Electronic Subcontracting Reporting System (eSRS) (www.esrs.gov), the Government-wide web-based system for small business subcontracting program reports. The Individual Subcontract Report is submitted semi-annually for the performance periods ending March 31 and September 30. A report is also required for each contract within 30 days of contract completion. The Summary Subcontract Report is also due semi-annually for DoD and NASA, but only at the end of the fiscal year for other civilian agencies.

An offeror of commercial products or services may also use its *commercial plan*, a subcontracting plan with goals that covers the offeror's fiscal year and applies to commercial items sold by the entire company or a portion thereof. The Government does not require another subcontracting plan from the same contractor while this commercial plan remains in effect and the product or service continues to qualify as a commercial item.

2.7.1.8 Contracting Officer Responsibilities Under Subcontracting Assistance

FAR 19.705

The contracting officer determines whether subcontracting possibilities exist by considering whether firms which furnish the required types of items customarily perform all work in-house or else contract-out part of the work to qualified vendors. The contracting officer reviews the subcontracting plan for adequacy and to ensure that the required information, goals and assurances are included. This review draws on previous involvement of small business concerns as prime contractors or subcontractors in similar acquisitions, and the relative success of methods to meet the goals and requirements of the plan. If a plan under a sealed bid does not cover each required element, the contracting officer requests submission of a revised plan by a specific date, or else the bidder is ineligible for award. If the plan demonstrates no intent to comply with its obligations under the Utilization of Small Business Concerns clause, the contracting officer may find the bidder to be nonresponsible.

In negotiated acquisitions, the contracting officer ensures that the offeror has not submitted unreasonably low goals to avoid the administrative burden of good faith efforts. Goals may be negotiated upward unless they would greatly increase cost. The contracting officer may encourage the offeror (except for SDBs) to increase subcontracting opportunities by providing monetary incentives for exceeding goals. Subcontracting can also be a factor in determining the award fee in a cost-plus-award-fee contract. When establishing goals, the contracting officer evaluates:

- achievability of goals based on available subcontractors and opportunities;
- capacity to provide specialized products or services through subcontracting;
- consistency with the offeror's cost or pricing data, and make-or-buy policy or program;
- known availability of socioeconomic concerns in the geographical area where the work will be performed;
- past performance of the offeror in fulfilling subcontracting plans;
- performance of other contractors on similar efforts; and
- the offeror's long-standing contractual relationship with its suppliers.

The contracting officer may advise the offeror of available sources of information on potential socioeconomic concerns, or specific concerns known by name, and recommendations from the SBA procurement center representative and the agency small business specialist. The contracting officer will then evaluate the plan as outlined above, perhaps with the help of the SBA procurement center representative. If a firm replies that it has no subcontracting opportunities when a plan is required, this position must be approved at a level above the contracting officer.

Letter contracts and similar undefinitized instruments contain at least a preliminary basic plan, and a final plan will be negotiated within 90 days after award or before definitization, whichever occurs first.

Liquidated damages are authorized when a contractor's *failure to make a good faith effort* to comply with the subcontracting plan reflects intentional failure to perform or frustrate the plan. The fact that the contractor failed to meet its subcontracting goals does not, by itself, constitute a failure to make a good faith effort. Instead, indicators of such a failure include lack of:

- company policies or procedures that support the objectives of the plan;
- designating a company official to administer the subcontracting program and monitor and enforce compliance with the plan;
- effort to identify, contact, solicit, or consider socioeconomic concern for award;
- Individual or Summary Subcontract Reports submitted to eSRS; or
- records or procedures of plan compliance.

If the contracting officer finds that the contractor failed to make a good faith effort to comply with its subcontracting plan, (s)he issues a final decision to the contractor and requires payment of liquidated damages. These damages will equal the actual dollar amount by which the contractor failed to achieve each subcontracting goal. This decision is subject to appeal under the Disputes clause.

Solicitation Provisions and Contract Clauses

FAR 52.219-8, Utilization of Small Business Concerns, if the contract amount is expected to exceed the simplified acquisition threshold. Do not use for personal services or performance outside of the United States and its outlying areas.

FAR 52.219-9, Small Business Subcontracting Plan, when subcontracting possibilities are expected to exceed $700,000 ($1,500,000 for construction of any public facility), and the Utilization of Small Business Concerns clause is included. Do not use if the acquisition is set aside or is to be accomplished under the 8(a) program. Use the clause with Alternate I when contracting by sealed bid. Use the clause with its Alternate II when contracting by negotiation, and subcontracting plans are required with initial proposals.

FAR 52.219-10, Incentive Subcontracting Program, when a monetary incentive is necessary to increase socioeconomic subcontracting opportunities.

FAR 52.219-16, Liquidated Damages – Subcontracting Plan, when including the Small Business Subcontracting Plan clause.

2.7.2 Small Disadvantaged Business Firms

For Federal contracting purposes, *disadvantage* is a long-term, chronic and substantial condition based on color, gender, national origin, or physical handicap. The cause of the disadvantage must arise from one of the above detriments within American society, not from a foreign nation. This detriment must then result in difficulty in gaining access to working capital, such as failure to obtain a loan from a lending institution. If all these conditions apply, then the firm can qualify under one or more of the disadvantaged categories.

FAR 19.8

Section 8(a) of the Small Business Act (15 U.S.C. 637(a)) authorizes the SBA to enter into contracts with other agencies and then subcontract to firms eligible for program participation, referred to as *8(a) contractors*. The SBA selects firms in which at least 51% of the ownership is held by socially and economically disadvantaged entrepreneurs. These firms typically spend four years in a developmental stage (often in a mentor-protégé relationship with an established firm) and then up to five years building the company to transition into self-sufficiency and graduate from the 8(a) program.

The SBA serves as prime contractor to the agency, and subcontracts the effort to an 8(a) contractor. These subcontracts may be awarded on either a sole-source or competitive basis. The SBA and agency cooperate, usually with the assistance of the SBA procurement center representative, to match the agency's requirements with the capabilities of 8(a) concerns. The SBA issues a search letter of an 8(a) firm's capabilities and asks the agency to identify acquisitions to support the firm's business plans. The SBA can also identify a specific requirement for a particular 8(a) firm(s), and agencies may review planned acquisitions to identify requirements to offer to the SBA. The size of an 8(a) contract cannot exceed $22 million, including all options.

After completing an annual evaluation, the agency notifies the SBA of its plans to place 8(a) contracts for specific quantities of items or work, plus award dates. The SBA will determine whether to accept the requirement for the 8(a) program within 10 working days of receipt (two days if the contract is at or below the simplified acquisition threshold). If the acquisition is accepted as a sole source, the SBA advises the contracting activity of the 8(a) firm selected for negotiation, which is often the contracting activity's recommended source. However, sometimes the SBA will wish to rotate the award to another firm that needs the business to survive and grow. Repetitive acquisitions awarded through the 8(a) program require separate offers and acceptances so that the SBA may determine competitiveness, a nominated firm's eligibility, and the effect of contract award on the equitable distribution of 8(a) contracts. Separate offers and acceptances are not made for individual orders under multiple awards or multi-agency contracts.

An 8(a) acquisition can be awarded based on a competition limited to eligible 8(a) firms if there is a reasonable expectation that at least two responsible 8(a) firms will submit offers and that award can be made at a fair market price. To establish a competitive acquisition, the anticipated total value of the contract, including options, must exceed $7 million for acquisitions with manufacturing NAICS codes and $4 million for all other requirements. An acquisition exceeding these thresholds can still be accepted as sole source if competition is not expected or if it is performed by an Indian tribe or Alaskan Native Corporation. An agency request for a competitive 8(a) award below the thresholds will be approved only where technical competitions are appropriate or if many responsible 8(a) firms are available for competition.

The negotiated contract price and the estimated fair market price are subject to the concurrence of the SBA. To determine a fair market price, the contracting officer may use a variety of data:

- commercial prices for similar products and services;
- cost or price analysis, including data submitted by the SBA or the 8(a) contractor;
- data from another agency;
- in-house cost estimates; and
- prior purchase history.

The estimated price is then adjusted for differences in packaging and packing, performance periods, quantities, specifications, transportation, and other terms and conditions. Price indices may be used as guides for revised labor and material costs.

The SBA Administrator may appeal to the agency head if the SBA and the contracting officer fail to agree on making a particular acquisition available for award under the 8(a) Program, or for rejecting a specific 8(a) firm for award after SBA's acceptance of the requirement for the 8(a) Program. An appeal can also occur if they fail to agree on pricing or terms and conditions of a proposed 8(a) contract. Notification of a proposed appeal must be received by the contracting officer within five working days after the SBA is formally notified of the contracting officer's decision. The contracting officer suspends action on the acquisition until the agency head makes a decision, unless (s)he determines in writing that urgent and compelling circumstances will not permit waiting. SBA's response is due within 15 days thereafter. Moreover, an 8(a) contract is normally terminated for convenience if the firm transfers ownership or control to another firm.

Solicitation Provisions and Contract Clauses

FAR 52.219-14, Limitations on Subcontracting.

FAR 52.219-17, Section 8(a) Award, in competitive solicitations and awards.

FAR 52.219-18, Notification of Competition Limited to Eligible 8(a) Concerns, in competitive solicitations and contracts. Use the clause with its Alternate I when competition is to be limited to 8(a) concerns within one or more specific SBA districts. Use the clause with its Alternate II when the acquisition is for a product in a class for which the SBA has waived the nonmanufacturer rule.

Contract Clauses

FAR 52.219-11, Special 8(a) Contract Conditions, in sole-source contracts.

FAR 52.219-12, Special 8(a) Subcontract Conditions, in competitive contracts.

2.7.3 Price Evaluation Adjustment for Small Disadvantaged Business Concerns

FAR 19.11 and 19.12

At times, discussion has arisen over how to favor SDBs who submitted offers in an unrestricted competition. At one time, Congress directed DoD and certain agencies to introduce an adjustment factor in price determinations by adding an amount to the evaluated price of non-SDBs. However, per the U.S. Court of Appeals, DoD contracting activities may not use such a price evaluation adjustment for SDBs in its procurements.[21] As such, use of a price adjustment factor is severely restricted. Only the Coast Guard and NASA may use a price evaluation adjustment in competitive acquisitions. However, even these agencies cannot use an adjustment factor if the acquisitions are:

- less than or equal to the simplified acquisition threshold;
- multiple award schedule contracts;
- not using price as a selection factor, which makes a price evaluation factor meaningless (e.g., architect/engineer services); or
- set aside for small business, 8(a), HUBZone or service-disabled veteran-owned small business concerns.

If using this factor, the contracting officer adjusts offers from SDBs by adding a price adjustment factor determined by the Department of Commerce to all offers. This factor is not applied to an offer from a historically black college or university or minority institution, nor to an SDB which has not waived the use of the evaluation adjustment.[22] Other evaluation factors such as transportation costs or rent-free use of Government property are added to the offers before applying the price evaluation adjustment. This adjustment cannot lead to award at a price that exceeds fair market price by more than the price adjustment factor.

In developing an SDB participation evaluation factor or subfactor for the solicitation, agencies may consider the extent of:

- commitment to use SDB concerns;
- complexity and variety of the work SDB concerns are to perform;
- past performance of offerors to comply with subcontracting plan goals and monetary targets for SDB participation; and
- specific identification of SDB concerns.

Solicitation Provisions and Contract Clauses

FAR 52.219-24, Small Disadvantaged Business Participation Program Targets.

FAR 52.219-25, Small Disadvantaged Business Participation Program—Disadvantaged Status and Reporting.

FAR 52.219-26, Small Disadvantaged Business Participation Program—Incentive Subcontracting, when using the Disadvantaged Status and Reporting clause. The clause is not used when an award-fee provision is used instead of the incentive.

2.7.4 Labor Surplus Area Set-asides

Labor surplus areas (LSAs) are communities and counties that have experienced severe unemployment, based on a yearly survey by the Department of Labor. An area receives an LSA designation when its average unemployment rate rises at least 20% above the national average over a two-year period. This implies that an area has more labor than needed, so an employer will find it easier and more economical to staff a contract. Executive Order 12073, Federal Procurement in Labor Surplus Areas, and Executive Order 10582, Implementing the Buy American Act, create procurement preferences for employers located in LSAs. As a result, LSAs are another source of socioeconomic preference. There are no prescribed FAR clauses for LSAs, however, and currently the program is just voluntary.

2.7.5 Service-Disabled Veteran-Owned Small Business Procurement Program

FAR 19.14

The Veterans Benefit Act of 2003 (15 U.S.C. 657f) created the Service-Disabled Veteran-Owned Small Business Program to provide Federal contracting assistance to service-disabled veteran-owned small business concerns. A joint venture may qualify if at least one member of the joint venture is a service-disabled veteran-owned small business concern and the other concerns are small businesses under the NAICS code for the procurement. The veterans' benefit does not apply to:

• awards to certain federally chartered nonprofit agencies;
• orders under indefinite-delivery contracts or Federal Supply Schedules;
• procurements below the micro-purchase threshold; or
• requirements accepted under the 8(a) Program (unless SBA has consented to release the requirements from the 8(a) Program).

The contracting officer must have a reasonable expectation of receiving offers from at least two service-disabled veteran-owned small business concerns, and award at a fair market price. Receiving only one offer at a fair price can still constitute award, however lack of any offers will lead to cancellation of the solicitation and reversion to a small business set-aside. A sole-source solicitation can be made if only one service-disabled veteran-owned small business concern can satisfy the requirement and the anticipated award price of the contract (including options) does not exceed $3 million ($5.5 million for manufacturing).

Contract Clause

FAR 52.219-27, Notice of Total Service-Disabled Veteran-Owned Small Business Set-Aside.

2.7.6 Indian Incentive Program

FAR 26.1

25 U.S.C. 1544 provides an incentive to prime contractors that use Indian-owned[23] organizations and economic enterprises as subcontractors. *Indian organizations* are any community, economic enterprise, group, pueblo, or village of natives recognized by the Federal Government as eligible for services from the Bureau of Indian Affairs (BIA) in the Department of the Interior. An *Indian* is a member of any tribe or community recognized as eligible for services from the BIA, plus any "native" as defined in the Alaska Native Claims Settlement Act (43 U.S.C. 1601). An *Alaska Native Corporation* (ANC) is a regional, urban or village corporation which is organized under the laws of the State of Alaska and is deemed a minority and economically disadvantaged concern. The Indian Incentive Program allows an incentive payment equal to 5% of the amount paid to an Indian organization or Indian-owned economic enterprise subcontractor.

Contracting officers and prime contractors may rely on the representation of an Indian organization or Indian-owned economic enterprise as to its eligibility, unless another potential offeror challenges its status prior to subcontract award or the contracting officer has independent reason to question that status. The contracting officer then refers the matter to the BIA, to determine the eligibility and notify the contracting officer of its decision. This process can take up to seven weeks. The prime contractor withholds award of the subcontract pending the determination by BIA, unless the prime contractor and contracting officer determine that award must be made in order to permit timely performance of the prime contract. Challenges received after award of the subcontract are referred to BIA, but its determination has prospective application only. If the BIA determination is not received within the prescribed time period, the contracting officer and the prime contractor may rely on the representation of the subcontractor.

Contract Clause and Solicitation Provision

FAR 52.226-1, Utilization of Indian Organizations and Indian-Owned Economic Enterprises, if subcontracting possibilities exist for Indian organizations or Indian-owned economic enterprises, and funds are available for any incentive payment.

2.7.7 Disaster or Emergency Assistance

FAR 26.2

The Robert T. Stafford Disaster Relief and Emergency Assistance Act (42 U.S.C. 5150) provides a preference for local firms, individuals and organizations when contracting for major disaster or emergency assistance activities, such as flood or hurricane recoveries. Agencies performing response, relief and reconstruction activities must transition to local firms any work performed under contracts which are in effect on the date on which the President declares a major disaster or emergency, unless the head of such agency determines in writing that transition is not feasible or practicable.

Preference may be given through a local area set-aside or an evaluation preference. The contracting officer may set aside solicitations to allow only local firms within a specific geographic area to compete, but must first define the specific geographic area. This geographic area may or may not include all the counties in the declared disaster/emergency area(s), but cannot go outside the area(s). The contracting officer also determines whether a local area set-aside should be further restricted to small business concerns in the set-aside area. Any decision against a set-aside requires written justification.

A list of prospective vendors voluntarily participating in the Disaster Response Registry can be retrieved using the SAM Search tool at https://www.acquisition.gov. Contractors must register with SAM in order to gain access to the Disaster Response Registry.

Solicitation Provision and Contract Clauses

FAR 52.226-3, Disaster or Emergency Area Representation.

FAR 52.226-4, Notice of Disaster or Emergency Area Set-aside.

FAR 52.226-5, Restrictions on Subcontracting Outside Disaster or Emergency Area.

2.7.8 Historically Black Colleges and Universities and Minority Institutions

FAR 26.3

Executive Order 12928, "Promoting Procurement with SDB-HBCU/MI," encourages procurements to historically black colleges and universities and minority institutions. There are no set-aside provisions to these entities, but they are included in an agency's goal of awards to SDBs (usually, at least 5% of total contract dollars).

Solicitation Provisions

FAR 52.226-2, Historically Black College or University and Minority Institution Representation, in solicitations exceeding the micro-purchase threshold, for research, studies, supplies, or services of the type normally acquired from higher educational institutions.

2.7.9 Food Donations to Nonprofit Organizations

FAR 26.4

The Federal Food Donation Act of 2008 (42 U.S.C.1792) encourages executive agencies and their contractors to donate excess food that would otherwise be discarded to nonprofit organizations that provide assistance to needy people in the United States. The food must meet all labeling and quality standards imposed by Federal, State and local laws and regulations. The Government will not reimburse any costs incurred by the contractor for donation of Federal excess foods.

Solicitation Provision and Contract Clause

FAR 52.226-6, Promoting Excess Food Donation to Nonprofit Organizations, if greater than $25,000 to provide, service, or sell food in the United States.

2.7.10 Historically Underutilized Business Zone (HUBZone) Program

FAR 19.13

The Historically Underutilized Business Zone (HUBZone) Act of 1997 (15 U.S.C. 631) created the HUBZone Program ("HUBZone Empowerment Contracting Program") to provide Federal contracting assistance for qualified small business concerns located in such geographic zones. The program is designed to increase economic development, employment and investment in those areas. The company must have its principal office in the HUBZone and at least 35% of its employees must live in any HUBZone (not necessarily the same zone as the office or of other employees).[24]

If the SBA determines that a firm (including a joint venture) qualifies, it issues a certification and adds the concern to the List of Qualified HUBZone Small Business Concerns on its Internet website at http://www.sba.gov/hubzone. A listed firm is eligible for HUBZone program preferences without regard to place of performance.

HUBZone preference does not apply to requirements:

- for commissary or exchange resale items;
- ordered against Federal Supply Schedules or indefinite-delivery contracts;
- that can be satisfied through award to FPI or Javits-Wagner-O'Day Act nonprofit agencies for the blind or severely disabled;
- that SBA has accepted for performance under the authority of the 8(a) Program, unless SBA releases the requirements; or
- within the micro-purchase threshold.

To set aside an acquisition for competition restricted to HUBZone small business concerns, the contracting officer must reasonably expect that offers will be received from two or more HUBZone small business firms, and award will be made at a fair market price. Any HUBZone small business concern proposing a product that it did not itself manufacture must furnish the product of another HUBZone small business concern manufacturer to receive the benefit. The HUBZone concern must perform at least half of the work in-house (for construction contracts, it must perform 15% in-house, or 25% for special trades).

As with other set-aside methods, if the contracting officer receives only one acceptable offer from a qualified HUBZone small business concern in response to a set-aside, award to that concern may proceed. If the contracting officer receives no acceptable offers from HUBZone small business concerns, the set-aside is withdrawn and the requirement is set aside for small business concerns.

A contracting officer may award contracts to HUBZone small business concerns on a sole-source basis without considering small business set-asides if:

- award can be made at a fair and reasonable price;
- only one HUBZone small business concern can satisfy the requirement, and has been determined to be a responsible contractor;
- the anticipated price of the contract, including options, will not exceed $5.5 million for a manufacturing requirement or $3.5 million otherwise; and
- the requirement is not currently performed by a non-HUBZone small business concern.

The SBA has the right to appeal the contracting officer's decision not to make a HUBZone sole-source award. The cognizant SBA official will decide within five business days, and the decision is final on all parties without appeal.

The contracting officer gives preference to offers from HUBZone small business by adding a 10% factor to all other offers except those from HUBZone small business concerns that have not waived the evaluation preference, and from otherwise successful offers from small business concerns. The factor is applied on a line item basis or to any group of line items. Other evaluation factors, such as transportation costs or rent-free use of Government property, are added to the offer price before adding the factor of 10%. The price evaluation preference for HUBZone small business concerns is used in full and open competition that exceeds the simplified acquisition threshold, where price is not a selection factor (e.g., architect/engineer acquisitions), or where all fair and reasonable offers are accepted (e.g., the award of multiple award schedule contracts).

A concern that is both a HUBZone small business concern and a small disadvantaged business concern will receive the benefit of both the HUBZone and the small disadvantaged business evaluation adjustments. Each price adjustment is calculated independently against an offeror's base offer, then added to the base offer to arrive at the total evaluated price.

Solicitation Provisions and Contract Clauses

FAR 52.219-3, Notice of Total HUBZone Set-Aside, for acquisitions that are set aside for HUBZone small business concerns. Use the clause with Alternate I if HUBZone firms cannot meet the 50% in-house rule.

FAR <u>52.219-4</u>, Notice of Price Evaluation Preference for HUBZone Small Business Concerns, if exceeding the simplified acquisition threshold. Use the clause with Alternate I if HUBZone firms cannot meet the 50% in-house rule.

2.7.11 Woman-Owned Businesses

FAR 19.15

Another size preference program covers firms where at least 51% is owned and controlled by one or more women. The SBA will determine those NAICS codes where such firms are underrepresented in Federal contracting. Such firms must be certified by an SBA-approved third-party certifier, however self-certification is acceptable if proper documentation has already been submitted but the SBA has not yet completed its review and no protest is filed. Again, a protest process through SBA exists which allows 15 days after receipt to respond to any protest. The contracting officer does have an appeal right and can maintain an award based on a written D&F to any adverse decision. However, no options or further orders may be placed.

Both sole-source and competitive awards are possible under this program. Competition is required for set-aside procurements of $6.5 million for manufacturing or $4 million for services. The set-aside may be further restricted to economically disadvantaged woman-owned businesses if sufficient competition is expected.

Solicitation Provisions and Contract Clauses

FAR <u>52.219-29</u>, Notice of Set-Aside for, or Sole Source Award to, Economically Disadvantaged Women-Owned Small Business Concerns.

FAR <u>52.219-30</u>, Notice of Set-Aside for, or Sole Source Award to, Women-Owned Small Business Concerns Eligible Under the Women-Owned Small Business Program.

2.7.12 Disabilities

Although no preference programs exist for commercial concerns run by non-service-disabled persons, all firms must comply with Section 508 of the Americans with Disabilities Act (42 U.S.C. 12101). A critical player in this program is the United States Access Board, an independent Federal agency which provides guidance on accessibility standards for people with physical disabilities. These include design criteria for buildings, classroom acoustics, computer systems, public transportation vehicles, and telecommunications equipment. The board provides technical assistance and training on these guidelines to firms, and enforces standards on federally funded construction projects. There are no FAR clauses for this program as of yet.

2.8 RESEARCH AND DEVELOPMENT

FAR Part 35

2.8.1 Policy

Government *research and development* (R&D) programs advance and apply scientific and technical knowledge to achieve agency and national goals. Unlike contracts for supplies and services, most R&D contracts have objectives for which the work or methods cannot be precisely described in advance, and may offer little or no assurance of full success.

Research and development consists of four stages:

- basic research;
- applied research;
- design; and
- development.

Basic research investigates a physical phenomenon in an effort to gain knowledge. It focuses on achieving specified objectives rather than predetermined end results written in a work statement. To pursue this focus, technical and contracting personnel consider:

- area of exploration and objectives;
- background information for the objective (e.g., known phenomena, methodology, techniques, or results of related work);
- contract type;
- design-to-cost requirements;
- for level-of-effort work statements, an estimate of applicable professional and technical effort involved;
- information on environment, interfaces and personnel that may constrain the results; and
- reporting requirements or deliverables due at specific intervals as the work progresses.

Applied research normally follows basic research, but may not always be severable. Designed to identify potential application of the knowledge, it attempts to determine and exploit the potential of scientific discoveries or improvements in devices, materials, methods, processes, techniques, or technology. The basic intent, of course, is to advance the state of the art.

Design uses creativity and problem-solving skills to explore possibilities and constraints to create a new or revised product or service. The firm will test and modify it until efficiently reaching full-scale operability at an acceptable cost. It may also prototype possible solutions, investigate external trends, and revise current specifications.

Development first reduces the potential application to a model, prototype or specification(s) to demonstrate its physical capability or operational feasibility. The firm then systematically uses the scientific and technical knowledge gained in the research phases to design, test and evaluate the target product or service to meet the performance requirements or objectives. This phase includes design engineering, prototyping and engineering testing. It does not include any subcontracted technical effort which would be designed solely to develop an additional source for an existing product. A program is said to reach *full-scale development* when the items have been designed, fabricated, tested, and evaluated. The production process should by now mimic full-scale production. Documented test results provide confidence that the final product will meet the requirements.

The absence of precise specifications and difficulties in estimating costs with accuracy normally precludes using fixed-price contracting for R&D. Hence, the use of cost-reimbursement contracts is usually appropriate, often with a completion arrangement. Whenever levels of effort can be specified in advance, a short-term fixed-price contract may be useful to develop system design concepts, resolve potential problems, and reduce Government risks. Fixed-price contracting may also be used in minor projects when the objectives of the research are well-defined and there is enough confidence in the cost estimate for price negotiations.

R&D projects with future production requirements normally move from cost-reimbursement to fixed-price contracts as designs become more firmly established and risks are reduced. Adopting a fixed-price contract will occur as production equipment, processes and tooling are developed and proven.

Corporate research and development activities may have a different objective, as they are intended to enhance the firm's competitive posture. Here, research entails discovering and expanding product and technological knowledge, including knowledge of competitors' products. Research can also lead to processes that reduce capital and operating costs, and improve performance of existing products and processes. Corporate development projects can find and create not only new products, but also new uses for existing products. The results can also provide technical expertise to the firm's other functional departments.

A firm often allocates a set percentage of projected revenue (say, 3%) to such effort, since such an investment is essential in this era of quickly evolving technology. The firm's management must decide on how to evaluate potential research and development projects. It may consider analysis of intrinsic worth, cost, literature and patent search, and usability within the firm's capabilities. Project selection methods are either qualitative (using checklists of evaluation factors) or quantitative (e.g., determining rate of return and present value using an index of relative worth or project value). Projects may also be selected to leverage off existing processes, software or technology. Decisions could also be driven by customer need or competitors' development projects.

New product development (NPD) is a process which emphasizes external interaction to reduce product cost and time-to-market. This idea is geared toward increasing innovation and profitability. For instance, some firms may wish to transfer design responsibility upstream to their suppliers. A firm can use techniques to speed up cycle time such as concurrent engineering and product simplicity. They may also employ integrated teams for design, development, manufacturing, marketing, and research. This development process also considers such areas as quality, reliability, responsiveness, robustness, service, and technology.

There are several ways in which a firm can decide to pursue development. It can be done sequentially using one approach at a time and then discarding it for another approach if it proves unworkable. Alternatively, development effort may be performed in parallel using multiple approaches. This *parallel development* method involves concurrent work on different products which may go into production at different times. Sometimes customizations can be done simultaneously to products that are otherwise unrelated to each other. Dependencies sometimes result where two teams implement components which are related to each other. This parallel approach avoids the need to choose a best solution upfront, however management must eventually decide when to focus on only one approach and drop the others. Further, the project must still set goals and furnish progress reports, evaluation and corrective actions, and follow-up activities. Liaison among departments is essential to smoothly transfer approaches into production and convert lab language into shop talk.

2.8.2 Solicitations

FAR 35.007

Contracting officers solicit only sources that are technically qualified to perform research or development in the specific field of science or technology. They rely on technical personnel to recommend potential sources that appear qualified based on their:

- ability to acquire and retain the professional and technical capability and facilities to perform the work;
- past and present performance of similar work;
- professional stature and reputation; and
- relative position in the field of study.

Solicitations require offerors to describe their technical and management approach, identify and propose resolution of any uncertainties, and include any planned subcontracting of scientific or technical work. They contain evaluation factors to determine the most technically competent offeror, e.g.:

- approach proposed to accomplish the scientific and technical objectives, or the merit of the ideas or concepts proposed;
- availability and competence of experienced engineering, scientific or technical personnel;
- availability of necessary laboratory, research, shop, or testing facilities;
- novel ideas in the specific branch of science and technology involved;
- past experience; and
- understanding of the scope of the work.

The contracting officer also considers management capability (including cost management techniques), past performance and subcontracting practices. Generally, an R&D contract is awarded to the firm that proposes the best ideas and has the highest competence in the specific field of science or technology. Although cost or price is not normally the controlling factor in selecting a contractor to perform R&D, it is considered for source selection.

R&D contracts require contractors to furnish scientific and technical reports as a permanent record of the work accomplished under the contract. Agencies provide R&D contract results to other Government activities and the National Technical Information Service, as well as the private sector.[25] Contracting officers follow agency regulations regarding data protection, national security and new-technology dissemination. As stated before, R&D contracts must specify the technical data to be delivered under the contract, since the FAR data clauses do not require delivery of any such data.

In planning a developmental program when subsequent production contracts are contemplated, program offices consider the need and time required to obtain a technical package (drawings, plans and specifications) to achieve competition for production. Sometimes, the developmental contractor may be in the best position to produce such a technical package.

If the contractor obtains the contracting officer's advance approval, it automatically acquires and retains title to any item of equipment costing less than $5,000 (or a lesser amount established by agency regulations). For a larger dollar value, title may vest in the contractor, either upon acquisition without further obligation to the Government, or subject to the Government's right to directly transfer title to the Government or to a third party within 12 months after contract completion or termination. If title to equipment is vested in the contractor, no charges for amortization, depreciation or use are allowable under any existing or future Government (sub)contract. If the contract is performed at a Government installation and there is a continuing need for the equipment after contract completion, the Government may choose to retain title.

An educational institution or other nonprofit organization performing R&D work bears primary responsibility for the research if it is not defined precisely, and the contract states only a period during which work is conducted. The contractor must obtain contracting officer approval to change the phenomenon under study, or the stated research objectives or methodology. The contractor also provides the name of the principal investigator or project leader who is continuously responsible for the conduct of the work, estimates the amount of time that individual will devote to the work, and advises the contracting officer if this person will, or plans to, either leave the contract or devote substantially less effort to the work than anticipated.

An advance procurement plan is developed to describe the procurement method, timetable and expected price. Advance notification of the acquisition should be given the widest practicable dissemination by publicizing through the GPE and distribution to educational institutions, FFRDCs, foreign sources, Government laboratories, nonprofit organizations, and small businesses. The Government can also encourage industry participation by using draft solicitations and presolicitation conferences with prospective offerors for comment and solicitation revision.

The contracting officer sends the final solicitation to all prospective offerors to:

- describe the required mission capabilities without reference to any specific systems;
- include selection requirements;
- indicate and explain the capability, cost objectives, known constraints, and schedule;
- provide or indicate how to access all Government data related to the acquisition;
- reflect (if required) the use of an Earned Value Management System; and
- state that each offeror is free to propose its own design features, subsystems, technical approach, and alternatives to capability, cost and schedule goals.

The solicitation does not reference or mandate Government specifications or standards, unless the agency is mandating a subsystem or other component as approved under agency procedures. Proposals should discuss the right to use technical data deliverables for competitive future acquisitions (including acquisition and usage costs), and development or qualification of multiple sources of supply for competitive future acquisitions.

2.8.3 Broad Agency Announcement

FAR 35.016

A *broad agency announcement* (BAA) may be used by agencies for scientific study and experimentation directed toward advancing the state of the art, or increasing knowledge rather than focusing on a specific system or hardware solution. The focus is on seeking new and innovative approaches and ideas to solve a specific problem. The BAA technique is only used when meaningful proposals with varying technical or scientific approaches can be reasonably anticipated. The BAA describes the agency's research interest, either for an individual program requirement or for broad areas of interest. Like any written solicitation, a BAA contains instructions for the preparation and submission of proposals, and describes the criteria for selecting proposals, their relative importance, and the method of evaluation. It also specifies the time period during which proposals will be accepted.

Availability of the BAA must be publicized through the GPE and may also be published in scientific, technical or engineering periodicals at least annually. Proposals are evaluated in accordance with the evaluation criteria through a peer or scientific review process. Written evaluation reports on each proposal are necessary, but proposals need not be evaluated against each other since they are not submitted in accordance with a common work statement. The primary bases for selecting proposals for acceptance are technical ability, importance to agency programs, and available funding. Cost realism and reasonableness are considered if appropriate. Synopsis of any awards is not required.

2.8.4 Grants and Cooperative Agreements

Per the Federal Grant and Cooperative Agreement Act of 1977 (PL 95-224), the Federal Government may not directly procure for a non-Federal entity, but rather must use an instrument of assistance such as a grant or cooperative agreement. *Grants* are awards of funding by the Government to a nonprofit entity, educational institution, firm, or individual. In order to receive a grant, an application or proposal is usually required. Often, a project office will fund multiple proposals through grants based solely on technical compliance, so price competition may not be present. Most grants fund a specific project and require some level of compliance and reporting. Grants have several unique features.

A *parent company guarantee* is used if the customer requires an awardee to provide a guarantee of its performance from its parent company. This document is drafted by the parent company and says that its liability only arises if its subsidiary commits a breach of contract and fails to rectify it. The parent's liability is limited to that of the subsidiary.

Grants may have a *long stop date* which sets a point in time where performance must end, regardless of where research stands or how promising it could be. Continuation of effort would require a new solicitation and consideration of other sources.

A *cooperative agreement* is similar to a grant in that a Government agency provides financial assistance to a commercial firm. However, the agency provides management support of the project collaboratively, often on a cost-sharing basis with the firm. In contrast, grants have little or no Federal involvement in their management.

Independent research and development consists of projects involving basic research, applied research, development, and systems or concept formulation studies. This effort is not directly reimbursed under a contract or grant (but may be to some extent allowable as an indirect expense), nor does it include development of technical data to support bid or proposal preparation. Some major contractors enter into agreement with a Federal agency (e.g., DoD) to be reimbursed a certain amount per year to cover IR&D expenses for projects of interest to that department.

2.8.5 Small Business Innovative Research

The *Small Business Innovation Research* program is coordinated by the SBA to reserve for small business 2.8% of any federal agency's extramural research budget in excess of $100 million.[26] The program funds early-stage innovation ideas that are too risky for private investors or venture capital firms. Recipient firms must have fewer than 500 employees to be eligible. Similarly, the *Small Business Technology Transfer Program* expands partnerships between small businesses and nonprofit U.S. research institutions, and is funded at 0.3% of the same agency's extramural research budgets.[27]

There are three phases in the SBIR Program. Phase I is intended to establish the technical merit, feasibility, and commercial potential of the proposed R&D efforts, as well as the quality of performance of the firm itself. SBIR Phase I awards are generally limited to $150,000 and 6 months of effort. Phase II continues the R&D efforts from Phase I; only

Phase I awardees are eligible for a Phase II award. Funding is based on the scientific and technical merit and commercial potential results achieved in Phase I. SBIR Phase II awards are usually limited to $1,000,000 and two years of effort. A Phase III award allows the small business to pursue commercialization based on the results from earlier phases. The SBIR program does not fund Phase III, however some Federal agencies may provide their own funding for processes, products or services intended for Government use.

2.8.6 Federally Funded Research and Development Centers

FAR 35.017

The Federal Government provides funding support for a number (currently 42 and growing) of licensed nonprofit organizations to conduct effort in specific initiatives of interest. Known as *Federally Funded Research and Development Centers*, these entities furnish state-of-the-art research and education, and seek discoveries, knowledge and technological innovation in such areas as astronomy, cybersecurity, defense, health, nanoscience and nanoengineering, and safety. FFRDCs are operated and managed by a university or consortium thereof, other nonprofit organization, or an industrial firm, as an autonomous or identifiable separate operating unit of the parent organization. A complete list of these centers is found on the National Science Foundation's website at www.nsf.gov/statistics/ffrdclist. Primary sponsors will provide information on each FFRDC, including funding data, mission statements, sponsoring agreements, and type of R&D being performed, to the Foundation upon its request.

An FFRDC meets a special long-term research or development need which is not achievable by existing in-house or contractor resources. FFRDCs allow agencies to use another set of private sector resources to accomplish tasks that are critical to their mission and operations. An FFRDC has access beyond what is common to the normal contractor to Government and supplier data (including proprietary and sensitive data), employees, installation equipment, and real property.[28] Therefore, the FFRDC is responsible to operate in the public interest independently and objectively, remain free from organizational conflicts of interest, and fully disclose its affairs to the sponsoring agency. It is not intended to use these special benefits to compete with the private sector.

Long-term relationships between the Government and FFRDCs provide the continuity that will attract high-quality personnel. This encourages the FFRDC to maintain currency in its field(s) of expertise, familiarity with the needs of its sponsor(s), and a quick response capability.

A written agreement of sponsorship is created with the Government when the FFRDC is established. A sponsor is the executive agency which administers, funds and monitors the overall use of an FFRDC. Multiple agency sponsorship is possible as long as one agency agrees to act as the *primary sponsor* or lead agency under a multiple sponsorship agreement. The following requirements are addressed in either a sponsoring agreement or sponsoring agency's policies and procedures:

- a purpose and mission of the FFRDC;
- considerations which will affect negotiation of any fees;
- cost elements which require advance agreement for cost-type contracts;
- identification of retained earnings and a plan for their use and disposition;
- orderly termination or nonrenewal of the agreement, including disposal of assets and settlement of liabilities;
- prohibition against the FFRDC competing with any non-FFRDC concern in response to a Federal solicitation, though any parent organization or other subsidiary is free to compete; and
- whether or not the FFRDC may accept work from other than the sponsor(s), and if so, the procedures and limits to the nonsponsors from which work can be accepted.

The term of the agreement will not exceed five years, but can be renewed, as a result of periodic review, in increments not to exceed five years.

To establish an FFRDC, or change its basic purpose and mission, the sponsor will:

- determine that existing alternative sources cannot effectively meet the special research or development needs;
- confirm that sufficient Government expertise is available to objectively evaluate the work to be performed by the FFRDC;
- ensure that all work placed with the FFRDC is within the purpose, mission, general scope, or special competency of the FFRDC;
- ensure that the FFRDC refrain from quantity production or manufacturing unless authorized by legislation;
- establish controls to ensure that the costs of the services are reasonable;
- maintain continuity in the level of support to the FFRDC, consistent with the agency's need for the FFRDC and the terms of the sponsoring agreement;
- notify the Executive Office of the President, Office of Science and Technology Policy;
- operate in the public interest, free from organizational conflict of interest;
- place notices required for publication;

- receive approval from the head of the sponsoring agency; and
- state the basic purpose and mission of the FFRDC to differentiate from work which should be performed by non-FFRDCs.

The head of the sponsoring agency, prior to extending the contract or agreement with an FFRDC, conducts a comprehensive review of the use and need for the FFRDC. The review is coordinated with any co-sponsors and may be performed in conjunction with the budget process. A negative decision requires the sponsor to allow other agencies which use the FFRDC to assume sponsorship, or else phase out operations. An FFRDC review should examine the:

- adequacy of the FFRDC management to ensure a cost-effective operation;
- alternative sources to meet the sponsor's needs;
- criteria for establishing the FFRDC;
- efficiency and effectiveness of the FFRDC in meeting the sponsor's needs;
- FFRDC's ability to maintain currency in its field(s) of expertise, familiarity with the sponsor's needs, independence, objectivity, and quick response capability; and
- sponsor's technical needs and mission requirements that are performed by the FFRDC to determine if and at what level they continue to exist.

2.9 SERVICE CONTRACTS

A *service* delivers value to customers by using the firm's employees to obtain or facilitate desired outcomes. A customer will contract out for services when it does not want to own the costs and risks of performance, or lacks the needed knowledge or technological expertise in-house. Moreover, the supplier of the service can spread its costs among multiple customers, which not only lowers prices but also allows each customer to focus on its specific needs. By definition, services are intangible and perishable if not delivered.

To deliver value, a firm must use its service assets, which are normally a capability or a resource. Examples of assets include:

- capital;
- information;
- infrastructure;
- knowledge;
- management;
- organization;

- people;
- processes; and
- software applications.

Services must have utility to support customer performance and remove some constraints. Services must also have the functionality to meet a need (also known as *fitness for purpose*). To ensure the functionality and utility of a service, the firm should:

- enable the customer to integrate the service into its business processes;
- minimize unpredictable impact on customer operations;
- reduce variation between predicted and actual value of services; and
- set customer expectations on performance and use of results.

Many service contracts (especially those in support of information systems) use *service level agreements* to define service targets and responsibilities of both parties, in an effort to enhance service performance. Tailored to the specific needs of the operation, service level agreements document customer needs and provider responses. Each service level requirement is based on a business objective and a target level of support. These requirements can be geared toward the customer or the service, or both.

Integral to proper operation of these agreements is the process of *continual service improvement*. This concept is intended to boost quality of services delivered, as well as both the return and value of the firm's investment to deliver these services. Continual service improvement examples include efforts to:

- assess and recommend areas for improvement;
- conduct customer satisfaction surveys;
- conduct internal audits to verify process compliance;
- furnish a benefit that exceeds the amount expended to achieve it;
- increase value of non-monetary or long-term outcomes;
- increase a desirable metric or reduce an undesirable metric; and
- review management information and trends.

Any improvements must be both objective and measurable, and must meet the firm's business strategy. Once the improvement is implemented, the firm must then measure its achievements, validate the action as being correct, and provide any necessary change in direction. These metrics can address improved process efficiency and effectiveness, or technology, or just achievement of a goal.

2.9.1 Federal Service Contracting

FAR 37.1

A *service contract* directly engages the time and effort of a contractor to perform an identifiable task rather than to furnish an end item of supply. A service contract can cover services performed by either professional or non-professional personnel on an individual or organizational basis. Some areas in which service contracts are found include:

- advice and assistance;
- architect-engineering;
- communications;
- housekeeping and base support;
- modernization, modification, overhaul, rehabilitation, repair, salvage, or servicing of equipment, supplies or systems;
- operation of Government-owned equipment, real property and systems;
- recurring maintenance of real property;
- research and development; and
- transportation.

As a special type of service, a *personal services contract* is characterized by the employer-employee relationship it creates between the customer and the contractor's personnel. Such a relationship occurs under a service contract when, as a result of contract terms or the manner of administration during performance, contractor personnel are subject to the relatively continuous supervision and control of a customer officer or employee.

The very nature of a personal services contract is inherently a real problem in Federal contracting. The Government is required to obtain its employees by direct hire. Obtaining personal services by contract circumvents those laws unless Congress has specifically authorized acquisition of the services through contracting. Hence, agencies do not award personal services contracts unless specifically authorized by statute. However, giving an order for a specific item or service, with the right to reject the finished product or result, is an acceptable action. Examples of situations which raise the spectre of personal services include:

- comparable services that meet similar needs performed in the same or similar agencies using civil service personnel;
- performance on-site;
- services integral to the agency mission;

- the nature of the service or its performance requires Government direction or supervision of contractor employees to retain Government control of the function;
- the need for the service is expected to last beyond one year; or
- tools and equipment are furnished by the Government.

On-site performance is an especially tricky situation. Government personnel must respect the need for distance between themselves and contractor employees. Even though many service contracts require on-site performance (especially where access to classified information is regularly required), it still presents an easy opportunity for Government personnel to "cross the line" and provide personal direction contrary to the arm's-length distance they are required to obey. This problem can best be avoided through constant vigilance by supervisors and the contracting officer.

For service contracts funded by annual appropriations, the term does not normally extend beyond the end of the fiscal year of the appropriation except when authorized by law. Nevertheless, an executive agency[29] may enter into a contract, exercise an option, or place an order for severable services for a period that begins in one fiscal year and ends in the next fiscal year if the total period of the contract, option or order does not exceed 12 months. Funds made available for the current fiscal year may be obligated for the total amount of such an action.

Award of contracts for recurring and continuing service requirements are often delayed due to circumstances beyond the control of contracting offices. To avoid recurring short contract extensions, the contracting officer may include an option clause to require continued performance of services within the limits and at the rates specified in the contract. However, these rates may be adjusted only as a result of revisions to prevailing labor rates provided by the Secretary of Labor. The option provision may be exercised more than once, but the total extension of performance may not exceed six months.

Contracting officers may enter into contracts with temporary help service firms for the brief use of private sector temporaries. These services are not regarded as personal services, but cannot be used in lieu of recruitment under civil service laws or to displace a Federal employee.

The head of any agency may waive the cost allowability limitations on severance payments to foreign nationals before awarding a contract performed in whole or in part outside the United States that provides significant support services for members of the armed forces or Federal employees stationed outside the United States. However, contracts are prohibited with organizations that offer quasi-military armed forces for hire, or with their employees. However, guard or protective services are not considered to be armed forces and may be covered by contract.

Any time the Government requires the contractor to provide advice, analyses, ideas, opinions, recommendations, or reports could influence the accountability, authority and responsibilities of Government officials. Hence, agencies must again ensure that qualified Government employees oversee contractor activities, especially to support Government policy or decision-making. All contract personnel who attend meetings and answer Government telephones, and whose contractor status is not obvious to third parties, must identify themselves as contractors to avoid creating an impression that they are Government officials, unless the agency decides that no harm can come if they fail to identify themselves. The Government ensures that all documents or reports produced by contractors are marked as contractor products.

Use of uncompensated overtime is a very controversial subject. In this situation, contract employees are working more than 40 hours per week with little or no pay or premium for their extra time.[30] This results in free labor to the Government, which is cost-effective but contrary to public labor policy. To address this two-sided problem, the Government has adopted the position that uncompensated overtime is neither encouraged nor prohibited. When professional or technical services are acquired by number of hours rather than task, the solicitation requires offerors to identify uncompensated overtime hours and the overtime rate for proposed personnel, including subcontractors. The use of uncompensated overtime cannot degrade the level of technical expertise required to meet Government requirements. Contracting officers conduct a risk assessment and look for unrealistically low labor rates and unbalanced distribution of uncompensated overtime.

Solicitation Provisions

FAR 52.237-1, Site Visit, for services performed on Government installations, except for construction.

FAR 52.237-8, Restriction on Severance Payments to Foreign Nationals, where the cost accounting standard for such payments has been waived. However, the clause is still required for military banking contracts or for certain work performed in the Philippines.

FAR 52.237-10, Identification of Uncompensated Overtime, if above the simplified acquisition threshold, for professional or technical services to be acquired based on the number of hours.

Solicitation Provisions and Contract Clauses

FAR 52.237-2, Protection of Government Buildings, Equipment, and Vegetation, for services to be performed on Government installations, except for construction.

FAR 52.237-3, Continuity of Services, for services vital to the Government that must continue without interruption and which, upon contract expiration, can be continued by either the Government or another contractor. It can also be used when the Government anticipates difficulties during the transition from one contractor to another or to the Government (e.g., services in remote locations or requiring personnel with special security clearances).

FAR 52.237-9, Waiver of Limitation on Severance Payments to Foreign Nationals, when the head of an agency has granted a waiver.

FAR 52.237-11, Accepting and Dispensing of $1 Coin, for services that involve business operations conducted in U.S. coins and currency, including vending machines, on any property owned by the United States or under the control of any agency or instrumentality of the United States.

FAR 4.17

All service contractors are required to submit an annual report for both the total dollars and direct labor hours charged to each of its Government contracts. First-tier subcontractors must report the same information to their prime contractors, unless their only contracts are fixed-price and below $500,000.

Contract Clauses

FAR 52.204-14, Service Contract Reporting Requirements.

FAR 52.204-15, Service Contract Reporting Requirements for Indefinite-Delivery Contracts.

2.9.2 Service Contract Act of 1965

FAR 22.10

Service employees are those persons performing in service contracts who are not administrators, executives or professionals. Contracts over $2,500 for services performed within the United States or its possessions require equivalent Federal employee classifications and wage rates (or minimum wages if no Federal classifications apply) and fringe benefits for service employees, plus safe and sanitary working conditions.[31] The firm must notify employees of same by posting notices addressing these requirements. Contracts for service employees may not exceed five years in length.

If a predecessor contractor had a collective bargaining agreement for substantially the same services performed in the same locality, the successor contractor must pay wages and fringe benefits (including accrued wages and benefits and prospective increases) at least equal to those contained in the agreement. If no predecessor contractor's collective bargaining agreement applies, then the Department of Labor may issue a wage determination to determine minimum wages and fringe benefits, based on employment of class(es) of service employees in the given locality. The contractor must then pay employees the amount set forth in the wage determination; otherwise, the minimum wage set forth in the Fair Labor Standards Act applies, based on a 40-hour workweek. The Service Contract Act does not apply to a contract for:

- agricultural, nursery and livestock products, and related work subject to 41 USC 65;
- calibration, maintenance or repair of the following types of equipment if used for non-Government purposes and sold in substantial quantities to the general public:[32]
  - automated data processing and information/word processing systems,
  - office or business machines serviced by the manufacturer or supplier, or
  - scientific and medical equipment using micro-electronic circuitry or similar sophisticated technology;
- construction of public buildings or works;
- direct services to a Federal agency by an individual(s);
- hotel/motel services for conferences, including lodging and/or meals;
- issuance and servicing of financial cards (credit, debit, purchase, and smart cards);
- operating postal contract stations or mail delivery service for the U.S. Postal Service;
- public utility services;
- radio, telegraph, telephone, or cable services;
- real estate and property appraisal services;
- transportation of persons or freight by common carrier (air, marine vessel, motor vehicle, or rail) or pipeline under published tariff rates; or
- vehicle maintenance services (unless to operate a Government motor pool).

The real estate and property appraisal services listed above must be related to housing or disposal of real property to be excluded from the Service Contract Act. This includes relocation services of real estate brokers and appraisers to assist Federal employees or military personnel in buying and selling homes. However, actual moving or storage of household goods and related services are subject to wage determinations.

Examples of services which are covered by the Service Contract Act include:

- aerial spraying and reconnaissance for fire detection;
- custodial and housekeeping services;
- data analysis, collection and processing;

- drafting, illustrating and graphic arts;
- electronic equipment maintenance and operation;
- engineering support;
- food service and lodging;
- grounds maintenance and landscaping;
- laundry, dry cleaning, linen supply, and clothing alteration and repair;
- maintenance and repair of equipment such as aircraft, construction equipment, electrical motors, electronic office equipment, engines, and vehicles;
- mortuary services;
- operation, maintenance or logistics support of a Federal facility;
- packing, crating and storage;
- repair of equipment other than remanufacturing or major overhaul;
- security guard services;
- snow and trash removal;
- stenographic reporting; and
- vehicle services such as ambulance, motor pool operation, parking, and taxi services.

Executive Order 13658, Establishing a Minimum Wage for Contractors, of February 12, 2014, may also apply to certain individuals who will be subject to minimum wage standards. These wage rates are set forth in an Executive Order. The minimum rate is currently $10.10 per hour, and may be adjusted either by law or annually based on the Consumer Price Index, rounded off to the nearest nickel. If the minimum wage rate is increased during performance, the contractor may be entitled to a price increase. There is no decrease if the minimum wage should go down (since the Government does not want to encourage wage cuts to individual contract employees). The Department of Labor will investigate any claims of below-minimum-rate payments, and may instruct the contracting officer to withhold payments.

To obtain the applicable wage determination from the Department of Labor, the contracting officer determines the following information concerning the service employees expected to be employed by the (sub)contractor:

- classes of service employees to be used in performing the contract;
- locality(ies) where the services will be performed;
- wage rate that would be paid each class if employed by the agency; and
- whether a predecessor contract is covered by the Act and if the incumbent (sub)contractor(s) and employees have a collective bargaining agreement.

If service employees of the incumbent (sub)contractor are represented by a collective bargaining agent, the contracting officer must receive a copy of the agreement (usually from the administrative contracting officer).

The contracting officer then provides both the incumbent contractor and its employees' collective bargaining agent with written notification of the upcoming successor contract or modification and critical acquisition dates (e.g., issuance of solicitation, bid opening, negotiations, contract award, start of performance, and contract anniversary date) at least 30 days before the acquisition or anniversary date.

The contracting officer must monitor the www.wdol.gov website to learn of any revisions to wage determinations, and incorporate them into the acquisition. Any revision at least 10 days before sealed bid opening or 30 days after award of a negotiated contract must be incorporated, with equitable adjustment if necessary.

Upon award, the contracting officer furnishes the contractor with a copy of Department of Labor Publication WH-1313, Notice to Employees Working on Government Contracts, for posting at the workplace in an accessible location. This poster addresses employee rights regarding:

• minimum wages (attaching a copy of any wage determination which dictates a higher pay rate);
• fringe benefits required by the wage determination;
• overtime pay (time-and-a-half for all effort in excess of 40 hours in a week);
• child labor (employees on a federal contract must be at least 16 years of age);
• safety and health (work conditions must be sanitary and not hazardous or dangerous for employees); and
• enforcement (e-mail addresses and phone numbers for Department of Labor and Occupational Safety and Health Administration).

If a contract is performed at a Federal facility where employees may be hired or retained by a succeeding contractor, the incumbent prime contractor furnishes a certified list of all service employees on the payroll and anniversary dates of employment to the contracting officer at least 10 days before contract completion. At the beginning of the succeeding contract, the contracting officer provides the list to the successor contractor to determine employee eligibility for vacation or other fringe benefits based upon length of service with predecessor contractors.

Any violations of the Service Contract Act render the contractor liable for the amount of any deductions, rebates, refunds, underpayments, or nonpayment of compensation due to contract employees. The contracting officer withholds (either on his/her own initiative or upon written request of the Department of Labor) the amount needed to pay such employees from accrued payments due to the contractor on any contract (whether subject to the Service Contract Act or not). Any contractor failure to comply with the requirements of the Service Contract Act contract clause may be grounds for termination for default.

A list of persons or firms found to be in violation of the Act is contained in the Excluded Parties List System. No Government (sub)contract may be awarded to any violator or entity in which the violator has a substantial interest, without the approval of the Secretary of Labor.

FAR 22.19

Executive Order 13658, Establishing a minimum wage for contractors, of February 12, 2014, establishes minimum wages for certain workers who are not administrative, executive or professional employees. The wage rate is subject to annual increases by an amount determined by the Secretary of Labor. These amounts may exceed a collective bargaining agreement wage or a minimum wage determination issued by the Department of Labor, in which cases this higher amount takes precedence. Any complaints lodged regarding violation of this Executive Order will be investigated by the Department of Labor, and the contracting officer will furnish information as requested by that Department. If a violation is found, the contracting officer may withhold payment or pursue debarment until the contractor fully pays the employee(s).

Solicitation Provisions

FAR 52.222-48, Exemption from Application of the Service Contract Act to Contracts for Maintenance, Calibration, or Repair of Certain Equipment–Certification, if applicability of the Service Contract Act of 1965 clause is unclear due to the exception for calibration, maintenance or repair of equipment.

FAR 52.222-52, Exemption from Application of the Service Contract Act to Contracts for Certain Services–Certification, if applicability of the Service Contract Act of 1965 clause is unclear due to the presence of another exception.

Solicitation Provisions and Contract Clauses

FAR 52.222-41, Service Contract Act of 1965, for services over $2,500, unless the solicitation includes either FAR 52.222-48 or FAR 52.222-52, Exemption from Application of the Service Contract Act to Contracts for Certain Services—Certification.

FAR 52.222-42, Statement of Equivalent Rates for Federal Hires, if expected to be over $2,500 and the Service Contract Act is applicable.

FAR 52.222-43, Fair Labor Standards Act and Service Contract Act – Price Adjustment (Multiple Year and Option Contracts), if fixed-price containing the Service Contract Act of 1965 clause, exceeds the simplified acquisition threshold, and could run longer than one year (including options).

FAR 52.222-44, Fair Labor Standards Act and Service Contract Act – Price Adjustment, if fixed-price containing the Service Contract Act of 1965 clause, exceeds the simplified acquisition threshold, and is not expected to run longer than one year.

FAR 52.222-49, Service Contract Act – Place of Performance Unknown.

FAR 52.222-51, Exemption from Application of the Service Contract Act to Contracts for Maintenance, Calibration, or Repair of Certain Equipment – Requirements (or FAR 52.222-53), if FAR 52.222-48 applies.

FAR 52.222-53, Exemption from Application of the Service Contract Act to Contracts for Certain Services—Requirements, if FAR 52.222-52 applies.

FAR 52.222-55, Minimum Wages under Executive Order 13658.

2.9.3 Advisory and Assistance Services

FAR 37-2

OMB Circular A-120, Guidelines for the Use of Advisory and Assistance Services, prohibits acquisition of professional and technical advice that is available within the agency, unless acquired through A-76 procedures. Agencies may contract for *advisory and assistance services* to obtain:

- advice regarding developments in foundation, industry or university research;
- operational support and improvement of an organization or its hardware or managerial systems;
- opinions, skills or special knowledge of noted experts;
- outside points of view to avoid too-limited judgment on critical issues; or
- understanding of, and developing alternative solutions to, complex issues.

Advisory and assistance services are not awarded for:

- architectural and engineering services;
- awards on a preferential basis to former Government employees;
- basic research of biological, medical, physical, psychological, or social phenomena;
- bypassing personnel ceilings, pay limitations or competitive employment procedures;
- influencing or enacting legislation;

- obtaining professional or technical advice which is readily available within the agency or another Federal agency;
- policy, decision-making or managerial effort which is a direct responsibility of agency officials;
- research on theoretical mathematics; or
- routine information technology services, unless integral to acquire advisory and assistance services.

Contractors (other than FFRDCs) may not be paid for services to evaluate a proposal submitted for an initial award unless no civil service or military personnel with adequate training and capabilities are readily available, including from other agencies. However, FFRDCs may evaluate proposals because they are not in direct competition with the offerors.

Contracts for health care providers require the contractor to indemnify the Government for any act or omission committed by itself, its employees or agents occurring during contract performance. Although the Government may evaluate the quality of professional and administrative services provided, it cannot retain control over their professional judgments or diagnosis for specific medical treatment. The contractor must maintain medical liability insurance, at least in the amount in the locally prevailing community.

Solicitation Provision and Contract Clause

FAR 52.237-7, Indemnification and Medical Liability Insurance.

2.9.4 Utility Services

FAR Part 41

Utility services include furnishing electricity, natural or manufactured gas, sewage, thermal energy, chilled or hot water, or steam. Other services such as rubbish or snow removal may be appropriate when the acquisition is not subject to the Service Contract Act of 1965. Utility services provisions do not apply to:

- cable television and telecommunications services;
- construction or maintenance of Government-owned equipment and real property;
- natural or manufactured gas when purchased as a commodity;
- rights in public utility facilities, real property and on-site equipment needed for the facility's own distribution system;
- third-party-financed shared-savings projects;[33]

- utility services in foreign countries; or
- utility services obtained by purchase or exchange by a Federal power or water marketing agency's distribution program, or provided by another Federal agency under interagency agreements.

The GSA prescribes policies and methods governing the acquisition and supply of utility services for Federal agencies. This includes managing public utility services and representing Federal agencies in proceedings before Federal and state regulatory bodies. GSA contracts for utility services for periods not exceeding 10 years. However, there are a couple of exceptions. DoD is authorized to acquire utility services for military facilities. Department of Energy is authorized to obtain electric services for up to 25 years for uranium-enrichment installations.

Requests for delegations of contracting authority from GSA must include a certification from the acquiring agency's Senior Procurement Executive that the agency has an established acquisition program, personnel technically qualified to deal with specialized utilities problems, and the ability to accomplish its own pre-award contract review.

Purchase of electricity must be consistent with state law governing the provision of electric utility service. This includes state utility commission rulings and electric utility franchises or service territories established pursuant to state regulation or statute, or territorial agreement. The contracting officer conducts a market survey of other qualified sources who can meet the Government's requirements, or consults with state officials before acquiring electric utility services on a competitive basis. If competition for an entire utility service (e.g., energy, sewage, transportation, water, standby or back-up service, or transmission and/or distribution service) or associated services (e.g., billing, metering, operation and maintenance, quality assurance, or system reliability) is not available, the market survey may be used to determine the availability of competitive sources for certain portions of the requirement.

GSA enters into an area-wide contract with a utility service supplier to cover needs of Federal agencies within the supplier's franchise territory. A *franchise territory* is a geographical area that a utility supplier has a right to serve based upon either a franchise or a certificate of public convenience and necessity. Each area-wide contract includes an authorization form to request service, (dis)connection, or change in service within the franchise territory or service area. Rates must be approved and/or established by a regulatory body and published in a tariff or rate schedule. Agencies are free to negotiate other rates and terms and conditions of service with the supplier, but may require the approval of the regulatory body to change them. Though these contracts normally run for just one year, they can last up to 10 years if the provider insists or can offer lower rates or charges. GSA will require at least four months to provide these services. The service request to GSA includes:

- accounting data for contractor payment;
- connection charges to be paid by the Government;
- date of service initiation;
- demand and consumption estimates (both initial and maximum, along with time frame to ramp up to maximum);
- meter and facility locations (including meter placement with regard to the transformer);
- necessary new connection facilities;
- termination liability; and
- twelve-month actuals for demand and cost.

Utility service contracts usually contain one or two unique charges. A *connection charge* covers all nonrecurring costs, whether refundable or not, to be paid by the Government to the utility supplier for the required connecting facilities which are installed, owned, operated, and maintained by the utility supplier. The *termination liability* is a contingent Government obligation to pay a utility supplier the unamortized portion of a connection charge and nonrefundable service charge if the Government terminates the contract before the utility supplier has recovered the cost of the connection facilities.

Agencies review utility service invoices on a monthly basis, and all utility accounts with annual values exceeding the simplified acquisition threshold on an annual basis. This ensures that the utility supplier is furnishing services under the most economical applicable rate, and permits examining competitive markets for more advantageous service offerings. The annual review is based upon the facility's usage, conditions, values, and characteristics of service at each delivery point collected for the most recent 12 months. If a more advantageous rate is appropriate, the Federal agency requests the supplier to change the rate immediately.

Any rate change by a regulatory body is added to the contract by unilateral modification or otherwise documented in accordance with agency procedures. The contractor need not sign the modification because it has been decreed by the applicable Government agency. The approved rate is effective on the date determined by the regulatory body.

Solicitation Provision

FAR 52.241-1, Electric Service Territory Compliance Representation, for utility services when proposals from alternative electric suppliers are sought.

Solicitation Provisions and Contract Clauses

FAR 52.241-2, Order of Precedence-Utilities.

FAR 52.241-3, Scope and Duration of Contract.

FAR 52.241-4, Change in Class of Service.

FAR 52.241-5, Contractor's Facilities.

FAR 52.241-6, Service Provisions.

FAR 52.241-7, Change in Rates or Terms and Conditions of Service for Regulated Services, when the utility services are subject to a regulatory body.

FAR 52.241-8, Change in Rates or Terms and Conditions of Service for Unregulated Services, when the utility services are not subject to a regulatory body.

FAR 52.241-9, Connection Charge, when the Government must pay a refundable connection charge to compensate the contractor for furnishing additional facilities necessary to supply service. Use Alternate I to the clause if a nonrefundable charge is to be paid.

FAR 52.241-10, Termination Liability, when the contractor will be paid upon termination of service, either with or in lieu of a connection charge upon completion of the facilities.

FAR 52.241-11, Multiple Service Locations, if possible alternative service locations or delivery points are considered, except under area-wide contracts.

FAR 52.241-12, Nonrefundable, Nonrecurring Service Charge, when the Government pays a nonrefundable and nonrecurring membership fee, a charge for service initiation, or a contribution for the cost of facilities construction. The Government may include this amount or fee in the connection charge, the initial payment for services, or as periodic payments to fulfill the Government's obligation.

FAR 52.241-13, Capital Credits, when the Federal Government is a member of a cooperative and is entitled to capital credits, consistent with the bylaws and governing documents of the cooperative.

2.9.5 Commercial Studies

It is clear from the previous discussion that the Federal Government relies on the private sector for commercial services. OMB has issued Circular A-76, Performance of Commercial Activities, of May 29, 2003, to govern how this process is executed. Each agency identifies all activities performed by government personnel as either commercial or inherently governmental, retaining the latter for government personnel. The agency then conducts studies to determine if government personnel should perform the former or if contractor performance is more cost-effective. The agency develops a cost estimate in accordance with Circular A-76 rather than traditional agency methods, and compares the estimate to competitive commercial offers to decide whether to retain the effort in-house or contract out.

A competition is not required for continued private sector performance of a commercial activity, a new requirement, or expansion to an existing commercial activity performed by government personnel.

FAR 7.306

For sealed bidding, the contracting officer opens and records commercial bids, then opens the sealed cost estimate of Government performance. After entering the price of the apparent low bidder on the cost comparison form, (s)he announces the result, subject to further evaluation and protest. Both the bid abstract and cost comparison form are available for public inspection, along with detailed data supporting the cost estimate for Government performance. The contracting officer determines responsibility of the apparent low bidder, while the preparer of the cost estimate completes a comparison with the apparent low bidder. The responsible agency official makes a final written determination for performance by the Government or contractor, and the contracting officer either awards a contract or cancels the solicitation.

For negotiated procedures, the contracting officer conducts negotiations as necessary and selects the most advantageous proposal. Before public announcement, however, the contracting officer opens the sealed estimate in the presence of the preparer, enters the amount of the most advantageous proposal on the cost comparison form, and returns the form to the preparer for completion. If the result of the cost comparison favors performance under contract and the responsible agency official approves the result, the contracting officer awards a contract and notifies the offerors of the cost comparison result and the winning offeror's name. (S)he then makes the cost comparison data available for review and awaits the public review period (15–30 working days) and any appeals. Should the result of the cost comparison favor Government performance, the contracting officer either notifies the incumbent contractor to stop work, or else cancels either performance or the solicitation.

Each agency establishes an appeals procedure for informal review of the initial cost comparison by an official at a higher level than the official who approved that result. This protects the rights of affected parties and ensures that final agency determinations are fair and equitable, and in accordance with established policy. Appeals address only questions concerning the calculation of the cost comparison, not the selection of one contractor over another (those questions are still treated under the Protests clause).

Solicitation Provisions

FAR 52.207-1, Notice of Standard Competition, or FAR 52.207-2, Notice of Streamlined Competition.

FAR 52.207-3, Right of First Refusal of Employment, if conversion from Government performance to contract performance is possible. Also use in resultant contracts. The 10-day period in the clause may be varied by the contracting officer up to 90 days.

2.9.6 Bundling

FAR 7.107

A special concern involves *bundling* services. This entails consolidating two or more procurement requirements for goods or services previously provided by separate contracts into a solicitation for a single contract that could be too large for a small business firm to perform. It also covers any procurement that is so large or diverse in terms of geography or skill sets that a small business (or team of small businesses) cannot expect to perform.

If an agency contemplates bundling, it consults with the local SBA procurement center representative with the anticipated benefits and cost savings. At least 30 days before solicitation or placing an order, the agency also notifies any affected incumbent small business concerns of the Government's intention to bundle the requirement, and how they can contact the SBA representative. Moreover, if the total value exceeds $2 million, the agency's senior procurement executive or chief acquisition officer must determine in writing that market research has been conducted, alternative approaches and negative impacts on small businesses have been considered, the SADBU or SBA representative has been consulted, and how small businesses will be included in the acquisition.[34] This determination is then posted on the agency's website.

Bundling may provide substantial benefits to the Government, but requires market research to justify its use. Benefits are often received in terms of cost, delivery, quality, and contract terms and conditions. Contracting offices are tempted to bundle to reduce their workload.[35] However, bundling gives rise to concern that small businesses will be unable to compete for the full requirement. Analysis should quantify and discuss cost savings or price reduction, improved terms and conditions, quality improvements, and reduced acquisition cycle times. As a rule of thumb, bundling is justified if analysis reveals 10% savings of estimated contract value if the total contract value is estimated to be below $94 million, or 5% savings (but not less than $9.4 million) if greater than $94 million. Reduced administrative or personnel costs are inadequate justification. The acquisition strategy must identify:

- benefits anticipated from bundling;
- impediments to participation by small business concerns as contractors, and actions designed to maximize small business participation as (sub) contractors; and
- strategies to reduce the scope of the bundling, and the rationale for not choosing these alternatives.

Solicitation Provision

FAR 52.207-6, Solicitation of Offers from Small Business Concerns and Small Business Teaming Arrangements or Joint Ventures (Multiple-Award Contracts), if exceeding prescribed dollar thresholds.

2.10 INFORMATION TECHNOLOGY

Computers and digital information have become critical aspects of Government operations and contract support. Although regulatory guidance is limited, it is essential that today's contracting professionals have a basic understanding of some key concepts in this area.

2.10.1 Information Management

The Federal Government probably produces, collects and distributes more information than any other American entity. Because of the import and scope of these information activities, the management of Federal information resources is a critical issue. In acquiring information technology products and services, agencies must comply with OMB Circular A-130, Managing Information as a Strategic Resource, of November 28, 2000, to consider:

- accommodations for individuals with disabilities;
- emergency preparedness;
- energy efficiency;
- environmental assessment of hardware;
- evolving information technology through market research and refreshment;
- national security;
- protection of privacy; and
- security of resources.

The Federal Government makes extensive use of *information systems* which process data, facts (often not for public release), and opinions, for a number of processes (e.g., audiovisual presentations, cartography, payment data, and reports). It has developed standards for its information systems to ensure security and interoperability. Known as the *Federal Information Processing Standards* (FIPS), they are approved by the Secretary of Commerce and issued by the National Institute of Standards and Technology (NIST). NIST is the organization which develops and maintains publications for national standards and measurements. FIPS are compulsory and binding for Federal contractors and agencies, which cannot waive their use. NIST has also issued a series of special publications which are gaining increasing utility throughout the Federal Government as de facto standards for information system security, as well as usage in the academic and corporate sectors. These standards provide technical controls to protect the confidentiality, integrity and availability of stored data, and prescribe automated procedures to analyze and remediate vulnerabilities and weaknesses. Contractors who manage information systems must therefore:

- control connections to external information systems;
- control information posted or processed on publicly accessible or web-based information systems;
- identify and authenticate identities of devices, processes or users requesting access;
- identify, report and correct information and system flaws;
- limit physical access to authorized information equipment, systems and their operating environments;
- maintain subnetworks for publicly accessible system components so that they are logically or physically separated from internal networks;
- monitor and protect communications at the system's external boundaries and key internal boundaries;
- monitor visitor activity and maintain audit logs of physical access;
- periodically scan the system and files from external sources as applications are downloaded or executed;
- protect the system from malicious code and update mechanisms when new releases are available; and
- sanitize or destroy media before disposal or reuse.

Agencies must also follow OMB Circular A-127, Financial Management Systems, of January 9, 2009, to acquire financial products and services. Any core financial management software to be acquired for Federal-only information systems (they do not apply to contractor systems) must be certified by the Financial Systems Integration Office (formerly the Joint Financial Management Improvement Program) within the Department of the Treasury. This office manages the Federal Financial Management System Requirements, which tie into business processes and apply to administrative and programmatic systems supporting financial management systems.[36] These requirements cover data input, processing and output, and are intended to focus on outcomes rather than process or technology.

In accordance with section 508 of the Rehabilitation Act of 1973 (29 U.S.C. 794d), Federal employees and citizens with disabilities must be able to access and use data to the same extent as their colleagues without disabilities.[37] However, these requirements do not apply to a:

- national security system;
- project or effort incidental to a contract;
- repair or occasional monitoring of equipment; or
- situation which would impose an undue difficulty or expense on the agency.

Concerns over software vulnerabilities and malicious code, and the risks they introduce to information systems, have promoted the concept of *software assurance*. This approach provides a level of confidence that the software operates as intended and is free from defects. Pioneered by the Departments of Defense and Homeland Security, a working group developed guidance on how to include software assurance considerations in the acquisition process and build security into the software.[38] This has now become a paramount concern in software development and operations to mitigate risk. This guidance is also intended to minimize harm that may result from the loss, misuse or unauthorized access to (or modification of) the system itself or the information it manages.

FAR 39.103

Modular contracting is a technique using one or more contracts to acquire information technology systems in successive, interoperable increments. It is designed to acquire rapidly changing information technology while minimizing program risk and incentivizing contractor performance. Contracts are normally awarded within six months of solicitation. The effort may be divided into several smaller acquisitions to:

- address objectives incrementally to improve likelihood of achievement;
- isolate impact of custom-designed components from the system;
- leverage off technology innovation or requirements changes that occur during implementation; and
- test solutions without dependence on other increments.

Software itself comes in many forms and flavors. There are several types of software that could be bought in the marketplace:

- *commercial off-the-shelf software* is proprietary to the producer and readily available to the general public;
- *custom software* is developed for the customer per his/her specifications;
- *embedded software* is part of a larger system and performs some system functions without user interface (e.g., an aircraft or traffic control system);
- *freeware* is copyrighted software available free of charge for an indefinite time period;
- *Government off-the-shelf software* is developed in-house by the agency's technical staff, or else by a contractor funded specifically under contract;
- *mobile code* is passed between systems to describe applets (e.g., Microsoft's ActiveX, Sun's Java or Netscape's JavaScript) within web browsers, and is strictly controlled in many Government sites;
- *modifiable off-the-shelf software* means the *source code* (computer or application instructions, usually written in plain text, to be transcribed into binary code for the computer to execute) can be modified by the buyer, producer or third party to meet customer requirements;
- *open source software* has source code available under a copyright license for users to study, improve and redistribute it; and
- *shareware* is a trial version of commercial software distributed free and in advance of mass distribution, with payment due after a set number of days or uses.

To comply with the Privacy Act (5 U.S.C. 552a), any design, development or operation of a system of records that uses commercial information technology services must include agency rules of conduct for the contractor and its employees, Government inspection requirements, and safeguards for the contractor to implement. The intent is to ensure the discovery and counter-measures of new threats and hazards. If a contractor is required to design, develop or operate a system of records, the contracting officer must ensure that the statement of work complies with agency reqirements.

Solicitation Provision and Contract Clauses

FAR 52.204-21, Basic Safeguarding of Covered Contractor Information Systems.

FAR 52.224-1, Provacy Act Notification.

FAR 52.224-2, Privacy Act.

FAR 52.239-1, Privacy or Security Safeguards.

2.10.2 Network Systems

Networked computers exchange information by cable or wireless connection between data links. As such, several aspects of networking become important to keep in mind. *Network architecture* is a framework to specify an information system's physical components and their configuration, data formats and operating principles and procedures. A telecommunications network architecture may also include a description of products and services delivered, and detailed rate and billing structures. Network architecture often includes the classification and structure of a distributed application architecture.

Network management covers the activities, methods, procedures, and tools that are designed to:

- configure network resources to support a given service;
- keep the network and its services up and running smoothly by monitoring the network to spot problems rapidly;
- perform corrective and preventive measures to improve network performance;
- repair and upgrade equipment; and
- track and assign network resources.

Network management includes effort to plan, allocate, deploy, coordinate, and monitor network features such as:

- bandwidth management;
- *configuration management* (document a system's physical and functional characteristics, and control and report any changes thereto);
- cryptographic key distribution authorization;
- frequency allocation;
- performance management;
- predetermined traffic routing to support load balancing and associated analytics;
- resources; and
- security management.

Data for network management is collected through automated hardware agents installed at key points throughout the infrastructure. These hardware agents provide monitoring services to simulate activity logs, business transactions, sniffers to analyze data packets for illegal activity, and user activities.

Network monitoring looks for slow or failing components and notifies the network administrator in case of outages. While an intrusion detection system monitors a network for threats from the outside, a network monitoring system looks internally for problems caused by overloaded and/or crashed servers or network connections. Commonly measured metrics in the network monitoring process are response time and availability. If a connection cannot be re-established or times-out, or a document or message cannot be retrieved, the monitoring system sends an alarm email to the administrator. An automatic failover system may be activated to remove the troubled server from operation.

All information systems require qualified people to serve as network administrators to monitor their performance, respond to security incidents, and update with patches. These services may be performed in-house or contracted out, since they are commercial in nature.

2.10.3 Telecommunications

Telecommunications involves transmitting communications over distances (whether across the room or cross-country). A basic system includes a transmitter, physical channel and receiver to translate the message into readable form. Communications signals can be either *analog* (the information is varied continuously) or *digital* (the information is encoded as a set of discrete values, such as ones and zeros). Some digital networks contain routers to transmit information to the correct user, whereas an analog communications network uses switches to establish a connection between users. Both types of network may use repeaters to amplify or recreate the signal when transmitted over long distances, and to combat physical noise.

Computer networks stack individual protocols to run independently of each other. This way, lower-level protocols can be customized for the network without changing how higher-level protocols operate. Most intercontinental communication uses the Asynchronous Transfer Mode (ATM) protocol (or a modern equivalent) on top of optic fiber.

As the most common wireless network, the *Internet* is a worldwide network of computers that communicate with each other using the Internet Protocol (IP). It has become a critical resource for buyers and sellers to do research and communicate with each other. Any computer on the Internet has a unique IP address that can be used by other computers to route information to it, and to send a message to any other computer by using its IP address. For the World Wide Web, these IP addresses are derived from a human readable form using the Domain Name System. We have already seen examples of this (e.g., www.unicor.gov).

2.10.4 System Enterprise Resource Planning

Enterprise Resource Planning is a method to manage both external and internal resources by improving the information flow between business functions in the organization, and manages the connections to outside stakeholders. Enterprise resource planning uses an integrated computer-based system to manage physical assets as well as financial and human resources. Some firms distribute the system across the network to minimize hardware expenses and communicate on a local area network. This second method lets a firm assemble modules from different vendors without buying expensive computer systems.

Enterprise resource planning is an adaptation of *integrated business planning* to technologically connect all stakeholders in the firm's planning functions. This approach integrates finance, marketing and operations to identify their interdependencies and make informed decisions regarding profitability and financial risk.

Commercial ERP applications include:

- access control: managing user privileges;
- customer relationship management: call center support, customer contact, sales and marketing, service visits, and tracking commissions;
- data services: self-service interfaces for customers, employees and suppliers;
- financials: accounts payable, accounts receivable, cash management, fixed assets, and general ledger;
- human resources: employee benefits, payroll, time and attendance, and training;
- manufacturing: bills of material, capacity planning, engineering tasks, quality control, scheduling, and workflow and process management;
- project management: activity sequencing, billing, costing, performance tracking, and time and expense records;
- supply chain management: claim processing, inspection, inventory, order entry, product configuration, purchasing, and supplier scheduling; and
- translating contract requirements into usable instructions for internal compliance systems.

2.10.5 Seat Management

This initiative allows the management, operation and support of a distributed computing environment by a service provider firm. Performance is based on predetermined and negotiated service levels that are monitored by designated performance metrics. Examples of metric goals include:

- 98% or more availability;
- 80% customer satisfaction rating;
- answer help desk calls in 30 seconds or less;

- resolve 80% of problems on the first call;
- respond to hardware problems within one hour; or
- return hardware to service within two hours.

Critical to this concept are incentives to the contractor for exceeding key metrics and penalties for failing to meet these metrics. Also, a subscriber may elect to receive tiered services, opting to pay more money for higher levels of service. Thus, pricing is affected by asset distribution, infrastructure, refresh rate service levels required, and type of support,

In conjunction with the Clinger-Cohen Act (the Information Technology Management Reform Act of 1996), 104 U.S.C. 106, the Government requires measurable improvements in efficiency and effectiveness of Federal IT operations. The seat management solution offered by the GSA and NASA's Outsourcing Desktop Initiative are examples of this initiative. This legislation has also led the private sector to assess seat management to improve their cost performance, end-user satisfaction, environment, performance, and support.

2.11 RISK

2.11.1 Risk Identification

Risk is a concept which addresses the impact of a given vulnerability. It can be mathematically calculated as the product of the probability and magnitude of the vulnerability's impact. Risk calculation is a method to envision this impact on future outcomes by first measuring how much the results deviate from expected values, then planning how to avoid or mitigate these risks. Although these deviations may be either positive or negative, most people focus on the negative ("downside risk") or failure to achieve sufficient beneficial outcome ("upside risk"). Risk can be measured in economic terms due to lower income or higher costs than anticipated, caused by such events as:

- arrival of a new market competitor;
- change in political party in power;
- higher prices for raw materials;
- loss of key personnel;
- natural disasters; and
- production stoppages.

Risk is not always about a technical issue. It can also be financial in nature; perhaps an investment's actual return will differ from that expected. Competitors may introduce technological breakthroughs, or the marketplace may take a negative turn. Also, the possibility of external hacking or fraudulent employee behavior is ever-present.

A fundamental idea in the financial world is the relationship between risk and return. The greater the potential return sought, the greater the risk assumed. This is why demand for a safer investment drives its price higher and its return lower, while weak demand for a riskier investment drives its price lower and its potential return higher. Management will first address the risks with the greatest loss and probability of occurrence, then analyze risks with lower probability of occurrence and loss in descending order.

Risk management should be an integral part of a firm's decision-making processes. A systematic structured approach is necessary, such as that spelled out in ISO 31000, "Risk management – Principles and guidelines on implementation."[39] The process must consider the human factors and interests of all affected parties, respond to change and continuous process improvement, and be tailored to the firm.

The risk management process contains several steps:

- define a framework and agenda for risk identification;
- develop an analysis methodology;
- identify risks:
- develop mitigation or solution strategies using human, organizational and technological resources; and
- identify stakeholders, evaluation schemes and any constraints.

Critical to this process is *risk identification*, a process to isolate a problem or its source. Risk sources may be internal or external to the system, such as:

- application error (e.g., computation or input errors or buffer overflows);
- data loss or destruction;
- data misuse (e.g., espionage, fraud, sharing trade secrets, and theft);
- human error;
- inside or outside attacks (e.g., cracking or hacking);
- physical damage; and
- system or peripheral device malfunction.

Common risk identification methods are based on checklists, questionnaires, scenarios, or threats to objectives. Once risks have been identified, they must then be assessed for both their potential severity of loss and their probability of occurrence. The order of basic steps in the process are to:

- assign value to information and assets;
- perform a threat analysis;

- derive overall loss potential per risk;
- choose remedial measures to counteract each risk; and
- decide whether to accept, reduce or transfer the risk.

The risk management process can be either qualitative or quantitative in nature. A qualitative method identifies possible scenarios, ranks threat seriousness and asset sensitivity based on judgment and experience, and then derives a score for each scenario. Alternatively, the widely accepted formula for risk quantification is:

Risk = Rate of occurrence * Impact of event.

Adding all risk calculations results in a Composite Risk Index.

The biggest difficulty in risk assessment could be determining the rate of occurrence if there is limited statistical information on past incidents. The impact of the risk event may be assessed on a scale of 0 to 10, and the probability of occurrence is on a percentage scale from 0 to 100. The overall risk assessment is then Low, Medium or High, depending on the calculated value of the Composite Risk Index. For instance, Low could be classified as a score between 0 and 3.5, Moderate between 3.6 and 7.0, and High any score over 7.0.

FAR 39.102

When planning an acquisition, agencies use the common security configurations available from NIST at http://checklists.nist.gov, and agency guidance pertaining to information technology standards. They analyze risks, benefits and costs during program investment and implementation. Types of risk include:

- contract type;
- cost;
- dependencies between a new project and other projects or systems;
- funding availability;
- impact of lack of protection or a security breach;
- program management;
- quantity of simultaneous high-risk projects to be monitored;
- residual risk after all mitigation actions are taken;[40]
- schedule; and
- technical feasibility and obsolescence.

Evaluation criteria can include development knowledge, process maturity, and use of testing tools and code vulnerability scanners. Proposals are rated on a scorecard using either qualitative or quantitative methods, or else by means of a "go–no go" decision. A due diligence questionnaire is often used as a tool to gain further input from offerors on the following:

- architecture and design;
- assurance claims and evidence;
- built-in software defenses;
- component assembly;
- concept and planning;
- development process management;
- financial history and status;
- foreign interests and influences;
- individual malicious behavior;
- installation and acceptance;
- licensing:
- operating environment for services;
- organizational history;
- past version support;
- security monitoring and performance history;
- security training and awareness;
- service confidentiality policies;
- software change management;
- software manufacturing and packaging;
- testing; and
- timeliness of vulnerability mitigation.

Risk management is not an easy process to execute. Risks must be correctly understood. Cost impact may not always be acceptable. Moreover, an opportunity cost arises by not spending resources on more profitable activities. Hence, risk management strives to minimize resource consumption and avoid the negative impact of events.

2.11.2 Risk Management

Once risks have been identified and assessed, they will be addressed by one of four treatment methods:

- avoidance:
- reduction:
- sharing; and
- retention.

The first option is avoidance. The organization can refrain from performing an activity that could carry risk. For example, the Navy could decide that the cost of complying with shock test standards so discourages a potential maritime product that it would rather forego a shipboard application for its commercial product. Avoidance also means losing out on the potential rewards and profits that could have resulted if the risk was accepted. If the elimination of hazards takes too long or is too costly, mitigation must be considered.

Second, the organization can reduce the severity or likelihood of the loss from occurring. However, it must carefully balance technical effectiveness with cost for the solution. Incremental development and delivery (also known as "build a little, test a little") is one option used in major system development.

Third, the firm or organization can share or transfer risk by purchasing insurance or outsourcing, even though the buyer is still legally responsible. Risk retention pools are another example of sharing by retaining the risk for a group of entities without paying an upfront premium, but rather by assessing losses to all group members.

Finally, any risk that does not fall into the other categories is retained by definition. The organization can accept the benefit or loss from a risk when it occurs through self-insurance if the cost of purchased insurance exceeds the total losses sustainable. Uninsurable risks or those with unaffordable premiums are also retained, such as war.

A *Risk Management Plan* should document the decisions about how each of the identified risks should be handled. This plan should propose controls and countermeasures (with supporting rationales) to manage these risks (e.g., buying and installing an antivirus software program). The plan should also contain an implementation schedule and identify responsible parties. Practice and experience (perhaps even an actual event) will dictate changes in the plan and revised decisions in confronting risks. The plan should be reviewed at least annually to evaluate the effectiveness of the selected security controls and possible risk level changes in the environment. This evaluation should also identify new threats and reconsider the severity of ongoing threats.

For all its benefits, risk management is a process that can go off-track. Risks can be improperly assessed and prioritized, thereby wasting time with unlikely results and resources that could be used more profitably. Also, qualitative risk assessment is subjective and inconsistent, and could be mired in legal and bureaucratic processes. An organization must also take care not to prioritize risks so highly that it cannot complete a project.

An enterprise can also use risk management to address risks to its customers, existence, human and capital resources, products and services, as well as from the external environment and society. The process includes the following activities:

- assign a risk officer to foresee potential project problems;
- create an anonymous risk-reporting channel;
- identify risk management activities, budget and responsibilities;
- maintain a current project risk database with an action officer, description, importance, probability, and due date for resolution;
- prepare a mitigation plan to describe how this particular risk will be handled; and
- summarize planned and faced risks, effectiveness of mitigation activities, and level of effort for risk management.

Risk mitigation techniques during contract performance include:

- acquisition planning tied to budgeting;
- continuous risk-based data collection and assessment;
- implementing identified security controls;
- modular contracting;
- post-implementation cost-benefit reviews;
- project management;
- prototyping before implementation;
- trade-offs between cost, operational effectiveness and risk; and
- transfer to or sharing with a third party.

All risks cannot be fully avoided or mitigated due to financial and practical limitations, hence the organization must accept some level of residual risks. *Business continuity planning* addresses these accepted residual risks by considering infrastructure issues such as data, facilities and hardware. This planning must also address less tangible elements such as crisis communication, key personnel, planning for resumption of applications, and reputation protection. Any of three types of control measures (corrective, detective and preventive) can be implemented to reduce risk:

- *corrective* – restore the process or system back to its previous state, or mitigate the impact of the threat (e.g., antivirus protection, backup data storage and operating system restoration);
- *detective* – monitor activity to determine where policies or procedures were not followed (e.g., audit trails, intrusion detection systems, job rotation, and network monitoring systems); and
- *preventive* – preclude the harm or loss from occurring (e.g., antivirus protection, biometrics, firewalls, guards, and security awareness training).

A *disaster recovery plan* should be created that includes metrics for the recovery point and time for business processes, information systems and supporting infrastructure. These metrics can then be used to develop budget justification to ensure an affordable level of protection. Common strategies for data protection are:

- antivirus software;
- fire alarms and extinguishers;
- high-availability systems to replicate both the data and system off-site, using storage area network technology to enable continuous access;
- local mirrors of data and/or systems, and disk protection technology (such as redundant array independent disks);
- surge protectors;
- tape backups sent off-site at regular intervals (daily for critical data and weekly for more routine information); and
- uninterruptible power supply and/or backup generator.

Continuity of operations (COOP) is a plan that outlines the steps needed to ensure that an agency can carry on all essential functions in case of a natural or man-made disaster. Agencies designate functions as either essential or nonessential, depending on how critical is their need for performance (e.g., communications, financial, health, safety, and security). This is why organizations ensure that resources or personnel involved in a critical function are geographically disbursed and not concentrated in one area should a disaster strike. Presidential Decision Directive 67, Enduring Constitutional Government and Continuity of Government Operations, requires agencies to develop COOPs, and the Federal Emergency Management Agency (FEMA) released Federal Preparedness Circular 65, Federal Executive Branch Continuity of Operations, to advise how they should develop their COOPs. These plans identify the order of succession for agency management (principally for their positions and responsibilities), alternate work locations, and internal and public communications. Agencies must conduct tests and training exercises to ensure that backup operations can support the regular workload if networks fail.

There is more Federal guidance to continuity planning. Homeland Security Presidential Directive 20, National Continuity Policy (also labeled as National Security Presidential Directive 51), mandates agencies to develop continuity plans to ensure that mission-critical functions continue during emergencies.[41] FEMA remains in charge of coordinating emergency activities under the National Response Framework, a plan to promote interdepartmental cooperation and continuity during a national emergency (such as attack or natural disaster). The Continuity Policy Implementation Plan provides guidance for agencies to identify those functions that are necessary to continue operating the government. FEMA's Federal Continuity Directive 1 sets criteria for continuity facility operations, communications requirements, and vital records management. FEMA's Federal Continuity Directive 2 provides guidance on how to identify mission-essential functions and the primary functions that must be resumed within 12 hours of a catastrophe, and requires agencies to conduct a risk management process to identify these functions and report them to the Department of Homeland Security.[42]

COOP also includes teleworking remotely from home or another location to perform critical job tasks at an alternate location. GSA has a goal of promoting more eligible employees teleworking (25% or maybe even 50%).[43]

FAR 4.402

The National Industrial Security Program (NISP) safeguards Federal Government classified information that is released to contractors, grantees and licensees of the U.S. Government. NISP's operating manual (NISPOM) chronicles the requirements of various executive orders into a coherent operating procedure. Identified within the Department of Defense as DoD 5220.22-M, and its accompanying regulation (DOD 5220.22-R), it requires use of the Contract Security Classification Specification, DD Form 254, to indicate security requirements of contract performance in terms of documentation, facility and personnel clearances.

2.12 INNOVATIVE CONTRACTING METHODS

2.12.1 Multi-Year Contracting

FAR 17.1

A *multi-year contract* allows for supplies or services purchases for up to five years. Performance during the second and subsequent years of the contract may be contingent upon the appropriation of funds, with a cancellation payment to the contractor if appropriations are not made. There is no need to exercise an option for each program year.

The contracting officer may enter into a multi-year contract if the head of the contracting activity determines that the need for the supplies or services is reasonably firm and continuing over the period of the contract, and that a multi-year contract will encourage full and open competition or promote economy in agency administration and operation. For DoD, the Coast Guard and NASA, the head of the agency must further determine that the:

- contract will lead to substantial program cost savings over annual contracts;
- design is stable and the technical risks are not excessive;

- estimates of both the cost and its avoidance through the use of a multi-year contract are realistic;
- head of the agency plans to have sufficient funding to avoid contract cancellation; and
- minimum procurement quantity is expected to remain substantially unchanged during the contract period.

Use of multi-year contracting can provide many benefits, such as:

- broadened competitive base for firms not otherwise willing or able to compete for lesser quantities (often due to high startup costs);
- enhanced standardization;
- established quality control techniques and procedures;
- incentives to improve productivity through investment in capital facilities, equipment and technology;
- realistic estimates of contract cost and savings (and, hopefully, lower costs);
- reduced administrative burden in contract placement and administration;
- stabilized contractor planning and workforces;
- stable design and funding; and
- substantial continuity of production or performance (thus avoiding annual startup, preproduction testing and phase-out costs).

If funds are not appropriated to support the succeeding years' requirements, the agency must cancel the contract. This means that all program years after the first are subject to cancellation. This cancellation must occur within a contractually specified time. The contracting officer either notifies the contractor of nonavailability of funds, or else fails to notify the contractor that funds are available for performance of the succeeding program year.

For each program year subject to cancellation, the contracting officer establishes a *cancellation ceiling*. This represents the Government's maximum liability to the contractor should the contract be cancelled. This ceiling amount (also called *cancellation charges*) covers the contractor's nonrecurring costs (and perhaps some recurring costs, such as economic order quantities) which would have been recouped through amortization over the full term of the contract. Ceilings exclude amounts for requirements included in prior program years because they are prospective only, and decrease for each program year in direct proportion to the remaining requirements which are subject to cancellation. This concept differs from *termination costs*, which can be imposed at any time during the life of the contract and can apply to partial or total quantities.

The Government can fully fund this ceiling and hold the funds in reserve, or it can create an unfunded contingent liability that must nonetheless be covered if termination occurs. The cancellation ceiling is not an evaluation factor in source selection.

In determining cancellation ceilings, the contracting officer estimates preproduction or startup costs, labor learning and other nonrecurring costs which can be amortized across multi-year requirements. *Nonrecurring costs* are generally incurred on a one-time basis, such as:

- facilities to be acquired or established;
- pilot runs;
- plant or equipment relocation or rearrangement;
- preproduction engineering;
- special tooling and special test equipment;
- specialized workforce training and transportation to/from the work site; and
- spoilage and rework.

Nonrecurring costs exclude any labor, material or other expenses which might be incurred to perform subsequent program year requirements.[44] The total estimate of these costs is then compared with the contract cost estimate (based on in-house engineering cost estimates and the effect of labor learning) to arrive at a reasonable percentage or dollar figure to derive a cancellation ceiling.

Solicitations for multi-year contracts reflect all the factors to be considered for evaluation, specifically including the Government's:

- acknowledgement that award cannot be made for less than the first program year requirements;
- administrative costs of annual contracting, if known upfront;
- criteria to compare the lowest evaluated proposal for the first-year requirements to that for the multi-year requirements;
- evaluated price or estimated cost and fee for the first year only;
- requirements for the first program year and estimates for the total multi-year period; and
- separate cancellation ceiling on a percentage or dollar basis for each program year subject to cancellation.

Funding of multi-year contracts must conform to OMB Circular A-11, Preparation and Submission of Budget Estimates, revised July 1, 2016, which is the Government's "cookbook" on developing budget projections for upcoming fiscal years.[45] Multi-year contracts to acquire fixed assets are either funded in full or in economic or programmatic stages. When the period of production is likely to warrant a labor and material cost contingency in the contract price, the contracting officer uses an economic price adjustment clause.

A multi-year contract which includes a cancellation ceiling in excess of $11.5 million ($114.5 million for DoD, NASA, and the Coast Guard) may not be awarded until the head of the agency gives written notification of the proposed contract and cancellation ceiling to the appropriations and departmental oversight committees of the Senate and House of Representatives, and allows 30 days before award.

Contract Clauses

FAR 52.217-2, Cancellation Under Multi-year Contracts.

FAR 52.222-43, Fair Labor Standards Act and Service Contract Act – Price Adjustment (Multiple Year and Option Contracts), if the contract includes the Service Contract Act of 1965 clause. This clause may be modified in overseas contracts when laws, regulations or international agreements require contractors to pay higher wage rates. The contract may include an economic price adjustment clause if potential fluctuations are not included in cost contingencies.

2.12.2 Options

FAR 17.2

Options are used when the foreseeable requirements involve minimum economic quantities which are large enough to permit recovery of startup and production costs at a reasonable price. Options are also appropriate when future requirements permit competitive acquisition, production and delivery. Service contracts may use options when the Government needs continuity of operations and the potential cost of disrupted support is unacceptable. Options are not appropriate when:

- known firm requirements are funded;[46]
- market prices for the supplies or services are likely to change substantially;
- procuring architect-engineer services;
- procuring the construction, alteration or repair of real property (i.e., buildings, bridges and roads); or
- the contractor will incur undue risks, such as uncertain availability or pricing of necessary materials or labor.

Solicitations containing option provisions state whether evaluation excludes or includes the option, and informs offerors that the Government may exercise the option at time of award. In this case, solicitations specify how the Government will evaluate the option (e.g., highest option price offered, or option price for specified requirements).

Solicitations normally allow option quantities to be offered without price restriction. However, the solicitation may instead require that options be offered at prices no higher than those for the initial requirement, such as when future competition for the option is impracticable. Such solicitations specify that the Government will accept an option price higher than the base price only if it does not prejudice any other offeror. Solicitations also limit option quantities to 50% or less of the initial quantity of the line item (a level above the contracting officer may approve a greater percentage).

The contract specifies the period within which the option may be exercised. This provides the contractor adequate lead time to ensure continuous production. This period may extend beyond the contract completion date for service contracts when the option requires obligation of funds that are not yet available in the future fiscal year. Unless otherwise approved in accordance with legislation or agency procedures, the total of the basic and option periods cannot exceed five years of requirements (though information technology contracts may run for a longer period of time).

Contracts may include options for increased amounts of supplies or services in terms of percentage, quantity or additional numbered line items. Contracts may express extensions of the contract length as a later completion date or additional time for performance. The contracting officer justifies in writing the quantities or the term under option, the notification period for exercising the option, and any limitation on option pricing.

In awarding the basic contract, the contracting officer evaluates offers for any option quantities or periods contained in a solicitation if (s)he determines prior to soliciting offers that the Government is likely to exercise the options. This determination is mandatory under sealed bidding and customary for negotiation, unless determined at a level above the contracting officer that evaluation would not be in the best interests of the Government (e.g., funds will likely be unavailable to permit exercise of the option).

When exercising an option, the contracting officer provides written notice to the contractor within the time period specified in the contract (usually 30 or 60 days before expiration of the current year). If the contractor requests an economic price adjustment per contract terms, the contracting officer must consider the effect of the adjustment on prices. The contracting officer may exercise options only after determining in writing that:

• a new solicitation fails to produce a better price or a more advantageous offer than that included in the option;

- an informal price analysis or market survey indicates that the option price is better than prices available in the market;[47]
- exercise of the option is the most advantageous method of fulfilling the Government's need (considering continuity of operations, costs of disrupting operations, effect on small business, and price);
- funds are available;
- the contractor is not listed on the Excluded Parties List System;
- the option was synopsized; and
- the requirement covered by the option fulfills an existing Government need.

Solicitation Provisions

FAR 52.217-3, Evaluation Exclusive of Options.

FAR 52.217-4, Evaluation of Options Exercised at Time of Contract Award, if the option clause will probably be exercised.

FAR 52.217-5, Evaluation of Options, if firm fixed-price with an option clause that will probably be exercised after contract award.

Solicitation Provisions and Contract Clauses

FAR 52.217-6, Option for Increased Quantity, for supplies with an option quantity expressed as a percentage of the basic contract quantity or an additional quantity of a specific line item.

FAR 52.217-7, Option for Increased Quantity – Separately Priced Line Item, for supplies with an option quantity identified as a separately priced line item having the same nomenclature as the basic contract line item.

FAR 52.217-8, Option to Extend Services.

FAR 52.217-9, Option to Extend the Term of the Contract, if the Government must give the contractor either a preliminary written notice of its intent to extend the contract or else a specified limitation on the total duration of the contract.

2.12.3 Leader Company Contracting

FAR 17.4

The Government may designate a developer or sole producer of a product or system as the *leader company* to furnish assistance and knowledge under contract to one or more designated *follower* companies, so they can become a future source of supply. This approach may be used to develop a second source for production. The objectives of this technique can include:

- economies in production;
- eliminating problems with proprietary data;
- equipment compatibility, reliability and uniformity, as well as interchangeable and standardized components;
- geographic dispersion of suppliers;
- maximized use of scarce tooling or special equipment;
- reduced delivery time; and
- transition from development to production and subsequent competitive acquisition of major end items or components.

Leader company contracting is to be used only when:

- assistance is limited to that necessary to enable the follower(s) to produce the items;
- no other source could meet the Government's requirements without the aid of a leader company;
- the contract contains a disclosure agreement of any proprietary data or software, trade secrets, and technical concepts or designs;
- the firm has the production knowledge and can furnish assistance to the follower(s);
- the Government reserves the right to approve subcontracts between the leader company and the follower(s); and
- use is authorized in accordance with agency procedures.

The contracting officer may award a contract to a leader company, obligating it to subcontract a designated portion of the end items to a specified follower company and to assist it in production. Alternatively, the contract may require the leader company to assist a follower company, and the follower to produce the items. There can also be a contract awarded to the follower company, obligating it to subcontract with a designated leader company for required assistance.

2.12.4 Interagency Acquisitions

FAR 17.5

The Economy Act (31.U.S.C. 1535) authorizes agencies to enter into mutual agreements to obtain supplies or services on an interagency basis. *Interagency acquisition* is a procedure by which an agency needing supplies or services (the *requesting agency*) obtains them from another agency (the *servicing agency*), or from a different unit within the same department or agency. Agency regulations prescribe procedures for such transactions. The Economy Act does not apply to:

- acquisitions conflicting with any other agency's authority or responsibility;
- circumventing conditions and limitations imposed on the use of funds;
- contracting out inherently governmental functions; or
- procurements which have separate statutory authority (e.g., Federal Supply Schedule contracts or Government-wide acquisition contracts).

The requesting agency writes a D&F which concludes that the use of an inter-agency acquisition represents the best procurement approach. It then obtains the concurrence of the requesting agency's contracting office in accordance with internal agency procedures. The determination for a *directed acquisition* (where an agency places an award against another agency's indefinite delivery contract) further includes an analysis that the acquisition services of another agency:

- has prudent procurement approaches;
- is cost-effective with its servicing fees;
- satisfies the requesting agency's:
  - customer satisfaction,
  - delivery requirements,
  - performance, and
  - schedule; and
- will legally use funds in accordance with appropriation restrictions and the requesting agency's laws and policies.

The D&F also states that the servicing agency has an existing contract, or has capabilities or expertise not available within the requesting agency to contract for such supplies or services, or is specifically authorized by law or regulation to purchase such supplies or services on behalf of other agencies. This D&F is included in the package sent to the servicing agency.

For an *assisted acquisition* (where one agency asks another to procure on its behalf), the analysis also addresses the expertise of the requesting agency to place orders and administer them, against the other agency's selected contract vehicle throughout the acquisition life cycle. The analysis must also assess the contract's suitability and value in terms of:

- administrative cost savings;
- greater number of vendors;
- lower prices; and
- reasonable vehicle access fees.

Before solicitation, the two agencies sign a written interagency agreement to establish the terms and conditions of their relationship, such as roles and responsibilities for acquisition planning, contract execution and administration. The requesting agency provides any unique terms or conditions, laws or regulations, directives, and requirements for the order or contract.[48] The two agencies should agree to procedures for resolving disputes between them. If they agree on third-party resolution, the third party should agree in writing. Work placed with an FFRDC is subject to acceptance by the sponsor and must fall within the mission, scope of effort or competency of the FFRDC without placing the FFRDC in direct competition with domestic private industry.

The servicing agency must also develop a D&F that provides a business case that its use is in the best interest of the Government, and that the supplies or services cannot be obtained as conveniently or economically by contracting directly with a private source. The D&F also addresses the following:

- costs to award and administer the contract;
- impact of award on Government purchasing power;
- need for the contract;
- roles and responsibilities of contract administration; and
- strategies for promoting the use of small businesses.

The servicing agency is responsible for generating any required J&A or additional D&F for the procurement action.

The order may be placed on any form or document that is acceptable to both agencies, and includes a(n):

- acquisition authority;
- delivery requirement(s);
- description of the supplies or services;
- funds citation; and
- payment provision.

Several specific procedures apply to contractor payment. The servicing agency may direct the requesting agency to fully fund the procurement in advance, with adjustment based on negotiated or actual cost. Or, the servicing agency may ask instead for reimbursement after contract completion. Advance payment requests and bills may not be audited or certified before payment. In addition, the servicing agency may charge the requesting agency the actual cost of award or administration, but not an arbitrary fixed fee. In fact, the servicing agency cannot compel the requiring agency to pay any fee in excess of the actual cost (or estimated cost if the actual cost is not known) of entering into and administering the contract.

If a civilian agency is asked to place an order on behalf of a Defense activity, it is still bound to comply with FAR, DFARS and class deviations. Further, the civilian agency must certify its compliance in writing to the Under Secretary of Defense (Acquisition, Technology and Logistics).

Often, however, interagency acquisitions simply utilize indefinite-delivery contracts for task and delivery orders. Most often, these are FSS, GWACs and multiagency contracts. In the past, agencies used an interagency acquisition to circumvent funding conditions and limitations. Certain restrictions are now in place to prevent this abuse, however it is still allowed routinely for orders of $550,000 or less issued against Federal Supply Schedules. These agreements are listed at https://www.contractdirectory.gov/contractdirectory/.

2.12.5 Management and Operating Contracts

FAR 17.6

A *management and operating contract* (also known as a *facilities* contract) covers effort to operate, maintain or support a Government-owned or -controlled research, development, special production, or testing establishment.[49] This facility is often owned by either the Department of Defense or Energy, but could be statutorily assigned to other agencies. These Government-owned or -controlled facilities are utilized to promote the national defense or mobilization readiness, or because private enterprise is unable or unwilling to use its own facilities for the work. The conduct of the work is separate from the contractor's other business, and is of a long-term or continuing nature. These precautions ensure both continuity of operations and an orderly transition of personnel and work should there be a change in contractors.

The Government is often limited in its ability to effect competition or to replace a contractor. Hence, contracting officers must ensure that the prospective contractor's technical and managerial capacity are sufficient, resolve organizational conflicts of interest, and retain for the Government continuing rights in technical and managerial decision-making regarding performance.

Management and operating contracts are not authorized for functions involving:

- authorizing use and rental of Government property;
- daily agency staff or management functions;
- determining Government policies;
- direction or control of Government personnel (unless incidental to training); or
- exercise of police or regulatory powers, other than guard services or plant protection.

The contracting officer reviews each management and operating contract at least once every five years to determine whether meaningful improvement in performance or cost might reasonably be achieved. Any extension or renewal is authorized at the same level within the agency as where the original contract was authorized. When reviewing contractor performance, contracting officers consider the incumbent contractor's overall performance (technical, administrative and cost) and the potential impact of a change in contractors or program needs (e.g., mobilization, national defense and safety) through competition.

2.12.6 Emergency Acquisitions

FAR 18

Emergency acquisitions are determined by the head of an executive agency in support of a contingency operation to facilitate the defense against or recovery from biological, chemical, nuclear, or radiological attack against the United States. They can also occur when the President declares an incident of national emergency or a major disaster (such as a hurricane) under the Robert T. Stafford Disaster Relief and Emergency Assistance Act (42 U.S.C. 5121).

Contractors are not required to be registered in SAM for contracts awarded to support unusual and compelling needs or emergency acquisitions, but must register with SAM in order to gain access to the Disaster Response Registry. Contracting officers will consult the Registry at www.acquisition.gov to determine the availability of contractors for debris removal, distribution of supplies, reconstruction, and other disaster or emergency relief activities inside the United States and outlying areas. The following changes to normal procurement procedures include:

- agencies may limit the number of sources;
- agencies need not enforce qualification requirements;
- authorization under the North American Free Trade Agreement prior to use of a patented technology may be waived;
- contracting officers are not restricted to an AbilityOne notification if changes in specifications or descriptions are required;
- contracting officers may solicit from only one source for purchases not exceeding the simplified acquisition threshold;
- contracting officers need not submit a synopsis notice;
- contracts may be awarded on a sole-source basis to HUBZone and service-disabled veteran-owned small business concerns;
- contracts to the SBA for 8(a) firms may be awarded on either a sole-source or competitive basis;
- electronic funds transfer payments may be waived;

- interagency acquisitions are authorized;
- letter contracts may be used;
- oral requests for proposals are authorized;
- overtime approvals may be retroactive if justified;
- preference in the form of local area set-asides or evaluation preference will be given to local firms, individuals and organizations;
- purchase from FPI is not mandatory and a waiver is not required;
- rental requirements do not apply to certain items of Government production and research property if approved by the Federal Emergency Management Agency;
- the chief of the contracting office may waive the requirement to obtain a bid guarantee when a performance bond is required;
- the contracting officer has the authority under PL 85-804 to amend contracts without consideration, authorize advance payments, correct or mitigate nonfraudulent mistakes in a contract, or formalize informal commitments in the interest of national defense;
- the head of the contracting activity may determine that the contracting process may continue after GAO has received a protest;
- the no-setoff provision for assignment of claims may be used; and
- trade agreement policies need not apply to acquisitions awarded noncompetitively.

The head of the contracting agency may determine in writing to increase the thresholds for micro-purchases, simplified acquisitions or the commercial items test program to facilitate defense against or recover from such attacks. Using the same procedure, the same official can also treat any acquisition of supplies or services as commercial items, or waive the provisions of the Cargo Preference Act of 1954 (46 U.S.C. 55305) that require use of American-flagged vessels to carry cargo.

On a broader scale, the National Response Framework establishes a comprehensive, national approach to domestic incident response by identifying key response principles, roles and structures. It describes how communities, state and Federal governments, the private sector, and nongovernmental partners apply these principles for a coordinated, effective national response. It also describes when the Federal Government exercises a larger role, such as catastrophic incidents where a state would require significant support. The Framework is available at http://www.fema.gov/emergency/nrf/.

2.12.7 Alpha Contracting

Alpha contracting is an acquisition process adopted to reduce the cycle time of sole-source acquisitions. It promotes use of contractor and government teaming without compromising acquisition goals. An approved acquisition plan is required. A Joint Government/Industry Team develops requirements, conducts an audit, determines the price, and drafts the contract. There is no solicitation or proposal; rather, the team addresses the technical and cost details to draft a model contract prior to final pricing. The team may even recommend changes to the program baseline to improve performance or to reduce cost or risk. The model contract is revised as technical and price details are resolved, and then becomes the official contract document.

Success requires open communications early in the process, mutual understanding of the statement of work, and agreement on appropriate scope and hours. The contractor and Government negotiating teams use the same cost and pricing data spreadsheet format and software version to facilitate negotiations and documentation.

2.12.8 Performance-Based Acquisition

FAR 37.6

A method of acquiring services by emphasizing output is known as *performance-based acquisition*. Initially defined in OFPP Policy Letter 91-2 (since rescinded), this approach is objective, measurable and mission-related. The solicitation describes what must be done, not how it will be done. This approach is intended to provide several benefits:

- better contractor performance;
- innovation;
- lower prices due to fewer government-unique specifications;
- reduced contract administration; and
- shorter procurement lead time.

There are seven prescribed steps to this process, most of which are already familiar from prior discussion:

- establish the acquisition team;
- decide what problem needs solving;
- examine private- and public-sector solutions;
- develop a performance work statement or statement of objectives;
- decide how to measure and manage performance;
- select the correct contractor(s); and
- manage their performance.

Agencies develop a *Statement Of Objectives* (SOO) to describe the work through required results rather than how the work is to be accomplished or the

number of hours to be provided. The SOO enables assessment of work performance against measurable standards, and encourages competitors to develop
and implement innovative and cost-effective methods to perform the work.
These standards are usually written agreements among multiple organizations
that define characteristics or specifications of specific operations. The SOO
does not become part of the contract. The SOO sets forth:

* purpose;
* scope or mission;
* period and place of performance;
* background;
* performance objectives results; and
* any operating constraints.

Proposals for performance-based services include a *performance work
statement* that describes the effort to be performed in detail, measurable
performance benchmarks or standards (e.g., quality, quantity and timeliness) and the method of assessing contractor performance (including any
performance incentives). The proposal also includes any data deliverables
and needed Government-furnished property and facilities. The offerors may
select any performance method, so long as they emphasize outcomes rather
than procedures. The statement should focus on factors that the contractor
controls without relying on Government processes or procedures. Agencies
evaluate the proposed performance standards to determine if they meet
agency needs.

The Government may either prepare a *quality assurance surveillance
plan*, or require the offerors to submit a proposed plan for Government
review. This plan describes a methodology to verify that the contractor's
quality control efforts are effective and timely, and deliver the specified
results. The plan indicates how contractor performance will be measured
and what performance standards will be used. During performance, the
contractor appraises its performance against these standards. These standards are known as *acceptable quality levels* and must be realistic, represent
minimum acceptable performance levels, and consider cost trade-offs and
market research. If a quality level is breached, the contractor calculates the
number of errors as a percentage of total measured events during the time
period, then applies it to the task value to derive the amount to be deducted
from the price.

The *contract management plan* describes how the Government will administer contract execution. It covers such topics as:

- acceptance criteria;
- changes in contractor personnel;
- communication process between parties;
- contract background, purpose and scope;
- contract changes and requests;
- contract closure;
- deliverables review and approval process;
- independent verification and validation;
- invoicing;
- performance metrics and milestones;
- program reviews;
- roles and responsibilities for each party; and
- status reporting and meetings.

Performance-based acquisition is not used to acquire:

- architect-engineer services;
- construction;
- services that are incidental to supply purchases; or
- utility services.

2.12.9 Economic Order Quantities

FAR 7.2

An *economic order quantity* is that amount which minimizes all associated costs by equating carrying and acquisition costs. Each solicitation for supplies invites the offeror to indicate if the solicited quantity of supplies is economically advantageous to the Government, and recommend an alternative quantity which includes a unit price and total amount.

Contracting officers take no action to revise quantities to be acquired on the instant procurement unless a significant price variation is evident from the offers and a potential for significant savings has arisen. Then, the contracting officer consults with the cognizant inventory manager or requirements development activity before proceeding.

Solicitation Provision

FAR 52.207-4, Economic Purchase Quantity – Supplies, except for a GSA multiple-award schedule, or if the data is already available to the Government.

2.12.10 Telecommuting

FAR 7.108

Telecommuting is actually a controversial subject in Government performance, especially in terms of contractor performance and Government oversight. Government managers will disagree on whether contract workers can be allowed to perform from home or a nearby telework center, or whether they must sit in spaces owned or rented by the Government (which are not free and raise the specter of personal services). Congress has stepped into this dispute by prohibiting an agency from discouraging a contractor who wishes to allow its employees to telecommute in the performance of Government contracts.[50] However, the contracting officer can determine that the requirements of the agency, such as frequent meetings or security requirements, cannot be met if telecommuting is permitted. There is no current program for either the Government or the contractor to encourage or discourage telecommuting among contract employees.

2.12.11 Equipment Lease or Purchase

Agencies consider whether to lease or purchase equipment based on a case-by-case evaluation of comparative costs and other factors, such as:

- availability of a servicing capability;
- availability of purchase options;
- cumulative rental payments for the estimated period of use;
- estimated length and extent of usage;
- financial and operating advantages of alternative types and makes of equipment;
- imputed interest;
- maintenance and other service costs;
- net purchase price;
- potential future use of the equipment by other agencies;
- potential obsolescence of equipment due to imminent technological improvements;
- trade-in or salvage value; and
- transportation and installation costs.

Generally, purchase is preferable to rental if the equipment will be used beyond the point in time when cumulative leasing costs exceed the purchase price. Alternatively, the lease method may be better when circumstances require immediate use of equipment to meet program or system needs but do not justify purchase for the long term. If a lease is justified, an option to purchase is preferable, specified in the contract as either a firm price or a formula for how the purchase price will be established at the time of purchase. Generally, a long-term lease should be avoided, unless an option to purchase or other favorable terms are included.

Solicitation Provision and Contract Clause

FAR 52.207-5, Option to Purchase Equipment.

2.12.12 Outsourcing

Outsourcing is the process of subcontracting effort to an outside firm. Outsourcing provides the prime contractor with benefits to:

- access intellectual property;
- catalyst for change;
- develop a core business;
- improve quality with a new service level agreement;
- make variable costs more predictable;
- manage a change in production level;
- promote risk management through a more capable source of supply;[51]
- reduce overall cost of the service;
- reduce time to market;
- standardize business processes and information technology services, especially when too difficult or time-consuming to develop in-house;
- supplement limited in-house capacity by accessing a larger talent pool of science and engineering skills; or
- use a contract with financial penalties and legal redress, which cannot be done if retained in-house.

The prime contractor must decide how to align its interests with its subcontractor to promote their common goals. This should lead to a governance structure that facilitates discussions between the parties to thoroughly understand the interests of both. A contract manager may be dedicated on a full-time basis to attend meetings, monitor operations for compliance with contract terms, review and maintain procedures, and track communications.

As a critical element of outsourcing, quality of service is measured through a service level agreement. Quality can be measured through customer satisfaction questionnaires which are professionally designed to capture an unbiased view of quality tracked over time and to identify corrective action to be taken.

Foreign sources provide challenges for outsourcing. Laws and taxes in foreign nations, as well as administrative procedures, must be followed. Labor unions, workforce structure and management control may also be different. Language barriers, especially where words may have different meanings, could be a problem (even between English-speaking countries). Sometimes, public opinion in the United States opposes offshoring because it leads to job displacement and workforce insecurity.[52]

Offshore outsourcing solely to save cost could diminish the real productivity of a company. Firms may reduce employment and outsource work to firms offshore that appear to be more productive simply because the workers are paid less. This may be illusory, however, since increased productivity often results from more productive tools or operating methods that make it possible for a worker to do more work in a given time period. Yet offshore outsourcing may reduce prices and provide greater economic benefit, so the controversy continues.

2.12.13 E-Procurement

E-procurement is a paperless, electronic form of procurement that involves B2B, B2C or B2G purchase and sale over the Internet. Typically, e-procurement Websites allow registered users to look for buyers or sellers to invite or submit offers. Repetitive purchases may qualify customers for volume discounts. E-procurement allows vendors to control inventories, reduce purchasing, payroll and manufacturing cycles, and obtain real-time information of customer needs. Both Government (through simplified acquisitions) and contractors may use e-procurement for commercial products.

There are at least seven versions of e-procurement:

- *e-informing*: gather and distribute purchasing information both from and to internal and external parties;
- *e-market sites*: buyers access suppliers' websites, add to shopping carts, create and approve requisitions, receive purchase orders, and process invoices;
- *e-MRO* (Maintenance, Repair and Overhaul): order goods and services that are not product-related;
- *e-reverse auctioning*: buy goods and services from a number of suppliers;
- *e-sourcing*: identify new suppliers;
- *e-tendering*: send and receive requests for information and prices to suppliers; and
- *Web-based Enterprise Resource Planning*: create and approve requisitions, place purchase orders, track deliveries, manage inventory, and receive goods and services.

Electronic contracting contains three main methods of transactions. A *shrink-wrap contract* purchases off-the-shelf products such as software, delivered with documented terms and conditions. This type of transaction has been around for some years, and exists in both paper and electronic environments. Secondly, a *click-wrap agreement* made on a website requires the buyer to click "I agree" before the transaction continues or the user gains access to the website. In the *browse-wrap transaction*, the user accesses a website where terms and conditions are posted but does not require the user to click assent to these terms before paying for the product.

All three methods have raised fundamental questions about what types of conduct constitute assent to terms and conditions. There have been concerns about how to treat terms that are not proposed or disclosed until after the user has already agreed to go forward with the transaction and made payment. One can also question whether there was assent, when it was manifested, and whether it covers terms about which the user had no knowledge or understanding. Fortunately, the incidence of unexpected terms should diminish as lawyers work to improve the focus of the terms and conditions which are acknowledged before purchase is completed.

Electronic Data Interchange is a structured transmission of business data in a standardized format between systems (known as *trading partners*) without human intervention. The documents are transmitted between sender and receiver via telecommunications over a third-party, value-added network, or else via electronic storage media. The sending computer connects to the Internet through a modulator-demodulator (*modem*) which converts computer-stored information into an audio tone that can pass over the telephone wire. Then at the receiving end, the tone can be reconverted into computer-readable data. This process is used for electronic commerce for a variety of business functions such as solicitation, award, modification, billing, and shipping.

The Government can also do electronic funds transfer between bank accounts to pay contractors via electronic bill payment or payment card. Although several sets of standards prescribe formats, character sets and data elements, the predominant formatting in North America is the American Standard Code for Information Interchange (X12).

These electronic transactions use an *encryption* algorithm to make the information in the electronic transfer unreadable to anyone who does not have the key to decrypt the cipher. Most firms encrypt data transfers and stored data. Messages use a message authentication code or digital signature to ensure they are genuine and to protect the validity of the data.

2.13 SUPPLY CHAIN MANAGEMENT

Supply chain management is the process of furnishing products and services to customers. This approach integrates inventory, logistics, performance measurement, procurement, production, and transportation, along with forecasts of suppliers and clients. This process designs, plans and monitors the storage and transportation of raw materials and parts, converts these materials into finished goods, manages work-in-process inventory, and transports finished goods to the point of consumption. Critical to the supply chain is *physical distribution*, a process which deals with packaging, shipping and warehousing.

The path by which these intermediary activities occur is the *supply chain*, since each link in the chain adds value to the process or final product. The supply chain is a bidirectional flow of products, services, funds, and information among participating firms and customers. Some links represent in-house effort in different departments, but many links connect needs which are contracted to other firms. By focusing in-house effort on core competencies and outsourcing other activities to sources that can perform them more efficiently, the firm tends to increase both source and distribution channels, reduce management control of daily logistics operations, and improve trust and collaboration among partners within the chain. Again, these activities are all in an effort to ultimately create user satisfaction.

2.13.1 Logistics

Logistics involves the flow management of goods and services (including people and data) between the points of origin and delivery to meet customer requirements. More colloquially, it means having the right item in the right quantity at the right time at the right place for the right price in the right condition to the right customer. Logistics integrates a great deal of information into the supply chain to add value, such as inventory, packaging, security, and transportation.

Logistics is closely tied with *production planning and control*, which coordinates supply and demand. The firm must tie together these functions so that finished goods are available from inventory, the production line or suppliers in time to fill orders. Whereas demand is a function largely filled by human performance (i.e., sales), the supply function lends itself to more automated means.

At the operational level, *production logistics* ensures that each machine and workstation is fed with the right product in the right quantity and quality at the right point in time. It strives to streamline and control the product flow and eliminate steps adding little or no value. Production logistics is a means to merge customer satisfaction with capital efficiency.

Even at the component level, logistics plays a key role in production planning. Each component must be compatible and interface with each other to ensure interchangeability. The firm can simplify this process by reducing the number and complexity of items in a product design, largely by eliminating unnecessary subitems or performance features. Another logistics technique is component redundancy, which utilizes multiple items or systems to overlap other parts or systems to increase *reliability* (the duration or probability of failure-free performance), though it also increases cost. Another technique is to standardize the number and size of parts and components used in production. This approach often leads to purchasing larger quantities, longer manufacturing runs, and reduced setup costs. However, this approach suffers if customers do not want standard parts for their custom-made items.

Another approach is *Integrated Logistics Support*, largely used in military industries to ensure customer service at the lowest cost and maximum reliability, availability and *maintainability* (using prescribed procedures and resources by skilled personnel to maintain and repair equipment or restore their working condition). This approach leads to systems components that function together effectively and efficiently, last longer with less support, increase customer value and contractor return on investment, and avoid proliferation of similar items. This process emphasizes off-the-shelf items produced and placed in stock by a manufacturer or distributor before receiving orders.

There are similarities between commercial and Government logistics problems. Both are concerned with efficiently acquiring material and services in the right price, quality, quantity, and time. Both want to develop good vendor relationships and interdepartmental communications, and ensure adequate training of personnel. However, the Government is also concerned with implementing socioeconomic issues, meeting more stringent requirements and properly accounting for spent public funds.

2.13.2 Supply Chain

Three models are used to depict the materiel management activities within the supply chain:

- Supply-Chain Operations Reference model (SCOR) from the Supply Chain Council;
- Supply Chain Management (SCM) from the Global Supply Chain Forum; and

- The American Productivity & Quality Center (APQC) Process Classification Framework from the Council of Supply Chain Management Professionals.

Since SCOR is the most commonly used, it will be the only method discussed in depth in this study.[53] SCOR strives to improve and communicate management practices between all parties within the supply chain, treating them like an extended enterprise. SCOR focuses on customer-focused interactions (from order entry through paid invoice), materials and services, and market (from understanding total demand to filling each order).

SCOR contains three basic pillars: process modeling, performance measurements and best practices. The *Process Modeling Pillar* uses building blocks and a prescribed set of definitions to model supply chains which describe the supply channel's breadth and depth. This pillar is based on five distinct management processes:

- *Plan* – balance aggregate demand and supply to optimally meet the requirements below;
- *Source* – procure goods and services;
- *Make* – transform product to a finished state;
- *Deliver* – manage distribution of finished goods and services; and
- *Return* – receive returned products.

This pillar defines scope, supply chain configuration, and attributes of process performance. To accomplish this approach, however, the firm must predefine its practices and strive to maximize its competitive advantage, while adapting to changing business conditions. The process modeling not only explains relationships between processes, but also enables collaboration between supply chain members. Further, it describes, measures and evaluates configuration alternatives, in an effort to support both continuous improvement and strategic planning.

The Performance Measurements Pillar reflects over 150 indicators of operations performance attributes of a supply chain operation. This promotes evaluation with other supply chains to measure success within the marketplace against competitors.

The *Best Practices Pillar* contains over 430 executable methods that are current, *structured* (have clearly stated goal, scope, process, and procedure), proven in a working environment, and repeatable elsewhere. These practices show either a gain in a positive metric or a reduction in an unfavorable metric.

SCOR modeling requires that a unit of supply engenders a unit of delivery, and vice versa. The model can be depicted in a labeled picture for any supply chain operation.

Critical to success of supply chain management is the use of *strategic sourcing*. Instead of buying tactically to meet a specific need, this approach encourages the firm to plan collaborative acquisitions by looking at its spending trends and future requirements. After the firm collects and standardizes its requirements, it conducts a total cost analysis of producing the needed supplies and services. The firm must then define the level of competition it feels comfortable with, and perhaps establish a formal concept of operations. Only then can it identify suitable suppliers to develop a sourcing strategy.

After negotiating with the chosen supplier(s), a supply structure is implemented and monitored. The firm may create permanent partnerships, and even centers of excellence based on core competencies or local practice. This approach should minimize dollar expenditure while maximizing use of resources and support. The Federal Government uses this approach sometimes to enhance interagency collaboration.

A firm practicing total supply chain management concentrates on those activities where it has knowledge and a distinctive advantage, and outsources everything else. The manufacturer will provide products to distribution channels based on past forecasts. Ideally, orders are filled just-in-time in minimum lot sizes, which leads to shorter cycle times and improved responsiveness to customer demand.

Another component of supply chain management addresses the customer. *Customer service* is designed to attain operational objectives, or perform an activity of value to the customer. Customer service can be provided in both wholesale logistics (e.g., weapon systems) or retail logistics (e.g., base services). Typically, customer orientation and warranties are hallmarks of customer service. Properly managed customer service should ultimately increase revenue and enhance profitability.

Possible scenarios that could disrupt the supply chain are created and resolved under *supply chain event management*. There are many challenges in supply chain management, including:

- aligning organizational and supply strategies;
- cash-flow and payment terms among firms (e.g., milestone payments);
- communication with partners of operational improvements and status updates;
- configuration of suppliers, production facilities, distribution centers, and customers, including any constraints imposed by same;
- consumption of raw materials;
- customer communication channels and service;
- demand forecasting, and sharing the results with all suppliers;
- developing strategic partnerships;
- distribution plans and schedules;

- flow of finished goods;
- globalization, which leads to issues of:
  ○ cross-border sourcing,
  ○ different tax laws,
  ○ different trading protocols,
  ○ global coordination and planning,
  ○ inconsistent treatment and lack of transparency of cost and profit,
  ○ longer lead time, and
  ○ multiple currencies;
- implementing best practices within the firm;
- inbound tracking and receipt from suppliers;
- integrating new and current products into the supply chain and capacity management;
- logistical coordination;
- long-lead procurements;
- make-or-buy decisions;
- manufacturing flow;
- market forces which lead to changes from customers and suppliers (which in turn impact the supply chain infrastructure, process configuration and work flows);
- need to improve trust and collaboration among partners during inventory movement;
- order fulfillment and shipments;
- product life-cycle management to integrate supplies and services into the supply chain;[54]
- production scheduling for each manufacturing facility in the supply chain;
- quantity, location and size of warehousing and distribution centers;
- replenishment strategy;
- returns and warranty management;[55]
- security management;
- sharing service centers for logistical and administrative functions;
- source selection;
- trade-offs to reduce total logistics cost;
- transportation routes, including frequency and modes; and
- updating, expanding and sharing information and its technology.

In a related vein, *Supply Chain Management 2.0* (SCM 2.0) is a term used to describe today's world of global and specialized supply chains. SCM 2.0 emphasizes creativity and web-based information sharing among partners in the supply chain in terms of processes, tools and delivery options.

2.13.3 Inventory

The *inventory* function includes several areas:

- design;
- disposal of excess items;
- materials requirements identification;
- ordering;
- packaging, storage and delivery;
- planning production and sourcing; and
- receiving and inspection.

Inventory products include the following:

- *raw materials* – substances and components scheduled for processing and consumption in the production process;
- *purchased parts* – components made by other firms to their own specifications;
- *subcontracted items* – components made by other firms to the customer's specifications;
- *work in process* – materials and components that are partially completed when transformed into finished goods. It allows production scheduling flexibility and provides a buffer against raw materials lead time and variation in demand;
- *safety stock* – a minimal amount of spare parts to cushion against stockout; used only if the cost of stockout exceeds carrying cost of the safety stock;
- *finished goods* – ready for sale to customers; and
- returned goods for resale.

Major materials functions are often assigned to a single materials management department. This unit manages cost control, production flow and control, use of capital resources, and interaction with vendors and suppliers. Many firms use a *material management and accounting system* to plan and control material acquisition, use and disposal. The system could be stand-alone, but often ties into other systems (e.g., accounting, engineering, estimating, planning, and purchasing). The materials system may be automated or manual.

A firm can use *materials requirements planning* to determine when and how much material to order based on customer demand. This methodology requires assessing delivery schedules, production activities and purchasing deadlines to ensure that materials are on hand when needed, though at minimal stocking levels. A computer program can use the master production schedule for a given item to estimate specific component or part requirements for the time period. Today's planning systems also consider capacities of labor, machine and suppliers. Of course, the firm must ensure that the inventory is available to the facility, rather than sitting in a warehouse across the country (if so, shipping cost and time must be included in the calculations).

Firms will record inventory using either a periodic or perpetual system. Some firms use a *periodic inventory method* to physically count at discrete times the units in raw material, work-in-process and finished goods states. Other firms use a *perpetual inventory method* to continuously track these items and update records whenever a unit is added or subtracted.

The program office develops a *bill of material* to list all raw material, parts and assemblies needed to fabricate the product. The list can be developed as requirements are designed, fabricated, maintained, or ordered. The list is often hierarchical in nature, with each assembly broken down into subassemblies and parts. This list is then used by the procurement department to purchase supplies for inventory.

The material system then develops an *economic order quantity* (EOQ), the number of units to be ordered that would minimize both ordering costs and carrying costs.[56] The *ordering costs* cover procurement expenses, while the *carrying costs* include inventory storage costs (which are often expressed as a percentage of the value of the material costs). EOQ is used to determine incremental impacts for both types of costs. This process assumes constant ordering cost and rate of demand, fixed lead time, instantaneous replenishment and delivery, and unit prices not wildly fluctuating.

This discussion means that the Total Cost (TC) of a given purchase is the sum of three cost components:

- *purchase price*: the product of unit price and demand quantity, or $P*D$;
- *ordering cost*: a fixed cost O for placing one order times the number of orders in a given time period (usually a year). This second number is derived by dividing the total annual demand quantity D by the order time frequency F. Hence, ordering cost = $O*D/F$;
- *holding cost*: carrying cost C times the average quantity in stock, which is midway between full and empty stock shelves, or $C*D/2$.

Hence, $TC = PD + OD/F + CD/2$.

As a result of mathematical manipulations beyond the scope of this book (by using basic calculus), EOQ = the square root of $2DO/C$.

Maintaining an inventory costs money, but lack of an item can stop a production line. Hence, production forecasts should include EOQs and order points. There are several formulas that tie into this approach:

- Maximum inventory = quantity at delivery + units on hand;
- Average inventory = ½ * (beginning inventory + ending inventory);
- Reorder point = lead time * average usage in the same period of time (e.g., months or weeks).

The *reorder point* is the level of inventory at which a new order must be placed to procure enough material to return to the EOQ. Ordering at this point in time ensures that inventory is never totally depleted (stockout), which runs the risk of customer dissatisfaction and lost sales. Since the procurement office must have sufficient lead time to place an order, the firm can identify the normal consumption during this lead time and add it to the safety stock level to obtain a realistic reorder level.

Safety stock quantities escalate throughout the supply chain because each vendor adds its own buffer stock to inventory. Common causes of safety stock are:

- anticipated shortages;
- consolidated demands and quantity discounts from vendors;
- forecasting errors (e.g., replenishment lead time);
- lost synchronization between lot sizes and ordering;
- misperceptions of the production process;
- panic ordering after unmet demand; and
- revised inventory projections.

These conditions can lead to more than just excessive or insufficient inventory. It can also cause inefficient production, inferior customer service, and poor utilization of the distribution channel. They can also cause a *bullwhip effect*, where an action downstream causes a response throughout the upstream supply chain, where each entity up the chain wishes to carry its own safety stock. The effect grows with each link of the supply chain, leading to unnecessary inventory on hand throughout the distribution system.

The length of the manufacturing cycle also affects materials accounts. The acquisition lead time begins with identifying a materials requirement and continues until award is made. At that point, production lead time commences until the day of delivery. Therefore, the concept of *lead time risk* is a factor in program impact due to failure of material to arrive on time, regardless of whether the delay is due to the acquisition process or vendor performance. This item may need to be included in the risk assessment for program management consideration.

Advance buys of long-lead items can protect production schedules by avoiding lengthy delays awaiting components. Some major programs with known or predictable future needs will execute an *advance acquisition contract* solely to obtain long-lead items as well as production planning and engineering effort. These contracts cover items that are either needed upfront or take a long time to fabricate or locate and then deliver. The end items will be fully funded in a future fiscal year, however long-lead funding is available in the current year. These long-lead contracts may then be converted into the final production contracts as funds become available and final end-item prices are definitized.

A controversial alternative is to order all raw material upfront, known as *forward buying*. Ordering upfront and receiving material only as needed will free up cash flow and minimize storage capacity used. However, this approach can lead to complex inventory management and higher storage costs, so it is usually practiced only in stable markets or when prices are rising.

The length of manufacturing time can also be a factor in deciding for forward buying. A long manufacturing cycle requires more complex management with a higher probability of schedule impacts. A short manufacturing cycle requires less complex management, but does not afford as much time for rework. Even for finished goods inventory, the length of a manufacturing cycle would impact the amount of inventory to satisfy demand. A long cycle would require more material and goods, while a short cycle would need less finished goods inventory.

Some entities may use a *systems contract* that authorizes designated employees (often from the user department) to place orders with the supplier for specific items at a specific time in a predetermined release system. Sometimes known as *stockless purchasing*, this approach reduces inventory to a minimal level while assuring continuity of supply.

As complicated as this process is, it is essential to expose customer demand back up the channel.[57] This requires investment in information technology and the embracement of flexibility and customer demand. It also requires all supply chain firms to share information with each other. Other methods to address customer demand include:

- discourage low-price promotions;
- limit customer returns and cancellations;
- prioritize orders based on past sales data;
- provide more frequent replenishments;
- reduce batch sizes; and
- spread out vendor deliveries.

Upon receipt, each item is bar-coded with an identification number (known as a *store keeping unit* identifier, or SKU) to track its presence in storage. These are the same bar codes read by the cash register at your favorite retail store.

Nontangible items such as warranties or delivery fees also bear SKUs on their written terms of service. SKUs are entered into a database for an information system to track physical features (e.g., size and color), as well as destination of a particular unit and stock on hand.

Inventory systems use bar codes and Radio Frequency Identification (RFID) tags to automate identification of inventory items (e.g., capital equipment, fixed assets, goods for sale, material, tools, etc.) A bar code scanner or RFID reader identifies the unit to collect information for display on terminals or mobile computers. This automates the process of filling sales orders. The system can also be programmed to alert managers when products reach a predetermined low level in order to prompt reordering.

Two major models to track inventory are *fixed-order quantity* to initiate an order at a specified reorder level, and *fixed-order period* (also known as *periodic*, or *interval system*) to order at a predetermined point in time. Both inventory models strive to minimize costs by either *deterministic* (where demand is certain) or *probabilistic* methods (where demand varies daily and requires either setting safety stock to meet customer desire, or else minimizing carrying cost of additional inventory). Input necessary to manipulate these models includes:

- frequency of review;
- order placement cost;
- order size;
- production setup cost;
- reorder point;
- shipping costs;
- storage cost; and
- vendor identity, lead time and pricing.

Other management methods can be used to track inventory. *Price-break models* measure quantity changes when unit price changes with order size, while *single-period models* (or *static models*) present a cost trade off for every order and stocking action.

Another option involves *ABC classification*, an implementation of the Pareto Rule (20% of the quantity provides 80% of the benefit) by stratifying inventory items. This approach is intended to set priorities among a number of issues, then focus priorities and resources on the most important ones. The technique lists the items into several categories, say A, B and C. Then category A reflects the largest 80% of cost, B represents the next 15% or so, and C includes the rest of the items. We can see the Pareto principle reflected in this scheme: 80% of the cost applies to a few items (category A), so they are the cost drivers and require more attention. Category B items require less attention and will undoubtedly be more numerous in number. Depending on the level of confidence in the firm's inventory management process, Category C items may be accepted without further review, or at most a sanity check. This process can also be used for customer prioritization, since for many firms, roughly 20% of the customers provide about 80% of the revenue.

After deriving the ABC data, a *Pareto diagram* can be prepared to graphically depict the results from this stratification. A bar chart can be developed to display a value for each object (e.g., number of times a problem occurs, sales per customer, or usage of an inventory item) in descending order to identify the most important problems. Then a line chart can display all bars to visually reflect the sum results of the data collection.

Material attrition is a net loss to the firm, and can manifest itself in several ways. *Shrinkage* is the loss of materials once they have reached the firm due to loss or damage. To reduce this risk, firms take loss prevention measures (e.g., bar coding, itemized product inventory, and security cameras). Other causes of material attrition include obsolescence and spoilage. *Loss through misplacement* is common in large organizations or warehouses where material is received at the entry point and then moved to an incorrect location by the distribution staff (or worse, stolen). This condition can be reduced through bar code scanning and a tracking system which records when and where items are stored.

Inventory that is not included in deliverable items is known by several names. *Rejects* are material that did not meet production standards. *Scrap* is material left over or discarded, but can be reprocessed, whereas *waste* is useless material created as a byproduct and must be disposed. *Surplus material* is inventory remaining after contract completion. Surplus material can be disposed in any of several methods:

• donation to an educational institution;
• return to the supplier;
• sale to employees or another firm; or
• use within the firm.

Commonality is another method to make inventory as efficient as possible. When separate materials or systems have similar and interchangeable characteristics, they may be charged out of stock for use on the other system. However, personnel who are trained to use one system may not work equally well with the other, so cross-training may be necessary.

Inventory costs include a variety of components:

• breakage and spoilage;
• depreciation;

- insurance;
- line cost for each item;
- obsolescence;
- *opportunity cost of capital*;[58]
- ordering cost;
- production setup;
- stockout;
- storage space; and
- taxes.

Cost of Goods Sold (CoGS) is a prime measure of a factory's productivity. It is calculated by deriving the cost of goods produced:

Cost of Beginning Inventory
+ Inventory Purchases
+ Production Cost
= Cost of Goods Produced.

This number absorbs production overhead and raw material costs into an inventory value. Then,

Cost of Goods Produced
− Cost of Ending Inventory
= Cost of Goods Sold.

CoGS can then be subtracted from the sales price to determine a sales margin figure.

Manufacturing management also uses formulas to measure inventory levels. One approach can derive a value for inventory turnover:

$$\text{Inventory turnover ratio} = \frac{\text{Cost of Goods Sold}}{\text{Average Inventory}}$$

where Average Inventory is the average of Beginning Inventory and Ending Inventory levels. This number tells us how much cash or goods are tied up waiting for the process and is a critical measure of process effectiveness and reliability. The time frame for turnover can be defined as follows:

$$\text{Average Days to Sell Inventory} = \frac{\text{Number of Days in a Year}}{\text{Inventory Turnover Ratio}}$$

When an item is issued from inventory, the value of the inventory account is reduced by CoGS.

Common methods to adjust inventory value are:

- *First-In-First-Out* (FIFO) matches the price of the first unit that arrived in inventory to the cost of the first unit sold. Many stock units actually do operate this way to avoid spoilage. Under this method, older costs are assigned to CoGS and newer costs are assigned to Inventory. Since costs generally rise over time, FIFO tends to increase the value of inventory and reduce CoGS.

- *Last-In-First-Out* (LIFO) matches the last arriving unit with the first one sold. As the mirror image of FIFO, LIFO tends to reduce the value of inventory and increase CoGS. Because material prices tend to rise over time, LIFO accounting often leads to lower net income[59] and lower *book value* (cost less depreciation, which is the asset value carried in the accounting books) because of inflation, and hence lower taxes.
- *Average Cost* of a unit in beginning inventory plus purchases made during the period helps to derive both the cost of sales and the ending inventory value.
- *Weighted Average Method* derives a unit average cost as follows:

Cost of purchases + cost of beginning inventory
units bought year-to-date + beginning # units
Then,
Unit cost * number of units in ending inventory = Inventory Cost.

Just-in-time inventory management was developed in Japan to ensure that inventory materials arrive at the plant only when needed for use on the production line. Parts and materials are bought in an exact quantity just as needed. It has changed the procurement function through:

- contingent liabilities if production is cancelled;
- frequent specification changes;
- increased transportation costs due to frequent delivery cycles;
- less inventory in the plant;
- multi-year relationships with fewer suppliers to promote their timely delivery; and
- price escalation protection.

Manufacturing firms are impacted by shortages of critical materials. They reconsider their inventory decision models and the significance of *make-or-buy* decisions (deciding whether to perform or make in-house or subcontract the effort to another firm). They strive to improve cooperation between purchasing and production departments, develop alternate sources of supply, consider backward and forward integration, and increase efficiencies. Inventory management also addresses:

- available physical space;
- cost control (start-up, facilities, tools, labor, training, transportation, and location);

- defective goods;
- demand forecasting;
- price forecasting;
- quality management;
- replenishment lead time; and
- visibility.

Methods to improve the inventory system include:

- accept partial deliveries on EOQs;
- negotiate shorter lead times;
- select local suppliers;
- set aside stocks at supplier facilities; and
- use formal agreements for recurring purchases.

2.14 INTERNATIONAL CONTRACTING

2.14.1 Agreements and Restrictions

FAR 25

The *Buy American Act* (41 U.S.C. 8301) advocates the purchase of *domestic end products*, as defined below. The Act restricts the purchase of non-domestic end products for use within the United States, unless the contracting officer determines that the price of the lowest domestic offer is unreasonable or if another exception applies. The Buy American Act uses a two-part test to define a domestic end product: it must be manufactured in the United States, and the cost of domestic components must exceed 50% of the cost of all the components. This second test is waived to acquire COTS items.

There are three key exceptions to the Buy American Act for supplies. The head of the agency may determine that domestic preference would be inconsistent with the public interest, such as an agreement with a foreign government that provides a blanket exception to the Buy American Act. Second, the Act does not apply to end items or components that are not mined or produced in the United States in sufficient commercial quantities and quality. Also, the Act does not apply to micro-purchases.

A nonavailability determination has been made for a variety of items listed in FAR 25.104, meaning that domestic sources can only meet half or less of total domestic demand. However, before acquiring an article on the list as either an end product or a component comprising over half the value of all components within an end product, the procuring agency must first conduct market research to seek domestic sources.

When the lowest offer in a competition is not a domestic item, the contracting officer must determine cost reasonableness by adding to its price any duty, plus a premium differential. The duty must be identified in the offer. The differential is six% of the offered price if the lowest domestic offer is from a large business concern, or 12% if the lowest domestic offer is from a small business concern. The head of the agency may increase these percentages. The socioeconomic status of the respective offerors is not relevant in this situation. Even if the acquisition is conducted under a small business set-aside, and even if the low offer is from a small business concern offering a nondomestic end product from another small business concern, a premium must be applied to the price. If the domestic offer does not exceed this adjusted price, it is deemed reasonable (a tie is decided in favor of the domestic product). The evaluation factor does not provide a preference for one foreign offer over another.

2.14.2 Buy American Act – Construction Materials

FAR 25

The Act also generally requires the use of domestic construction materials in contracts for construction within the United States. *Construction material* is an article or supply brought to the construction site by a (sub)contractor to be incorporated into the building or work. It could be either preassembled or incorporated on the site. However, there are special exceptions for safety systems: audio evacuation, emergency lighting and fire alarm systems are evaluated as a single construction material regardless of when or how the individual parts or components are delivered to the site. Also, this policy does not include materials bought directly by the Government – they are considered supplies rather than construction material. Other exceptions for construction contracts are for:

- impracticability or inconsistency with the public interest, such as an agreement with a foreign government that bears a blanket exception to the Buy American Act;
- information technology that is a commercial item;
- nonavailability within the United States (the same exception as for supply contracts); or
- unreasonable cost.

A D&F is necessary to invoke any of these exceptions.

The contracting officer reviews any allegations of Buy American Act violations. If a positive finding results, (s)he notifies the contractor of the apparent unauthorized use of foreign construction material and requests a reply, to include a proposed corrective action (unless fraud is suspected, in which case [s]he must follow agency procedures). The contracting officer may:

- direct replacement of the foreign material without causing delay;
- determine not to remove the material but not waive the Act, thereby preserving the right to further punitive action;
- reduce the contract price;
- suspend or debar the (sub)contractor; or
- terminate for default.

Certain trade agreements waive the Act below a specified dollar value. In these cases, end products and construction materials from specified countries receive nondiscriminatory evaluation.

2.14.3 Performance Outside the United States

FAR 25.3

Contractors usually provide their own logistic and security support. The Government can do so if it has available resources to ensure continuation of contract performance and the contractor cannot obtain them at a reasonable cost. This would occur most often in contingency, housekeeping or peacekeeping missions. The contracting officer must specify in the solicitation what support it will provide and whether the contractor shall reimburse the Government.

Contractors providing security services overseas have the additional responsibility of informing their employees about compliance with:

- accident reporting;
- accounting for weapons;
- keeping appropriate personnel records;
- registering and identifying armored vehicles, helicopters and other military vehicles;
- relevant directives, instructions and orders, including those of the theater military commander; and
- reporting incidents involving personnel performing private security functions.

Failure to comply with the above could lead to a negative report in the past performance database and reduced award fee. If the failure is long term, suspension or debarment may be called for.

Solicitation Provisions and Contract Clauses

FAR 52.225-19, Contractor Personnel in a Designated Operational Area or Supporting a Diplomatic or Consular Mission outside the United States. The contract must require contractor personnel to perform in a designated operational area during contingency operations (including humanitarian, peace-keeping or military operations), or when supporting a diplomatic or consular mission designated by the Department of State as a danger pay post. Do not use for personal service contracts with individuals.

FAR 52.225-26, Contractors Performing Private Security Functions Outside the United States, for performance in a combat area or in support of foreign military operations. Do not use if the contract supports intelligence activities or temporarily uses indigenous personnel unaffiliated with a local security company.

2.14.4 Trade Agreements

FAR 25.4 and 5

This subpart does not apply to acquisitions:

- from FPI and SourceAmerica;
- in support of national security (including war materiel);
- of end products for resale;
- of sole-source or limited-source nature; or
- under small business set-asides.

The Trade Agreements Act (19 U.S.C. 2501, et seq.) authorizes the President to waive the Buy American Act and other provisions for eligible products from countries with which the United States has an international trade agreement or designation of preference. This provision extends to the World Trade Organization Government Procurement Agreement and our nation's Free Trade Agreements. Offers of these eligible products receive equal consideration with domestic offers. However, the country of origin must be where material incurs "substantial transformation" into a new and different article, with a different character, name or use. Dollar thresholds are revised by the U.S. Trade Representative for different nations roughly every other year, and are summarized at FAR 25.402.

The contracting officer must determine the origin of supplies or services by the country in which the firm is established, though (s)he may rely on the offeror's certification of end product origin. To evaluate offers, the contracting officer first eliminates offers deemed unacceptable due to nonprice issues, such as nonresponsiveness or prohibited sources. Then the remaining offers are ranked by price. Any other nonprice evaluation factors are then considered. To break any ties, preference is given to a domestic offer if nonprice factors were considered, or drawing lots if no such preferences were involved.

To derive the evaluated price of the domestic product, the contracting officer adds the value of all options and invoke the following rules:

- If a fixed-term contract of 12 months or less is contemplated, use the total estimated value of the acquisition.
- If a fixed-term contract of more than 12 months is contemplated, use the total estimated value of the acquisition plus the estimated residual value of any leased equipment at the end of the contract.
- If an indefinite-term contract is contemplated, use the estimated monthly payment multiplied by the total number of months for ordering (i.e., the initial ordering period plus any optional ordering periods).
- If there is any doubt as to the contemplated term of the contract, use the estimated monthly payment multiplied by 48.
- If, in any 12-month period, recurring or multiple awards for the same type of product or products are anticipated, use the total estimated value of these projected awards. The acquisition should not be divided with the intent of reducing the estimated value of the acquisition below the dollar threshold of the Agreement.

Should one or more offers call for award by lot or on an all-or-none basis, the contracting officer may need to first apply evaluation factors by line item for any portion that does not so restrict award, then evaluate the lots which are restricted. Unless the restricted lot price is lower overall, award is made to the most favorable unrestricted offer. For offers of both domestic and foreign items, whichever constitutes the majority of the price for the given lot determines whether to treat the offer as domestic or foreign.

Solicitation Provisions

FAR 52.214-34, Submission of Offers in the English Language.

FAR 52.214.35, Instruction to Offerors—Competitive Acquisitions.

2.14.5 American Recovery and Reinvestment Act

FAR 25.6

The American Recovery and Reinvestment Act (7 U.S.C. 2036, previously introduced as the Recovery Act) is intended to finance a project to alter, construct, maintain, or repair a public building or work that is located in the

United States. It includes only manufactured goods such as iron and steel that are produced or manufactured in the United States. This restriction does not apply if the:

- contracting officer determines that a certain construction material is not mined, produced or manufactured in the United States in sufficient and available commercial quantities of a satisfactory quality;
- cost of domestic construction material is unreasonable (i.e., would raise the evaluated contract price more than 25% for a manufactured item or 6% for unmanufactured material);
- steel or iron is used as a component of other manufactured construction material (such as a window frame), which need not be domestic; or
- restriction would be impracticable or inconsistent with public interest.

Allowable countries of origin are a World Trade Organization Government Procurement Agreement country, a Free Trade Agreement country, or a least developed country as designated in FAR 25.003. Prohibited sources of supply are listed at http://www.treas.gov/offices/enforcement/ofac. Current prohibited sources are Cuba, Iran, Sudan, Myanmar (imports only), and North Korea (imports only). Any instances of contractor noncompliance with the Recovery Act are handled by the contracting officer in the same manner as the Buy American Act.

An offeror may request from the contracting officer a determination concerning the inapplicability of section 1605 of the Recovery Act or the Buy American Act for specifically identified construction materials. FAR 52.225-22 or -24 (whichever applies to the solicitation) paragraph (b) describes the timing for such a request, and FAR 52.221-21 or -23 (whichever applies to the solicitation) paragraphs (c–d) describes the information to be furnished.

If the contracting officer has determined that an exception applies because the cost of certain domestic construction material is unreasonable, then (s)he adds an evaluation factors to the offered price in the same manner as described earlier for the Buy American Act. The factor is 25% to the offer including foreign iron, steel or other manufactured goods, or 6% to the cost of foreign unmanufactured construction material. Once again, if two or more offers are equal in price, the contracting officer gives preference to an offer that does not include foreign construction material.

Offerors may submit alternate offers based on use of equivalent domestic construction material to avoid possible rejection of the entire offer, in case the Government determines that no exception permits use of a particular foreign construction material. The alternate offer may not be a very attractive price, but at least the firm is still under consideration for award.

Although uncommon, the contracting officer might grant a request to determine inapplicability after award. However, (s)he must negotiate adequate consideration in this case and modify the contract to allow use of the foreign construction material. Again, the 25% and 6% factors may be used if a domestic material is found to be unreasonably priced.

2.14.6 Other International Issues

FAR 25.9

U.S. laws impose duties on foreign supplies imported into the customs territory of the United States, as implemented at 19 CFR 10.100. Certain exemptions from these duties are available to Government agencies by contracting officer petition to the Commissioner of Customs. Subchapters VIII and X of Chapter 98 of the Harmonized Tariff Schedule of the United States (19 U.S.C. 1202) list supplies for which exemptions may be obtained.[60]

The solicitation will specify the currency of offers and payment, either U.S. dollars or local currency. If offers come in terms of multiple currencies, the contracting officer must convert the offered prices to U.S. currency for evaluation purposes. This requires using the current market exchange rate from a commonly used source (e.g., http://www.federalreserve.gov/releases/g5/current/) in effect on the date of bid opening for sealed bidding, or the date specified for receipt of offers or any final revisions for negotiated acquisitions.

Solicitation Provisions and Contract Clauses

FAR 52.215-2, Audit and Records–Negotiation, and paragraph (d) of the clause at 52.212-5, Contract Terms and Conditions Required to Implement Statutes or Executive Orders–Commercial Items, with foreign contractors to authorize examination of records by the Comptroller General. If they object, the contracting officer may use 52.215-2 with its Alternate III or 52.212-5 with its Alternate I after negotiations fail, no other sources of supply can be found in a reasonable time at reasonable cost, and the head of the agency has executed a D&F with the concurrence of the Comptroller General. Such concurrence is not required if the contractor is a foreign government or agency, or prevented by native law from providing records for examination.

FAR 52.225-1, Buy American Act—Supplies and 52.225-2, Buy American Act Certificate, when greater than $25,000 and no alternative clauses apply. The clauses are not used if restricted to domestic end products, for supplies for use outside the United States, or for supplies to be used within the United States and an exception to the Buy American Act applies (e.g., nonavailability, public interest, or information technology that is a commercial item).

FAR 52.225-3, Buy American Act–Free Trade Agreements–Israeli Trade Act, and 52.225-4, Buy American Act–Free Trade Agreements–Israeli Trade Act Certificate for use within the United States, and the acquisition value is between $25,000 and $191,000. Use both clauses with Alternate I if the acquisition value is between $25,000 and $50,000. Use both clauses with Alternate II if the acquisition value is between $50,000 and $77,533. Use both clauses with Alternate III if the acquisition value is between $77,533 and $100,000. Do not use for information technology that is a commercial item.

FAR 52.225-5, Trade Agreements, and 52.225-6, Trade Agreements Certificate, if valued at $194,000 or more, the acquisition is covered by the WTO GPA, and the Buy American Act does not apply.

FAR 52.225-7, Waiver of Buy American Act for Civil Aircraft and Related Articles, for civil aircraft and related articles, if the acquisition value is less than $191,000.

FAR 52.225-8, Duty-Free Entry, for supplies that may be imported into the United States and for which duty-free entry may be obtained, if the value of the acquisition exceeds the simplified acquisition threshold, or if the savings from waiving the duty exceed the administrative cost of the duty.

FAR 52.225-9, Buy American Act–Construction Materials, for construction that is performed in the United States valued at less than $7,358,000.

FAR 52.225-11, Buy American Act–Construction Materials under Trade Agreements, for construction that is performed in the United States and valued at $7,358,000 or more. Use the clause with Alternate I if the acquisition value is between $7,358,000 and $10,079,365.

When using funds appropriated under the Recovery Act for construction, use the following (with appropriate Alternates) in lieu of the provisions and clauses 52.225-9, 52.225-10, 52.225-11, or 52.225-12, respectively:

- FAR 52.225-21, Required Use of American Iron, Steel, and Manufactured Goods–Buy American Statute–Construction Materials.
- FAR 52.225-22, Notice of Required Use of American Iron, Steel, and Manufactured Goods–Buy American Statute–Construction Materials.
- FAR 52.225-23, Required Use of American Iron, Steel, and Manufactured Goods–Buy American Statute–Construction Materials Under Trade Agreements. List all foreign construction materials excepted from the Buy American Act or Section 1605 of the Recovery Act.
- FAR 52.225-24 Notice of Required Use of American Iron, Steel, and Manufactured Goods–Buy American Statute–Construction Materials Under Trade Agreements.

FAR 52.225-13, Restrictions on Certain Foreign Purchases, unless an exception applies.

FAR 52.225-14, Inconsistency Between English Version and Translation of Contract, if anticipating translation into another language.

Solicitation Provisions

FAR 52.225-10, Notice of Buy American Act Requirement–Construction Materials, in solicitations containing the clause at 52.225-9. Use the provision with Alternate I if insufficient time is available before receipt of offers to process a determination of inapplicability of the Buy American Act.

FAR 52.225-12, Notice of Buy American Act Requirement–Construction Materials under Trade Agreements, if containing the clause at 52.225-11. Use the provision with its Alternate I if insufficient time to process a Buy American Act determination. Use the provision with its Alternate II for acquisitions between $7,358,000 and $10,079,365.

FAR 52.225-17, Evaluation of Foreign Currency Offers, to permit the use of an unspecified currency. Insert in the provision the source of the rate to be used in the evaluation of offers.

FAR 52.225-18, Place of Manufacture, for manufactured end products whose estimated value exceeds that of other items to be acquired as a result of the solicitation.

FAR 52.225-20, Prohibition on Conducting Restricted Business Operations in Sudan—Certification, except for commercial items.

FAR 52.225-25, Prohibition on Contracting with Entities Engaging in Certain Activities or Transactions Relating to Iran-Representation and Certifications.

2.14.7 Export Controls

An *export* is a product, software or technology sent from the United States to a foreign nation. An item is also considered an export if it leaves the United States to a wholly owned U.S. subsidiary in a foreign country. Even a foreign-origin item is treated as an export if it is trans-shipped through the United States, or returns from the United States to its foreign country of origin.

The Department of State controls some commodity exports by means of the International Traffic in Arms Regulation. All other exports are controlled by the Department of Commerce through the Export Administration Regulations (EAR), usually under a general license. Releasing technology or source code to a foreign national within the United States is considered an export to the home country of the foreign national under the EAR.

License requirements depend on an item's technical characteristics, destination, end user, and purpose. If an exported item has both commercial and military or space usage, it requires a validated license to protect a national security or foreign policy interest. The item is given a specific Export Control Classification Number that describes both the item and the controls placed on that item. All such numbers are listed in the Commerce Control List, available at http://www.access.gpo.gov/bis/ear/ear_data.html#ccl.

2.14.8 Foreign Military Sales

The DoD runs a Foreign Military Sales (FMS) program to facilitate sales of U.S. arms and defense equipment (including from defense stockpiles), services, and military training to foreign governments. This program implements the Foreign Assistance Act of 1961 (22 U.S.C. 2301) and the Arms Export Control Act (22 U.S.C. 2778). The foreign buyer does not deal directly with the defense contractor. Rather, the Defense Security Cooperation Agency serves as an intermediary for procurement, logistics and delivery support, and often provides product support and training. FMS requires the foreign nation to place a deposit in a U.S. trust fund or else demonstrate appropriate credit and approval. Funding can also come from congressional appropriation or grants under the Military Assistance Program.[61]

The foreign nation can dictate a sole source. The United States charges the foreign nation an administrative fee and nonrecurring costs to place and administer the contract. Note that any unusual costs of doing business in the foreign country (e.g., government brokerage fees) could raise the price.

In addition to goods, knowledge may also be shared with foreign nations. A good example is *international coproduction*, a method by which technical information and procedures are transferred to other nations to produce or assemble military items domestically.

2.14.9 Priority Delivery

Mutual interdependence of supplies is necessary to achieve national security, interoperability and timely delivery between the United States and its allies. DoD has entered into arrangements with several NATO nations to request priority delivery for (sub)contracts or orders from companies in these countries. DoD program managers and contractors acquiring materials and services from participating firms may request priority delivery for their (sub)contract or order to meet U.S. defense requirements. Partner nations are instituting government-industry codes of conduct for firms to help provide priority support on a voluntary basis.

NOTES

1. In this regard, *horizontal marketing* describes the process of selling goods and services between entities. This effort manifests itself when firms pursue subcontracting opportunities with Federal contractors.

2. A *broker* is a third-party entity authorized to negotiate with potential vendors but not authorized to make a commitment or contract.

3. 41 UCC 253, Competition in Contracting Act of 1984, requires the use of advance procurement planning and market research for all major procurements, and commercial products wherever practicable.

4. Rewards or penalties may be involved with the original vendor in second-source development.

5. Some agencies may establish procedures to obtain advance approval, on a case-by-case basis.

6. National Institute of Standards and Technology, "Special Publication 500-267: A Profile for IPV6 in the U.S. Government," National Institute of Standards and Technology, Gaithersburg, Md., 2008.

7. See OMB Memorandum M-05-22, Transition Planning for Internet Protocol Version 6, dated August 2, 2005. The agency Chief Information Officer may waive the requirement.

8. The *system acquisition process* begins with requirements definition in terms of capabilities, priorities and resources, and ends when the system enters operational use.

9. Support Anti-terrorism by Fostering Effective Technologies Act of 2002 (6 U.S.C. 441).

10. OMB, "OMB Circular A-109, Major Systems Acquisition," OMB, Washington, D.C., April 5, 1976.

11. *Value engineering* is a similar activity also used by firms to find opportunities for cost cutting.

12. Modifying the product itself would constitute re-engineering.

13. DoD, "DoD Instruction 4200-15, Manufacturing Technology (Mantech) Program," DoD, Washington, D.C., September 19, 2002. This program is fully discussed at www.dodmantech.com.

14. This is done through quantitative and qualitative analysis to determine the probability that a specific interaction of performance, schedule and cost will or will not be attained due to a planned course of action.

15. Small Business Administration, Office of Advocacy, "Frequently Asked Questions About Small Businesses," Washington, D.C., September 2012, page 1.

16. Such components then become Government Furnished Equipment to the systems manufacturer.

17. A partial set-aside cannot be used in construction contracts, since there is only one prime contractor per job.

18. However, for competitive 8(a) contracts, only the contracting officer may challenge the firm's status. The protest goes to the SBA Government Contracting

Area Office for the geographical area covering the principal office of the challenged concern.

19. If the firm is determined by the chief of the contracting office to be unqualified, or is suspended or debarred, no referral to the SBA is necessary.

20. Specific results must be reported for subcontracts exceeding $150,000 in value.

21. *Rothe Development Corp. v. Dept. of Defense* (545 F. 3d 1023).

22. This exclusion includes an SDB from a particular region if the price differential is applied on a regional basis.

23. Despite any concerns over political correctness, the term "Indian" was used in the original statute and has never been changed by Congress, hence the term will be used in this book.

24. This program was inspired by E.O. 13005, Empowerment Contracting, May 24, 1996.

25. This agency within the Department of Commerce emphasizes new ways to use data in solving problems. It is the largest data repository of federally sponsored research, dating back to World War II, and promotes new ways to collect, store and analyze data. Its website is https://www.ntis.gov.

26. More information on the SBIR program can be found at https://www.sbir.gov/.

27. This is not to be confused with the Stevenson-Wydler Technology Innovation Act (15 U.S.C. 3701), which reserves 0.5% of each agency's research budget to fund technology transfer between laboratories and industry.

28. Recall that real property includes land and rights in land, buildings and other structures, ground improvements, and utility distribution systems. It does not include foundations and other work necessary to install plant equipment or special tooling or test equipment.

29. NASA is the sole agency which does not have this authority.

30. An *overtime premium* is the difference between the regular rate of pay and the higher payment rate for the overtime period. It is not a *shift premium*, which is paid merely for working unusual hours such as nights or weekends.

31. This dollar threshold was imposed in the legislation (41 U.S.C. 351) when it was written in 1965, and has never been modified by Congress. Hence, we have the odd situation where requirements for service employees might fall below the simplified acquisition threshold, but still require a formal contract and wage determination.

32. However, the installation is subject to the Davis-Bacon Act if the services are obtained from the manufacturer or supplier of the equipment on a sole-source basis.

33. Although these projects may include energy savings or purchased utility service due to a third-party-financed shared-savings project for periods not to exceed 25 years.

34. At higher dollar values (which vary by agency), this determination requires further explanation of anticipated small business participation, since at this point we have substantial bundling.

35. Agencies may not consider savings in procurement operations or manpower when justifying bundling. Ironically, this was the very reason why some agencies were blamed for promoting the use of bundling in the first place.

36. The Department of the Treasury periodically updates these requirements for annual reporting purposes. The current version, issued for Fiscal Year 2014, is in the Treasury Financial Manual, Chapter 9500, found at http://tfm.fiscal.treasury.gov/v1/p6/c950.pdf.

37. See also Department of Energy, Architectural and Transportation Barriers Compliance Board Electronic and Information Technology (EIT) Accessibility Standards (36 CFR 1194), Department of Energy, Washington, D.C., June 2005.

38. Detailed guidance is found in "Software Assurance in Acquisition: Mitigating Risks to the Enterprise" at https://buildsecurityin.us-cert.gov/swa/downloads/SwA_in_Acquisition_102208.pdf. This is issued by the United States Computer Emergency Readiness Team within the Department of Homeland Security.

39. Published in 2009 by ISO in Geneva, Switzerland. *ISO* stands for the International Organization for Standardization, a multinational collection of quality and safety experts who pool their knowledge to develop voluntary consensus-based standards to promote international trade.

40. DoD program managers develop an information assurance strategy to describe how information protection and security requirements will be incorporated into their program.

41. FEMA, "Homeland Security Presidential Directive 20, National Continuity Policy," Washington, D.C., May 4, 2007.

42. FEMA, Federal Continuity Directive 1, "Federal Executive Branch National Continuity Program and Requirements," updated July 14, 2014, and "Federal Continuity Directive 2, Federal Executive Branch Mission Essential Functions and Candidate Primary Mission Essential Functions Identification and Submission Process," updated December 9, 2013.

43. An OPM report to Congress, "2014 Status of Telework in the Federal Government," dated November, 2015, says that only about 17% of all employees in the Executive Branch regularly telework, primarily nonsupervisors. This number rises to 46% during snowstorms and other crises.

44. Such *recurring costs* also include operating and maintenance costs that vary with production operations and recur repeatedly during the life cycle of the product or service.

45. OMB Circular A-11, Preparation and Submission of Budget Estimates, July 1, 2016, OMB, Washington, D.C.

46. However, if the basic quantity is for learning or testing purposes and competition for the option is impracticable after initial contract award, then an option amount may not be appropriate.

47. This method is often used when the option date is shortly after initial award.

48. An excellent resource to do this is the OFPP document "InteragencyAcquisitions" available at http://www.whitehouse.gov/omb/assets/procurement/iac_revised.pdf.

49. These are known as *Government-owned contractor-operated* (GOCO) facilities. They differ from COCO or GOGO facilities, where the acronym identifies the owner and operator of the facilities. Hence, contractors own and operate COCOs and the Government does both duties for GOGOs.

50. National Defense Authorization Act, Section 1428, 41 U.S.C. 403.

51. This is generally referred to as *acquisition risk*, the chance that a (sub)contract will produce an unintended impact on system availability, cost, effectiveness, or maintainability.

52. This could become especially critical as public opinion seems to be turning against sending jobs out of the country.

53. For further information, consult the Supply Chain Council's website at http://www.apics.org/sites/apics-supply-chain-council/frameworks/scor.

54. This work can be done by an *integrator*, a third-party firm that combines products of multiple other firms to produce a final product or system. They are often used to assemble information systems, but can be used in other types of endeavor.

55. This is known as *reverse logistics* involving customer returns of merchandise and warranty services, both of which drain funds from revenue or warranty services reserve, respectively.

56. Some people make the mistake of trying to equate these two values. That is not the goal of this ordering process; rather, the objective is to minimize both inventory carrying and ordering costs.

57. One method to send demand upchannel is *kanban*, a Japanese approach to schedule what, when and how much to produce. This approach gained prominence in Toyota Motor Corp., and is now used by other distributed firms such as Wal-Mart, where point-of-sale information is sent to a central data point to assess customer demand and inventory movement.

58. This is the maximum alternative earnings that might have been obtained if the item had been put to another use. It is the real cost of an alternative that is not pursued.

59. *Net income* (also called *net profit* or, more colloquially, *the bottom line*) is the sum of total revenue and gains, minus expenses and losses for the accounting period. It is often paid out as dividends or else classified as retained earnings.

60. U.S. International Trade Commission, "Harmonized Tariff Schedule of the United States." 19 U.S.C. 1202. U.S. International Trade Commission, Washington, D.C., October 1, 2015. Although the Trade Commission publishes and maintains the schedule, the actual legwork and rulings are performed by the Customs and Border Protection unit out of the Department of Homeland Security.

61. Guidance is at Under Secretary of Defense (Comptroller), DoD Financial Management Regulation 7000.14-R, Volume 15, DoD, Washington, D.C., December 15, 2013. See also http://www.defenselink.mil/comptroller/fmr/15/index.html.

Chapter 3

Placement

Procurement operations commence when the program office or requirements office submits a procurement package with all information and technical description necessary to commence the solicitation process. This includes a purchase request that describes the requirement to tell prospective offerors what is required. The procurement action then goes through a series of steps until an award is finally made. This chapter addresses the many steps involved in the placement process.

3.1 SOURCE SELECTION PLAN

The *source selection plan* documents how the Government will conduct a competition and find a contractor that fully meets its needs. The plan lists the organization, membership and responsibilities of the source selection team, and contains the process and evaluation criteria for selection. It is prepared by the program manager, reviewed by the contracting officer, and approved by the source selection authority. This may well be the contacting officer on routine procurements, but on major acquisitions it will be a designated agency official.The content is dictated by agency directive rather than Federal regulation, often in a free-form template. The plan will certainly include:

- background information on the procurement;
- communications protocols among the procurement officials;
- evaluation factors;

- how each factor will be evaluated and addressed in final reports;
- how the different steps in the procurement process will be achieved;
- membership and responsibilities of the source selection groups;
- organizational chart;
- organizational conflict of interest;
- ratings;
- risk analysis;
- schedule milestones; and
- use of non-Government personnel.

The evaluation factors may be tailored to the particular acquisition, but must have meaningful impact on source selection. Cost or price is always included, along with any of the following as appropriate:

- cost realism;
- experience;
- management capability;
- past performance;
- personnel qualifications;
- schedule; and
- technical excellence.

Usually these criteria are grouped into technical, management and cost categories.

Once the criteria have been selected, their relative importance must be measured and set forth in the solicitation. This process is usually based on judgment, priority or trade-off. Technical and management factors must be expressed in terms of more, less or equal in importance to cost. Importance can be scored by several methods:

- adjectives – excellent, good, fair, poor (with a narrative description of findings);
- binary – either acceptable or unacceptable;
- lowest-priced technically acceptable offer;
- numerically – by score;
- trade-offs – score the management and technical proposals, then trade off the differences against the prices offered; or
- varied – cost becomes more important as technical proposals become more equal to each other.

3.2 DESCRIBING AGENCY NEEDS

3.2.1 General Specifications

FAR 11.0 through 11.1

Specifications are particulars that describe technical requirements for the deliverable item or service. There are three basic types. *Functional specifications* describe performance characteristics and intended use of a product with only a general end result. They will include the minimum essential characteristics to satisfy the product's intended use. In contrast, *performance specifications* describe operational characteristics and end results of the item. This approach allows contractor use of judgment and discretion to design and engineer the product as it sees fit to meet the performance requirements. They tend to be more restrictive than functional specifications because they limit alternatives and set definite performance standards that the contractor must meet, or else risk nonperformance. This type of specification is best left to experienced contractors or special-use military items of high performance and low volume, but also fits well with commercial items.

Design specifications prescribe key characteristics of the item to be produced or delivered. They include measurements and tolerances for inspection and quality control, or mandatory material composition requirements. This approach leaves the Government responsible for any errors and omissions, as well as accepting the risk of nonperformance if the product is built to specification. In effect, the Government provides an implied warranty through its design specifications that the contractor will deliver an acceptable product by following these specifications.[1] Hence, the Government must take care that the specifications are current, reasonably flexible and specific, and do not limit competition.

DoD has *military specifications* which depict standards and requirements that are unique to military application and needs. They can be either design or performance in nature, and are stored in the DoD Index of Specifications and Standards.[2] This index works in conjunction with the Military Standard Requisitioning and Issue Procedures (MILSTRIP) to issue material by standardized methods.[3]

As often as possible, requirements for contractor performance must be expressed in a way to encourage offerors to supply commercial or nondevelopmental items, and to require (sub)contractors to incorporate such items as components of their deliverable products. Specifications should not be more restrictive or detailed than necessary to meet the minimum needs of the Government. Too much detail or "gold-plated" specifications could restrict competition and frustrate the most reasonable pricing. To avoid this problem, the specifications should not contain unnecessary design requirements, arbitrary requirements unrelated to needs, or bias toward a specific product. However, they can be tailored to meet specific needs of the requestor or to adjust minimum requirements. In fact, there is a prioritization scheme for setting requirements:

• statute-specified documents;
• performance work specifications and statements of objectives;
• design specifications and Federal or DoD standards or specifications; and
• nonmandatory standards and specifications.

The Metric Conversion Act of 1975 and the Omnibus Trade and Competitiveness Act of 1988 (both at 15 U.S.C. 205a, et. seq.) designate the metric system of measurement as the preferred system of weights and measures for U.S. commerce. Each agency uses the metric system of measurement in its acquisitions unless impracticable or likely to cause significant inefficiencies or loss of market.

Whenever possible, agencies use voluntary consensus standards in lieu of Government-unique standards, unless they are impractical or illegal. The private sector manages and administers consensus standards (e.g., ISO 9000 and IEEE 1680).[4] The Federal specifications which do exist are available from GSA's Index of Federal Specifications, Standards and Commercial Item Descriptions (https://www.gsa.gov/portal/content/100847), and DoD specifications are available online at https://assist.dla.mil/online/start. Solicitations should specify the document version and effective date.

Potential offerors may recommend including and tailoring requirements documents and alternative approaches. Requiring agencies should then make a final decision on the use or modification of these documents for the design and development process. For a negotiated procurement, this process may continue through the proposal and evaluation steps.

Section 8002(c) of 41 U.S.C. 22 provides that an agency may require offerors to demonstrate that the items offered have either achieved commercial market acceptance (except for new or evolving items) or been supplied to an agency under current or recent contracts for the same or similar requirements. Otherwise, offered items must meet the item description or specifications prescribed in the solicitation. This means that the contracting officer must ensure that the solicitation criteria:

• are supported by market research;
• consider items supplied satisfactorily under prior contracts;
• consider the entire relevant commercial market, including small business concerns;
• reflect minimum needs of the agency; and

- show an item's performance and intended use rather than an offeror's capability.

Brand name or equal purchase descriptions are sometimes used when the Government can cite one or several specific make and model numbers that will meet its requirements. These descriptions include functional, performance or physical characteristics of the brand-name item that an "equal" item must meet to be acceptable. Offerors submit literature describing their offered product, and the Government determines whether the product meets the needed characteristics.

Solicitations citing requirements documents listed in the GSA Index of Federal Specifications, Standards and Commercial Item Descriptions, the DoD Acquisition Streamlining and Standardization Information System (ASSIST; http://assist.daps.dla.mil), or other agency index must identify each document's approval date and any applicable amendments and revisions.[5] Contracting offices will not normally furnish these cited documents with the solicitation. Any other documents not listed in these indices are furnished with the solicitation, or else specific instructions to obtain or examine them are included.

Under the Information Technology Management Reform Act (40 U.S.C. 25), the Department of Commerce issues standards and guidelines for Federal computer systems that are developed by NIST. These standards and guidelines are issued as FIPS for use government-wide (e.g., interoperability and security) and as industry standards. FIPS standards are located at http://www.itl.nist.gov/fipspubs, or purchased from the Superintendent of Documents, U.S. Government Printing Office.

When acquiring commercial items, the contracting officer considers the customary practices in the industry. (S)he may require offerors to provide information on any proposed supplies that are used, reconditioned or remanufactured, as well as unused former Government surplus property.

Section 505 of Executive Order 13101, "Greening the Government through Waste Prevention, Recycling, and Federal Acquisition," September 14, 1998, establishes minimum recovered material content standards to purchase printing and writing paper. It includes *postconsumer fiber* such as used corrugated boxes, old newspapers and magazines, paper, paperboard, and other fibrous materials.[6] The fiber definition also includes *manufacturing wastes* (dry paper and paperboard waste generated after completion of the papermaking process, and obsolete inventories of commercial paper and paperboard). Agencies do not normally require supplies composed of virgin material unless directed by law or regulation, or if vital for safety or performance requirements. If so, the offeror must acknowledge the presence of virgin material in the proposal.

Solicitation Provisions

FAR 52.211-1, Availability of Specifications Listed in the GSA Index of Federal Specifications, Standards and Commercial Item Descriptions, FPMR Part 101-29.

FAR 52.211-2, Availability of Specifications, Standards, and Data Item Descriptions Listed in the Acquisition Streamlining and Standardization Information System (ASSIST).

FAR 52.211-3, Availability of Specifications Not Listed in the GSA Index of Federal Specifications, Standards and Commercial Item Descriptions.

FAR 52.211-4, Availability for Examination of Specifications Not Listed in the GSA Index of Federal Specifications, Standards and Commercial Item Descriptions.

FAR 52.211-5, Material Requirements, for supplies that are not commercial items.

FAR 52.211-6, Brand Name or Equal.

FAR 52.211-7, Alternatives to Government-Unique Standards, if using Government-unique standards when the agency reports its use of voluntary consensus standards to NIST per OMB Circular A-119, "Federal Participation in the Development and Use of Voluntary Consensus Standards and in Conformity Assessment Activities" (2016).

3.2.2 Delivery or Performance Schedules

The time of delivery or performance is stated in solicitations and must meet the realistic requirements of the Government. Short or difficult schedules tend to restrict competition, conflict with small business policies, and may increase contract prices. Factors to consider when setting delivery schedules include:

- administrative time to obtain and evaluate offers and award contracts;
- capacity and capabilities of potential contractors;
- industry practices and market conditions;
- production lead time;
- time for compliance with any conditions precedent to contract performance (e.g., furnishing Government property);
- transportation time; and
- urgency of need.

For construction contacts, additional considerations include availability of materials, milestone completion dates and seasonality.

The contracting officer may express contract delivery or performance schedules in terms of:

- effective date of the contract (e.g., award a contract in September for effort to begin in October);
- days after receipt of award by the contractor;
- periods of time after the date of award; or
- specific calendar dates.

Solicitation Provisions and Contract Clauses

FAR 52.211-8, Time of Delivery, other than construction and architect-engineering, if the Government requires delivery by a particular time and the delivery schedule is based on the contract date. Use the clause with its Alternate I if the delivery schedule is expressed in terms of specific calendar dates or specific periods and is based on an assumed date of award. Use the clause with its Alternate II if the delivery schedule is expressed in terms of specific calendar dates or specific periods and is based on an assumed date the contractor will receive notice of award. Use the clause with its Alternate III if the delivery schedule is to be based on the actual date the contractor receives a written notice of award.

FAR 52.211-9, Desired and Required Time of Delivery, other than construction and architect-engineering, if the Government desires delivery by a certain time but requires delivery by a specified later time, and the delivery schedule is to be based on the date of the contract. The Alternate versions are used in the same manner as FAR 211.8.

FAR 52.211-10, Commencement, Prosecution, and Completion of Work, when a fixed-price construction contract is contemplated. Use the clause with its Alternate I if the completion date is expressed as a specific calendar date, based on the contractor receiving the notice to proceed by a certain day.

3.3 ACQUISITION OF COMMERCIAL ITEMS

3.3.1 General

FAR Part 12

Buying commercial products rather than specially designed and manufactured items is often a good idea because they:

- are faster to acquire;
- cost less due to competition;
- reduce inventory costs, with fewer items stocked due to plentiful availability; and
- travel quickly through established distribution systems.

However, commercial items will not meet all requirements and may require additional contractor maintenance. Items bought commercially include auto parts, drugs, food, office supplies, and tools. Items least susceptible to commercial acquisition include MIL-SPEC or Government-only items and military aircraft components.

Agencies conduct market research to determine whether commercial or nondevelopmental items could meet the agency's requirements. They also require prime contractors and subcontractors at all tiers to incorporate, to the maximum extent practicable, commercial or nondevelopmental items as components of deliverable items. This policy does not apply to acquisitions at or below the micro-purchase threshold or from another Federal agency.

A solicitation for a commercial item describes the product or service to be acquired, how the agency plans to use it, and its functionality, performance requirement or essential physical characteristics. The contracting officer uses the Standard Form 1449, Solicitation/Contract/Order for Commercial Items, for an acquisition exceeding the simplified acquisition threshold (and may use it for lower-value acquisitions) and usually allows 15 days to notify the marketplace before soliciting.

Offers are evaluated in accordance with the criteria contained in the solicitation. For many commercial items, the criteria need not be more detailed than technical, price and past performance. Technical capability may be evaluated by how well the proposed products meet the Government requirement and their intended use. A technical evaluation would normally include examination of such things as product literature describing product characteristics or operation, product samples, technical features, and warranty provisions. If an agency decides during their market research that technical information is necessary to evaluate offers, agencies review literature of products available in the industry to determine its adequacy. Offerors may propose more than one product that will meet a Government need in response to solicitations for commercial items, and each product is evaluated as a separate offer.

Contracts for commercial items rely on contractors' existing quality assurance systems instead of Government inspection and testing, unless customary market practices for the commercial item include in-process inspection.

The parties presume that data delivered under a contract for commercial items was developed exclusively at private expense. Commercial computer software and documentation are acquired under licenses customarily provided to the public if consistent with Federal law and otherwise satisfy the Government's needs. Generally, offerors and contractors need not furnish noncustomary technical information or provide the Government any further rights to such software or documentation.

Firm-fixed-price contracts or fixed-price contracts with economic price adjustment are normally used for the acquisition of commercial items. A time-and-materials contract or labor-hour contract (including an indefinite-delivery contract) may be used to acquire commercial services; however, the contracting officer must write a D&F justifying the contract type and establish a ceiling price that can only be changed by writing another D&F. The D&F describes the market research, explains the impossibility of estimating work extent or duration and/or cost uncertainty, and discusses the likelihood of using the preferred contract types in future acquisitions for the same supplies or services. These alternative contract types may also include an award fee using performance or delivery incentives rather than cost.

Contracting officers may use a combined synopsis/solicitation procedure to streamline the process. In this case, no separate written solicitation is used. Because the synopsis and solicitation are contained in a single document, it is not necessary to separately synopsize 15 days before the issuance of the solicitation. A reasonable response time must be set based on availability, commerciality, complexity, and urgency.

FAR 15.403-1

Services that are offered and sold competitively in substantial quantities in the commercial marketplace may be considered commercial items regardless of quantity actually sold. The contracting officer must sign a D&F stating that the offeror has submitted sufficient information to evaluate (through price analysis) that the price of such services is reasonable. The contracting officer may request price information (or if not available, then cost information) from the offeror to make this determination. DoD, NASA and the Coast Guard are exempt from this requirement for any modifications of a commercial item that do not exceed 5% of total contract price (up to the certified cost or pricing data threshold).

3.3.2 Warranties

FAR 12.404

The Federal Acquisition Streamlining Act of 1994 (41 U.S.C. 264) requires contracting officers to use commercial warranties whenever possible. Solicitations for commercial items require offerors to furnish the same warranty terms offered to the general public in commercial practice. However, they may also include express warranties (perhaps covering a minimum duration) appropriate for the Government's intended use of the item. However, the express warranty must be cost-effective, protect the Government's needs, and allow post-award administration (e.g., collect product performance information, identify warranted items, and set forth procedures to return warranted items to the contractor for repair or replacement).

In some markets, contractors may customarily exclude or limit the implied warranties. If so, the contracting officer must still ensure that the express warranty provides for repair or replacement of defective items discovered within a prescribed time period after acceptance.

The Government relies on the contractor's assurances that the commercial item tendered for acceptance conforms to the contract requirements. Government inspection of commercial items does not prejudice its other rights, since it always has the right to refuse acceptance of nonconforming items.

3.3.3 Impact on Regulations

FAR 12.5

The following laws do not apply to contracts for commercial items:

- 41 U.S.C. 65, Contracts for Materials, Supplies, Articles, and Equipment Exceeding $15,000;
- 41 U.S.C. 254(a) and 10 U.S.C. 2306(b), Contingent Fees;
- 41 U.S.C. 416(a)(6), Minimum Response Time for Offers under Office of Federal Procurement Policy Act;
- 41 U.S.C. 701, et seq., Drug-Free Workplace Act of 1988;
- 31 U.S.C. 1354(a), Limitation on use of appropriated funds for contracts with entities not meeting veterans' employment reporting requirements;
- 31 U.S.C. 6101 note, Federal Funding Accountability and Transparency Act of 2006, requirement to report subcontract data;
- Section 806(a)(3) of Public Law 102-190, as amended at 10 U.S.C. 2302, Payment Protections for Subcontractors and Suppliers; and
- 41 U.S.C. 254d(c)(1) and 10 U.S.C. 2313(c)(1), GAO Access to Contractor Employees, Section 871 of Public Law 110-417.

Certain requirements of the following laws are not applicable to contracts for commercial items:

- 40 U.S.C. 3701, et seq., requirement for a certificate and clause under the Contract Work Hours and Safety Standards Act;
- 41 U.S.C. 57(a)-(b) and 58, requirements for a clause and other issues related to the Anti-Kickback Act of 1986; and
- 49 U.S.C. 40118, requirement for a clause under the Fly American provisions.

Certain laws have been modified for contracts for the acquisition of commercial items:

- 41 U.S.C. 253g and 10 U.S.C. 2402, Prohibition on Limiting Subcontractor Direct Sales to the United States; and
- 41 U.S.C. 254(d) and 10 U.S.C. 2306a, Truth in Negotiations Act, 41 U.S.C. 422, Cost Accounting Standards (48 CFR chapter 99).

The following laws do not apply to subcontracts for commercial items or components:

- 10 U.S.C. 2631, Transportation of Supplies by Sea, except that the clause does apply to items resold or distributed to the Government without adding value (either under f.o.b. destination shipment or shipped in direct support of U.S. military contingency operations, exercises, or humanitarian or peacekeeping operations);
- 15 U.S.C. 644(d), requirements for labor surplus areas under the Small Business Act;
- 41 U.S.C. 65;
- 41 U.S.C. 253d, Validation of Proprietary Data Restrictions;
- 41 U.S.C. 254(a) and 10 U.S.C. 2306(b), Contingent Fees;
- 41 U.S.C. 254d(c) and 10 U.S.C. 2313(c), Examination of Records of Contractor, when a subcontractor is not required to provide cost or pricing data, unless using funds appropriated or otherwise made available by the Recovery Act;
- 41 U.S.C. 416(a)(6), Minimum Response Time for Offers under Office of Federal Procurement Policy Act;
- 41 U.S.C. 418a, Rights in Technical Data;
- 41 U.S.C. 701, et seq., Drug-Free Workplace Act of 1988;
- 46 U.S.C. App. 1241(b), Transportation in American Vessels of Government Personnel and Certain Cargo, except for the types of subcontracts listed under the Transportation of Supplies by Sea clause above;
- 49 U.S.C. 40118, Fly American provisions;
- Section 806(a)(3) of Public Law 102-190, as amended by Sections 2091 and 8105 of Public Law 103-355, Payment Protections for Subcontractors and Suppliers (10 U.S.C. 2302);
- 41 U.S.C. 10a, portion of first sentence that reads "substantially all from articles, materials, or supplies mined, produced, or manufactured, as the case may be, in the United States," Buy American Act—Supplies, component test;
- 41 U.S.C. 10b, portion of first sentence that reads "substantially all from articles, materials, or supplies mined, produced, or manufactured, as the case may be, in the Unites States," Buy American Act—Construction Materials, component test; and

- 42 U.S.C. 6962(c)(3)(A), Certification and Estimate of Percentage of Recovered Material.

The requirements for a certificate and clause under the Contract Work Hours and Safety Standards Act, 40 U.S.C. 3701, et seq., do not apply to subcontracts for commercial items or commercial components.

The applicability of the following laws has been modified in regards to subcontracts for commercial items or components:

- 41 U.S.C. 253g and 10 U.S.C. 2402, Prohibition on Limiting Subcontractor Direct Sales to the United States;
- 41 U.S.C. 254(d) and 10 U.S.C. 2306a, Truth in Negotiations Act; and
- 41 U.S.C. 422, Cost Accounting Standards (48 CFR chapter 99).

Solicitation Provisions and Contract Clauses

When acquiring commercial items, contracting officers use only these provisions and clauses:

FAR 52.212-1, Instructions to Offerors – Commercial Items.

FAR 52.212-2, Evaluation – Commercial Items, when the use of evaluation factors is appropriate.

FAR 52.212-3, Offeror Representations and Certifications – Commercial Items. Use the provision with its Alternate I in solicitations issued by DoD, NASA, or the Coast Guard. Use the provision with its Alternate II in solicitations for small disadvantaged business procurements on a regional basis.

FAR 52.212-4, Contract Terms and Conditions – Commercial Items. Use this clause with its Alternate I when a time-and-materials or labor-hour contract will be awarded. The contracting officer may tailor this clause except for the following topics:

- assignments;
- disputes;
- payment;
- invoice;
- other compliances, including with laws unique to Government contracts; and
- unauthorized obligations.

FAR 52.212-5, Contract Terms and Conditions Required to Implement Statutes or Executive Orders–Commercial Items. Use the clause with its Alternate I when the head of the agency has waived the need for examination of records by the Comptroller General. Use the clause with Alternate II if using funds appropriated by the Recovery Act. The contracting officer may not use Alternate I when Alternate II applies.

FAR 52.244-6, Subcontracts for Commercial Items and Commercial Components. Use the clause with its Alternate I when the head of the agency has waived the examination of records by the Comptroller General. Use the clause with its Alternate II if the acquisition will use funds appropriated or otherwise made available by the Recovery Act.

The contracting officer may include in solicitations and contracts by addendum other FAR provisions and clauses, and agency-unique statutes as approved by the agency senior procurement executive. Any tailoring of the above clauses is by addenda to the solicitation and contract.

3.4 UNIFORM CONTRACT FORMAT

FAR 14.201

The Uniform Contract Format is as follows:

Part I – The Schedule

A Solicitation/contract form
B Supplies or services and prices
C Description/specifications
D Packaging and marking
E Inspection and acceptance
F Deliveries or performance
G Contract administration data
H Special contract requirements

Part II – Contract Clauses

I Contract clauses

Part III – List of Documents, Exhibits, and Other Attachments

J List of documents, exhibits, and other attachments

Part IV – Representations and Instructions

K Representations, certifications, and other statements of bidders
L Instructions, conditions, and notices to bidders
M Evaluation factors for award

The contracting officer prepares the schedule as follows:

- *Section A, Solicitation/contract form.* Use SF 33, Solicitation Offer and Award, or 1447, Solicitation/Contract. The alphanumeric contract number will follow a format prescribed in agency regulations, beginning with a six-digit identifier of the procurement office which issues the contract or agreement, the last two digits of the fiscal year of award, a letter which indicates the type of procurement instrument, and a serial number of between four and eight digits assigned by the department or agency. It then depicts such basic information as name and address or issuing office and bid room, dates of issuance and bid opening, and address blocks for the bidder and payment.
- *Section B, Supplies or services and prices.* Include a brief description of the supplies or services (e.g., item or part number, national stock number, title or name, and quantities).[7] Use Optional Form 336 or Continuation Sheet.
- *Section C, Description/specifications.*
- *Section D, Packaging and marking.* Include packing and preservation requirements.
- *Section E, Inspection and acceptance.* Include quality assurance and reliability requirements.
- *Section F, Deliveries or performance.* Specify the requirements for time, place and method of delivery or performance.
- *Section G, Contract administration data.* Include accounting and appropriation data and instructions.
- *Section H, Special contract requirements.* Include requirements not listed elsewhere.
- *Section I, Contract clauses.*
- *Section J, List of documents, exhibits, and other attachments.* List the title, date and number of pages for each attached document.
- *Section K, Representations, certifications, and other statements of bidders.* Include solicitation provisions that require bidders to fill in representations and certifications.
- *Section L, Instructions, conditions, and notices to bidders.* Insert the time and place for bid openings, and submission information.
- *Section M, Evaluation factors for award.* Include price-related factors to be considered in evaluating bids and awarding the contract.

The contracting officer may use the simplified contract format instead, consisting of:

- *Solicitation/contract form.* Standard Form (SF) 1447.
- *Contract schedule.* Include the following for each contract line item:
  - contract line item number;
  - description of supplies or services;
  - quantity and unit of issue;
  - unit price and amount;
  - packaging and marking requirements;
  - inspection and acceptance, quality assurance, and reliability requirements;
  - place of delivery, performance and delivery dates, period of performance, and f.o.b. point; and
  - other item-specific information (e.g., individual fund citations).
- Clauses. Include only the clauses required by FAR and agency supplement, adding clauses only when considered absolutely necessary to the particular acquisition.
- List of documents and attachments.
- Representations and instructions:
  - *Representations and certifications.* Insert provisions that require representations, certifications or other information by offerors.
  - *Instructions, conditions, and notices.* Include the required provisions and any other instructions to guide offerors.
  - *Evaluation factors for award.*

Upon award, the contracting officer need not include the representations and certifications in the resulting contract, but does retain them in the contract file.

The clauses and provisions below are required for all Federal solicitations or contracts:

Solicitation Provisions

FAR 52.252-3, Alterations in Solicitation, in solicitations in order to revise or supplement, as necessary, other parts of the solicitation that apply to the solicitation phase only, except for any provision authorized for use with a deviation.

FAR 52.252-5, Authorized Deviations in Provisions, in solicitations that include any FAR or supplemental provision with an authorized deviation. The contracting officer identifies the deviation by the same number, title, and date assigned to the provision when it is used without deviation, including regulation name for any supplemental provision, but inserts "(DEVIATION)" after the date of the provision.

Solicitation Provisions and Contract Clauses

FAR 52.252-1, Solicitation Provisions Incorporated by Reference.

FAR 52.252-4, Alterations in Contract, to revise or supplement, as necessary, other parts of the contract, or parts of the solicitations that apply to the contract phase, except for any clause authorized for use with a deviation.

FAR 52.252-6, Authorized Deviations in Clauses, if including any FAR or supplemental clause with an authorized deviation. The contracting officer identifies the deviation by the same number, title, and date assigned to the clause when it is used without deviation, including regulation name for any supplemental clause, but inserts "(DEVIATION)" after the date of the clause.

Contract Clauses

FAR 52.252-2, Clauses Incorporated by Reference.

3.5 CONTRACT TYPES

FAR 16.1 through 16.3

A wide variety of contract types is available to provide flexibility in cost management and profit incentive. The objective in selecting contract type is to negotiate a price arrangement that will result in reasonable contractor risk and maximize incentive for efficient and economical performance. The contract types are grouped into two broad categories: *fixed-price* and *cost-reimbursement*.

Fixed-price contracts establish a ceiling beyond which the Government is not responsible for payment, no matter what the contractor's cost incurrence is. By contrast, cost-reimbursement contracts pay a contractor's allowable incurred costs based on an upfront estimate of total cost to establish a maximum amount that the contractor exceeds at its own risk. They are used when uncertainties in performance do not permit cost estimates sufficient to use a fixed-price contract. Government surveillance during performance provides reasonable assurance that efficient methods and cost controls are used. Once the money runs out, the contractor may stop performance unless the Government provides additional funds to cover further costs on a no-fee basis. No further consideration is needed because the original contract amount was merely an estimate.

There are many factors that the contracting officer considers in selecting and negotiating contract type:

- adequacy of the contractor's accounting system to develop valid cost data for a flexibly priced arrangement;
- complex requirements often result in greater cost risk assumption by the Government (e.g., research and development), whereas a recurring requirement or production shifts cost risk to the contractor and a fixed-price contract is more appropriate;
- concurrent contracts and their pricing arrangements;
- contractor's financial responsibility to control costs;
- cost analysis and the Government cost estimate provides baselines to negotiate contract pricing to ensure the contractor bears a fair degree of cost responsibility;
- extent of proposed subcontracting that could reduce risk to the prime contractor;
- period of performance or length of production run may require economic price adjustment terms;
- price analysis (price competition often leads to realistic pricing, so a fixed-price contract may be in the Government's best interest);
- stability of labor and material prices that could argue for flexible pricing; and
- urgency of the requirement may lead the Government to assume more risk or offer incentives to ensure timely performance.

The contractor faces many risk elements that will influence its desired contract type, including:

- cost (mitigated by proper contract type);
- exotic specifications;
- first-time use;
- hazardous components;
- performance;
- program termination;
- schedule; and
- sophisticated hardware.

Many, though not all, contract types require the contracting officer to develop and sign a D&F to justify use of the chosen contract type. The D&F must identify added risks in terms of their mitigation and management, complexity of requirements, cost analysis if competition is limited or non-existent, contractor's technical capability and financial responsibility (including its accounting system), contract administration, and effort to make follow-on contracts of a more favorable type. This document must be executed before solicitation.

FAR 17.1

One way to mitigate risk is by use of multiyear contracting. *Multiyear contracting* is a means to obtain quantity price discounts for requirements lasting up to four outyears after the base year without full funding. This is accomplished by issuing a fixed-price contract with a cancellation ceiling for each year should the funding not come through. This ceiling should bear some relationship to the proportionality of estimated contract cost, such that the ceiling rises in any given year with anticipated heavy expenditures, and drops in a year with lighter expenditures. Calculation for ceiling amounts may also need to reflect such considerations as startup and learning costs and amortization of facilities and equipment. Civilian agencies may use cost-type of fixed-price contracting methods for multi-year contracts, but DoD, the Coast Guard and NASA must stay with fixed-price methods only. Benefits of multi-year contracting include:

- broaden the competitive base with firms not otherwise willing or able to compete for lesser quantities, particularly in cases involving high startup costs;
- incentivize contractors to improve productivity through investment in capital facilities, equipment and advanced technology;
- lower costs;
- maintain the same quality control techniques and procedures each year;
- reduce contract administrative burden;
- stabilize contractor workforces;
- standardization; and
- substantial continuity of production or performance, thus avoiding annual startup costs, preproduction testing costs and phaseout costs.

Solicitation Provisions and Contract Clauses

FAR 52.217-2, Cancellation Under Multi-Year Contracts.

FAR 52.222-43, Fair Labor Standards Act and Service Contract Labor Standards- Price Adjustment (Multiple Year and Option Contracts), if the contract is subject to the Service Contract Act.

Solicitation Provisions

FAR 52.216-1, Type of Contract, except for a fixed-price acquisition made under simplified acquisition procedures, or for information or planning purposes.

3.5.1 Firm Fixed Price

FAR 16.202

A *firm-fixed-price contract* cannot be adjusted due to the contractor's cost experience. The contractor bears total cost risk and responsibility, and therefore a maximum incentive to control costs and perform effectively. Therefore, care should be taken before award to ensure there is reasonable certainty of cost, product performance and schedule achievement.

A firm-fixed-price contract is used to acquire commercial items and other supplies or services with definite functional specifications. Prior cost history is usually available. There is usually adequate price competition or comparison with prior competitive purchases of the same or similar supplies or services. Nearly all contracts resulting from sealed bidding are firm-fixed-price contracts. A written D&F that justifies contract type is not required.

Both parties have minimal administrative burden. The contractor need not have an approved cost accounting system. The contract can include an award-fee incentive to address performance or delivery incentives rather than cost.

3.5.2 Firm Fixed Price with Economic Price Adjustment

FAR 16.203

A *fixed-price contract with economic price adjustment* is set up like a firm-fixed-price contract, but with a twist. The contract provides for up-or-down price revision upon the occurrence of specified contingencies. The price adjustment is based on a prescribed level in published industry prices, labor or material cost standards, or indexes beyond the contractor's control. This contract type may include an award-fee adjustment based on performance or delivery incentives rather than cost. The contractor need not have an approved cost accounting system, though the contracting officer must execute a D&F justifying the use of a price adjustment clause to protect the Government and/or contractor from market fluctuations.

Use of an adjustment based on cost indexes of labor or materials may be appropriate when the period of performance exceeds one year and the economic variables for labor and materials are too unstable to equitably divide risk between the Government and contractor. The agency prepares and approves the price adjustment clause. It specifies labor rates and material unit prices subject to adjustment, and their quantities allocable to each deliverable unit. If adjustment is only to a unit price, then the catalog or price list (plus any discount) must be included in the contract file.

Solicitation Provisions and Contract Clauses

FAR 52.216-2, Economic Price Adjustment – Standard Supplies, for standard supplies with catalog or market prices.

FAR 52.216-3, Economic Price Adjustment – Semistandard Supplies, for semistandard supplies related to the prices of standard supplies with catalog or market price.

FAR 52.216-4, Economic Price Adjustment – Labor and Material, when labor or material cost factor(s) are subject to change.

3.5.3 Firm Fixed Price, Level-of-Effort Term

FAR 16.207

A *firm-fixed-price, level-of-effort term contract* is used to investigate a specific research and development area and produce a report showing the results achieved by the level of effort. Payment is based on the effort expended rather than on the results achieved. This contract type is usually at a price below $150,000, unless the chief of the purchasing office agrees to a higher amount. The contractor will accept cost risk in this instance because it is confident in its cost estimate and willing to accept what little risk exists.

3.5.4 Fixed Price Incentive

FAR 16.205-206 and 16.402-403

Incentive contracts are used to obtain supplies or services (often with improved delivery or technical performance) by relating the amount of profit or fee to contractor performance. An incentive arrangement includes predefined relationships of cost, schedule and/or technical performance to motivate the contractor to meet or even exceed the Government's desired outcomes. Increased profit or fee dollars are earned for exceeding performance targets (not just minimum requirements), and decreases are imposed for missing targets. The contractor is thereby motivated to improve performance and mitigate waste and inefficiency. The contracting officer must first execute a D&F to justify contract type.[8]

Incentive contracts can be either fixed-price or cost-reimbursement in nature. Incentives should be:

- able to motivate the contractor toward a desired level of performance;
- communicating what is desired;
- quantitatively measurable; and
- realistic for contractor performance.

Many incentive contracts include only cost incentives, which take the form of a profit adjustment formula to motivate the contractor to effectively manage costs. No incentive contract may provide for other incentives without also providing a cost incentive or constraint to avoid paying more than the value of a performance or technical improvement. The parties negotiate a share ratio which shows the relative level of responsibility of costs which deviate from the target. If the ratio is 80/20 for example, the Government pays every dollar of cost overrun but reduces the profit by 20 cents for each dollar of overrun. If the contractor underruns, the government accepts the cost savings and adds to the profit amount 20 cents for each dollar underrun. In effect, the Government bears 80% of the cost risk and the contractor bears 20%.

To implement this pricing approach, in lieu of a firm fixed price, these contracts include a target cost, a target profit and an adjustment formula. This formula is designed to ensure that actual cost at target will result in the target profit, cost overruns will result in downward adjustment of profit, and cost underruns will result in a higher final profit. The final price is subject to a negotiated price ceiling; however, there is no limit on the final profit rate. This contract type insures that the contractor's assumption of some cost responsibility will motivate a profit incentive to manage cost and performance. Billing prices are established as an interim basis for payment and are adjusted within the ceiling limits upon request of either party, once it is obvious that final negotiated cost will differ from target cost.

Added incentives on technical performance and/or delivery can positively impact the contractor's management of the work. Performance incentives may be used in connection with performance characteristics in major systems contracts (e.g., missile range, aircraft speed, engine thrust, or vehicle maneuverability), both in development (when performance objectives are known and fabrication of prototypes for test and evaluation is required) and in production (if improved performance is desired and attainable). Positive and negative performance incentives can also be considered for service contracts to perform objectively measurable tasks. Because technical performance incentives may involve a variety of characteristics that contribute to the overall performance of the end item, the incentives must be balanced to avoid exaggerating one characteristic to the detriment of overall performance. The contract establishes test criteria (e.g., conditions, data interpretation, instrumentation precision, etc.) and performance standards (such as the quality levels of services to be provided). The incentive itself is calculated based on a formula included in the contract (e.g., a test speed which is 10 miles per hour faster than specification earns 1% profit, whereas a speed which is 10 miles slower loses 1% of profit).

Delivery incentives are used when the Government desires improvement from its required delivery schedule (e.g., earliest possible delivery or earliest quantity production). The contract specifies the rewards and penalties for Government-caused delays or other delays beyond the control of the contractor or subcontractor. A delivery incentive might reward 1% of profit for delivery 30 days early, or deduct 1% for every 10 days late.

A properly structured multiple-incentive arrangement should motivate the contractor to strive for outstanding results in all incentive areas. It will compel trade-off decisions among the incentive areas, consistent with the Government's overall objectives for the acquisition. The incentive plan includes the *point of total assumption* (PTA), where the sum of actual cost and earned profit will equal the ceiling price. Beyond this point, the contractor absorbs total responsibility for cost growth.

For example, suppose the parties negotiate a target cost of $100,000, a target profit of $10,000 and a ceiling price of $125,000, plus a share ratio of 70/30. The PTA is calculated as follows:

$$PTA = \frac{Ceiling\ Price - Target\ Price}{Government\ Share} + Target\ Cost$$

$$PTA = \frac{\$125,000 - (100,000 + 10,000)}{0.70} + \$100,000$$

$$= \frac{\$15,000}{0.70} + \$100,000 = \$121,429$$

This allows the contractor to incur a cost overrun of over 21% before all profit erodes; beyond that point, the contractor earns no more profit dollars and has no motivation to control costs. Since delivery is required in a fixed-price environment, the contactor is now unable to cover any additional costs, but must still perform. However, the PTA shows that there is still plenty of room for cost growth, which hopefully will result in better technical performance and/or early delivery.

Now, assume that final cost is $95,000, a 5% underrun. Then:

$$Final\ Profit = \frac{(Target\ Cost - Final\ Cost)}{Government\ Share} + Target\ Profit$$

$$= \frac{\$5,000}{0.70} + \$10,000 = \$17,143$$

Then the final price is $95,000 + $17,143 = $112,143. The effective profit rate is

$$\frac{\$17,143}{\$95,000} = 18.05\%$$

Since the target profit rate was only 10%, one can see the benefit the contractor gains through motivation to control costs.

Because performance incentives present complex problems in contract administration, the contracting officer negotiates them in full coordination with Government engineering and pricing specialists. The parties must also remain aware of the effect that any contract changes pursuant to the Changes clause will have on performance incentives.

There are four different methods used to price changes in FPI contracts. The *Individual Adjustment* method means the parties negotiate separately each component of the incentive package. This approach maximizes tailoring the change to the circumstances but is time-consuming and administratively burdensome, and could permit a poorly performing contractor to get well. The *Severable Change* method negotiates price adjustment separately to be added to the contract as a package, but the costs must be segregable. The *Constant Dollar* method increases ceiling price by the same dollar amount as target price. This approach significantly increases profit at the point of total assumption, and is used when small changes do not greatly affect program uncertainty. The *Constant Percentage* method ignores the dollar relationships of these values by adjusting the ceiling price to be the same percentage of target cost, and can be used to combine multiple changes.

To further complicate the subject of fixed-price incentive contracts, there are five different variations that are authorized for use. Each will now be examined.

3.5.4.1 Fixed Price Incentive (Firm Target) Contract

FAR 16.403-1

A *fixed-price incentive (firm target) contract* includes a target cost, target profit, price ceiling (but not a profit ceiling or floor), and profit adjustment formula. This is the predominant form of fixed-price incentive contract and incorporates the features just discussed. The price ceiling is the maximum that may be paid to the contractor. As we saw in the mathematical example above, once the contractor completes performance, the parties negotiate the final cost and apply the formula to establish the final price. If the final cost is less than the target cost, the final profit will exceed the target profit, whereas a final cost above the target cost results in a final profit below the target profit. If the final negotiated cost exceeds the price ceiling, the contractor absorbs the difference as a loss and earns no profit. Because profit varies inversely with cost, this contract type provides a profit incentive for the contractor to control costs.

3.5.4.2 Fixed Price Incentive (Successive Targets) Contract

FAR 16.403-2

A *fixed-price incentive (successive targets) contract* specifies an initial target cost and profit, and a ceiling price as above, but adds an initial profit adjustment formula to establish the firm target profit (including a ceiling and floor), and the production point at which the firm targets (cost and profit) will be negotiated (usually before delivery or completion of the first item). When the production point is reached, the parties negotiate the firm target cost based on cost experience under the contract to date. Applying the formula establishes the firm target profit. The parties may decide to negotiate a firm fixed price at this point by adding together the firm target cost and target profit, or else negotiate a formula to establish the final cost at completion and then apply the formula to set the final profit. This contract type is appropriate when enough information becomes available early in contract performance to negotiate either a firm fixed price or firm targets and a final profit formula to incentivize the contractor.

3.5.4.3 Fixed Price with Prospective Price Redetermination

FAR 16.205

A *fixed-price contract with prospective price redetermination* provides a firm fixed price for an initial period of contract performance, and prospective redetermination at a stated time(s) (at least annually) to price-out subsequent periods of performance. The contract may provide for a ceiling price based on evaluation of performance uncertainties and their possible cost impact, and assumption of a reasonable amount of risk by the contractor. However, the ceiling price may be adjusted only by equitable adjustment or as specified in the contract.

Contract Clause

FAR 52.216-5, Price Redetermination – Prospective.

3.5.4.4 Fixed Price with Retroactive Price Redetermination

FAR 16.206

A *fixed-price contract with retroactive price redetermination* provides for price adjustment within the ceiling price after contract completion. It is used for research and development contracts valued at $150,000 or less when a firm fixed price cannot be negotiated at the outset and the short performance period make the use of any other contract type impracticable. The contract requires a negotiated billing price. The ceiling price is adjusted equitably or as specified in the contract. The ceiling price is really the only cost control motivator for the contractor in this variation.

Contract Clause

FAR 52.215-6, Price Redetermination – Retroactive.

3.5.4.5 Fixed Price Contract with Award Fees

FAR 16.404

Award-fee provisions may be used in fixed-price contracts when the Government wishes to motivate a contractor but contractor performance cannot be measured objectively to allow for other incentive arrangements. Such contracts establish a fixed price for satisfactory contract performance, and an award fee for above-target performance. A special board of Government officials is convened to determine the award fee. This variation uses award-fee provisions to be discussed thoroughly in an upcoming section.

3.5.5 Time-and-Materials Contract

FAR 16.601

A *time-and-materials contract* is based on direct labor hours at specified fixed hourly rates. It reimburses actual costs for materials, subcontracts and other direct costs. It is not possible at the time of placing the contract to either estimate accurately the extent or duration of the work, or to anticipate costs with any reasonable degree of confidence. It provides no positive profit incentive to the contractor for cost control or labor efficiency, so Government surveillance of contractor performance must give reasonable assurance that efficient methods and effective cost controls are being used.

The contract specifies separate fixed hourly rates for each labor category. These rates can also cover services transferred between divisions, subsidiaries or affiliates of the contractor under a common control. They do not include profit for the transferring organization, but may include profit for the prime contractor. Any commercial services carry the established catalog or market rate per the established pricing practice of the transferring organization. Material handling costs are excluded from the labor-hour rate and allocated to direct materials per the contractor's usual accounting procedures.[9]

The contract includes a ceiling price that the contractor exceeds at its own risk. Contractors under this contract type are not motivated toward effective cost control. It is commonly used for engineering and design services, repair and maintenance and overhaul, and emergency work.

The contracting officer's D&F of contract type must be approved by the head of the contracting activity if total length (including option periods) exceeds three years. The D&F reports on efforts to develop a firm-fixed-price contract.

Solicitation Provisions

FAR 52.216-29, Time-and-Materials/Labor-Hour Requirements—Non-Commercial Item Acquisitions With Adequate Price Competition, for non-commercial items where price is based on adequate price competition.

FAR 52.216-30, Time-and-Materials/Labor-Hour Proposal Requirements—Non-Commercial Item Acquisitions without Adequate Price Competition, for noncommercial items if the price is not based on adequate price competition.

FAR 52.216-31, Time-and-Materials/Labor-Hour Proposal Requirements—Commercial Item Acquisitions.

3.5.6 Labor-Hour Contract

FAR 16.602

A *labor-hour contract* is a variation of the time-and-materials contract, differing only in that materials are not supplied by the contractor. The same restrictions for usage apply.

3.5.7 Cost Plus Incentive Fee

FAR 16.304 & 16.405

Once we encounter contracts without a ceiling price, we introduce the concept of fee. A *fee* is the same as profit, namely the amount of revenue that exceeds cost. It is merely a change in terminology to differentiate from fixed-price contracts, which include profit rather than fee. Also, cost-plus contracts do not use the term "price," but rather talk in terms of estimated cost and fee.

A *cost-plus-incentive-fee contract* has a negotiated fee to be adjusted later by a formula based on the relationship of total allowable costs to total target costs. This contract type specifies a target cost and three different fee numbers (target, minimum and maximum), and a fee-adjustment formula. Note the differences from fixed-price incentive contracts: the firm ceiling price concept is gone (replaced by an estimate), and now we see minimum and maximum restrictions on the fee rate.

After contract performance, the final fee is determined in accordance with the formula. The fee amount increases above target when total allowable costs are less than the target cost, and decreases below target when total allowable costs exceed the target cost. When total allowable cost is greater than the range of costs within which the fee-adjustment formula operates, the contractor is paid total allowable costs, plus the minimum fee. By contrast, if total cost is below the cost range, the contractor receives all allowable costs plus maximum fee.

Assume a target cost of $500,000, target fee of $50,000 (10%), minimum fee of 5% ($25,000), maximum fee of 15% ($75,000), and an 80/20 share ratio. Now let us assume a 2% overrun, which means the final cost is

$500,000 + 2% = $500,000 + $10,000 = $510,000

The contactor's share of the overrun is 20% * $10,000 = $2,000. Subtracting this result from the target fee of $50,000 leaves a final fee of $48,000. Added to the final cost of $510,000, this yields a final contract amount of $558,000. The final fee rate is:

$$\frac{\$48,000}{\$510,000} = 9.4\%$$

Note that this total amount is below the maximum possible amount of $500,000 + $75,000 = $575,000, so it is allowable. Also, note that the final fee rate is below the target of 10% because the contractor incurred cost growth and was therefore penalized.

Alternatively, assume the contractor underruns cost estimate by 15%. Then,

$500,000 − $75,000 = $425,000 final cost
Contractor share = 20% * $75,000 = $15,000
Final fee = $50,000 + $15,000 = $65,000
Final amount = $425,000 + $65,000 = $490,000
Final fee rate = $\frac{\$65,000}{\$425,000} = 15.3\%$

Note the higher calculated fee rate because the contractor is rewarded for a significant cost underrun.

But wait! Now we have a problem. This result exceeds the legally permitted maximum fee rate of 15%, hence the final fee rate must be restricted to 15% * $425,000 = $63,750. This is because the actual result lies outside the *range of incentive effectiveness*, the set of probable costs over which the incentive arrangement works. The delta of $65,000 − $63,750 = $1,250 is not recovered by the contractor, not as lost cost but rather as unrealized profit.

In this example, the range of incentive effectiveness lies between the outcomes which produce a 5% and 15% final fee. It equates to a maximum allowable cost figure of $547,619 (plus $27,381 fee) and a minimum allowable cost figure of $478,261 (plus a 15% fee of $71,739).[10]

Notice that there is more room for the incentive fee to work for an overrun than underrun. This is due to the cost uncertainty of a cost contract environment being reflected in this example, where the target fee is midway between the minimum and maximum fees. These numbers can be adjusted in negotiations if the Government wishes a different result, such as more seriously motivating the contractor to control costs.

As with fixed-price incentives, the contract may include technical performance incentives if required development of a major system is feasible, and the use of both cost and technical performance incentives is desirable. Schedule performance incentives may also be used to reward early and/or penalize late delivery. The fee adjustment formula provides an incentive over the full range of foreseeable variations from target cost. If a high maximum fee is negotiated, the contract also provides for a low minimum fee that could conceivably be zero or negative.

Changes can be priced out using the same methods as FPI contracts. The *Constant Dollar* method maintains the dollar relationships between minimum, maximum and target fees (and therefore the range of incentive effectiveness), with a certain increase in minimum fee, but assumes little technical uncertainty associated with the changed effort. The *Constant Percentage* method ignores the dollar relationships of these values and instead preserves the percentage relationships between minimum and maximum fees. This method increases the minimum fee less than the Constant Dollar method and thereby increases the range of incentive effectiveness due to greater uncertainty for cost overrun, and can also be used to combine multiple changes.

Solicitation Provisions and Contract Clauses

FAR 52.216-7, Allowable Cost and Payment, for a cost-plus-incentive-fee or a cost-plus-award-fee contract.

FAR 52.216-10, Incentive Fee, for cost-plus-incentive-fee arrangements.

FAR 52.216-16, Incentive Price Revision – Firm Target. Use the clause with its Alternate I to order supplies or services under a provisioning document or Government option and include the prices in the incentive arrangement.

FAR 52.216-17, Incentive Price Revision – Successive Targets. Use the clause with its Alternate I for the same circumstance as FAR 52.216-16.

3.5.8 Cost Plus Award Fee Contract

FAR 16.305 & 16.401

A *cost-plus-award-fee contract* provides two fees: a base amount (which may be zero) fixed at contract inception, and an award fee based upon a judgmental evaluation by the Government to motivate excellence in contract performance. It may be used in combination with other types of incentive fee contracts. Periodic evaluations by the Government help determine award amounts by providing feedback to the contractor to enable improved motivation, performance, responsiveness, and visibility. Or, it can lead to contractor frustration at perceived Government unfairness, since the contractor has no basis for appeal of award fee decisions.

Performance factors must be meaningful, demonstrate effective management control over each factor and its results, and clearly described with measurement criteria. Evaluation may include assessment of personnel usage or ability to plan work, as well as timely and acceptable test results. Management controls could include:

- business management;
- corporate support;
- cost management;
- customer relationships;
- mission enhancement; and
- planning and scheduling.

Award-fee contracts are used when predetermined objective incentive targets are not possible. The contract arrangement should provide the Government with the flexibility to evaluate both performance and the conditions under which it was achieved. The Government bears additional administrative effort and cost to monitor and evaluate performance, so the D&F justifying contract type addresses the expected benefits by a risk and cost-benefit analysis. The Government determination and its methodology are documented in the contract file. The determination is a unilateral decision solely within the discretion of the Government and not subject to dispute or appeal.

All contracts providing for award fees are supported by an award-fee plan that establishes the procedures to evaluate award fee. There may also be a formal award review board. An *Award-Fee Board* is a team identified by name or position in the award-fee plan to evaluate performance and recommend the award-fee amount. The *Fee-Determining Official* reviews the Board's recommendations to determine the amount of award fee to be earned by the contractor for each evaluation period. Award-fee plans:

- are approved by the Fee Determining Official;
- identify the award-fee evaluation criteria and how they link to the acquisition objectives in terms of contract cost, schedule and technical performance;
- provide for evaluation period(s) at stated intervals during the period of performance (e.g., quarterly, every 6 or 12 months, or at specific milestones) to inform the contractor of performance quality and the areas in which improvement is expected; and
- specify the total award-fee pool amount and its allocation across each evaluation period.

Award-fee pools use an adjectival rating and award-fee pool earned percentages such as shown below (contracting officers may supplement the adjectival rating description):

Award Fee Rating	Award-Fee Pool Available to Be Earned
Excellent	91%–100%
Very Good	76%–90%
Good	51%–75%
Unsatisfactory	50% or less

The Government may unilaterally change evaluation weights during the contract, to take effect with the subsequent rating period, if it desires to change management emphasis as the contract progresses. A significant amount of the fee pool must be retained, however, for the final evaluation period to maintain contractor incentive.

The Government does not rollover unearned award-fee dollars, which is a process that would transfer unearned fee in one evaluation period to a subsequent period to allow the contractor an additional opportunity to earn fee dollars. Prohibiting rollover imposes a penalty of sorts in terms of lost fee dollars, but alerts the contractor to improve performance in future evaluation periods. Similarly, any award-fee plan must allow for the possibility of zero fee dollars when a contractor's overall cost, schedule and technical performance is below satisfactory.

Each agency collects data on award fees, incentive fees and performance measures to determine their effectiveness as a tool to improve contractor performance and achieve desired program outcomes. This information should be included in the acquisition planning process to determine the appropriate type of contract for future acquisitions.

3.5.9 Cost Plus Fixed Fee Contract

FAR 16.306

A *cost-plus-fixed-fee contract* has a negotiated fee that does not vary with actual cost, but may be adjusted as a result of changes in the work to be performed under the contract. This arrangement covers efforts that present great risk to contractors but only a minimum incentive to control costs. It is suitable for research, preliminary exploration or study, or for development and test, provided that the required *level of effort* (the quantity of hours to be procured over a stated period of time) is unknown. It is not used to develop major systems after preliminary exploration, studies and risk reduction indicate that development can be achieved and reasonably firm performance objectives and schedules are available. All allowable costs are reimbursed up to the estimated cost level. The fee dollars are fixed regardless of cost performance. The Government is free to add funding to cover additional costs, but the fee dollars remain unchanged (hence the final fee rate would drop). There is no guarantee of results, only the contactor's best efforts. This contract type will generate unpopularity with some members of the public and Congress due to many instances of cost growth and overrun.

A cost-plus-fixed-fee contract may take one of two basic forms – completion or term. The *term* form describes the scope of work in general terms and requires the contractor to devote a specified level of effort for a stated time period. The *completion* form contains a definite goal or target and end product, and normally requires the contractor to complete and deliver the specified end product (often a final research report) as a condition for payment of the entire fixed fee. If the end item is not delivered in time, the contractor may be directed by the Government to continue performance until delivery is made, and if additional time is necessary and provided, the work must be under a cost-only basis without additional fee dollars. Because the delivery requirement imposes a certain amount of risk on the contractor, fee rates tend to be slightly higher under this method than the term format.

For both contract forms, if performance is satisfactory to the Government, the fixed fee is paid at the end of the contract period. Should the work not be completed within the estimated cost, the Government may increase the contract amount to require more effort and cover the cost without increasing the fee.

The cost-plus-a-percentage-of-cost contract is prohibited in all prime and subcontracts (except under firm-fixed-price contracts, where subcontract approval is not required).

Solicitation Provisions and Contract Clauses

FAR 52.216-7, Allowable Cost and Payment. Use the clause with Alternate I for a construction contract. Use the clause with Alternate II for an educational institution contract. Use the clause with Alternate III for a contract with a state or local government. Use Alternate IV for a nonprofit organization if it is not an educational institution, is a state or local government, or is exempted under OMB Uniform Guidance at 2 CFR Part 200, Appendix VIII.

FAR 52.216-8, Fixed Fee, for a cost-plus-fixed-fee contract other than a construction contract.

FAR 52.216-9, Fixed-Fee – Construction, for a cost-plus-fixed-fee construction contract.

3.5.10 Cost-Only Contract

FAR 16.302

In a *cost-only contract*, the contractor receives no fee. It is used for research and development work with nonprofit educational or other nonprofit organizations.

Solicitation Provisions and Contract Clauses

FAR 52.216-11, Cost Contract – No Fee. Include Alternate I for a research and development contract with an educational institution or nonprofit organization and no withholding of allowable costs.

FAR 52.216-15, Predetermined Indirect Cost Rates, for a research and development contract with an educational institution using predetermined indirect cost rates.

3.5.11 Cost-Sharing Contract

FAR 16.303

For a *cost-sharing contract*, the contractor receives no fee and is reimbursed only for an agreed-upon portion of its allowable costs. It is used when the contractor expects compensating benefits in future business, either Government or commercial, and wishes to obtain defrayment of its development costs. This would most likely be an educational or nonprofit organization.

Solicitation Provisions and Contract Clauses

FAR 52.216-12, Cost-Sharing Contract – No Fee. Include Alternate I for research and development with an educational institution or a nonprofit organization and no withholding of allowable costs.

3.5.12 Letter Contract

FAR 16.603

A *letter contract* is a written preliminary contractual instrument that authorizes the contractor to begin immediately to manufacture supplies or perform services. A letter contract is used when the contractor receives a binding commitment to start work immediately, and negotiating a definitive contract is not yet possible.[11] However, a letter contract is as complete and definite as possible. If award is based on price competition, the contracting officer includes an overall price ceiling in the letter contract.

Each letter contract contains a negotiated definitization schedule including dates for:

- submission of the contractor's price proposal and required cost or pricing data;
- any required make-or-buy and subcontracting plans;
- the start of negotiations; and
- definitization within 180 days after the date of the letter contract or before completion of 40% of the work to be performed, whichever occurs first.

If the contracting officer and the contractor cannot reach agreement as to price or fee, the contractor proceeds with the work and the contracting officer may, with the approval of the head of the contracting activity, determine a reasonable price or fee, subject to appeal under the Disputes clause.

A letter contract requires the head of the contracting activity or a designee to determine in writing that no other contract is suitable. Letter contracts do not commit the Government to a definitive contract in excess of the funds available at the time of execution. The maximum liability of the Government is the estimated amount necessary to cover contractor requirements for funds before definitization, but not over 50% of the estimated cost of the definitive contract, unless approved in advance by the official that authorized the letter contract.

Contract Clauses

FAR 52.216-23, Execution and Commencement of Work.

FAR 52.216-24, Limitation of Government Liability.

FAR 52.216-25, Contract Definitization, with its definitization schedule completed. Add Alternate I if the letter contract is being awarded on the basis of price competition.

FAR 52.216-26, Payments of Allowable Costs Before Definitization, if cost reimbursement, except for ship conversion, alteration or repair.

3.5.13 Indefinite Delivery/Indefinite Quantity Contract

3.5.13.1 Policy

FAR 16.5

Indefinite delivery contracts provide for issuing orders during the contract period without specifying a firm delivery schedule. Likewise, *indefinite quantity contracts* have no firm quantities in the contract, other than a minimum or maximum quantity. *Delivery order contracts* cover supplies, while *task order contracts* cover services. These contracts have the following advantages:

- limit the Government's obligation to the minimum quantity specified in the contract;
- may provide for any appropriate cost or pricing arrangement;
- permit flexible quantity and delivery scheduling after requirements are firm; and
- permit Government stocks to be maintained at minimum levels and ship directly to users.

There are three types of indefinite-delivery contracts: definite-quantity, requirements and indefinite-quantity contracts, each of which will be discussed in detail below. They are used when the exact times of future deliveries are not known at the time of contract award. Whether the quantity is known in advance dictates whether a definite- or indefinite-quantity contract is used.

The contracting officer does not synopsize orders under indefinite-delivery contracts, unless funded in whole or in part by the Recovery Act. Performance-based acquisition methods are used whenever possible for services orders.

Delivery and task orders contain the following information:

- accounting and appropriation data;
- contract line-item number, description, quantity, and unit price or estimated cost and fee;
- contract number and order number;
- date of order;
- delivery or performance schedule;
- method of payment and payment office, if not specified in the contract;
- packaging, packing and shipping instructions; and
- place of delivery or performance.

Some agencies issue *Governmentwide Agency Contracts* (GWAC) for multiple agencies to place orders against. These are multiple-award procurements to promote competition and reduce delivery times for repetitive or common requirements, both supplies and services. Orders placed under an indefinite-delivery contract awarded by another agency or a GWAC still have an acquisition plan if otherwise required, and cannot circumvent regulations for bundling requirements or funding obligations. Orders placed under multi-agency contracts for architect-engineer services require direct supervision by a professional architect or engineer licensed in the state or area where the services are to be performed.

Protests for an order are only allowed if the order increases the scope, period of performance or maximum value of the contract. Protests of orders in excess of $10 million may only be filed with the Government Accountability Office.

The Government may place multiple contracts with different firms for the same family of supplies or services, with the intent of generating competition among these firms. The contracting officer provides each awardee a *fair opportunity* to submit an offer for each order exceeding $3,500 (below that amount, a sole-source award is acceptable). The contracting officer has broad discretion to develop order-placement procedures, including streamlined procedures such as oral presentations. The contracting officer need not contact any awardee which does not respond to the fair opportunity notice.

For task or delivery orders in excess of $5 million, the requirement to provide all awardees a fair opportunity for each order includes:

- a notice of the agency's requirements;
- a reasonable response period;
- evaluation factors and subfactors, including cost or price, and their relative importance;
- the basis for award if best value; and
- an opportunity for a post-award debriefing.

Each agency has an ombudsman (often the agency's competition advocate) to review complaints from contractors and ensure they are afforded a fair opportunity for consideration. The fair opportunity process is not required when:

- a single source is required by statute;
- only one awardee is capable of providing the required quality of supply or service;
- the agency need for the supplies or services is too urgent to permit delay;
- the order satisfies a minimum guarantee; or
- the requirement is a logical follow-on to an order already issued under the contract and must be awarded on a sole-source basis to promote economy and efficiency.

The ordering period of a task-order contract for advisory and assistance services, including all options or modifications, normally may not exceed five years unless specifically authorized by a statute. The contracting officer may extend the contract on a sole-source basis only once for a period not to exceed six months. This action requires a determination that the award of a follow-on contract is delayed by unforeseeable circumstances and extension is necessary to ensure continuity of services.

There are dollar limits on these contracts. Requirements contracts cannot exceed $112 million in total estimated value. If any indefinite contract covers advisory and assistance services, it normally cannot exceed three years in length and $13.5 million in value unless multiple awards are made.

Solicitation Provisions

FAR 52.216-27, Single or Multiple Awards, if solicitation may result in multiple contract awards.

FAR 52.216-28, Multiple Awards for Advisory and Assistance Services, instead of FAR 52.216-27 for advisory and assistance services that exceed three years and $11.5 million (including all options). The estimated number of awards must be specified.

Solicitation Provisions and Contract Clauses

FAR 52.216-18, Ordering.
FAR 52.216-19, Order Limitations.

3.5.13.2 Definite Quantity Contract

FAR 16.502

A *definite-quantity contract* provides for specific supplies or services to be delivered over a fixed period scheduled at designated locations upon order. It is used when a firm quantity of supplies or services will be required during the contract period, and the supplies or services are regularly available or will be available after a short lead time.

Solicitation Provisions and Contract Clauses

FAR 52.216-20, Definite Quantity.

3.5.13.3 Requirements Contract

FAR 16.503

A *requirements contract* provides for a contractor to fill all actual purchase requirements of designated Government activities for supplies or services during a specified contract period. The contract guarantees the contractor all orders and obligates some funding upfront to motivate the contractor to keep a quantity on hand for the Government customer. Requirements contracts encourage faster deliveries for long-lead time items because a contractor is more willing to maintain limited stocks when it has status as the sole source of supply. This contract type is used when the Government cannot predetermine the precise quantities of supplies or services that designated activities will need during a definite period.[12]

The contracting officer develops a realistic estimated total quantity based on records of previous requirements and consumption. The contract states the maximum quantity for the contract, the maximum or minimum quantities for each order, and the maximum amount to be ordered during a specified period of time.

No requirements contract over $100 million (including all options) may be awarded to a single source unless the agency head so determines in writing and notifies Congress within 30 days.

When a requirements contract is used to repair, modify or overhaul Government property, the Government furnishes such items in "estimated" or "maximum" amounts and will not entitle the contractor to any equitable adjustment in price under the Government Property clause.

Any requirements contract principally for advisory and assistance services in excess of three years and $11.5 million (including all options) requires a contracting officer determination that the services required are so unique or highly specialized that it is not practicable to make multiple awards.

Solicitation Provisions and Contract Clauses

FAR 52.216-21, Requirements. Use the clause with Alternate I for nonpersonal services and related supplies. Use the clause with Alternate II to acquire subsistence products for both Government use and resale on a brand-name basis. Use the clause with Alternate III for a partial small business set-aside. Use the clause with Alternate IV if both conditions for Alternates II and III apply.

3.5.13.4 Indefinite Quantity Contract

FAR 16.504

An *indefinite-quantity contract* provides for the Government placing orders for individual requirements, stating quantity limits as number of units or as dollar values. The contract requires the Government to order (and the contractor to furnish) at least a stated minimum quantity of supplies or services. The contracting officer establishes a maximum quantity based on market research, trends on recent contracts for similar supplies or services, or a survey of potential users. The minimum quantity must be more than a nominal quantity, but not in excess of the amount that the Government is fairly certain to order. The contract may also specify maximum or minimum quantities that the Government may order under each task or delivery order and the maximum that it may order during a specific period of time.

An indefinite-quantity solicitation and contract specifies:

- a description of the activities authorized to issue orders;
- a statement of work or specifications;
- authorization for placing oral orders, if appropriate;
- contact information of the agency task- and delivery-order ombudsman;
- if multiple awards may be made, how the Government will provide awardees a fair opportunity to be considered for each order;
- procedures that the Government will use in issuing orders, and the ordering media;
- the period of performance, number of options and the period for which the Government may extend the contract under each option; and

- the total minimum and maximum quantity of supplies or services the Government will acquire under the contract.

An indefinite-quantity contract is used when the Government cannot predetermine, above a specified minimum, the precise quantities of required supplies or services for the contract period, but the Government is willing to commit itself for more than a minimum quantity.

The Government prefers to make multiple awards of indefinite-quantity contracts for the same or similar supplies or services, except for advisory and assistance services. The number of contracts to be awarded is a function of scope and complexity, expected duration and frequency of orders, mix of contractor resources, and ability to maintain competition among the awardees. The multiple-award approach is not appropriate if:

- more favorable terms and conditions and pricing will be provided for a single award;
- only one contractor is capable of performance due to unique or highly specialized supplies or services, or because the projected orders are integrally related (in which case a requirements contract would be more appropriate);
- the administrative cost of multiple contracts outweighs their expected benefits; or
- the total estimated value of the contract is below the simplified acquisition threshold.

No task- or delivery-order contract in excess of $100 million (including all options) may be awarded to a single source unless the head of the agency determines in writing (and notifies Congress within 30 days) that:

- only one source is qualified and capable of performing the work at a reasonable price to the Government;
- the public interest requires a single source due to exceptional circumstances; or
- the task or delivery orders are so integrally related that only a single source can reasonably perform the work.

Here again, unless incidental to contract performance, an indefinite-quantity contract for advisory and assistance services exceeding three years and $11.5 million, including all options, requires multiple awards unless the sole-source conditions outlined above are present or only one offer is received.

Solicitation Provision and Contract Clause

FAR 52.216-22, Indefinite Quantity.

3.6 AGREEMENTS

3.6.1 Basic Agreement

FAR 16.702

A *basic agreement* is not a contract, but rather a written instrument of understanding between an agency and a contractor that contains contract clauses to be applied to future contracts between the parties by reference or attachment. Also known as a *master agreement*, it is used when numerous separate contracts may be awarded to a contractor during a particular period and significant recurring negotiating problems may have been experienced. These separate orders or contracts contain the specifics as to performance and price.[13] Basic agreements may be used with negotiated fixed-price or cost-reimbursement contracts. Each basic agreement is reviewed annually before the anniversary of its effective date and modified as necessary to conform to regulations. Either party may cancel the agreement with 30 days written notice. Modifying an agreement does not retroactively affect orders previously issued under it. Contracting officers often obtain and use existing basic agreements of another agency.

Each contract incorporating a basic agreement includes a scope of work and price, and delivery and other terms that apply to the particular contract. The basic agreement is incorporated into the contract by specific reference or attachment. A basic agreement does not cite appropriations or obligate funds, but rather states an agreement by the Government to place future contracts or orders with the contractor.

3.6.2 Basic Ordering Agreement

FAR 16.703

A *basic ordering agreement* is likewise not a contract, but rather an agreement with terms and clauses applying to future orders between the parties during its term, a description of supplies or services to be provided, and methods for pricing and issuing future orders under the basic ordering agreement. It contains the same qualities and restrictions as a basic agreement. Each basic ordering agreement specifies the point where each order becomes a binding contract (e.g., date of issuance, acceptance of order, or specified number of days afterward to allow for rejection by the contractor). A basic ordering agreement may be used to expedite contracting for uncertain requirements when specific items, prices and quantities are unknown at the time the agreement is executed, but numerous requirements are anticipated to be purchased from the contractor. These procedures can reduce administrative lead time, inventory investment and obsolescence from design changes.

The contracting officer cannot make any final commitment or authorize the contractor to begin work on an order under a basic ordering agreement until prices have been established, unless the order establishes a ceiling price limiting the Government's obligation. In this case, either the basic ordering agreement provides adequate procedures for timely pricing of the order early in its performance period, or else the need for the supplies or services is unusually urgent. The contracting officer prices the order as soon as practical, but not retroactively. Failure to reach agreement on negotiated price for any order is a dispute under the Disputes clause.

3.7 SEALED BIDDING

FAR 14.101 and .201

Sealed bidding is a contracting method that uses public solicitation, bid opening and award. *Invitations for bids* are publicized by mailing to prospective bidders, posting in public places, and transmission to www.fedbizopps.gov. The Government provides enough time for prospective bidders to prepare and submit bids, which are opened publicly at the time and place stated in the solicitation. Bids are evaluated without discussions between parties or permitting the offeror to revise its offer. Award is made to the responsible bidder whose bid is most advantageous to the Government, considering only price and those factors specified in the invitation. An *Order of Precedence* provision sets priorities to resolve any contradictions within the solicitation. Only firm-fixed-price contracts or fixed-price contracts with economic price adjustment clauses are subject to sealed bidding. Contracting officers solicit sealed bids if:

- award will be made on the basis of price and other price-related factors;
- discussions with the responding offerors are not necessary;
- there is a reasonable expectation of receiving more than one sealed bid; and
- time permits the solicitation, submission and evaluation of sealed bids.

Award is made by acceptance of a bid on the award portion of Standard Form 33, 26, or 1447, incorporating the bidder's Representations and Certifications, and other statements of the bidder.

Solicitation Provisions

FAR 52.214-3, Amendments to Invitations for Bids.

FAR 52.214-4, False Statements in Bids.

FAR 52.214-5, Submission of Bids.

FAR 52.214-6, Explanation to Prospective Bidders.

FAR 52.214-7, Late Submissions, Modifications, and Withdrawals of Bids.

FAR 52.214-10, Contract Award – Sealed Bidding (except for construction contracts).

FAR 52.214-12, Preparation of Bids.

FAR 52.214-13, Telegraphic Bids, in invitations for bids if the contracting officer decides to authorize telegraphic bids. Use the provision with its Alternate I for perishable subsistence, and when offerors might be unwilling to provide acceptance periods long enough to allow written confirmation.

FAR 52.214-14, Place of Performance – Sealed Bidding, unless the place of performance is specified by the Government.

FAR 52.214-15, Period for Acceptance of Bids, for nonconstruction solicitations not issued on SF 33 or SF 1447, unless the Government specifies a minimum acceptance period.

FAR 52.214-16, Minimum Bid Acceptance Period, for nonconstruction solicitations when a minimum acceptance period must be specified.

FAR 52.214-18, Preparation of Bids – Construction, for construction work.

FAR 52.214-19, Contract Award – Sealed Bidding – Construction, for construction work.

FAR 52.214-20, Bid Samples, if bid samples are required. Use the provision with its Alternate I if the nature of the required product permits a waiver to a product produced at a different plant from where the product previously acquired or tested was produced. Use the provision with its Alternate II if the waiver must restrict award to a product produced at the same plant in which the product previously acquired or tested was produced.

FAR 52.214-21, Descriptive Literature, if the required descriptive information will not be readily available unless it is submitted by bidders. Use the provision with its Alternate I if the contracting officer may waive the requirement for furnishing descriptive literature for a bidder offering a previously supplied product that meets current specification requirements.

FAR 52.214-22, Evaluation of Bids for Multiple Awards, if multiple awards might be made if economically advantageous to the Government.

FAR 52.214-23, Late Submissions, Modifications, Revisions, and Withdrawals of Technical Proposals under Two-Step Sealed Bidding, for technical proposals in step one of two-step sealed bidding.

FAR 52.214-24, Multiple Technical Proposals, for technical proposals in step one of two-step sealed bidding if the contracting officer permits the submission of multiple technical proposals.

FAR 52.214-25, Step Two of Two-Step Sealed Bidding, for step two of two-step sealed bidding.

FAR 52.214-31, Facsimile Bids, if authorized.

FAR 52.214-34, Submission of Offers in the English Language, if including any Buy American Act clause.

FAR 52.214-35, Submission of Offers in U.S. Currency, if including any Buy American Act clauses unless the Evaluation of Foreign Currency Offers clause is included.

Solicitation Provisions and Contract Clauses

FAR 52.214-26, Audit and Records – Sealed Bidding, if submission of cost or pricing data is required. Use the clause with its Alternate I if the acquisition will use funds appropriated by the Recovery Act.

FAR 52.214-27, Price Reduction for Defective Cost or Pricing Data – Modifications – Sealed Bidding, if cost or pricing data are required, unless waived by the head of the contracting activity for a contract with a foreign government or agency.

FAR 52.214-28, Subcontractor Cost or Pricing Data – Modifications – Sealed Bidding, if cost or pricing data are required, unless waived by the head of the contracting activity for a contract with a foreign government or agency.

FAR 52.214-29, Order of Precedence – Sealed Bidding, if the uniform contract format applies.

3.7.1 Rules for Solicitation

FAR 5.3

The procurement must be advertised through FedBizOpps by means of a brief write-up known as a *synopsis*. This step is important to broaden competition and assist small businesses in obtaining Government contracts and subcontracts. A synopsis is required for all solicitations exceeding the simplified purchase threshold unless:

- awarded under the Small Business Innovation Development Act;
- for perishable subsistence supplies;
- for utility services to one source (although telecommunications services must still be synopsized);
- national security precludes public announcement of the requirement;
- the result of an unsolicited proposal with a unique and innovative research concept; or
- to support the Government in a dispute or litigation.

FAR 14.2

The time frame between issuance of the solicitation and opening of bids is at least 30 calendar days when a synopsis is required. To avoid unduly restricting competition or paying higher prices, the following factors are considered to set a reasonable bid time:

- anticipated extent of subcontracting;
- complexity of requirement;
- degree of urgency;
- geographic distribution of bidders; and
- transmittal time for invitations and bids.

As a rule, solicitations estimated between $15,000 and $25,000 can be synopsized for up to 10 days. Such a notice may go to FedBizOpps or can be posted at a convenient public location near the Procurement office. Synopsis for solicitations below this amount is discretionary. Presolicitation notices are often considered as well.

Telegraphic bids and mailgrams are authorized only when the opening date will not allow bidders enough time to submit bids in the prescribed format, or if prices change frequently (e.g., bulk fuels).

The Government may require bid samples to assess a product's balance, color, ease of use, or feel that cannot be described adequately in the specification.[14] Invitations for bids set forth the number and size of sample submissions, and also state the characteristics to be examined. The requirement for bid samples may be waived when a bidder offers a product previously or currently contracted for or tested by the Government and found to comply with current specifications.

Bid samples merely determine the responsiveness of the bid, not a bidder's ability to produce the required items. Bids will be rejected as nonresponsive if the sample fails to conform to each of the characteristics listed in the invitation. Unrequested bid samples are usually disregarded, unless the bid is qualified for their acceptance.

Bidders need not furnish descriptive literature unless required before award to determine whether the products offered meet the specification. The invitation states what descriptive literature to furnish and why it is needed. Further, the solicitation must specify the extent of consideration in bid evaluation and the impact of any failure to furnish the literature before bid opening or not complying with the requirements of the invitation.

As with bid samples, the contracting officer may waive the requirement to furnish descriptive literature if the bidder states that the product being offered is the same as one previously or currently furnished to the contracting activity, and the product complies with the current requirement. The bid may be based on either descriptive literature or a previously furnished product, but not both. Unsolicited descriptive literature is treated the same as unsolicited bid samples.

Contracting officers may authorize facsimile bids based on urgency, price change frequency or administrative inability to handle bid volume and protection. Contracting officers will then request the apparently successful offeror to provide the complete, original signed bid subsequent to the opening date. Contracting officers may authorize use of electronic commerce to submit bids, but must specify in the solicitation the electronic method(s) to use.

In lieu of initially forwarding complete bid sets, the contracting officer may send presolicitation notices to potential bidders. The notice specifies the final date for receipt of requests for a complete bid set and describes the requirement. It also furnishes other information for firms to determine whether they have an interest in the invitation. Bid sets are sent to concerns that request them in response to the notice.

A prebid conference may be used before bid opening in a complex acquisition to brief prospective bidders and explain complicated requirements and clear up any ambiguities. This ensures that all potential bidders have a common understanding of the goods or services required. However, it is not a substitute for amending a defective or ambiguous invitation.

Any changes in opening date, quantity, schedule, specifications, or a defective or ambiguous invitation are accommodated by amending the invitation for bids using Standard Form 30. Amendments are sent before bid opening to every solicited firm and are also displayed in the bid room. If it is appropriate to extend the period of time remaining until bid opening, bidders should be notified by telegram or telephone and confirmed in the amendment.

Any information given to a prospective bidder is furnished promptly to all other prospective bidders as an amendment to the invitation, especially if the lack of such information would be prejudicial to uninformed bidders. This provides prospective bidders with enough time to decide on or modify their bids. General information that would not be prejudicial to other prospective bidders may be furnished upon request (e.g., explaining a clause or a condition in the invitation for bids).

Invitations for bids should never be cancelled unless the requirement ends or the amendment is so extensive that a new solicitation package is cleaner. The reason for cancellation is announced electronically, any electronic bids received are deleted without viewing, and any paper bids are returned unopened.

Information concerning proposed acquisitions is not released outside the Government before solicitation except for presolicitation notices, long-range acquisition estimates or synopses. Within the Government, such information is restricted to those with a legitimate interest. Releases of information are made simultaneously to all prospective bidders, so that one prospective bidder does not have an unfair advantage over another.

3.7.2 Submission of Bids

FAR 14.3

To be considered for award, a bid must comply in all material respects with the invitation for bids. This approach places all bidders on an equal footing and maintains the integrity of the sealed-bidding system. Telegraphic, electronic or facsimile bids are not considered unless permitted by the solicitation. Bids are filled out, executed and submitted in accordance with the instructions in the invitation. A bidder's own bid form or letter may be considered only if the bidder accepts all terms and conditions of the invitation and does not vary from the invitation.

Bids may be modified or withdrawn by any method authorized by the solicitation, if notice is received in the designated bidding office not later than the exact time set for opening of bids. If no time is specified in the solicitation, then the time for receipt is 4:30 p.m., local time, on the date that bids are due. Otherwise, the bid is late and will not be considered unless received before award is made without unduly delaying the acquisition, and it was received either at the initial point of entry to the Government infrastructure by 5:00 p.m. on the working day prior to the date specified for receipt of bids, or at the Government installation and under Government control prior to the hour set for receipt of bids. This means that a delivery man delayed at the gate to obtain permission to enter the installation is not a legitimate excuse for missing the deadline.

A late modification of a successful bid that makes its terms more favorable to the Government will be considered at any time it is received and may be accepted. Evidence to establish the time of receipt at the Government installation includes the time/date stamp on the bid wrapper or oral testimony or statements of Government personnel. If an emergency or unanticipated event (e.g., a snowstorm or natural disaster) interrupts normal Government processes to prevent bid receipt at the Government office by the exact time specified in the solicitation, the time specified for receipt of bids will be extended to the same hour on the first work day on which Government processes resume.

Late bids and modifications that are not considered are held unopened (except for identification) until after award and then retained with other unsuccessful bids. However, any bid bond or guarantee is returned.

3.7.3 Opening of Bids and Award of Contract

FAR 14.4

All bids received before the time set for opening are securely stored. Envelopes that do not identify the bidder or the solicitation are opened solely for identification by a designated official. This official immediately writes on the envelope an explanation of the opening, the date and time opened, the invitation number, and signature, then reseals the envelope.

Bid openings are open to the general public, usually representatives of the bidding firms. The bid-opening officer announces when the time set for opening bids has arrived, personally and publicly opens all bids received by that time, reads the bids aloud, and records them on an abstract sheet. The original copy of each bid is examined by the public only under the immediate supervision of a Government official to prevent alteration or substitution in the bid. The abstract of offers is available for public inspection at this time but does not indicate such things as apparent collusion of bidders, failure to meet responsibility, or information exempt from public disclosure.

The general public may not attend bid openings for classified acquisitions; only a bidder or representative with the appropriate security clearance may attend. No public record is made of bids or bid prices received in response to classified invitations for bids.

If only one or two bids are received, the contracting officer should research why competition was so limited to broaden the bidding base or eliminate any procedural problems. This research should in no way delay award, however.

Award is made to the responsible bidder who submitted the lowest responsive bid, unless there is a compelling reason to reject all bids and cancel the invitation. The contracting officer tries to anticipate requirement changes before the opening date and notifies all prospective bidders of any resulting modification or cancellation, so they can change their bids and avoid unnecessary exposure of bid prices.

Sometimes delivery is expressed in terms of days after award. In such cases, the contracting officer evaluates the bid by adding five calendar days for arrival through ordinary mail. If the solicitation states that the contract or notice of award will be transmitted electronically, the contracting officer adds one working day to the proposed delivery schedule based on the date of contract receipt or notice of award. Solicitations also inform bidders or offerors how their bids or proposals will be evaluated with respect to time of delivery or performance.

3.7.4 Rejection of Bids

FAR 14.404 through 14.406

Cancelling an invitation for bids is discouraged because it means lost time, effort and money by both Government and bidders. Invitations may only be cancelled and all bids rejected after opening when the agency head determines in writing that any of the following events has occurred:

- a cost comparison as prescribed in OMB Circular A-76 shows that performance by the Government is more economical;
- all bids received are at unreasonable prices;
- bids indicate that the needs of the Government can be satisfied by a less expensive article or manner than specified;
- bids were not independently priced in open competition or were submitted in bad faith;
- cancellation is clearly in the public's interest;
- no bidder is deemed responsible;
- only one bid is received and the contracting officer cannot determine the reasonableness of the bid price;
- specifications were ambiguous, inadequate or outdated;
- the invitation did not include all cost evaluation factors; or
- the supplies or services are no longer required.

Bids are returned unopened to the bidders and notice of cancellation is sent to all prospective bidders to whom invitations were issued. Electronic bids remain unopened and are purged from data storage systems. The cancellation notice identifies the solicitation number and subject matter, states the reason for cancellation, and assures prospective bidders that they will have an opportunity to bid on any presolicitation or future requirements for the same type of supplies or services.

Should administrative difficulties be encountered after bid opening that may delay award beyond bidders' acceptance periods (which are normally

60 days after bid opening date), the several lowest bidders whose bids have not expired are requested to extend in writing the bid acceptance period (with consent of sureties, if any) to avoid presolicitation. The number of bidders requested in this instance depends on the bid pricing; the contracting officer need not contact any bidders who clearly will not receive an award, but must ensure that those with a reasonable chance are requested to extend their bid expiration dates.

When the agency head determines that an invitation for bids should be cancelled in favor of negotiations, the contracting officer may award without a new solicitation if each responsible bidder is given notice that negotiations will be conducted and an opportunity to participate in negotiations.

A bid must be rejected when it:

- comes from a bidder determined to be not responsible (but if a bidder is a small business concern, a certificate of competency could be in order);
- comes from any person or firm that is debarred, proposed for debarment, suspended, or otherwise declared ineligible as of the bid-opening date;
- contains materially unbalanced prices for any line items or subline items;[15]
- fails to conform to the delivery schedule or any alternates stated in the invitation;
- fails to conform to the essential requirements of the invitation for bids, unless the solicitation authorized submission of alternate bids and the supplies offered meet the requirements;
- fails to furnish a required bid guarantee;
- imposes conditions that would modify requirements of the invitation or limit the bidder's liability to the Government, since to allow the bidder to impose such conditions would be prejudicial to other bidders;
- is from a firm which transfers its assets during the time period between the bid opening and the award, unless the transfer is effected by merger or operation of law;
- is unreasonable as to price, either in total amount or by individual item;
- limits the rights of the Government under any contract clause;
- prohibits the disclosure of information to permit competing bidders to know the nature and type of the products offered or elements of the bid related to quantity, price and delivery terms;
- protects against future changes in conditions, such as cost-escalation clauses;
- qualifies its price as being subject to what is in effect at time of delivery;
- qualifies that it is to be considered only if the bidder receives (or does not receive) award under a separate solicitation before date of award; or
- requires the Government to determine that the bidder's product meets applicable Government specifications.

The contracting officer may request a low bidder to delete objectionable conditions from a bid if they do not go to the substance of the bid (i.e., not affect price, quantity, quality, or delivery, or create injustice on other bidders). If the condition goes to the heart of the bid, however, it must be rejected.

Unless the solicitation provides otherwise, a bid may be responsive notwithstanding that the bidder specifies that award will be accepted only on all, or a specified group, of the items. The contracting officer could find during price evaluation that an all-or-none bid might be in the Government's best interest.

A *minor informality* or irregularity is merely a matter of form and not of substance, an immaterial defect in a bid or a variation of a bid that can be corrected or waived without prejudicing other bidders. The defect or variation has no impact on delivery, price, quality, or quantity compared with the total cost or scope of the supplies or services acquired. The contracting officer either gives the bidder an opportunity to cure any deficiency resulting from a minor informality or irregularity or else waives the deficiency, whichever is to the Government's advantage. Examples include failure of a bidder to:

- acknowledge receipt of an amendment to an invitation for bids if the bid clearly indicates its acceptance by another action (e.g., only a matter of form or has no or only negligible effect on the bid);
- execute the representations with respect to equal opportunity and affirmative action programs, previous contracts and compliance reports, and affirmative action compliance;
- furnish required information concerning the number of its employees;
- return the number of copies of signed bids required by the invitation; and
- sign its bid if a cover letter or bid guarantee indicates the bidder's intention to be bound by the unsigned bid. Otherwise, an unsigned bid must be rejected because it is not a binding offer.

If a bid received at the Government facility by electronic data interchange is so unreadable that conformance to the essential requirements of the invitation for bids cannot be ascertained, the contracting officer immediately notifies the bidder that the bid will be rejected unless the bidder provides clear and convincing evidence of the original bid's content. In order to be excused, the unreadable condition of the bid must be caused by Government software or hardware error, malfunction or mishandling. A bidder mistake or transmission error is not acceptable to excuse an unreadable bid.

The originals of all rejected bids, and any written findings with respect to such rejections, are preserved in the acquisition file.

3.7.5 Mistakes in Bids

FAR 14.407

Contracting officers examine all bids for mistakes before award. Mistakes differ from minor informalities because they do affect the bid pricing or terms. If a mistake is found, the contracting officer requests from the bidder a verification of the bid and calls attention to the suspected mistake.

Any obvious clerical mistake may be corrected by the contracting officer before award after obtaining from the bidder a verification of the bid intended (e.g., misplaced decimal point, reversed discounts or FOB prices, etc.). The verification must be attached to both copies of the bid and award, since the Government may not change the face of the submitted bid.

If a bidder requests permission to correct a mistake and evidence clearly establishes both the existence of the mistake and the bid actually intended, the agency head may determine that the bidder may correct the mistake. However, if the correction displaces any lower bids, the existence of the mistake and the bid actually intended must be obvious from the invitation and the bid itself.

If a bidder requests permission to withdraw rather than correct a bid, and the evidence of the mistake is clear and convincing, and the bid is still the lowest price, the agency head may determine to correct the bid and not permit its withdrawal. If on the other hand, the evidence that a mistake exists is clear and convincing but not as to the intended bid price, an official above the contracting officer may determine to allow the bidder to withdraw the bid. If the evidence does not warrant any determination, the agency head may decide to neither correct nor withdraw the bid.

If the bid is verified, the contracting officer considers the bid as originally submitted. If the time for acceptance of bids is likely to expire before a decision can be made, the contracting officer requests all bidders eligible for award to extend the acceptance time for their bids. If the bidder whose bid is believed erroneous does not extend the time, the bid shall be considered as originally submitted.

On the other hand, if the bidder admits a mistake, the contracting officer advises the bidder to make a written request to withdraw or modify the bid, including evidence that establishes the existence of the error, how it occurred, and the intended bid. If the bidder fails or refuses to furnish evidence in support of a suspected or alleged mistake, the contracting officer considers the bid as submitted.

3.7.6 Mistakes After Award

FAR 14.407-4

When a mistake in a contractor's bid is not discovered until after award, it may be corrected by contract modification if favorable to the Government without changing the essential requirements of the specifications. The contracting officer may also rescind the contract or reform it to delete the items involved in the mistake or increase the price if it does not exceed that of the next lowest acceptable bid under the original invitation for bids (if it does exceed another bid price, it would damage the integrity of the bidding process and cannot be done). The mistake must be either mutual or else so obvious that the contracting officer should have noticed it.

The contracting officer requests the contractor to support the alleged mistake by submitting written statements and pertinent evidence (e.g., contractor's file copy of the bid, original worksheets and other data used in preparing the bid, subcontractor quotes, published price lists, etc.). The case file concerning an alleged mistake contains this contractor evidence plus a signed statement by the contracting officer that describes the action taken.

FAR 14.408-4

When a solicitation does not contain an economic price adjustment clause but a bidder proposes one with a ceiling that the price will not exceed, the bid is evaluated on the basis of the maximum possible economic price adjustment of the quoted base price. Prior to award, the contracting officer requests the bidder to agree to the inclusion in the award of an approved economic price adjustment clause subject to the same ceiling, or else awards the bid as originally submitted. If the proposed clause has no ceiling, the bid must be rejected.

When a solicitation contains an economic price adjustment clause and no bidder takes exception to the provisions, bids are evaluated on the basis of the quoted prices without the allowable economic price adjustment being added. The bid is rejected if the bidder increases the maximum percentage of adjustment or deletes the clause. If the bidder proposes decreasing the maximum percentage, the bid is be evaluated at the base price and, if awarded, reflects the lower ceiling.

3.7.7 Price Related Factors

FAR 14.201-8

If bids are on an f.o.b. origin basis, transportation costs to the designated points shall be considered in determining the lowest cost to the Government.

Changes made or requested by the bidder in any provisions of the invitation for bids may be considered if the change does not constitute a basis for rejection. The contracting officer may also need to consider taxes and origin of supplies and, in case of foreign origin, application of the Buy American Act or any other prohibition on foreign purchases.

Sometimes a solicitation for multiple line items might lead to multiple awards. The contracting officer considers advantages or disadvantages to the Government that might result from making more than one award. (S)he uses $500 as the cost to the Government for issuing and administering each separate award.

3.7.8 Award

FAR 14.408

The contracting officer issues a contract award by written or electronic notice within the time for acceptance specified in the bid or extension. Award is made to that responsible bidder whose bid, conforming to the invitation, will be most advantageous to the Government, considering only price and the price-related factors included in the invitation. All solicitation provisions and changes made by a bidder are set forth (either expressly or by reference) in the award document. Because the award is an acceptance of the bid, both the bid and the award constitute the contract. Award is generally made by using SF 33 or 1447.

Prompt payment discounts are not considered in evaluating bids. However, any discount offered will form a part of the award, and will be taken by the payment center if payment is made within the discount period specified by the bidder.

In case of a tie bid, preference is shown for a small business in a labor-surplus area, and if none, then a small business. If a tie remains, then lots may be drawn with at least three witnesses, including the bidders if feasible.

The contracting officer notifies each unsuccessful bidder in writing or electronically within three days after contract award that its bid was not accepted. When award is made to other than a low bidder, the notice states the reason for rejection in the notice to each of the unsuccessful low bidders. When a nonbidder requests information of an unclassified award, the contracting officer may furnish the names of successful bidders and the award prices. No such information is provided for a classified award.

FAR 5.2

Whenever exceeding the simplified acquisition threshold, the contracting officer then issues a synopsis to FedBizOpps in the same manner as the solicitation. However, a synopsis of award is not required when the award is:

- acceptance of a Small Business Innovation Development proposal;
- acceptance of an unsolicited research proposal, to prevent disclosure of the originality, innovativeness or proprietary information, unless award is based solely upon the unique capability of the source to perform the particular research;
- an order under a previously synopsized contract, such as an indefinite-delivery contract;
- for brand-name commercial items for authorized resale;
- for DoD work performed outside the United States and its possessions and only local sources will be solicited;[16]
- for perishable subsistence supplies;
- for the services of an expert to support the Federal Government in any current or anticipated litigation or dispute;
- made through another Government agency, including an 8(a) or Committee for Purchase from People Who Are Blind or Severely Disabled award;
- made under unusual and compelling urgency;
- sole source for utility services other than telecommunications services;
- such that synopsis would result in disclosure of classified information;
- the head of the agency determines in writing, after consultation with OFPP and SBA, that advance notice is not appropriate or reasonable; or
- to a source directed by a foreign government or treaty.

3.7.9 Two-Step Sealed Bidding

FAR 14.5

Two-step sealed bidding permits a description of the Government's requirements, including a technical data package, so that future acquisitions may be made by conventional sealed bidding. This method is used in acquisitions for complex items requiring technical proposals. Step one consists of a request for technical proposals, which calls for solicitation, submission, evaluation, and any discussion of an unpriced technical proposal. This step determines the acceptability of the proposed supplies or services and clarifies technical questions (e.g., engineering approach, manufacturing processes and testing techniques). The Government may request no further information from any offeror, even if considered to be reasonably susceptible of being made acceptable, nor can it discuss proposals with all offerors. The contracting officer notifies any offeror if its proposal is deemed unacceptable. When specifications permit different technical approaches, the Government often permits multiple proposals.

Proposals are categorized as acceptable, reasonably susceptible of being made acceptable, or unacceptable. Any proposal which modifies or does not conform to the essential requirements or specifications of the solicitation is considered nonresponsive and rejected as unacceptable. When a technical proposal is found unacceptable, the contracting officer notifies the offeror of the basis of the determination and that a revision of the proposal will not be considered. The contracting officer debriefs unsuccessful offerors at their written request.

The contracting officer may proceed directly with Step Two if sufficient acceptable proposals ensure adequate price competition and the Government lacks the time or desire to make additional proposals acceptable. At this point, the contracting officer requests any bidders who are susceptible to becoming acceptable to submit additional clarifying information by a fixed time.

Sealed-bidding procedures continue throughout Step Two except that invitations for bids are issued only to those offerors submitting acceptable technical proposals in Step One, and are not synopsized through FedBizOpps. However, the names of firms that submitted acceptable proposals in Step One will be listed through FedBizOpps for the benefit of prospective subcontractors.

Step Two is the submission of sealed-price bids by those who submitted acceptable technical proposals in Step One. These bids are evaluated and awards are made in the same manner as sealed bidding. Each bid in the second step is based on the bidder's own technical proposals. The Government could decide to accept an initial proposal, so the bidder must bid its most favorable terms. If Step One results in no acceptable technical proposal or only one acceptable technical proposal, the acquisition may be continued by negotiation.

Two-step sealed bidding is preferred to negotiation when:

- a firm-fixed-price contract or a fixed-price contract with economic price adjustment will be used;
- at least two technically qualified sources are available;
- available specifications or purchase descriptions are not definite or complete, or may be too restrictive without technical evaluation;
- definite criteria exist for evaluating technical proposals; and
- sufficient time will be available for use of the two-step method.

3.8 COMPETITIVE NEGOTIATIONS

3.8.1 Solicitation of Proposals and Information

FAR 15.2

Unlike sealed bidding, competitive negotiations promote discussions between Government and offerors. Information should be freely shared, from the earliest identification of a requirement through receipt of proposals, among all interested parties (e.g., potential offerors, end users and Government acquisition personnel). This improves the understanding of Government requirements and industry capabilities, so that potential offerors may judge how they can satisfy the Government's requirements. An early exchange of information can identify and resolve concerns regarding the acquisition strategy, contract type, reference documents, requirements, schedules, suitability of the proposal instructions and evaluation criteria, and terms and conditions. Common techniques to promote early exchanges of information are:

- draft solicitations;
- industry or small business conferences;
- market research;
- one-on-one meetings with potential offerors;
- prequalification of offerors;
- presolicitation notices;
- presolicitation or preproposal conferences with potential offerors to discuss technical issues and gauge the level of market interest;
- public hearings;
- requests for information; and
- site visits.

Prequalification is used when the procurement office wishes to announce an upcoming requirement to assess the level of interest in the marketplace. The announcement will include criteria for selecting proposals and request the participation of all offerors capable of meeting the requirements. This action is intended to reduce the solicitation list to only the most interested and qualified parties. It can be used when solicitation packages are quite voluminous with extensive drawings and specifications.

A *Request For Information* (RFI) is used when the Government does not necessarily intend to award a contract, but rather wants to obtain price, delivery or market information or capabilities for planning purposes. It can also be used to announce an upcoming solicitation and request firms to participate in the procurement. Responses to these notices are not offers and cannot be the basis for a binding contract. There is no required format for RFIs.

The agency may publish a presolicitation notice to invite potential offerors to submit information so that the Government may advise the offerors about their potential as viable competitors (and if not, why not). The presolicitation notice includes a general description of the scope or purpose of the acquisition, information that must be submitted, and the criteria to make the initial evaluation. Information sought may be limited to a statement of qualifications, proposed technical concept, past performance, and limited pricing information. All respondents may participate in the resultant acquisition, even if advised by the Government that they are not viable competitors.

The Government may issue a *master solicitation* with clauses and provisions essential for repetitive procurements of supplies or services. An agency may decide to maintain a master solicitation by updating it with changes in laws, regulations or policies.

After release of the solicitation, the contracting officer is the focal point of any exchange with potential offerors. Any information about a proposed acquisition disclosed to one or more potential offerors is furnished to all as soon as practicable to avoid creating an unfair competitive advantage.

3.8.2 Requests for Proposals

Requests for proposals (RFPs) are used in negotiated acquisitions to submit Government requirements to prospective contractors and to solicit proposals. If facsimile proposals are authorized, contracting officers may request offeror(s) to provide the complete, original signed proposal at a later date. Not all RFPs are formal solicitations. Letter RFPs may be used in sole-source acquisitions. Oral RFPs are authorized when processing a written solicitation would create a delay to the Government's detriment (e.g., perishable items and support of contingency operations or other emergency situations).

In addition to the Uniform Contract Format used for formal bids, two more sections are added to the solicitation. Section L, Instructions to Offerors, will provide formal directions on proposal preparation and may require organization of proposals into sections (e.g., Administrative, Management, Technical, Past Performance, and Cost and Pricing Data). Section M, Evaluation Factors for Award, will identify all factors used to evaluate offers.

3.8.3 Amending the Solicitation

If the Government changes its requirements or terms and conditions, the contracting officer issues amendments to all parties solicited or still under consideration for award. This is the same process used in sealed bidding.

If a proposal of interest to the Government departs from the stated requirements, the contracting officer amends the solicitation but must withhold from the other offerors the alternate solution proposed. Even so, the solicitation may be cancelled if this amendment would so greatly change the solicitation as to permit additional firms to propose. Oral notices may be used in case of urgency. The amendment may revise the solicitation closing date.

The procurement office physically safeguards all proposals and RFI responses from unauthorized disclosure throughout the source selection process. Any proposal or modification received at the designated Government office after the exact time specified for receipt of proposals is considered late. It cannot be considered unless received before award is made, the contracting officer determines that accepting it would not unduly delay the acquisition, or a late modification of an otherwise successful proposal makes its terms more favorable to the Government. Of course, if it is the only proposal received, then even a late proposal may be considered.

Proposals may be withdrawn by written notice at any time before award. Oral proposals in response to oral solicitations may be withdrawn orally.

Prescribed forms are not required for RFPs, but generally are the SF30, SF33 and OF-17.

Solicitation Provisions

FAR 52.215-1, Instructions to Offerors – Competitive Acquisition, where the Government intends to award a contract without discussions. Use the provision with its Alternate I if the Government intends to make award after discussions with offerors within the competitive range. Use the provision with its Alternate II if the Government would be willing to accept alternate proposals.

FAR 52.215-3, Request for Information or Solicitation for Planning Purposes.

FAR 52.215-5, Facsimile Proposals.

FAR 52.215-6, Place of Performance, unless the place of performance is specified by the Government.

Solicitation Provisions and Contract Clauses

FAR 52.215-2, Audit and Records-Negotiation, unless below the simplified acquisition threshold, utility services at rates not exceeding those applied uniformly to the general public (plus any applicable reasonable connection charge), or commercial items where cost or pricing data submission is exempted. Use the provision with its Alternate I when using funds appropriated or made available by the Recovery Act. Use the clause with its Alternate II for cost-reimbursement contracts with state and local governments, educational institutions, and other nonprofit organizations. Use the clause with its Alternate III when the head of the agency has waived the examination of records by the Comptroller General.

FAR 52.215-8, Order of Precedence – Uniform Contract Format.

3.8.4 Unsolicited Proposal

FAR 15.6

An *unsolicited proposal* occurs when the business concern submits a proposal on its own initiative rather than in response to a solicitation. Knowledge of an unannounced need may result from work on another contract, broad agency announcement or knowledge of a contractor employee. An unsolicited proposal must be innovative and unique, individually developed without Government assistance or endorsement, and demonstrate benefit to the agency (especially in research or development). It cannot be merely an advance proposal for a future known requirement. The proposal must be detailed enough to permit a determination that Government support could benefit the agency's research and development or other mission responsibilities. Ideally, it leads to sole-source negotiation.

The Government encourages the submission of new and innovative ideas in response to Broad Agency Announcements, Small Business Innovation Research, and Small Business Technology Transfer Research, Program Research and Development Announcements. On the other hand, unsolicited proposals often represent a substantial investment of time and effort by the offeror to provide unique and innovative ideas or approaches to the Government with the intent to enter into contract.

Agencies must furnish firms which are considering unsolicited proposals with the following information:

- agency points of contact for information;
- definition and content necessary for formal evaluation;
- information sources on agency objectives and areas of potential interest;
- instructions to identify and mark proprietary information;
- procedures to submit and evaluate unsolicited proposals; and
- requirements concerning responsibility and organizational conflicts of interest.

Unsolicited proposals should contain the following information:

- concise title and abstract (approximately 200 words) of the proposed effort;
- date of submission;

- description of the organization, previous experience, relevant past performance, and facilities to be used;
- desired Government property or personnel;
- identification of proprietary data to be used only for evaluation purposes;
- names and biographical information on the proposed key personnel;
- names and telephone numbers of technical and business personnel for
  evaluation or negotiation;
- names of other Federal, State or local agencies receiving or funding the
  proposed effort;
- objectives, method of approach, duration, anticipated results, contract type,
  and how it helps accomplish the agency mission;
- offeror's name and address and type of organization (e.g., profit, nonprofit,
  educational, small business, etc.);
- organizational conflicts of interest, security clearances and environmental
  impacts;
- period of time for proposal validity;
- proposed price or total estimated cost; and
- signature of a person authorized to represent and contractually obligate the
  offeror.

Before initiating a comprehensive evaluation, the agency contact point shall
determine if the proposal:

- complies with marking requirements;
- contains sufficient technical information and cost or price information for
  evaluation;
- has been approved by a responsible official to obligate the offeror
  contractually;
- has overall scientific, technical or socioeconomic merit related to the
  agency mission; and
- is a valid unsolicited proposal suitable to an existing agency requirement.

Evaluators consider the following proposal elements:

- capabilities, experience and qualifications of the proposed principal investigator, team leader or key personnel;
- cost realism;
- offeror's capabilities, experience, facilities, and techniques to achieve the
  objectives;
- overall scientific, socioeconomic and technical merits;
- potential contribution to the agency's specific mission; and
- unique, innovative and meritorious methods, approaches, or concepts.

The evaluators notify the agency point of contact of their recommendations upon completion of evaluation. The agency point of contact returns an unsolicited proposal to the offeror with reasons if it:

- covers an approach available to the Government from another source;
- does not demonstrate an innovative and unique approach, concept or method;
- does not relate to the activity's mission;
- is not deemed a meritorious proposal; or
- resembles a pending competitive acquisition requirement.

The contracting officer may begin negotiations on a sole-source basis only after an unsolicited proposal has received a favorable comprehensive evaluation, a J&A has been signed, funding has been provided, and the requirement has been synopsized.

Government personnel may not use any data or unsolicited proposal as the basis to solicit or negotiate with any other firm unless the offeror is notified of and agrees to the intended use. No information bearing restrictive markings may be disclosed, including a Use and Disclosure of Data restriction printed on the title page and referred to in a header or footer of affected pages.

3.9 SIMPLIFIED ACQUISITION PROCEDURES

FAR Part 13

3.9.1 Theory

Simplified acquisition procedures reduce administrative costs, increase socio-economic contracting opportunities, and create a more efficient and economic contracting process. They are used for purchases above the micro-purchase threshold of $3,500 ($20,000 for contingency or emergency operations domestically and $30,000 overseas) up to $150,000 ($300,000 for the same exceptions). The threshold for contingency operations contracts awarded and performed outside the United States has been raised to $1 million. The agency head must approve any such increases above the basic threshold.

All simplified acquisitions are reserved for small businesses. There may be further set-asides for HUBZone or service-disabled veteran-owned small business concerns within the contracting officer's discretion, without further review by the procurement center representative.

The contracting officer should not split a requirement greater than the simplified acquisition or micro-purchase threshold into several purchases below the applicable threshold merely to avoid using regular contracting procedures.

On the other hand, contracting officers are encouraged to combine requirements to promote quantity discounts and economic order quantities, award
orders on an "all-or-none" basis instead of split awards, and use bulk funding
by obligating funds from a lump sum rather than pursue individual appropriations for each order.

An agency that has specific statutory authority to acquire personal services
may use simplified acquisition procedures to do so. Also, certain conditions
are lifted for commercial buys up to $7 million ($13 million in support of
contingency operations or defense against attack). Agencies use the Government-wide commercial purchase card and electronic purchasing techniques
to the maximum extent practicable in conducting simplified acquisitions.
Drawings and lengthy specifications can be provided off-line in hard copy.

If the contracting officer has determined through market research that
only commercial items will be offered in response to a solicitation, simplified procedures may be used if the acquisition does not exceed $6.5 million.
This threshold rises to $12 million for defense or recovery from a biological,
chemical, nuclear, or radiological attack.

An agency may issue a Request for Quotation using SF18; however, a
quotation is not an offer. It is instead a statement of price, either oral or written, issued by a seller at the request of the buyer. It may describe the product
or service, delivery, payment, period of performance, and/or terms of sale. It
cannot be accepted by the Government to form a binding contract, but may be
used as the basis for an ensuing contract or for obtaining market information.

The following clauses do not apply to (sub)contracts at or below the simplified acquisition threshold:

- FAR 52.203-5, Covenant Against Contingent Fees;
- FAR 52.203-6, Restrictions on Subcontractor Sales to the Government;
- FAR 52.203-7, Anti-Kickback Procedures;
- FAR 52.215-2, Audits and Records – Negotiation, except it can be used
  with its Alternate I if funds are appropriated or available by the Recovery
  Act;
- FAR 52.222-4, Contract Work Hours and Safety Standards Act – Overtime
  Compensation;
- FAR 52.223-6, Drug-Free Workplace, except for contracts with individu-
  als; and
- FAR 52.223-9, Estimate of Percentage of Recovered Material Content for
  EPA-Designated Items.

3.9.2 Procedures

FAR 13.1

Contracting officers use the System for Award Management database to find vendor information. Offices that maintain additional vendor source files or listings should identify the status of each source in the following categories:

- HUBZone small business;
- service-disabled veteran-owned small business;
- small business only;
- small disadvantaged business;
- veteran-owned small business; and
- women-owned small business.

A combined synopsis and solicitation may be used for commercial items or supplies or services. A current price list that reflects proper discounts may be used in lieu of obtaining a new quote.

The contracting officer does not solicit quotations based on personal preference, nor restrict solicitation to suppliers of well-known and widely distributed makes or brands. (S)he considers solicitation of at least three sources to promote competition to the maximum extent practicable, and tries to request quotations or offers from two sources that were not included in the previous solicitation (the third source may be the previous successful offeror). Very often, these are firms within the local trade area.

In soliciting competition, the contracting officer considers whether the requirement is highly competitive and readily available, dollar value, urgency, and past experience concerning specific dealers' prices. The contracting officer notifies potential offerors of the basis on which award will be made (price alone or price and other factors). Contracting officers may solicit from one source only after signing a J&A that only one source is available.

If obtaining electronic or oral quotations is uneconomical or impracticable, the contracting officer issues paper solicitations for contract actions likely to exceed $25,000 (or construction requirements exceeding $2,000).

The contracting officer has broad discretion in establishing evaluation procedures. Such a solicitation does not require formal evaluation plans, competitive range, discussions, or scoring. Past performance evaluation may be based on contracting officer knowledge and prior experience with the supply or service being acquired, customer surveys, past performance questionnaire replies, and the Government-wide Federal Awardee Performance and Integrity Information System (FAPIIS) at www.ppirs.gov.[17] This system also includes information regarding defective cost or pricing data and terminations for default.

Before making award, the contracting officer must determine that the proposed price is fair and reasonable. Whenever possible, competition should be the basis for reasonableness. If only one response is received, the contracting officer must include a statement of price reasonableness in the contract file that is based on:

- comparison with prices found reasonable on previous purchases;
- comparison with similar items in a related industry;
- current price lists or catalogs;
- independent Government estimate;
- market research; and
- personal knowledge of the item being purchased.

If award is based on nonprice factors, an explanation must be included.

Notification to unsuccessful suppliers is given only if requested, subcontracting opportunities are present, or the procurement is subject to the World Trade Organization Government Procurement Agreement or a Free Trade Agreement.

3.9.3 Actions at or Below the Micro-Purchase Threshold

FAR 13.2

The Government-wide commercial purchase card is the preferred method to purchase and to pay for micro-purchases. These purchases do not require provisions or clauses. The supplier must be listed in the System for Award Management, and be able to accept electronic funds transfer for payment. The threshold limit for contingency operations or in defense or recovery from attack is $20,000 for domestic award or performance and $30,000 for international award or performance.

To the extent practicable, micro-purchases are distributed equitably among qualified suppliers. Micro-purchases may be awarded without soliciting competitive quotations if the price is reasonable. Action to verify price reasonableness need only be taken if the contracting officer believes that the price may not be reasonable (e.g., comparison to the previous price paid or personal knowledge of the supply or service), or no comparable pricing information is readily available.

An unusual problem occurs with supplier license agreements or terms of service, especially for computer software and web-delivered services, since they often have indemnification clauses that are inconsistent and unenforceable under Federal law and could therefore violate the Anti-Deficiency Act. The following clause is prescribed to avoid this problem.

Contract Clause

FAR 52.232-39, Unenforceability of Unauthorized Obligations.

3.9.4 Purchase Orders

FAR 13.3

The Government sends the supplier an offer in the form of a purchase order to buy certain supplies or services upon specified terms and conditions. A contract is established only when the supplier accepts the offer. The contracting officer may ask the supplier to indicate acceptance of an order by written notification to the Government. Otherwise, the supplier indicates acceptance of the order by furnishing the supplies or services ordered, or else proceeding with the work until it has complied with all major aspects of contract performance requirements. This differs from the norm where the contractor signs the document before the Government does. In this case, the contracting officer signs the delivery order without contractor signature. In effect, the purchase order is not a contract because the supplier did not sign it, but instead manifests agreement by performance.

Purchase orders are usually firm-fixed-price written instruments. They specify the quantity of supplies or scope of services ordered, contain a definite delivery date or period of performance, and include any offered trade and prompt payment discounts. Generally, inspection and acceptance should be at destination. Shipping costs are typically included for supplies delivered within the continental United States. Facsimile and electronic signatures are both allowed, and electronic funds transfer is required.

An unpriced purchase order is used when the price is not established at the time of the order. This is fairly common for equipment repairs requiring disassembly to determine the nature and extent of repairs, or items for which exact prices are not known (e.g., repair parts). A monetary limitation is placed on each unpriced purchase order (either in total or by line item), which is adjusted when a firm price is established. The contracting officer reviews the invoice price for reasonableness and processes it for payment.

The Government may (by written notice to the supplier, at any time before acceptance) withdraw, amend or cancel its offer.

Contract Clauses

FAR 52.213-2, Invoices, to authorize advance payments for subscriptions for newspapers, magazines, periodicals, or publications.

FAR 52.213-3, Notice to Supplier, in unpriced purchase orders.

FAR 52.213-4, Terms and Conditions – Simplified Acquisitions (Other Than Commercial Items), if exceeding the micro-purchase threshold for non-commercial items.

FAR 52.225-3, Buy American Act—Free Trade Agreements—Israeli Trade Act, with Alternate I or Alternate II, if appropriate, for supplies to be used within the United States that cannot be set aside for small business concerns and trade agreements apply. Do not use FAR 52.225-1, Buy American Act—Supplies, whenever acquiring supplies for use outside the United States.

3.9.5 Blanket Purchase Agreements

FAR 8.405-3

If the supplies or services are repetitive in need, the ordering activity may decide to establish an unpriced blanket purchase agreement with each supplier. *Blanket Purchase Agreements* (BPAs) are designed to fill repetitive needs with one or more contractors. BPAs are useful when the quantities and delivery requirements are not known in advance and may vary considerably, and for offices that do not have the authority to purchase. The BPA process avoids the need to write numerous purchase orders.

The number of BPAs to establish is a function of administrative costs within the purchasing office, contractor technical qualifications, requirement scope and complexity, and need for technical or price completion. BPAs set forth terms for:

- authorized ordering agencies;
- delivery locations and times;
- discounts;
- estimated quantities;
- invoicing instructions;
- ordering frequency and procedures; and
- type of work.

If the ordering activity has only one BPA, authorized users may place orders directly under it to fill requirements. If the ordering activity awards multiple BPAs, however, any order exceeding the micro-purchase threshold requires solicitation among multiple BPA holders for competitive quotes and a best-value determination before award.

BPAs generally run a maximum of five years, but may go longer to meet program requirements. However, the ordering activity reviews the BPA annually to verify that the schedule contract is still in effect and represents best value, that estimated amounts have not been exceeded, and whether additional price reductions can be obtained. The office should pursue price reductions when the supply or service is available elsewhere at a lower price, or if the potential volume of orders (regardless of the size of individual orders) could lead to greater discounts. Any price reductions obtained on a single order are not binding on either the contractor or customer for future orders.

Although BPAs may fall outside the socioeconomic preference programs, orders placed against schedule contracts may be credited toward the ordering activity's small business goals. Small business set-asides are encouraged. Ordering activities rely on the small business representations made by schedule contractors. Hence, socioeconomic status may be a factor when selecting a source for award of an order or BPA, especially for orders exceeding the micro-purchase threshold when two or more items at the same delivered price will satisfy the requirement. Nonetheless, an ordering activity must still justify its action when considering only one source for any acquisition above the micro-purchase level.

For brand-name purchases between $25,000 and $100,000, the contracting officer will post to e-Buy the RFQ and the reason(s) for restricting competition. For actions over $100,000, the J&A information is also posted. As with delivery orders, posting is not necessary in case of national security or file size or format, or if the agency's senior procurement executive determines that access through e-Buy is not in the Government's interest.

The ordering activity contracting officer refers any disputes regarding contract terms and conditions to the schedule contracting officer for resolution under the Disputes clause, and so notifies the schedule contractor. Ordering activities also evaluate contractor performance for each order that exceeds the simplified acquisition threshold.

An ordering activity contracting officer may terminate individual orders for cause, and so notify the schedule contracting office. Only the schedule contracting officer may terminate a BPA for cause, in which case no further orders may be placed for those items. Nonetheless, orders placed prior to termination must still be fulfilled by the contractor.

FAR 13.303

Contracting officers establish any necessary parameters to limit purchases to individual items or commodity groups or classes. They also consider suppliers of proven past performance with consistently lower prices, especially at or below the simplified acquisition threshold. Additional benefits of BPAs include maximum discounts and consolidated billings. BPAs require the following:

- the vendor must furnish supplies or services when requested during a specified period and within any stipulated aggregate amount;

- the Government is obligated only to the extent of authorized purchases made under the BPA;
- the dollar limitation for each individual purchase under the BPA;
- a list of individuals authorized to purchase under the BPA, identified either by title of position or by name of individual, organizational component, and the dollar limitation per purchase for each; and
- all shipments under the agreement (except periodicals such as newspapers or magazines) must be accompanied by delivery tickets or sales slips.

Purchases generally are made electronically or orally. Individual purchases cannot exceed the simplified acquisition threshold unless for commercial items. A paper purchase document may be issued only to ensure that the supplier and purchaser agree on the transaction. An informal memorandum records the date, supplier, supplies or services, price, delivery date, and accounting data on the purchase requisition. Upon delivery or performance, the supplier's sales or delivery document or invoice may record receipt and acceptance of the supplies or services.

The contractor must submit either a summary or itemized invoice monthly for all deliveries made during a billing period by listing the delivery tickets, total dollar value, and receipt copies of the tickets. Alternatively, an itemized invoice can be submitted monthly for all deliveries during a billing period for which payment has not been received (copies of delivery tickets are not required). All individual invoices for a delivery may be accumulated if a single payment is made for each specified period. The discount period begins on either the last date of the billing period or receipt of invoices for accepted deliveries, whichever occurs later. For subscriptions or other periodicals, an invoice can show the starting and ending dates and state that ordered subscriptions are in effect, or will be upon receipt of payment.

If the fast payment procedure is used, supplies must be shipped prepaid, and invoices must be submitted directly to the finance office designated in the order (or in the case of unpriced purchase orders, to the contracting officer).

The ordering officer reviews a random sample of the BPA files at least annually to ensure that authorized procedures are being followed. This review includes updating the BPA and maintaining awareness of changes in market conditions and sources of supply. The results of this review may warrant making new arrangements with different suppliers or modifying existing arrangements.

An individual BPA is considered complete when the purchases under it equal any total dollar limitation or when its stated time period expires.

Contract Clause

FAR <u>52.213-4</u>, Terms and Conditions – Simplified Acquisitions (Other Than Commercial Items).

3.9.6 Imprest Funds and Third Party Drafts

FAR 13.305

An *imprest fund* is a fixed amount of cash without appropriation, but rather advanced from a financial or disbursing officer to a duly appointed cashier. They are used to pay cash for relatively small dollar amounts for incidental items. Each agency using imprest funds and third-party drafts periodically reviews accounts to determine whether there is a continuing need for each fund or draft account. They also designate personnel to make purchases using imprest funds or third-party drafts, accept supplies and services for the Government, receive cash or third-party draft payments by suppliers, and make cash advances and reimbursements. Agency regulations may require that these personnel be bonded, since they do disburse cash with limited oversight.

Imprest funds may be used for purchases up to $500, and third-party drafts up to $2,500, or as set by agency or Treasury restrictions. Each purchase using these simple methods is based upon an authorized purchase requisition or contracting officer funds verification statement. These purchases are placed orally and without soliciting competition if prices are considered reasonable. No clauses are involved because ordering and delivery are simultaneous.

3.9.7 Forms

* SF 1449, Solicitation/Contract/Order for Commercial Items;
* SF 18, Request for Quotations;
* OF 336, Continuation Sheet, when additional space is needed;
* OF 348, Order for Supplies or Services Schedule – Continuation, when additional space is needed for clauses;
* SF 30, Amendment of Solicitation/Modification of Contract;
* SF 44, Purchase Order – Invoice – Voucher, for on-the-spot or over-the-counter purchases of supplies and services while away from the purchasing office or at isolated activities. It also can be used as a receiving report, invoice and public voucher; and
* SF 1165, Receipt for Cash – Subvoucher, for purchases using imprest funds or third-party drafts.

3.9.8 Fast Payment Procedure

FAR 13.4

The fast payment procedure allows payment under limited conditions before verification that supplies have been received and accepted. This procedure provides for payment based on the contractor's invoice that certifies delivery to a common carrier, post office or point of first receipt by the Government (with transportation prepaid). The invoice also certifies that the contractor shall replace or repair supplies not received at destination, damaged in transit or not conforming to the agreement, with the contracting officer determining any debt due from the contractor. The conditions for use are as follows:

- documentation exists of contractor prior performance under fast payment purchases;
- Government receiving and disbursing activities are apart from each other and lack communications to make timely payment;
- individual actions do not exceed $30,000, unless increased by agency regulations;
- invoices are submitted directly to the finance or other office designated in the order, or, in the case of unpriced purchase orders, to the contracting officer;
- supplies are shipped transportation or postage prepaid;
- the consignee notifies the purchasing office within 60 days after the date of delivery of supplies not received, damaged in transit or not conforming to specifications;
- the purchase instrument is a firm-fixed-price contract, purchase order or delivery order; and
- timely feedback of any deficiency is provided to the contracting officer.

Solicitation Provision and Contract Clause

FAR 52.213-1, Fast Payment Procedure.

FAR 52.253-1, Computer Generated Forms, when the contractor must submit data on Standard or Optional Forms prescribed by FAR and agency supplements.

3.10 RESPONSIBLE OFFERORS

3.10.1 Responsibility

FAR 9.104

The contracting officer must determine responsibility for any contractor other than another government entity, source furnished through NIB or SourceAmerica, or firm covered by an SBA Certificate of Competency. To be determined responsible, an offeror must have:

- a satisfactory record of performance and of integrity and business ethics;
- ability to comply with the delivery or performance schedule, considering current customer commitments;
- adequate financial resources to perform the contract, or the ability to obtain them;
- compliance with all applicable laws and regulations; and
- the ability to obtain the necessary equipment and facilities, experience, organization, technical skills, and controls (accounting, operations, production, property, quality assurance, and safety).

A prospective contractor seriously deficient in past or present contract performance is presumed to be nonresponsible, unless the contracting officer determines that the circumstances were beyond the contractor's control, or that the contractor has taken appropriate corrective action. Past failure to apply tenacity and perseverance to perform acceptably or meet quality requirements is strong evidence of nonresponsibility. Compliance with subcontracting plans under recent contracts is also considered.

A prospective contractor may be required to provide written evidence of a proposed subcontractor's responsibility. The contracting officer may directly determine a prospective subcontractor's responsibility by using the same standards as for a prime contractor's responsibility.

The contracting officer notifies the agency official responsible for initiating debarment or suspension action if an offeror indicates the existence of a charge, indictment, conviction, civil judgment, or Federal tax delinquency, or has been convicted within the past 24 months of a Federal felony. Each offeror must so affirm in its representations.

Lack of relevant performance history is not a basis for nonresponsibility. In making the determination of responsibility, the contracting officer considers a variety of information, including:

- business and trade associations;
- commercial sources of supplier information;

- financial institutions;
- FAPIIS (www.ppirs.gov), a warehouse of performance and integrity information on government contractors;[18]
- other Government agencies;
- pre-award survey reports from the offeror's cognizant contract administration office;
- proposal certifications and financial data;
- records within the contracting office, audit offices, contract administration offices, and other contracting offices;
- suppliers and customers of the prospective contractor; and
- the Excluded Parties List System.

A pre-award survey is normally required only when available information is not sufficient to make a determination regarding responsibility. It is usually performed by the contract administration office which is cognizant of the offeror's geographic area. When a pre-award survey discloses previous unsatisfactory performance, the surveying activity specifies the extent to which the prospective contractor plans or has taken corrective action. The report addresses any persistent pattern of need for costly and burdensome Government assistance (e.g., technical, testing or excessive inspection assistance).

Recall that if a small business concern is to be rejected because of a determination of nonresponsibility, the contracting officer refers the matter to the SBA, which will decide whether or not to issue a Certificate of Competency.

FAR 9-106

The contracting officer's signing of a contract constitutes a determination that the prospective contractor is responsible with respect to that contract. If the offeror is found to be nonresponsible, the contracting officer signs and places in both the contract file and FAPIIS a determination of nonresponsibility.

Solicitation Provisions

FAR 52.209-5, Certification Regarding Responsibility, where the estimated value exceeds the micro-purchase threshold.

FAR 52.209-7, Information Regarding Responsibility Matters, where the estimated value exceeds $500,000.

FAR 52.209-9, Updates of Publicly Available Information Regarding Responsibility Matters, when award is anticipated to exceed $500,000 and the offeror has active Federal contracts and grants totaling at least $10,000,000.

FAR 52.209-11, Representation by Corporations Regarding Delinquent Tax Liability or a Felony Conviction under any Federal Law.

FAR 52.209-12, Certification Regarding Tax Matters, in all solicitations over $5 million in estimated value by the specific departments and agencies listed in FAR 9.104-7(e).

FAR 52.222-57, Representation Regarding Compliance with Labor Laws, for acquisitions expected to exceed $500,000 (and discretionary for smaller-value solicitations).

Contract Clause

FAR 52.222-59, Compliance with Labor Laws, for acquisitions expected to exceed $500,000 (and discretionary for smaller-value contracts).

3.10.2 Teams and Pools

FAR 9.6 and 9.7

Partnering is a technique used by contractors who cannot provide all deliverables in-house, and need one or more firms to join them to develop a top-notch team. It entails a voluntary cooperative agreement to work together and share the resources, responsibilities, risks, and rewards of performance. Successful partnering creates a synergistic arrangement where each party can leverage off its own strengths to succeed beyond its own capabilities, often for cost reduction and greater competitiveness.

A *team arrangement* involves at least two firms who form a partnership to act as a single entity (either prime or subcontractor) to perform a contract. Often used in complex research and development projects, such an arrangement is established before the offer is made. A teaming arrangement can be mutually exclusive, where the parties pledge neither to seek other sources for the work kept in-house nor to remove resources to work on other projects. They can be of either a repetitive or one-time-only nature. Prospective team members must consider several factors about each other before entering an agreement:

- bonding capability and track record;
- compensating strengths in terms of:
  - past performance with the same customer,
  - personnel resources,
  - possession of required equipment,
  - proximity to the project site,
  - technical knowledge, and

- ∘ unique capabilities;
- cultural fit and values;
- customer satisfaction;
- Dun & Bradstreet rating;
- ethics compliance;
- financial resources;
- OSHA safety record; and
- willingness to take risks.

A *joint venture* is an association of persons or concerns engaged in a specific business venture for joint profit, but not on a continuing or permanent basis. They combine their efforts, money, property, and skills or knowledge. It is considered a business entity with the power of management.

A *pool* is a group of firms that agree to perform together by formally chartering their organization and procedures. Formal approval must be obtained from the small and disadvantaged business utilization specialist or other designated official. The pool submits an offer in its own name with written concurrence of all pool members. The contracting officer verifies pool status with the SBA and obtains from each pool member a certified power of attorney of signature status, which is physically attached to the signed copy of the contract. Any pool member is free to submit an independent offer on any solicitation on which the pool is not offering, but any such proposal is rejected if submitted for the same requirement where the pool is offering.

A *memorandum of agreement* (MOA) or *cooperative agreement* is a written agreement between parties to cooperatively work together on a project or meet an objective. An MOA can be used between agencies, or between agencies on different government levels. An MOA can set forth the cooperative procedures, terms and responsibilities of the partner entities, sometimes with an obligation of funds.

3.10.3 Prohibition on Contracting With Inverted Domestic Corporations

An *inverted domestic corporation* was incorporated in the United States or in a partnership in the United States at one time, but now is either incorporated in a foreign country or is a subsidiary whose parent corporation is incorporated in a foreign country (usually to obtain more favorable tax treatment). A foreign corporation is treated as an inverted domestic corporation rather than as a foreign corporation if at least 80% of the stock is now held by former shareholders or partners of the domestic entity, and the foreign entity does not have substantial business activities in the foreign country. Contracting with such a corporation is prohibited. Any agency head may waive the requirement for a specific contract by determining in writing that the waiver is required in the interest of national security, documents the determination, and reports it to the Congress.

Solicitation Provision

FAR 52.209-2, Prohibition on Contracting with Inverted Domestic Corporations—Representation.

FAR 52.209-10, Prohibition on Contracting with Inverted Domestic Corporations.

3.10.4 Qualifications Requirements

FAR 9.2

Occasionally, production items may need to be formally qualified as a requirement for award. Before establishing a pre-award qualification requirement, the agency head or designee justifies in writing the need and reason to establish the qualification requirement, estimates testing costs to be incurred by the potential offeror to become qualified, and specifies all requirements that a potential offeror (or its product) must satisfy in order to become qualified. Potential offerors are provided upon request all requirements to satisfy the qualification and a prompt opportunity to demonstrate their abilities to meet these standards. A potential offeror seeking qualification is promptly informed of qualification results and reasons for any failure. If successful, the offeror is placed on a Qualified Bidders List (QBL), Qualified Manufacturers List (QML) or Qualified Products List (QPL), and cannot be denied the opportunity to submit and have considered an offer for a contract. The qualification decision and its requirements are not subject to a certificate of competency. Nor is the qualification process an opportunity to delay an award merely because a potential offeror wishes to be qualified for the instant procurement. Qualification requirements are reviewable every seven years.

If a qualification requirement applies, the contracting officer need consider only those offers identified as meeting the requirement or included on the applicable QBL, QML or QPL, unless an offeror can satisfactorily demonstrate to the contracting officer that the product to be produced either by itself or its subcontractor can meet the standards established for qualification before the date specified for award.

A QPL specifies the manufacturers and products that have passed qualification tests. It saves time, provides a quick reference list, eliminates the need to qualify for new procurement, is tightly controlled, and gives a high degree of confidence that the product will meet requirements. Testing can be a lengthy process, however, could lead to protests due to limiting competition, takes time to maintain, and has high laboratory costs.

The contracting officer promptly report to the agency activity which established the qualification requirement any conditions which may merit removal or omission from a qualified list, such as:

- a condition of meeting the qualification requirement was violated;
- a firm has discontinued its manufacture of a qualified product;
- a revised specification imposes a new qualification requirement;
- a source requests removal from a QBL, QML or QPL;
- a supplier fails to request reevaluation after moving or changing ownership of the plant where the product was manufactured;
- defects of rejected products or services were not corrected;
- manufacturing or design changes are made to the qualification requirement;
- performance subject to a qualification requirement is unsatisfactory;
- products or services submitted for inspection or acceptance do not meet the qualification requirement; or
- the source is on the Excluded Parties List System.

Solicitation Provision and Contract Clause

FAR 52.209-1, Qualification Requirements.

3.10.5 First Article Testing and Approval

FAR 9.3

First article testing and approval ensures that the contractor can furnish a product that conforms to all contract requirements for acceptance. This idea entails preproduction models, test and initial production samples, and first lots. First article testing is appropriate when the contractor has not previously furnished the product to the Government, specifications or manufacturing processes have changed, production has been discontinued for a long time, or the product performed below expectation. First article testing is also appropriate if a manufacturing standard must be established. It is not appropriate for research or development, product qualification, commercial items, or validating technical specifications. Before imposing such a requirement, the contracting officer considers the impact on cost or time of delivery, risk of foregoing such a test, and availability of less costly methods to ensure desired quality before requiring such a test. The solicitation provides performance characteristics, technical requirements and deliverable data.

When the Government is responsible for the first article approval testing, the solicitation includes performance characteristics and tests necessary to obtain approval. An offeror may submit alternate offers with one unapproved item and one approved product. The delivery schedule can provide for earlier delivery when testing and approval is waived and the Government desires earlier delivery (though this cannot be an evaluation factor). However, the Government's estimated testing costs will be a factor for use in evaluating offers. The contracting officer must ensure that prices for first articles and tests in relation to production quantities are not materially unbalanced when separately priced.

Solicitation Provisions and Contract Clauses:

FAR 52.209-3, First Article Approval – Contractor Testing, when the contractor will be required to conduct the first article testing.

FAR 52.209-4, First Article Approval – Government Testing, when first article approval under Government test is required.

For either First Article Approval clause, use the clause with its Alternate I if the contractor is required to produce the first article and the production quantity at the same facility. Use the clause with its Alternate II to authorize the contractor to purchase material or commence production before first article approval.

3.10.6 Excluded Parties List System

GSA operates the web-based Excluded Parties List System of names and addresses of all contractors debarred, suspended, proposed for debarment, or ineligible, with cross-references when more than one name is involved in an action. They could also be ineligible through the *Nonprocurement Common Rule*, the procedures used by executive agencies to suspend, debar or exclude individuals or firms from participation in nonprocurement transactions under Executive Order 12549, Debarment and Suspension, of February 18, 1986. Examples of nonprocurement transactions are:

- contracts of assistance;
- cooperative agreements;
- donation agreements;
- fellowships;
- grants;
- insurance;
- loan guarantees;

- loans;
- payments for specified use;
- scholarships; and
- subsidies.

Any debarment, suspension or other Government-wide exclusion of an offeror applies to all Federal executive agencies. Contractors debarred, suspended or proposed for debarment may not receive contracts, represent other contractors, act as a surety, or be solicited unless the agency head determines that there is a compelling reason for such action. Otherwise, any offers from such firms are not considered. Immediately prior to award, the contracting officer again reviews the List to ensure that no award is made to a listed contractor. Agencies may continue (sub)contracts in existence at the time the contractor was debarred, suspended or proposed for debarment unless the agency head directs otherwise. Contractors may not enter into any subcontract in excess of $30,000 with a firm that has been debarred, suspended or proposed for debarment unless there is a compelling reason to do so.

3.10.7 Debarment

FAR 9.4

Debarred firms are listed in the System for Award Management (SAM) managed by GSA and available at https://www.acquisition.gov. Once a firm is debarred or proposed for same, it can no longer receive solicitation or awards, nor can it act as a surety. Subcontracts can only be awarded for standard commercial items or for awards below $35,000 in value. This is why the contracting officer must check SAM before award. However, ongoing contracts continue to completion unless the agency head determines otherwise. Agencies establish their own debarment procedures. Before arriving at any debarment decision, the debarring official designated by the agency head considers if the contractor:

- brought the activity to the attention of the Government agency in a timely manner;
- cooperated fully with Government agencies during the investigation and any court or administrative action;
- fully investigated the circumstances and provided the results to the debarring official;
- had enough time to eliminate the circumstances within its organization;
- had effective standards of conduct and internal control systems in place at the time of the activity under investigation;

- implemented or agreed to implement remedial measures and revised review and control procedures and ethics training;
- paid or agreed to pay all criminal, civil, and administrative liability for the improper activity, including any investigative or administrative costs incurred by the Government, and has made or agreed to make full restitution;
- recognizes and understands the seriousness of the misconduct; and
- took appropriate disciplinary action against the individuals responsible for the activity.

If a cause for debarment exists, the contractor has the burden of demonstrating, to the satisfaction of the debarring official, its present responsibility and that debarment is not necessary. Debarment applies to all divisions or other organizational elements of the contractor, unless limited by its terms to specific divisions, organizational elements, or commodities.

The debarring official may debar a contractor for:

- a knowingly false statement of a material element of a certification concerning the foreign content of an item of supply;
- commission of an offense indicating a lack of business integrity or honesty, such as an unfair trade practice;
- conviction of or civil judgment for committing fraud, or a criminal offense;[19]
- delinquent Federal taxes exceeding $3,500;
- failure by a principal, until three years after final payment, to timely disclose to the Government evidence of bribery, conflict of interest, fraud, or gratuity; False Claims Act violations; or significant contract overpayments (other than from contract financing payments);
- failure to comply with the requirements of FAR 52.223-6, Drug-Free Workplace;[20]
- intentionally affixing a label bearing a "Made in America" inscription to a product sold in or shipped to (but not made in) the United States or its outlying areas;
- noncompliance with Immigration and Nationality Act employment provisions based on a determination by the Secretary of Homeland Security or the Attorney General of the United States;[21]
- violation of any agreement of the Coordination Committee under the Export Administration Act of 1979 (50 U.S.C. App. 2401, et seq.) or any similar bilateral or multilateral export control agreement;
- violation of Federal or State antitrust statutes relating to the submission of offers;

- violation of Section 337 of the Tariff Act of 1930 (19 U.S.C.1337) as determined by the International Trade Commission; or
- willful failure to perform in accordance with the terms of one or more contracts.

Debarment is for a period commensurate with the seriousness of the cause(s), normally not to exceed three years. However, there are many exceptions to this rule. Debarment lasts five years for conviction of violating the Drug-Free Workplace Act of 1988 and one year where no conviction is involved. The debarring official may extend the debarment for an additional period if necessary to protect the Government's interest. Alternatively, the debarring official may reduce the period or extent of debarment upon contractor request for reasons such as:

- bona fide change in ownership or management;
- elimination of causes for which the debarment was imposed;
- newly discovered material evidence; or
- reversal of the conviction or civil judgment.

The criminal, fraudulent or improper conduct of any director, employee, officer, partner, or shareholder associated with a contractor may be imputed to the contractor when the conduct occurred in connection with the individual's performance of duties for or on behalf of the contractor, or with the contractor's approval or knowledge. Contractor acceptance of the benefits derived from this conduct is evidence of such approval or knowledge.

3.10.8 Suspension

FAR 9.407

An alternative form of discipline is suspension, which can be imposed more immediately than debarment. As a general rule, suspension is imposed if a contractor is indicted for a crime, and debarment occurs if a conviction ensues. Suspension is imposed on the basis of adequate evidence, pending investigation or legal proceedings (including appeals) when necessary to protect the Government's interest against many of the grounds for debarment. Agencies consider the amount of available information, its credibility, corroboration of allegations, and drawn inferences. The suspending official (the agency head or designee) may consider remedial measures or mitigating factors. A contractor has the burden of promptly presenting evidence of remedial measures or mitigating factors when it has reason to know that a cause for suspension exists.

Suspension covers all divisions or organizational elements of the contractor, unless limited by its own terms. The suspending official may extend the suspension decision to include any affiliates of the contractor if they are given written notice of the suspension and an opportunity to respond. *Affiliates* are business concerns, organizations or individuals where either one controls or has the power to control the other, or a third party controls or has the power to control both. Indications of control include:

- common use of employees;
- identity of interests among family members;
- interlocking management or ownership; or
- shared facilities and equipment.

A business entity organized after the debarment, suspension or proposed debarment of a contractor, which bears the same or similar management, ownership or principal employees is probably an instance of control that would lead to suspension.

Agencies establish procedures governing the decision-making process that are as informal as practicable, while maintaining fairness. Suspension is for a temporary period pending the completion of investigation and any legal proceedings. If legal proceedings are not initiated within 12 months after the date of the suspension notice, the suspension ends automatically unless an Assistant Attorney General requests a six-month extension. A suspension cannot exceed 18 months without legal proceedings underway.

Solicitation Provision and Contract Clause

FAR 52.209-6, Protecting the Government's Interests when Subcontracting with Contractors Debarred, Suspended, or Proposed for Debarment, where the contract value exceeds $35,000, except for COTS items.

3.11 PROPOSAL PREPARATION

3.11.1 Proposal Preparation

Every contractor has its own methodology to develop proposals. In general, however, major proposals follow these steps:

- evaluate the opportunity;
- decide to bid or no-bid;

- develop a capture strategy;
- develop a compliance matrix;
- draft a proposal outline;
- prepare a storyboard outline;
- write and edit proposal;
- review proposal; and
- submit proposal.

Offerors will develop a compliance matrix to list all solicitation requirements, specifications and evaluation criteria. A compliance matrix can cross-reference requirements, reveal inconsistencies in the solicitation, provide organization to the proposal writers, and ensure responsiveness to requirements. They will also use the matrix to assess their competitive strengths and weaknesses, as well as to ensure completeness of their proposal. A storyboard serves to focus the proposal team on the objective of the exercise – a winning proposal. The review is sometimes called "white glove" because it not only reviews the write-up but also adds polish.

3.11.2 Bid or No-Bid Decision

Upon receipt of the solicitation, a firm thoroughly reads it (especially the statement of work or specifications, and special provisions) and decides whether it makes sense to submit an offer by examining the evaluation factors, risk and potential benefits. The bid–no bid decision is critical because it preserves resources for those opportunities with a higher win probability and thereby raises the firm's win-ratio of winning to total proposals. Factors which the firm must consider in this decision include:

- ambiguities;
- availability of resources;
- capability and qualifications to perform;
- competitiveness and probability of winning;
- contract type;
- difficulty of performance;
- importance to firm's business line and market posture;
- incumbency or presence of competitor incumbent contractor;
- need to maintain workforce employment;
- possibility of cost overrun;
- potential for follow-on work;
- potential gains (experience, financial and knowledge);
- prior customer dealings;

- profitability;
- program stability;
- restrictive provisions or specifications; and
- schedule.

As a rule of thumb, a firm would like at least a one-in-three chance of winning to decide to develop an offer. If the firm decides not to offer, it should notify the agency in writing, either by letter or by filling out the cover page of the SF-18, with a brief reason why (such as inability to meet the requirements), and that it wishes to remain on the mailing list to compete for future agency requirements.

3.11.3 Proposal Volumes

The Instructions to Offerors will specify the content structure of the submission, as well as more mundane but still critical directions such as maximum page count. More complicated requirements and evaluations will require more detailed proposals with multiple binders, whereas more routine requirements may require nothing more than a handful of pages stapled together.

The submission often includes:

- binders and covers;
- introduction stating corporate commitment to performance;
- executive summary of the highlights;
- index to cross-reference the proposal to the statement of work;
- page limit consistent with the instructions to offerors;
- table of contents;
- list of exhibits;
- section dividers;
- references; and
- page numbers.

The *technical proposal* is designed to convince the Government that the firm understands what the Government wants and has developed an effective and efficient solution. It often includes a detailed description of the firm's background and approach, related past performance, task breakdown, and biographies of key personnel and consultants.

The *management proposal* (if one is required) explains how the firm will manage the work and organize human and materiel resources to reach a successful conclusion. It should also identify any necessary facilities or equipment to be furnished by the Government. The *cost proposal* is submitted in a separate volume and contains all cost and pricing information requested in the solicitation.

3.12 EVALUATION OF OFFERS

3.12.1 Evaluation Process

The Source Selection Evaluation Board contains a variety of specialists who advise the contracting officer in developing the source selection plan. They evaluate proposals in accordance with the plan. Most boards contain subgroups for evaluation: one for technical aspects of the proposal, one to assess any management aspects of the proposal, and one to analyze proposed cost and price.

Complex procurements may add a Source Selection Advisory Council to review the Board's final report and to assist in comparative analysis of the proposals. This council may include budget, legal, logistics, and security specialists. The contracting officer serves as a business advisor to this council. The final report is then submitted to the Source Selection Authority, who makes the final selection decision.

All reviewers must sign an agreement to not disclose any offeror's technical solutions, prices and past performance references without permission of the contracting officer.

FAR 15.3

The contracting officer is designated as the source selection authority, unless the agency head appoints another individual for a particular acquisition(s). The source selection authority will:

- establish a comprehensive evaluation team;
- approve the source selection strategy or acquisition plan before solicitation release;
- ensure consistency among the contract clauses, data requirements, evaluation (sub)factors, notices to offerors, proposal preparation instructions, and solicitation provisions;
- ensure that proposals are evaluated based solely on the (sub)factors contained in the solicitation;
- consider the recommendations of any advisory boards or panels; and
- select the source(s) proposing the best value to the Government.

After release of a solicitation, the contracting officer serves as the focal point for inquiries from actual or prospective offerors.

The award decision is based on evaluation factors and subfactors that are tailored to the acquisition. Evaluation factors represent the key areas of importance in the source selection decision, and support meaningful comparison and discrimination between and among competing proposals. These factors must reflect the important issues in selecting the best offer and support meaningful discriminators between offers. All factors and significant subfactors and their relative importance are stated in the solicitation, usually in descending order of importance.[22] Common factors include:

- cost (mandatory as a factor);
- management approach;
- past performance;
- personnel qualifications; and
- technical approach.

Proposal evaluation assesses the offeror's ability to perform the prospective contract successfully based solely on the (sub)factors specified in the solicitation. The applicability and sufficiency of the proposed approach is reviewed to determine if it will meet contract requirements. The board's report documents the relative strengths, deficiencies, weaknesses, and risks supporting proposal evaluation.

Evaluations may use any rating method or combination of methods – and there are many of them. Some agencies use adjectives (e.g., Outstanding, Good, Susceptible to Becoming Acceptable, and Unacceptable). Other offices use a similar approach by substituting colors for adjectives (e.g., Blue, Green, Yellow, and Red). Still other offices use numerical weights or ordinal rankings (first, second, third, etc.). A fourth option is to conduct trade-offs between cost and technical factors, although the board must justify why additional technical merit is worth the additional cost (which is subject to frequent protests). Alternatively, the board can select to use technical factors solely to determine an acceptable proposal without trade-offs, then award to the lowest-priced technically acceptable offeror. A sixth approach was previously discussed as performance-based contracting, where the requirements are described in terms of results rather than work processes, using measurable performance standards (and perhaps incentives to motivate contractor performance).

Past performance is evaluated in all source selections for negotiated competitive acquisitions expected to exceed the simplified acquisition threshold, unless the contracting officer documents why it is not an appropriate evaluation factor.[23] The currency and relevance of past performance information are considered. This comparative assessment of past performance information is separate from the responsibility determination. The solicitation describes the approach for evaluating past performance, including for offerors with no relevant performance history, and allows offerors to identify past or current contracts (including Federal, State and local government and the private sector) for efforts similar to the Government requirement. The solicitation authorizes offerors to provide information on problems encountered on the identified contracts and corrective actions.

Prior customers identified in the proposal are contacted to learn about the firm's performance in terms of complexity, contract type, similarities in size and scope, and technology. A negative reference will not downgrade the offeror's evaluation, but will cause it to lose a chance to score points with the evaluators. If a contractor has no past performance record, it receives a neutral rating – neither positive nor negative.

The evaluation may consider past performance information regarding predecessor companies, key personnel who have relevant experience, or subcontractors that will perform major or critical aspects of the requirement. The evaluation includes the past performance of offerors in complying with subcontracting plan goals for small disadvantaged business concerns.

For solicitations involving bundling that offer a significant opportunity for subcontracting, the contracting officer includes a factor in the past per-formance evaluation that assesses the extent to which the offeror attained applicable goals for small business participation. The extent of participation of small disadvantaged business concerns in performance of the contract is normally evaluated in unrestricted acquisitions expected to exceed $550,000 ($1,000,000 for construction).

When trade-offs are performed, the source selection team assesses each offeror's ability to accomplish the technical requirements and summarizes (both quantitatively and in words) each technical proposal using the evalua-tion factors.

When contracting on a firm-fixed-price or fixed-price with economic price adjustment basis, comparison of the proposed prices usually satisfies the requirement to perform a price analysis by examining the price itself without evaluating separate cost elements, and a cost analysis need not be performed. Sometimes a cost analysis may establish reasonableness of the otherwise suc-cessful offeror's price. When contracting on a fixed-price incentive or cost-reimbursement basis, evaluations include a cost realism analysis to determine what the Government should realistically expect to pay for the proposed effort, the offeror's understanding of the work, and the offeror's ability to perform the contract.

There are several techniques used to estimate cost without obtaining detailed breakdowns from offerors. A *bottoms-up* estimate can be made at the lowest possible level (provided that detailed data exists at such a level) using engineering expertise, then aggregated and adjusted to account for integration and indirect expenses. One could draw an *analogy* by collecting cost data on similar systems and modify to reflect variations in the evaluated system. A third method is to *extrapolate* from actual costs. Finally, *parametric analysis* of cost data can develop cost-estimating relationships between cost elements and system or process characteristics. The bottoms-up approach is most accurate but consumes more time and labor than the others. The two comparison methods establish an initial baseline and calibrate other methods. Parametric analysis will be more accurate based on data quality, representative cost estimating relationships and the strength of the derived relationships.

The cost evaluator (usually the contracting officer or procurement analyst) looks at the offeror's cost estimates and metrics to ensure they are credible and logical. (S)he also assesses whether all proposed effort is priced out and traceable to the cost proposal (and vice versa). Finally, (s)he must determine if the cost estimate is realistic and shows a clear understanding of the requirements.

The total cost is evaluated as well as its *reasonableness* (level of proposed effort) and *realism*. The concept of cost realism addresses risk of contractor buy-in at low cost in hopes of getting well either during performance or receiving follow-on contracts on a sole-source basis at artificially high prices. Cost information may be provided to the technical evaluation team in accordance with agency procedures.

The source selection authority may reject all proposals received in response to a solicitation, if doing so is in the best interest of the Government.

3.12.2 Exchanges with Offerors

FAR 15.3

It is possible that the contracting officer can talk to offerors without commencing formal discussions. *Clarifications* are limited exchanges between the Government and offerors that may occur when award without discussions is contemplated. Offerors may be given the opportunity to clarify aspects of proposals or resolve minor or clerical errors. Award may then be made without discussions if the solicitation states the Government intends to make award without discussions.

The contracting officer decides during the proposal evaluation process whether to award without negotiations or else address the various offerors in an effort to clear up ambiguities and pursue improved proposals. A *competitive range* includes all offerors who have a reasonable chance of receiving award (when in doubt, include them in the range) based on responsiveness, technical acceptability and possible price reductions. Communications are limited to the offerors within the range, and any offerors facing elimination due solely to past performance. Such communications may be conducted to enhance Government understanding of proposals or facilitate the Government's evaluation process. These communications may address ambiguities in the proposal or other concerns (e.g., perceived deficiencies or weaknesses, errors, omissions, and past performance information). However, communications are not used to cure proposal deficiencies or material omissions which increase risk of unsuccessful performance, or to materially alter the technical or cost elements of the proposal.

If the solicitation permits, the contracting officer may limit the number of proposals in the competitive range to permit an efficient competition among the most highly rated proposals. If the contracting officer decides that an offeror's proposal should no longer be included in the competitive range, the proposal is eliminated by written notice to the offeror, who may then request a debriefing. If an offeror's proposal is eliminated or otherwise removed from the competitive range, no further revisions to that offeror's proposal are accepted or considered.

Negotiations are exchanges (in either a competitive or sole-source environment) between the Government and offerors to allow the offeror to revise its proposal. These negotiations may include *bargaining*, such as persuasion, changing assumptions and give-and-take. Bargaining may apply to contract type or terms, price, schedule, or technical requirements.

When negotiations are conducted in a competitive acquisition, they take place after establishment of the competitive range and are called *discussions*. These are tailored to each offeror's proposal, and must be conducted by the contracting officer with each offeror within the competitive range to maximize the Government's ability to obtain best value, based on the requirement and the evaluation factors set forth in the solicitation. The contracting officer must discuss with each offeror under consideration for award any deficiencies, significant weaknesses and adverse past performance information to which the offeror has not yet had an opportunity to respond, but need not discuss every area where the proposal could be improved. The scope and extent of discussions are a matter of contracting office judgment. (S)he may negotiate for increased performance beyond any mandatory minimums, and may suggest to offerors that have exceeded any minimums that their proposals would be more competitive if the excesses were removed and the offered price decreased. If discussions result in an offeror originally in the competitive range no longer considered to be among the most highly rated offeror, that offeror may be eliminated from the competitive range even if all material aspects of the proposal were not discussed, and whether or not the offeror has been afforded an opportunity to submit a proposal revision.

Auctioneering is a controversial part of contracting. Here, a contracting officer shops around among offerors offering lower prices than bid in the hope that somebody will lower their price without sacrificing quality or delivery terms merely to obtain the contract. When used in Government contracting, it gives rise to two competing schools of thought. On the one hand, it reflects the sworn duty of the contracting officer as a wise steward of the tax dollar to obtain as low a price as possible; on the other hand, it raises concern about the integrity of the competitive procurement process and could make a mockery of the system by which the Federal Government spends its money. Because this philosophical argument has no resolution, the Government takes the official position that it cannot discourage the use of auctioneering.

The contracting officer may inform an offeror that its price is considered to be too high or too low, and may reveal the results of the analysis supporting that conclusion, including a Government cost or price estimate. However, the Government cannot reveal the names of individuals providing reference information about an offeror's past performance. The contracting officer may request or allow proposal revisions to clarify and document understandings reached during negotiations.

However, care must be taken not to share technical information between offerors. Such *technical transfusion* would expose a firm's confidential approach and information to other offerors, which is expressly forbidden in Government contracting. Similarly, the contracting officer may not reveal price or technical features of one proposal to another firm. This is known as *technical leveling* because it gives an offeror inside knowledge of a competitor's proposal and an opportunity to improve its own approach. This activity is strictly prohibited, as it precludes a firm's technical originality and pricing position. The contracting officer also may not reveal the relative strengths and weaknesses of any proposal, as that would also lead to leveling. Also, the contracting officer may not help an offeror upgrade its proposal by conducting multiple rounds of negotiations. This would be the result of discussing the offeror's lack of competence, diligence or inventiveness, and is also expressly forbidden in Government contracting.

At the conclusion of discussions, each offeror still in the competitive range has an opportunity to submit a *best and final offer*, with the contracting officer establishing a common cut-off date only for receipt of final proposal revisions. Requests for final proposal revisions advise offerors that the final proposal revisions be in writing and that the Government intends to make award without further revisions.

The source selection authority's (SSA) decision is based on the evaluation board's comparative assessment of proposals against all source selection criteria in the solicitation. The report addresses all elements of technical, past performance and cost evaluations, as well as the results of any competitive negotiations. While the SSA may use reports and analyses prepared by others, the source selection decision represents the SSA's independent judgment.

The source selection decision is documented, including the rationale for any business judgments and trade-offs made or relied on by the SSA. The documentation need not quantify the trade-offs that led to the decision.

Unfortunately, mistakes can and are made at this point, such as incorrect price evaluations, evaluation board oversights or outright rejection by the selection authority. In such a case, the contracting officer may need to contact remaining offerors for a revised best and final offer, then reconvene the evaluators and SSA. It is hard to put a positive face on this event – to put it bluntly, someone goofed! It is embarrassing for the Government to do this, creates unnecessary stress among all parties, and impacts the agency's reputation. But it does happen.

3.12.3 Best Value Continuum

FAR 15.1

The concept of *best value* contracting entails trading off evaluation factors to obtain the best contract performance, including but not limited to cost. It reflects a life-cycle cost analysis and a marginal analysis of cost versus technical performance trade-off for each offeror. Price and related factors cannot be the dominant concern in best value procurements. Evaluators compare proposals and look for relative advantages (*discriminators*) held by one or more proposals that tie into specified evaluation factors or system capabilities. Discriminators should be quantified in dollar terms whenever possible, so that a cost-benefit trade-off may be conducted. The common method for conducting such trade-offs is to estimate the cost if the lowest-priced offeror provided the benefit, adjusted for cost realism and discounted cash flow, and add to its evaluated price. If the lowest-priced offer is still low, then the added benefit is not cost-effective. Alternatively, the Government can quantify the benefit using an index, methodology or model. Third, the agency can compare benefits between a specific pair of offers and then rank the results ordinarily.

Assigning points to price and technical proposals is an old approach which does not quantify the benefits and still requires using the second or third option. Consequently, point systems are not recommended.

In acquisitions where the requirement is clearly definable and the risk of unsuccessful contract performance is minimal, cost or price may play a dominant role in source selection. Prospective pricing decisions made prior to contract performance are based on analyzing comparative prices, price estimates, past costs, or all of the above. Where the requirement is less definitive, more development work is required, or more performance risk is present, then technical or past performance considerations will be more significant in source selection. A *trade-off process* is used when it may be in the best interest of the Government to consider award to other than the lowest-priced or highest technically rated offeror. All evaluation factors and significant subfactors that will affect contract award and their relative importance are stated in the solicitation. The solicitation also states whether all evaluation factors other than cost or price, when combined, are significantly more important than, approximately equal to, or significantly less important than cost or price. This process permits trade-offs among cost or price and noncost factors, and allows the Government to accept other than the lowest-priced proposal. However, the perceived benefits of the higher-priced proposal must merit the additional cost and be documented in the file.

Alternatively, the lowest-priced technically acceptable source selection process is appropriate when best value is expected to result from selection of the technically acceptable proposal with the lowest-evaluated price. Solicitations specify that award will be made on the basis of the lowest-evaluated price of proposals meeting or exceeding the acceptability standards for non-cost factors. Past performance need not be an evaluation factor. Trade-offs are not permitted in this approach. If the contracting officer finds that a small business's past performance is not acceptable, the matter is referred to the SBA for a Certificate of Competency determination. Proposals are evaluated for acceptability but not ranked using non-cost/price factors.

Oral presentations by offerors may be requested by the Government to replace or supplement written information. Oral presentations may occur at any time in the acquisition process, and are subject to the same restrictions as written information regarding timing and content. Oral presentations provide an opportunity for dialogue among the parties. Pre-recorded videotaped presentations that lack real-time interactive dialogue are not considered oral presentations, although they may be included in offeror submissions. Representations and certifications are submitted with a signed offer sheet (including any exceptions to the Government's terms and conditions). Additional information (e.g., an offeror's capability, past performance, work plans or approaches, staffing resources, transition plans, or sample tasks) may be suitable for oral presentations. In deciding what information to obtain through an oral presentation, the contracting officer considers the Government's ability to adequately evaluate the information, incorporate any information into the resultant contract, impact on the acquisition process, and impact (including cost) on small businesses. The solicitation may describe the types of information to be presented orally (e.g., personnel qualifications), any requirements or limitations on the use of written material or other media, and any restrictions governing the time length. The solicitation should also address the scope and content of exchanges between the Government's and offeror's representatives, including whether or not discussions will be permitted during oral presentations.

The contracting officer maintains a record of oral presentations to document what the Government relied upon in making the source selection decision. The source selection authority will determine the level of detail for the record. An oral presentation including information that the parties intend to include in the contract as material terms or conditions should then be put in writing. Incorporation by reference of oral statements is not permitted.

3.13 NEGOTIATION

3.13.1 Cost/Price Analysis

FAR 15.4

Contracting officers must purchase supplies and services from responsible sources at fair and reasonable prices. In establishing the reasonableness of the offered prices, the contracting officer must focus on obtaining only the information that is necessary. Unless cost or pricing data are required, the contracting officer usually uses the following order of preference in determining the type of information required:

- no additional information from the offeror, if the price is based on adequate price competition;
- established catalog or market prices or previous contract prices;
- information available within the Government;
- information obtained from third parties;
- information obtained from the offeror on the prices at which the same or similar items have been sold previously; and
- cost breakdown information.

The contracting officer prices each contract separately without using proposed price reductions under other contracts as an evaluation factor, or considering losses or profits realized or anticipated under other contracts. Nor does (s)he include in a contract price any amount for a specified contingency if the contract provides for a price adjustment based upon the occurrence of that contingency.

Detailed cost or pricing data is not requested for acquisitions in any of the following circumstances:

- priced at or below the simplified acquisition threshold;

- based on adequate price competition. This means at least two responsible offerors compete independently and submit priced offers that satisfy the Government's expressed requirement;
- a reasonable expectation that adequate price competition would exist, even though only one offer is received from a responsible offeror. Based on the offer received, the contracting officer could reasonably conclude that the offer was submitted with the expectation of competition, approved at a level above the contracting officer;
- price analysis demonstrates that the proposed price is reasonable in comparison with current or recent prices for the same or similar items, adjusted to reflect changes in market or economic conditions, quantities, or terms and conditions under contracts that resulted from adequate price competition;
- prices set by law or regulation, or by review or ruling by a governmental body. A firm need not charge the same price as for intrastate commerce if it does not limit competition, established lower prices in good faith, or sees changed conditions in delivery, manufacturing, market, or sales; or
- commercial items, if the offeror has submitted sufficient information to evaluate, through price analysis, price reasonableness. The contracting officer may request the offeror to submit prices paid for the same or similar commercial items under comparable terms and conditions by both Government and commercial customers. (S)he may also consider information on labor costs, material costs and overhead rates.

Additionally, the head of the contracting activity may waive the requirement for submission of cost or pricing data in exceptional cases if the price can be determined to be fair and reasonable without data submission. Award of any lower-tier subcontract expected to exceed the cost or pricing data threshold requires the submission of cost or pricing data to the prime contractor and thence to the Government unless an exception or waiver applies. If the contracting officer has sufficient information available to determine price reasonableness, then (s)he should consider requesting a waiver if the price does not exceed $750,000. On the other hand, the head of the contracting activity may authorize the contracting officer to obtain cost or pricing data for pricing actions below this threshold but over the simplified acquisition threshold.

When cost or pricing data are required, the offeror includes a certificate of current cost or pricing data that to the best of its knowledge and belief, the cost or pricing data were accurate, complete, and current as of the date of agreement on price, or an earlier date agreed upon between the parties that is as close as practicable to the date of agreement on price. This disclosure ensures compliance with the Truth in Negotiations Act (10 U.S.C. 2306a) to ensure the Government does not pay excessive prices.

The exercise of an option at the price established at contract award or initial negotiation does not require submission of cost or pricing data. Also, cost or pricing data are not required for proposals solely for overrun funding or interim billing price adjustments.

3.13.2 Sole-Source Negotiation

Negotiation is a communications process by which the Government and firm work to reach a mutually satisfactory agreement. A meeting of the minds is necessary. Negotiations do not mean mutual sacrifice just to reach agreement, but rather a process by which both parties can maximize their interests. Successful negotiations are a function of reasonable goals and positions, negotiating skill and the willingness to make concessions.

Before entering formal negotiations, the Government determines the factual basis and estimating assumptions used by the offeror to create the proposal. This may include production problems and delivery impact, and perhaps data requirements.

A formal procedure highlights the pre-negotiation position of the Government, which may be a formal flip-chart presentation, oral briefing with spreadsheet, or a written description of each cost element and topic for negotiation. The objective is to obtain management approval for negotiation objectives. Each agency determines the depth of this process.

The ideal outcome of negotiations is a "win-win" situation where both parties achieve long-term satisfaction. This result increases trust and reduces competition, while promoting a fair and reasonable price and long-term success of the contractor. Undesirable outcomes include "win-lose," which may happen in one-time transactions where one party does much better than the other, and "lose-lose" relationships where a deadlock often occurs.

3.13.3 Strategy and Tactics

The Government maintains the initiative throughout negotiations, since it has the power of the purse. Negotiations are led by the contracting officer or a procurement specialist. Technical specialists may participate, especially in sole-source negotiations. After nonprice issues are resolved, the Government makes a counteroffer within its approval threshold. Over time, the goal is to reach an agreement on a fair and reasonable price, as individual cost elements need not be agreed to by the parties.

Sole-source negotiations for major procurements often include fact-finding meetings, either at the contracting office or at the contractor's facility. Cost auditors and program engineers may be present to lend their expertise.

Assumptions and judgments made by the contractor will be questioned and either accepted or contested. Afterward, the contractor may need to revise its proposal assumptions and costing, while the contracting officer digests all this input to develop a coherent position, either as a counteroffer or justification for the proposed amount. The wise contracting officer will develop a range of acceptable positions to provide negotiating room, and will also brief office management on the proposal, recommendations received from other team members and an objective position.[24]

Negotiation techniques vary depending on the situation. In a sole-source environment, the negotiator must evaluate the proposal in depth and take care not to authorize work until price agreement is reached. In a competitive environment, no single firm can influence the market price, so the buyer uses the supply-demand force to drive closer to the market price, considering nonprice aspects of competition for a standardized product. In an oligopoly with few firms who consider reactions of the others to set their pricing policy, the buyer will focus on their mutual interdependence, inflexible prices and critical nonpricing competition. In a regulated market, the buyer will try to maximize benefits such as favorable terms, free services, price breaks, and quantity buys.

Negotiation features bargaining or discussion, flexibility, a lack of competition, and a time deadline. They may be written or oral, or both. Some specific stratagems and tactics that are commonly used (not always successfully or even wisely) include:

- adopt and maintain high aspiration levels;
- ask for an additional concession;
- ask questions to uncover any avoided topic;
- announce all your demands at once;
- avoid controversy;
- avoid showing any weaknesses;
- be patient, polite and respectful;
- be prepared to walk away, but also to return;
- concede slowly in small amounts, in trade for a concession from the other side;
- create doubts in the other party's mind to lower their expectations;
- create options for mutual gain through brainstorming ideas aloud;
- derive the true cost of a concession rather than conceding a given quantity;
- describe the problem in one's own words before offering a solution;
- discuss each other's perceptions;
- do not blame the other party;
- establish a deadline to pressure the other party;

- focus on interests rather than positions;
- imagine yourself in the other party's position to understand their concerns, interests and constituents;
- insist that everything is negotiable;
- invite criticism and advice rather than defending your ideas;
- list and prioritize the other party's interests;
- listen actively;
- maintain room to compromise;
- narrow down the issues to learn what is essential to the other party;
- negotiate agreeable items before differences;
- never volunteer weaknesses;
- not yield to perceived prestige of other side;
- pause to create an effective silence;
- prioritize negotiation objectives to separate must-haves from give points;
- provide counteroffers which contain new conditions or prices, in effect rejecting the previous offer by the other party;
- recognize emotions of both parties;
- review previous negotiations to identify past problems and negotiation flexibility;
- satisfy the other side without sacrificing one's own goals;
- separate the people from the problem;
- speak in first rather than second person;
- stand firm on your position without anger or fear;
- stay calm and professional;
- think before you speak;
- trade a decoy for a concession of value;
- use alternative pricing packages; and
- wait out a party who breaks off negotiations to see how they respond.

Parties should identify the opportunity cost of not reaching agreement (known as the *best alternative to a negotiated agreement*). Hopefully, this won't lead to a breakdown in negotiations and no resulting contract, though this does sometimes happen. The desired solution for both parties should reflect a mutual agreement which satisfies both their interests.

After negotiations conclude, the contracting officer writes a post-negotiation memorandum that explains why the price is fair and reasonable. It discusses what facts were relied on, what new data was presented by the offeror during negotiations, and how these new facts changed the Government's judgment. The memorandum explains why the contracting officer considers the price to be fair and reasonable. Format for this memorandum is dictated by the agency and procurement office.

3.13.4 Notifications to Unsuccessful Offerors

FAR 15.503

The contracting officer notifies offerors promptly in writing when their proposals are excluded from the competitive range, with the basis for the determination, and that no proposal revision will be considered. For a competitive socioeconomic set-aside, the contracting officer notifies each offeror upon completion of negotiations of the identity of the successful offeror, that the Government will not consider any revisions to proposals, and that they may challenge the apparent successful offeror's socioeconomic status. This notice is not required when the contracting officer determines in writing that the urgency of the requirement necessitates award without delay.

Within three days after the date of contract award, the contracting officer notifies each offeror whose proposal was in the competitive range but was not selected for award:

- number of offerors solicited;
- number of proposals received;
- name and address of each offeror receiving an award;
- items, quantities and any stated unit prices of each award; and
- reason(s) the offeror's proposal was not accepted, unless the price of the successful offeror is clearly the reason for award.

The same information may be provided to unsuccessful offerors where simplified acquisition procedures are used only upon request of the offeror(s), as well as to unsuccessful offerors that received a pre-award notice of exclusion from the competitive range.

The contracting officer awards a contract to the successful offeror by furnishing the executed contract or other notice of the award. If the award document includes information that is different than the latest signed proposal, both the offeror and the contracting officer sign the contract, creating a *bilateral award*.

3.13.5 Debriefing

FAR 15.505 and .506

Offerors excluded from the competitive range or before award may request a debriefing before award by written request to the contracting officer within three days after receipt of the notice of exclusion from the competition. At the offeror's request, this debriefing may be delayed until after award. The contracting officer may refuse the request for a debriefing if, for compelling reasons, it is not in the best interests of the Government to conduct a debriefing at that time. Debriefings may be done orally or in writing. Pre-award debriefings include the agency's evaluation of the offeror's proposal, the rationale for eliminating the offeror from the competition, and answers to questions about whether source selection procedures contained in the solicitation and applicable regulations were followed. Pre-award debriefings do not disclose:

- commercial and financial information that is confidential (e.g., cost breakdowns, indirect cost rates and profit);
- content of other offerors proposals;
- identity or number of other offerors;
- names of individuals providing reference information about an offeror's past performance;
- point-by-point comparisons of the debriefed offeror's proposal with other offerors;
- privileged or confidential manufacturing processes and techniques;
- ranking and evaluation of other offerors; and
- trade secrets.

Post-award debriefings do include:

- a summary of the rationale for award;
- evaluation of the significant weaknesses or deficiencies in the offeror's proposal;
- for acquisitions of commercial items, the make and model of the item to be delivered by the successful offeror;
- overall evaluated cost or price (including unit prices), and any technical rating of the successful offeror and the debriefed offeror;
- overall ranking of all offerors;
- past performance information on the debriefed offeror; and
- whether source selection procedures contained in the solicitation and applicable regulations were followed.

Debriefings can be anticipated with dread, but should be construed as a meaningful learning experience by all parties. Positive strengths should be emphasized as well as negative weaknesses. Questions about the process and interpretation of the regulations should be freely answered. The offeror should feel that it is taking home something positive and be wiser than when they started the proposal. This approach precludes protests and may widen the competitive base for future requirements.

3.14 PROTESTS

FAR 33.1

A *protest* is a written objection by an interested party to a solicitation or award, or cancellation thereof, requesting specific relief.[25] An *interested party* is an actual or prospective offeror whose direct economic interest would be affected by the award of a contract or the failure to award a contract. Protests usually claim either improper or illegal procedures or unfair treatment. Protests based on alleged apparent improprieties in a solicitation must be filed before bid opening or the closing date for receipt of proposals.

Contracting officers consider all protests and seek legal advice. (S)he will withhold award unless performance is urgently required or otherwise in the Government's best interest. Offerors will be requested to extend their validity dates. The impact of a protest is delayed award with mission impact, administrative time and expense, and notice that the process did not flow smoothly (either the agency or the protestor is wrong). The protestor may fear informal blacklisting for causing trouble, but more likely feels that it has been denied a deserved award.

The contracting officer may suspend performance of a contract within 10 days after contract award or within five days after a debriefing date offered to the protestor. This decision requires a written determination that a protest is likely to be filed by an interested party, and delay of performance is in the best interest of the United States.

3.14.1 Protests to the Agency

FAR 33.103

The agency provides for protest resolution that is expeditious, inexpensive, informal, and simple. All protests filed directly with the agency are addressed to the contracting officer. Alternative dispute resolution techniques or third-party neutrals are both acceptable protest resolution methods. Interested parties may request an independent review of their protest at a level above the contracting officer.

Upon receipt of a protest before award, a contract may not be awarded, pending agency resolution of the protest, unless contract award is justified in writing for urgent and compelling reasons or is otherwise determined to be in the best interest of the Government. Such justification or determination is approved at a level above the contracting officer. The contracting officer informs the offerors who might become eligible for award of the protest. If appropriate, the offerors should be requested to extend the time for acceptance. In the event of failure to obtain such extension of offers, consideration should be given to proceeding with award.

Agencies try to resolve agency protests within 35 days after filing. The parties may exchange relevant information. The protest decision is provided to the protestor with evidence of receipt.

If the head of an agency determines that a solicitation or a proposed award or actual award violates law or regulation, the head of the agency may reimburse the protestor for costs and require the awardee to reimburse the Government's costs due to the awardee's intentional or negligent miscertification, misrepresentation or misstatement. The Government may collect this debt by offsetting the amount against any payment due the awardee under any contract.

If the contractor is unsuccessful in protesting to the department or agency, it can always file in the United States Court of Claims. The Court will accept the administrative determination of fact (as prescribed in the Wunderlich Act, 41 U.S.C. 321), and focus on whether the contracting officer or department review is supportable. This process is expensive and time-consuming, and not used very often (perhaps because it is difficult for the contractor to prevail at this point).

3.14.2 Protests to GAO

FAR 33.104

An interested party is encouraged to seek resolution with the agency before filing a protest with the GAO, but may protest directly to the GAO. GAO has jurisdiction because it is charged with examining the use of public funds and evaluating Federal Government activities. However, no protest may be filed at GAO for a procurement integrity violation unless that person reported the incident to the contracting officer within 14 days after first discovering the possible violation. The agency, for good cause or when a protest raises a significant issue, may consider the merits of any protest which is not timely filed.

GAO has four options in a decision:

- declare the contract illegal and void;
- direct termination for convenience and award to the proper offeror;
- issue a letter of criticism to the agency; or
- notify the protestor that the award was properly made.

Procedures for protests to GAO are found at 4 CFR Part 21 (GAO Bid Protest Regulations). A protestor furnishes a copy of its complete protest to the contracting officer or official and location designated in the solicitation within one day after the protest is filed with the GAO. The GAO may dismiss the protest if it is late. Immediately after receipt of the GAO's written notice of a protest, the agency notifies the contractor (if award has been made) or all parties who appear to have a reasonable prospect of receiving award. The contracting officer immediately begins compiling the information necessary for a report to the GAO within 30 days after the GAO notifies the agency that a protest has been filed, or within 20 days after receipt if the GAO determines to use its express option (which compresses time deadlines for less complicated protests).

When a protest is filed with the GAO, and an actual or prospective offeror so requests, the procuring agency provides actual or prospective offerors reasonable access to the protest file. At least five days prior to the filing of the report, the agency provides to all parties and the GAO a list of documents that the agency has released to the protestor or intends to produce, and those documents that it intends to withhold from the protestor with the reasons. Any objection to the scope of the agency's proposed (non)disclosure of documents must be filed with the GAO and the other parties within two days after receipt of this list. At the same time it submits its report to the GAO, the agency furnishes copies of its report to the protestor and any interveners. The GAO process for adjudicating protests is the same as for agencies, both before and after award.

The GAO may issue protective orders which establish terms, conditions and restrictions to provide any document to an interested party, especially for procurement-sensitive information, trade secrets, proprietary research or development, or commercial information. Protective orders do not authorize withholding any documents or information from Congress or an executive agency.

In accordance with agency procedures, the head of the contracting activity may authorize contract performance, notwithstanding the protest, for the same reasons as with an agency protest. Contract performance shall not be authorized until the agency has notified the GAO of same. If instead it is decided to suspend performance or terminate the awarded contract, usually because an award may be invalidated and a delay in receiving the supplies or services is not prejudicial to the Government's interest, the contracting officer attempts to negotiate a no-cost mutual agreement. The contracting officer also gives written notice of the decision to the protestor and other interested parties.

Any agency appellate review of the contracting officer's decision on the protest will not extend GAO's timeliness requirements, so any subsequent protest to the GAO must be filed within 10 days of knowing about an initial adverse agency action.

GAO issues its recommendation on a protest within 100 days from the date of filing of the protest, or within 65 days if it chooses an express option. The head of the contracting activity must report any failure to implement the GAO findings within five days of the expiration of a 60-day period. The protestor may file for reconsideration if it believes GAO has made a factual or legal error. However, the ultimate decision by GAO is final and not subject to court challenge by either party (again, because Congress has the ultimate power of the purse).

If the GAO determines that a solicitation or award does not comply with a statute or regulation, it may recommend that the agency pay to a protestor the cost, exclusive of profit, of filing and pursuing the protest. This cost may include reasonable attorney, consultant and expert witness fees, as well as bid and proposal preparation costs. The agency uses funds available for the procurement to pay the costs awarded. The protestor files its claim for costs with the contracting agency within 60 days after receipt of the GAO's recommendation that the agency pay the protestor its costs. Failure to file the claim within that time may result in forfeiture of the right to recover its costs. If the agency and the protestor are unable to agree on the amount to be paid, the GAO may, upon request of the protestor, recommend to the agency the amount of costs that the agency should pay.

Solicitation Provisions and Contract Clauses

FAR 52.233-2, Service of Protest, if expected to exceed the simplified acquisition threshold.

FAR 52.233-3, Protest After Award. Use the clause with its Alternate I if a cost-reimbursement contract is contemplated.

3.15 CONSTRUCTION CONTRACTS

3.15.1 Policy

FAR 36.2

Contracts to build real property such as a building, road or other public work have a mind-set all their own. *Design-bid-build* is the traditional delivery method, where design and construction are sequential and contracted for separately with two contracts and two contractors. The design process defines the construction requirement, functional relationships and technical systems to be used (e.g., architectural, electrical, environmental, fire protection, mechanical, and structural), producing the technical specifications and drawings, and preparing the construction cost estimate. Offers are then solicited to obtain a separate builder firm. A construction contract is not awarded to the firm that designed the project or its subsidiaries or affiliates, except with the approval of the head of the agency or authorized representative.[26]

An independent Government cost estimate is prepared and furnished to the contracting officer for each proposed contract or modification antici- pated to exceed the simplified acquisition threshold, or greater if requested by the contracting officer. The estimate is prepared in such detail as though the Government were competing for award. When two-step sealed bid- ding is used, the independent Government estimate is prepared when the contract requirements are definitized. Access to information concerning the Government estimate is limited to authorized Government personnel, although the contracting officer might need to disclose the associated cost breakdown figures in the Government estimate of a specialized task during negotiations.

The overall amount of the Government's estimate is not disclosed except as permitted by agency regulations. Advance notices and solicitations state the magnitude of the requirement in terms of physical characteristics and estimated price range, as follows:

- under $25,000;
- $25,000 to $100,000;
- $100,000 to $250,000;
- $250,000 to $500,000;
- $500,000 to $1,000,000;
- $1,000,000 to $5,000,000;
- $5,000,000 to $10,000,000; and
- over $10,000,000.

Contracts for construction must comply with any statutory cost limitations (with allowances for Government-imposed contingencies and overhead), unless applicable limitations are waived in writing for the contract.[27] Solicita- tions containing one or more items subject to statutory cost limitations spec- ify the applicable cost limitation for each affected item in a separate schedule, and that an offer which does not contain separately priced schedules will not be considered. The solicitation also states that the price on each schedule shall include an approximate apportionment of all estimated direct costs, allocable indirect costs and profit.

The Government rejects an offer if its prices are materially unbalanced, even if within statutory limitations. An offer is unbalanced if its prices are significantly below cost for some work, and overstated for other work.

Firm-fixed-price contracts are usually used to acquire construction. They may be priced on either a lump-sum or unit-price basis, or both. Lump-sum pricing is preferred. Unit-price basis is used only when:

- estimated quantities of work may change significantly during construction;
- large quantities of work such as building outside utilities, grading, paving, or site preparation are involved;
- offerors would have to expend unusual effort to develop adequate estimates; or
- quantities of work, such as excavation, cannot be estimated to develop a lump-sum offer without a substantial contingency.

Fixed-price contracts with economic price adjustment may be used if customary in contracts for the type of work being acquired, or when omission of an adjustment provision would either preclude many firms from submitting offers or cause offerors to include unwarranted contingencies in proposed prices. Cost-type or price-incentive contracts are not permitted concurrently at the same work site with firm-fixed-price contracts (to avoid concerns over mischarging costs to the wrong contract) without the prior approval of the head of the contracting activity.

The contracting officer arranges for prospective offerors to inspect the work site and to examine available data which may provide information concerning the performance of the work (e.g., boring samples and records, plans of previous construction, utilities to be furnished during construction, etc.). A record is maintained of the identity and affiliation of all offerors' representatives who attend a site visit or examine the data.

Advance notices and solicitations are distributed to as many prospective offerors as practicable. Contracting officers may send notices and solicitations to organizations that maintain free display rooms for prospective offerors, subcontractors, and material suppliers. If requested by such organizations, this may be done for construction projects on an annual or semiannual basis. Contracting officers may determine the geographical extent of distribution of advance notices and solicitations on a case-by-case basis.

FAR 36.5

To assure adequate interest in and supervision of all work involved in larger projects, the contractor must perform a significant part of the contract work with its own workforce. The contract states a minimum percentage of work that must be performed in-house. This percentage is as high as the contracting officer considers appropriate for the project, consistent with customary or necessary specialty subcontracting and the complexity and magnitude of the work. This number is usually around 12% unless a greater percentage is required by law or agency regulation. Specialties such as electrical, heating and plumbing work are usually subcontracted, and should not normally be considered in establishing the amount of work required to be performed in-house.

If a contractor discovers *differing site conditions* that are latent (not obvious) or subsurface, it is entitled to equitable adjustment of price and/or schedule. Such conditions are categorized as either I or II. Category I conditions differ from what is specified in the contract, while Category II conditions differ from what is usually encountered in such work.

Forms used for construction, demolition, dismantling, or removal of improvements contracts are:

- Standard Form 1442, Solicitation, Offer, and Award (Construction, Alteration, or Repair), if expected to exceed the simplified acquisition thresholds;
- Optional Form 347 (Order for Supplies or Services) or SF 1442, if at or below the simplified acquisition threshold; or
- Optional Form 1419, Abstract of Offers – Construction, and Optional Form 1419A, Abstract of Offers – Construction, Continuation Sheet, for sealed bidding (and optional for negotiations).

Solicitation Provision and Contract Clause

FAR 52.237-4, Payment by Government to Contractor, for demolition, dismantling or removal of improvements if the Government will pay the contractor and take title to any property it received under the contract.

FAR 52.237-5, Payment by Contractor to Government, for demolition, dismantling or removal of improvements whenever the contractor is to receive title to dismantled or demolished property and a net amount of compensation is due to the Government.

FAR 52.237-6, Incremental Payment by Contractor to Government, for demolition, dismantling or removal of improvements if the contractor is to receive title to dismantled or demolished property and a net amount of compensation is due the Government. The contracting officer must determine that it would be advantageous for the contractor to pay in increments and the Government to transfer title to the contractor for increments of property only upon receipt of those payments.

3.15.2 Sealed Bidding Procedures

FAR 36.213

Contracting officers may use sealed bid procedures when appropriate for a construction contract performed within the United States and its outlying areas. The contracting officer issues presolicitation notices on any construction requirement exceeding the simplified acquisition threshold, and may do so below the threshold. These notices are issued in advance of the invitation for bids to stimulate the interest of prospective bidders. They include the:

- amount (if any) to be charged for solicitation documents;
- deadline to submit requests for the invitation for bids;
- location of the work;
- nature and volume of work (i.e., physical characteristics and estimated price range);
- place where plans will be available for inspection without charge;
- publication through a GPE;
- restriction to small businesses (if any); and
- tentative dates for issuing invitations, opening bids and completing contract performance.

Each invitation for bids includes the following information, when applicable:

- any facilities (e.g., utilities, office or storage space) to be furnished during construction;
- appropriate wage determination, or a notice that the schedule of minimum wage rates to be paid under the contract will be issued as an amendment to the invitation for bids before the opening date for bids;
- arrangements for bidders to inspect the site and examine data concerning performance of the work;
- FAR 52.236-1, Performance of Work by the Contractor clause;
- instructions concerning bids and award;
- magnitude of the proposed project;
- period of performance;
- prebid conference information;
- reporting requirements; and
- special qualifications or experience requirements to be considered in determining the responsibility of bidders.

If any proposed cost element differs significantly from the Government estimate (e.g., material estimates, wage rates, etc.), the contracting officer requests the offeror to submit cost information concerning that element. When a proposed price is significantly lower than the Government estimate, the contracting officer ensures that both the offeror and the Government estimator completely understand the scope of the work. If negotiations reveal errors in the Government estimate, the estimate is corrected and the changes are documented in the contract file. Proposed prices may be compared to current prices for similar types of work, adjusting for differences in the work site and the specifications. Rough yardsticks may be used (e.g., cost per cubic foot for structures, cost per linear foot for utilities, and cost per cubic yard for excavation or concrete).

3.15.3 Two-Phase Design-Build Selection

FAR 36.303

A *two-phase design-build selection procedure* is used to select a limited number of offerors during Phase One to submit detailed proposals for Phase Two. These procedures are used for the design and construction of a public building, facility or work, if the contracting officer makes a determination that the procedures are appropriate for use. These procedures are used based on the following:

- at least three offers are anticipated from capable offerors;
- design work must be performed by offerors before developing price or cost proposals;
- offerors will incur a substantial amount of expense in preparing offers;
- project requirements are adequately defined;
- the delivery schedule allows for an extra phase of evaluation; and
- the Government agency is capable of managing a two-phase selection process.

The agency develops a scope of work that defines the project and states the Government's requirements. The scope of work may include criteria and preliminary design, budget parameters, and schedule or delivery requirements.

One solicitation may be issued covering both phases, or two solicitations may be issued in sequence. Proposals will be evaluated in Phase One to determine which offerors will submit proposals for Phase Two, if only one contract will be awarded.

Phase One of the solicitation(s) includes:

- scope of work;
- Phase One evaluation factors, including:

- ◦ technical approach (but not detailed design or technical information);
- ◦ technical qualifications:
  - · specialized experience and technical competence;
  - · capability to perform;
  - · past performance of the offeror's team (including the architect-engineer and construction members); and
- ◦ other appropriate factors (excluding cost or price related factors);
- • Phase Two evaluation factors; and
- • the maximum number of offerors that will be selected to submit Phase Two proposals.

After evaluating Phase One proposals, the contracting officer selects the most highly qualified offerors (usually not more than five) and requests that only those offerors submit Phase Two proposals.[28] Examples of potential Phase Two technical evaluation factors include design concepts, key personnel, management approach, and proposed technical solutions. Phase Two requires submission of technical and price proposals, which are evaluated separately.

Solicitation Provisions and Contract Clauses

FAR 52.236-1, Performance of Work by the Contractor, if fixed-price unless awarded under socioeconomic preference programs, when the contract amount is expected to exceed $1,500,000.

FAR 52.236-2, Differing Site Conditions, if fixed-price and exceeding the simplified acquisition threshold.

FAR 52.236-3, Site Investigation and Conditions Affecting the Work, if fixed-price and exceeding the simplified acquisition threshold.

FAR 52.236-4, Physical Data, if fixed-price construction and physical data (e.g., test borings, hydrographic data, weather conditions data) will be furnished or made available to offerors.

FAR 52.236-5, Material and Workmanship, for construction only.

FAR 52.236-6, Superintendence by the Contractor, if fixed-price and exceeding the simplified acquisition threshold.

FAR 52.236-7, Permits and Responsibilities, if fixed-price (or cost-reimbursement for construction only).

FAR 52.236-8, Other Contracts, if fixed-price and exceeding the simplified acquisition threshold.

FAR 52.236-9, Protection of Existing Vegetation, Structures, Equipment, Utilities, and Improvements, if fixed-price and exceeding the simplified acquisition threshold.

FAR 52.236-10, Operations and Storage Areas, if fixed-price and exceeding the simplified acquisition threshold.

FAR 52.236-11, Use and Possession Prior to Completion, if fixed-price construction and exceeding the simplified acquisition threshold.

FAR 52.236-12, Cleaning Up, if fixed-price and exceeding the simplified acquisition threshold.

FAR 52.236-13, Accident Prevention, if fixed-price and exceeding the simplified acquisition threshold. Use the clause with its Alternate I if the work is of a long duration or hazardous nature. Alternate I is optional if services will be performed at Government facilities and technical representatives advise that special precautions are appropriate.

FAR 52.236-14, Availability and Use of Utility Services, if fixed-price and exceeding the simplified acquisition threshold, the existing utility system(s) is adequate for both the Government and the contractor (and listed in the contract), and furnishing it is in the Government's interest.

FAR 52.236-15, Schedules for Construction Contracts, if fixed-price construction and exceeding the simplified acquisition threshold. The period of actual work performance usually exceeds 60 days.

FAR 52.236-16, Quantity Surveys, if fixed-price construction with unit pricing of items and payment based on quantity surveys. Use the clause with its Alternate I if determined at a level above the contracting officer that Government personnel cannot perform the original and final surveys, and the contractor must do so.

FAR 52.236-17, Layout of Work, if fixed-price construction and accurate work layout and site verification during work performance are necessary.

FAR 52.236-18, Work Oversight in Cost-Reimbursement Construction Contracts, if cost-reimbursement construction.

FAR 52.236-19, Organization and Direction of the Work, if cost-reimbursement construction.

FAR 52.236-21, Specifications and Drawings for Construction, if fixed-price and exceeding the simplified acquisition threshold. When the Government needs *record drawings* (drawings submitted by a [sub]contractor to show the construction of a particular structure or work as actually completed under the contract), use the clause with its Alternate I if reproducible shop drawings are needed, or with its Alternate II if reproducible shop drawings are not needed.

FAR 52.236-26, Preconstruction Conference, if fixed-price and a preconstruction conference is desired.

Additional Solicitation Provisions

FAR 52.236-27, Site Visit (Construction), if using the Differing Site Conditions and Site Investigations and Conditions Affecting the Work clauses. Use Alternate I if a site visit will be conducted.

FAR 52.236-28, Preparation of Offers – Construction, for negotiated construction.

3.15.4 Davis-Bacon Act

The *Davis-Bacon Act* (40 U.S.C. 3141, et seq.) requires any laborer or mechanic employed at the work site on a Federal construction contract over $2,000 within the United States to receive at least the prevailing local wage rate. To implement the Davis-Bacon Act, the Department of Labor issues *wage determinations* for individual contracts to reflect prevailing wages and fringe benefits, applied only to laborers and mechanics employed by a contractor on the work site, including drivers who transport materials and equipment to or from the site. A *general wage determination* contains prevailing wage rates for the types of construction (e.g., building, heavy, highway, and residential) designated for the contract and specific geographical area. General wage determinations do not expire until canceled, modified or superseded by the Department of Labor, or the contracting officer exercises an option to extend the period of performance. The determinations are published on-line at http://www.wdol.gov/sca.aspx.

A *project wage determination* is issued at the specific request of a contracting agency when no general wage determination applies, and is effective for 180 calendar days. However, if a determination expires before contract award, an extension to the 180-day determination is possible to cover the life of the contract, unless the contracting officer exercises an option to extend the term of the contract.

If a general wage determination on the WDOL website applies to the project, the agency may use it without notifying the Department of Labor. Otherwise, the contracting agency submits requests for project wage determinations on SF 308 to the Department of Labor at least 45 days before issuing the solicitation or exercising an option to extend the term of a contract. Subsequently, some very situation-specific procedures come into play.

In a sealed bid process, bids are not opened until after the wage determination (or modification) for the primary work site is furnished to all bidders. If necessary, the contracting officer postpones the bid-opening date to obtain the determination, amends the solicitation, and permits bidders to revise their bids. If the new determination does not change the wage rates, the amendment merely cites the number and date of the new determination.

If a project wage determination expires after bid opening but before award, the contracting officer requests an extension of the current wage determination expiration date and, if necessary, delays award to permit receipt. Otherwise, the contracting officer may award the contract and incorporate the new determination (or modification) to take effect on the contract award date, with an equitable adjustment to the contract price for any change in resultant cost.

In negotiated acquisitions, the contracting officer may open proposals and conduct negotiations before obtaining the wage determination (or modification), but must incorporate it before submission of best and final offers. If a project wage determination expires before contract award, the contracting officer requests a new determination and delays award until obtained, requesting offerors to extend the period for acceptance of proposal if necessary. If the new determination (or modification) changes any wage rates, the contracting officer amends the solicitation to incorporate the new determination and provide offerors an opportunity to amend their proposals. If the new determination (or modification) does not change any wage rates, then (as with sealed bidding) the amendment only includes the number and date of the new determination.

The Department of Labor may modify a wage determination by either specifying only the items being changed or else reissuing the entire determination. The need to modify a general wage determination for a solicitation is based on either the date the modified wage determination is published on the WDOL, or the date the agency (not the contracting officer) receives actual written notice of the modification from the Department of Labor, whichever occurs first. During the course of the solicitation, the contracting officer monitors the WDOL website to determine whether the applicable wage determination has been revised, and amends the solicitation if warranted.

The contractor must post a copy of the applicable wage determination and any added classifications at the work site so the workers can easily see it.

The Secretary of Labor has established an Administrative Review Board to hear appeals concerning Davis-Bacon Act wage determinations. A contracting agency or other interested party may file a petition for review if reconsideration by the Administrator has been sought and denied.

Whenever the contracting officer exercises an option to extend the term of a construction contract, (s)he modifies the contract and any task orders to incorporate the most current wage determination, which becomes effective for the complete period of performance of those task orders. However, the contracting officer may not further adjust the contract price or extend the term of the contract. Generally, this method is used in construction-only contracts with options to extend the term up to three years.

The contract may include a method to adjust the price upon exercise of each option. At the time of option exercise, the contracting officer incorporates a new wage determination into the contract and applies the specific pricing method to calculate the contract price adjustment. One such method is to include a clause which designates what percentage of the contract is subject to the provision of the Davis-Bacon Act (the default portion is 50%), then apply a percentage rate using a published economic indicator to that portion of the contract. Another technique is to arithmetically adjust the price to reflect the contractor's actual increase or decrease in wages and fringe benefits due to the new or revised wage determination upon exercise of the option.

In computing wages paid, the contractor may include only the amounts paid in cash to the laborer or mechanic, and irrevocable contributions to a trustee or a third party under a plan or program to provide a *fringe benefit*. Examples of such benefits include compensation for occupational injuries or illness, life insurance, medical or hospital care, pensions for accident disability or sickness, and unemployment benefits.

The contractor computes required overtime payments (i.e., 1 1/2 times the basic hourly rate of pay) using either the wage determination basic hourly rate or the actually paid rate, if higher. The basic rate of pay includes employee contributions to fringe benefits, but excludes the contractor's contributions or costs of cash equivalents for fringe benefits. The contracting officer rejects any misclassified apprentices or helpers, and requires the contractor to pay the affected employees at the rates for the classification of the work actually performed.

Within seven calendar days after the payment date of each payroll week, the contractor submits copies of weekly payrolls for itself and all subcontractors, along with statements of compliance. The contracting officer withholds funds from any payment should the contractor fail to do so. The contracting agency retains payrolls and statements of compliance for three years after contract completion and furnishes them upon request to the Department of Labor, the (sub)contractor who submitted them, or any higher-tier (sub)contractor.

The contracting officer periodically checks to ensure compliance with the labor standards requirements of the contract. Regular compliance checking includes:

- daily inspector's report and logs of construction, to ensure consistency;
- employee interviews to determine correctness of classifications, fringe benefits payments, hours worked, and rates of pay;
- on-site inspections to check type of work performed, number and classification of workers, and posting of notices; and
- payroll reviews to ensure timely submissions and completeness.

The contracting officer reports to the Wage and Hour Division of the Department of Labor on SF 1446, Labor Standards Investigation Summary Sheet, upon finding the (sub)contractor has:

- committed aggravated or willful violations;
- disregarded its obligations to employees and subcontractors under the Construction Wage Rate Requirements statute;
- not assured future compliance;
- not made restitution; or
- underpaid a subcontractor by $1,000 or more.

If a contractor or subcontractor fails or refuses to comply with the Davis-Bacon Act and related statutes, the agency suspends payment or guarantee until either the violations cease or the agency has withheld sufficient funds to compensate employees for back wages and any liquidated damages.

Executive Order 13502, Use of Project Labor Agreements for Federal Construction Projects, encourages the use of a *project labor agreement* to promote economy and efficiency in the performance of Federal construction projects where the total cost is more than $25 million. The agency may require that every (sub)contractor engaged on a construction project agree, for that project, to negotiate or become a party to a project labor agreement with one or more labor organizations. This approach is appropriate if:

- a project labor agreement will promote the agency's long-term program interests, such as facilitating the training of a skilled workforce to meet the agency's future construction needs;
- completion of the project will require an extended period of time;
- project labor agreements have been used on comparable projects undertaken by Federal, State, municipal, or private entities in the geographic area of the project;
- the agreement may be developed with the input of potential bidders and labor union officials;
- the project will require multiple construction (sub)contractors employing workers in multiple crafts or trades; or
- there is a shortage of skilled labor in the region in which the construction project will be sited.

The agreement will:

- allow all (sub)contractors to compete for (sub)contracts without regard to whether they are otherwise parties to collective bargaining agreements;

- bind all (sub)contractors engaged in construction on the project to comply with the project labor agreement;
- contain guarantees against job disruptions such as lockouts and strikes;
- include any additional requirements as the agency deems necessary to satisfy its needs;
- provide other mechanisms for labor-management cooperation on matters of mutual interest and concern, including health, productivity, quality of work, and safety; and
- set forth effective, prompt, and mutually binding procedures for resolving labor disputes arising during the term of the project labor agreement.

Solicitation Provision

FAR 52.222-33, Notice of Requirement for Project Labor Agreement. Use the provision with its Alternate I if the agency decides to require the submission of a project labor agreement, from only the apparent successful offeror, prior to contract award. Use the provision with its Alternate II if an agency allows submission of a project labor agreement after contract award.

Contract Clauses

The following FAR clauses are used in solicitations and contracts over $2,000 for construction within the United States:

- 52.222-5, Davis Bacon Act—Secondary Site of the Work;
- 52.222-6, Davis-Bacon Act;
- 52.222-7, Withholding of Funds;
- 52.222-8, Payrolls and Basic Records;
- 52.222-9, Apprentices and Trainees;
- 52.222-10, Compliance with Copeland Act Requirements;
- 52.222-11, Subcontracts (Labor Standards);
- 52.222-12, Contract Termination-Debarment;
- 52.222-13, Compliance with Davis-Bacon and Related Act Regulations;
- 52.222-14, Disputes Concerning Labor Standards;
- 52.222-15, Certification of Eligibility; and
- 52.222-16, Approval of Wage Rates, except for contracts with a State or political subdivision.

FAR 52.222-30, Davis-Bacon Act–Price Adjustment (None or Separately Specified Pricing Method), if subject to the Davis-Bacon Act and option provisions may extend the term of the contract.

FAR 52.222-31, Davis-Bacon Act—Price Adjustment (Percentage Method), if fixed-price, subject to the Davis-Bacon Act, and contains option provisions to extend the term of the contract and adjust the price for a revised age determination.

FAR 52.222-32, Davis-Bacon Act—Price Adjustment (Actual Method), if fixed-price, subject to the Davis-Bacon Act, and contains option provisions to extend the term of the contract and adjust the price for a revised age determination.

FAR 52.222-34, Project Labor Agreement. Use the clause with its Alternate I if an agency allows submission of the project labor agreement after contract award.

3.16 ARCHITECT/ENGINEERING SERVICES

FAR 36.6

Architect-engineer services are professional services which are associated with design or construction of real property, and are performed by registered architects or engineers or their employees (sometimes so mandated by state law), such as:

- comprehensive planning;
- conceptual designs;
- construction services;
- consultations;
- drawing reviews;
- mapping;
- preparing operating and maintenance manuals;
- program management;
- soils engineering;
- specifications development;
- studies and investigations;
- surveying;
- tests and evaluations; and
- value engineering.

3.16.1 Source Selection

FAR 36.602 through .603

Agencies evaluate each offeror for its:

- capacity to accomplish the work in the required time;
- location in and knowledge of the geographical area of the project;
- past performance (e.g., cost control, compliance with performance schedules, customer satisfaction, integrity, incentive-fee performance, quality of work, and small business subcontracting;[29]
- professional qualifications necessary for satisfactory performance; and
- specialized experience and technical competence in the type of work required (e.g., energy conservation, pollution prevention, use of recovered materials, or waste reduction).

For facility design contracts, the statement of work requires the architect-engineer to maximize use of recovered materials (consistent with the performance requirements, availability, price reasonableness, and cost-effectiveness) and, if appropriate, energy conservation, pollution prevention and waste reduction. The contractor must identify hazardous material and use safety data sheets.

To be considered for architect-engineer contracts, a firm must file with the appropriate office or board an SF 330, "Architect-Engineer Qualifications," using Part I to provide information about the firm's specific qualifications for the contract and Part II to discuss the firm's general professional qualifications. These offices or permanent evaluation boards maintain an architect-engineer qualifications data file. After reviewing the SF 330, they classify the firm with respect to capacity of work that can be undertaken, experience in computer-assisted design, location, professional capabilities, and specialized experience.

Agencies may evaluate firms on the basis of their conceptual design of the project. Design competition may be used for prestige projects (e.g., memorials), when sufficient time is available for the production and evaluation of conceptual designs, and when beneficial to the project.

The architect-engineer evaluation board is composed of representatives from the acquisition, architecture, construction, and engineering fields. Members are appointed from among highly qualified professional employees of the agency or other agencies, and (if authorized by agency procedures) private practitioners. One Government member of each board is designated as the chairperson. No firm may be awarded an architect-engineer contract during the period in which any of its principals or associates are participating as members of the awarding agency's evaluation board. The evaluation board will:

- evaluate the responding firms and their current data files;
- hold discussions with at least three of the most highly qualified firms about concepts and relative utility of alternative methods of furnishing the required services; and

- prepare a selection report for the agency head or designated selection authority recommending, in order of preference, at least three firms that are the most highly qualified to perform the required services. The report describes the board's discussions and evaluation.

The selection authority reviews the recommendations of the evaluation board and makes the final selection by listing, in order of preference, the firms (s)he considers most highly qualified to perform the work. If the firm listed as the most preferred is not the firm recommended as the most highly qualified by the evaluation board, the selection authority explains in writing the reason for the preference. All firms on the final selection list are considered "selected firms" with which the contracting officer may negotiate.

The selection authority cannot add firms to the selection report. If the firms recommended in the report are not deemed to be qualified or the report is considered inadequate, the selection authority records the reasons and returns the report to the evaluation board for revision.

Two shorter processes may be used to select firms for contracts not expected to exceed the simplified acquisition threshold. In one method, the board's selection report becomes the final selection list and is provided directly to the contracting officer. Or, if the board decides that formal action is not necessary for selection, the board chairperson performs the selection functions, submits a report to the agency head or designated selection authority, and, upon approval, sends the report to the contracting officer as authorization to begin negotiations.

3.16.2 Negotiations

FAR 36.606

Architect-engineer services are always acquired by negotiation, not by sealed bidding. An independent Government estimate of the cost of architect-engineer services is prepared and furnished to the contracting officer before beginning negotiations for each proposed contract or contract modification expected to exceed the simplified acquisition. The Government estimate is based on a detailed analysis of the required work as though the Government were submitting its own proposal.

Unless otherwise specified by the selection authority, the final selection authorizes the contracting officer to begin negotiations with the most preferred firm in the final selection. The contracting officer should seek advance agreement on any charges for computer-assisted design, and discuss with the offeror appropriate modern and cost-effective design methods (e.g., computer-assisted design) if not addressed in the proposal. Subcontractors must be specifically agreed to at this time, since qualifications are a critical element of selection.

If a mutually satisfactory contract cannot be negotiated, the contracting officer obtains a written final proposal revision from the firm, and notifies the firm that negotiations have been terminated. The contracting officer then initiates negotiations with the next firm on the final selection list. This procedure is continued until a mutually satisfactory contract has been negotiated. If negotiations fail with all selected firms, the contracting officer refers the matter to the selection authority, who may direct the evaluation board to recommend additional firms.

Contracting officers solicit offers using SF 1442 and award using either Optional Form 347 (if under the simplified acquisition threshold) or SF 252, Architect-Engineer Contract, to award fixed-price contracts for architect-engineer services if performed in the United States or its outlying areas.

3.16.3 Design Within Funding Limitations

FAR 36.609-1

The Government may require the architect-engineer contractor to design the project so that construction costs will not exceed a contractually specified dollar limit or funding limitation. If the construction price proposed exceeds the construction funding limitation in the architect-engineer contract, the firm is solely responsible for redesigning the project within the funding limitation. However, if the cost of proposed construction is affected by events beyond the firm's reasonable control (e.g., unanticipated increase in material costs or undue Government delay in issuing a construction solicitation), the firm is not obligated to redesign without cost to the Government. The amount of the construction funding limitation is established during negotiations. The estimated construction contract price takes into account any statutory or other limitations and excludes any allowances for contingencies, overhead or Government supervision. The contracting officer furnishes to the contractor the information upon which the Government based its initial construction estimate and any subsequently acquired information that may affect the construction costs.

3.16.4 Responsibility for Design Errors or Deficiencies

FAR 36.609-2

Architect-engineer contractors make necessary corrections at no cost to the Government when their designs, drawings, specifications, or services contain any deficiencies, errors or inadequacies. If the Government does not require a firm to correct such errors, the contracting officer documents the contract file with the reasons for that decision.

Architect-engineer contractors may also be liable for Government costs resulting from problems in designs furnished under its contract. When a construction contract must be modified because of a deficiency or error in the services provided, the contracting officer considers the extent to which the contractor may be reasonably liable. The contracting officer then issues a demand for payment of the amount due, if the recoverable cost will exceed the administrative cost involved or is otherwise in the Government's interest.

Contract Clauses

FAR 52.236-22, Design Within Funding Limitations, if fixed-price unless the:

- design effort involved is minimal;
- design is for a standard structure and is not intended for a specific location; or
- head of the contracting activity or a designee determines in writing that cost limitations are secondary to performance considerations and additional project funding can be expected, if necessary.

FAR 52.236-23, Responsibility of the Architect-Engineer Contractor, if fixed-price.

FAR 52.236-24, Work Oversight in Architect-Engineer Contracts.

FAR 52.236-25, Requirements for Registration of Designers, unless the design is to be performed outside the United States and its outlying areas, or in a state or outlying area of the United States that does not require registration for the particular field.

NOTES

1. This concept is based on the *Spearin Doctrine* set forth by the Supreme Court in *United States v. Spearin*, 248 U.S. 132 (1918), which holds the contractor without liability in such cases.
2. Department of Defense, "DoD Index of Specifications and Standards," 41 CFR 101-29.216, DoD, Washington, D.C., 2012.
3. Defense Logistics Management Standards Office, "Military Standard Requisitioning and Issue Procedures," Defense Logistics Agency, Alexandria, Va., 2016.
4. *ISO* stands for the International Standards Organization. Based in Geneva, Switzerland, it is composed of representatives from many national standards

organizations to develop and issue worldwide industrial and commercial standards. *IEEE* is the Institute of Electrical and Electronics Engineers and develops standards in a variety of technological fields (e.g., energy, health, information technology, and transportation) to foster innovation and excellence.

5. General Services Administration, Federal Management Property Regulation, Part 101-29, General Services Administration, Washington, D.C., 1992.

6. This definition does not include converter scrap, over-issue publications and printer over-runs.

7. A *National Stock Number* is a 13-digit number assigned to each part in a Government inventory.

8. This and other flexibly priced contracts contain *framework pricing arrangements,* which are definitive in all respects except pricing. They include a predetermined framework (e.g., algorithm, formula or index) to calculate price at time of completion.

9. In a related vein, a *fixed-rate contract* requires product delivery for a period of time at a fixed price.

10. This concept also applies to some extent to fixed-price incentive contracts, where the point of total assumption coincides with the top end of the range (one could argue that there is no bottom end).

11. A letter contract is an example of a *gap filler,* an interim agreement to define the rights and obligations of the parties and the basis to conduct business before establishing a formal contract. Other examples of gap fillers are memoranda of understanding and teaming or short-term agreements.

12. Alternatively, an agency can issue a *letter of intent* to obligate funds while protecting price and availability of long-lead items, then convert the letter to another contract type upon definitization.

13. In a similar vein, European governments use a *framework pricing agreement* between contractor and agency to establish terms (especially price and quantity) for the parties to enter into contracts with each other during a specified time period.

14. However, when these characteristics are extensive, two-step sealed bidding or negotiation is used.

15. This would occur if a bidder charges too much for one item and not enough for another, such as not increasing the price for an item with greater requirements.

16. However, it must still be synopsized if covered by the World Trade Organization Government Procurement Agreement or a Free Trade Agreement.

17. FAPIIS was replaced by the Past Performance Information Retrieval System (PPIRS), however the website name still follows the old name.

18. The contracting officer must use some judgment in evaluating FAPIIS data, since it is up to five years old and contains contracts irrelevant to the current acquisition.

19. The list of specified felonies is long: bribery, embezzlement, falsification or destruction of records, forgery, illegally obtaining or attempting to obtain a Federal contract or subcontract, making false statements, receiving stolen property, tax evasion, theft, or violating Federal criminal tax laws.

20. This also applies if a number of contractor employees are convicted of violations of criminal drug statutes occurring in the workplace, which indicates that the contractor has failed to make a good faith effort to provide a drug-free workplace.

21. Such a determination is automatically accepted without further review in the debarment proceedings.

22. The solicitation will also include such mundane topics as page limits and font size. Though seemingly silly, the Government is serious about reducing proposal expenses and the amount of material that evaluators must sift through. The evaluators may stop reading a 15-page proposal at page 10 if that was the limit set forth in the solicitation, meaning that the last third of the proposal is totally ignored.

23. Past performance need not be evaluated for construction contracts below $550,000 in value (and architect-engineering services below $30,000 in value) unless the offeror was previously terminated for default.

24. It is a proven axiom that these presentations, either oral or written, provide the negotiator and contracting officer with an opportunity to demonstrate their talents to management and enhance their careers.

25. A contractor may also protest a decision to terminate a contract for default, arguing that it should rather be terminated for convenience. Success in such a protest will ensure a contractor gets paid for its effort while maintaining its reputation in past performance. The procedures are the same as for protesting a solicitation or award. However, a termination for convenience is not protestable because it is the Government's right to do so without contractor approval.

26. *Design-build* is an alternative method which combines design and construction into a single contract with one contractor. This approach means one award instead of two, which save the contracting office much time and effort. However, it is not very popular with contractors because so much design work must be done before realistic build costs can be derived.

27. For example, 33 U.S.C. 624 prohibits the Army Corps of Engineers from awarding a contract for harbor or river improvement that exceeds the Government cost estimate by more than 25%.

28. A D&F is required if the contracting officer desires to consider more than five offerors for Phase Two. If the acquisition exceeds $4 million, the D&F must be approved by the head of the contracting activity or designee, such as the competition advocate.

29. The contracting officer then enters these evaluations into the Contractor Performance Assessment Reporting System at www.cpars.gov.

Chapter 4

Pricing

Pricing defines the income which a firm will receive for its products. Pricing factors include manufacturing or services cost and profit goal. Pricing can be either market-based or cost-based.

4.1 MARKET-BASED PRICING

Price should match market reality in terms of competitor prices and how much customers value the products and services that it provides. This requires the firm to set an *efficient price* (the highest amount that customers are willing to pay) to maximize its return. Pricing is a balancing act, striving for equilibrium between a price floor (below which the organization loses money) and a price ceiling (beyond which demand sinks toward zero).

One can imagine three different pricing levels. Pricing at the *industry* level focuses on changes in both supplier prices and customer demand. This activity is often based on raw material or commodity futures, or else economic trends. The price we pay at the gasoline pump behaves in this manner. By contrast, pricing at the *market* level focuses on competitive pricing rather than competitor products. This results in matching competitor pricing behavior, either raising or lowering prices based on what the competition does. Retail stores operate on this approach. Finally, pricing at the *transaction* level focuses on discounts from list price, and is unique to each customer based on frequency or quantity of purchase, or importance of retaining its business. Volume discounts such as in public warehouses are a classic example of transaction pricing.

A firm will estimate the potential market price of its offering (also known as its *fair value*) by examining those features that enhance profits and help the firm maintain a competitive advantage in the marketplace. It will consider such factors as:

* cost of close substitute products;
* costs of acquisition, production and distribution;
* interaction of supply and demand;
* perceived utility by customer;
* return on capital; and
* risk.

Several different types of markets can be described in economic terms. A *monopoly* involves one supplier with so much market control that it in effect dictates the terms of sale to multiple customers, who find no effective alternative source of supply.[1] A regulated utility or raw material supplier can be an example, and there is not much the Government or prime contractor can do to obtain a price reduction. In fact, any firm guilty of price-fixing can be accused of being a monopoly. However, even a complete monopoly must be aware of potential alternative products that could cost it customers, such as a regulated landline telephone utility facing the challenge of wireless telephone carriers.

A *monopsony* is the opposite of a monopoly, in which one customer has control of the marketplace. For example, the Federal Government has monopsonistic control over the American aircraft carrier and submarine industries. In all Federal contracts in fact, certain clauses are certainly monopsonistic (e.g., Cost Accounting Standards, disputes, socioeconomics clauses, and termination for convenience). Some laws and regulations seem monopsonistic (e.g., percentage of profit limits, restrictive bidding rules, and truth in negotiation). One could argue that the Government tends to rely heavily on certain product lines, perhaps because commercial competitors refuse Government contract terms, which also leads to monopsonistic tendencies.

In contrast, an *oligopoly* is an industry with a few firms producing most of the industry output in identical form. Basic commodity industries such as aluminum or nylon would be oligopolies because they contain a few large firms producing homogeneous products. An oligopoly would also describe markets with a few sellers of differentiated products such as automobiles, cigarettes and heavy machinery. Government contracting officers may obtain some competition within an oligopoly market, but the number of offerors will be limited.

Another market type involves *differentiated sellers*. Here there may be many sellers who try to create an impression in the minds of potential customers that their products are better than their competitors. This market includes common consumer items in stores.

The contrasts between oligopolies and monopolies are significant. Oligopolies include interdependent decision-making, intense competition and relative price stability. If one firm lowers its price, others match the reduction in a "price war." Alternatively, a price increase by one may not create any response from competitors other than price maintenance to gain any customers upset with the price increase. Hence the actions of one firm can influence the behavior of other firms in the industry. Monopolies and oligopolies have significant barriers of entry due to control of natural resources, high start-up costs or technological superiority, intellectual property rights, and/or lack of substitute goods. They tend to be price-setters and can run abnormally high profits over a long term. By contrast, monopsonistic markets have more price-takers and lower barriers to entry.

4.2 COST-BASED PRICING

4.2.1 Managerial Accounting

Unlike market-based pricing, the cost-based method makes heavy use of accounting. Individual cost elements must be projected and tracked. A bottoms-up approach is used to project prices. It identifies both direct costs assignable to a specific contract and indirect costs allocated across several contracts.

Management is heavily involved in reviewing reports of these numbers. This is why cost-based pricing feeds directly into *managerial accounting* to develop numbers for reports which management can then use in developing strategies and making decisions.

Two managerial uses of cost analysis are activity-based and life-cycle costing. *Activity-based costing* correlates costs of each production activity based on their actual consumption. It sums direct and indirect costs to help estimate the total costs of products or services. This method emphasizes production efficiency such as scheduling production runs or equipment idle time when no useful work is performed. Activity-based accounting helps to identify inefficient activities and departments, so it can be used to support resource allocation and cost-control initiatives. It is quite useful in production plants where multiple products share common costs.

Life-cycle (or *whole-life*) *costing* is more comprehensive in scope because it examines total costs over the life of the program or asset, sometimes colloquially referred to as "cradle-to-grave" cost. Frequently used in Federal programs, this process recognizes that the best time to influence the cost of manufacturing is in the design stage, since small changes to the product design may lead to significant savings in manufacturing cost. Individual cost components of life-cycle costing may include:

- acquisition;
- construction;
- depreciation;
- design;
- development;
- financing;
- maintenance;
- operations;
- planning;
- production;
- renewal or rehabilitation;
- replacement or disposal;
- research; and
- training.

Total life-cycle cost is the sum of the costs for all phases of a program. Lower life-cycle costs reduce proposed price and thereby increase the chance for award, although losses may result if cost projections are too low. This process can also be used to assess lease-or-buy options by considering cost elements rather than price to derive total cost of ownership.

Life-cycle costing can also be used to cost out alternative purchase choices, which are then used in a benefit-cost analysis to select the best option. The benefit and cost of each option is calculated and then discounted into a present value. Each option (including the null option of doing nothing) receives a benefit-cost ratio, and the highest ratio is chosen.

4.2.2 Cost Accounting

Cost accounting is used to determine budgeted and actual costs of departments, operations and products. Managers use cost accounting to support decisions to cut costs and improve profitability. Cost accounting is primarily used for internal managers rather than outside users, and management decides what to compute based on its own objectives. There are so many varieties of cost accounting in use that even managers can become confused (much less you, the reader). Nonetheless, some of the common techniques will be described here.

The nature of a given cost depends on the reason for its incurrence. *Fixed costs* are incurred without regard to production volume, whereas *variable costs* are caused by production activities. Fixed costs are often a function of time because they are incurred to maintain operations (e.g., depreciation, insurance and property taxes). Over time, the law of diminishing returns will tend to reduce the extra output produced when adding more variable production factors such as labor and material. Hence, although the cost of further production increases for each succeeding item, the marginal cost of production falls. This is why quantity discounts are often feasible.

Costs are collected through the life of the project and summarized at its end point. Costs are collected either by job order or by process. *Job order costing* collects costs assigned to a specific job by reference number. Direct costs are recorded at their actual value. In contrast, *process costing* collects costs continuously for high-volume, homogeneous, standardized products when unit costs cannot be developed until after the work is completed. Dividing total costs by units of work performed yields a process cost. Both of these methods collect historical costs of the product, which can then be adjusted to allow for changes in such factors as equipment, manufacture methods, materials, plant layout, working conditions and efficiency, and even uncontrollable factors such as time and weather. Alternatively, the firm can develop *cost-estimating relationships* to apply historical costs to a performance or physical feature of the end product, such as cost per pound. Use of these relationships is quick and easy, and quite objective, however they do not allow history to reflect the factor changes cited above, and could be too simplistic or even inaccurate.

To project what a cost should be, the department may develop *standard costs,* which are expected values used as goals or baselines. Standard costs are derived through engineering studies, efficiency reviews and actual working conditions. The accounting system captures and analyzes variances from standards for material, labor hours and overhead costs. The difference between planned and actual cost is a *variance*, which can be analyzed by dividing the actual cost into its components (e.g., labor, material, etc.) to determine why costs differ from their planned level. The standard costs for each factor of production are then added to overhead to derive the cost of the finished unit. Note that overhead is not a standard cost, but rather a period cost for a set time frame, often a month.

Yet another choice for product costing is to use either the absorption or direct costing method. *Absorption costing* assigns costs to production units as they progress through stages, from Work in Process through Finished Goods to Cost of Goods Sold. Indirect costs are added to direct labor and material costs to yield the total unit cost. If standard costing is used, then the product cost is the sum of standard allowances for each factor of production. This method recognizes that unit cost will vary with production volume. A variation of this approach is the *normal cost* approach, which takes the actual labor and material costs of a production item and adds a predetermined estimate of overhead cost derived from the average production schedule.

By contrast, *direct costing* classifies all costs as either fixed or variable regardless of volume or production stage. It assigns all variable costs to production accounts and all fixed costs to an expense account which is then allocated across all production units. Because the direct costing method separates fixed and variable costs from overhead, it can more easily identify key pricing factors and ignore any variations in overhead costs. Direct costing data is especially useful to determine lot sizes and economical production runs, and is typically used in pricing proposals. However, direct costing may miss some production and inventory costs and does not consider charges against revenue for the period, and is therefore not widely used to measure earnings.

Accountants use several more terms to describe types of costs. *Discretionary* or *managed costs* are fixed costs which reflect management policies, such as advertising or research and development. The opposite would be *avoidable costs,* those not incurred due to management decision to change or delete a given operation (e.g., shutting down a department to avoid salary expenses). *Joint costs* are common to multiple business segments of the firm and must be allocated to a collection pool. Joint costs could be assigned to multiple units without identification to a specific unit until they reach a later *split-off point* where the individual units can again be identified.

Time is an element that is reflected in several costing terms. *Unexpired costs* are carried forward to a future accounting period and treated as an asset, such as inventory. *Recurring costs* occur period after period. *Nonrecurring costs* are one-time expenses such as plant or equipment setup or moving, preproduction engineering, special tooling and test equipment, spoilage and rework, and workforce training.

Capital expenditures benefit future periods, such as investing in new equipment or plant, whereas *revenue expenditures* only benefit the current period (such as maintenance of equipment). An expenditure which requires current or future resource utilization is an *out-of-pocket cost* and thus an impending cash outflow. By contrast, a *sunk cost* is a past commitment of funds (e.g., depreciation) and may be irrelevant to future decision-making.

Incremental costs result from a decision to do or not do something, such as to increase or change production. Incremental costing can be used for quantity buys or options where fixed costs were covered during the initial production run. This process can also be used in make-or-buy decisions to provide an alternative method to decide whether to preserve labor or a production line, such as to fabricate a component when demand is down and buy it when demand is up.

A firm can also use *throughput accounting* to allocate variable costs to products and services, which are then deducted from sales revenue to determine actual throughput. This method is based on cash receipts and may not allocate all fixed costs or overhead. It seeks to maximize throughput (and reduce inventory and operating costs) rather than profit.

Finally, *lean accounting* is an approach that eliminates traditional costing procedures and budgeting, instead focusing on:

- box scores for decision-making;
- desire to free up capacity;
- eliminating transactional control systems;
- eliminating waste;
- performance measurements;
- simple financial reports;
- speeding up the process;
- summarizing direct costs; and
- value-based pricing.

4.2.3 Auditing

An *audit* systematically evaluates a firm, system, process, or project. Audits review the validity and reliability of information by developing a formal written opinion based on testing (often statistical sampling) and then assessment of the results. Audits adhere to generally accepted standards set by governing bodies to provide sufficient confidence that the opinions are arrived at professionally and reasonably error-free. Auditors can review financial systems and records, information system performance and security risks. An *integrated audit* goes one step further, in that auditors express a written opinion on a firm's internal control over financial reporting. Auditors validate reported cost savings and cost reduction reports by selectively reviewing the reports and supporting documents.

The accountant for the firm is under a professional obligation for *full disclosure* of all relevant information to promote a clear understanding and avoid errant implications. Accountants use the *objectivity test* to ensure that information is verifiable and can be reproduced for independent reviewers who use the same set of facts and assumptions.

Quality audits review a quality management system, usually in accordance with ISO 9001 (which will be discussed later). Quality audits assess if processes achieve their targets, are properly implemented and reduce problem areas. Such audits can also look at monitoring procedures, but are primarily concerned with program effectiveness.

Audits should not be confused with assessments. Audits are independent evaluations involving quantitative and qualitative analysis, whereas an *assessment* tends to be less independent and more consultative in nature. Generally, consultants conduct assessments and independent third parties run audits.

4.2.4 Chart of Accounts

Every firm keeps a list of the various accounts in which it accumulates costs. This is necessary for both proposals and cost accounting. Assets, liabilities and expenses are maintained in separate sections, with numerous accounts treated as "buckets" into which accountants drop specific debits and credits ("plusses" and "minuses"). Set forth in Table 4.1 is a sample chart listing typical accounts with assigned code numbers.

Table 4.1   Chart of Accounts

ASSETS (0-199)
CASH (100-129)
101 Petty Cash
110 Bank Savings Account
112 Payables Checking Account
115 Payroll Checking Account
120 Money Market Account
RECEIVABLES (130-139)
131 Customer Accounts Receivable
INVENTORIES (140-149)
140 Purchased Materials
145 Subassembly Inventory
146 Work-in-Process Inventory
147 Finished Product Inventory
PREPAID EXPENSES (150-159)
151 Rent
154 Advertising
155 Insurance
FIXED ASSETS (160-199)
161 Land
162 Buildings
169 Buildings Depreciation
170 Machinery & Equipment
179 Machinery & Equipment - Depreciation
180 Furniture & Fixtures
188 Leasehold Improvements
189 Furniture & Fixtures - Depreciation
190 Transportation Equipment
199 Transportation Equipment - Depreciation
LIABILITIES & EQUITY (200-299)
PAYABLES (200-229)
220 Accounts Payable

225 Commissions Payable
229 State Sales/Use Tax Payable
PAYROLL & WITHHOLDINGS (230-239)
231 Accrued Wages
232 Vacation
234 Withholdings - FIT (federal income tax)
235 Withholdings - FICA (social security)
236 Withholdings - FICM (Medicare)
237 Withholdings - SIT (state income tax)
ACCRUED EXPENSES (240-249)
240 Federal Unemployment Tax
241 State Unemployment Tax
249 Property Tax
OTHER LIABILITIES (250-259)
250 Bank Loan
251 Mortgage
EQUITY (280-289)
280 Common Stock
285 Paid-In Capital
289 Retained Earnings
NET EARNINGS (290-299)
290 Domestic Revenue
297 Exports

EXPENSES (300-999)

MANUFACTURING EXPENSE (300-399)
320 Labor - General
325 Overtime
326 Bonuses
335 Vacation
336 Holidays
340 Material Discounts
349 Manufacturing Supplies
355 Heat, Light, Power
361 Freight Out
362 Freight In
370 Outside Services
ENGINEERING EXPENSE (400-499)
420 Labor
425 Overtime
426 Bonuses
435 Vacation
436 Holidays
460 Supplies
470 Outside Services
495 Royalties
SELLING EXPENSE (600-699)
620 Labor
625 Overtime
626 Bonuses
629 Commissions

(Continued)

Table 4.1 Chart of Accounts (Continued)

635 Vacation
636 Holidays
640 Air Travel
641 Auto Expense
642 Parking and Tolls
650 Advertising
660 Supplies
669 Postage
670 Outside Services
680 Travel & Entertainment
690 Bad Debts
696 Sales Allowances
ADMINSTRATIVE EXPENSE (700-799)
720 Labor
725 Overtime
735 FICA
738 Federal Unemployment Tax
739 State Unemployment Tax
741 Workers Compensation
745 Employee Insurance
751 Sick Leave
752 Vacation
753 Holidays
760 Benefits
765 Commissions
771 Equipment Maintenance
772 Facility Maintenance
775 Supplies
778 Telephone
780 Outside Services
782 Legal & Audit
785 Travel & Entertainment
786 Automotive
787 Depreciation
789 Corporate Insurance
792 Real Property Tax
793 Personal Property Tax
795 Sales/Use Tax
OTHER EXPENSE (900-999)
940 Loan Interest

Note the broad headings in the chart above. Assets include permanent physical attributes such as equipment, facilities and land. Liabilities include payable accounts such as material inventory, prepaid benefits and work in process. Next come accrued liabilities such as payroll and associated taxes due, then loans and mortgages which raise operating capital. Equity such as stock and bond issues, as well as net earnings, are treated as liabilities by accountants. The rest of the accounts address operating expenses such as labor, selling and other administrative activities.

4.2.5 Direct Costs

Direct costs (or *prime costs*) are traced logically and entirely to a final cost objective (e.g., job or contract), such as direct labor or material. This reflects the matching concept in accounting theory that aligns expenses with the revenue they generate.

Labor costs are the salaries paid to employees who charge to a given job. Often these are engineers who develop solutions to specific issues on a contract, manufacturing people on the assembly line, or professional and technical personnel who provide services as subject matter experts.

There are several broad categories of engineering labor. Design engineers are paid to turn concepts into drawings and procedures. They specify the physical characteristics of the product and develop drawings (assemblies and tooling), parts lists, schematics, and technical manuals (installation, repair, training, and users). This may also include engineers who develop reliability and repair documentation, and schedules to ensure maintainability.

Manufacturing engineers plan labor activities to produce the item by writing manufacturing instructions and process sheets, organizing work stations and scheduling production activities. Manufacturing labor examples include:

- assembly of components;
- fabrication of parts from raw material;
- inspection of assemblies and fabrications;
- machine operators;
- mechanical and system testers; and
- painting and engraving.

Quality assurance engineers develop specifications for test equipment and procedures to test the end product for compliance and performance. Field engineers support deployed end items through a variety of maintenance and testing tasks.

Some job-shop factories collect costs under a *job order* system against a specific contract or production run. This technique is chosen because the runs are short-term and designed to customer specifications, which makes cost forecasting a difficult task. By contrast, continuous manufacturers and mass producers of a single product use a *process cost* system which collects all costs over an accounting period (usually a month). Costs travel with the product from one process center to another until recorded in the final center.

Sometimes, direct laborers support multiple contracts in the course of a week or month, and therefore may be charging their time to several contracts. Because it is often impossible to predict who will charge how much time to a specific contract, much less track their actual payroll cost to each contract, firms will create *labor categories* of similar labor types and responsibilities in which to accumulate salary expenses. Within a given project or contract, there may be different labor categories. The projected salaries for the upcoming year are averaged out to create an hourly *labor rate* for each category, which is then used to price out labor projections in proposals and to bill for hours incurred on contracts.

Material costs are frequently spelled out in a *bill of materials* that describes and quantifies by listing all items necessary to fabricate the final end item. Each item on the list includes a part number and name or similar identification, required quantity per unit and in total, unit price, and extended cost (quantity multiplied by unit price).

Raw material quantity estimates must allow for scrap and shrinkage incurred during production. Parts may be consumed during trial-and-error testing during machine setup. Machine tolerance and sheet cutting may create unusable overage and hence scrap.[2]

Material costs consist of three different types. *Raw material* includes the purchase of any substance that is transformed during manufacture into a different form, such as aluminum or solder. *Purchased parts* are commercial items that are often listed and priced in a vendor's catalog. If they prove defective during contract performance, the subcontractor bears the responsibility to remedy the problem at its own cost. *Subcontracted items* are bought from vendors based on the buyer's specifications, often made to order rather than pulled from stock. If they prove defective, the buyer bears the responsibility for correction and may need to fund any rework out of its own pocket. This is another manifestation of the *contra preferentum* concept, which we have seen before.

Material can be issued from stock using either a First-In-First-Out (FIFO) or Last-In-First-Out (LIFO) method. For most firms, the actual flow of materials follows FIFO, where the oldest items are sold first while newer items are kept in stock. If costs are increasing, the first items sold are therefore the least expensive, so the cost of goods sold decreases, thereby increasing profits (and income taxes). Under LIFO, the newer items are more expensive, so as the cost of goods sold increases, both profits and income taxes decrease. Of course, if costs are decreasing, the opposite effects occur.

Other direct costs sometimes appear in proposals. These are pass-through costs that are incurred solely for the contract and do not bear any overhead. Examples include:

- computer processing time at a corporate or independent server;
- consultant services;
- federal excise taxes;
- interdivisional transfers from another unit in the corporation;[3]
- royalty expense;
- special tooling and test equipment; and
- travel and seminar attendance at customer direction.

4.2.6 Indirect Costs

FAR 31.201-6

After direct costs have been determined and charged appropriately, *indirect costs* are those remaining to be allocated to intermediate or multiple final cost objectives. Indirect costs cannot be identified with just one final cost objective and are therefore collected into *cost centers* or expense pools. At the end of the accounting period, they are allocated based on logical and causal relationships that reflect the department responsible for their incurrence. The logic here is that the department would not have incurred the expense if it did not wish to receive the benefit. Examples of indirect costs include:

- building maintenance and repair;
- depreciation;
- insurance:
  - accident,
  - fire,
  - flood, and
  - personal liability;
- office equipment and furniture;
- rent;
- travel;
- utilities:
  - electricity,
  - fuel,
  - telephone, and
  - water and sewage.

Depreciation requires a definition of what constitutes a capital expense, since one could go crazy depreciating every pen or coffeemaker in the plant. So most firms use a rule of thumb that they will only capitalize and depreciate major items (usually over $5,000 in purchase price) and expense the smaller-value items to current-year cost centers. In fact, the contractor may treat any small direct cost as an indirect cost if consistently applied to all final cost objectives and resulting in substantially the same results as if it treated the cost as direct.

A *base period* to allocate indirect costs is the time frame when costs are incurred and accumulated to allocate work performed. This is usually a 12-month period of time coinciding with the contractor's *fiscal year*, the accounting period for which annual financial statements are regularly prepared.

The firm cannot split the base by removing individual elements; all items within the base bear a pro rata share of indirect costs. The allocation method may be revised due to change in the business, extent of subcontracting, fixed-asset improvements, inventory, manufacturing processes, and sales and production volume. The end result is a series of rates to equitably allocate costs. Equitability is important because a pool which is either under- or overabsorbed could cause the firm's competitive posture to suffer. Moreover, indirect costs are harder to control in the short run than direct costs because so many of them are fixed costs in nature.

Overhead is the term that covers indirect expenses incurred to support direct costs. Hence, there are *material overhead* and *labor overhead* pools. *Material overhead* comprises those expenses covering direct material charged to contracts:

- inspection;
- insurance;
- inventory;
- issuance;
- procurement operations;[4]
- receiving; and
- stockroom storage.

Labor overhead includes salaries of employees who spread their time among numerous contracts to such an extent that their time cannot be parsed to a level of detail where it could be allocated to a specific contract. This includes such labor types as clerical, maintenance and supervisors (and, with some firms, quality control).

Labor overhead covers a number of expenses in support of contract labor:

- depreciation of manufacturing equipment;
- employee benefits, e.g.:
  - awards,
  - bonuses,

- ○ leave (annual, educational and sick),
- ○ unemployment programs, and
- ○ workman's compensation;
- equipment maintenance and insurance;
- payroll taxes;
- time card maintenance; and
- utilities.

Labor categories may be accrued into several clusters, each to bear its own overhead rate. This occurs when overhead expenses vary widely between clusters. This approach also serves to make services contracts more competitive by eliminating the need to include manufacturing costs that are unrelated to the end objective of a services contract. Common cluster names are engineering, field engineering or on-site support, manufacturing, and quality assurance.

General and Administrative (G&A) expenses are incurred to manage and administer the whole business unit. They are collected in a separate indirect cost pool for allocation to final cost objectives through a G&A base. Examples of G&A costs include:

- accounting;
- computer operations;
- conventions and seminars;
- depreciation;
- entertainment;
- executive management;
- Federal income tax;
- home office;
- human resources;
- insurance;
- interest;
- legal;
- memberships and professional society dues;
- office equipment and supplies;
- parking;
- postage;
- printing;
- recruiting;
- relocation;
- rent;
- salaries and benefits;
- sales;

- subscriptions;
- telephone;
- tools;
- training;
- transportation; and
- utilities.

The cost input base to allocate G&A expense includes all elements of the business unit's activity. The cost input base may use a total cost, value-added or single-element method. However, any changes from one type of input base to another due to a business circumstance are subject to equitable adjustment, provided that the contractor has notified the contracting officer of the change.

Total cost is the most common method, since it simply adds up all the direct and overhead costs of the business unit. However, the other two methods can be used if a particular final cost objective or contract would receive a disproportionate allocation of G&A expenses by using the total cost input base. This is because the cost accounting standard does not permit the use of an abated or reduced rate for many costs.

Large subcontracts that do not require close supervision by the prime contractor could absorb G&A on a *value-added* base, which includes only labor and its overhead costs and excludes material and subcontract costs. Service contractors with major purchasing and subcontracting responsibility on a pass-through basis could allocate G&A as either the value-added or single-element method.

A *single-element* cost input base may be used only when the base dollars are significant. This could occur with a services contractor which has heavy labor costs but very little material expense or other direct costs.

Any work on stock or product inventory items is considered a productive activity and therefore receives a G&A allocation only for the period(s) in which the items are produced or worked on. No additional G&A is applied when these items are finally issued.

The cost element known as *cost of capital* is the expected return on financing that reflects the cost of debt and equity. This is a technique to evaluate potential new projects by deriving the minimum return that investors expect for providing capital to the company. This is the logic behind Facilities Capital Cost of Money recognition used in DoD contracts, due to the need for heavy investment in facilities for military-unique production. It is not recognized for civilian agencies or departments.

A *directly associated cost* is generated solely because of incurring another cost (e.g., salary of personnel incurred while generating unallowable costs). When an unallowable cost is incurred, its directly associated costs are also unallowable and so identified in any billing, claim or proposal to the Government. If a directly associated cost is included in a cost pool allocated over a base that includes an unallowable cost, the Government will disallow both the unallowable costs and their allocable share of costs from the indirect cost pool if they are material. *Materiality* is a function of the actual dollar amount, cumulative effect of all directly associated costs in a cost pool, and ultimate effect on total contract cost.

Statistical sampling is a valid way to account for unallowable costs if it results in an unbiased sample of the universe that permits audit verification. Any large dollar-value or high-risk transaction is removed from the universe and separately reviewed. An advance agreement specifies the basic characteristics of the sampling process, or else the burden of proof is on the contractor to establish that its method meets these criteria. The sampling process may be *probability sampling* (selecting sample units according to chance) or *nonprobability sampling* (selecting sample units based on personal choice or expert judgment).

Solicitation Provisions and Contract Clauses

FAR 52.215-9, Changes or Additions to Make-or-Buy Program, when a make-or-buy program is contemplated for the contract. If a less economical "make" or "buy" categorization is selected for one or more items of significant value, use the clause with Alternate I for a fixed-price incentive contract, or Alternate II for a cost-plus-incentive-fee contract.

FAR 52.215-10, Price Reduction for Defective Cost or Pricing Data, when cost or pricing data will be required from the contractor or any subcontractor.

FAR 52.215-11, Price Reduction for Defective Cost or Pricing Data – Modifications, if cost or pricing data will be required from the contractor or any subcontractor to price contract modifications, and FAR 52.215-10 is not used.

FAR 52.215-12, Subcontractor Cost or Pricing Data, when FAR 52.215-10 is included.

FAR 52.215-13, Subcontractor Cost or Pricing Data – Modifications, when FAR 52.215-11 is included.

FAR 52.215-14, Integrity of Unit Prices, if greater than the simplified acquisition threshold except for:

- commercial items;
- construction or architect-engineer services;
- petroleum products;
- services where supplies are not required; and
- utility services.

Use the clause with its Alternate I when contracting without adequate price competition or when prescribed by agency regulations.

FAR 52.215-15, Pension Adjustments and Asset Reversions, when cost or pricing data will be required.

FAR 52.215-16, Facilities Capital Cost of Money, in solicitations with commercial organizations subject to cost principles. If so, the contract will replace this provision with the clause at FAR 52.215-17, Waiver of Facilities Capital Cost of Money.

FAR 52.215-18, Reversion or Adjustment of Plans for Postretirement Benefits (PRB) Other Than Pensions, when cost or pricing data will be required.

FAR 52.215-19, Notification of Ownership Changes, when cost or pricing data will be required.

FAR 52.215-21, Requirements for Cost or Pricing Data or Information Other Than Cost or Pricing Data – Modifications, if cost or pricing data or other information will probably be required for contract modifications. This clause also provides instructions to contractors on how to request an exception. Use the clause with its Alternate I to specify an alternative format for cost or pricing data. Use the clause with its Alternate II if copies of the proposal are to be sent to the contract administration office and contract auditor. Use the clause with its Alternate III if submission via electronic media is required. Replace the basic clause with its Alternate IV if cost or pricing data are not expected to be required because an exception may apply, but other pricing information is required.

FAR 52.215-22, Limitation on Pass-Through Charges—Identification of Subcontract Effort, for a cost-reimbursement contract over the simplified aaquisition threshold.[5]

FAR 52.215-23, Limitations on Pass-Through Charges, when using FAR 52.215-22. Use the clause with its Alternate I when the prospective contractor has demonstrated that its functions provide added value to the contracting effort and there are no excessive pass-through charges.

Solicitation Provision

FAR 52.215-20, Requirements for Cost or Pricing Data or Information Other Than Cost or Pricing Data, in solicitations if cost or pricing data will be required. This provision also provides instructions to offerors on how to request an exception. The contracting officer uses Alternate forms in the same manner and conditions as FAR 52.215-21.

4.3 COST PRINCIPLES

FAR 31

Federal contractors use cost accounting procedures governed by *generally accepted accounting procedures* (GAAP) issued by the Financial Accounting Standards Board, a private institution of the accounting trade. GAAP is not accounting theory, but rather a collection of agreements based on custom, experience, practical necessity, and reason. These practices have the authoritative support of the accounting trade and are accepted practices within the profession. The U.S. Government does not impose any financial reporting regulations on its contractors, believing that the private sector is in a better position to understand the needs of the users of financial information.

In view of GAAP, the Government issues *cost principles* to equitably treat similar firms doing similar work. Cost principles and procedures are used in contracts with commercial firms to:[6]

- calculate the cost-reimbursement portion of time-and-materials contracts;
- definitize changes and contract modifications and terminations;
- negotiate indirect cost rates; and
- revise fixed-price incentive contracts.

The accounting profession has a mindset of exactitude which is reflected in its treatment of costs. Accountants generally use a policy of conservatism to avoid overstating assets and income. Costs must be treated the same in successive years to ensure consistency over time.

The contractor submits a description of any proposed change to its accounting process at least 60 days before implementation. If the description is adequate and compliant with cost accounting principles, the contracting officer requests the contractor to submit a general dollar magnitude proposal of the estimated overall impact on affected (sub)contracts based on the previous cost accounting practice, or else the fiscal year(s) in which the costs are incurred. The parties then negotiate any cost or price adjustments. If the request is denied, the change might still be implemented unilaterally by the contractor.

The Government may not object as long as the change complies with GAAP, and will certainly be happy if it deems the change to be desirable. A *desirable change* is any unilateral change to a disclosed cost accounting practice that the contracting officer finds beneficial to the Government. The contractor elects to make the change voluntarily and the Government pays no aggregate increased costs. To be deemed desirable, the contracting officer must consider how the change will maintain compliance with cost accounting principles and promote cost savings through forward pricing rates. If the change leads to a cost increase, availability of funds is necessary.

Individual deviations concerning cost principles require advance approval of the agency head or designee. Class deviations require advance approval of the Civilian Agency Acquisition Council for civilian agencies, NASA's Deputy Chief Acquisition Officer, and the Director of Defense Procurement in the Office of the Under Secretary of Defense for Acquisition, Technology and Logistics.

Administrative contracting officers and contractors may seek advance agreement on the treatment of special or unusual costs. Advance agreements are negotiated before incurrence of these costs. The agreements must be in writing and executed by both parties before being incorporated into applicable current and future contracts. Advance agreements may cover a single contract or group of contracts, or for all the contracts of a contracting office or agencies. Examples for which advance agreements may be useful are:

- compensation (e.g., incentive pay, living differential, relocation, severance, or termination of defined benefit pension plans;
- construction plant and equipment costs;
- deferred maintenance costs;
- general and administrative costs for architect-engineer, construction or job site, facilities, and GOCO plant contracts;
- idle facilities and idle capacity;
- independent research and development, and bid and proposal costs;
- plant reconversion;
- precontract costs;
- professional services (e.g., accounting, engineering, or legal);
- public relations and advertising;
- royalties;
- selling and distribution costs;
- statistical sampling methods;
- training and education;
- travel; and
- usage charges for fully depreciated assets.

Any generally accepted method to determine or estimate future costs may be used if it is equitable and consistently applied. The contractor must account for costs and maintain supporting documentation. A cost is *allowable* only when allocable, compliant with GAAP, permitted by contract terms, and reasonable. The contracting officer may disallow any unsupported cost or portion thereof. This is why flexibly priced contracts require certification of the indirect cost rates to initiate final payment. If unallowable costs are included in final indirect cost settlement proposals after contract termination, penalties may be assessed.

A cost is *reasonable* if it does not exceed that which would be incurred by a prudent person in the conduct of competitive business. No presumption of reasonableness is attached to a cost just because it was incurred. Once challenged by the contracting officer, the burden of proof is upon the contractor to establish that the cost is reasonable. What is reasonable depends upon:

- contractor responsibilities to employees, the Government, other customers, owners, and the public;
- deviations from the contractor's established practices;
- Federal and State laws and regulations;
- general recognition of a cost as ordinary and necessary to conduct business or perform the contract; and
- generally accepted sound business practices and arm's-length bargaining.

A cost is *allocable* if appropriately assigned to one (or more) cost objective. Allocation includes both direct assignment of cost and the reassignment of a share from indirect cost pools. A cost is allocable if:

- assignable or chargeable to one or more cost objectives based on relative benefits received or other equitable relationship;[7]
- benefiting both the contract and other work;
- distributed to work in reasonable proportion to the benefits received;
- incurred specifically for the contract; and
- necessary to the overall operation of the business.

The Government receives a credit for the applicable portion of any income, rebate or allowance relating to any allowable cost that is received by or accrues to the contractor. This credit is taken either as a cost reduction or a cash refund.

Direct costs are charged directly to the contract. All costs specifically identified with other final cost objectives of the contractor are direct costs of those cost objectives and therefore are not charged to the contract, either directly or indirectly. If a cost was previously incurred for the same purpose in like circumstances and included in an indirect cost pool, the contractor must treat the cost as indirect to be consistent with past practice. Of course, the contractor may treat any small direct cost as indirect if the accounting treatment is consistently applied to all final cost objectives and results in the same outcome as if it were treated as a direct cost.

After direct costs have been determined and charged directly to the contract, indirect costs must then be allocated to intermediate or multiple final cost objectives. To do this, the contractor accumulates these indirect costs by logical cost groupings based on the reasons for their incurrence. The contractor then determines an allocation base that is common to all cost objectives. The base must then allocate the grouping to intermediate and final cost objectives based on the accrued benefits.

Once an appropriate base for allocating indirect costs has been accepted, the contractor cannot remove individual elements. All items includable in an indirect cost base must bear a pro rata share of indirect costs, regardless of whether they are acceptable as Government contract costs. If unallowable, the Government will recalculate the rate by excluding these costs and negotiate a lower rate.

The base period for allocating indirect costs is the same as the accounting period during which the costs are incurred and accumulated. The base period is usually the contractor's fiscal year used for financial reporting purposes. The fiscal year will normally be 12 months, but a different period may be appropriate (e.g., a change in fiscal year due to a business combination).

4.3.1 Advertising and Public Relations Costs

FAR 31.205-1

Advertising costs cover use of communications media to promote sales. These media include billboards, broadcasting, business cards, conventions, magazines, and samples. These costs cover not only the actual expense of buying time and space, but also associated salaries, fringe benefits and travel. Advertising costs are allowable if required by (or arising from) the contract to acquire scarce items or dispose of scrap or surplus materials acquired for contract performance. Costs to promote exports of products sold to the U.S. Government, including trade shows, are allowable except for alcoholic beverages, entertainment and memorabilia.

Public relations expenses are incurred to promote a favorable image of the company and its products among the public. Allowable public relations costs include:

- participation in community service activities (e.g., blood bank, charity and savings bond campaigns, disaster assistance, etc.);
- plant tours and open houses;
- public communications (e.g., creditors, customers, press, stockholders, etc.);
- responding to inquiries on company policies and activities; and
- roll-out ceremonies specifically provided for by contract (e.g., keel laying, ship launching or commissioning, etc.).

Other advertising and public relations costs not listed above are disallowed. This includes corporate celebrations, donation of excess food, dues for joining community activities, product promotional material, and special events that do not disseminate technical information.

4.3.2 Bad Debts

FAR 31.205-3

Bad debts, collection costs and legal costs from uncollectable accounts receivable are unallowable.

4.3.3 Bonding Costs

FAR 31.205-4

Bonding costs are allowable when the Government requires assurance against financial loss to itself or others caused by contractor act or default. This covers bid, payment and performance bonds. Any bonding costs to cover general conduct of a business are also allowable where customary for the trade.

4.3.4 Compensation for Personal Services

31.205-6

Compensation covers the total amount of wages, bonuses, deferred compensation, and employer contributions to defined contribution pension plans. Allowable compensation costs must be for work performed by the employee in the current year, not a retroactive adjustment of prior years' wages. The total compensation must conform to the terms and conditions of the contractor's implemented compensation plan or practice. Distribution of profits is not an allowable cost. Table 4.2 gives a comparison of allowable and unallowable costs.

Reasonable tests for compensation involve looking at similar firms of the same size and industry, perhaps in the same geographic area, engaged in similar non-Government work.

Incentive pay systems which offer more money for more labor are controversial because they create several problems. They may tend to sacrifice quality for quantity, can lead to friction between labor and management, and may divert the latter's attention from improving organization and operations. Incentive rates are rather inelastic and hard to charge as time rates. Incentive plans may be unusable in new operations or by beginning workers. They could increase supervision of employees. Finally, it is hard to change from a time-rate to incentive wage system.

Table 4.2

Allowable Costs	Unallowable Costs
Compensation costs established under "arm's length" labor-management agreements	Compensation costs unjustified by the nature of the work, discriminatory, or exceeding that paid for similar commercial work by other firms of the same size, industry and geographic area
Corporate stocks and bonds assessed at the fair market value on the date when the number of shares awarded is known	---
Income taxes and reimbursed relocation costs due to foreign assignments	Differential income tax allowances from domestic assignments
Bonuses and incentive compensation paid or accrued under an agreement pre-dating the services rendered, or pursuant to an established plan or policy	---
Severance pay to workers if involuntarily terminated, required by law, employer-employee agreement, established contractor policy, or circumstances of employment	Payments to a replacement contractor to continue employment at another facility or entity of the firm
Normal turnover severance payments based on past experience at the contractor's plant	Mass severance pay, though case-by-case exceptions may be granted
Severance payments to foreign nationals employed under a service contract performed outside the United States	Severance payments to the same foreign nationals that exceed amounts typically paid to domestic employees providing similar services in the same industry within the United States, or if the facility is closed by direction of the host government
Back pay (a retroactive adjustment of prior years' salaries or wages) for underpaid work required by a negotiated settlement or court decree, or to union employees (and to nonunion employees under a firm's policy or practice) incurred during labor-management negotiations while no labor agreement is in force	All other forms of back pay, including changes in the price of corporate securities, dividend or cash payments to an employee in lieu of receiving or exercising an unallowable benefit, option or right
Year-end accruals for salaries, wages or bonuses paid within a reasonable time after the end of a cost accounting period	Deferred compensation to award an employee in a future cost accounting period(s) for services rendered in a prior period

---	Termination payments to employees after a change in management control or ownership of the firm or its assets
---	Payments to employees under plans introduced by a management change which are contingent upon the employee remaining with the firm for a specified period of time
An early retirement incentive plan if the plan benefits only active employees. The firm must measure, assign and allocate the costs in accordance with its accounting practices.	The present value of the total incentives in excess of the employee's annual salary for the fiscal year before retirement
Fringe benefits – allowances and services provided by the firm to its employees in addition to regular wages and salaries (e.g., employee insurance, holidays, vacations, sick and military leave, and supplemental unemployment benefit plans). These costs must be required by law, employer-employee agreement, or the firm's established policy.	The cost of company-furnished automobiles for personal use by employees, including transportation to and from work
---	Rebates and purchase discounts granted to employees on products or services produced by the firm or its affiliates
Employee stock ownership plans (ESOP) – a stock bonus plan designed to invest primarily in the stock of the employer. Pension costs must be funded by the time set for filing the Federal income tax return or any extension.	Contributions by the firm in any one year that exceed the deductibility limits of the Internal Revenue Code (26 U.S.C. et seq.) for that year
ESOP stock contributions limited to the fair market value of the stock on the date that title is effectively transferred to the trust.	Stock purchases by the ESOP in excess of fair market value. The excess amount must be credited to the same indirect cost pools charged for the ESOP contributions in the year in which the stock purchase occurs.

Post-retirement benefit plans are very complicated in their cost treatment, yet are a critical element in an employee's compensation package and therefore require some discussion. A *pension plan* is a deferred compensation method established and maintained by employers to pay benefits to plan participants after their retirement. They may include additional benefits (e.g., permanent and total disability payments, and survivorship payments to beneficiaries of deceased employees). A *pension plan participant* is a current or former employee or beneficiary who is or may become eligible to receive a benefit from a pension plan by meeting its participation requirements.

A *qualified pension plan* is a written program to benefit employees that meets the Internal Revenue Code criteria for preferential tax treatment regarding contributions, investments and distributions. Any other plan is deemed a *nonqualified pension plan.*

For most pension plans, the contractor must fund pension costs by the deadline to file the Federal income tax return or any extension thereto. Traditionally, most companies fund these costs within 30 days of the end of the quarter. But for defined-contribution pension plans, where the company sets aside a specific amount or percentage every year, allowable pension cost is limited to the net contribution for the cost accounting period (after considering dividends and other credits).

Pension payments require an agreement between the contractor and employees before the work is performed. Most one-time-only pension supplements unavailable to all participants of the basic plan are not allowable unless they represent a separate pension plan and the benefits are payable for life at the employee's option. However, the Government will allow increased payments for cost-of-living adjustments to previously retired plan participants.

A firm using the pay-as-you-go method allocates pension costs in the cost accounting period to which they are assigned. Any excess funded amount is assigned to a future period. For defined-benefit plans, a pension cost exceeding the amount required to be funded pursuant to a waiver granted under the Employee Retirement Income Security Act of 1974 (29 U.S.C. 1001) is allowable in those future accounting periods to which the funding is assigned.

Indemnifying the Pension Benefit Guaranty Corporation due to terminating an employee deferred compensation plan is allowable if the indemnification payment is not recoverable under insurance.

An advance agreement is required to recognize increased pension costs if assets are withdrawn from a pension fund and transferred to another employee benefit plan fund or related account. The advance agreement states the portion of the Government's equitable share in the amount withdrawn or transferred. Unless otherwise specified by law or regulation, the Government may direct refund or credit of its equitable share of any assets that revert to the contractor. Excise taxes on pension plan asset reversions or withdrawals are unallowable.

Certain fringe benefits are strictly disallowed. Deferred bonuses are not allowable – only a bonus paid in the current year is recognized. Payments to terminated workers in excess of normal company severance payments are also disallowed. In the opposite sense, a payment to remain with the company when taken over by new management will be disallowed. Use of company cars is allowable to the extent they are used for company business, but not that part attributed to personal use. Employee rebates and purchase discounts are also unallowable.

Post-retirement benefits other than pensions (PRB) cover all benefits (other than cash and life insurance paid by pension plans) provided to employees, their beneficiaries and covered dependents during the period following the employees' retirement. Examples of PRB include day care, health care, housing subsidies, legal services, life insurance, and tuition assistance. PRB costs must be incurred pursuant to law, employer-employee agreement or an established contractor policy. There are three different types of PRB plans:

- *Accrual basis.* PRB costs are accrued during the working lives of employees and are paid to an insurer or trustee to establish and maintain a fund or reserve solely to provide PRB to retirees. They are measured and assigned in accordance with either GAAP or the Internal Revenue Code.
- *Pay-as-you-go.* This is the opposite approach – PRB costs are not accrued during the working lives of employees. Costs are assigned to the period in which benefits are actually provided or paid to an insurer or provider for current year benefits or premiums.
- *Terminal funding.* Again, PRB costs are not accrued during the working lives of the employees. The entire PRB liability is paid in a lump sum upon employee termination (or conversion to a terminal-funded plan) to an insurer or trustee to establish and maintain a fund reserve for PRB payments to retirees. Terminal funded costs are amortized over a period of 15 years.

As with pension plans, PRB costs must be funded or paid to the insurer or provider by the time set for filing the Federal income tax return or any extension thereof, and are not allowable in any subsequent year. Similarly, increased PRB costs due to delay of more than 30 days after each quarter are not allowable. The Government receives a fair share of any previously funded PRB costs which revert or inure to the firm.

Compensation in excess of the benchmark amount determined for the fiscal year by OFPP is unallowable. Although this policy at one time applied just to the most highly compensated executives, it now applies across the board to all employees.

4.3.5 Contingencies

FAR 31.205-7

A *contingency* is a possible future event or condition arising from presently known or unknown causes, with an unknown outcome. Such costs are generally unallowable except for contract termination, where a contingency factor may be recognized for a past period to recognize minor unsettled factors. This is permitted to expedite contract settlement.

Future cost contingencies may arise from presently known and existing conditions, such as anticipated costs of rejects and defective work, in which case they are included in the estimates of future costs. They could also arise from presently unknown conditions that cannot be measured precisely, such as results of pending litigation. These contingencies are excluded from cost estimates and separately disclosed, including their basis of computation.

4.3.6 Contributions or Donations

FAR 31.205-8

Contributions or donations of cash, property and services (other than charity drives) are unallowable.

4.3.7 Cost of Money

FAR 31.205-10

Facilities capital reflects the net book value of depreciable capital assets, both tangible and intangible. Because actual interest cost is unallowable, *facilities capital cost of money* is recognized as an imputed cost of borrowings to finance facilities and other capital assets used in contract performance. It is considered an "incurred cost" under cost-reimbursement contracts and for progress payments under fixed-price contracts. The cost of money rate is established by the Department of the Treasury and adjusted twice a year.

4.3.8 Depreciation

FAR 31.205-11

Depreciation is a common fixed cost that is based on the *going-concern concept* that a firm will continue indefinitely and therefore use up the depreciable asset over its full lifetime. Depreciation allocates an asset's cost over its useful life on an annualized basis. American firms use the Modified Cost Recovery System to recover the capitalized cost of tangible property over a specified period of years that represents its usable lifetime. This calculation need not consider the asset's level of output. Annual depreciation rates are specified in tables issued and maintained by the Internal Revenue Service.

Capital costs are one-time expenditures to purchase land and improvements thereto (i.e., buildings and equipment) and will be depreciated over 15 to 20 years for the equipment, 27.5 years for real property, and 39 years for business property. Personal property lifetimes range between 3 and 20 years.

A *tangible capital asset* has physical substance and is expected to be held for continued use beyond the current accounting period. Generally, only estimated residual values that exceed 10% of the asset's capitalized cost are used to establish depreciable costs, and are not deducted from capitalized cost.

Depreciation on a contractor's plant, equipment and other capital facilities is allowable. However, depreciation cost is disallowed if it significantly reduces the book value of a tangible capital asset below its residual value.

Four common methods of depreciation are used. A common one is known as *straight-line*, deriving equal periodic charges during the life of the item. The depreciation amount for each period equals the cost of salvage or service life. So if a lathe costs $40,000 and is expected to last five years, and has a $4,000 salvage value, the annual depreciation cost is

$$\frac{\$40,000 - \$4,000}{5} = \$7,200$$

Second, the *unit of production* method relates an item's depreciation to estimated productive capacity. The purchase cost less salvage value is divided by the number of production units expected during its lifetime to derive a depreciable cost per unit. The unit cost is multiplied by total production volume for a given year. If our lathe can process 9,000 items, then:

$$\frac{\$40,000 - \$4,000}{9,000 \text{ units}} = \$4 \text{ per unit}$$

And if the 9,000 units are equally spread over the five-year service life mentioned above, then $9,000/5 = 1,800$ units per year can be expected. So, 1,800 units x $4/unit = $7,200. This is not a remarkable result and indicates that the purchase price is fair related to its productive value.

The *sum of the years digits* approach is an accelerated method that charges depreciation heavily to the early years, providing greater income tax savings in early years. The years of service life are added up and used as the denominator, which in our case is $1 + 2 + 3 + 4 + 5 = 15$. The numerator will be the sum of the years of remaining life. So in the first year of operation:

$$\frac{5}{1 + 2 + 3 + 4 + 5} = 33.3\%$$

Using this method, the second year would be 4/15 or 26.7%, the third year is 20%, year four is 13.3%, and the final year is 6.7%. Note as a check that these percentages do add up to 100%. This demonstrates how this method to value depreciation starts out high in early years, then diminishes over time.

Finally, *double declining balance* is another accelerated method based on twice the number derived in straight line method. For our lathe, 2 x $7,200 = $14,400 per year.

One concern with buyers is that using an accelerated method means they bear the brunt of investment, while subsequent buyers pay less for the same item. Nonetheless, it is an accepted accounting practice to reflect greater value of an asset early in its life cycle, and to treat depreciation accordingly.

The value of an asset or liability is based on its current market price, known as *fair value accounting*. This approach requires an unbiased estimate of an asset's market price based on alternatives cost, its utility and the interaction of supply and demand. Whenever market conditions affect the value of the asset or liability, the firm changes the balance sheet entry. However, this approach is not accurate if the market price differs greatly from the *book value* (historical or purchase cost). This problem occurs if the marketplace cannot value future assets and liabilities (due to excessive optimism or pessimism), or else lacks information to make informed pricing decisions. However, unless the Government can demonstrate that the book value or purchase price is unreasonable, it will accept the asset price.

Depreciation, rental or use charges are unallowable on property acquired from the Government at no cost. Allowable depreciation for contractor-owned property usually does not exceed the amount used for financial accounting purposes, and is determined by the same depreciation policies and procedures used on non-Government business.

No depreciation or rental is allowed on property which is already fully depreciated. However, a usage charge may be allowed based on cost, decreased efficiency due to age, increased maintenance charges, or total estimated useful life.

A lease of capital equipment is usually capitalized as a purchased asset and distributed over either the asset's useful life as a depreciation charge, or over the leased life as an amortization charge. Should the contractor reacquire property in a sale and leaseback arrangement, allowable depreciation is based on the asset's net book value on the date of its first lease.

4.3.9 Economic Planning Costs

FAR 31.205-12

Economic planning costs for the contractor's future overall business development, including market changes and resultant company changes, are allowable.

4.3.10 Employee Activity Costs

FAR 31.205-13

Costs to improve employee working conditions, employer-employee relations, morale, and performance (excluding any income generated by these activities) are allowable. For example, this includes company-sponsored employee counseling services, fitness centers, health clinics, in-house publications, and sports teams. Contributions to an employee organization and vending machine receipts are allowable only if directly incurred by the firm. Cost of gifts is disallowed, though the cost of performance awards is allowable. Food and dormitory services are only allowable if the company tries to break even in their operation, so undercharging for a company cafeteria and residence is a clear sign that such costs should be disallowed.

4.3.11 Entertainment Costs

FAR 31.205-14

The following entertainment costs are unallowable:

- gratuities;
- lodging;
- meals;
- membership in country, dining or social clubs;
- rentals;
- social activities;
- tickets to shows or sports events; or
- transportation related to entertainment.

4.3.12 Fines, Penalties and Mischarges

FAR 31.205-15

Costs of fines and penalties resulting from violations of Federal, State, local, or foreign laws and regulations are unallowable unless incurred to comply with contract terms and conditions, or under written instructions from the contracting officer.

Effort related to mischarging costs on Government contracts is unallowable when the costs result from:

- alteration or destruction of records;
- determining magnitude of the improper charge;
- false or improper charges or records; or
- records review and reconstruction.

4.3.13 Disposition or Impairment of Depreciable Property or Other Capital Assets

FAR 31.205-16

Gains and losses from the sale or retirement of depreciable property are assigned in the year incurred to the applicable cost grouping(s). However, no gain or loss is recognized from transfer of assets in a business combination.

When costs of depreciable property are subject to sale and leaseback limitations, the gain or loss is the difference between the net amount realized and the asset's undepreciated balance on the date the lease begins. Of course, if the fair market value exceeds the undepreciated balance, no cost is allowable.

Gains and losses on disposition of tangible capital assets are measured the same as other depreciation costs. The amount realized is the difference between the acquisition cost of the asset and its undepreciated balance (or for assets acquired under a capital lease, the value at which the leased asset is capitalized). If the asset is replaced, the contractor can either adjust the basis of the new asset by the amount of the gain or loss, or else can recognize the gain or loss in the period of disposition. If the asset is not replaced, the gain or loss is recognized in the period of disposition.

An insurance award is allowable if property is destroyed by uncontrollable events (e.g., accident, fire, flood, theft, windstorm, etc.). However, a contractor cannot reflect a loss for assets written-down from carrying value to fair value due to environmental damage.

FAR 31.205-52

Depreciation and cost of money for tangible capital assets, when the purchase method of accounting for a business combination is used, is allowable if based on the capitalized asset values. *Intangible capital assets* have no physical substance or substantial value, and will be held by an enterprise for continued use beyond the current accounting period for the benefits it yields. For intangible capital assets under the purchase method of accounting, amortization and cost of money is limited to what would have been allowed had the combination not taken place.

4.3.14 Idle Facilities and Idle Capacity Costs

FAR 31.205-17

The costs of idle facilities cover equipment, land and plant in terms of:

- depreciation;
- housing;

- insurance;
- maintenance;
- property taxes;
- rent; and
- repair.

These costs are unallowable except to meet fluctuations in workload or due to unforeseen changes in production economies and requirements, or company reorganization. Even these costs are normally allowable for one year only.

Idle capacity means the facilities are not used for a work shift (or multiple shifts if customary for the facility). These costs are allowable if full capacity was necessary or reasonable under normal circumstances and cannot be rented out or sold. A separate agreement is necessary to cover reimbursement for any idle capacity reserved for defense mobilization production.

4.3.15 Independent Research and Development and Bid and Proposal Costs

FAR 31.205-18

Independent research and development (IR&D) is effort which is not sponsored by a grant or contract, and is categorized as basic research, applied research, development, or *systems and other concept formulation studies* (analyses and study efforts related to specific IR&D efforts, or effort to identify or modify systems [current or new] or their components or equipment). IR&D does not include technical effort to develop and prepare technical data specifically to support a bid or proposal.

IR&D costs incurred in previous accounting periods are normally unallowable, unless a contractor has developed a specific product at its own risk in anticipation of recovering the development costs in the sale price of the product. To be allowable in such a case, the contractor must have either had no Government business during the time of cost incurrence, or else did not allocate IR&D costs to Government contracts. If this is true, then the total amount of IR&D costs applicable to the product must be prorated over time. When deferred costs are recognized, the contract (except firm-fixed-price and fixed-price with economic price adjustment) specifies the allocable amount of deferred IR&D costs.

IR&D costs may be incurred by contractors working jointly with non-Federal entities pursuant to a cooperative arrangement (e.g., collaboration and consortium arrangements, joint ventures, limited partnerships, teaming arrangements). In these cases, IR&D costs are allowable if the work performed would have been allowed as contractor IR&D.

Bid and proposal (B&P) costs are incurred to prepare, submit and support bids and proposals (whether or not solicited) on potential contracts. The term does not include any effort sponsored by a grant or cooperative agreement, or required by contract (they might be allowable as an IR&D expense if for a collaboration or consortium). This concept is intended to motivate Federal contractors to maintain continued interest in the industrial base.

IR&D and B&P costs are allocated to final cost objectives on the same basis used for the G&A expense grouping of the profit center. A *profit center* is the smallest organizationally independent segment charged by management with profit and loss responsibilities. If the expenses benefit other profit centers or the entire company, they are allocated through either their own G&A or corporate G&A.

4.3.16 Insurance and Indemnification

FAR 31.205-19

Insurance is the undertaking of one party to indemnify another against a certain eventuality, in exchange for a premium payment. There is a transfer of risk manifested in a bilateral contract, namely the insurance policy itself. Purchased insurance costs are allowable. Actual losses are unallowable unless expressly provided for in the contract, incurred under the deductible provisions of purchased insurance, or minor losses in the ordinary course of business. In fact, losses might not be covered by insurance (e.g., spoilage, breakage, disappearance of hand tools, etc.).

Insurance by purchase or self-insurance includes coverage that the contractor is required to carry under the contract terms. A *self-insurance charge* is the projected average loss under a self-insurance plan, and allowable if not exceeding the cost of comparable purchased insurance (including associated insurance administration expenses). Self-insurance is allowable unless paid insurance is available, in which case self-insurance is disallowed. Even if the latter is the case, charges for risks of catastrophic losses are unallowable.

Insurance administration expenses include operating an insurance or risk-management department. This also includes such costs as actuarial fees, processing claims and service fees paid to insurance companies, technical consultants or trustees. Costs of insurance maintained by the contractor in connection with the general conduct of its business are allowable. Business interruption insurance costs are also allowable except for coverage of profit.

Many property insurance costs are allowable. If property insurance premiums exceed the assets' acquisition cost, the written policy must state that the new asset bears the book value of the replaced asset, adjusted for insurance proceeds and actual replacement cost. Costs of insurance for the risk of loss, damage, destruction, or theft of Government property are allowable only if the contractor is liable, the contracting officer has not revoked Government assumption of risk, and the insurance excludes willful misconduct or lack of good faith by contractor management. Costs of insurance on the lives of officers, owners or employees are allowable as additional compensation.

Several insurance costs are unallowable. The expense of insurance to correct the contractor's own defects in materials and workmanship is unallowable, except for fortuitous or casualty losses. Premiums for retroactive or backdated insurance written to cover known losses are unallowable. Late premium payment charges for employee deferred compensation plan insurance are also unallowable.

4.3.17 Interest on Other Financial Costs

FAR 31.205-20

Unless assessed by State or local taxing authorities, the following financial costs are unallowable:

- bond discounts;
- capital financing;
- interest on borrowings;
- legal and professional fees to prepare a prospectus; and
- preparing and issuing stock rights.

4.3.18 Labor Relations Costs

FAR 31.205-21

Costs to maintain satisfactory relations between the contractor and its employees, including costs of employee publications, labor management committees and shop stewards, are allowable. However, costs dealing with efforts to persuade employees to either create or turn down the right to collective bargaining are not allowable (e.g., information materials, legal counsel and meetings).

4.3.19 Lobbying and Political Activity Costs

FAR 31.205-22

The Government takes a hard line against political activities and their associated costs, on the theory that contractors must secure and perform contracts in an unbiased mode. Efforts to influence the introduction or outcome of any Federal, state or local election or referendum are unallowable. This includes cash or in-kind contributions, endorsements or publicity with a legislator or Government official. Similarly, costs incurred to influence a Federal employee on a contract or regulatory matter are unallowable. Also prohibited are costs to operate or contribute to a political campaign, party or political action committee. Also, a contractor must disclose any person hired or expected to be hired with private funds.[8]

The Government is more lenient if the contractor is addressing contract matters before a legislature. In response to a documented request, contractor costs will be allowed when incurred to present information regarding contract performance in a formal statement or testimony, or in a letter to the Congress or a state legislature member or cognizant staff member. Costs for transportation, lodging or meals are allowable only if incurred to offer testimony at a scheduled congressional hearing, again pursuant to a written request by the chairman or ranking minority member of the committee or subcommittee.

Lobbying costs are allowable only to influence state or local legislation to directly reduce contract costs or avoid material impairment of contractor authority to perform the contract.

4.3.20 Losses on Other Contracts

FAR 31.205-23

Any cost in excess of income under any other contract is unallowable. A contractor cannot charge for a loss incurred on another contract.

4.3.21 Manufacturing and Production Engineering Costs

FAR 31.205-25

Costs to analyze, develop and deploy new or improved production methods and pilot production lines (e.g., materials, systems, processes, methods, equipment, tools, and techniques) are allowable. This includes plant layout, production scheduling and control. Also allowable are inspection techniques, tooling design and improvements, and analyses to optimize manufacturing suitability.

4.3.22 Material Costs

FAR 31.205-26

Material costs include components, parts, raw materials, sub-assemblies, and supplies, whether purchased or manufactured by the contractor, plus inbound transportation, in-transit insurance overruns, spoilage, and defective work. The contractor adjusts the material costs for income credits, trade discounts from list price, refunds, rebates, allowances, cash discounts, and credits for scrap, salvage, and material returned to vendors. Credits are charged either directly to the material account or to material overhead. Differences between periodic physical inventories and book inventories may be included.

Allowance for all materials, services and supplies sold or transferred between any affiliates, divisions or subsidiaries is normally on a cost-incurred basis, but may be included at price for a commercial item or service, or as a competitive award.

4.3.23 Organization Costs

FAR 31.205-27

Costs are unallowable to plan, execute or resist a business reorganization or takeover (including mergers and acquisitions). Such expenditures include changes in the contractor's financial structure, costs of employees or outside experts, and incorporation fees. However, administrative costs of short-term borrowings for working capital are allowable, regardless of whether additional capital is raised.

4.3.24 Other Business Expenses

FAR 31.205-28

The following types of recurring costs are allowable:

- incidental costs of directors, committee and shareholder meetings;
- preparing and publishing shareholder reports and forms to regulatory and taxing bodies;
- proxy solicitations; and
- registration and transfers for changes in ownership of contractor-issued securities.

4.3.25 Plant Protection Costs

FR 31.205-29

Guard equipment, uniforms and wages are allowable. Depreciation on plant protection capital assets, and compliance with military requirements, are likewise allowable.

4.3.26 Patent Costs

FAR 31.205-30

Allowable costs include those to prepare invention disclosures and reports, search for invention disclosures, file and prosecute a U.S. patent application to convey title or a royalty-free license to the Government, and general counseling services on patent laws and employee agreements.

4.3.27 Plant Reconversion Costs

FAR 31.205-31

Plant reconversion costs restore or rehabilitate contractor facilities to the same approximate condition as before the contract start, except for fair wear and tear. Reconversion costs are unallowable except to remove Government property and associated restoration or rehabilitation costs.

4.3.28 Precontract Costs

FAR 31.205-32

Precontract costs are incurred before the effective date of the contract when necessary to comply with the proposed contract delivery schedule. These costs are allowable as if incurred after the date of contract. However, a clause must be included in the contract expressly allowing precontract costs, along with a not-to-exceed amount.

4.3.29 Professional and Consultant Services

FAR 31.205-33

Professional and consultant services are rendered by members of a profession who possess a special skill and are not contractor employees. Usually economic, financial, legal, or technical in nature, they furnish analyses, evaluations, information, recommendations, studies, or training. They may also include liaison with Government officials. These costs are generally allowable. Factors to help determine cost reasonableness and allowability include:

- impact of Government contracts on the contractor's business;
- nature and scope of the service rendered;
- past pattern of acquiring such services and their costs;
- qualifications of the individual or firm rendering the service and the customary fee charged on non-Government contracts;

- terms of the contract (e.g., description, estimate of time required, compensation rate, termination provisions); and
- whether the service can be performed more economically in-house.

Professional and consultant services to illegally use protected data, implement an improper business practice or conflict of interest, or influence solicitation content or source selection are unallowable.

Retainer fees are allowable only if:

- consultants submit work products and related documents (e.g., meeting minutes, trip reports, etc.);
- invoices submitted by consultants include the time expended and nature of the actual services provided;
- supported by evidence that the services are necessary and customary;
- the level of any past services justifies the amount of the retainer fees;
- the retainer fees are reasonable compared to maintaining an in-house capability to perform the covered services; and
- work requirements and rate of compensation are documented.

4.3.30 Recruitment Costs

FAR 31.205-34

The following costs are allowable:

- employment agencies;
- help-wanted advertising that describes specific positions;
- operating an aptitude and educational testing program;
- operating an employment office;
- travel of applicants for interviews; and
- travel of employees to recruit personnel.

4.3.31 Relocation Costs

FAR 31.205-35

Relocation costs arise from an employee's permanent change of work location for at least a year, or upon recruitment of a new employee. The following relocation costs are allowable:

- advance trips by employee and/or spouse to locate living quarters;
- canceling an unexpired lease;
- closing costs to sell the employee's residence (i.e., appraisal, broker, financing, and legal fees, and points), up to 14% of the sales price;

- costs of family and personnel movements of a special or mass nature;
- home acquisition costs in the new work location for previous homeowners only, up to 5% of the purchase price;
- increased employee income or Federal Insurance Contributions Act taxes incident to allowable reimbursed relocation costs;
- mortgage interest differential payments for previous homeowners only;
- mortgage title insurance policy if the employee had a policy in the former home;
- ownership costs of a vacant residence (e.g., maintenance of building and grounds, mortgage interest, property insurance, taxes, and utilities) after the settlement or lease date of a new permanent residence, up to 14% of the sales price;
- relocation expenses (e.g., automobile registration, cutting and fitting rugs and draperies, (dis)connecting household appliances, driver's license and use taxes, forfeited utility fees and deposits, and insurance premiums for loss or damage to personal property);
- rental differential payments when retaining ownership in the old location and renting at the new location;
- spouse employment assistance;
- temporary lodging during the transition period for the employee and immediate family; and
- travel of the employee, immediate family members, and household and personal effects to the new location.

The reimbursable costs above must meet the following criteria to be considered allowable:

- be in accordance with an employer's established policy or practice designed to motivate employees to relocate promptly and economically;
- to find a new home, travel to the new location (but not to transport household goods) and temporary lodging;
- cannot exceed the employee's actual expenses; and
- the move must be for the benefit of the employer.

The following types of costs are unallowable:

- continuing mortgage principal payments on a residence being sold;
- costs to acquire a home in the new location (i.e., brokers' fees and commissions, litigation, mortgage life insurance, operating or maintenance costs, property insurance against damage or loss, and property taxes);

- furnishing equity loans to employees or arranging with lenders for employees to obtain below market rate mortgage loans; and
- loss on sale of a home.

If relocation costs for an employee have been allowed and the employee resigns within 12 months for reasons within the employee's control, the contractor refunds or credits the relocation costs to the Government. Companies may in turn impose this same policy on their employees.

4.3.32 Rental Costs

FAR 31.205-36

Rental costs under operating leases are allowable. Rental costs under a sale and leaseback arrangement are limited to the net book value of the asset on the lease date, adjusted for any gain or loss. Rental charges for property between any divisions or subsidiaries are allowable up to the annual ownership costs as of the valuation date, excluding any unfunded actuarial liability.

4.3.33 Royalties and Other Patent Use Costs

FAR 31.205-37

Royalties or amortization of patent cost or rights for the contract are allowable unless the Government has a license or the right to free use of the patent. Costs are unallowable if the patent is expired, invalid or unenforceable. A royalty for a patent formerly owned by the contractor cannot exceed the cost which would have been allowed had the contractor retained title.

4.3.34 Selling Costs

FAR 31.205-38

Direct selling efforts are those acts or actions to induce particular customers to purchase particular products or services of the contractor. Direct selling is characterized by person-to-person contact and familiarizing a potential customer with the contractor's products or services, conditions of sale, service capabilities, etc. It also includes individual demonstrations, liaison, negotiation, technical and consulting discussions, and any other efforts intended to apply or adapt the contractor's products or services to a particular customer's use. The cost of these direct selling efforts is allowable.

Sellers' or agents' compensation, fees, commissions, percentages, retainers, or brokerage fees are allowable only when paid to bona fide employees or established commercial or selling agencies.

4.3.35 Service and Warranty Costs

FAR 31.205-39

Allowable service and warranty costs include installation, refunds for inadequate performance, repair of product defects, replacing defective parts, and training.

4.3.36 Special Tooling and Special Test Equipment Costs

FAR 31.205-40

The cost of special tooling and test equipment is allowable and allocated to the specific Government contract or contracts for which acquired. Special tooling includes items such as dies, fixtures, gauges, and molds that can only be used (unless greatly modified) for development or production of particular items or parts. Special test equipment is designed to assess interconnected and interdependent items or assemblies. The cost of items acquired by the contractor before the effective date of the contract, and items which the contract schedule specifically excludes, are allowable only as depreciation or amortization. The cost of adapting the items for use under the contract and returning them to their prior configuration is also allowable.

4.3.37 Taxes

FAR 31.205-41

Federal, State and local taxes paid or accrued in accordance with GAAP are allowable. If the contracting officer directs the contractor not to pay a given tax for any reason, then interest or penalties incurred by the contractor for nonpayment are allowable. However, the following taxes are not allowable:

* accruals for the differences between taxable income and pretax income;
* excise tax (e.g., qualified pension plans, welfare plans, and deferred compensation plans);
* Federal income and excess profits taxes;
* financing, refinancing, refunding operations, or reorganizations;

- real or personal property (including possession, sales, usage, or value taxes) used solely in connection with non-Government contracts;
- special land assessments that represent capital improvements; and
- taxes where exemptions are available to the contractor.

Property taxes must directly apply to the respective work category to be allowable, except for insignificant amounts or if comparable results would otherwise be obtained. Tax or penalty refunds that were previously allowed must be remitted to the Government.

4.3.38 Termination Costs

FAR 31.205-42

The costs of items which are usable on other contract work are only allowable if the contractor submits evidence that the items could not be retained at cost without sustaining a loss (e.g., contemporaneous purchases of common items by the contractor).

Costs which cannot be discontinued immediately after the effective date of termination are generally allowable, unless due to negligent or willful failure of the contractor to discontinue the costs.

Starting load costs are also recognized. They result from inexperienced labor (such as spoilage and subnormal production and techniques) and training. Unless fully absorbed because of termination, these costs are allowable as nonrecurring labor, material and related overhead costs.

Initial plant rearrangement and alterations, personnel organization and production planning costs are allowable. Loss of useful value of special equipment, machinery and tooling is generally allowable if not capable of use in other work. However, title must be transferred to the Government if the contracting officer requests. Loss of acquisition cost is limited to the percentage of contract value terminated.

Rental costs under unexpired leases less residual value are generally allowable if the contractor makes all reasonable efforts to assign, reduce, settle, or terminate the lease. The cost of alterations and restorations required by the lease may be allowed.

Accounting, clerical and legal costs are allowable to prepare and present settlement claims to the contracting officer. This includes protection, storage, transportation, and disposition of property acquired or produced for the contract. Indirect costs related to salary and wages are limited to fringe benefits, occupancy, payroll taxes, and supervision costs.

Subcontractor claims are generally allowable. A share of the contractor's indirect expense may be allocated to the subcontractor claim, but not claimed as settlement expenses.

4.3.39 Trade, Business, Technical and Professional Activity Costs

FAR 31.205-43

Memberships in these organizations are allowable, as are subscriptions to their periodicals. Also allowable are certain costs of a conference, convention, meeting, seminar, or symposium to disseminate business, professional, technical, or trade information or stimulate production or productivity. Allowable costs include attendance, organization, rental of meeting facilities, setup, sponsorship, subsistence, transportation, and travel costs by contractor employees. Also allowable is attendance by non-employees if they are not reimbursed by the employing company or organization and the individual's attendance is essential to the event.

4.3.40 Training and Education Costs

FAR 31.205-44

Costs of training and education related to the field in which the employee is working are generally allowable, including contributions to college savings plans for employee dependents. However, the following costs are unallowable:

- contributions to college savings plans for employee dependents;
- grants to educational or training institutions, including donation of facilities, fellowships and scholarships;
- overtime compensation for training and education;
- payments for full-time graduate education (e.g., fees, materials and textbooks, subsistence, salary, and tuition) after two school years;
- salary cost for attending undergraduate-level classes or part-time graduate-level classes during working hours, except when unusual circumstances do not permit attendance outside of regular working hours; and
- training or education costs for non-employees, except for employee dependents in a foreign country where public education is not available (these costs may be included in overseas differential pay).

4.3.41 Travel Costs

FAR 31.205-46

Costs incurred by contractor personnel on official company business are allowable and may be based on mileage rates and/or actual costs incurred. Costs for lodging, meals, and incidentals may be based on actual expenses and/or maximum per diem rates set forth in departmental regulations, e.g., GSA's *Federal Travel Regulation* (September 14, 2016), DoD's *Joint Travel Regulations* (December 4, 2016), or Department of State's *Standardized Regulations* (April 2, 1961, as amended).

Higher amounts must be approved by an officer of the contractor's organization per established practice, and all expenditures over $75 must be supported by receipt. Contracting officer approval is necessary if this is done on a continual basis. Airfare costs above the lowest-priced rates are only allowable when avoiding excessive delays or physical impact to the traveler. So a more expensive direct flight to make a meeting is allowable, as is a first-class ticket for a physically challenged passenger. Costs of contractor-owned or -leased automobiles (including lease, operation, maintenance, depreciation, insurance) are allowable.

4.3.42 Legal and Other Proceedings Costs

FAR 31.205-47

Legal costs are incurred before, during and after a judicial or administrative proceeding which bears a direct relationship to the proceeding. They include accountants or consultants retained by the contractor, administrative and clerical expenses, employee and director salaries, and legal services (either in-house or private counsel).

Costs incurred in connection with any government proceeding or investigation for violation of or failure to comply with a law or regulation are unallowable if the result is a finding of contractor liability with penalty. Should the proceeding result in a consent agreement or compromise between the contractor and the United States, such costs are allowable as agreed to between the parties. Costs incurred in an action brought under the False Claims Act by a third party that would have failed on its merits are allowable.

Up to 80% of legal costs are allowable if an action is brought by a State, local or foreign government due to a Federal contract's terms and conditions, or by specific written direction of the cognizant contracting officer. This reflects the *Boyle Rule*, which allows a Government contractor to escape liability from state law that conflicts with a unique Federal interest, provided the contractor conformed to precise contract specifications approved by the Federal Government, and warned the Government of potential damages.[9]

The following actions will create legal costs that are unallowable:

- defense of suits for antitrust claims or brought by employees or ex-employees of the contractor where the contractor was found liable or settled;
- defense or prosecution against Federal Government claims or protests;

- lawsuits or appeals between contractors arising from joint or teaming arrangement, dual sourcing or coproduction (unless in accordance with the contract or agreed to in writing by the contracting officer);
- organization, reorganization or resisting mergers and acquisitions;
- patent infringement litigation; or
- representing or assisting groups, individuals or legal entities convicted of violating a law or regulation, or found liable in a civil or administrative proceeding.

Legal costs which may be unallowable are segregated and separately accounted for by the contractor. The contracting officer generally withholds payment of such costs until the legal proceeding is concluded.

4.3.43 Goodwill

FAR 31.205-49

Goodwill is an unidentifiable intangible asset arising during a business combination when the price paid by the acquiring company exceeds the fair value sum of identifiable individual assets acquired, less liabilities assumed. Any costs for amortization, expensing, write-off, or write-down of goodwill are unallowable.

4.3.44 Costs of Alcoholic Beverages

FAR 31.205-51

Costs of alcoholic beverages are unallowable.

4.3.45 Contracts with Non-Profit Entities

OMB Circular A-21, Cost Principles for Educational Institutions (2012), provides rules to determine the costs for research and development, training, and other work performed by educational institutions under contracts with the Government.[10] OMB Circular A-122, Cost Principles for Nonprofit Organizations (2009), sets forth all principles to determine the costs applicable to work performed by nonprofit organizations under contracts and grants with the Government. These nonprofit organizations exist for charity, education or science instead of private gain.

FAR 31.6

OMB Circular A-87, Cost Principles for State and Local Governments, Revised, provides principles to determine allowable contract and subcontract costs with State, local and Indian tribal governments. The following costs are unallowable:

- advertising designed to promote the contractor or its products;
- alcoholic beverages;
- commercial insurance that protects against the costs to correct the contractor's own defects in materials or workmanship;
- contributions or donations;
- civil, criminal or administrative proceedings commenced by the United States or a state;
- defense of any civil or criminal fraud proceeding brought by the United States where the contractor is found liable or pleads *nolo contendere* to a charge of fraud;
- entertainment, amusement, diversion, and social activities;
- fines and penalties resulting from violations of, or failure to comply with, laws and regulations, unless incurred to comply with contract terms and conditions or written instructions from the contracting officer;
- influencing legislative action before Congress or a state legislature;
- membership in any dining or social organization, including a country club;
- payment to an employee in excess of normal severance pay upon termination of employment (also known as a *golden parachute* payment) after a change in management control over the firm or assets;
- promotional items such as gifts, memorabilia, models, and souvenirs;
- severance pay to foreign nationals under a service contract performed outside the United States which exceeds the customary or prevailing practice for firms in that industry providing similar services in the United States. This also applies if employment termination of the foreign national is due to the closing or curtailment of activities at a U.S. facility;
- tickets to shows or sports events;
- travel by commercial aircraft which exceeds the standard commercial fare; and
- travel costs such as gratuities, lodging, meals, rentals, and transportation.

4.4 COST ACCOUNTING STANDARDS

FAR 30

Public Law 100-679 (41 U.S.C. 422) requires that the policies and procedures to apply the Cost Accounting Standards Board (CASB) rules and regulations (48 CFR Chapter 99 (FAR Appendix)) apply to negotiated contracts and subcontracts with large businesses.[11] CASB promotes uniform accounting procedures and cost treatment by contractors. It is not affiliated with the Financial Accounting Standards Board, which develops generally accepted accounting practices for commercial firms. The CASB is chaired by OFPP and has representatives from the Defense Contract Audit Agency (DCAA), GSA, industry, and the private sector. The Cost Accounting Standards (CAS) issued by CASB are set forth in Table 4.3.

Applicability of CAS rules and regulations is governed by a CAS clause in the contract and the requirements of the standards themselves.

The contractor develops a *Disclosure Statement,* a written description of a contractor's cost accounting practices and procedures. Completed Disclosure Statements are required for any business unit that receives a CAS-covered (sub)contract of $50 million or more (for educational institutions, the threshold is $25 million). A separate Disclosure Statement is submitted for each segment whose costs included in any CAS-covered (sub)contract exceed $650,000, unless the (sub)contract is exempted or the segment's CAS-covered awards are less than 30% of total segment sales and less than $10 million.

Federal agencies assign a contracting officer to determine if a Disclosure Statement has adequately disclosed the practices required to be disclosed

Table 4.3

CAS Number	CAS Title
401	Consistency in Estimating, Accumulating, and Reporting Costs
402	Consistency in Allocating Costs Incurred for the Same Purpose
403	Allocation of Home Office Expenses to Segments
404	Capitalization of Tangible Assets
405	Accounting for Unallowable Costs
406	Cost Accounting Period
407	Use of Standard Costs for Direct Material and Direct Labor
408	Accounting for Costs of Compensated Personal Absence
409	Depreciation of Tangible Capital Assets
410	Allocation of Business Unit General and Administrative Expenses to Final Cost Objectives
411	Accounting for Acquisition Costs of Material
412	Composition and Measurement of Pension Cost
413	Adjustment and Allocation of Pension Cost
414	Cost of Money as an Element of the Cost of Facilities Capital
415	Accounting for the Cost of Deferred Compensation
416	Accounting for Insurance Costs
417	Cost of Money as an Element of the Cost of Capital Assets under Construction
418	Allocation of Direct and Indirect Costs
419	Reserved (not in use)
420	Accounting for Independent Research and Development and Bid and Proposal Costs

by CASB rules and standards.[12] This contracting officer determines when a proposed contract may require CAS coverage and ensures that Disclosure Statements have been submitted and audited to verify compliance with CAS and cost principles. Either party may submit amendments and revisions to Disclosure Statements at any time, along with a general dollar magnitude or detailed cost impact proposal. Revisions could be due to an accounting system or CAS change, and could result in a net cost benefit to the Government. The assigned contracting officer reviews proposed changes for adequacy and materiality. Any decision of noncompliance must be returned to the contractor within 15 days, after which (s)he has 60 days for rebuttal. The process to approve a request often takes longer.

Offerors state whether contract award requires a change to an established cost accounting practice affecting existing (sub)contracts, and submit a description of the changed cost accounting practice as pricing support for the proposal.

The contractor or higher-tier subcontractor is responsible for administering the CAS requirements contained in subcontracts.

The head of the agency may waive the applicability of CAS for a particular (sub)contract, and may delegate this waiver authority to the senior contract policy-making level. The (sub)contract value must be less than $15 million, and the firm must be primarily engaged in the sale of commercial items with no (sub)contracts that are subject to CAS.

FAR Appendix B – 9903.201

The following categories of (sub)contracts are exempt from all CAS requirements:

- contractors or business units not currently performing any CAS-covered (sub)contracts valued at $7.5 million or greater;
- firm-fixed-price and fixed-price with economic price adjustment contracts and subcontracts for commercial items;
- firm-fixed-price (sub)contracts awarded on the basis of adequate price competition without submission of cost or pricing data;
- foreign governments or their agents;
- foreign subcontractors under the NATO PHM Ship program if performance outside the United States for negotiated contracts and subcontracts not in excess of $650,000;
- prices set by law or regulation;
- sealed-bid contracts; and
- small businesses.

Full coverage requires that the business unit comply with all CAS in effect on the date of the contract award and with any CAS that become applicable because of subsequent award of a CAS-covered contract. Full coverage applies to contractor business units that receive a CAS-covered award of at least $50 million, or received at least $50 million in net CAS-covered awards during its preceding cost accounting period.

Modified CAS coverage may be applied to a covered contract below the thresholds for full coverage. Modified CAS coverage requires only that the contractor comply with the standards for:

- 401 - Consistency in Estimating, Accumulating, and Reporting Costs;
- 402 - Consistency in Allocating Costs Incurred for the Same Purpose;
- 405 - Accounting for Unallowable Costs; and
- 406 - Cost Accounting Period.

Once a business entity receives a contract with modified coverage, all CAS-covered contracts awarded to that business unit during that cost accounting period must also have modified coverage until it receives a $50 million award, in which case both the award and all subsequent contracts will be subject to full CAS coverage. However, no current contract is upgraded from modified to full coverage.

Coverage for educational institutions applies to business units that receive negotiated contracts in excess of $650,000, however FFRDCs operated by an educational institution are subject to the full or modified CAS coverage.

Subcontracts subject to CAS require the same type of CAS coverage as would prime contracts awarded to the same business unit.

Contracts with foreign concerns are only subject to Standards 401 and 402: Consistency in Estimating, Accumulating, and Reporting Costs; and Consistency in Allocating Costs Incurred for the Same Purpose.

The head of an executive agency may waive CAS applicability for a (sub)contract with a value of less than $15 million upon written determination that the business unit would not otherwise be subject to CAS, or when necessary to meet the needs of the agency.

Within 15 days of receiving a report of alleged CAS noncompliance from the auditor, the contracting officer either notifies the auditor of disagreement stating the reasons for same, or else issues a notice of potential noncompliance to the contractor, allowing 60 days for the contractor to agree or submit rationale of immateriality. The contracting officer reviews the contractor's response and notifies both the contractor and auditor in writing of the determination of compliance or noncompliance.

Naturally, there are several criticisms of CAS. The contractor may in fact use different methods for commercial and Government business. Most standards were unilaterally developed by the Government with minimal industry input. Often expensive to implement, CAS arguably reflects Government intervention in contractor business management, and may encourage firms to leave the Government supplier base.

Solicitation Provisions

FAR 52.230-1, Cost Accounting Standards Notices and Certification.

FAR 52.230-7, Proposal Disclosure–Cost Accounting Practice Changes.

Contract Clauses:

FAR 52.230-2, Cost Accounting Standards, unless the contract is exempted or subject to modified coverage.

FAR 52.230-3, Disclosure and Consistency of Cost Accounting Practices, if over $750,000 but less than $50 million, and the offeror certifies it is eligible for and elects to use modified CAS coverage.

FAR 52.230-4, Disclosure and Consistency of Cost Accounting Practices for Contracts Awarded to Foreign Concerns, with foreign concerns (not including foreign governments or their agents), unless the contract is otherwise exempt from CAS. FAR 52.230-2 and -3 are not included in these contracts.

FAR 52.230-5, Cost Accounting Standards – Educational Institution, if awarded to educational institutions, unless the contract is exempted or performed by an FFRDC.

FAR 52.230-6, Administration of Cost Accounting Standards, except for contracts which do not contain FAR 52.230-2, 3, 4, and 5.

4.5 COST PROPOSAL

FAR 15.408

FAR Table 15-2—Instructions for Submitting Cost/Price Proposals When Cost or Pricing Data Are Required, provides instructions to prepare a pricing proposal when cost or pricing data are required. The offeror submits cost or pricing data that are verifiable and factual to explain the estimating process, including judgmental factors and mathematical or other methods used in the estimate, and those used to project from known data. It also discusses the nature and amount of any contingencies included in the proposed price. The offeror shows the relationship between contract line-item prices and the total contract price, and attaches cost-element breakdowns for each proposed line item. When more than one contract line item is proposed, summary total amounts covering all line items for each element of cost are included. The proposal identifies any incurred costs for work performed before proposal submission.

Use of forward pricing rates/factors negotiated with the Government is described in the proposal. Contracting officers use forward pricing rates for pricing all contracts, modifications and other contractual actions to be performed during the period covered by the agreement. These agreements with major Federal contractors or offerors reflect current and complete cost or pricing data to establish rates to price out proposals. They can be canceled by either party at any time. Certification is not required at the time of agreement for data supplied in support of advance agreements.

The offeror must provide breakdowns for the following basic cost elements:

- *Materials and services:* individual material quantities and the basis for pricing (e.g., vendor quotes and invoice prices) for raw materials, purchases, parts, components, assemblies, and services. The proposal identifies each item, source, quantity, and price. Cost or price analysis is required for all subcontracts and included with the offeror's cost or pricing data submissions. *Interorganizational transfers* (work assigned from the seller to another division or profit center within the same corporate entity, also known as *interdepartmental transfers* or *work authorizations*) priced at other than commercial price are explained. The prime contractor is responsible for updating a prospective subcontractor's data.
- *Direct Labor*: a time-phased (e.g., monthly, quarterly, etc.) breakdown of labor hours, rates, and cost by appropriate category, with bases for estimates. The amount of engineering labor is a function of product complexity and age (state-of-the-art products require much more work than proven products) as well as the manufacturer's technology and previous production experience. Sometimes a complexity factor can be used to increase or decrease prior experience to reflect the change in projected workload. Labor can be of a recurring nature if the process is identical to that done on prior contracts, or nonrecurring (such as preproduction effort).
- *Indirect Costs*: the basis for computing and applying indirect costs, including cost breakdowns. The proposal includes trends and budgetary data to evaluate the reasonableness of proposed rates.
- *Other Costs*: e.g., special tooling, travel, computer and consultant services, preservation, packaging and packing, spoilage and rework, and Federal excise tax. The bases for pricing are included.[13]
- *Facilities Capital Cost of Money*: if selected by the contractor, then Form CASB-CMF must be submitted to show the calculation of the proposed amount.

If the offeror intends to subcontract more than 70% of the total cost, it must identify the amount of its indirect costs and profit/fee applicable to the subcontracted effort, and describe the added value it provides to the subcontracted effort. The same requirements apply to any subcontractor proposing to send more than 70% of its effort to lower-tier subcontractor(s). In this case, the contracting officer must investigate whether direct contracting with one or more subcontractors is feasible. If not, (s)he prepares a written D&F for the file.

4.6 COST ANALYSIS

4.6.1 Analysis Techniques

FAR 15.404

The contracting officer evaluates the reasonableness of the offered prices. The complexity and circumstances of each acquisition determine the level of detail of analysis required.[14] *Fair and reasonable price* is based on current market conditions, fairness to the seller because it covers full costs plus a reasonable profit, and fairness to the buyer based on value and utility.

The purpose of performing cost or price analysis is to develop a negotiation position that permits the contracting officer and the offeror an opportunity to reach agreement on a fair and reasonable price. A fair and reasonable price does not require that agreement be reached on every element of cost, nor is it mandatory that the agreed price be within the contracting officer's initial negotiation position. The contracting officer is responsible for exercising the judgment to reach a negotiated settlement with the offeror and is solely responsible for the final price agreement. However, when significant audit or other specialist recommendations are not adopted, the contracting officer provides rationale to support the result in the price negotiation documentation.

Price analysis is the process of examining and evaluating a proposed price without evaluating its separate cost elements and proposed profit. Analysis techniques include comparisons (more or less in order of preference):

- of proposed prices from all offerors (competition is always the first choice);
- of previous Government and commercial contract prices with current proposed prices for the same or similar items (the preferred technique if no competition exists);
- with competitive published price lists, market prices of commodities, similar indexes, and discount or rebate arrangements;
- with prices obtained through market research for the same or similar items;
- with independent Government cost estimates; and
- by parametric estimating methods (e.g., dollars per pound or per horsepower) to highlight inconsistencies that warrant additional pricing inquiry.

The contracting officer can also measure any variance between the actual and standard prices, multiplied by the number of units to be bought. Traditionally, this term applies to direct materials and "rate variance" is used for assessing labor rates.

Except for commercial items, contracting officers require that offerors identify in their proposals those items of supply that they will not manufacture or contribute significant value to, unless adequate price competition is expected. Such information is used to determine whether the intrinsic value of an item was distorted through application of overhead and should be considered for breakout.

Cost analysis is the review and evaluation of the separate cost elements and profit in a proposal and the application of judgment to determine how well the proposed costs represent what the cost of the contract should be, assuming reasonable economy and efficiency. The Government may use various cost analysis techniques and procedures to ensure a fair and reasonable price, including:

- analysis of make-or-buy program reviews to evaluate subcontract costs;
- audited or negotiated indirect cost rates, labor rates and cost of money factors;
- comparison with actual costs previously incurred by the same offeror;
- comparison with previous cost estimates from the same or other offerors for same or similar items;
- evaluating cost necessity allowing for contingencies;
- evaluating the effect of the offeror's current practices on future costs;
- forecasts of planned expenditures;
- independent Government cost estimates by technical personnel;
- necessity and reasonableness of proposed costs and allowances for contingencies;
- projection of the offeror's cost trends based on current and historical cost or pricing data;
- reasonableness of estimates generated by parametric models or cost-estimating relationships;
- trend analysis of basic labor and materials;
- verification of cost data;
- verification that the offeror's cost submissions are in accordance with the contract cost principles and procedures; and
- whether any cost or pricing data necessary to make the contractor's proposal accurate, complete and current have not been either submitted or identified by the contractor.

The contracting officer's objective is to negotiate a contract type and price that provides the contractor the greatest incentive for economical and efficient performance. Therefore, the contracting officer does not become preoccupied with any single element and should balance the contract type, cost, and profit or fee to achieve a total price that is fair and reasonable to both parties. Because profit or fee is only one of several interrelated variables, the contracting officer does not agree on profit or fee without concurrent agreement on cost and type of contract.

Several variations of cost analysis are employed by the Government or higher-tier contractors. *Parametric cost estimating* involves collecting historical cost data and using mathematical and statistical methods to relate to the contemplated work output. An estimating relationship must be derived to connect a physical characteristic of the work output to the cost or labor hours needed to produce it. Examples of these characteristics include power, size, volume, or weight. They can provide a quick estimate even when nothing is known about the work output other than its physical characteristics. Similarly, *cost estimating relationships* compare historical costs with performance or technical characteristics. The danger is that reliance on historical experience could lead to false cost trends. However, these methods can help determine a realistic cost in these days where weapon system overruns are common.

There are other cost analysis methods that can be useful. *Value analysis* objectively and systematically evaluates a product's function to its cost, in an effort to derive the product's inherent worth. *Will cost* is a different technique that evaluates a cost estimate for a future task by the best estimate that uses current methods, historical costs and forecasting future costs.

Cost realism analysis is the process of independently reviewing and evaluating specific elements of the proposed cost estimate to determine whether they are sensible for the work to be performed, reflect a clear understanding of the requirements, and are consistent with the materials and methods of performance described in the offeror's technical proposal. The *probable cost* reflects the Government's best estimate of the most likely cost of the offeror, and is used to determine the best value. The probable cost is determined by adjusting each offeror's proposed cost and fee to reflect any additions or reductions in cost elements to realistic levels based on the results of the cost realism analysis. Cost realism analyses may also be used on competitive fixed-price incentive contracts when new requirements may not be fully understood by competing offerors, or past experience indicates that proposed costs have resulted in quality or service shortfalls.

Unbalanced pricing may increase performance risk and could result in payment of unreasonably high prices. Unbalanced pricing exists when, despite an acceptable total evaluated price, the price of one or more contract line items is significantly over- or understated. No method to distribute costs to line items may distort unit price. The greatest risks associated with unbalanced pricing occur with separate line items for startup work, mobilization or first articles.

Likewise, when base quantities and option quantities are separate line items, or the evaluated price is the aggregate of estimated quantities to be ordered under separate line items of an indefinite-delivery contract, unbalanced pricing may result. An offer may be rejected if the contracting officer determines that the lack of balance poses an unacceptable risk to the Government. Except for adequate price competition or catalog or market price, unit prices must reflect the intrinsic value of an item or service and be proportionate to an item's manufacturing or acquisition costs.

The proposal for a complex project will include a *work breakdown structure* (WBS) to decompose the project into its components in a tree-like structure or hierarchical chart. The WBS is used both to describe the statement of work and to create work packages for the cost proposal. The WBS must cover all the work and deliverables within the scope of the contract, without overlap between work packages. This means that each package should depict a desired outcome or result, without dwelling on actions or methods. Each package must be estimated realistically, not subject to further breakdown, and be measurable and unique. The packages are identified using the same numerical structure as in this book, broken down into successively lower levels (though not usually more than four levels). Less complicated tasks such as systems engineering and project management may only need two levels. As a rule of thumb, a work package at the lowest level comprises no more than 80 hours of work and can be performed within a single reporting period (usually a month).

For material, the analysts would look at:

- bill of material;
- catalog or market prices;
- competition obtained among suppliers;
- duplication of costs;
- effective planning and use of material;
- estimating methods;
- kinds and quantities;
- make-or-buy decisions;
- prior purchase history (quantities and prices);
- price breaks and economic purchase sizes;
- residual inventory;
- shrinkage or scrap factor, compared to industry average; and
- subcontractor proposals.

The analysis of direct labor would assess:

- actual hours incurred for previous effort;

- complexity factor applied to previous similar effort;
- design data package for engineering drawings and product specifications;
- estimating methodology;
- experience or learning curve data;
- historical costs;
- job descriptions;
- labor efficiency and performance factors;
- labor mix and types;
- labor standards compared to industry norms for fabrication and assembly hours;
- management ratio;
- number of hours;
- organization chart;
- process sheets; and
- rework history.

Engineering labor is often proposed on a level-of-effort basis, meaning it is man-loaded by projecting the number of people or hours to accomplish the task. This effort is a function of product complexity and prior production, as well as the contractor's readiness and technology.

Manufacturing labor is largely nonrecurring in nature and therefore may be more difficult to analyze. It covers operating machinery such as drills, lathes, mills, and punch presses. It also includes associated tools such as clamps, gages, vises, and wrenches. Also, cutting machines must not only be operated, but also removed and replaced or sharpened.[15] This type of effort consists of:

- machine setup and teardown time and housekeeping;
- measuring;
- operation time for machine positioning, part handling and cutting;
- personal allowance, fatigue and delay; and
- tool changing and sharpening.

The material to work with also impacts labor-hour projections. Steel is heavier than copper and much heavier than aluminum, and therefore takes longer to cut or fabricate. Both cut length and feed rate also affect labor hours. Hence, a manufacturing outline sheet or routing sheet is compiled by an industrial estimator from blueprints to detail the operations in sequence and select the machine and needed tools.

Manufacturing labor may be estimated in several ways by using labor standards. One option is to collect historical actual amounts for continuous observations of a person of average talent under average conditions without a break, known as *leveled time*. Another method is to break down a process into basic motions and time several iterations of each, calculating an average time for the process. A hybrid of these methods is the *predetermined-leveled-time technique*, used in high-volume production plants. A *work sampling* technique uses random sampling rather than continuous observations of an individual, especially if work cycles are lengthy in time. The problem with leveled time is that it does not allow for personal breaks, so an industrial engineer would increase the calculated time by adding a *personal, fatigue and delay* allowance to cover bathroom breaks, drinking water, material replenishment, minor repairs to equipment and tools, oiling machinery, and end-of-day cleanup. When all this idle time is added up, it is expressed as a percentage of either 60 minutes or 8 hours to derive an allowance, which is then added to estimated work hours to derive a proposed amount. Similarly, a rework factor may be added based on historical data for inspection-rejected components. Also, test station setup time may need to be added as a discrete number, again based on historical data.

Yet another option is to create a *realization factor* by deriving the ratio of actual time to standard time, thereby reflecting the effects of such factors as fire, flood or obsolete equipment. The reciprocal of this factor is an *efficiency factor*. So if a process has a standard time of 10 minutes but actually takes 12 1/2 minutes, the realization factor is 1.25 and the efficiency factor is 0.8. If the factor calculations show a wide gap before standard and actual times, inefficiency is present and should be investigated, such as cramped work stations, employee abuse or morale, excessive housekeeping or personal breaks, lack of storage space, or poor tool crib management.

To project the difference between standard and actual performance into the future for proposal purposes, the firm will develop an *experience curve* (better known as a *learning curve*). The theory here is that performance improves with repetition because machines are broken in, designs are stabilized, workers become efficient, and material-handling methods improve. In theory, the labor or product cost decreases by a constant amount as the quantity of product doubles. By recording historical data, this relationship can be plotted on a graph to develop a learning curve whose slope represents an experience curve. The steeper the slope, the greater the learning. So if we have a curve of 80% and a cost at unit 1 of $10, the cost for unit 2 will be 10 x 0.8 = $8, for unit 4 will be $6.40, and for unit 8 will be $5.12. Note that the difference between these cost figures is shrinking, which means that the curve slopes toward an asymptote with a long tail when it reaches a certain point. This shows us that the impact of learning is shrinking as experience grows.

The cost analyst will look to ensure that proposed Other Direct Costs are not also included elsewhere, such as an overhead account, to avoid double charging. Special tooling and test equipment must be dedicated to this contract, or else an appropriate pro rata share of cost should be used (or the item should be expensed). Government-furnished equipment should not be available in this circumstance. Travel plans should be spelled out by trip and include airfare, car rental, per diem, and other incidentals (such as parking and tolls).

4.6.2 Information to Support Analysis

The contracting officer may request that personnel with specialized experience, knowledge or skills in engineering, management or science perform a *technical analysis* of direct costs. Often, a cost analyst or procurement analyst performs this task. (S)he will review the proposal in detail to understand how each cost element was developed, and then determine how best to evaluate them. Complex proposals will include a description page for each work package to identify hours and any material cost, with a written explanation to justify these numbers.

The contracting officer requests field pricing assistance when the information available at the buying activity is inadequate to determine a fair and reasonable price. (S)he tailors the type of information and level of detail requested to the minimum necessary to help determine reasonableness. Such assistance normally includes:

- business, production or technical capabilities and practices of an offeror;
- identifying customarily granted or offered discounts;
- identifying general market conditions affecting determinations of commerciality and price reasonableness;
- information on related pricing practices and history;
- audit and technical reports on the cost elements of a proposal, including subcontracts;
- verifying historical data for an item previously not commercial that the offeror is now trying to qualify as a commercial item;
- verifying sales history; and
- verifying the proposed catalog or price list.

Within DoD, the contracting officer may ask DCAA for rate information or, if the estimated price is large enough, for a full pricing report (this service is also available to civilian agencies, for a fee). The completed field pricing assistance need not reconcile the audit recommendations and technical recommendations. General access to the offeror's books and financial records is limited to the auditor, however the contracting officer may request the offeror provide or make available any data or records necessary to analyze the offeror's proposal.

The contracting officer considers whether a (sub)contractor has an approved purchasing system, has performed cost or price analysis of proposed subcontractor prices, or has negotiated the subcontract prices before negotiation of the prime contract. The prime contractor or subcontractor conducts appropriate cost or price analyses to establish the reasonableness of proposed subcontract prices, includes the results of these analyses in the price proposal, and submits any required subcontractor cost or pricing data with its own cost or pricing data. The contractor submits, or directs the subcontractor(s) to submit, cost or pricing data to the Government for subcontracts that are either $13.5 million in value or in excess of both the certified cost or pricing data threshold and 10% of the prime contractor's proposed price, unless the contracting officer believes such submission is unnecessary. The contracting officer may require subcontractor cost or pricing data below these thresholds if necessary to adequately price the prime contract. Subcontractor cost or pricing data is also certified as current, accurate and complete as of the date of price agreement. The contractor updates subcontractor data during source selection and negotiations. If there is more than one prospective subcontractor for any given work, the contractor need only submit to the Government cost or pricing data for the prospective subcontractor most likely to receive award.

After this initial review, a list of questions should be sent to the offeror's contracts representative. On major procurements, a fact-finding session will be held face to face to explore the proposal in more depth. Often, this is at the contractor's facility because the answers may not lie with the attendees, but rather with a person elsewhere in the facility who might not otherwise travel to the contracting office. The offeror is responsible for making available all facts which would contribute to the validity of both incurred costs and future costs. Fact-finding sessions should result in learning much more about the contractor's estimating assumptions and methodology, and identifying areas which need further clarification or revision. Upon return to the office, the cost analyst will review his/her notes to begin developing a prenegotiation position as to what a reasonable pricing structure should be.

Normally, for contractors other than educational institutions and nonprofit organizations, DCAA is the responsible Government audit agency to service both military and civilian agencies to:[16]

- audit progress payments;
- examine defective pricing proposals;
- examine reimbursement vouchers for cost-type contracts;
- provide recommendations to procurement and contract administration personnel;
- review contractor estimating systems and procedures;

- review cost proposals to ensure economy, effectiveness and efficiency, and submit field pricing reports to document their findings;
- review ongoing contracts for allocability, allowability and reasonableness; and
- review the financial and accounting aspects of the contractor's cost-control systems and proposed and incurred costs.

The auditor may inspect the books under a cost-type contract at the plant or a subcontractor, with penalties for contractors who impede free access thereto. The auditor has the authority to decide what (s)he needs. In DoD, this requirement extends up to three years after final payment and includes the right to reproduce records.

FAR 42.707

Cost-sharing arrangements may call for indirect cost rates lower than the anticipated actual rates. In such cases, a negotiated indirect cost rate ceiling may be incorporated into the contract for prospective application. These cases include a new or recently reorganized company with no past or recent record of incurred indirect costs, a contractor with rapidly increasing indirect cost rates due to a declining volume of sales, or a contractor trying to enhance its competitive position by proposing indirect cost rates lower than those that may reasonably be expected to occur during contract performance (thereby causing a cost overrun). In such cases, an equitable ceiling covering the final indirect cost rates may be negotiated and specified in the contract. When ceiling provisions are utilized, the Government will not be obligated to pay any additional amount should the final rates exceed the negotiated ceiling rates, but any final rates below the negotiated ceiling rates will lead to rate reductions.

FAR 15.4

For contracts above the simplified acquisition threshold, the contracting officer will determine whether the price is based on competition, regulation or a commercial catalog or price list. If none of these apply, then the offeror will need to certify the cost or pricing data submitted with the proposal.[17]

4.7 PROFIT

When price negotiations are not based on cost analysis, contracting officers need not analyze profit. When the price negotiation is based on cost analysis, contracting officers in agencies that have a structured approach use it to analyze profit; if not, then the guidelines discussed below are sufficient.

Elements of profit are subjective, but are intended to tie a greater profit opportunity to outstanding performance of more demanding tasks. They are based on contract type motivating the contractor to incur greater cost risk and input into performance. Hence, neither predetermined or historical rates nor unreasonably low rates are valid profit policies.

Contracting officers use the prenegotiation cost objective amounts as the basis to calculate the profit or fee prenegotiation objective. Before applying profit or fee factors, the contracting officer excludes any facilities capital cost of money included in the cost objective amounts, since the Government will not allow profit on top of the cost of money. If the prospective contractor does not propose facilities capital cost of money for a contract that will be subject to the cost principles, a contract clause will be necessary to make it an unallowable cost.

The contracting officer does not negotiate a profit or fee rate that exceeds the following statutory limitations per 10 U.S.C. 2306(d) and 41 U.S.C. 254(b):

- for experimental, developmental, or research work performed under a cost-plus-fixed-fee contract, 15% of the estimated cost;
- for architect-engineer services for public works or utilities designs, plans, drawings, and specifications, 6% of the estimated cost of construction; and
- for other cost-plus-fixed-fee contracts, 10% of the contract's estimated cost.

The offeror need not submit breakouts or supporting rationale for its profit or fee objective, but may do so voluntarily for the contracting officer to consider.

Three factors considered by the contracting officer in developing a profit or fee objective are contractor effort, contract cost risk and management.

Contractor effort measures the complexity of the work and the resources required for contract performance. Greater profit opportunity is provided under contracts requiring a high degree of managerial and professional skill and to prospective contractors whose facilities, skills and technical assets indicate economical and efficient contract performance. Subfactors include:

- *Material acquisition* – purchased parts, raw material and subcontracted items. This includes the complexity of the items required, the number of purchase orders and subcontracts to be awarded and administered, whether established sources are available or new or alternate sources must be developed, and whether material will be obtained through routine purchase orders or complex subcontracts requiring detailed specifications.

- *Conversion direct labor* – the contribution of direct engineering, manufacturing, and other direct labor to convert data, raw materials and subcontracted items into the contract. Considerations include the diversity of engineering, manufacturing and scientific labor skills required and the amount and quality of supervision and coordination.
- *Conversion-related indirect costs.* The labor elements in the allocable indirect costs receive the profit consideration they would earn if treated as direct labor. Other elements of indirect costs are evaluated to determine their level of merit based on either routine nature or significant contribution to the proposed contract.
- *General management* – G&A expense and how much they contribute to contract performance. Considerations include how overhead labor would be treated as if direct, whether elements within the pools are routine expenses or contribute significantly to the proposed contract, and whether the elements require routine or unusual managerial effort and attention.

The *Contract cost risk* factor measures the degree of cost responsibility and associated risk that the prospective contractor will assume as a result of the contract type contemplated. It considers the reliability of the cost estimate in relation to the complexity and duration of the contract task. This factor compensates contractors proportionately for assuming greater cost risks. The contractor assumes the greatest cost risk in a closely priced firm-fixed-price contract to perform a complex undertaking on time at a predetermined price. If the contract task is less complex or many of the contractor's costs are known at the time of price agreement, the risk factor is reduced accordingly. The contractor assumes the least cost risk in a cost-plus-fixed-fee, level-of-effort contract because it is reimbursed for all costs determined to be allocable and allowable, plus the fixed fee. Time-and-materials, labor-hour, and firm-fixed-price, level-of-effort term contracts are treated the same as cost-plus-fixed-fee contracts in this regard.

There are four different *management* factors used in setting a profit objective for the Government negotiator to achieve during negotiations. The *Federal socioeconomic programs* factor measures the degree of support given by the prospective contractor to such programs. Greater profit opportunity is provided to contractors that have displayed unusual initiative in these programs. The *Capital investments* factor considers the contribution of contractor investments to efficient and economical contract performance. A *Cost-control and other past accomplishments* factor recognizes a contractor's success in performing similar tasks effectively and economically, productivity improvements, and other cost-reduction accomplishments that will benefit the Government in follow-on contracts. Finally, an *Independent development* factor recognizes efforts for the contract end item without Government assistance, especially if the development cost was not recovered from Government sources.

Each agency may include additional factors in its structured approach or take them into account in the profit analysis of individual contract actions.

Excess profits are controversial because they are not subject to external evaluation in nongovernment industries. This concept developed during World War II out of fear that Federal dollars would be lost to excess profit. Under the Renegotiation Act of 1951 (50 U.S.C. App. 1211), these fears were revived due to the noncompetitive nature of defense procurement. The Renegotiation Board had authority to reset profits under Federal contracts but suffered from vague regulations and lack of resources, and lapsed in 1976. Efficient low-cost producers could have been penalized for excess profits. Fortunately, increased professionalism of government personnel and more stringent regulations led to better contract pricing and less risk of excess profits. This topic remains subject to lobbying on both sides of the issue.

4.8 DOCUMENTATION

The prenegotiation objectives establish the Government's initial negotiation position to assist in the contracting officer's determination of fair and reasonable price. They are based on the results of the contracting officer's analysis of the proposal, taking into consideration audit reports, fact-finding, field pricing assistance, independent Government cost estimates, price histories, and technical analysis. The scope and depth of the analysis supporting the objectives is directly related to the dollar value, importance and complexity of the pricing action.

The contracting officer and contractor are encouraged to reach a prior agreement on criteria for establishing closing or cutoff dates to minimize delays associated with proposal updates. Before agreement on price, the offeror updates data to the latest closing or cutoff dates for which the data are available.

The contracting officer documents in the contract file the principal elements of the negotiated agreement in a price negotiation memorandum, such as:

- purpose of the negotiation;
- description of the acquisition;
- name, position and organization of each person representing the contractor and the Government in the negotiation;

- current status of any contractor systems (e.g., accounting, compensation, estimating, and purchasing);
- if applicable, the exception used and the basis for not requiring cost or pricing data if above the data threshold;
- the extent to which the contracting officer relied on cost or pricing data in negotiations and any inaccuracy, incompleteness or nonoccurrence (including actions taken for resolution and effect on negotiated price);
- summary of the contractor's proposal, any field pricing assistance recommendations, reasons for any pertinent variances from them, the Government's negotiation objective, and the final settlement. This includes discussing each major cost element (if using cost analysis) or source and type of data used to support price analysis;
- factors controlling the establishment of the prenegotiation objectives and the negotiated agreement, and an explanation of significant differences between the two positions;
- quantification of the impact of direction given by Congress, other agencies, and higher-level officials;
- basis for the profit or fee prenegotiation objective and the amount negotiated; and
- statement that price is fair and reasonable.

4.9 DEFECTIVE COST OR PRICING DATA

When a noncompetitive negotiation exceeds $750,000, the offeror will need to certify that to his/her best knowledge and belief, the cost and pricing data submitted is accurate, complete and current as of the date when negotiations were completed. The certificate of current cost or pricing data is not a representation as to the accuracy of the contractor's judgment on the estimate of future costs or projections, but rather to data upon which the judgment or estimate was based. If the contractor had information reasonably available at the time of agreement showing the contrary, it is responsible for disclosure and is not limited by any lack of personal knowledge on the part of its negotiators.

If the contracting officer learns that any cost or pricing data submitted are inaccurate, incomplete or noncurrent, (s)he immediately brings the matter to the attention of the prospective offeror, and considers the matter when negotiating the contract price. The price negotiation memorandum includes any adjustments made to the data used to negotiate the contract price.

If such a finding occurs after award and was in error on or before the date of final agreement, the Government is entitled to a price adjustment of any significant amount by which the price was increased because of the defective data, including subcontractor data. The contracting officer offsets, for any understated cost or pricing data submitted in support of price negotiations, the amount of the Government's claim for overstated pricing data arising out of the same pricing action. An offset is allowed only if the contractor certifies that, to the best of its knowledge and belief, it is entitled to the offset in the amount requested, and proves that the cost or pricing data were available before the "as of" date specified on the Certificate of Current Cost or Pricing Data but were not submitted. In addition to the price adjustment, the Government is entitled to recovery of any overpayment plus interest or penalty, provided that payment has been made for supplies or services accepted by the Government (overpayments do not result from contract financing, by definition).

The contracting officer may not reprice the contract solely because the profit was greater than forecast or because a contingency specified in the submission failed to materialize.

NOTES

1. The act of maintaining or expanding a large market share illegally or through threats is called *monopolization*, and is often the subject of investigation by the Federal Trade Commission.

2. This introduces a choice the contractor must make – either invest in more precise equipment and highly trained machinist labor, or else settle for higher overage.

3. Unless they are standard commercial items or acquired competitively, interdivisional transfers should not bear any profit. Although really another type of material, they do not bear overhead and are therefore listed as an Other Direct Cost.

4. Some large firms have procurement personnel dedicated to a large program. In such cases, the buyers may become direct labor charged to the program.

5. DoD has certain prescribed further exceptions to use of the -22 and -23 clauses.

6. OMB Uniform Guidance at 2 CFR part 200, appendix VIII, specifically exempts 32 organizations from the use of cost principles, principally nonprofit organizations which are not affiliated with educational institutions. Also exempted are state and local governments.

7. This is sometimes referred to as a *separable cost*.

8. These restrictions derive from the *Byrd Amendment*, 31 U.S.C. 1352.

9. *Boyle v. United Technologies Corp.*, 487 U.S. 500 (1988).

10. All three OMB circulars mentioned here are dated May 10, 2004.

11. A firm which only contracts on a firm-fixed-price basis does not need to comply with CASB. Any large firm using a more flexibly priced contract does. Small businesses are exempt from compliance.

12. Often this is the cognizant administrative contracting officer assigned by DoD.

13. If the cost is a royalty exceeding $1,500, additional information is needed to assess each separate royalty or license fee.

14. An excellent source of information is the Contract Pricing Reference Guides from the Air Force Institute of Technology and the Federal Acquisition Institute, http://www.acq.osd.mil/dpap/cpf/contract_pricing_reference_guides.html.

15. In general, the harder-surface cutter will be more efficient in time but also be more expensive. The trade-off here is labor cost versus purchase cost.

16. Cognizance of educational and nonprofit institutions is assigned to whichever service or agency has the most negotiated dollars awarded to the entity. With some medical institutions, this is the Department of Health and Human Services.

17. The Head of the Contracting Activity may waive the requirement for certified cost or pricing data in exceptional cases, such as when the contractor previously furnished such data and it was deemed adequate and remains current.

Chapter 5

Post-Award

5.1 CONTRACT ADMINISTRATION SERVICES

5.1.1 Duties

FAR 42.0

Contract administration is the process whereby the parties ensure that the results or performance match the contract. Emphasis is placed on progress toward meeting delivery and schedule, invoicing and payment, and fulfilling contract conditions. On major contracts, this process often begins with a kickoff meeting to discuss the requirements and approach, and address administrative concerns. Subcontractor post-award conferences are also sometimes held.

Contracting officers may delegate contract administration or specific support services, either through interagency agreements or by direct request, to the cognizant *contract administration office* (CAO) listed in the Federal Directory of Contract Administration Services Components, available at https://pubapp.dcma.mil/CASD/main.jsp. Most of these offices are part of the Defense Contract Management Agency (the others are located within the individual DoD services). These offices have either geographic jurisdictions or corporation assignments, and accept contracts for administration based on these jurisdictional rules.

Assignment is based on the identity of the prime contractor's location. Since the prime contractor is responsible for managing its subcontracts, the CAO's review of subcontracts is normally limited to evaluating the prime contractor's oversight process and results. Therefore, supporting contract administration is not used for subcontracts unless the Government would either incur undue costs due to subcontract performance or else raise concern about successful completion of the prime contract.

The contracting officer normally delegates to the CAO the following contract administration functions, which are performed by contract administrative officers (ACOs), who often have contract administrators on their staff to perform many of these functions (though only the ACO has a warrant to bind the Government to a position):

- accomplish administrative closeout procedures;
- administer the industrial security program;
- advise and assist contractors on priorities and allocations responsibilities;
- analyze quarterly limitation on payment statements and recover overpayments;
- approve final vouchers;
- assess compliance with cost, schedule and technical requirements for design, development and production;
- assist contracting offices to request special assistance and obtain priority ratings for privately owned capital equipment;
- cancel unilateral purchase orders when notified of nonacceptance by the contractor;
- conduct post-award orientation conferences for Government and contractor personnel to understand contract requirements and resolve potential problems;
- consent to the placement of subcontracts (but not if the prime contact is firm-fixed-price);
- coordinate the removal of urgently required material from a strikebound contractor's plant upon contracting officer authorization;
- deobligate excess funds after final price determination;
- determine adequacy of contractor's accounting system;
- determine allowability of costs;
- determine that the contractor has a drug-free workplace and awareness program;
- determine the adequacy of the contractor's disclosure statements and compliance with CAS and disclosure statements;
- determine the allowability of costs, and suspend or disapprove their payment;
- ensure contractor compliance with safety and quality assurance requirements;
- ensure contractor payment of rent;
- ensure processing and execution of duty-free entry certificates;
- ensure timely contractor notification of any anticipated cost overrun or underrun under cost-reimbursement contracts;

- ensure timely submission of reports;
- establish final indirect cost and billing rates;
- evaluate and monitor contractor procedures for restrictive markings on data;
- evaluate and recommend acceptance or rejection of waivers and deviations;
- evaluate contractor engineering efforts and management systems;
- evaluate contractor requests for Government property, and changes to existing property;
- evaluate use of Government property on a noninterference basis;
- issue administrative changes which do not require additional contract funds;
- issue and control Government bills of lading and other transportation documents;
- issue no-cost administrative changes;
- issue Notices of Intent to Disallow or not Recognize Costs;
- issue tax-exemption forms;
- issue work requests under maintenance, modification and overhaul contracts;
- maintain documentation of contractor performance under subcontracting plans and requirements;
- manage special bank accounts and make contractor payments;
- modify contracts to cover screening, redistribution and disposal of excess Government property;
- monitor commercial financing provisions and contractor security to ensure adequacy to cover outstanding payments;
- monitor contractor compliance with the delivery or use of products that are biobased, environmentally preferable, energy-efficient, or possess recovered materials;
- monitor contractor environmental practices for adverse impact on contract performance or cost, and for compliance with environmental requirements, and request environmental technical assistance;
- monitor contractor ethics code;
- monitor contractor industrial labor relations and apprise the contracting officer and cognizant labor relations advisor of actual or potential labor disputes;
- monitor the contractor's financial condition and advise the contracting officer when it jeopardizes contract performance;
- monitor the contractor's value engineering program;
- negotiate and execute supplemental agreements to extend delivery schedules up to 90 days on contracts with an assigned Criticality Designator of C;[1]

- negotiate forward pricing rate agreements and advance agreements regarding treatment of costs in future time periods;
- negotiate price adjustments and execute supplemental agreements;
- negotiate prices and execute supplemental agreements for spare parts and provisioning;[2]
- perform engineering analyses of contractor cost proposals;
- perform pre-award surveys to evaluate a prospective contractor's ability to perform a given contract. This entails examining the firm's physical, technical, managerial, and financial capability, as well as its systems, procedures and past performance record;
- perform production surveillance and report delivery performance and slippages;
- perform property administration;
- process and execute novation and change of name agreements;
- provide appropriate recommendations to the contracting officer;
- release shipments from contractor's plants according to the shipping instructions, and review price adjustment proposals for amended shipping instructions;
- report items no longer needed for Government production;
- report to the contracting office any specification inadequacies;
- review all amended packaging and shipping instructions to ensure timely adjustments;
- review and (dis)approve contractor requests for payments under the progress payments or performance-based payments clauses;
- review and evaluate contractor logistics support, maintenance and modification;
- review and evaluate contractors' proposals (including engineering and design studies) and furnish comments and recommendations to the contracting officer;
- review and evaluate preservation, packaging and packing;
- review contractor compensation structure and insurance plans;
- review contractor insurance plans;
- review engineering change proposals for classification and need, producibility and technical adequacy of design, plus impact on cost, quality, reliability, and schedule;
- review the adequacy of the contractor's traffic operations;
- review the contractor's compensation structure;
- review, (dis)approve and monitor the contractor's purchasing system;
- review, evaluate and approve plant or division-wide socioeconomic master subcontracting plans, including compliance with similar plans under prior contracts;

- screen Government property before contractor acquisition;
- screen, redistribute and dispose of contractor inventory;
- settle cancellation charges under multiyear contracts;
- settle contract terminations for convenience;
- support the program offices in program reviews, such as performance status and actual or anticipated problems;
- survey flight operations; and
- try to resolve disputes.

If authorized by the contracting officer, the ACO may negotiate and execute supplemental agreements to:

- adjust prices due to exercise of an economic price adjustment clause;
- amend shipping instructions;
- change interim billing prices;
- definitize unpriced orders;
- deobligate unexpended dollar balances exceeding known contract requirements;
- permit a change in place of inspection at origin specified in firm-fixed-price supply contracts with nonmanufacturers;
- price out change orders;
- reduce line-item quantities and deobligate excess funds on firm-fixed-price supply contracts due to delivery shortage (up to $250 or 5% of the contract price); and
- revise contract delivery schedules.

5.1.2 Corporate ACO

FAR 42.6

Major Federal contractors with more than one operational location often have corporate-wide activities, policies and procedures requiring Government review and approval that affect the work of multiple ACOs. To maintain consistent contract administration may require a corporate administrative contracting officer to deal with corporate management and to perform selected contract administration functions on a corporate-wide basis. Typically, corporate ACOs administer CAS to corporate accounting practices, determine final indirect cost rates for flexibly priced contracts, and establish advance recommendations or agreements on corporate and home office expense allocations.

5.1.3 Contracting Officer's Representative

The program office will assign a Contracting Officer's Representative (COR, or sometimes COTR for a technical representative) to provide program knowledge assistance to the contractor and contracting officer during contract performance.[3] The COR monitors specific facets of the contract under the direction of the contracting officer, such as:

- advise the contracting officer on any claims and remedies therefore;
- complete past performance evaluations;
- conduct site visits;
- conduct property management;
- inspect and accept deliverables;
- interpret technical requirements;
- monitor and evaluate contractor performance to identify any problems or noncompliance;
- monitor contractor use of Government-furnished property;
- prepare procurement and option requests;
- recommend changes and corrective actions; and
- review invoices and contractor status reports.

The contracting officer will issue a designation letter to the COR immediately upon award. This letter manifests the duties of the COR and asserts that (s)he is qualified and trained to perform the duties.

The COR is a Government employee who is very familiar with the program and statement of work, but not necessarily savvy with contract terms and conditions. In short, the COR can tell the contractor what to do (within the scope of work, of course) but not how to do it. The COR has no authority to commit the Government to a position, direct changes or authorize subcontract placement. The COR cannot authorize overtime (only the contracting officer may do so), but can examine time cards and authorized overtime, as well as any expenses.

5.2 LABOR

5.2.1 Labor Laws

FAR Part 22

Collective bargaining and freedom of association for labor was ensured by the *National Labor Relations Act* (29 U.S.C. 151), which prohibits a firm from discriminating against employees regarding activities for or against a labor union, or who file charges or testify against the firm. The firm cannot interfere with labor union operations or refuse to bargain collectively with union representatives. Finally, the firm cannot coerce or restrain employees from association, mutual aid or self-organization to bargain collectively for wages and better working conditions.

Agencies must remain impartial concerning any dispute between labor and contractor management without resort to conciliation, mediation or arbitration. However, they will exchange information with other agencies to ensure a uniform Government approach concerning a labor-management dispute. The contracting officer may seek a voluntary agreement between management and labor to permit uninterrupted acquisition of supplies and services, but cannot become involved in the merits of the dispute. Normal plant inspection continues without regard to the existence of a labor dispute, strike or picket line, unless personal safety is threatened. The head of the contracting activity may designate programs or requirements where contractors must notify the Government of actual or potential labor disputes that could delay timely contract performance.

Contractors are responsible for reasonably avoidable delays, and must file a charge with the National Labor Relations Board to seek injunctive relief in court. They should try to use private boards or organizations to settle disputes. Beyond this, however, contractors are not held responsible if their diligent efforts fail to end the dispute.

Contract labor normally uses a 40-hour workweek, or, if outside the United States, the normal workweek for the area without a premium rate for more than 40 hours per week. Contractors do not use overtime, especially as a regular employment practice, unless lower overall costs result or if necessary to meet urgent program needs. Therefore, solicitations normally do not specify delivery or performance schedules that require overtime at Government expense. During contract performance, the agency approving official must determine in writing that overtime is necessary to meet essential delivery or performance schedules, compensate for delays beyond the control and without the fault or negligence of the contractor, or eliminate extended production bottlenecks.

Contractor employees must record on their timecards all hours worked, including unbillable direct labor and any indirect labor. Managers with timecard approval authority review the accuracy of charge numbers and the hours charged at the end of the pay period. They should approve the timecard only after the employee has done so, and are accountable for timecard accuracy.

When an employee changes any recorded hours, the reason code becomes part of the timecard's audit trail, providing an auditor with a comprehensive picture of the employee's labor charging during the pay period.

Solicitation Provisions and Contract Clauses

FAR 52.222-1, Notice to the Government of Labor Disputes, when designated by the agency head.

FAR 52.222-2, Payment for Overtime Premiums, if a cost-reimbursement contract is expected to exceed the simplified acquisition threshold. This does not apply to contracts to operate vessels or a cost-plus-incentive-fee contract that provides a target fee swing of at least plus or minus 3% and a contractor's share of at least 10%.

5.2.2 Convict Labor

FAR 22.2

The Federal Government encourages developing the occupational and educational skills of prison inmates.[4] A contractor may hire past or present Federal prisoners or parolees. State or local prisoners may also be hired if authorized to work for pay in the community in a voluntary approved work training program. However, to avoid unfair competition with salaried labor:

- employed workers cannot be displaced;
- local union representatives must be consulted (if applicable);
- no existing services contracts can be impaired;
- the pay rate must be that for similar work in the region; and
- the trade must have a surplus of available labor in the locality.

Solicitation Provision and Contract Clause

FAR 52.222-3, Convict Labor, if above the micro-purchase threshold for performance in the United States and outlying areas, unless subject to 41 U.S.C. 65, with Federal Prison Industries, Inc., or involving the purchase from a State prison of finished supplies that may be secured in the open market or from existing stocks.

5.2.3 Contract Work Hours and Safety Standards Act

FAR 22.3

The Contract Work Hours and Safety Standards Act (40 U.S.C. 3701) applies to contracts for laborers or mechanics (but not seamen). *Laborers* or *mechanics* include:

- apprentices, helpers and trainees;
- firefighters;

- foremen who devote more than 20% of their time during a workweek performing duties of a laborer or mechanic;
- guards and watchmen; and
- those who perform manual or physical duties, rather than mental or managerial.[5]

No laborer or mechanic under the contract may work more than 40 hours in any workweek unless paid for all overtime hours at least 1 1/2 times the basic pay rate, regardless of whether the employer required or permitted the employee to do so.

When a computation discloses underpayments, the responsible (sub)contractor pays the affected employee any unpaid wages and then pays liquidated damages to the Government at the rate of $10 per affected employee per day worked.

If the (sub)contractor fails or refuses to comply and the funds withheld do not cover the unpaid wages, the Government pays laborers the wages owed (or a prorated amount if sufficient funds are not available) plus liquidated damages. If the agency head finds that the violation was inadvertent, (s)he can waive liquidated damages if below $500.

Solicitation Provision and Contract Clause

FAR 52.222-4, Contract Work Hours and Safety Standards Act – Overtime Compensation, if employing laborers or mechanics. Do not use if:

- exempt under Department of Labor regulations;
- for commercial items;
- for supplies with only incidental services that do not require substantial employment of laborers or mechanics;
- for transportation or transmission of intelligence;
- to be performed outside the United States or outlying areas; or
- valued at or below $150,000.

5.2.4 Labor Standards for Construction

FAR 22.4

We have seen several statutes and executive orders prescribe labor requirements for contracts to construct, alter or repair public buildings and public works. A *construction, alteration or repair* contract addresses laborers and mechanics on a building or work site who:

- alter, install or remodel items that were fabricated off-site;
- furnish or manufacture equipment, materials or supplies on the work site;

- decorate and paint; or
- transport materials and supplies between the work site and a facility dedicated to the construction project.

These labor standards apply only to:

- construction work at a site where wage rates can be determined for the locality;
- dismantling, demolition or removal of improvements;
- manufacture or fabrication at the work site of construction materials and components by the (sub)contractor; and
- painting public buildings or works, either during original construction or as alteration or repair of an existing structure.

Recall that the Davis-Bacon Act (40 U.S.C. 3141) requires wage determinations to be issued by the Department of Labor for such contracts over $2,000. Also, the *Copeland (Anti-Kickback) Act* (18 U.S.C. 874 and 40 U.S.C. 3145) prohibits inducement, intimidation, surrender of compensation due, or threat of dismissal of any person employed under Federal construction contracts. This statute also requires each (sub)contractor to furnish a weekly statement of compliance for wages paid each employee during the preceding week.

5.2.5 Contracts for Materials, Supplies, Articles, and Equipment Exceeding $15,000

FAR 22.6

Replacing the Walsh-Healey Public Contracts Act, this long-titled legislation is perhaps better known by its legal citation of 41 U.S.C. 65. It addresses performance within the United States and certain possessions, in any amount exceeding $15,000, and includes or incorporates by reference provisions regarding child and convict labor, maximum hours, minimum wages, and safe and sanitary working conditions. Contracts to acquire the following supplies are exempt from the Act:

- agricultural or farm products processed for sale by the original producers or purchased by the Department of Agriculture;
- items where immediate delivery is required by the public exigency;
- newspapers, magazines or periodicals from sales agents or publisher representatives;
- perishables, including dairy, livestock and nursery products;
- public utility services;

- purchases against a defaulting contractor if the contract was itself exempt; or
- supplies manufactured outside the United States, Puerto Rico and Virgin Islands.

Upon the request of the agency head, the Secretary of Labor may exempt specific contracts or classes of contracts from application of one or more of the Act's stipulations when the conduct of Government business will be seriously impaired.

The $15,000 threshold applies to any subcontract and indefinite-delivery contract or agreement (in terms of total orders placed thereunder), but ceases to apply if a contract is modified to an amount below the threshold.

Solicitation Provision and Contract Clause

FAR 52.222-20, Contracts for Materials, Supplies, Articles, and Equipment Exceeding $15,000.

5.2.6 Equal Employment Opportunity

FAR 22.8 through 22.9

Everyone has the right to be considered for employment without discrimination due to age, creed, color, gender identity, handicap (mental or physical), national origin, race, or sexual orientation. No contract or modification can be awarded to an entity found to be noncompliant with the requirements of Executive Orders 11246, Equal employment opportunity (October 5, 1978), and 13672, Prohibiting discrimination based on sexual orientation and gender identity (July 21, 2014). Each nonconstruction (sub)contractor with 50 or more employees and a (sub)contract of $50,000 or more (or totaling $50,000 or more or in any 12-month period) must develop a written affirmative action program for each of its establishments within 120 days from beginning its first such Government (sub)contract or bill of lading.

For construction contracting, each agency maintains a listing of geographical areas that are subject to affirmative action requirements, and specifies goals for minorities and women in covered trades. If a contracting officer anticipates an award over $10,000 in an area which is not covered, (s)he must request instructions from the Office of Federal Contract Compliance Programs (OFCCP) regional office. Contracting officers give written notice to OFCCP within 10 working days of award of a construction contract. If the estimated amount of the (sub)contract is $10 million or more, the contracting officer requests clearance from the appropriate OFCCP regional office 30 days before the proposed award date or modification for new effort. If

OFCCP does not respond within 15 days or a mutually agreed time frame, approval is assumed. The contracting officer need not request a pre-award clearance if the specific proposed contractor is listed in OFCCP's National Preaward Registry at http://www.dol-esa.gov/preaward/pa_reg.html, and the projected award date is within 24 months of its Notice of Compliance completion date in the Registry.

To demonstrate compliance, the contracting officer furnishes to the contractor multiple copies of the poster entitled "Equal Employment Opportunity Is The Law." Many firms post this and similar notices on a bulletin board in the coffee mess, where it can be easily seen by all employees.

Using contract awards as a tool to enforce civil rights legislation may seem controversial and costly, but OFCCP has insufficient resources to enforce implementation in any other way. Moreover, the Supreme Court decided that contractors may be treated differently when Congress says so, and that a remedial program to place minorities on an equal footing for public contracting opportunities is valid.[6] Nonetheless, all or part of these requirements of Executive Order 11246, Equal employment opportunity (October 5, 1978), may be excluded for:

- contracts with religious entities (e.g., corporation, association, educational institution, or society) or with State or local governments;
- effort for national security;
- facilities not connected with contracts;
- indefinite-quantity contracts if the amount to be ordered in any year is not expected to exceed $10,000. The Equal Opportunity clause is applied once a single order exceeds $10,000, and continues in force for the contract's duration regardless of the amounts ordered, or expected to be ordered, in any future year;
- special circumstances of national interest;
- transactions of $10,000 or less (Government bills of lading are not exempt, regardless of amount);
- work on or near Indian reservations to prefer employment to Indians living on or near a reservation (however, the contractor must still comply with Executive Order 11246); or
- work outside the United States by employees who were not recruited within the United States.

Per Executive Order 11141, Declaring a public policy against discrimination based on age, of February 12, 1964, (sub)contractors may not discriminate against persons because of their age in terms of employment, promotion or discharge. No contract clauses are required.

Solicitation Provisions

FAR 52.222-22, Previous Contracts and Compliance Reports, unless completely exempt from Executive Order 11246.

FAR 52.222-23, Notice of Requirement for Affirmative Action to Ensure Equal Employment Opportunity for Construction, if expected to exceed $10,000.

FAR 52.222-24, Preaward On-Site Equal Opportunity Compliance Evaluation, if non-construction (unless completely exempt from Executive Order 11246) and expected to be $10 million or more.

FAR 52.222-25, Affirmative Action Compliance, if nonconstruction (unless completely exempt from Executive Order 11246).

Solicitation Provisions and Contract Clauses

FAR 52.222-21, Prohibition of Segregated Facilities.

FAR 52.222-26, Equal Opportunity, unless exempt from Executive Order 11246. Use the clause with its Alternate I if the contract is exempt from one or more, but not all, of the requirements of Executive Order 11246.

FAR 52.222-27, Affirmative Action Compliance Requirements for Construction, if non-construction (unless completely exempt from Executive Order 11246) and expected to be in excess of $10,000.

Contract Clause

FAR 52.222-29, Notification of Visa Denial, if nonconstruction (unless completely exempt from Executive Order 11246) and performed in or on behalf of a foreign country.

5.2.7 Professional Employee Compensation

FAR 22.11

A *professional employee* is a person whose livelihood is based upon acquiring specialized knowledge through prolonged study. Professions include:

- accountants;
- actuaries;
- architects;
- dentists;
- engineers;

- lawyers;
- physicians;
- nurses;
- pharmacists; and
- scientists.

When the contract amount is expected to exceed $750,000 and the services will require numerous professional employees, offerors must submit for evaluation a total compensation plan of proposed salaries and fringe benefits for all professional employees working on the contract.

Solicitation Provision

FAR 52.222-46, Evaluation of Compensation for Professional Employees, when the negotiated contract amount is expected to exceed $750,000 and the services will require numerous professional employees.

5.2.8 Non-Displacement of Qualified Workers

FAR 22.12

When the Government awards a follow-on service contract to a firm that is not the incumbent contractor, the successor firm must offer all service employees currently working under the prior contract a right of first refusal for employment under the new contract in positions for which they are qualified. This requirement does not apply to (sub)contracts awarded:

- below the simplified acquisition threshold;
- for vending facilities;
- for service employees working under both a Federal and one or more non-Federal service contracts;
- to SourceAmerica; or
- to sheltered workshops employing severely handicapped persons (this primarily occurs for custodians, elevator operators, messengers, or security guards).

At least 30 days before completion of the contract, the predecessor contractor must furnish to the contracting officer a certified list of the names of all service employees working under the contract and its subcontracts, along with anniversary dates of employment of each service employee. Any updated changes are due 10 days before contract completion. The contracting officer will furnish the final list to the successor contractor and, if requested, to the employees themselves or their authorized representatives. All current employees are notified of their rights in writing, either by personal letter or by posting a notice at the workplace, including their possible right to an offer of employment with the successor contractor. Failure to do so could result in suspension of payment by the contracting officer, as well as possible suspension or debarment.

Any job offer by the new contractor must give the employee 10 days to respond. An offer is not required when the employee will stay with the predecessor contractor on another assignment or has failed to show adequate work performance. Also, the successor contractor need not offer employment to all prior workers if it plans to reduce the workforce; however, it must then wait 90 days to attract new talent (otherwise, it must first offer the position to displaced former employees).

The agency's senior procurement executive may waive this provision upon written determination that it would impair the ability of the Federal Government to economically or efficiently procure the services. The agency must provide the Department of Labor its waiver decision and analysis within five business days after the solicitation issuance date. Within the same time frame, the contracting officer must direct the contractor to notify affected workers and their collective bargaining representative in writing.

Contract Clause

FAR 52.222-17, Nondisplacement of Qualified Workers, for follow-on service contracts.

5.2.9 Veterans Affairs

FAR 22.13

In accordance with several statutes and an executive order,[7] (sub)contractors must list all employment openings for service labor lasting more than three days, unless filled from within the organization. They must take affirmative action to promote employment of qualified disabled veterans without discrimination to their disability or veteran's status. The Act applies to all (sub)contracts for personal property and nonpersonal services (including construction) of $150,000 or more, unless waived by the Secretary of Labor. The Act requires (sub)contractor submission of the VETS-4212 Report, except for awards to state and local governments and foreign organizations where the workers are recruited outside of the United States. To verify if a proposed contractor has submitted a current VETS-4212 Report, the contracting officer either emails or consults the Department of Labor's database at www.dol.gov/vets/vets4212.htm.

The head of the agency may waive these requirements upon determination that the contract is essential to the national security, and that its award without complying with such requirements is necessary to the national security.

Possible sanctions for violation include withholding progress payments, contract suspension or termination, or debarment.

Solicitation Provision

FAR 52.222-38, Compliance with Veterans' Employment Reporting Requirements, if exceeding the simplified acquisition threshold and the contract is not for COTS.

Solicitation Provisions and Contract Clauses

FAR 52.222-35, Equal Opportunity for Special Disabled Veterans, Veterans of the Vietnam Era, and Other Eligible Veterans, if the expected value is $150,000 or more, unless the work is performed outside the United States by employees recruited outside the United States, or the Deputy Assistant Secretary of Labor has waived the clause. Use the basic clause with its Alternate I if only part of the clause is waived.

FAR 52.222-37, Employment Reports on Special Disabled Veterans, Veterans of the Vietnam Era, and Other Eligible Veterans, if containing FAR 52.222-35.

5.2.10 Employment of Disabled Workers

FAR 22.14

Per Section 503 of the Rehabilitation Act of 1973 (Rehabilitation Act of 1973) and Executive Order 11758 (Delegating authority of the President under the Rehabilitation Act of 1973) (January 15, 1974), Government contractors must take affirmative action to employ and advance qualified individuals with disabilities, without discriminating against their mental or physical disability. If notified by the appropriate agency official of violations, the contracting officer may withhold payments or institute sanctions, suspend or terminate the contract, or begin debarment proceedings. The agency head, with the concurrence of the OFCCP, may waive any or all requirements if a waiver is deemed to be in the national interest.

Solicitation Provision and Contract Clause

FAR 52.222-36, Affirmative Action for Workers with Disabilities, if the expected value is $15,000 or more, unless the work is performed outside the

United States by employees recruited outside the United States or OFCCP has waived the clause. Use the basic clause with its Alternate I if only part of the terms of the clause is waived.

5.2.11 Products Produced by Forced or Indentured Child Labor

FAR 22.15

When solicitting for supplies expected to exceed the micro-purchase threshold, the contracting officer must check the List of Products Requiring Contractor Certification as to Forced or Indentured Child Labor at https://www.dol.gov/ilab/reports/child-labor/list-of-products/. The List contains products which may have been mined, produced or manufactured by forced or indentured child labor under age 18 in a specified country. The offeror must certify in its offer that it will not supply any end product manufactured in a country identified on the List for that product, or that it is not aware of any such child labor in use. The Government may impose remedies if the contractor:

- failed to cooperate with an investigation of the use of forced or indentured labor by any Inspector General or the Department of Justice or Treasury;
- furnished an end product or component using forced or indentured child labor; or
- submitted a false certification regarding knowledge of the use of forced or indentured child labor.

Contract termination is the only available remedy for furnishing an end product or component using forced or indentured child labor. For the other situations, suspension or debarment for up to three years is authorized (as is contract termination).

Solicitation Provision

FAR 52.222-18, Certification Regarding Knowledge of Child Labor for Listed End Products, if expected to exceed the micro-purchase threshold and are for the type of end products identified by country of origin on the List of Products Requiring Contractor Certification as to Forced or Indentured Child Labor. It is not used in solicitations for commercial items that include the provision at FAR 52.212-3, Offeror Representations and Certifications—Commercial Items. The contracting officer identifies whichever provision is used, the applicable end products, and countries of origin from the List.

Solicitation Provision and Contract Clause

FAR 52.222-19, Child Labor—Cooperation with Authorities and Remedies, if expected to exceed the micro-purchase threshold.

5.2.12 Notification of Employee Rights Under the National Labor Relations Act

FAR 22.16

Executive Order 13496, Notification of Employee Right Under Federal Labor Laws, of January 30, 2009, requires (sub)contractors that exceed the simplified acquisition threshold to post a notice informing employees of their rights to collective bargaining, and to include this requirement in subcontracts over $10,000 (unless performed solely outside the United States). The Department of Labor may investigate any (sub)contractor to determine violation of any of the requirements. If a violation is found, the Department of Labor may direct that the contract be canceled, suspended or terminated (in whole or in part), and declare the contractor ineligible for further Government contracts. The Secretary of Labor may grant exemptions, including deleting or modifying the prescribed clause in contracts.

Solicitation Provision and Contract Clause

FAR 52.222-40, Notification of Employee Rights Under the National Labor Relations Act, unless below the simplified acquisition threshold, for work solely outside the United States, or exempted by the Secretary of Labor.

5.2.13 Combating Trafficking in Persons

FAR 22.17

(Sub)contractors and their employees cannot engage in the following activities during the period of performance of the contract:

- charging recruiting fees to employees;
- destroying immigration documents;
- failing to provide a written contract of employment where required by law;
- failing to provide transportation to departing employees from foreign countries;
- misleading job applicants about the terms of employment;
- procuring commercial sex acts;
- providing unsafe housing;

* trafficking persons involuntarily; and
* using forced labor in the performance of the contract.

The successful offeror must certify before award over $500,000 for non-COTS supplies or services to be performed outside the United States that it has a compliance plan and is not in violation, or else has corrected any violation. The contractor must collect the same certification from any subcontractor meeting the same criteria. The contracting officer notifies his agency Inspector General of any violations.

Solicitation Provision

FAR 52.222-56, Certification Regarding Trafficking in Persons Compliance Plan, if over $500,000 and performed outside the United States, and not for commercial products.

Solicitation Provision and Contract Clause

FAR 52.222-50, Combating Trafficking in Persons. Use the basic clause with its Alternate I when the contract will be performed outside the United States.

5.2.14 Employment Eligibility Verification

FAR 22.18

Under the Department of Homeland Security (DHS), the United States Citizenship and Immigration Service's employment eligibility verification program (E-Verify) is the means to verify employment eligibility. Contractors may employ only individuals who are eligible to work in the United States. Contractors must enroll as Federal contractors in E-Verify, using it to verify employment eligibility of all new hires working in the United States. However, it can restrict such a review to Federal contract hires only if it is a Government agency (state, local or Indian), institution of higher education, or a surety performing under a takeover agreement entered into with a Federal agency pursuant to a performance bond.

The same requirement applies to subcontracts for services (unless part of a COTS item or service) and construction. The contractor need not verify employment eligibility of employees who hold an active security clearance, or for whom background investigations have been completed and credentials issued per Homeland Security Presidential Directive (HSPD)-12 of August 5, 2005.

DHS and the Social Security Administration may terminate a contractor's memorandum of understanding and deny access to the E-Verify system. The terminating agency refers the matter to a designated agency official for possible suspension or debarment action.

Solicitation Provision and Contract Clause

FAR 52.222-54, Employment Eligibility Verification, if exceeding the simplified acquisition threshold, except for:

- a period of performance less than 120 days;
- commercial services that are part of a COTS item or performed by the COTS provider;
- COTS items; or
- work performed outside the United States.

5.2.15 Safe Workplaces

FAR 22.20

In solicitations exceeding $500,000, offerors must reveal any labor law decisions rendered against them within the past three years. The contracting officer must investigate any affirmative response by requesting mitigating factors and remedial measures taken by the firm. SAM and FAPIIS should be updated with contractor disclosures of labor law decisions, and the contracting officer should consult those databases.[8] The agency may have a labor expert on staff who consults with the Department of Labor and may submit analysis and advice to the contracting officer to help make the responsibility determination, such as requiring the firm to enter into a labor compliance agreement. The requirement also applies to subcontracts exceeding $500,000. For all covered (sub)contracts, the firm must also provide wage statements (such as pay stubs) for all employees performing work thereon.[9]

   Executive Order 13673, Fair pay and safe workspaces, of February 12, 2014, requires all contracts over $1 million to obtain voluntary consent of employees or subcontractors before deciding to arbitrate claims or torts regarding sexual assault or harassment. Collective bargaining agreements often cover this point, in which case no contract clause is necessary. Also, wage statements must be transparent by specifying hours worked (and identifying how many were overtime), hourly pay rate, gross pay, and itemized additions to or deductions from gross pay.[10]

Solicitation Provisions

FAR 52.222-57, Representation Regarding Compliance with Labor Laws, if the estimated value exceeds $500,000.
FAR 52.222-58, Subcontractor Responsibility Matters Regarding Compliance with Labor Laws, if the estimated value exceeds $500,000.

Solicitation Provisions and Contract Clauses

FAR 52.222-59, Compliance with Labor Laws, if the estimated value exceeds $500,000.

FAR 52.222-60, Paycheck Transparency, if the estimated value exceeds $500,000.

FAR 52.222-61, Arbitration of Contractor Employee Claims, if the estimated value exceeds $1 million and is not for commercial items.

5.2.16 Executive Compensation

FAR 4.14

Section 2 of the Federal Funding Accountability and Transparency Act of 2006, as amended by section 6202 of the Government Funding Transparency Act of 2008 (31 U.S.C. 6101), requires most contractors to report the total compensation of the five most highly compensated executives of itself and any first-tier subcontractor when the subcontract equals or exceeds $30,000 in value. The first-tier subcontract award data is available at www.usaspending.gov, managed by the Department of Treasury. Any classified contracts and contracts with individuals are not included, nor are simplified acquisitions. Agencies review contractor reports on a quarterly basis to ensure that the information is consistent with contract information. The agency informs the contractor of any inconsistencies with the contract information and requires the contractor to correct the report, or else explain why it believes the information is correct. Agencies review the reports at www.fsrs.gov.[11] (Sub)contractors who had gross income in the previous tax year under $300,000 are exempt from the reporting requirement.

Contract Clause

FAR 52.204-10, Reporting Executive Compensation and First-Tier Subcontract Awards, in all solicitations and contracts unless classified or a simplified acquisition.

5.3 QUALITY

5.3.1 Quality Assurance

FAR 46.1 and .2

Quality assurance is a systematic process approach to provide confidence that supplies, services or data conform to requirements and achieve satisfactory performance.[12] A successful quality assurance program specifies quality requirements, determines supplier capability, inspects deliveries, and motivates suppliers. When acquiring commercial items, the Government relies on contractor quality assurance systems before acceptance unless in-process inspection by the customer is customary in the market. This process includes testing parts and material, both before ordering and during use to ensure that the required level of quality is met. This is typically completed before a purchase order is issued, to ensure that the supplier has met the requirements.

There is more to this concept than mere inspection of parts. Quality assurance looks at the contractor's systems and procedures to control quality and quantity in the plant, while *inspection* assures that products conform to specifications. The former intends to prevent quality problems while the latter looks only for nonconformities. A quality assurance program emphasizes feedback and corrective actions to correct process-driven failures. Quality control techniques include attribute sampling, random statistical sampling, and regression and correlation analysis. Statistical quality control is useful for prediction, testing output, detecting causes of variation, and analysis of same.

Acceptance sampling can be done based on either attributes or variables. Sampling by attributes is a statistical method based on sample size and aids a yes-or-no decision on acceptability. By contrast, acceptance sampling by variables records actual measurements, sets a range of tolerable limits, and then determines a percentage of defectives. It requires fewer samples and less inspection than the attribute method.

Material quality management is a joint function of engineering, production and purchasing departments. Engineering develops specifications and drawings, testing methods and procedures, and a range of acceptable qualities. Production considers cost constraints, inventory adequacy and manufacturing techniques. Purchasing handles order placement, performance monitoring, quality control, and sampling. These departments decide what level of detail should be used to assure vendor compliance. It can also help the production department to lower costs and find materials that are easy to work with.

The contracting officer will include specifications for inspection, testing and other quality requirements in the contract. (S)he will issue instructions to the contract administration office and act on their recommendations or, if contract administration is retained, verify that the contractor fulfills the contract quality requirements. The contracting officer also ensures that nonconformances are identified and considered when determining the acceptability of supplies or services which do not meet contract requirements.

The Government may rely on the contractor to accomplish all inspection and testing at or below the simplified acquisition threshold to ensure conformance with contract quality requirements. The contractor's inspection system or program covers:

- drawings, specifications and engineering changes;
- fabrication and delivery of products;
- manufacturing processes;
- preservation, packaging, packing, and marking;
- reliability and maintainability assessment;
- technical documentation (e.g., drawings, specifications, handbooks, manuals, and other technical publications); and
- testing and examination.

The extent of contract quality requirements and inspection for a given contract is based upon the technical description of the contract supply or service (i.e., commercial, Federal or military), and its complexity and criticality. Complex items have quality characteristics requiring assembly, manufacturing, measurement, performance, and test operations. Noncomplex items require only simple measurement and testing the end item to determine conformance to contract requirements. The manufacturer may institute a process quality team or quality improvement team to maintain ongoing quality reviews and process improvements.[13]

Sometimes the Government must test the supplies or services before tender for acceptance, or must pass judgment upon the adequacy of the contractor's internal work processes. This would be due to:

- cost of detailed Government inspection;
- nature of the supplies and services and their intended use;
- potential losses in the event of defects; or
- probability of uncontested replacement or correction of defective work.

The ACO maintains records of Government contract quality assurance actions, including the number of observations and defects, any decisions regarding the acceptability of the products, processes and requirements, and actions to correct defects. (S)he reports to the contracting office any defects observed in design or technical requirements (including quality), implements any written instructions from the contracting office, and recommends any changes necessary to the contract (as well as instructions or specifications) that will provide more effective operations or eliminate unnecessary costs.

Government quality assurance often requires performing inspection and related functions to see if a contractor has fulfilled the contract obligations regarding quality and quantity. It is conducted before acceptance by or under the direction of Government personnel. The Government can run a *physical configuration audit* to examine the item against its technical baseline (usually specifications or drawings) to verify that it conforms to the item's technical documentation. This is often done with items that are hard to manufacture, are being built by a new contractor, or come off a production line that was shut down for some time.

Nonconforming supplies or services are classified as critical, major or minor. *Critical nonconformance* means a deficiency that is likely to result in hazardous or unsafe conditions for individuals using, maintaining or relying upon the supplies or services, or is likely to prevent performance of a vital agency mission. *Major nonconformance* means a noncritical deficiency that is likely to result in failure of the supplies or services, or to materially reduce the usability of the supplies or services for their intended purpose. *Minor nonconformance* means a deficiency that is not likely to materially reduce the usability of the supplies or services for their intended purpose, or is a departure from established standards with little impact on the effective use or operation of the supplies or services. Minor nonconformities are often accepted, perhaps with a price adjustment, but major or critical nonconformances are usually rejected.

When a contract is assigned for administration to a Government office located at a contractor's plant, the office verifies whether the supplies or services conform to contract quality requirements, and reports to the contracting office any defects observed in design, quality or technical requirements. The office will also recommend any changes to the contract, specifications or instructions to improve effective operations or eliminate unnecessary costs.

Requiring compliance with higher-level quality standards is appropriate for complex or critical items when the technical requirements of the contract require control of work operations, in-process controls and inspection. *Critical items* are components, material or subsystems that must be available at a specific time in production or else jeopardize cost, quality or schedule. They could also be used to provide more attention to documentation, organization, planning, and work instructions. Examples of higher-level quality standards are:

- ANSI/ASME NQA-1 (National Quality Assurance – 1, 2015);
- ANSI/ASQC E4– *A Quality System Standard for Environmental Data Collection and Technology*;
- ANSI/ASQC Q9001 (*Quality Management Systems – Requirements*, 2008), Q9002 (*Quality Systems – Model for Quality Assurance in Production, Installation, and Servicing*, 1994), or Q9003 (*Quality Systems – Model for Quality Assurance in Final Inspection and Test*, 1994); and
- ISO 9001, *Quality management systems*, 2015.[14]

The International Organization for Standardization's (ISO) 9001 publication sets forth standards for a quality management system by stating principles and processes to design, develop and deliver a product or service. A firm can participate in a continuing certification process under ISO 9001 to show its compliance with the standard and its requirement for planned quality improvement.

FAR 46.402 and .403

Quality assurance may be performed either at *origin*, where the work is performed, or at *destination*, where delivery will be made. The decision of where to perform quality assurance is based on a number of factors. It will be performed at source if:

- considerable loss would result from the manufacture and shipment of unacceptable supplies, or from the delay in making necessary corrections;
- Government inspection during contract performance is essential;
- performance at any other place would require uneconomical disassembly or destructive testing, or costly special packing and packaging; or
- special required instruments or facilities are available only at source.

Quality assurance that can be performed at destination is normally limited to inspection of the supplies or services if the following occurs:

- necessary testing equipment is located only at destination;
- supplies are purchased off-the-shelf and require no technical inspection;
- the contract is for services performed at destination; or
- the products are processed under direct control of the National Institutes of Health or the Food and Drug Administration of the Department of Health and Human Services.

Brand-name products purchased for authorized resale through commissaries or similar facilities are normally inspected at destination. However, supplies destined for direct overseas shipment may be accepted by the contracting officer or an authorized representative by a tally sheet showing receipt of shipment signed by the port transportation officer or other designated official at the transshipment point. Overseas inspection of supplies shipped from the United States is only required in unusual circumstances if the contracting officer determines in advance that overseas inspection can be performed or makes necessary arrangements for its performance.

Simplified acquisitions are generally limited in quality control to verifying count and item number, damage and packaging.

FAR 46.405

The contract administration office may determine the conformance of subcontracted supplies or services with contract requirements, but does not relieve the prime contractor of any responsibilities under the contract. The Government performs quality assurance at the subcontract level when required at source.

The program office may establish *critical success factors* to indicate the defect-free character of a product or service. More formally, the program office can conduct a *critical design review* to ensure the product meets the engineering and functional requirements, and that the specification ensures design compatibility between the item and such considerations as computer programs, equipment, facilities, and personnel. This review also assures that the design assesses producibility and risk areas, and reviews the preliminary product specification.

5.3.2 Inspection

FAR 46.4

Inspection involves testing and examining supplies or services to ensure they meet contract requirements. The Government has the right to make inspections and tests while work is in process, and to require the contractor to maintain and provide records of its inspection work. Inspections can be performed on-line to avoid impacting the flow of items through the production line. The firm may also submit an item for examination and testing for Government test or witness before starting production to ensure that its methods can produce items that fulfill the contract's technical requirements.

Each contract designates the place(s) where the Government reserves the right to inspect, by or under the direction or supervision of Government personnel. Government inspection may also be done concurrently with contractor inspection. Government inspection is documented on an inspection or receiving report form, or commercial shipping document/packing list.

There are numerous methods of inspection that could be used by either the contractor or Government, each with its own uses and benefits. The Government usually inspects deliverables at or below the simplified acquisition threshold at destination by visual analysis for type and quantity, as well as damage, operability, preservation, packaging, packing, and marking. When repetitive purchases of the same item are made from the same manufacturer with a history of defect-free work, Government inspection may be reduced to a periodic check of occasional purchases.

Inspection at source allows use of contractor facilities to test and make corrections. Most complex hardware is inspected at source where Government in-plant inspectors are available. It is easier to hold contractors liable, although it could be a disadvantage if an inspector must be brought in from afar or is not familiar with the product. Inspection at destination means readily available Government personnel can ensure that the product works in less-than-ideal conditions and reveals damage in transit. However, this approach lacks the availability of contractor personnel and precludes inspection of packaging, preservation or shipping methods prior to shipment. If the contract provides for inspection at source, the place(s) of performance may not be changed without the authorization of the contracting officer.

The Government can physically inspect or test a product after contractor inspection, a process known as *product verification inspection.* Alternatively, *floor inspection* is done at the work station during assembly and fabrication. It minimizes material handling, storage and delay in process. However, it is not common because it is mostly informal in nature, slows piece work processing and creates too much idle time for the inspector.

Similarly, *flow* or *process inspection*:

- detects adverse quality trends promptly to introduce rapid corrective measures;
- easily identifies defective production to the operator;
- prevents excessive accumulation of spoiled work; and
- prevents more work on parts already found defective.

On the other hand, flow inspection requires more people and equipment at more cost.

In contrast, *central inspection* has a location to take items for fine-tuned formal and impartial inspection that fully utilizes inspectors' time and improves supervision of them. But it does not eliminate gross errors or identify adverse trends or the responsible worker or equipment. Moreover, it requires rework on parts with minor defects, and increases material handling and cost.

Agencies prescribe procedures and instructions to use, prepare and distribute material inspection and receiving reports that validate Government receipt and inspection/acceptance. These procedures can also validate commercial shipping document/packing lists to show Government inspection and acceptance.

The contracting officer has several avenues of recourse if products or services fail inspection:

- address a dispute;
- consider latent defect, fraud or gross mistake;
- replace or correct at contractor's expense;
- require delivery and equitably adjust the process; or
- terminate for default.

Solicitation Provisions and Contract Clauses

FAR 52.246-1, Contractor Inspection Requirements, for supplies or services at or below the simplified acquisition threshold due to agency procedures, to ensure an explicit understanding of the contractor's inspection responsibilities, or the Government need to test the supplies or services in advance of acceptance or to pass judgment upon the adequacy of the contractor's internal work processes.

FAR 52.246-2, Inspection of Supplies – Fixed-Price, for supplies, or services that involve the furnishing of supplies, when a fixed-price contract is contemplated and the contract amount is expected to exceed the simplified acquisition threshold. Use the clause with Alternate I if a fixed-price incentive contract is contemplated. Use the clause with Alternate II if a fixed-ceiling-price contract with retroactive price redetermination is contemplated.

FAR 52.246-3, Inspection of Supplies – Cost-Reimbursement, for supplies, or services that involve the furnishing of supplies, when a cost-reimbursement contract is contemplated.

FAR 52.246-4, Inspection of Services – Fixed-Price, for services, or supplies that involve the furnishing of services, when a fixed-price contract is contemplated and the contract amount is expected to exceed the simplified acquisition threshold.

FAR 52.246-5, Inspection of Services – Cost Reimbursement, for services, or supplies that involve the furnishing of services, when a cost-reimbursement contract is contemplated.

FAR 52.246-6, Inspection – Time-and-Material and Labor-Hour, for a time-and-material contract or a labor-hour contract. Use the clause with its Alternate I if Government inspection and acceptance are to be performed at the contractor's plant.

FAR 52.246-7, Inspection of Research and Development – Fixed-Price, if fixed-price research and development exceeding the simplified acquisition threshold when the primary objective of the contract is the delivery of end items other than designs, drawings or reports.

FAR 52.246-8, Inspection of Research and Development – Cost-Reimbursement, if cost-reimbursement research and development when the primary objective of the contract is the delivery of end items other than designs, drawings, or reports. Use the clause with its Alternate I if the contract will be on a no-fee basis.

FAR 52.246-9, Inspection of Research and Development (Short Form), when neither FAR 52.246-7 nor FAR 52.246-8 is used.

FAR 52.246-11, Higher-Level Contract Quality Requirement, when the inclusion of a higher-level contract quality requirement is appropriate.

FAR 52.246-12, Inspection of Construction, if fixed-price for construction exceeding the simplified acquisition threshold.

FAR 52.246-13, Inspection – Dismantling, Demolition, or Removal of Improvements, for dismantling, demolition or removal of improvements.

FAR 52.246-14, Inspection of Transportation, for freight transportation services (including local drayage) by rail, motor (including bus), domestic freight forwarder, and domestic water carriers (including inland, coastwise and intercoastal). Do not use the clause to acquire transportation services by air carriers or international ocean carriers. Do not use for freight services which are provided under bills of lading or negotiated for reduced rates.

FAR 52.246-16, Responsibility for Supplies, for supplies, services involving the furnishing of supplies, or fixed-price research and development exceeding the simplified acquisition threshold.

5.3.3 Acceptance

FAR 46.5

Acceptance acknowledges that the supplies or services conform to applicable contract quality and quantity requirements. The Government assents to ownership of the supplies delivered, or consents to the services rendered. Acceptance may take place before, during or after delivery, depending on the contract terms and conditions. Supplies or services are ordinarily not accepted before completion of Government contract quality assurance actions. Acceptance is usually evidenced by a certification on an inspection/receiving report form or commercial shipping document or packing list.

Each contract specifies the place of acceptance, which is usually the same place where Government contract quality assurance occurs. Acceptance of supplies or services is the responsibility of the contracting officer, or ACO when this responsibility is assigned to a contract administration office.

A certificate of conformance may be used in certain instances instead of source inspection at the discretion of the contracting officer if in the Government's best interest, small losses would be incurred in the event of a defect, or the contractor's reputation or past performance makes it likely that the supplies or services furnished will be acceptable and any defective work would be corrected, repaired or replaced without contest.

Solicitation Provision and Contract Clauses

FAR 52.246-15, Certificate of Conformance.

5.3.4 Liquidated Damages

FAR 11.2

The contracting officer considers the potential impact on pricing, competition and contract administration before using a liquidated damages clause. When delivery or timely performance is so important that the Government expects to suffer damage if the contractor is delinquent, and the damage would be difficult or impossible to estimate accurately or prove, then liquidated damages may be prudent. Liquidated damages are neither punitive nor negative performance incentives, but rather are compensation to the Government for probable damages. The liquidated damages rate reasonably forecasts compensation for these damages. The contracting officer may use more than one liquidated damages rate when the probable damage to the Government may change over the contract period of performance.

Construction contracts with liquidated damages provisions describe the rate(s) of liquidated damages assessed per day of delay, the estimated daily cost of Government inspection and superintendence, and an amount for other expected expenses associated with delayed completion, such as renting substitute property or paying for extended per diem expenses.

Solicitation Provisions and Contract Clauses

FAR 52.211-11, Liquidated Damages – Supplies, Services, or Research and Development, if fixed-price for supplies, services, or research and development when the contracting officer determines that liquidated damages are appropriate.

FAR 52.211-12, Liquidated Damages – Construction, for construction (other than cost-plus-fixed-fee) when the contracting officer determines that liquidated damages are appropriate. It can be modified to reflect multiple liquidation rates for multiple stages of work.

FAR 52.211-13, Time Extensions, for construction that uses the Liquidated Damages – Construction clause, when FAR 52.211-12 has been revised.

5.3.5 Variation in Quantity

FAR 11.3

A fixed-price supply contract may authorize Government acceptance of a variation in the quantity of items called for if caused by packing, loading or shipping, or by allowances in manufacturing processes. Any permissible variation is stated as a percentage increase, decrease or both. It is based upon the normal commercial practices of a particular industry for a particular item. The permissible variation does not exceed plus or minus 10% unless a different limitation is established in agency regulations. Excess quantities of items totaling up to $250 in value may be retained without compensating the contractor, and excess quantities over $250 in value may, at the Government's option, be either returned at the contractor's expense or retained and paid for at the contract unit price.

Construction contracts may authorize a variation in estimated quantities of unit-priced items. If the variation between the estimated and actual quantity of a unit-priced item is more than plus or minus 15%, an equitable adjustment in the contract price is made if requested by either the Government or the contractor. The contractor may request an extension of time if the quantity variation requires it to complete performance. The contracting officer may extend this time limit before the date of final settlement of the contract.

Solicitation Provisions and Contract Clauses

FAR 52.211-16, Variation in Quantity, for fixed-price supplies or services.

FAR 52.211-17, Delivery of Excess Quantities, for fixed-price supplies.

FAR 52.211-18, Variation in Estimated Quantity, for fixed-price construction.

5.3.6 Transfer of Title and Risk of Loss

FAR 46.505

Regardless of when or where physical possession occurs, title for supplies passes to the Government upon formal acceptance. Unless the contract specifically provides otherwise, risk of loss of or damage to supplies remains with the contractor until delivery to a carrier if transportation is f.o.b. origin. Risk transfers upon acceptance by or delivery to the Government at the destination specified in the contract if transportation is f.o.b. destination.

The risk of loss or damage to nonconforming supplies remains with the contractor until cure or acceptance. The contractor is not liable for loss or damage to supplies caused by the negligence of Government agents, employees or officers acting within the scope of their employment.

Contract Clause

FAR 52.246-16, Responsibility for Supplies.

5.3.7 Nonconforming Supplies or Services

FAR 46.407

The contracting officer gives the contractor an opportunity to correct or replace nonconforming supplies or services within the required delivery schedule without additional cost to the Government. In fact, the Government may charge the contractor the cost of Government reinspection and retests because of prior rejection. The contracting officer ordinarily rejects supplies or services when the nonconformance is critical or major, or the supplies or services are otherwise incomplete. However, economy or urgency may require conditional acceptance of supplies or services to be in the best interest of the Government. If the nonconformance is minor, the contract administration office may accept or reject, except where this authority is withheld by the procuring contracting office.

When supplies or services are accepted with critical or major nonconformances, the contracting officer modifies the contract to provide for an equitable price reduction or other consideration. For conditional acceptance, amounts withheld from payments must be sufficient to cover the estimated cost and profit to correct deficiencies and complete unfinished work. For minor nonconformances, the contract need not be modified unless the savings to the contractor in fabrication or performance exceed the Government's cost of processing the modification.

Notices of rejection include the reasons therefore and are furnished to the contractor to avoid the possibility of acceptance being implied as a matter of law.

Government-wide responsibility for quality assurance support for acquisitions of biologics, drugs and other medical supplies is assigned to the Food and Drug Administration. Responsibility for food lies with the Department of Agriculture, except that seafood is assigned to the National Marine Fisheries Service of the Department of Commerce.

5.3.8 Production Surveillance and Reporting

FAR 42.11

Production surveillance is a function of contract administration to determine contractor progress and to identify any factors that may delay performance. Production surveillance involves Government review and analysis of contractor industrial processes and controls, performance, plans, and schedules. Simplified acquisitions should not normally require production surveillance. The contract administration office determines the extent of production surveillance based on:

- any supplementary written instructions from the contracting office;
- contractor financial capability;
- contractor performance history;
- criticality;
- performance schedule;
- prior experience with the supplies or services;
- production plan; and
- reporting requirements for production progress and performance.

Contracting officers may require contractors to submit production progress reports from their own management systems.

Solicitation Provision and Contract Clause

FAR 52.242-2, Production Progress Reports, when production progress reporting is required, unless a construction contract or a Federal Supply Schedule contract is contemplated. The contracting officer specifies reporting instructions in the Schedule.

5.3.9 Defense Priorities and Allocations System

FAR 11.6

Title I of the Defense Production Act of 1950 (50 U.S.C. App. 2061, et seq.) requires preferential acceptance and performance of contracts and orders supporting certain national defense and energy programs. These include programs for military and energy production or construction, military assistance to any foreign nation, stockpiling, and space exploration and support. It also applies to emergency preparedness activities conducted pursuant to title VI of The Robert T. Stafford Disaster Relief and Emergency Assistance Act (42 U.S.C. 5195, et seq.). The agency allocates facilities, materials and services to promote these programs.

The Defense Priorities and Allocations System (DPAS) is a Department of Commerce process to address approved national defense, emergency preparedness, and energy programs. Two levels of priority for rated orders are established by the DPAS, identified by the rating symbols "DO" and "DX." All DX-rated orders have equal priority with each other and take preference over DO-rated and unrated orders. All DO-rated orders take preference over unrated orders. Contracting officers follow agency procedural instructions concerning the use of rated orders. Contracting officers assign a criticality designator to each contract over the simplified acquisition threshold as follows:

- "A" for critical contracts and DX-rated contracts for unusual and compelling urgency, or for major systems;
- "B" for other items needed to maintain a production or repair line, preclude out-of-stock conditions, or meet user needs for nonstock items; and
- "C" for all contracts other than those designated "A" or "B."

Solicitation Provision

FAR 52.211-14, Notice of Priority Rating for National Defense, Emergency Preparedness, and Energy Program Use, when the award will be a rated order.

Contract Clause

FAR 52.211-15, Defense Priority and Allocation Requirements, in rated orders.

5.4 WARRANTY

FAR 46.7

A *warranty* provides a contractual right to correct defects based on a stated period of time or use, or the occurrence of a specified event. It is the seller's promise to the buyer regarding the condition, nature or usefulness of the supplies or services furnished under the contract. Generally, a warranty's purpose is to delineate the rights and obligations for defective items and services, and to foster quality performance. The benefits from a warranty must be commensurate with their cost to the Government. Factors to select the use of a warranty for a given contract include:

- complexity and function;
- contractor's charge to accept the deferred liability created by the warranty;
- degree of development;
- difficulty in detecting defects before acceptance;
- end use;
- Government administration and enforcement of the warranty;
- potential harm to the Government if the item is defective;
- reduced Government contract quality assurance requirements (if the warranty provides adequate assurance of a satisfactory product);
- state of the art; and
- trade practice (i.e., the cost of an item to the Government might be the same whether or not a warranty is included).

A warranty can be either express or implied in its nature. An *express warranty* includes specifications and descriptions which can be included in technical literature. An express warranty makes the seller responsible when the buyer relies on the warranty and always nullifies an implied warranty. By contrast, an *implied warranty* is conducted through discussion or observation as the buyer relies on the vendor's skill in selecting a specific product, such as merchantability and fitness for a particular purpose. For an implied warranty, knowledge of both parties is critical and the seller is responsible only if the buyer could not determine the facts from the specifications.

The use of a warranty in an acquisition is approved in accordance with agency procedures. They are usually discouraged for use in cost-reimbursement contracts. Warranty clauses do not limit the Government's rights under an inspection clause regarding latent defects, fraud or gross mistakes that amount to fraud. Except for warranty clauses in construction contracts, warranties apply notwithstanding inspection and acceptance clauses or other terms of the contract. Warranty clauses clearly state the nature of the item and its characteristics to be warranted, contractor obligations to the Government for breach of warranty, remedies available to the Government, and warranty scope and duration.

Contractor obligations under warranties extend to all defects discovered during the warranty period, but not to damage caused by the Government. A warranty may be required for any aspect that requires special protection (e.g., accessories, components, installation, packaging, packing, and preservation). If the Government specifies the end item's design, inspection requirements, materials, measurements or tolerances, or tests, the contractor's obligations for correction of defects are usually limited to defects in material and workmanship or failure to conform to specifications. If the Government does not specify the design, then the warranty extends also to the design's usefulness.

In case of defect, the Government normally may either obtain an equitable adjustment of the contract or direct the contractor to repair or replace the defective items at contractor expense. Alternate remedies include the Government retaining the defective item and reducing the contract price, or repair or replacement of the defective item by another source at contractor expense (and perhaps with contractor-furnished parts or instructions). Repair may be possible at the contractor's facility at contractor expense. In any event, the contractor is usually responsible for the cost of all labor and material to repair or replace, retransport, reinspect, retest, repack, and remark any defective items.

The time period or duration of the warranty is clearly specified after consideration of estimated useful life, storage or shelf life, and trade practice. This period does not extend the contractor's liability for patent defects beyond a reasonable time after acceptance by the Government. The warranty specifies a reasonable time for furnishing notice to the contractor regarding the discovery of defects.

Warranties help ensure that the product works correctly for a guaranteed period of time. They are used to enforce design and manufacturing requirements, combat defects in materials and workmanship, and achieve essential performance requirements. They may be tailored for the individual contract, but must be affordable. The Government has a self-insurance policy that applies after acceptance and warranty periods expire to any contract (other than firm-fixed-price), though the Government pays for the cost of correction.

Warranties should not be used if their costs exceed the value of protection to the Government, but should be used if the Government cost for corrections exceeds contractor cost. They should be used in cases of high logistics support costs or low administrative and enforcement costs.

Warranty cost should also be compared to risk. It should incentivize the contractor to produce higher-quality products in light of its current quality assurance procedures. In this vein, reliability improvement or failure-free warranty of equipment motivates contractors to improve their equipment during the warranty period through no-cost engineering change proposals, and is usually used during an initial production run.

Solicitation Provisions and Contract Clauses

Because so many situations influence warranty conditions, the contracting officer may vary the terms and conditions of the clauses as needed.

FAR 52.246-17, Warranty of Supplies of a Noncomplex Nature, for noncomplex items when a fixed-price supply contract is contemplated and the use of a warranty clause has been approved under agency procedures. Use the clause with its Alternate II (there is no Alternate I) to specify that necessary transportation to correct or replace the item will be at Government expense.[15] Use the clause with its Alternate III if the supplies cannot be obtained from another source. Use the clause with its Alternate IV if a fixed-price incentive contract is contemplated. Use the clause with its Alternate V if recovery of the warranted items may involve considerable Government expense for disassembly and/or reassembly of larger items.

FAR 52.246-18, Warranty of Supplies of a Complex Nature, for deliverable complex items when a fixed-price supply or research and development contract is contemplated. The same conditions for Alternatives II through IV apply as in FAR 52.246-17.

FAR 52.246-19, Warranty of Systems and Equipment under Performance Specifications or Design Criteria, when performance specifications or design are of major importance, and a fixed-price supply, service, or research and development contract for systems and equipment is contemplated. The same conditions for Alternatives II and III apply as in FAR 52.246-17.

FAR 52.246-20, Warranty of Services, for services when a fixed-price contract for services is contemplated, unless FAR 52.246-19 is used.

FAR 52.246-21, Warranty of Construction, when a fixed-price construction contract is contemplated. Use the clause with its Alternate I if the Government specifies in the contract the use of any equipment by brand name and model.

5.5 INDEMNIFICATION

FAR 46.8

Indemnification is an agreement by one party to compensate the other party for any loss suffered during contract performance. The loss can be caused by either party or by a third party. It is not appropriate for:

- architect-engineer services;
- commercial items;
- construction;
- information technology and telecommunications;
- maintenance and rehabilitation of real property; and
- simplified acquisitions.

The Government will generally act as a self-insurer by relieving contractors of liability for loss of or damage to Government property that occurs after acceptance of supplies delivered or services performed under a contract, and results from defects or deficiencies in the supplies or services.

However, the Government will not relieve the contractor of liability for loss of or damage to the contract end item itself, except for *high-value items*, which have a unit cost designated by the contracting officer (normally $100,000 per unit). Examples of such items include an aircraft or its engine, communications or computer system, missile, or ship. In contracts requiring delivery of high-value items, the Government relieves contractors of contractual liability for loss of or damage to those items. However, the Government retains its rights to correct, repair or replace a defective item or component if discovered before the loss of or damage to a high-value item occurs. It also retains its right to equitable relief if discovered after loss or damage occurs, rather than repair or replacement. The Government will not provide any contractual relief when contractor liability can be preserved without increasing the contract price. Moreover, this relief does not apply if:

- any contractor insurance or self-insurance reserve covers liability for loss or damage suffered by the Government through purchase or use of the supplies or services;
- contractor liability is expressly provided under a contract clause; or
- willful misconduct or lack of good faith by the contractor's management causes a defect or deficiency in the supplies or services, or Government's acceptance.

Contract Clauses;

FAR 52.246-23, Limitation of Liability, for delivery of end items that are not high-value items.

FAR 52.246-24, Limitation of Liability – High Value Items, for delivery of high-value items.

FAR 52.246-25, Limitation of Liability – Services, for the performance of services. In contracts requiring both the performance of services and the delivery of end items, use all three Limitation of Liability clauses and identify in the contract schedule any high-value line items.

5.6 FINANCIAL PROTECTIONS

5.6.1 Bonds

FAR 28.1

The *Miller Act* (40 U.S.C. 3131) requires bonds for any construction contract exceeding $100,000. *Bonds* are written instruments executed by a bidder or contractor (known as the *principal*), and a second party (the *surety*) to warrant fulfillment of the principal's obligations to a third party (the *obligee*, in this case the Government). If the principal's obligations are not met, the bond assures payment by the surety of the specified amount of loss incurred by the obligee. Bonds are regularly used in construction contracting, and may be used for supplies and services. The bonding requirement can be waived by the contracting officer for work to be performed in a foreign country where it is impracticable for the contractor to furnish a bond. The Government determines the correct amount of the bond. There are six types of bonds:

- A *payment bond* assures contractor payments to all laborers and suppliers during contract performance. A payment bond is required only when a performance bond is required for this contract size, and only if its use is in the Government's interest. The bond amount is usually 100% of the contract amount.

- An *advance payment bond* secures fulfillment of contractor obligations under an advance payment clause of the contract. The contracting officer determines the amount of the advance payment bond to protect the Government against liens.
- A *performance bond* secures performance and fulfillment of contractor obligations under a given contract. They usually equal the amount of the contract, and replace the advance payment bond. The bond amount is usually 100% of contract amount.
- An *annual bid bond* secures all bids to be submitted during a specific fiscal year on contracts that would otherwise require their own bonds. Unlike the previously mentioned entries, this type of bond is not used in construction contracts.
- An *annual performance bond* also covers all bids to be submitted during a specific Government fiscal year, by securing fulfillment of contractor obligations on contracts that would otherwise require their own bonds. They provide a gross penal sum applicable to the total amount of all covered contracts. As with annual bid bonds, this type of bond is not used in construction contracts.
- A *patent infringement bond* secures fulfillment of contractor's obligations under a patent clause of the contract. No performance bond is furnished. The contractor's financial responsibility is often unknown or doubtful in these cases.

Though uncommon, performance bonds may be required for nonconstruction contracts exceeding the simplified purchase threshold to protect the Government's interest, such as:

- contractor asset sales or merger, and the Government desires assurance that the new entity is financially capable;
- contracts to dismantle, demolish or remove improvements;
- increase in contract price;
- providing Government property or funds to the contractor as partial compensation (e.g., retention of salvaged material); or
- substantial progress payments begun before delivery.

For construction contracts between $35,000 and $150,000, the contracting officer does not usually insist on performance bonds, but will instead select at least two of the following payment protections:

- a payment bond;
- a tripartite escrow agreement with a federally insured financial institution as escrow agent for all suppliers. The escrow agreement sets forth the terms

of payment and resolution of disputes among the parties. The Government tenders payment to the escrow account rather than the contractor, and the escrow agent distributes the payments in accordance with the agreement;

- an irrevocable letter of credit from a financial institution (the preferred method);
- certificate of deposit from a federally insured financial institution;
- common payment method such as bank draft, certified or cashiers' check, currency, or money order; or
- United States bonds or notes.

A bond must include a *penal sum* or *penal amount* as a maximum amount (or a percentage of the bid price for a bid bond) for which the surety is obligated. If there is no individual surety, then this is the amount of security to be pledged to the Government.

The agent or underwriter authorized to bind the surety is an attorney-in-fact. An original, or a photocopy or facsimile of an original, power of attorney is included with the bid. The contracting officer treats the failure to provide a proper power of attorney at the time of bid opening as a matter of responsiveness, and addresses any concerns about the authenticity and enforceability of the power of attorney as a matter of contractor responsibility.

A *bid guarantee* is assurance that the bidder will not withdraw a bid before acceptance, will execute a written contract, and will furnish required bonds and insurance agreements within the time specified in the bid. A bid guarantee must be accompanied by a performance bond (perhaps along with a payment bond), and is usually required whenever these bonds are required. This requirement can be waived by the chief of the contracting office (allowing submission of just the bond[s] without the guarantee) if in the best interest of the Government. These waivers are usually for overseas construction or emergency acquisitions, and are often sole-source contracts with proven contractors. Class waivers may be authorized by the agency head or designee.

In sealed bidding, noncompliance with a solicitation requirement for a bid guarantee requires rejection of the bid unless waived by the chief of the contracting office. For a negotiated procurement, noncompliance with a solicitation requirement for a bid guarantee will result in rejection of an initial proposal as unacceptable if award is based on initial proposals without discussion (unless waived). If discussions do occur, deficiencies in bid guarantees from offerors in the competitive range are addressed during discussions and the offeror has an opportunity to correct the deficiency.

The surety, upon its written request, may be furnished information on work progress, payments and the estimated percentage of completion, concerning the contract for which the bond was furnished. The same information may be furnished to persons who have provided labor or materials and have not been paid. The contracting officer shall, upon request, furnish the name and address of the surety(ies) of a payment bond to a subcontractor.

The head of the agency or designee will furnish a certified copy of the payment bond and the contract to any subcontractor who states by affidavit that it has supplied labor or materials for such work and either has not been paid or is being sued on the bond. The requestor may need to pay preparation costs.

During contract performance, the Government cannot withhold payments due to contractors or assignees merely because they have not been paid. However, after completion of the contract work, if the surety notifies in writing about the contractor's failure to meet its obligation to its subcontractors or suppliers, the contracting officer does withhold final payment. However, the surety must agree to hold the Government harmless from any liability resulting from withholding the final payment. The contracting officer will authorize final payment upon agreement between the contractor and surety or upon a judicial determination of the rights of the parties.

Solicitation Provisions and Contract Clauses

FAR 52.228-1, Bid Guarantee. The contracting officer inserts an amount for the bid guarantee which is adequate to protect the Government from loss should the successful bidder fail to execute bonds and contractual documents. This amount is normally at least 20% of the bid price, up to $3 million. Both a percentage and a maximum dollar limitation may be specified.

FAR 52.228-2, Additional Bond Security.

FAR 52.228-12, Prospective Subcontractor Requests for Bonds, when a payment bond will be furnished per the Miller Act, except for commercial items.

FAR 52.228-13, Alternative Payment Protections, if between $35,000 and $150,000. The contracting officer may establish a lower percentage for the bonds.

FAR 52.228-15, Performance and Payment Bonds – Construction, if over $150,000 and requires performance and payment bonds. The contracting officer may establish a lower percentage for the bonds. If no bid guarantee is involved, the contracting officer sets a period of time to return executed bonds.

FAR 52.228-16, Performance and Payment Bonds – Other than Construction. The contracting officer inserts the bond amount and a period of time (usually 10 days) to return executed bonds. Use Alternate I when only performance bonds are required.

5.6.2 Sureties and Bond Security

FAR 28.2

For a contract modification, the contracting officer must obtain *consent of surety*, an acknowledgment by a separate party that its bond given in connection with a contract continues to apply, unless an additional bond is obtained from another surety. Acknowledgement is not required if a contract modification is either beyond the scope of the contract or else changes the contract price more than either 25% or $50,000. A new surety may be necessary in these cases. Consent of surety is always required for a novation agreement.

Corporate sureties offered for contracts performed in the United States or its outlying areas must appear in the Department of the Treasury Circular 570, *Surety Companies Acceptable on Federal Bonds* (July 2016). This circular includes a maximum underwriting limit for each surety. The penal amount could exceed the underwriting limit only if the excess amount is coinsured or reinsured, and even then cannot exceed the underwriting limit of the coinsurer or reinsurer. For contracts performed in a foreign country, the contracting officer may accept a surety not appearing on Treasury Department Circular 570 if (s)he determines that it is impracticable for the contractor to use Treasury-listed sureties.

Agencies always obtain adequate security for bonds, including coinsurance and reinsurance agreements when necessary. *Reinsurance* provides that a surety, for financial consideration, agrees to indemnify another surety against loss that could result from a bond it has issued. Acceptable forms of security include corporate or individual sureties, U.S. bonds or notes, and other negotiable instruments as previously listed for construction contracts. The contractor must execute and submit reinsurance agreements to the contracting officer within the time specified on the bid form, but no more than 45 calendar days after the bond execution.

If an amendment to Circular 570 terminates a company's authority to qualify as a surety on Federal bonds, the contracting officer must review the outstanding contracts and take any action necessary to protect the Government. This could mean securing new bonds with other acceptable sureties.

The unencumbered value of the assets (excluding all outstanding pledges for other bond obligations) pledged by the individual surety equals or exceeds the penal amount of each bond. An offeror may submit up to three individual sureties for each bond, such that their combined value equals or exceeds the penal amount of the bond. Each individual surety accepts both joint and several liability up to the penal amount of the bond. Upon written request, the contracting officer may release the security interest on the surety's assets in support of a bid guarantee for an unsuccessful offer.

The contracting officer may grant a contractor a reasonable time to either add or substitute an acceptable surety if a current surety is determined to be unacceptable. However, if the contracting officer determines that no individual surety is acceptable to support a bid guarantee, the offeror is rejected as nonresponsible. If a small business, this decision is not referred to the SBA for a competency review, since the issue is strictly financial in nature.

An individual surety may be accepted only if a security interest is furnished with the bond. It may be provided by an escrow account with a federally insured financial institution in the name of the contracting agency, or by a lien on real property. The escrow account provides the contracting officer the sole and unrestricted right to draw upon all or part of the funds deposited in the account by written demand to the financial institution. This institution is in turn authorized to release to the surety all or part of the balance of the escrow account, including any accrued interest, upon written authorization by the contracting officer. The Government is not responsible for any costs to establish, maintain or administer the account. The terms of the escrow account cannot be amended without the consent of the contracting officer.

The Government accepts from individual sureties only cash, readily marketable assets or irrevocable letters of credit from a federally insured financial institution to satisfy the underlying bond obligations. For a bond with a security interest in real property, the individual surety provides a mortgage title insurance policy equal to the amount of the lien, plus either a copy of the current real estate tax assessment or an appraisal dated within the past six months. The property is then valued at either its tax appraised value or 75% of its market value. The surety may request the contracting officer to accept a substitute asset for what is currently pledged.

The contracting officer releases the security interest on the individual surety's assets as soon as possible. The assets pledged in support of a payment bond may be released to a subcontractor upon receipt of either a Federal district court judgment or a sworn statement by the subcontractor (and notarized by the surety) that the claim is correct. The security interest is maintained for one year after final payment (90 days if the contract is not subject to the Miller Act), or for a longer period until all claims against the payment bond are resolved (or longer, if a performance bond has a longer warranty period).

Upon written request by the individual surety, the contracting officer may release a portion of their assets based upon substantial performance of the contractor's obligations under its performance bond. However, the unreleased portion of the lien must cover the remaining contract obligations, including payments to subcontractors and potential liabilities.

An individual may be excluded from acting as a surety by the agency head or designee for failure to fulfill or disclose obligations under a prior bond, or for misrepresenting either the value of available assets or outstanding liabilities. The surety is then listed in the SAM. Contracting officers cannot accept the bonds of listed sureties without written approval of the agency head or designee.

Any deposited United States bonds or notes include an executed power of attorney and agreement authorizing the collection or sale of these bonds or notes in case the bond's principal defaults. The contracting officer may either turn securities over to the authorized agency official, or else deposit them with a Federal Reserve Bank.

A separate irrevocable letter of credit may be furnished for each bond, requiring only a written demand and any letter of confirmation. If used as a bid guarantee, the irrevocable letter of credit expires at least 60 days after close of the bid acceptance period. If used as an alternative to corporate or individual sureties to secure a performance or payment bond, the letter's initial expiration date is at least one year from the date of issuance. The letter of credit automatically extends for one year until the period of required coverage ends and the contracting officer provides the financial institution with a written statement waiving the right to payment. However, the issuer may provide the beneficiary written notice of nonrenewal at least 60 days in advance of the current expiration date.

The irrevocable letter of credit must be issued or confirmed by a federally insured financial institution rated "investment grade" or higher. Letters of credit over $5 million must be confirmed by a second acceptable financial institution that had letter of credit business of at least $25 million in the past year, unless the issuer itself had that much business. The contracting officer must verify the presence of federal insurance from the Federal Depositors Insurance Corporation and current credit rating from the Securities and Exchange Commission. If the contracting officer learns that a financial institution's rating has dropped below investment grade, (s)he will either give the contractor 30 days to substitute an acceptable irrevocable letter of credit, or else begin to draw on the line of credit.

Solicitation Provisions and Contract Clauses

FAR 52.228-11, Pledges of Assets.

FAR 52.228-14, Irrevocable Letter of Credit.

5.6.3 Insurance

FAR 28.3

Contractors provide insurance for workers' compensation, commingling property, or when directed by the Government due to contract terms or type of operation and ownership. The minimum amounts of insurance may be reduced when a contract is to be performed outside the United States and its outlying areas. Contractors for health care nonpersonal services must maintain medical liability insurance and indemnify the Government for liability-producing acts or omissions by the contractor, its agents and employees.

The policies contain an endorsement that precludes any cancellation or material change in the coverage adversely affecting the Government's interest, unless the insurer or the contractor so notifies the contracting officer in writing.

If the Government requires insurance to cover loss or damage to Government-furnished property, the contractor may either obtain a separate policy or include the risks in its existing policies. In either event, the policies must disclose the Government's interest in the property. Otherwise, the Government reserves the right to disapprove the purchase of any insurance coverage.

The Government considers several factors to set up an insurance program. Cost-type contracts impose insurance requirements on contractors such as injury and traffic accident liability, however fixed-price contractors only require insurance if performing on a Government installation. Fire, flood and theft liability coverage is common. Insurance costs and premiums are allowable, but not losses due to willful neglect.

By contrast, cost-reimbursement (sub)contracts usually require group insurance and liability protection. The contractor submits the group insurance plan for approval per agency regulations, including any change in benefits that could increase the cost to the Government. Aircraft and passenger liability insurance coverage in conjunction with contract performance should be at least $200,000 per person and $500,000 per occurrence for bodily injury (other than passenger liability), and $200,000 per occurrence for property damage. Coverage for passenger liability bodily injury must be at least $200,000 multiplied by the number of seats or passengers (whichever is greater). Bodily injury and property damage liability covering the operation of all automobiles used in contract performance should cover at least $200,000 per person, $500,000 per occurrence for bodily injury, and $20,000 per occurrence for property damage. Employer's liability coverage should be at least $100,000, except in states with exclusive or monopolistic funds that prohibit workers' compensation written by private carriers. Other desirable features include:

- occupational diseases are not compensated under Federal or state statutes, unless contract operations are too commingled with a contractor's commercial operations to make this practical;
- property damage liability insurance for circumstances determined by the agency;

- the Government shares in any premium refunds or credits paid or allowed to the contractor; and
- vessel collision liability and protection, and any indemnity liability insurance.

Self-insurance is permitted. If at least half of the self-insurance costs at a contractor's business segment will be allocable to negotiated Government contracts (and equals at least $200,000 per year), the contractor submits information on its proposed self-insurance program or changes thereto for ACO approval. To qualify for a self-insurance program, a contractor demonstrates the ability to sustain the potential losses, such as:

- compliance with Federal and State laws and regulations;
- geographic dispersion of assets to avoid a single loss depleting them all;
- history of previous losses, including frequency of occurrence and the financial impact of each loss;
- sound financial condition, including available lines of credit; and
- type and magnitude of risk (e.g., minor coverage for a deductible, or major coverage for hazardous risks).

The ACO will not approve a program of self-insurance for catastrophic risks, but may agree to indemnify the contractor or recognize an appropriate share of premiums for purchased insurance. Self-insurance programs to protect a contractor against the costs of correcting its own defects in materials or workmanship also are not approved, however rework estimates and warranty costs are acceptable.

5.6.4 Overseas Workers Compensation and War Hazard Insurance

FAR 28.305

The Defense Base Act (42 U.S.C. 1651) extends the Longshoremen's and Harbor Workers' Compensation Act (33 U.S.C. 901) to employees working outside the United States on public works or contracts that are approved or financed under the Foreign Assistance Act of 1961 (22 U.S.C. 2151). A *public-works contract* is for a fixed improvement for the public use of the United States or its allies that involves on-site work such as:

- alteration;
- construction;
- dams;
- dredging;
- harbor improvements;

- housing;
- removal;
- repair; and
- roadways.

Similarly, the War Hazards Compensation Act (42 U.S.C. 1701) protects employees against the risk of war hazards (injury, death, capture, or detention). When a contractor's insurance policy or self-insurance program provides the workers' compensation coverage required by the Defense Base Act, the employees automatically receive war-hazard risk protection. If the Secretary of Labor waives applicability of the Defense Base Act to any (sub)contract, work location, or classification of employees, the benefits of the War Hazards Compensation Act are automatically waived for those employees, and the contractor provides workers' compensation coverage against the risk of work injury or death. The contractor then assumes liability toward the employees and their beneficiaries for war-hazard injury, death, capture, or detention. These liability or insurance costs are allowable. This is one instance where agencies may specify insurance requirements under fixed-price contracts.

Solicitation Provisions and Contract Clauses

FAR 52.228-3, Workers' Compensation Insurance (Defense Base Act), when the Defense Base Act applies and either the contract is for a public work performed outside the United States, or will be approved or financed under the Foreign Assistance Act of 1961 (32 U.S.C. 2151).

FAR 52.228-4, Worker's Compensation and War-Hazard Insurance Overseas, for a public work performed outside the United States and the Secretary of Labor waives use of the Defense Base Act.

FAR 52.228-5, Insurance – Work on a Government Installation, for fixed-price contracts exceeding the simplified acquisition threshold on a domestic Government installation (unless work is minimal). The contracting officer may require additional coverage and higher limits, or may reduce or eliminate coverage.

FAR 52.228-7, Insurance – Liability to Third Persons, if cost-reimbursement, other than construction and architect-engineer services.

FAR 52.228-8, Liability and Insurance – Leased Motor Vehicles.

FAR 52.228-9, Cargo Insurance, for transportation or related services, except when freight is shipped under rates subject to released or declared value.

FAR 52.228-10, Vehicular and General Public Liability Insurance, for transportation or related services if public vehicular liability insurance required by law is not sufficient.

5.7 VALUE ENGINEERING

FAR 48.1

Value engineering is a program designed to eliminate anything that increases costs (acquisition, operation or support) without impairing essential functions or characteristics. There are two value engineering approaches. One is an incentive approach in which a contractor voluntarily uses its own resources to develop and submit value engineering change proposals (VECPs). The contract provides for sharing savings and paying the contractor's allowable development and implementation costs only if a VECP is accepted. This voluntary approach should not increase costs to the Government.

The second approach is a mandatory program in which the Government requires and pays for a specific value engineering program effort of a defined scope and level of effort as a separately priced contract line item. The contractor shares in savings on accepted VECPs, but at a lower rate than under the voluntary approach. This mandatory approach ensures that the contractor's value engineering effort is applied where opportunities may arise for considerable savings, consistent with the functional requirements of the end item. This approach is not permitted in architect-engineering contracts.

The contract under which the VECP is submitted is known as the *instant contract*. The VECP does not include quantity increases which could occur after acceptance due to additional orders, contract modification, exercise of options, or (if a multiyear contract) quantities funded after VECP acceptance. In a fixed-price contract with prospective price redetermination, the VECP refers to the period only for which firm prices are established.

The contracting officer must accept or reject the VECP within 45 days of receipt, or else notify the contractor promptly in writing with the reasons for delay and the anticipated decision date. The contractor may withdraw, in whole or in part, a VECP not accepted within the time period. Any VECP may be approved, in whole or in part, by a contract modification incorporating the VECP. Until the effective date of the contract modification, however, the contractor performs in accordance with the existing contract. If the Government accepts the VECP but rejects subsequent deliveries (or the contractor fails to deliver), the contractor reimburses the Government for its proportionate share of payments. If the VECP is not accepted, the contracting officer notifies the contractor in writing of the reasons for rejection. Agencies establish guidelines for processing VECPs, and may require incorporation of value engineering clauses in appropriate subcontracts.

Contracting officers must determine for each VECP the *sharing period*, which begins with acceptance of the first unit incorporating the VECP, and ends on a specific calendar date that is either set by the contracting officer (between 36 and 60 consecutive months) after the first unit affected by the VECP is accepted, or else the last scheduled delivery date of an item affected by the VECP. In establishing a sharing period, the contracting officer considers the:

- complexity and extent of the change;
- contractor's financial risk;
- development cost;
- number of units affected;
- performance and/or reliability impact; and
- remaining production period.

For contracts containing engineering development or low-rate-initial-production or early-production units, the end of the sharing period is based not on a calendar date. Rather, the period is based on acceptance of the number of future contract units affected by the VECP and scheduled to be delivered during the time frame that spans the highest planned production rate. This time frame runs somewhere between 36 and 60 consecutive months, and is set by the contracting officer. Agencies may prescribe sharing future contract savings on all future deliverable units under any or all contracts awarded within the sharing period, even if the scheduled delivery date is outside the sharing period.

The Government may benefit from more savings than just a single contract. *Acquisition savings* result from applying a VECP to multiple contracts awarded by the same contracting office for the same unit. Acquisition savings include three components. Again we have *instant contract savings,* the net cost reductions on the contract under which the VECP is submitted and accepted. They equal the *instant unit cost reduction* of performance due to using the VECP on the instant unit, multiplied by the number of instant contract units affected by the VECP. This calculation is then reduced by the contractor's costs to develop, test, prepare, and submit the VECP and make the contractual changes required by Government acceptance. In service contracts, the instant unit cost reduction is the number of hours per line-item task saved by using the VECP on the instant contract, multiplied by the contract labor rate.

A second savings component is the *concurrent contract savings,* the net reductions in the prices of other contracts that are ongoing at the time the VECP is accepted. Third is the *future contract savings,* the product of the future unit cost reduction and the number of future contract units in the sharing base. For these savings calculations, *future unit cost reduction* is the instant unit cost reduction adjusted for projected learning or quantity changes

Table 5.1

	Sharing Agreement	
Contract Type	Incentive (Voluntary)	Program Requirement (Mandatory)
Firm-Fixed-Price	50/50	75/25
Incentive	Per current contract arrangement; 50/50 on concurrent and future contracts	Per current contract arrangement; 75/25 on concurrent and future contracts
CPFF and CPAF	75/25	85/15

during the sharing period. The *sharing base* is the number of affected end items on contracts of the contracting office accepting the VECP.

Net acquisition savings include instant, concurrent and future contract savings, less Government costs, shared between the parties as seen in Table 5.1.

Government/Contractor Shares of Net Acquisition Savings (Figures in Percentages)

The contractor is entitled to a percentage share of any net acquisition savings which exceed the sum of Government costs and negative instant contract savings. *Government costs* address increases in logistics, maintenance, operations, and testing support, but exclude administrative costs to process the VECP and negative instant contract savings. *Negative instant contract savings* comprise the instant contract cost or price increases because development and implementation costs now exceed the instant contract savings.

If the instant contract is not incentivized, the contractor's share of net acquisition savings is calculated and paid each time savings are realized. This will occur either once or several times. When the instant contract is incentivized, the contractor shares in instant contract savings through the contract's incentive structure. In either event, the contractor shares in the savings on all affected units scheduled for delivery during the sharing period. The contractor must maintain, for three years after final payment on the contract, records to identify the first delivered unit incorporating the applicable VECP.

Agencies establish procedures to fund and pay the contractor's share of *collateral savings* (measurable savings in the agency's overall projected collateral costs, excluding acquisition savings) and future contract savings.[16] Contractor shares of savings are paid through the contract under which the VECP was accepted. On incentive contracts, the contractor's share of all savings are paid as a separate firm-fixed-price contract line item on the instant contract within three months after concurrent contracts are modified to reflect price reductions due to use of the VECP. The parties agree whether the contractor's share of future contract savings is paid as subsequent contracts are awarded or in a lump-sum payment at the time the VECP is accepted. The lump-sum method is easier if a good estimate exists of how many items will be purchased for delivery during the sharing period, and if the funding is available.

Sharing on construction contracts applies only to savings on the instant contract and to collateral savings. The Government's share of savings is determined by subtracting Government costs from instant contract savings and multiplying the result by either 45 percent for fixed-price contracts or 75% for cost-reimbursement contracts. Value engineering sharing does not apply to incentivized construction contracts.

The Government shares collateral savings with the contractor, unless the head of the contracting activity has determined that the cost of calculating and tracking collateral savings will exceed the benefits to be derived. The contractor's share of collateral savings may range from 20% to 100% of the estimated savings to be realized during a typical year of use, up to $100,000, but may not exceed the contract's estimated target cost or firm-fixed-price at the time the VECP is accepted.

Profit or fee is excluded when calculating instant or future contract savings because incentive payments do not constitute profit or fee. Generally, profit or fee on the instant contract is not adjusted downward as a result of accepting a VECP.

A no-cost settlement may be used if reliance on other VECP approaches likely would not be more cost-effective. The contractor would keep all of the savings on the instant contract, and all savings on its concurrent contracts only. The Government would keep all savings resulting from concurrent contracts placed with other sources, savings from all future contracts, and all collateral savings. Use of this method must be by mutual agreement of both parties.

Incentivized performance or design-to-cost targets are not adjusted because of VECP acceptance. The only benefits of an accepted VECP which are rewarded under a value engineering clause are those not rewardable under other incentives.

The following unilateral decisions are made solely at the discretion of the Government:

- accept or reject a VECP;
- collateral costs of agency operation, maintenance, logistic support, or Government-furnished property;
- collateral savings;
- duration of the sharing period; and
- contractor's sharing rate.

Solicitation Provisions and Contract Clauses

FAR 52.248-1, Value Engineering, in excess of the simplified acquisition threshold, but not for:

- commercial products that do not involve special requirements or specifications;
- contracts exempted by the agency;
- engineering services from nonprofit organizations;
- personal services;
- product or component improvement; or
- research and development, other than full-scale development.

Use the clause with its Alternate I if substantial savings to the Government may result from a sustained value engineering effort. Use the clause with its Alternate II if both a value engineering incentive and a mandatory program requirement are used. Use the clause with its Alternate III if the head of the contracting activity determines that the cost of computing and tracking collateral savings will exceed the benefits to be derived and a value engineering incentive is used. Use Alternates I and III if a value engineering program requirement is used, or Alternates II and III if both an incentive and a program requirement are used.

FAR 52.248-2 Value Engineering – Architect-Engineer, when the Government requires and pays for a specific value engineering effort in architect-engineer contracts.

FAR 52.248-3, Value Engineering – Construction, when the contract amount is estimated to exceed the simplified acquisition threshold, unless an incentive contract is contemplated. The contracting officer may include the clause in contracts of lesser value if the contracting officer sees a potential for significant savings. The contracting officer does not include the clause in incentive-type construction contracts. If the head of the contracting activity determines that the cost of computing and tracking collateral savings for a contract will exceed the benefits to be derived, use the clause with its Alternate I.

5.8 SUBCONTRACTING

5.8.1 Privity of Contract

The doctrine of *privity of contract* precludes granting any rights or obligations to a person or firm which is not a party to the contract. Only parties to contracts may enforce their rights or claim damages. Hence, the Government cannot impose itself into dealings between a prime and subcontractor; they must work out their disagreements themselves. For instance, if the prime contractor withholds payment to the subcontractor, the Government cannot (in most cases) get involved to mediate the dispute. Likewise, a subcontractor cannot bring suit against the Government; it must go through its prime contractor (or higher-tier subcontractor) for relief.

This could become a concern when responsibility for a key area of performance flows down from prime to subcontractor. In such a case, requirements are transferred and translated from a party to which the Government has recourse to another party whom the customer cannot legally touch. However, the contracting officer may withhold final payment if the surety agrees to hold the Government harmless from any resulting liability.

5.8.2 Make-or-Buy Program

FAR 15.407-2

When make-or-buy programs are required, the Government may reserve the right to review and agree on the contractor's make-or-buy program.[17] Contracting officers may require prospective contractors to submit make-or-buy program plans for negotiated acquisitions requiring cost or pricing data that are at least $11.5 million in value, except for research or development effort. Contracting officers may require prospective contractors to submit make-or-buy programs for lower-value negotiated acquisitions only upon written determination that the information is necessary. The solicitation includes a statement that the program and required supporting information must accompany the offer and describes evaluation factors for the proposed program, such as:

- availability of socioeconomic businesses for subcontracting;
- capability;
- capacity;
- control of technical and schedule interfaces;
- delivery or performance schedules;
- proprietary processes;
- technical risks; and
- technical superiority or exclusiveness.

The contractor's proposal discusses major items or work efforts that require company management review of the make-or-buy decision because they are complex, costly, needed in large quantities, or require additional equipment or real property to produce. Normally, make-or-buy programs should not include items or work efforts estimated to cost less than 1% of the total estimated contract price or any minimum dollar amount set by the agency.

The contracting officer may incorporate the make-or-buy program in negotiated contracts for major (sub)systems or their components, regardless of contract type. The program can also be used in a cost-type contract in which the contractor's share of the cost is less than 25% and technical or cost risks justify Government review and approval of changes or additions to the make-or-buy program.

Contracting officers normally do not agree to proposed "make items" when the products or services are not regularly manufactured or provided by the contractor, or are available from another firm at lower prices. However, the contracting officer may agree to these as "make items" if it is in the best interest of the Government. Possible reasons include design secrecy, direct control over production and/or quality, integrating plant operations, overall lower Government-wide cost, unreliable suppliers, and using excess capacity to absorb fixed overhead.

By contrast, reasons to buy from vendors include:

- available vendor supplies and schedules;
- cost of specialty machinery;
- desire to maintain a stable workforce;
- desire to maintain multiple sources;
- labor and facilities specialization;
- limited in-house production facilities;
- lower cost;
- lower risk of quality or schedule problems;
- materials complexity;
- small volume requirements; and
- suppliers' research and knowledge.

Using a standard cost system to make this decision can identify inefficient suppliers or provide a critical look at the production process. This in turn provides both a negotiation tool and a quantitative basis for making a decision. The disadvantages of a standard cost-based decision process are calculation error, ignoring nonfinancial considerations, misinterpreting technical know-how and managerial expertise, and over-optimism.

Unlike contractors, the Government does not have a make-or-buy decision to make. Public policy requires it to buy unless industry cannot produce the item, production is limited, or the specification must remain under tight control.

5.8.3 Consent to Subcontract

FAR 44.2

If the contractor has an approved purchasing system, consent is required only for subcontracts specifically identified by the contracting officer in the contract. The contracting officer may require consent to subcontract if required to protect the Government due to subcontract complexity, type, value, or need for special surveillance. These subcontracts are usually for critical components, services or (sub)systems.

If the contractor does not have an approved purchasing system, consent to subcontract is required for cost-reimbursement, labor-hour, time-and-materials, and letter contracts. Consent is also required for unpriced modifications and delivery orders under fixed-price contracts that exceed either the simplified acquisition threshold or 5% of the total estimated contract cost. For DoD, NASA and the Coast Guard, the greater of these two parameters governs the need for consent.

The ACO provides consent to subcontracts, except when the contracting officer retains the contract for administration or withholds the consent responsibility from delegation to the ACO. The following are considerations in this determination:

- adequate consideration obtained for any proposed subcontract that will involve the use of GFP and equipment;
- appropriate subcontract type for the risks involved;
- assessment of alternate subcontractor proposals;
- availability of property from Government sources;
- compliance with applicable cost accounting standards for awarding the subcontract;
- compliance with socioeconomic plans;
- consistency with the contractor's approved make-or-buy program;
- flowdown of required clauses;
- performing adequate cost or price analysis and obtaining accurate, complete and current cost or pricing data and certifications;
- presence of adequate price competition or sole-source justification;
- review of information in SAM; and
- translation of prime contract technical requirements into subcontract requirements.

Contracting officers do not consent to:

- cost-reimbursement subcontracts if the fee exceeds statutory fee limitations;
- repetitive use of cost-reimbursement, labor-hour or time-and-materials subcontracts;

- subcontracts obligating the contracting officer to deal directly with the subcontractor;
- subcontracts providing for cost-plus-a-percentage-of-cost payments; or
- subcontracts that impose on the Government the results of arbitration, judicial decision or voluntary settlement between the prime contractor and subcontractor.

Subcontractors may insist on the right of indirect appeal to an agency board of contract appeals if affected by a dispute between the Government and the prime contractor. In such cases, the prime contractor and subcontractor are equally bound by the contracting officer's or board's decision. However, the contracting officer or the appeals board are not obligated to decide questions that do not arise between the Government and the prime contractor or are not cognizable under the Disputes clause.

Contractors may try to pass risk on to subcontractors due to market risk, production uncertainties from labor or material deficiencies, or social or personal hazards. Prudent contractors will minimize these issues by negotiating firm-fixed-price subcontracts before settling with the Government, and authorizing work only on a not-to-exceed basis. However, the contractor should pass along risk through correction-of-defects clauses and proper inspection techniques.

Solicitation Provisions and Contract Clauses

FAR 52.244-2, Subcontracts, when contemplating a:

- cost-reimbursement contract;
- fixed-price contract that exceeds the simplified acquisition threshold under which unpriced contract actions (i.e., modifications or delivery orders) are anticipated;
- labor-hour contract that exceeds the simplified acquisition threshold;
- letter contract that exceeds the simplified acquisition threshold; or
- time-and-materials contract that exceeds the simplified acquisition threshold.

For a cost-reimbursement contract for civilian agencies other than the Coast Guard and NASA, the contracting officer uses the clause with its Alternate I. Use of this clause is not required in fixed-price architect-engineer contracts, or contracts for mortuary, refuse, or shipment and storage (of personal property) services when an agency-prescribed clause or approval of subcontractors' facilities is required.

FAR 52.244-4, Subcontracts and Outside Associates and Consultants (Architect-Engineer Services).

FAR 52.244-5, Competition in Subcontracting, if negotiated and the contract amount is expected to exceed the simplified acquisition threshold,
except for an architect-engineer, firm-fixed-price (awarded competitively or
whose prices are set by law or regulation), labor-hour, or time-and-materials
contract.

5.8.4 Contractor's Purchasing System Review

FAR 44.3

A *contractor purchasing system review* (CPSR) evaluates the efficiency and
effectiveness of the contractor to subcontract and comply with Government
policy. The review provides the ACO a basis to grant, withhold or withdraw
approval of the contractor's purchasing system.

The ACO determines the need for a CPSR based on the past performance
of the contractor and the volume, complexity and dollar value of the subcontracts. If a contractor's Government sales (excluding competitively awarded
firm-fixed-price and fixed-price with economic price adjustment prime contracts, and sales of commercial items) are expected to exceed $25 million
during the next 12 months, a CPSR is usually needed (although the agency
head for contract administration may adjust this figure up or down). A CPSR
is not performed for a specific contract. This decision for a review must be
revisited at least every three years.

Special attention during a CPSR is given to:

- compliance with Cost Accounting Standards in awarding subcontracts;
- degree of price competition obtained;
- management control systems and internal audit procedures for progress
  payments;
- market research;
- methods of evaluating subcontractor responsibility, including use of SAM;
- obtaining accurate, complete and current cost or pricing data and
  certification;
- planning, award and post-award management of major subcontract programs;
- pricing policies and techniques;
- quality standards invoked;
- socioeconomic subcontracting policies and procedures;
- treatment of affiliates and other concerns who work with the contractor; and
- use of appropriate contract types.

Surveillance is in accordance with a plan developed by the ACO with the assistance of audit, pricing, subcontracting, and technical specialists. The plan covers pre-award, post-award, performance, and contract completion that affect the contractor's purchasing and subcontracting. The plan should also provide for reviewing the effectiveness of the contractor's corrective actions taken as a result of previous Government recommendations.

The ACO approves a purchasing system only after determining that the contractor's purchasing policies and practices are efficient and provide adequate protection of the Government's interests, and promptly notifies the contractor in writing of the granting, withholding or withdrawal of approval. The notification granting system approval will:

- apply to all Federal Government contracts at that plant;
- waive the contractual requirement for advance notification in fixed-price contracts, but not for cost-reimbursement contracts;
- waive the contractual requirement for consent to subcontracts unless selected for special surveillance; and
- be subject to withdrawal at any time at the ACO's discretion.

Consent to certain subcontracts or classes of subcontracts may still be required even though the contractor's purchasing system has been approved. This is usually because the CPSR or continuing surveillance has revealed sufficient weaknesses in a particular area of subcontracting to warrant special attention by the ACO.

The ACO withholds or withdraws approval of a contractor's purchasing system for major weaknesses when the contractor fails to provide sufficient information upon which to make an affirmative determination, or if the contractor's purchasing system has so deteriorated as to threaten the Government's interest. Approval is withheld or withdrawn when there is a recurring noncompliance with requirements (e.g., advance notification, Cost Accounting Standards, cost or pricing data, or small business subcontracts).

5.8.5 Subcontracts for Commercial Items and Commercial Components

FAR 44.4

Prime and subcontractors at all tiers incorporate commercial items or nondevelopmental items as components, and impose on their subcontractors only clauses that implement laws or executive orders applicable to subcontractors furnishing commercial items or commercial components, or else are consistent with customary commercial practice.

Contractors who purchase supply items from NIB or SourceAmerica must go through the Defense Logistics Agency, the General Services Administration, and the Department of Veterans Affairs (if available through their distribution facilities) before placing an order with the central nonprofit agency.

In each authorization to the contractor, the contracting officer may include any other limitations or conditions deemed necessary, such as:

- authorize purchases from Government supply sources of overhead supplies, but not production supplies;
- limit the authorization requirement for Government sources to a specific dollar amount, allowing the contractor to make smaller purchases from other sources;
- restrict the authorization to certain facilities or specific contracts; or
- specify if vesting of title will differ from other property acquired or furnished by the contractor for use under the contract.

The contracting officer may authorize cost-reimbursement contractors to obtain interagency fleet management system vehicles for short-term use and related services, such as:

- fuel and lubricants;
- inspection;
- maintenance;
- repair; and
- storage.

FAR Part 51

The contracting officer may authorize contractor use of Government sources of supply based on a written D&F due to lower cost, delivery or suitability. Certain procedures are prescribed for obtaining an address activity code and GSA ordering. For vehicle rental, the contractor must furnish motor vehicle liability insurance covering bodily injury and property damage.

Solicitation Provisions and Contract Clauses

FAR 52.244-6, Subcontracts for Commercial Items, unless the prime contract is for commercial items.

FAR 52.251-1, Government Supply Sources, when the contracting officer authorizes the contractor to acquire supplies or services from a Government supply source.

FAR 52.251-2, Interagency Fleet Management System (IFMS) Vehicles and Related Services, when a cost-reimbursement contract is contemplated and the contracting officer may authorize the contractor to use IFMS vehicles and related services.

5.9 PROPERTY

5.9.1 Property Administration

FAR 45

Contractors are ordinarily required to furnish all property necessary to perform Government contracts. The Government furnishes property (GFP) to contractors only when the overall benefit to the contract outweighs the increased risk and cost of property administration, or if the Government requirements cannot otherwise be met. Agencies:

• avoid requiring contractors to maintain a separate management system for GFP;
• encourage contractors to use voluntary consensus standards and industry best practices to manage Government property in their possession;
• ensure maximum reutilization of contractor inventory, such as property acquired by and in the possession of a (sub)contractor for which title is vested in the Government and is not needed to complete performance;
• minimize any competitive advantage a prospective contractor could have by using Government property; and
• require contractors to declare as excess (or justify retaining) any Government property not needed for contract performance.

Contractors are not liable for damage, loss or theft of GFP except under fixed-price contracts that are not subject to submission of cost or pricing data. However, the contracting officer may revoke the Government's assumption of risk when the property administrator determines that the contractor's property management practices are inadequate and/or present an undue risk to the Government. Moreover, the Government may seek damages if it can show lack of good faith or willful misconduct, or improper consumption during contract performance.

All GFP is administered by tracking against a specific contract. A prime contractor that provides property to a subcontractor is still accountable to the Government for the GFP under the same contract. GFP is transferred from one contract to another only when firm requirements exist under the gaining contract. Such transfers are documented by modifications to both gaining and losing contracts.

If GFP is delivered late or defective, the contractor is entitled to an equitable adjustment in price or schedule. The contractor may also be instructed to sell or scrap the property after contract performance.

The Government may also furnish information or data to assist the contractor in performance. Since the Government is presumed to have *superior knowledge* in light of having custody of this information, it has a duty to disclose any information vital to cost proposal preparation or contract performance. This concept is similar to the ideas of good faith and fair dealing. However, this duty does not transfer between agencies, meaning that one agency is not held liable just because another agency had superior knowledge.

Solicitation Provisions and Contract Clauses

FAR 52.245-1, Government Property, when the Government will provide property and the procurement exceeds the simplified acquisition threshold. Use the clause with its Alternate I in contracts other than those identified in FAR 45.104(a), Responsibility and Liability for Government Property. Use the clause with its Alternate II for a contract to conduct basic or applied research at nonprofit institutions either of higher education or conducting scientific research.

FAR 52.245-2, Government Property (Installation Operation Services), in service contracts to be performed on a Government installation, GFP will be provided for initial provisioning only and the Government is not responsible for repair or replacement.

FAR 52.245-9, Use and Charges, when the Government Property clause is included.

5.9.2 Solicitation and Evaluation Procedures

FAR 45.2

The contracting officer lists in the solicitation the GFP to be offered. In a competitive acquisition, the contractor is responsible for all installation, rehabilitation or transportation costs to make the property available for use. The solicitation describes the evaluation procedures to be followed, including rental charges and other costs or savings to be evaluated. Offerors must list or describe all Government property that it or its subcontractors propose to use on a rent-free basis, along with the accountable contract under which the property is held and the contracting officer authorization for its use.

The contracting officer considers any potentially unfair competitive advantage that may result from the contractor possessing Government property by applying, for evaluation purposes only, a rental equivalent evaluation factor. The contracting officer ensures the offeror's property management plans or procedures for property accounting are consistent with the requirements of the solicitation.

5.9.3 Authorizing the Use and Rental of Government Property

FAR 45.3

Government property is normally provided on a rent-free basis. Any rental charges do not apply to Government property that is left in place or installed on contractor-owned property for mobilization or future Government production purposes. The contractor may request approval to use Government property under fixed-price contracts other than the contract to which it is accountable. If approved, the contracting officer obtains a fair rental or other adequate consideration.

5.9.4 Title to Government Property

FAR 45.4

The Government retains title to all GFP until properly disposed. Under cost-type and time-and-material contracts, the Government acquires title to all property for which the contractor is reimbursed. Under fixed-price contracts, the contractor retains title to all property acquired for use on the contract, unless identified as a deliverable end item. The Government acquires title to property acquired or fabricated by the contractor in accordance with the financing provisions or other contract requirements. If a deliverable item is retained by the contractor for use after inspection and acceptance by the Government, it is accountable to the contract through a contract modification listing the item as GFP.

5.9.5 Inventory Disposal Schedules

FAR 45.602-1

A contractor obtains the plant clearance officer's approval to remove Government property from an inventory disposal schedule when it:

- can return unused property to the supplier at fair market value and credit the contract (less any restocking fee);
- has requested continued use of Government property (and the plant clearance officer has consulted with program and technical personnel);
- is authorized to use the property on another Government contract; or

- wishes to purchase or produce an item at acquisition cost and credit the contract. *Acquisition cost* includes the purchase price of a capital asset and costs to position and prepare it for use.

Plant clearance officers initiate reutilization actions in the following order:

- reuse within the agency;
- (if educationally useful equipment and with GSA approval only) to other Federal agencies with a need for the property;
- transfer to schools and nonprofit organizations;
- reuse within the Federal Government; and
- donate as designated by GSA.[18]

The screening period begins upon the plant clearance officer's acceptance of an inventory disposal schedule. The plant clearance officer determines whether standard or special screening is appropriate (the standard screening period is 46 days).

Upon approval at a higher level, plant clearance officers may abandon, destroy or donate to public bodies any surplus property that is not *sensitive property* (which is potentially dangerous to the public safety or security if stolen or lost, or subject to exceptional physical accountability, control, protection, and security). Examples of sensitive property include ammunition, controlled substances, explosives, hazardous materials or wastes, precious metals, radioactive materials, and weapons. The property also cannot require *demilitarization* which would render it unusable for, and not restorable to, the purpose for which it was designed or is customarily used. Sensitive property not requiring demilitarization may be abandoned with contractor consent, but instructions are necessary for its proper care, handling and disposal.

The contractor may dispose of scrap resulting from production or testing without Government approval. However, if the scrap requires demilitarization or is sensitive property, then the contractor must submit the scrap on an inventory disposal schedule.

5.10 INTERNATIONAL CONSIDERATIONS

5.10.1 Trade

FAR 25.4

The following regulations govern the export of commercial and defense articles:

- *The International Traffic in Arms Regulations* (22 CFR 120-130), issued by the Department of State, control the export of defense-related articles, services and technical data, ensuring compliance with the Arms Export Control Act. The U.S. Munitions List identifies these items.

- *The Export Administration Regulations (15 CFR 730-774)*, issued by the Department of Commerce, control the export of dual-use commodities, software and technology. They are listed by Export Control Classification Number on the Commerce Control List.
- *National Security Decision Directive (NSDD) 189, National Policy on the Transfer of Scientific, Technical and Engineering Information*, directs that products of fundamental research be unrestricted as much as possible. Contracts for unclassified fundamental research generally do not involve any export-controlled items, information or technology.

Trafficking persons for involuntary servitude and debt bondage is forbidden to DoD contractor employees, with penalties imposed by agency regulation. If the contracting officer receives information of such an event, (s)he must immediately notify the Combatant Commander responsible for the geographical area in which the incident has occurred. No comparable policy applies to civilian agencies.

The contracting officer may direct the contractor to litigate the applicability of a foreign tax if the contract is cost-reimbursable, or a fixed-price type with a tax escalation clause. In fact, some international treaties may exempt the United States from paying specific taxes. The Department of State publishes a list of treaties on its website at www.state.gov.

5.10.2 SAFETY Act

FAR 50.2

The Support Anti-terrorism by Fostering Effective Technologies Act of 2002 (SAFETY Act, 6 U.S.C. 441) has liability protections to promote development and use of anti-terrorism technologies to protect the nation, while providing risk and litigation management protections for (sub)contractors. An *act of terrorism* means any unlawful act determined to use or attempt to use weapons or other methods intended to cause mass destruction, injury or other loss to citizens or institutions of the United States. It can also be an event which causes harm, including financial harm, to an entity, person or property in the United States, or in the case of a domestic U.S. air carrier or a U.S.-flag vessel,[19] in or outside the United States.

Agencies determine whether the technology to be procured is appropriate for SAFETY Act protections, send determinations to DHS to support contractor application(s) for SAFETY Act protections, and encourage offerors to seek SAFETY Act protections for their offered technologies (even in advance of a solicitation). The processing times vary for issuing determinations of applications, so this issue must be planned early in the acquisition cycle.

DHS will issue a *SAFETY Act certification* that a product has been approved for homeland security (i.e., that it conforms to the seller's specifications, will perform as intended, and is safe for use as intended). It will issue a *Qualified Anti-Terrorism Technology* (QATT) for any technology designed, developed, modified, procured, or sold for the purpose to detect, deter, identify, or prevent acts of terrorism or limiting the harm such acts might cause. A technology can include a:

- consulting service;
- design service;
- engineering service;
- equipment;
- information technology;
- product;
- service (including support services);
- software development or integration service;
- threat assessment; or
- vulnerability study.

DHS also issues a *block certification* for a technology class that it designates as approved for homeland security, and a *block designation* when the class is determined to be a QATT.

There is a preliminary step before obtaining either a SAFETY Act certification or QATT. A *pre-qualification designation notice* states that the technology to be procured either affirmatively or presumptively satisfies the technical criteria necessary to be deemed a QATT. The designation notice authorizes offeror(s) to submit streamlined applications for SAFETY Act designation and receive expedited processing of those applications.

Contracting officers may authorize contingent offers only if DHS issued a pre-qualification designation notice or a block designation or certification. The Government does not provide advance notice merely if potential offerors could obtain SAFETY Act designations or certifications for their offered technologies before release of a solicitation. Market research must show that there will be insufficient competition without SAFETY Act protections, or the subject technology would be sold to the Government only with SAFETY Act protections.

Contracting officers may award contracts presuming that DHS will issue a SAFETY Act designation and certification to the contractor, but only with approval of the chief of the contracting office. The contracting officer advises

DHS of the timelines for potential award and consults DHS as to when it could complete evaluations of offerors' applications.

Solicitation Provisions

FAR 52.250-2, SAFETY Act Coverage Not Applicable, if the agency consulted with DHS on a questionable case of SAFETY Act applicability and then determined that SAFETY Act protection is not applicable for the acquisition; or DHS has denied approval of a pre-qualification designation notice.

FAR 52.250-3, SAFETY Act Block Designation/Certification, if DHS has issued a block designation/certification for the solicited technologies. Use the provision with Alternate I when contingent offers are authorized. Use the provision with Alternate II when offers are authorized to presume SAFETY Act designation or certification. The contracting officer may increase the number of days within which offerors must submit their SAFETY Act application.

FAR 52.250-4, SAFETY Act Pre-qualification Designation Notice, if DHS has issued a pre-qualification designation notice. Use the provision with its Alternate I when contingent offers are authorized. Use the provision with its Alternate II when offers presuming SAFETY Act designation or certification are authorized. The contracting officer may increase the number of days within which offerors must submit their SAFETY Act application.

FAR 52.250-5, SAFETY Act–Equitable Adjustment, in a solicitation, if either FAR 50.205-3 or 52.250-4 is used with its Alternate II; and in any resultant contract if DHS has not issued SAFETY Act designation or certification to the successful offeror before contract award.

5.11 ENVIRONMENTAL ISSUES

5.11.1 Energy and Water Efficiency

FAR 23.2

Federal Government procurement policy implements numerous environmental protections and initiatives. One such initiative is to purchase items which meet the Federal Energy Management Program (FEMP) standby power wattage recommendation, or else document the reason for not purchasing such items. This applies to products delivered for use by the Government, or by a contractor at a Federal facility, or incorporated into a building or public work during construction or maintenance. If FEMP has listed a product without a corresponding wattage recommendation, the contracting officer purchases items which use only one watt in their standby power-consuming mode.

An agency is not required to procure an ENERGY STAR® or FEMP-designated product if the head of the agency determines in writing that no such product is reasonably available that meets the functional requirements of the agency, or is not cost-effective over the life of the product (taking energy cost savings into account).

Another initiative is an *energy-savings performance contract* which reduces energy use and cost in facilities and operations for up to 25 years. The energy service company finances the capital to implement energy conservation measures, and receives in return a negotiated share of cost savings. The contracting officer uses the selection method and terms and conditions in 10 CFR 436, Subpart B (www.eren.doe.gov/femp/resources/legislation. html), and may use the "Qualified List" of energy service companies from the Department of Energy.

Contract Clause

FAR 52.223-15, Energy Efficiency in Energy-Consuming Products.

5.11.2 Hazardous Material Identification

FAR 23.3

Another initiative addresses use of hazardous materials in deliverables or during performance per Federal Standard 313E (Material Safety Data Sheet, Preparation and Submission of) of July 2014. These Material Safety Data Sheets are submitted by the apparent successful offeror prior to contract award. For civilian agencies, a data sheet must be submitted again with the supplies upon delivery.

The contractor notifies the contracting officer prior to delivery of radioactive materials, who then notifies receiving activities so that appropriate safeguards can be taken.

Contract Clauses

FAR 52.223-3, Hazardous Material Identification and Material Safety Data. Use the clause with its Alternate I if the contract is awarded by an agency other than the Department of Defense.

FAR 52.223-7, Notice of Radioactive Materials.

5.11.3 Use of Recovered Materials

FAR 23.4

Both the Environmental Protection Agency and the Department of Agriculture have developed special rules to promote the use of recovered materials if either the item price or the aggregate amount paid in the prior fiscal year exceeds $10,000. An EPA-designated product is (or can be) made with recovered material listed in a procurement guideline (40 CFR Part 247) and subject to EPA's purchasing recommendations. These recommendations are set forth in a *Consolidated Recovered Materials Advisory Notice (RMAN) for the Comprehensive Procurement Guideline (CPG)*, (November 9, 2016). Likewise, a USDA-designated item is part of a generic grouping of products that are (or can be) made with biobased materials and listed in a procurement guideline (7 CFR Part 2902, Subpart B) and subject to USDA purchasing recommendations at https://www.biopreferred.gov/BioPreferred/.

Agencies create their own programs to assure the use of products containing recovered materials and biobased products to the maximum extent without jeopardizing their intended use. Customarily, the agency will estimate, certify and verify the amount of recovered material for EPA-designated products. Both the recovered material content and biobased programs require pre-award certification that the products meet EPA or USDA recommendations. A second certification is required at contract completion for recovered material content. EPA and USDA may provide categorical exemptions for items they designate when procured for spacecraft system and launch support equipment, and military equipment for combat or related missions. The policy does not apply if the item cannot meet performance, delivery or cost requirements.

When both the USDA-designated item and the EPA-designated item could meet the agency's needs, the agency purchases the EPA-designated item.

Solicitation Provisions

FAR 52.223-1, Biobased Product Certification, to require the delivery or specify the use of USDA-designated items, unless including the clause at 52.223-2.

FAR 52.223-4, Recovered Material Certification, if requiring the delivery or specifying the use of EPA-designated items, or include the clause at 52.223-17. The provision does not apply to COTS items.

Solicitation Provisions and Contract Clauses

FAR 52.223-2, Affirmative Procurement of Biobased Products Under Service and Construction Contracts, for services or construction unless the contract will not involve the use of USDA-designated items.

FAR 52.223-9, Estimate of Percentage of Recovered Material Content for EPA-Designated Items, if exceeding $150,000 or using EPA-designated products containing recovered materials. Use the clause with its Alternate I if technical personnel advise that estimates can be verified. The clause does not apply to COTS items.

FAR 52.223-17, Affirmative Procurement of EPA-Designated Items in Service and Construction Contracts, for services or construction unless not using EPA-designated items.

5.11.4 Drug-Free Workplace

FAR 23.5

The Drug-Free Workplace Act of 1988 (41 U.S.C. 8102) applies to all contracts and modifications above the simplified acquisition threshold unless:

- for commercial items;
- performed in part outside the United States and its outlying areas;
- the agency head or designee determines that application would conflict the agency's undercover operations; or
- where application would be inconsistent with either the international obligations of the United States or with the laws and regulations of a foreign country.

The offeror must agree to notify its employees that the unlawful manufacture, distribution, dispensing, possession, or use of a controlled substance is prohibited in the contractor's workplace, and to specify the actions that will be taken against employees for violations of such prohibition.

After determining in writing that adequate evidence exists to suspect noncompliance, the contracting officer may suspend contract payments, terminate a contract for default, or pursue suspension and debarment. Likewise, if contractor employees have been convicted of violations of criminal drug statutes occurring in the workplace, the contractor may be found to have failed to make a good faith effort to provide a drug-free workplace.

Contract Clause

FAR 52.223-6, Drug-Free Workplace.

5.11.5 Environmental Improvements

The term *green procurement* has come to mean purchasing products or services with minimal environmental impact. This includes eliminating risks to human health and the environment, such as preventing pollution. Green products consume less energy in their fabrication and usage, and contain fewer hazardous materials. They may be recycled, use less expendable packaging, and incur little or no disposal cost to the environment. Their usage requires fewer natural resources such as energy or water. ISO 14001:2015, Environmental management systems – Requirements with guidance for use, is the certification program for facilities to achieve green operating conditions.

However, green procurement faces some challenges:

- availability and delays in delivery;
- difficulty in implement a program;
- lack of clear specifications;
- need for corporate commitment;
- purchasing habits; and
- sometimes higher prices, though this may be offset by less packaging, lower life-cycle cost, and recyclability.

FAR 23.7

To promote the use of green contracting, Federal acquisition environmental objectives are to:[20]

- eliminate or reduce the generation of hazardous waste and the need for special material processing (such as handling, storage, treatment, and disposal). This also includes creating plans, drawings, specifications, standards, and product descriptions to authorize material substitutions, extensions of shelf life and process improvements;
- give preference to procuring chemicals, products and processes that minimize the depletion of ozone in the atmosphere;
- maximize the use of environmentally preferable products and services;
- promote energy efficiency and water conservation;
- promote the use of biobased products and nonhazardous and recovered materials;
- purchase only degradable plastic ring carriers; and
- realize life-cycle cost savings.

To comply with Executive Order 13693, *Planning for Sustainability in the Next Decade* (March 19, 2015), agencies must meet at least 95% of their annual acquisitions for domestically used electronic products with Electronic Product Environmental Assessment Tool (EPEAT)–registered products. These products include computers, imaging equipment (such as copiers and fax machines), and televisions. The requirement does not apply only if there is no EPEAT standard for the specific product or the agency head determines that no such product meets agency requirements or is cost-effective. A list of EPEAT-registered products that meet IEEE 1680 can be found at www.epeat.net.

FAR 23.8

Federal agencies try to cost-effectively minimize procurement of materials and substances that contribute to the depletion of stratospheric ozone and/or result in the use, release or emission of hydrofluorocarbons (which have the potential for high-altitude global warming).[21] They aspire to give preference to the procurement of acceptable alternative chemicals, products and processes. They will specify that contractors use an acceptable alternative to these hydrofluorocarbons in products and services where identified by EPA's Significant New Alternatives Policy (SNAP) program (www.epa.gov/snap). Examples of hydrofluorocarbon products include:

- aerosol lubricants;
- air-conditioning equipment;
- bulk refrigerants and fire suppressants;
- clean agent fire suppression systems/equipment;
- preservative or sealing compounds such as aerosol mold release agents, corrosion prevention compounds, and foam sealants;
- refrigeration equipment; and
- solvents, dusters and freezing compounds.

In addition to transitioning to SNAP-approved alternatives, the contractor must maintain equipment to prevent and repair refrigerant leaks, and recover and dispose of any equipment that emits or leaks hydrofluorocarbons (and reclaim same where possible). If the equipment contains at least 50 pounds of hydrofluorocarbons, the contractor must track annually this amount to maintain.

Additionally, SAM-registered contractors who received at least $7.5 million in Federal contract awards in the prior Federal fiscal year must state if they publicly disclose greenhouse gas emissions and an emissions reduction goal, along with the website for any such disclosures.

FAR 36.2

Good environmental practices also apply to building (de)construction, and operation and maintenance. The Federal Government implements high-performance sustainable practices to ensure:

- all new construction, major renovation, repair, and alteration of Federal buildings complies with the Guiding Principles for Federal Leadership in High-Performance and Sustainable Buildings (available at www.wbdg.org/pdfs/hpsb_guidance.pdf);
- alternatives to renovation that reduce existing assets' deferred maintenance costs;

- cost-effective, innovative strategies (e.g., highly reflective and vegetated roofs) to minimize consumption of energy, water and other materials;
- pollution prevention and waste elimination by diverting at least 50% of construction and demolition materials and debris; and
- rehabilitation of Federally owned historic buildings utilize best practices and technologies in retrofitting to promote long-term viability of the buildings.

Solicitation Provisions and Contract Clauses

FAR 52.223-10, Waste Reduction Program, for contractor operation and support services of Government-owned or -leased facilities.

FAR 52.223-11, Ozone-Depleting Substances, for supplies that may contain ozone-depleting substances, except for performance outside the United States and its outlying areas.

FAR 52.223-12, Refrigeration Equipment and Air Conditioners, for the maintenance, repair or disposal of any equipment using ozone-depleting substances as a refrigerant (e.g., air conditioners, refrigerators, chillers, or freezers), except for performance outside the United States and its outlying areas.

FAR 52.223-13, Acquisition of EPEAT®-Registered Imaging Equipment, for contractor operation and support services of Government-owned or -leased facilities.

FAR 52.223-14, Acquisition of EPEAT-Registered Televisions.

FAR 52.223-16, IEEE 1680 Standard for the Environmental Assessment of Personal Computer Products, for personal computer products, services that require furnishing of personal computer products for use by the Government, or contractor operation of Government-owned facilities. Use the clause with its Alternate I when sufficient EPEAT Silver registered products are available to meet agency needs.

FAR 52.223-20, Aerosols, for products containing hydrofluorocarbons or for maintenance or repair of electronic or mechanical devices.

FAR 52.223-21, Foams, for products containing hydrofluorocarbons or for insulation construction.

FAR 52.223-22, Public Disclosure of Greenhouse Gas Emissions and Reduction Goals-Representation, if the contractor is in SAM.

5.11.6 Pollution Prevention

FAR 23.9 and .10

Government policy is to purchase supplies and services in accordance with an environmental management system, and to specify how the contractor must comply. Every contract for performance on a Federal facility requires the contractor to provide information necessary to ensure Federal compliance with the emergency planning and toxic release reporting requirements.

Solicitation Provision

FAR 52.223-13, Compliance With Environmental Management Systems, in all solicitations for competitive contracts expected to exceed $100,000 and competitive 8(a) contracts, except for acquisitions of commercial items or where impractical.

Solicitation Provision and Contract Clause

FAR 52.223-5, Pollution Prevention and Right-to-Know Information, for performance, in whole or in part, on a Federal facility. Use with Alternate I if for contractor operation or maintenance of a Federal facility which implemented or plans to implement an environmental management system. Use the clause with its Alternate II if the agency has determined that the contractor activities should be included within the facility compliance audit.

FAR 52.223-29, Compliance With Environmental Management Systems, for operating Government-owned or -leased facilities or vehicles within the United States, and is discretionary for use outside the United States.

5.11.7 Text Messaging

(Sub)contractors must develop policies which ban text messaging while driving on Government business in a Federal, company or privately owned vehicle.

Solicitation Provision and Contract Clause

FAR 52.223-18, Encouraging Contractor Policies to Ban Text Messaging While Driving.

5.12 TRANSPORTATION

Transportation is critical to efficient distribution of supplies. The traffic or transportation manager has numerous major concerns:

- carrier selection (including use of company-owned assets);
- equipment scheduling;
- expediting shipments;
- lease-or-buy analysis;

- most advantageous rate, including special charges or discounts;
- routing shipments; and
- tracing lost shipments.

The basic modes of transportation are:

- commercial air transport: air freight and forwarders;
- motor freight: contract carrier, private trucking and small-shipment carriers;
- pipelines;
- railroads; and
- water transportation: overseas operations, intercoastal service or coastal trade.

Carriers can be common, contract, owner-operated, or private. These carriers interact through competition, and each has its own advantages in cost, reliability and speed.

5.12.1 Bill of Lading

FAR 47.001 through 47.1

A *bill of lading* is a transportation document used to evidence a contract of carriage, customs clearance, receipt, and title. The contracting officer authorizes domestic shipments on commercial bills of lading. Government bills of lading (executed by a Government official and bearing accounting data) may be used for international shipping, or for noncontiguous domestic trade shipments subject to regulation by the Surface Transportation Board involving traffic from or to Alaska, Hawaii or a territory or possession of the United States.

The preferred method of transporting supplies is by commercial carriers. However, Government-owned, -leased or -chartered vehicles, aircraft and vessels may be used if they are not otherwise fully utilized and result in substantial economies. In such cases, these modes of transit would most often be used for emergencies, local transportation between Government installations, or pickup and delivery for line-haul transportation that commercial carriers do not perform. Also, in these cases the Government generally acts as self-insurer without buying insurance and retains the risk of loss and/or damage to its property that is not the legal liability of commercial carriers.

Household goods are personal effects and property used in a dwelling. Transportation of such effects or property is usually arranged and paid for by the householder. It does not include property moving from a factory or store, or what the householder has purchased for use in the new dwelling and requested for transport. The contracting officer must specify in the contract all contractor liability for injury to people or damage to property, and how much insurance the contractor must maintain.

Solicitation Provisions and Contract Clauses

FAR 52.247-67, Submission of Transportation Documents for Audit, if cost-reimbursement and the prime or first-tier cost-reimbursement subcontract will authorize reimbursement of transportation as a direct charge to the contract or subcontract.

FAR 52.247-1, Commercial Bill of Lading Notations, when the contract will be either fixed-price f.o.b. origin greater than the simplified acquisition threshold, or a cost-reimbursement contract which may involve the movement of household goods.

5.12.2 Transportation and Related Services

FAR 47.2

It is generally more economical and efficient for most agencies to make use of term contracts and basic ordering agreements that have been executed by DoD and GSA to take advantage of personnel experienced in contracting for transportation and related services. If these instruments are not available, then agencies may obtain transportation or related services for which the cost does not exceed the simplified acquisition threshold.

The solicitation must include a time schedule, origin points, destination points, freight description, exclusions (e.g., bulk or heavy or hazardous shipments), and quantity.

Storage and distribution points, depots and other receiving activities require advance notice of shipments en route from contractors' plants for:

- certain hazardous materials and explosives;
- classified, controlled or sensitive material;
- minimum carload or truckload shipments; or
- selected shipments requiring movement control.

This process allows the destination to arrange for labor, materials handling equipment, space, and transportation control. This method also avoids incurring demurrage and vehicle detention charges.

The contracting officer specifies the contractor's liability for injury to persons or damage to property other than the freight being transported, and for loss of and/or damage to the freight being transported. The contracting officer also includes the amount of insurance the contractor is required to maintain.

Solicitation Provision

FAR 52.247-20, Estimated Quantities or Weights for Evaluation of Offers, when quantities or weights of shipments between each origin and destination are not known, but the provision states estimated quantity or weight for each origin/destination pair.

Solicitation Provisions and Contract Clauses

FAR 52.228-9, Cargo Insurance, when freight is not shipped under rates subject to the declared or released value of the cargo for reimbursement purposes. Released value is the maximum amount that could be recovered by the agency in the event of loss or damage for the shipments of freight and household goods, and may be more or less than the actual value of the cargo.

FAR 52.228-10, Vehicular and General Public Liability Insurance, when vehicular liability and/or general public liability insurance required by law are not sufficient for a contract.

FAR 52.247-2, Permits, Authorities, or Franchises, when regulated transportation is involved.

FAR 52.247-3, Capability to Perform a Contract for the Relocation of a Federal Office. Use Alternate I to maintain a facility within the state and not require State authority to operate.

FAR 52.247-4, Inspection of Shipping and Receiving Facilities, when it is desired for offerors to inspect the shipping, receiving or other sites to ensure realistic bids.

FAR 52.247-5, Familiarization with Conditions, to ensure that offerors become familiar with conditions and location of services to be performed.

FAR 52.247-6, Financial Statement, to ensure that offerors are prepared to furnish financial statements.

FAR 52.247-7, Freight Excluded.

FAR 52.247-8, Estimated Weights or Quantities Not Guaranteed.

FAR 52.247-12, Supervision, Labor, or Materials.

FAR 52.247-13, Accessorial Services – Moving Contracts, for the transportation of household goods or office furniture.

FAR 52.247-14, Contractor Responsibility for Receipt of Shipment.

FAR 52.247-15, Contractor Responsibility for Loading and Unloading.

FAR 52.247-16, Contractor Responsibility for Returning Undelivered Freight.

FAR 52.247-17, Charges. The charges may not exceed the contractor's charges for the same service that is available to the general public or otherwise tendered to the Government. The contracting officer includes in the solicitation a tabulation listing each required service and the basis for the rate (e.g., "unit of weight" or "per work-hour," leaving space for offerors to insert the rates offered for each service).

FAR 52.247-21, Contractor Liability for Personal Injury and/or Property Damage.

FAR 52.247-22, Contractor Liability for Loss of and/or Damage to Freight other than Household Goods.

FAR 52.247-23, Contractor Liability for Loss of and/or Damage to Household Goods, for the transportation of household goods, including the rate per pound appropriate to the situation.

FAR 52.247-24, Advance Notification by the Government, when the Government is responsible for notifying the contractor in advance when hazardous materials are included in a shipment, and for specific service times or unusual shipments.

FAR 52.247-25, Government-Furnished Equipment With or Without Operators. Insert the kind of equipment and the locations where the equipment will be furnished.

FAR 52.247-26, Government Direction and Marking, when office relocations are involved.

FAR 52.247-27, Contract Not Affected by Oral Agreement.

FAR 52.247-28, Contractor's Invoices, in drayage or other term contracts. The contracting officer states the responsibilities of the contractor, contracting agency and consignee to annotate and distribute shipping and billing documents.

FAR 52.247-68, Report of Shipment (REPSHIP), when advance notice of shipment is required for safety or security reasons, or where carload or truckload shipments will be made to Government facilities.

Contract Clauses

FAR 52.247-9, Agreed Weight—General Freight, when the shipping activity determines the weight of shipments of freight other than office furniture.

FAR 52.247-10, Net Weight—General Freight, when the weight of shipments of freight other than household goods or office furniture is not known at the time of shipment and the contractor is responsible for determining the net weight of the shipments.

FAR 52.247-11, Net Weight—Household Goods or Office Furniture, when movements of Government employees' household goods or relocations of Government offices are involved.

FAR 52.247-18, Multiple Shipments, when multiple shipments are tendered at one time to the contractor for transportation from one origin to two or more consignees at the same destination.

FAR 52.247-19, Stopping in Transit for Partial Unloading, when multiple shipments are tendered at one time to the contractor for transportation from one origin to two or more consignees along the route between origin and last destination.

5.12.3 Standard Delivery Terms

There are a multitude of ways in which shipping charges are paid. Consequently, the Government has developed a multitude of clauses to cover each situation. These situations vary in terms of *f.o.b.* ("free on board") to indicate at what point the cost and risk of shipment passes from buyer to seller. Up to that point, delivery expense and risk is borne by the contractor.

FAR 47.303

F.o.b. origin covers up to delivery and placement on board the carrier (or its wharf or freight station) in the city from which the shipment will be made and from which line-haul transportation service (as distinguished from switching, local drayage, or other terminal service) will begin. This type of delivery would also allow for delivery to a U.S. Postal Service facility, or any Government-designated point located within the same city or commercial zone as the f.o.b. origin point specified in the contract.

Despite the early transfer of cost and risk to the Government, the contractor still has several responsibilities. It must pack and mark the shipment to comply with contract specifications or carrier requirements to protect the goods and minimize transportation charges. It must order carrier equipment requested by the Government or, if left to its own responsibility, of proper capacity. It must deliver the shipment undamaged to the carrier and secure it (i.e., block, brace, load, stow, and trim) on the carrier's vehicle. Finally, the contactor must complete the Government bill of lading prescribed by the contract administrator or the appropriate agency transportation office, or else a commercial bill of lading or other transportation receipt, and distribute as directed by the ordering agency.

There are several variations to f.o.b. origin regarding point of risk transfer, but contractor responsibilities remain the same unless otherwise indicated below.

F.o.b. origin, contractor's facility means the delivery is covered only until on board the conveyance of the contractor (or of the Government if specified) at the designated facility or address of shipment.

F.o.b. origin, freight allowed deducts from the contract price an allowance for freight, based on applicable published tariff rates (or Government rate tenders) between the points specified in the contract.

Under *F.o.b. origin, freight prepaid*, the cost of transportation is ultimately the Government's obligation but is prepaid by the contractor to the point specified in the contract. The contractor does not prepare commercial bills of lading under this method.

F.o.b. origin, with differentials adds to the contract price costs for place of delivery, transportation mode or vehicle type, as indicated in the contractor's offer.

F.o.b. destination is the opposite of f.o.b. origin. It means free of expense to the Government, with the contractor bearing cost and risk of delivery on board the carrier's conveyance to the consignee's facility.[22] The Government is not liable for delivery, demurrage or storage charges involved before the actual delivery of the supplies to the destination, unless caused by an act or order of the Government.[23] The contractor must do the following:

• be responsible for loss or damage to the goods before receipt by the consignee;
• deliver the shipment in good condition to the point of delivery specified in the contract;
• furnish a delivery schedule and designate the mode of delivering carrier;
• pack and mark the shipment to comply with contract or carrier requirements;
• pay and bear all charges to the specified point of delivery; and
• prepare and distribute commercial bills of lading.

F.o.b. destination, within consignee's premises passes cost and risk to the Government upon delivery within the consignee's room. The contractor's responsibilities are the same as for f.o.b. destination.

Next, we have some intermediate methods of transport. Not quite the same as origin or destination, they require the contractor to bear cost and risk part way through the shipping process, then convert to Government responsibility the rest of the way.

F.a.s. vessel, port of shipment means "free alongside ship" and within reach of the vessel's loading tackle at the specified port. There is no expense to the Government until delivered alongside the ocean vessel. The contractor must:

• be responsible for any loss or damage occurring before delivery of the shipment to the point specified in the contract;

- pack and mark the shipment to comply with contract or carrier requirements to protect the goods and minimize transportation costs;
- pay and bear all transportation costs (including handling, heavy lifting and wharfage charges) up to this point;
- provide a clean dock or ship's receipt; and
- provide assistance at the Government's request and expense to obtain the documents required for export or import at destination.

Under *f.o.b. vessel, port shipment*, the only difference is that the contractor actually places the shipment on board the vessel and need not provide clean bills of lading.

F.o.b. inland carrier, point of exportation differs only in that the conveyance is an inland carrier, not necessarily an ocean vessel.

F.o.b. inland point, country of importation is delivered to the specified inland point where the consignee's facility is located (again, this may not be an ocean vessel). Beginning with this method and for the rest of the methods below, the contractor does not provide documentation for export or import at destination.

Ex dock, pier, or warehouse, port of importation differs only in that the Government designates a dock or warehouse at the specified port.

C.&f. (cost & freight) destination means the contractor bears the cost and risk on board the ocean vessel to the specified point of destination. The contractor also obtains and submits to the Government clean onboard ocean bills of lading to the specified point of destination. Further, at the Government's request and expense, the contractor provides certificates of origin and consular invoices issued in the country of origin or of shipment, or both, that may be required for importation into the country of destination.

C.i.f. (Cost, insurance, freight) destination adds to the c.&f. contractor duties the responsibility to pay for transportation and marine insurance. The contractor also obtains and submits to the Government an insurance policy or certificate providing the amount and extent of marine insurance coverage specified in the contract or agreed upon by the contracting officer.

F.o.b. designated air carrier's terminal, point of exportation is no different from f.o.b. inland point, except that the shipment is loaded aboard an aircraft, or delivered to the custody of the air carrier, at the air terminal specified in the contract. An air waybill may fulfill the need for a bill of lading.

F.o.b. designated air carrier's terminal, point of importation covers delivery only to the air carrier's terminal at the point of importation specified in the contract, and the Government bears the cost and risk of loading. The contractor does not normally obtain export paperwork under this method.

If it is advantageous to the Government, the contracting officer may authorize the contractor to ship supplies acquired f.o.b. origin to domestic destinations, including DoD air and water terminals, by common carriers on commercial bills of lading. Such shipments may not exceed 1,000 pounds (150 pounds by commercial air) and must be unclassified. No contract modification is necessary because the Government takes responsibility at time of loading on the carrier. The contractor is then reimbursed for transportation charges.

Contract Clauses

FAR 52.247-29, F.o.b. Origin.

FAR 52.247-30, F.o.b. Origin, Contractor's Facility.

FAR 52.247-31, F.o.b. Origin, Freight Allowed.

FAR 52.247-32, F.o.b. Origin, Freight Prepaid.

FAR 52.247-33, F.o.b. Origin, with Differentials, when it is likely that offerors may include in f.o.b. origin offers a contingency to compensate for unfavorable routing conditions by the Government at the time of shipment.

FAR 52.247-34, F.o.b. Destination.

FAR 52.247-35, F.o.b. Destination, within Consignee's Premises.

FAR 52.247-36, F.a.s. Vessel, Port of Shipment.

FAR 52.247-37, F.o.b. Vessel, Port of Shipment.

FAR 52.247-38, F.o.b. Inland Carrier, Point of Exportation.

FAR 52.247-39, F.o.b. Inland Point, Country of Importation.

FAR 52.247-40, Ex Dock, Pier, or Warehouse, Port of Importation.

FAR 52.247-41, C.&f. Destination.

FAR 52.247-42, C.i.f. Destination.

FAR 52.247-43, F.o.b. Designated Air Carrier's Terminal, Point of Exportation.

FAR 52.247-44, F.o.b. Designated Air Carrier's Terminal, Point of Importation.

FAR 52.247-65, F.o.b. Origin, Prepaid Freight-Small Package Shipments.

5.12.4 Determination of Delivery Terms

FAR 47.304 and 47.4

The contracting officer determines f.o.b. terms on the basis of overall costs. Solicitations state whether offerors must submit offers f.o.b. origin or destination, or both; or whether offerors may choose the basis on which they make an offer. The contracting officer considers the most advantageous delivery point. F.o.b. origin contracts present some desirable traffic management features:

- diversions to new destinations without price adjustment for transportation;
- flexibility when destinations are unknown or changeable:
- Government-controlled transportation;
- lower freight rates through Government rate tenders;
- premium cost transportation;
- small shipment consolidation stations;
- special routings or equipment (e.g., oversize shipments or circuitous routing); and
- use of transit privileges.

When destinations are tentative or unknown, the solicitation is f.o.b. origin only. When the size or quantity of supplies with security classification requires commercial transportation services, the solicitation is also likely to specify f.o.b. origin.

Solicitations with the following conditions are normally on an f.o.b. destination only basis:

- acceptance must be at destination;
- bulk supplies (e.g., coal) that require other than Government-owned or -operated handling, storage and loading facilities, and are destined for shipment outside CONUS;
- forest products such as lumber;
- perishable or medical supplies subject to in-transit deterioration; or
- evaluation of f.o.b. origin offers is anticipated to result in increased administrative lead time or administrative cost that would outweigh the potential advantages of an f.o.b. origin determination.

Solicitations for transportation within CONUS may permit offers on the basis of either or both f.o.b. origin and f.o.b. destination, and are evaluated on the basis of the lowest overall cost to the Government.

When Government acquisitions involve shipments from CONUS to overseas destinations, delivery f.o.b. origin is used due to lower freight rates and flexibility to select both port of export and ocean transportation.

When supplies are acquired for known destinations outside CONUS but originate within CONUS, the contracting officer (for transportation evaluation purposes) notes in the solicitation the CONUS port of loading or point of exit and the water port of debarkation that serves the overseas destination. The contracting officer may also list in the solicitation other CONUS ports that meet the eligibility criteria so that offerors that are geographically remote from the regular port may be competitive for transportation costs. Unless logistics requirements limit the ports of loading to those listed in the solicitation, the solicitation permits offerors to nominate additional U.S. ports more favorably located to their shipping points that possess all requisite capabilities to be considered in the evaluation of offers.

The requiring activity considers the acquisition of carload or truckload quantities. Perhaps additional quantities of the supplies can be transported at lower unit costs or at a small increase in total transportation costs, without impairing the program schedule. In such a case, the contracting officer ascertains from the requiring activity if a known requirement for additional quantities could profitably be stored by the activity for future use, or to several using activities on the same transportation route or in the same geographical area. Because consolidation of small shipments into larger lots frequently results in lower transportation costs, the contracting officer, after consulting with the requiring activity and transportation office, may revise the delivery schedules to provide for consolidated deliveries.

Contracts include complete consignment and marking instructions at the time of award to ensure that supplies are delivered to proper destinations without delay. If supplies cannot be properly classified through reference to freight classification tariffs, the contracting officer obtains the applicable freight classification from the transportation office. If complete consignment information is not initially known, the contracting officer amends delivery instructions under the Changes clause once the information is known. Marking and consignment instructions for military shipments conform to MIL-STD-129 (Military Standard Marking for Shipment and Storage) (October 29, 2004), while shipments for civilian agencies are marked per Federal Standard 123H, Marking for Shipment (Civil Agencies), of June 6, 1997.

When evaluating offers, contracting officers consider transportation and transportation-related costs, and the offerors' shipping and receiving facilities. The transportation officer provides the lowest available freight rates and related incidental charges that are or will be in effect on the expected date of the initial shipment, and on file or published on the date of bid opening. If rates or related charges become available after the bid opening or the due date of offers, they are not used in the evaluation unless they are brand-new rates or access costs.

If a U.S.-flag air carrier cannot provide the international air transportation needed, or its use would not accomplish an agency's mission, foreign-flag air carrier service may be deemed necessary. Agencies disallow costs for U.S. Government–financed commercial international air transportation on foreign-flag air carriers unless the voucher contains a memorandum explaining why service by U.S.-flag air carriers was not available, or why it was necessary to use foreign-flag air carriers.

The contracting officer specifies the contractor's liability for injury to persons or damage to property other than the freight being transported, and for loss of and/or damage to the freight being transported. The contracting officer also includes the amount of insurance the contractor is required to maintain.

The contracting officer may wish to include transit arrangements in the solicitation so that a carload can be stopped at an intermediate point for storage or processing. A transit charge is added to the single through rate rather than citing multiple rates. The contractor may have earned commercial transit credits with the carriers, which can be used in f.o.b. origin offers to reduce transportation costs on a commercial bill of lading.

Federal employees and their dependents, consultants, contractors, and grantees must use U.S.-flag air carriers for U.S. Government–financed international air travel and transportation of their personal effects or property, if available. There is some flexibility if air travel is between two points outside the United States. Similarly, U.S.-flag ocean vessels are required for use in ocean transportation for supplies owned by the Government or (sub)contractor, unless the rates are unreasonable.

Solicitation Provisions

FAR 52.247-46, Shipping Point(s) Used in Evaluation of F.o.b. Origin Offers.

FAR 52.247-47, Shipping Point(s) Used in Evaluation of F.o.b. Origin Offers.

FAR 52.247-49, Destination Unknown, when destinations are tentative and only for the purpose of evaluating offers.

FAR 52.247-50 No Evaluation of Transportation Costs.

FAR 52.247-51, Evaluation of Export Offers, when supplies are to be exported through CONUS ports and offers are solicited on an f.o.b. origin or f.o.b. destination basis. Use the clause with its Alternate I when the CONUS ports of export are DoD water terminals. Use the clause with its Alternate II when offers are solicited on an f.o.b. origin only basis. Use the clause with its Alternate III when offers are solicited on an f.o.b. destination only basis.

FAR 52.247-53, Freight Classification Description, when the supplies being acquired are new to the supply system, nonstandard, or modifications of previously shipped items, and different freight classifications may apply.

FAR 52.247-56, Transit Arrangements.

Solicitation Provisions and Contract Clauses

FAR 52.247-45, F.o.b. Origin and/or F.o.b. Destination Evaluation, when offers are solicited on the basis of both f.o.b. origin and f.o.b. destination.

FAR 52.247-48, F.o.b. Destination – Evidence of Shipment, when supplies will or may be purchased f.o.b. destination but inspection and acceptance will be at origin.

FAR 52.247-55, F.o.b. Point for Delivery of Government-Furnished Property, when Government property is to be furnished under a contract and the Government will be responsible for transportation arrangements and costs.

FAR 52.247-57, Transportation Transit Privilege Credits.

FAR 52.247-59, F.o.b. Origin—Carload and Truckload Shipments, when it is contemplated that they may result in f.o.b. origin contracts with shipments in carloads or truckloads. This will facilitate realistic freight cost evaluations of offers and ensure that contractors produce economical shipments of agreed size.

FAR 52.247-60, Guaranteed Shipping Characteristics, when shipping and other characteristics are required to evaluate offers as to transportation costs for all contracts above the simplified acquisition threshold. The contracting officer deletes unrequired shipping characteristics from paragraph (a) of the clause. The award document shows the shipping characteristics used in the evaluation.

FAR 52.247-61, F.o.b. Origin—Minimum Size of Shipments, when volume rates may apply.

FAR 52.247-63, Preference for U.S.-Flag Air Carriers, if greater than the simplified acquisition threshold (not for commercial items) when the U.S. Government–financed international air transportation of personnel (and their personal effects) or property might occur in the performance of the contract.

FAR 52.247-64, Preference for Privately Owned U.S.-Flag Commercial Vessels, if performance may involve ocean transportation of supplies subject to the Cargo Preference Act of 1954 (46 U.S.C. 1241). Use the clause with its Alternate I if the supplies are transported exclusively in privately owned U.S.-flag commercial vessels. Use the basic clause with its Alternate II for commercial items shipped for contingency operations (including UN or NATO humanitarian or peacekeeping operations), but not for ocean transportation services or construction.

FAR 52.247-66, Returnable Cylinders, whenever the contract involves the purchase of gas in contractor-furnished returnable cylinders and the contractor retains title to the cylinders.

5.13 COST MANAGEMENT

5.13.1 Earned Value Management

FAR 34.2

OMB Circular A-11 (Preparation, Submission and Execution of the Budget) 2015, requires an *Earned Value Management System* (EVMS) for major acquisitions in development (generally over $20 million in value), and can be directed by an agency for other acquisitions. EVMS strives to integrate cost, schedule and technical performance (including personnel, facilities and equipment) with risk management to objectively measure program progress and make program management more efficient. This approach provides an early warning of performance deficiencies and helps to prevent unwarranted expansion in scope of work (colloquially known as *scope creep*). The contractor develops or chooses a system to provide accurate and timely data, but must eventually comply with the American National Standards Institute/Electronics Industries Alliance (ANSI/EIA) Standard 748, Earned Value Management Systems, dated June 1998. Contractors submit EVMS monthly reports (including subcontractors). The Government will conduct an Integrated Baseline Review to verify the technical content and realism of the related performance budgets, resources and schedules. Measuring actual values against these objective baselines will determine the earned value of performance. This review provides a mutual understanding of the inherent risks in contractor performance plans and underlying management control systems, and should lead to developing a risk management plan.

Solicitation Provisions

FAR 52.234-2, Notice of Earned Value Management System - Pre-Award IBR, to require the contractor to use an EVMS and for which the Government requires an IBR prior to award.

FAR 52.234-3, Notice of Earned Value Management System - Post-Award IBR, to require the contractor to use an EVMS and for which the Government requires an IBR after contract award.

Contract Clause

FAR 52.234-4, Earned Value Management System, to require a contractor to use an EVMS.

5.13.2 Should-Cost Review

FAR 15.407-4

Should-cost reviews do not assume that a contractor's historical costs reflect efficient and economical operation, but rather evaluate the economy and efficiency of the contractor's existing equipment, management, materials, methods, operating systems, real property, and workforce. These reviews are accomplished by a multi-functional team of Government contracting, contract administration, audit, engineering, and pricing representatives. The reviews promote both short- and long-range economies and efficiencies to reduce the cost of performance, either by program or company-wide.

A *program should-cost review* evaluates direct cost elements such as labor and material, and associated indirect costs, usually associated with the production of major systems, when the:

- contract will be a sole-source award;
- future year production requirements are expected for large quantities of like items;
- initial production has already taken place;
- items have a history of increasing costs;
- personnel with the required skills are available for the duration of the review;
- time is available to plan and adequately conduct the should-cost review; and
- work is so defined to permit an effective analysis and major changes are unlikely.

Accounting, management, manufacturing, and subcontract management are normally reviewed in a should-cost review. The contracting officer considers the findings and recommendations in the review team report when negotiating contract price, and establishes a follow-up plan to monitor the correction of uneconomical or inefficient practices. These reviews are usually mentioned in the program's acquisition plan.

An *overhead should-cost review* evaluates indirect costs (e.g., depreciation, fringe benefits, G&A, plant maintenance and security, real property and equipment, shipping and receiving, and taxes). A separate audit report is required. The following factors are considered when selecting contractor sites for overhead should-cost reviews:

- changes in accounting systems, management or business activity;
- corporate reorganizations, mergers, acquisitions, or takeovers;

- dollar amount of Government business;
- importance of system or program;
- level of Government participation;
- level of noncompetitive Government contracts; and
- volume of proposal activity.

The objective of the overhead should-cost review is to evaluate significant indirect cost elements in depth, and identify and recommend corrective actions regarding inefficient and uneconomical practices. The ACO should use this information to form the basis for the Government position in negotiating a forward pricing rate agreement with the contractor.

5.13.3 Billing Rates

FAR 42.704

A *billing rate* is an indirect cost rate established temporarily for interim reimbursement of incurred indirect costs and adjusted as necessary pending establishment of final indirect cost rates.

The contracting officer or auditor ensures that the billing rates are as close as possible to the final indirect cost rates anticipated for the contractor's fiscal period, adjusted for unallowable costs. When the contracting officer or auditor determines that the dollar value of contracts does not warrant submission of a detailed billing rate proposal, the rates may be set by adjusting the prior year's indirect cost experience to eliminate nonrecurring and unallowable costs and reflect new or changed conditions.

Once established, billing rates may be prospectively or retroactively revised by mutual agreement of the parties to prevent substantial overpayment or underpayment. When agreement cannot be reached, the billing rates may be unilaterally determined by the contracting officer.

When the contractor provides the contracting officer with the certified final indirect cost rate proposal, the parties may mutually agree to revise billing rates to reflect the proposed indirect cost rates, reflecting historically disallowed amounts from prior years' audits, until the proposal has been audited and settled. The historical decrement is determined by either the contracting officer or the auditor.

Similarly, final indirect cost rates are established by either the contracting officer or auditor. Within 120 days (or longer, if approved in writing by the contracting officer) after settlement of the final annual indirect cost rates for all years of a physically complete contract, the contractor submits a completion invoice or voucher reflecting the settled amounts and rates. If the contractor fails to do so on time, the contracting officer may determine the amounts due to the contractor and issue a unilateral contract modification as a final decision. In simple cases for contractors without an ACO, DCAA can establish final billing rates.

Under cost-reimbursement research and development contracts with universities or other educational institutions, payment for reimbursable indirect costs may be made using predetermined final indirect cost rates. Unless their use is approved at a level higher than the contracting officer, such rates are not used when there has been no recent audit of the indirect costs, frequent or wide fluctuations in the indirect cost rates and their bases over a period of years, or the estimated reimbursable costs for any given contract are expected to exceed $1 million annually.

OMB Circular A-87, Cost Principles for State, Local, and Tribal Governments, 2012, concerns cost principles for contracting with state and local governments. It establishes procedures for a cognizant agency to approve indirect costs associated with federally funded programs and activities. The indirect cost rates negotiated by the agency are used by all Federal agencies. Other nonprofit organizations are covered by OMB Circular A-122, Cost Principles for Nonprofit Organizations, May 10, 2004.

5.13.4 Indirect Cost Rates

FAR 42.7

Establishing final indirect cost rates provides a uniform approach with a contractor supporting multiple contracts or agencies, and timely settlement of cost-reimbursement contracts. Billing rates provide a method for interim reimbursement of indirect costs at estimated rates, subject to adjustment during contract performance and at the time the final indirect cost rates are established.

A single agency is responsible for establishing final indirect cost rates for each business unit. These rates are binding on all agencies and contracting offices, unless otherwise prohibited by law or the contracting officer determines that an audit conducted by another agency is acceptable.

Established final indirect cost rates are used to negotiate the final price of fixed-price incentive and fixed-price redeterminable contracts, and cost-reimbursement contracts, unless the quick-closeout procedure is used. In accordance with 10 U.S.C. 2324(h) and 41 U.S.C. 256(h), a proposal is not accepted and no agreement is made to establish final indirect cost rates unless the costs have been certified by the contractor. The agency head may waive the certification requirement when determined to be in the interest of the United States if the contract is with a foreign government or international organization, state or local government, educational institution, or nonprofit organization.

If the contractor has not certified its proposal for final indirect cost rates and a waiver is not appropriate, the contracting officer may unilaterally establish the rates. Such rates are based on audited historical data and set low enough to ensure that unallowable costs will not be reimbursed.

Solicitation Provision and Contract Clause

FAR 52.242-4, Certification of Indirect Costs, for establishment of final indirect cost rates.

5.13.5 Disallowance of Costs

FAR 42.8

At any time during the performance of a contract other than firm-fixed-price contract (with or without an economic price adjustment clause), the ACO may issue the contractor a written notice of intent to disallow specified costs incurred or planned. A notice of intent to disallow such costs usually results from monitoring contractor costs. In the event of disagreement, the contractor may submit to the contracting officer a written response. The ACO then either withdraws the notice or make a written decision within 60 days.

FAR 42.803

When contracting officers receive vouchers directly from the contractor and approve or disapprove them, the process follows agency procedures. If the examination of a voucher raises a question regarding the allowability of a cost under the contract terms, the auditor may issue a notice of contract costs suspended and/or disapproved simultaneously to the contractor and the disbursing officer, with a copy to the cognizant contracting officer, requesting deduction from current payments of all costs claimed but not considered reimbursable. If the contractor disagrees with the deduction from current payments, it may request the contracting officer to pay the unreimbursed costs and to discuss the findings and/or file a claim under the Disputes clause.

Solicitation Provision and Contract Clause

FAR 52.242-1, Notice of Intent to Disallow Costs, unless firm-fixed-price or fixed-price with an economic price adjustment clause.

5.13.6 Resolving Cost Impacts

FAR 30.606

If a contract or modification represents at least $100,000 in total impact to other contracts, the contracting officer will coordinate with other affected contracting officers before negotiating and resolving the cost impact, and prepare a negotiation memorandum to send to the auditor and the other contracting officers. Adjustments reflect a *pro rata* share of the cost impact. For unilateral changes and noncompliances, the contracting officer does not adjust the price for fixed-price contracts, and does not increase the aggregate price of all contracts, but must individually adjust cost-type contracts.

For noncompliances that involve estimating costs, the contractor corrects the noncompliance and adjusts any paid invoices to reflect the adjusted contract prices. The contractor also corrects noncompliant contract cost accumulations for any affected contracts and adjusts interim payment requests and final vouchers to reflect the costs that should have been paid using the compliant practice.

For a CAS price adjustment or determination of noncompliance of a subcontractor, the chief financial officer for the subcontractor furnishes a copy of the negotiation memorandum or determination to the counterpart for the next higher-tier subcontractor.

Under a quick closeout procedure, the contracting officer negotiates the settlement of indirect costs for a specific contract, in advance of determining final rates. In this case, the contract must be physically complete and agreement must be reached on a reasonable estimate of allocable dollars. The amount of unsettled indirect cost to be allocated to the contract must not exceed $1 million or 10% of the estimated total value of the contract or order. The contracting officer must assess the risk of settlement based upon the contractor's accounting, estimating and purchasing systems.

Determining final indirect costs under the quick-closeout procedure does not affect any other contracts for over- or under-recoveries of costs allocated or allocable to the subject contract. Indirect cost rates used in quick closeout are not considered a binding precedent when establishing final indirect rates for other contracts.

Penalties are assessed against contractors which include unallowable indirect costs in either final indirect cost rate proposals or the final statement of costs incurred or to be incurred under a fixed-price incentive contract. This provision applies to all contracts in excess of $750,000, except fixed-price contracts without cost incentives.

If the indirect cost is unallowable under a cost principle, the penalty equals the disallowed costs plus interest on any paid portion of the disallowance.

If the indirect cost was determined to be unallowable before proposal submission, the penalty is doubled. These penalties are in addition to any other administrative, civil and criminal penalties. It is not necessary for unallowable costs to have been paid to the contractor in order to assess a penalty. The contracting officer may also need to refer the matter to a criminal investigative organization for further review and remedy.

The contracting officer waives penalties when the contractor withdraws the proposal before the Government formally initiates an audit, then submits a revised proposal, and the amount of the unallowable costs is $10,000 or less. The contractor must provide its established policies, evidence of personnel training, and an internal control and review system that assures precluding unallowable costs from being included in final indirect rate proposals. An acceptable self-governance program will outline specific accounting controls and compliance tests for indirect costs. Finally, any unallowable costs subject to the penalty must have been erroneously incorporated into the proposal.

Solicitation Provisions and Contract Clauses

FAR 52.242-3, Penalties for Unallowable Costs, if over $750,000, except fixed-price contracts without cost incentives or any firm-fixed-price contract for the purchase of commercial items.

5.13.7 Cost As an Independent Variable

Cost As an Independent Variable (CAIV) is a DoD strategy that entails setting aggressive yet realistic cost objectives when defining and managing operational requirements to acquire defense systems. Cost objectives must balance mission needs with projected out-year resources, taking into account existing technology, maturation of new technologies and anticipated process improvements in both DoD and industry. As system performance and cost objectives are decided based on cost-performance trade-offs, cost becomes more of a constraint and less of a variable. CAIV principles apply throughout a system's life cycle. The key principles of CAIV are:

- requirements are stated in terms of capabilities and may be exchanged, substituted or adjusted (capabilities are established at the system level only);
- early and continuous customer participation in setting and adjusting program goals throughout the program;
- trade space (i.e., cost with respect to performance) around the cost objective; and
- realistic but aggressive cost objectives are set early and updated for each phase of an acquisition program.

5.14 CONTRACT FINANCING

5.14.1 Invoicing

FAR 32.905

A contractor requests payment by submitting an *invoice*. Authorized payments are processed for:

- final cost or fee payments;
- interim payments under a cost-reimbursement contract for services;
- lease and rental payments; and
- partial deliveries accepted by the Government.

Payment is based on receipt of a proper invoice and satisfactory contract performance. A proper invoice must include the following items:

- contract number (including order number) and contract line-item number;
- contractor name and address;
- description, quantity, unit of measure, unit price, and extended price;
- discount for prompt payment terms;
- electronic funds transfer banking information, if required by the agency;
- invoice date and number;
- name and address of contractor official to whom payment is to be sent;
- point of contact (name, title, mailing address, and phone number) to notify in case of a defective invoice;
- shipping and payment terms (e.g., shipment number and date, bill of lading number and weight of shipment on Government bills of lading); and
- Taxpayer Identification Number (TIN), if required by agency procedures.

If the invoice does not comply with these requirements, the designated billing office returns it within seven days after receipt with the reasons for rejection. However, a defective invoice must be returned within three days on contracts for fish, meat or meat food products; and within five days on contracts for perishable agricultural or dairy products, and food products prepared from edible fats or oils.

The invoice must match up with a receiving report which cites:

- contract or order number;
- date supplies were delivered or services performed;
- date the designated Government official accepted the supplies or services or approved the progress payment request;
- description of supplies delivered or services performed;

Chapter 5

- quantities of supplies received and accepted or services performed; and
- signature, printed name, title, mailing address, and telephone number of the designated Government official responsible for acceptance or approval functions.

The Government will not make invoice payment more than seven days prior to the due date unless the agency head determines otherwise. Payment is made via electronic funds transfer.

All invoice payments, except on cost-reimbursement contracts for services, are supported by a receiving report or other Government documentation authorizing payment. The contractor is entitled to payment for accepted partial deliveries of supplies or partial performance of services that comply with all applicable contract requirements, provided that prices can be calculated from the contract items.

If determined necessary to withhold payment to protect the Government's interests, the contracting officer may unilaterally modify the contract to require the contractor to withhold up to 5% of the amount due, up to a maximum of $50,000. This happens in shipbuilding contracts, and sometimes in contracts with major corporations to facilitate final cost and rate settlement.

Solicitation Provision

<u>52.204-3</u> Taxpayer Identification.

5.14.2 Financing Methods

FAR 32.1

Contract financing payment is an authorized Government disbursement of monies to a contractor prior to acceptance of noncommercial supplies or services. They are not the same as invoice payments because they address other purposes:

- advance payments;
- interim payments under a cost-reimbursement contract;
- performance-based payments; or
- progress payments based on partial delivery or a percentage or stage of completion.

These methods are expected to be self-liquidating through contract performance. The intent is to finance contractor working capital, not facility expansion. The contract price should show a commensurate reduction to reflect the more favorable payment terms.

There is a prescribed order of preference of contract financing methods:

- private financing without Government guarantee. The contractor arranges through a private lender, such as a bank, to obtain necessary working capital without asking the Government for assistance;
- *customary contract financing* without specific reviews or approvals by higher management. This method includes both customary progress payments and performance-based payments.[24] *Performance-based payments* rely on either objective quantifiable methods or accomplishment of defined events. Both versions of contract financing payments may be used if the contractor cannot bill for the first delivery until well after work begins (normally at least four months for small businesses and at least six months for large firms). These payments cover expenditures during the predelivery period that would severely impact the contractor's working capital. The payment rate is 80% for large businesses and 85% for small businesses;
- *loan guarantees* made by a Federal Reserve Bank on behalf of a designated guaranteeing agency to enable contractors to obtain financing from private sources;
- *unusual contract financing* requires specific reviews or approvals by the head of the agency or as provided for in agency regulations; and
- *advance payments* which are *liquidated* (set-off) from future payments due to the contractor. Advance payments are generally used only in the following circumstances:
  - acquiring property for the Government,
  - financially weak contractors (or those who cannot receive finances),
  - Government-Owned-Contractor-Operated facilities,
  - national security,
  - nonprofit firms,
  - payments to subcontractors, or
  - small businesses.

The value of contract financing to the contractor is reflected in a reduced bid or negotiated price, or else contract terms and conditions that are more beneficial to the Government than usual. However, adequate new consideration is required for changes or additions to contract financing after award. This consideration could be a price adjustment reflecting the value of the anticipated amount and duration of contract financing at the imputed financial costs of equivalent working capital. Or it could be the estimated profit rate to be earned during the contract.

The contracting officer may reduce or suspend contractor payments when the agency head determines there is substantial evidence of a fraudulent request for advance, partial or progress payments for a contract or group of contracts. This authority does not apply to commercial interim payments or performance-based payments.

The due date for making contract financing payments is normally the 30th day (never less than the 7th day) after the billing office receives a proper contract financing request. The Government does not pay an interest penalty to the contractor due to delayed contract financing payments.

The contracting officer provides Government financing only to the extent needed for prompt and efficient performance. To determine this, (s)he considers the availability of private financing, predelivery expenditures, impact of production lead times on working capital, and the contractor's financial status. Because these financing methods are intended to be self-liquidating through contract performance, they are not intended for expanding contractor-owned facilities or acquiring fixed assets.

The contractor's need for contract financing is not a responsibility factor or evaluation criterion for contract award. Likewise, a Certificate of Competency from the SBA has no bearing on the contractor's need for or entitlement to contract financing.

If the contracting officer confirms a subcontractor claim that it has not been paid in accordance with the payment terms of the subcontract, (s)he may reduce or suspend progress payments.

Upon receipt of accelerated payments from the Government, prime contractors must pay small business subcontractors on an accelerated timetable to the maximum extent practicable, and upon receipt of accelerated payments from the Government.

Contract Clauses

FAR 52.232-1, Payments, for fixed-price supplies or services, or nonregulated communication services.

FAR 52.232-2, Payment under Fixed-Price Research and Development Contracts.

FAR 52.232-3, Payments under Personal Services Contracts.

FAR 52.232-4, Payments under Transportation Contracts and Transportation-Related Services Contracts.

FAR 52.232-5, Payments under Fixed-Price Construction Contracts.

FAR 52.232-6, Payments under Communication Service Contracts with Common Carriers.

FAR 52.232-7, Payments under Time-and-Materials and Labor-Hour Contracts. The contracting officer can require the contractor to withhold 5% of amounts due, up to a maximum of $50,000.

FAR <u>52.232-8</u>, Discounts for Prompt Payment, for a fixed-price supply or service contract.

FAR <u>52.232-9</u>, Limitation on Withholding of Payments, if two or more terms authorize temporary withholding of amounts payable to the contractor.

FAR <u>52.232-10</u>, Payments under Fixed-Price Architect-Engineer Contracts.

FAR <u>52.232-11</u>, Extras, for fixed-price supplies, services or transportation.

Solicitation Provision and Contract Clause

FAR <u>52.232-40</u>, Providing Accelerated Payments to Small Business Subcontractors.

5.14.3 Commercial Item Purchase Financing

FAR 32.2

For purchases of commercial items, contract financing is normally a contractor's responsibility. However, in some markets financing by the buyer is a commercial practice, so the contracting officer may include financing terms in such contracts when, in the best interest of the Government, the:

- contract is awarded competitively or, if sole-source, adequate consideration is obtained based on the time value of the additional financing, because it could be more advantageous to the offeror than its normal method of customer financing;
- contract price exceeds the simplified acquisition threshold;
- Government's best interest is served;
- need for adequate security is met;
- payment office concurs with using liquidation provisions; and
- sum of commercial advance payments before performance begins does not exceed 15% of the contract price.

The solicitation should specify what type of security is acceptable for Government financing. If the Government is willing to accept other forms of security, the offeror specifies the form it will provide, and the resulting contract will so specify. Contractor net worth and liquidity may be sufficient by itself to match the maximum unliquidated amount of contract financing payments. If not, then a lien against the plant, inventory or work-in-process is possible. The Government has the right to verify the existence and value of contractor assets, and whether they are already covered by a lien.

Subject to agency regulations, the contracting officer may determine the offeror's financial net worth and liquidity to be adequate security.

Nonetheless, the value of the security equals or exceeds the maximum unliquidated amount of contract financing payments due to the contractor. The value of security may be adjusted periodically during contract performance. Other acceptable forms of security include a(n):

- guarantee of repayment from a person or corporation of proven liquid net worth;
- irrevocable letter of credit from a federally insured financial institution;
- surety bond that guarantees repayment of the unliquidated contract financing; or
- title to identified contractor assets of adequate worth.

The Government's lien takes priority to all other liens and is effective immediately upon the first payment, without any filing or notice by the United States. The contract specifies what the lien is upon (e.g., inventory, plant or work-in-process). The Government has the right to verify the existence and value of the assets. The contractor certifies that the assets subject to the lien are free from any prior encumbrances (e.g., capital equipment loans, installment purchases, lines of credit, revolving credit arrangements, or working capital loans).

The contracting officer may either specify the financing terms in the solicitation or permit each offeror to propose its own customary financing terms. If specified in the solicitation, contract financing cannot be an evaluation factor of proposals, and proposals of alternative financing terms are not accepted. However, an offer may state that contract financing terms will not be used by the offeror. Unlike other financing methods, contract financing is not a basis for adjusting offerors' proposed prices because the effect of contract financing is already reflected in the pricing.

On the other hand, if an offeror proposes financing terms, the contracting officer must specify the invoice dates and interest rate, then adjust the proposed price for evaluation purposes to reflect the cost of providing the proposed financing. This is done by computing the imputed cost of financing payments and adding it to the proposed price. This adjustment is the product of payment amount, annual interest rate and number of years or fraction thereof.

Commercial financing payments are liquidated by deduction from these payments. Interest is calculated at the nominal discount rate specified in Appendix C of the Office of Management and Budget (OMB) Circular A-94, "Guidelines and Discount Rates for Benefit-Cost Analysis of Federal Programs" (2004). Financing payments computed on a whole contract basis are liquidated using a uniform percentage. Payment computed on a line-item basis is liquidated only against that item.

A variant of this approach is also available. *Installment payment financing* includes a fixed number of equal interim financing payments (usually on a monthly basis) prior to delivery and acceptance of a contract item, at a 70% financing rate (or lower in accordance with agency procedures). The amount paid upon acceptance is reduced by the amount of installment payments made for the item.

Contract Clauses

FAR 52.212-4, Contract Terms and Conditions – Commercial Items, "Payment."

FAR 52.232-29, Terms for Financing of Purchases of Commercial Items.

FAR 52.232-30, Installment Payments for Commercial Items.

FAR 52.232-31, Invitation to Propose Financing Terms, if the offeror proposes commercial financing. The contracting officer inserts conditions of contractor entitlement, description of the computation method of payment amounts, frequency and form of payment, and security provided by the contractor.

5.14.4 Loan Guarantees for Defense Production

FAR 32.3

Section 301 of the Defense Production Act (50 U.S.C. 4558) authorizes loan guarantees for contract performance related to national defense. Unlike conventional loans from private institutions, Federal Reserve Banks serve on behalf of the guaranteeing agency (any of five designated Departments plus GSA and NASA) to purchase a stated percentage of the loan and share any losses up to the guaranteed percentage. The guarantee is less than 100% of the loan, unless the agency determines that contractor performance is vital to the national defense and no other means of financing is available. The financial institution collects and disburses funds and administers the loan. A (sub)contractor that needs operating funds to perform a contract may always apply to a financial institution for a loan, which may then apply to its district Federal Reserve Bank for a guarantee before it extends credit. This means the Government will back the full value of the loan.

The contracting officer prepares a certificate of eligibility for a contract deemed to be of material consequence, when requested by the contract financing office or other interested agency, or if the application for a loan guarantee relates to a (sub)contract within his/her cognizance. This certificate and associated data on the contractor's financial status and performance is reviewed to determine whether authorization of a loan guarantee would be in the

Government's interest. If the contractor has several major national defense contracts, then relatively minor contracts need not be reviewed. However, if the contracting officer determines that a certificate of eligibility is not justified, (s)he must document the facts and reasons supporting that conclusion and furnish them to the agency contract finance office.

Any certificate of eligibility must discuss the contractor's past performance and the relationship to performance schedules. The certificate must then determine that the supplies or services to be acquired are essential to the national defense, and that the contractor has the facilities and the technical and management ability required for performance.

If the contractor is not a small business, the certificate must also determine that there is no practicable alternate source for the acquisition without prejudice to the national defense. This analysis must discuss the following factors:

- comparative prices available from other sources;
- disruption of established subcontracting arrangements;
- extent to which other sources would need contract financing to perform;
- prejudice to the national defense if a contract with another source conflicts with a major defense acquisition policy (e.g., mobilization base);
- technical ability and facilities of other potential sources;
- time and expense involved in repurchasing for contracts or parts thereof, such as potential claims under a termination for convenience or delays incident to any future default;
- urgency of performance schedules; and
- willingness of other sources to enter into contracts.

The guaranteeing agency evaluates the contractor's financial status and performance to determine if a loan guarantee is in the Government's interest. If this evaluation is favorable, it then sets both the maximum dollar amount and maturity date of the loan, then completes a standard form of authorization as prescribed by the Federal Reserve Board. The agency then transmits the authorization through the Federal Reserve Board to the nearest Federal Reserve Bank. The Bank then executes and delivers to the financing institution a guarantee agreement, with the terms and conditions approved for the particular case. The financing institution will then make the loan.

Note that the agency does not consider the percentage of guarantee requested by the financing institution in determining the contractor's eligibility. The agency usually employs an asset formula to limit the guarantee to 90% (or less if the contractor has inadequate working capital or credit) of the contractor's investment (e.g., payrolls and inventories). The formula excludes:

- amounts for which the contractor has not done any work or made any expenditure;
- amounts that would become due as the result of later performance under the contracts;
- cash collateral or bank deposit balances; and
- progress payments.

The agency usually requires a contractor under a guaranteed loan to execute an assignment of claims under defense production contracts. This includes any contracts entered into during the term of the guaranteed loan that are eligible for financing. This approach is not required (but still permitted) if the:

- assignment of claims would create an undue administrative burden (e.g., the contractor has many smaller dollar-value contracts);
- contractor's financial condition is strong enough that an assignment of claims is unnecessary to protect the Government; or
- increased protection of the loan provided by assignments under smaller contracts is not considered necessary by the agency.

A subcontract or purchase order subject to notice of assignment is problematic. It is not eligible for financing under guaranteed loans if the prime contractor reserves the right to pay the assignor directly (or jointly to the assignee). Nor is the contractor eligible if it reduces or sets off assigned proceeds under defense production contracts due to claims against the borrower.

If a substantial share of the contractor's defense contracts are covered by surety bonds, or the bond amount is substantial related to contractor net worth, the agency will not authorize a loan guarantee unless the surety subordinates its rights and claims to the loan to the financing institution. However, the loan guarantee agreement gives the financing institution the benefit of contract payments proportionate to its loans before any notice of default. Borrowings outside the guaranteed loan are discouraged but not prohibited by the Government.

5.14.5 Advance Payments for Non-Commercial Items

FAR 32.4

A Government agency is the least preferred method of contract financing, and used only when the agency head or designee determines in writing that the advance payment is necessary either to the public interest or to facilitate the national defense. Advance payments cannot exceed the contractor's interim cash needs based on its own working capital and cash flow analysis required for contract performance or reimbursements. Nonetheless, advance payments may be appropriate for:

- acquisition at cost of property for Government ownership;
- classified actions where the agency does not desire assignment of claims;
- experimental, research or development work with nonprofit educational or research institutions;
- financially weak contractors whose technical ability is essential to the agency, and whose performance and financial controls are closely monitored;
- management and operation of Government-owned plants;
- small business concerns; and
- when a loan by a private financial institution is not practicable even with a loan guarantee, often due to remote geographic performance.

Sealed bidders may request advance payments before or after award, even if the invitation for bids does not contain an advance payment provision. However, any bid that requires advance payments as a basis for acceptance is rejected.

The agency will submit a letter of credit for a 12-month or longer contract totaling at least $120,000; otherwise a check directly from the Treasury is in order. Interest is computed at the end of each month on the daily unliquidated balance of advance payments. The interest is computed at the higher of two rates: either the published prime rate of the financial institution holding the special bank account, or the rate established semiannually by the Secretary of the Treasury.

Interest-free advance payments may be authorized by the agency head or delegee for contracts with nonprofit education or research institutions (such as demographic surveys or research studies), to operate Government-owned plants, or with a state or local government (on a cost-reimbursement basis). If a contract provides interest-free advance payments, the contracting officer may require the contractor to charge interest on advances or down payments to subcontractors and then credit the Government for the amount. Interest is also allowed on advance payments to acquire property for Government ownership, if in combination with supply (sub)contracts. Interest charges are not allowed for cost-reimbursement contracts.

If advance payments are approved, the contracting officer provides for a paramount lien in favor of the Government to cover deliverable supplies, any credit balance for advance payments, and property that the contractor acquires for contract performance to which the Government has valid title. The agency may waive the need to deposit the advances in a special account and the countersignature requirement due to the contractor's financial strength, good performance record and minimal history of cost disallowances.

Contract Clause

FAR 52.232-12, Advance Payments. Use the clause with its Alternate I to waive the countersignature requirement. Use the clause with its Alternate II for a cost-reimbursement contract. Use the clause with its Alternate III to use for a more rapid liquidation. Use the clause with its Alternate IV for advance payments at no interest. Use the clause with its Alternate V if the requirement for a special account is eliminated.

5.14.6 Progress Payments Based on Costs

FAR 32.5

Progress payments are made based on costs incurred by the contractor as contract work progresses, to reflect the fair value of work performed. They do not include payments based on percentage or stage of completion accomplished, partial deliveries accepted by the Government, or submission of a contract termination proposal.

Progress payments may be customary or unusual. *Customary progress payments* use a rate of 80% of the total contract cost (85% for small businesses). For undefinitized contract actions, the rate is always 80% regardless of size status. The contracting officer rejects as nonresponsive any bids conditioned on progress payments when the solicitation did not provide for them. Similarly, an invitation for bids may restrict the availability of progress payments to small business concerns only.

The contracting officer may provide *unusual progress payments* at higher rates only if the contractor will bear predelivery expenditures that are large in relation to contract price and the contractor's working capital and credit. The contractor's request must be approved by the head of the contracting activity or a designee.

If the contract requires separate progress payment rates for separate portions of work, the contractor submits separate progress payment requests and separate invoices for the severable portions of work.

Progress payments are generally approved for a contractor that the ACO has found by previous experience or recent audit review (within the last 12 months) to be reliable and competent (and therefore capable of satisfactory performance). Also, the contractor must have an adequate accounting system and controls to properly administer progress payments, and be in sound financial condition. Otherwise, the ACO must first determine that the contractor will be capable of liquidating any progress payments or that the Government is otherwise protected against loss by additional protective provisions. The responsible audit agency or office is consulted as part of this process, thought the auditor may have sufficient information on hand so that a complete audit may not be necessary.

Postpayment reviews or audits are sometimes performed by the ACO to determine if the:

- contractor's accounting system, controls and certification are adequate and reliable;
- limitation on progress payments in the Progress Payments clause has been exceeded;
- unliquidated progress payments are supported by the value of the work accomplished on the undelivered portion of the contract; and
- unpaid balance of the contract price is adequate to cover the anticipated cost of completion, or if the contractor has adequate resources to complete the contract.

When satisfactory progress has not been achieved by a contractor during any period for which a progress payment is to be made, the contracting officer may retain up to 10% of the progress payment. Moreover, progress payments can be suspended by the contracting officer if the contractor is delinquent in payments to subcontractors, in a weakened financial condition, not maintaining a reliable accounting system and controls, or has been overpaid.

The contracting officer adjusts progress payments when necessary to ensure that the fair value of undelivered work equals or exceeds the amount of unliquidated progress payments. If the sum of the total costs incurred under a contract plus the estimated costs to complete the performance are likely to exceed the contract price, the contracting officer computes a loss ratio factor and adjusts future progress payments to exclude the element of loss. This sum of costs is the denominator in the ratio. The numerator is a revised contract price used in progress payment computations (the current ceiling price under fixed-price incentive contracts), plus the not-to-exceed amount for any pending change orders and unpriced orders. The contracting officer then divides the revised contract price by this sum of costs to derive the loss ratio factor.

If the contracting officer believes a loss is probable, future progress payment requests are modified by calculating the revised contract price and loss factor ratio as above, then determining the total costs eligible for progress payments. To find this number, (s)he multiplies the sum of paid costs eligible for progress payments by the loss ratio factor. The contracting officer must ensure that the costs applicable to items delivered, invoiced and accepted do not exceed the contract price.

If the contracting officer concludes that the contractor's figures in its progress payment request are not correct, (s)he shall prepare a supplementary analysis to be attached to the contractor's request, notify the contractor in writing of the differences, and adjust all further progress payments with the revised figures until the difference is resolved.

The Government recoups progress payments by deducting liquidation amounts from payments for completed contract items. The contracting officer applies a liquidation rate (usually the same as the progress payment rate) to the contract price of contract items delivered and accepted. This is easily calculated by dividing the progress payments amount by the contract price, rounding the resultant percentage up to the next highest tenth. The contracting officer may adjust the estimated cost and the contract price to include the estimated value of any authorized work not yet priced and any projected economic adjustments. Here again, this total cost number cannot exceed either the Government's estimated price of all authorized work or the amount of funds obligated for the contract.

An alternate liquidation rate method is available for the contractor to retain the earned profit element of the contract prices for completed items. The alternate rate can be used if the:

- contract delivery schedule is at least 18 months long;
- contractor would not be paid for more than the costs of items delivered and accepted (less allocable progress payments) and the earned profit on those items;
- data on actual costs are available for the products delivered, or for a performance period of at least 12 months;
- rate has not been reduced in the preceding 12 months;
- the Government can recoup under each invoice the full extent of the applicable progress payments; and
- unliquidated progress payments would not exceed the limit prescribed in the Progress Payments clause.

The contractor must agree to certify annually, or more often if requested by the contracting officer, that the alternate rate continues to meet these conditions (with adequate supporting information).

The contracting officer may increase the liquidation rate for both previous and subsequent transactions, if the contractor experiences a lower profit rate than anticipated at the time the liquidation rate was established, for both items already delivered and subsequent progress payments. Moreover, the rate can be raised or lowered to be consistent with any successive changes to the contract price or target profit (under a fixed-price incentive contract with successive targets), or for a redetermined price under a contract with prospective price redetermination at stated intervals. Once the liquidation rate is changed, the contracting officer issues a contract modification to specify the new rate in the Progress Payments clause. No additional consideration for these contract modifications is necessary.

Excess unliquidated progress payments over the contract limit can be corrected by increasing the liquidation rate, decreasing the progress payment rate, or suspending progress payments. This would most likely happen in a cost overrun, poor contractor performance or high rejection or spoilage rate.

Once the title to materials or other inventories is vested in the Government under the Progress Payments clause, the contractor must obtain contracting officer approval to transfer the inventory items from the contract for either disposition or its own use. If the contracting officer grants this request, associated costs are eliminated from progress payments (thereby reducing progress payments outstanding), and billings are reduced to increase liquidation. The contractor cannot bill for the costs allocable to the transferred property, and must credit to or repay the Government the unliquidated progress payments allocable to the transferred property.

Once contract performance is complete and all contractor obligations under the contract are satisfied, including full liquidation of progress payments, any remaining excess property is outside the scope of the Progress Payments clause. Therefore, the contractor holds title to it.

Solicitation Provisions

FAR 52.232-13, Notice of Progress Payments.

FAR 52.232-14, Notice of Availability of Progress Payments Exclusively for Small Business Concerns.

FAR 52.232-15, Progress Payments Not Included.

Contract Clauses

FAR 52.232-16, Progress Payments. The contracting officer inserts any unusual progress payment rate or liquidation rate that has been approved for the prime contractor or subcontractor. Use the clause with its Alternate I if the contractor is a small business concern. Use the clause with its Alternate II if the contract is a letter contract. Use the clause with its Alternate III if the contractor is not a small business firm and the award is an indefinite-delivery contract or basic ordering agreement.

5.14.7 Payment Adjustments

FAR 32.503

Periodic post-payment reviews assess the validity of progress payments by determining that the:

- applicable limitation on progress payments has been met or exceeded;
- contractor has adequate resources to complete the contract;
- contractor provides no reason to doubt the adequacy and reliability of its accounting system, controls and certification;
- unliquidated progress payments are fairly supported by the value of the work accomplished on the undelivered portion of the contract; and
- unpaid balance of the contract price will cover the anticipated cost of completion.

Under indefinite-delivery contracts, the contracting officer administers progress payments for each individual order as if each were a separate contract, unless agency procedures provide otherwise.

The Government has the right to reduce or suspend progress payments, or to increase the liquidation rate. Such actions are taken only after notifying the contractor of the intended action and providing an opportunity to discuss and evaluate the effect on the contractor's credit arrangements, financial condition, operations, or projected cash requirements. Even after full liquidation of progress payments, if the contracting officer finds that contract performance is endangered by the contractor's financial condition or failure to make progress, (s)he can direct the contractor to make additional operating or financial arrangements without loss to the Government.

Except for normal spoilage, the contractor bears the risk for property damage, destruction, loss, or theft, even though title is vested in the Government, unless the Government has expressly assumed this risk. If a loss occurs, the contractor must repay to the Government the amount of unliquidated progress payments based on costs allocable to the property. If Government title to property (including finished goods, materials and work-in-process) under the contract is compromised, the ACO may suspend or reduce progress payments. The contractor is not obligated to pay for the loss of property for which the Government has assumed the risk of loss.

Subcontracts may include either performance-based payments or progress payments, but not both. Subcontracts for commercial purchases may include commercial item purchase financing terms. Contracting officer review or consent is not required merely because the subcontract includes financing payments, so long as the prime contractor has installed the necessary management control systems and audit procedures.

If the contracting officer finds the contractor to be delinquent in paying the costs of contract performance but the contractor's financial condition is satisfactory, the contracting officer may continue progress payments if the contractor agrees to cure the payment delinquencies, avoid further delinquencies and arrange to complete the contract without loss to the Government.

If the contractor has, in good faith, disputed amounts claimed by subcontractors, the contracting officer cannot consider the payments delinquent until these amounts are established through arbitration or litigation. However, the amounts are excluded from costs eligible for progress payments so long as they are in dispute.

5.14.8 Contract Debts

FAR 32.6

Contract debts are amounts paid to or due from a contractor who is not entitled to them under the terms and conditions of the contract. They include:

- billing and price reductions due to price redetermination or defective cost or pricing data;
- breach of contract obligations for contract financing or GFP;
- damages or excess costs related to defaults;
- deficiencies in quality;
- delinquency in contractor payments for deferred or postponed collections;
- duplicate or erroneous payments;
- errors in quantity or billing;
- financing payments determined to be in excess of the contract limitation;
- Government expense of correcting defects;
- increased financing payment liquidation rates;
- overpayments disclosed by quarterly statements under price redetermination or incentive contracts;
- price adjustments due to CAS noncompliances or changes in cost accounting practices;
- reimbursing Government protest costs; and
- reinspection costs for nonconforming supplies or services.

The contracting officer demands repayment of any contractor debts (unless due to payment office error) because (s)he is not allowed to offset the debt amount against future payments. The payment office collects any contract debts, plus any duplicate and erroneous payments, and authorizes debt liquidation per agency procedures.

For debts resulting from specific contract clause provisions, the contracting officer notifies the contractor that payment should be made promptly, and that interest is due in accordance with the terms of the contract. Interest is computed from the date specified in the applicable contract clause until repayment by the contractor. The interest rate is specified in the applicable contract clause. However, for a debt arising from a price reduction for defective pricing or specified in a CAS clause in the contract, interest is computed from the date of overpayment by the Government until repayment by the contractor at the underpayment rate established by the Secretary of the Treasury, for the periods affected.

Additional interest charges usually apply to any debt unpaid after 30 days from the issuance of a demand. If the debt remains unpaid, the contracting officer issues a final decision by certified mail, return receipt requested, and a copy to the payment office. The payment office will then begin to withhold payments. If the debt continues beyond 180 days, it is referred to the Department of the Treasury for collection.

Each agency has an official authorized to grant deferment or installment payments; the contracting officer does not have this authority. Such a request might be granted if the contractor cannot pay in full at once or is deemed essential to the national defense. If the request is granted, a payment schedule is required, including interest, along with periodic financial reviews. For debts under $100,000 (excluding interest), the designated agency official may compromise the debt, though most agencies do not authorize contracting officers to do so.

In contrast, an equitable interest credit is applied when the:

- amount of debt initially determined is subsequently reduced through appeal;
- amount collected by the Government exceeds that assessed on appeal under the Disputes Clause;
- collection procedures result in over-collection of the debt due; or
- Government unduly delayed payments to the contractor during the period to which the interest charge applied (unless an interest penalty was paid for late payment).

Solicitation Provision and Contract Clause

FAR 52.232-17, Interest, if:

- at or below the simplified acquisition threshold;
- for paid advertisements;
- with a foreign government or instrumentality;
- with a State or local government or instrumentality;

- with Government agencies; or
- without any provision for profit or fee with a nonprofit organization.

5.14.9 Contract Funding

FAR 32.7

Per the Anti-Deficiency Act 31 U.S.C. 1341, no Government employee may create or authorize an obligation in excess of the funds available, or in advance of appropriations. Before signing a contract, the contracting officer obtains written assurance that adequate funds are available, or else conditions the contract upon availability of funds. This assurance is in the form of a financial accounting data sheet which specifies the budgeted allocation and other financial details, including amount obligated, and is attached as the last page of the contract or modification.[25]

The contracting officer may initiate a contract action to be funded in the new fiscal year (before funds are available) for operation and maintenance or for continuing services (e.g., rentals, utilities, and supply items not financed by stock funds) necessary for normal operations and consistently covered in the past by appropriated funds. However, the Government may not accept supplies or services under a contract conditioned upon the availability of funds until the funds are actually available.

A one-year indefinite-quantity or requirements contract for services funded by annual appropriations may extend into the next fiscal year if any specified minimum quantities will be ordered in the current fiscal year. Likewise, a contract funded by annual appropriations may not cross fiscal years except under statutory authorization or when the contract calls for an end product that cannot be subdivided for separate performance in each fiscal year (e.g., expert or consultant services). An agency (except NASA) may contract, exercise an option or place an order for severable services that begin in one fiscal year and end in the next fiscal year if the period of the award does not exceed 12 months. In this case, funds for the initial fiscal year may cover the total amount.

If the contract is limited in funds and the contractor approaches the funding limit (normally if 75% of the ceiling will be reached within the next 60 days), the contracting officer must notify the contractor in writing that either the:

- contract is terminated;
- contract will not be further funded;
- Government is still considering a funding increase, in which case the contractor is free to stop work when funding ends or work further only at his own risk; or
- specific amount of additional funds allotted or the estimated increased cost.

Funding instability is a serious problem for major systems acquisition professionals. Three ways a contracting officer can mitigate funding instability are by using Cost As an Independent Variable, multiyear procurement authority and priced options.

Some supplies or services must be acquired subject to supplier license agreements, such as computer software and services. Many of these agreements contain indemnification clauses that conflict with Federal law and could violate the Anti-Deficiency Act. The final clause in this list is intended to avoid this problem by expressly voiding such an agreement.

Contract Clauses

FAR 52.232-18, Availability of Funds, if the contract will be chargeable to next fiscal year's funds and contract action will initiate before availability.

FAR 52.232-19, Availability of Funds for the Next Fiscal Year, if a one-year indefinite-quantity or requirements contract for services is contemplated and the contract is funded annually and will extend beyond the initial fiscal year.

FAR 52.232-20, Limitation of Cost, for a fully funded cost-reimbursement contract.

FAR 52.232-22, Limitation of Funds, for an incrementally funded cost-reimbursement contract.

FAR 52.232.39, Unenforceability of Unauthorized Obligations, in all solicitations and contracts.

5.14.10 Assignment of Claims

FAR 32.8

Under the Assignment of Claims Act (31 U.S.C. 3727), a contractor may assign funds due under a contract if the:

- assignee sends a written notice of assignment to the contracting officer, bond surety and disbursing officer;
- assignment covers all unpaid amounts due under the contract;
- assignment is made only to one bank or other financing institution (if multiple parties finance the contract, only one party may be their agent or trustee) without further assignment;
- contract does not prohibit the assignment; or
- contract specifies payments aggregating $1,000 or more.

No payments to the assignee may be recovered due to contractor liability to the Government. Assignments can be reassigned unless prohibited if it is not in the Government's best interest. The Government may apply any liability against payments due, especially if the assignee has not made a loan or commitment to do so, or if the amount due on the contract exceeds the loan amount made or expected. Nonetheless, a no-setoff provision can be placed in the contract (which requires a determination by the head of the agency due to national defense or emergency and publication in the Federal Register). A no-setoff provision applies for any contractor liability to the Government, such as fines or penalties, payroll withholds or taxes payable. Once these obligations are satisfied, any balance due under the contract may be paid if the assignment is released by the assignee.

Contract Clauses

FAR 52.232-23, Assignment of Claims, if expected to exceed the micro-purchase threshold, unless the contract will prohibit the assignment of claims. Use the clause with its Alternate I if no-setoff commitment has been authorized.

FAR 52.232-24, Prohibition of Assignment of Claims, where in the Government's interest.

5.14.11 Prompt Payment

FAR 32.9

The *due date* to pay an invoice payment is the 30th day after either the billing office receives a proper invoice from the contractor or Government acceptance of supplies or services, whichever is later. For a final invoice after contract settlement, the time for acceptance begins on the effective date of the settlement. The due date for cost-reimbursement contracts for services is 30 days after receipt of a proper invoice, provided that some work has been done. For food products, payment must be made not later than the 7th day after delivery for meat or fish, and the 10th day for perishable agricultural commodities or dairy products.

To compute an interest penalty due to the contractor, Government acceptance is deemed to occur on the 7th day after the contractor delivers supplies or performs services, unless there is a disagreement over quality, quantity or contractor compliance. If actual acceptance occurs within this time frame, the Government bases the determination of an interest penalty on the actual date of acceptance. The contracting officer may specify in the contract a longer period to inspect and test the supplies furnished or to evaluate the services performed (except for commercial items).

For construction contracts, the due date for making progress payments is 14 days after the designated billing office receives a proper payment request.

The due date for payment of Government reserves is 30 days after approval by the contracting officer for release (or else as specified in the contract) based on satisfactory progress in contractor performance.

If the contractor owes interest on unearned amounts, the Government recovers this interest from subsequent payments to the contractor, which reverts to the Unites States Treasury.

When a discount for prompt payment is taken, the designated payment office will pay the contractor as close as possible to, but not later than, the end of the discount period. The payment office pays an interest penalty automatically, without request from the contractor, when all of the following conditions have been met:

- billing officer received a proper invoice;
- designated payment office paid the contractor after the due date;
- Government processed a receiving report authorizing payment, and there was no disagreement over quantity, quality or contractor compliance;
- Government takes a discount for prompt payment improperly;
- interim payment on a cost-reimbursement contract for services is made more than 30 days after the designated billing office receives a proper invoice; and
- payment amount for a final invoice is not subject to further contract settlement action.

Contract Clauses

FAR 52.232-25, Prompt Payment, for commercial items or when payment terms and late payment penalties are established by another governmental authority (e.g., tariffs). Use the clause with its Alternate I if the contract is a cost-reimbursement contract for services.

FAR 52.232-26, Prompt Payment for Fixed-Price Architect-Engineer Contracts.

FAR 52.232-27, Prompt Payment for Construction Contracts.

5.14.12 Performance-Based Payments

FAR 32.10

Performance-based payments are contract financing payments and therefore not subject to the interest-penalty provisions of prompt payment. They are made in lieu of progress payments, but not for architect-engineer services or construction contracts (including shipbuilding or ship conversion, alteration, or repair) that provide for progress payments based upon a percentage or stage of completion. This type of payment is not used for cost-reimbursement line items or contracts awarded through sealed bidding.

Unless agency procedures prescribe the bases for establishing performance-based payment amounts, the contracting officer may establish them on any rational basis, usually based either on objective, quantifiable methods or accomplishing defined events. Common examples of estimates include stages of completion, hours needed to achieve an event or criterion, or projected cost of performance of particular events. The payments may be made either on a whole contract or by deliverable item, but not due merely to the passage of time. Events or criteria may be either cumulative or severable, but not until a dependent event or criterion has occurred.

If a contract action significantly affects the price, event or performance criterion, the contracting officer adjusts the performance-based payment schedule appropriately. Total performance-based payments may not exceed 90% of the contract price or item price. The contract specifies the amount of each performance-based payment as a dollar amount or percentage of the contract price or item unit price.

Performance-based amounts are liquidated by deducting a percentage or a designated dollar amount from the delivery payments, ensuring complete liquidation by the time of final payment.

The contracting officer ensures that the Government title is not compromised by other encumbrances. Ordinarily, (s)he may rely upon the contractor's certification contained in the payment request. The existence of any such encumbrance violates the contractor's obligations under the contract, and (s)he may suspend or reduce payments under the Performance-Based Payments clause. Also, the contractor must repay any performance-based payments related to damaged or lost property.

Solicitation Provisions

FAR 52.232-32, Performance-Based Payments.

FAR 52.232-28, Invitation to Propose Performance-Based Payments, if inviting offerors to propose performance-based payments. Use the provision with its Alternate I in competitive negotiated solicitations if the Government intends to adjust proposed prices for evaluation purposes.

5.14.13 Electronic Funds Transfer (EFT)

FAR 32.11

The Government provides all contract payments through EFT unless:

- a contract is paid in foreign currency;
- for contingency or emergency operations;

- it would compromise classified information;
- the agency does not expect to make multiple payments to the recipient within a year;
- the payment is to a location outside the United States or Puerto Rico;
- the payment office loses the ability to release payment by EFT;
- there is only one source of supply or service and the Government would be seriously injured without using another payment method; or
- urgency dictates another payment method.

A Government-wide commercial purchase card charge authorizes a third-party financial institution that issued the purchase card to immediately pay the contractor. The Government reimburses the third party at a later date. The contract identifies the third party and the particular purchase card to be used but does not cite the purchase card account number, which is provided separately to the contractor to ensure privacy. If the payment exceeds the micro-purchase threshold, the contracting officer must first consult SAM for any delinquent contractor debt subject to collection.

Contract Clauses

FAR 52.232-33, Payment by Electronic Funds Transfer–Central Contractor Registration, unless payment is made through a third-party arrangement.

FAR 52.232-34, Payment by Electronic Funds Transfer–Other than Central Contractor Registration, if a nondomestic EFT mechanism is used and identified in the contract, or if the contractor is not required to be enrolled in SAM.

FAR 52.232-35, Designation of Office for Government Receipt of Electronic Funds Transfer Information, if EFT information is to be submitted to other than the payment office in accordance with agency procedures.

FAR 52.232-36, Payment by Third Party, if payment is made by a charge to a Government account with a third party such as a Government-wide commercial purchase card.

FAR 52.232-37, Multiple Payment Arrangements, if the contract or agreement includes delivery orders and the ordering office will designate the method of payment for individual orders.

FAR 52.232-38, Submission of Electronic Funds Transfer Information with Offer, if FAR 52.232-34 is included, a nondomestic EFT is used, and an offeror is required to submit EFT information prior to award.

5.15 PAST PERFORMANCE INFORMATION

FAR 42.15

Past performance information for future source selection purposes regards a contractor's actions under previously awarded contracts. It includes the contractor's record of:

- accurate billings;
- adherence to contract schedules, including the administrative aspects of performance;
- commitment to customer satisfaction;
- conforming to contract requirements and to standards of good workmanship;
- forecasting and controlling costs;
- integrity and business ethics;
- performance to achieve small business subcontracting goals (excluding awards to NIB or SourceAmerica);
- personnel knowledge and experience;
- quality of service;
- reasonable and cooperative behavior;
- reliability;
- responsiveness to customer direction;
- subcontract management; and
- timely submission of reports.

Upon contract completion, the COR and contracting officer complete a past performance survey for use on future proposal evaluations. Past performance evaluations are also prepared for each construction contract of $750,000 or more (or less if desired). Evaluations are also done for each construction contract terminated for default, regardless of contract value. The same principles apply to architect-engineer services contracts of $35,000 or more.[26]

Past performance evaluations are prepared once the work under the contract or order is completed. Interim evaluations are prepared annually (or more often if specified by the agency) to provide current information for contracts or orders whose period of performance (including options) exceeds one year. The content of the evaluations is tailored to contract complexity, complexity and size. Agencies evaluate contractor performance for each contract or order exceeding the simplified acquisition threshold, including the following:

- cost control (but not for firm-fixed-price or fixed-price with economic price adjustment arrangements);

- management;
- quality of product or service;
- schedule and timeliness;
- small business subcontracting; and
- any negative findings (e.g., defective cost or pricing data, failure to meet contractual reporting requirements, late payments to subcontractors, suspension and debarments, tax delinquency, terminations, trafficking violations, etc.).

Each factor is rated on a five-point scale (exceptional, very good, satisfactory, marginal, and unsatisfactory). Incentive and award-fee data must be entered into CPARS at www.cpars.gov, which will transmit the data to PPIRS at www.ppirs.gov. The contractor receives a draft copy of the evaluation and has 14 days to review and rebut the data. Any disagreements must be resolved at a level above the contracting officer. Agencies use the PPIRS information for any contract completed within the past three years (six for construction and architect-engineer contracts).

5.16 CONTRACT CHANGES/MODIFICATIONS

5.16.1 Modifications

FAR 43.1

Only contracting officers acting within the scope of their authority may execute contract modifications on behalf of the Government. No other Government personnel may direct or encourage the contractor to perform additional work, or create the impression that they have authority to bind the Government.

Contract modifications are priced before their execution unless this would adversely affect the interest of the Government. Otherwise, a ceiling price is negotiated.

Contract modifications may be unilateral or bilateral. A *unilateral* modification is signed only by the contracting officer. It covers administrative changes that do not affect the substantive rights of the parties (e.g., a change in the paying office or appropriation data), change orders and termination notices.

A *bilateral* modification, also known as a *supplemental agreement*, is signed by both the contractor and the contracting officer. It covers negotiated equitable adjustments due to the issuance of a change order, definitizes letter contracts, and reflects agreements of the parties that modify the terms of contracts. These instruments include a not-to-exceed price that caps contractor expenditures while price negotiations are underway.[27]

The *effective date* is when the modification or amendment goes into force. For a solicitation amendment, change order or administrative change, the effective date is the issue date of the document. For a supplemental agreement, the effective date is the date agreed upon by the contracting parties. For a modification that confirms a termination for the convenience of the Government, the effective date of the confirming notice is the same as the effective date of the initial notice. For a modification converting a termination for default to a termination for convenience, the effective date is the same as that for the termination for default. The same dating logic applies to a letter determination of the amount due in settlement of a contract termination for convenience.

Contract Clause

FAR 52.243-7, Notification of Changes, in negotiated research and development or supply contracts to acquire major weapon systems or subsystems. If the contract amount is expected to be less than $1 million, the clause is used only if the contracting officer anticipates that the contractor may allege that the Government has effected changes not identified in writing and signed by the contracting officer.

5.16.2 Change Orders

FAR 43.2

Government contracts contain a Changes clause that permits the contracting officer to make unilateral changes within the general scope of the contract by issuing a Standard Form 30 to modify the contract. Subject matter for changes includes:

- contract period;
- delivery point;
- price;
- provision of an existing contract;
- quantity;
- rate of delivery; or
- specifications.

The contractor continues performance of the contract as changed, except that in cost-reimbursement or incrementally funded contracts the contractor is not obligated to continue performance or incur costs beyond the limits established in the Limitation of Cost or Limitation of Funds clause. This allows the parties to plan a course of action in case additional funds are not forthcoming. The contractor files a claim for any price adjustment within 30 days, and can also claim in writing that the change is out-of-scope for the contract.

Although contractor accounting systems are seldom designed to segregate the costs of performing changed work, they must be prepared to revise their accounting procedures to comply with the Change Order Accounting clause. These include nonrecurring costs (e.g., engineering labor and obsolete or reperformed work), distinct new work caused by the change order (e.g., prototypes or backfit or retrofit kits), and recurring work (e.g., labor and material).

Price changes need not be increases. Price decreases do occur as a result of relaxing specifications, level of effort or delivery time. These are known as *deductive changes*.

When change orders are not forward priced, they require a supplemental agreement reflecting the equitable adjustment. If an equitable adjustment in the contract price and/or delivery terms can be agreed upon in advance, only a supplemental agreement need be issued. Changes issued pursuant to a clause giving the Government a unilateral right to make a change (e.g., an option clause) require only one document, as do administrative changes.

A change is *in-scope* if it affects drawings, packing, shipment, specifications, or time/place of delivery or performance. It must be reasonable to conclude that the subject matter was within the contemplation of the parties when the contract was executed. Otherwise, it is out-of-scope and requires a negotiated settlement with the contractor, which could result in a price increase. The contractor should always verify a direction that represents potential change with the contracting officer. Such a change can include a direction by the contracting officer to accelerate performance (known as *constructive acceleration*) when a schedule slip is due to an excusable delay.

Changes are priced out using specific costs to be incurred in performance, rather than after-the-fact costs or total cost of performance. Although interest is generally unallowable for ongoing business operations, a contractor may recover interest cost to a third party on borrowing when necessary to process a change order. This includes an imputed interest expense for an unfunded unilateral change or wrongful withholding of progress payments.

Constructive changes occur where the Government impacts the contract by an oral or written act without following procedures. This could occur if the contracting officer omitted an action or an authorized official issued a directive. An informal requirement to perform produces a formal requirement.

The *cardinal change* doctrine has therefore been created to provide a remedy when contractors are directed by the Government to perform work which is outside the general scope of the contract. A cardinal change is not covered by the Changes clause because it fundamentally alters the work from that bargained for when the contract was awarded. Deciding if a change is within the general scope of the contract is affected by the character and magnitude of the change, and its cumulative effect upon the project (known as the *Wunderlich rule* after the court case which gave rise to this judicial ruling).[28] For example, a change incorporating extensive redesign effort due to defective specifications is beyond the scope of the contract and therefore constitutes a cardinal change.

Solicitation Provisions and Contract Clauses

FAR 52.243-1, Changes – Fixed-Price, when a fixed-price contract for supplies is contemplated. Use the clause with its Alternate I if the requirement is for services, other than architect-engineer or other professional services, and no supplies will be furnished. Use the clause with its Alternate II if the requirement is for services (other than architect-engineer services, research and development, or transportation) and supplies are to be furnished. Use the clause with its Alternate III if the requirement is for architect-engineer or other professional services. Use the clause with its Alternate IV if the requirement is for transportation services. Use the clause with its Alternate V if it is desired to include the clause in solicitations and contracts when a research and development contract is contemplated.

FAR 52.243-2, Changes – Cost-Reimbursement, when a cost-reimbursement contract for supplies is contemplated. Use the clause with its Alternate I for services and no supplies will be furnished. Use the clause with its Alternate II for services and supplies are to be furnished. Use the clause with its Alternate III for construction. Use the clause with its Alternate V for research and development. Note that Alternate IV is not in use.

FAR 52.243-3, Changes – Time-and-Materials or Labor-Hours, when a time-and-materials or labor-hour contract is contemplated.

FAR 52.243-4, Changes, to dismantle, demolish or remove improvements; and fixed-price construction contracts in excess of the simplified acquisition threshold.

FAR 52.243-5, Changes and Changed Conditions, for construction below the simplified acquisition threshold.

FAR 52.243-6, Change Order Accounting, for supply and research and development contracts of significant technical complexity, if numerous changes are anticipated. The clause may be used in construction contracts, too.

5.16.3 Delays and Suspensions

FAR 42.13

If performance is late, the contracting officer assesses actual need and the reason for lateness, such as:

- contractor's past performance;
- contractor's potential to deliver to a revised schedule;
- cost;
- excusability;
- impact on other Government programs;
- need for additional testing or material; or
- party of cause – Government or contractor.

Based on the concept of *force majeure*, delay is excusable if due to acts of God or nature, external labor strikes or Government action. The contractor is protected from default, excess reprocurement costs or liquidated damages.

A *suspension of work* under an architect-engineer or construction contract may be ordered by the contracting officer for a reasonable period of time. Otherwise, the contractor may submit a written claim for increased cost of performance, excluding profit.

Stop-work orders may be used in negotiated contracts if work stoppage may be required for reasons such as advancement in the state of the art, production or engineering breakthroughs, or realignment of programs. Generally, a stop-work order will be issued only if advisable to suspend work pending a Government decision and a supplemental agreement is not feasible. Issuance of a stop-work order is approved at a level above the contracting officer. Stop-work orders are not used instead of a termination notice if a termination decision is made. As soon as feasible after a stop-work order is issued, the contracting officer should discuss the matter with the contractor and, before its expiration, either cancel the stop-work order (subject to the same approvals as for its issuance), extend the period of the stop-work order if both parties agree by supplemental agreement, or terminate the contract.

Government Delay of Work provides for administrative settlement of contractor claims that arise from delays and interruptions in the contract work caused by the acts, or failures to act, of the contracting officer. This clause does not apply if another contract clause provides for an equitable adjustment because of the delay or interruption (e.g., the Changes clause). This is not considered a delay, interruption or suspension of the contract work.

Solicitation Provisions and Contract Clauses

FAR 52-242-14, Suspension of Work, for fixed-price construction or architect-engineer services.

FAR 52.242-15, Stop-Work Order, for supplies, services or research and
development. Use the clause with its Alternate I if a cost-reimbursement
contract is contemplated.

FAR 52.242-17, Government Delay of Work, for supplies other than commercial or modified-commercial items. Use is optional for services or for
commercial or modified-commercial items.

5.16.4 Novation and Change-of-Name

FAR 42.12

A *novation agreement* is a three-way agreement between a contractor, successor in interest and the Government. The contractor guarantees contract
performance, the successor is a transferee to assume all contractual obligations, and the Government is the buyer recognizing the roles of the other
parties.

A contractor must request the contracting officer in writing to recognize a
successor in interest to its contracts or a name change. The responsible contracting officer then notifies each contract administration office and contracting office affected by such a proposed agreement (with a list of all affected
contracts) and requests submission of any comments or objections to the
proposed transfer within 30 days after notification.

The request must include the:

• balance sheets of both parties, evidence that security requirements have
  been met;
• certified copy of decision by board of directors and/or stockholders
  concurrence;
• consent of sureties;
• evidence of transferee's capability to perform;
• list of all affected contracts between transferor and Government (along with
  contract numbers and types, contracting office identity, dollar amounts, and
  remaining unpaid balances);
• purchase or sale agreement or memorandum of understanding; and
• transferee's certificate and articles of incorporation.

Upon receipt of the necessary information, the contracting officer determines
whether it is in the Government's interest to recognize the proposed successor

in interest on the basis of comments received and the proposed successor's responsibility and performance on prior Government contracts.

The novation agreement references any agreement between the transferor and transferee regarding the assumption of liabilities and obligations (e.g., CAS noncompliances, environmental cleanup costs, final overhead costs, or long-term incentive compensation plans). The guarantor may obtain a performance bond or else guarantees performance. Cost allocability provisions apply, except that a cutoff provision segregates government obligations before novation from those after. The Government does not pay cost increases due to the transfer.

Because 41 U.S.C. 15 prohibits transfer of Government contracts from the contractor to a third party, it may recognize a third party as the successor in interest to a Government contract due to transfer of all contractor assets or those assets involved in performing the contract. This would include incorporation of a proprietorship or partnership, sale of assets with assumption of liabilities, or transfer of assets due to a merger or corporate consolidation. A novation agreement is unnecessary when there is a change in the ownership due to a stock purchase without legal change in the contracting party or control of the assets.

If the contracting officer concurs with the successor, (s)he executes a novation agreement with the transferor and the transferee. It ordinarily provides that the transferee assumes all the transferor's obligations under the contract and waives all rights under the contract against the Government. The agreement also guarantees performance by the transferee (a performance bond may suffice).

If only a name change is involved and the Government's and contractor's rights and obligations remain unaffected, the parties execute an agreement to reflect the name change.

When it is in the Government's interest not to concur in the transfer of a contract from one company to another, the original contractor remains under contractual obligation to the Government, and the contract may be terminated for default if the original contractor cannot perform.

5.17 EXTRAORDINARY CONTRACT ACTIONS

FAR 50.1

Public Law 85-804 empowers the President to authorize agencies operating in connection with the national defense to enter into, amend and modify contracts, without regard to other provisions of law, whenever such action would facilitate the national defense. Requirements to implement Public Law 85-804's authority include the:

- action cannot obligate the Government to more than $34 million without notifying the Senate and House Committees on Armed Services in writing of the proposed obligation, and 60 days of continuous session of Congress have passed since the transmittal of such notification;
- approving authority finds that the action will facilitate the national defense. The authority is vested within the Secretary of the Department, but can be delegated to another official for actions up to $70,000;
- contractor submits a written request for payment within six months after furnishing, or arranging to furnish, supplies or services in reliance upon an informal commitment, and the approving authority finds that, at the time the commitment was made, it was impracticable to use normal contracting procedures (a process known as *ratification*);
- cost is within the limits of the amounts appropriated and the statutory contract authorization;
- other legal authority within the agency is lacking or inadequate; and
- resultant contract cites the law or executive order, the circumstances justifying the action, and states that the action will facilitate the national defense.

Indemnification agreements authorized by an agency head are not limited by appropriated amounts and do not require congressional notification.

Public Law 85-804 is not authority for:

- awarding a cost-plus-a-percentage-of-cost contract;
- making a contract that violates existing law limiting profit or fees;
- providing for other than full and open competition; or
- waiving any bid bond, payment bond or performance bond required by law.

Indemnification is not normally available for any supply or service that has been, or could be, designated by DHS as a QATT. An exception occurs if the Secretary of Defense has determined that the exercise of authority under Executive Order 10789[29] is necessary for the timely and effective conduct of U.S. military or intelligence activities. Another exception would be if DHS has advised whether the use of the authority under the SAFETY Act would be appropriate and the Director of OMB has approved the exercise of authority under the Executive Order.

FAR 1-602.3 and 50.103-2

Under rare circumstances, the Government can amend a contract without consideration to ensure fairness and the national interest, such as when a loss under the contract will impair the contractor's ability to perform on an essential contract, or the contractor's continued operation as a source of supply is found to be essential to the national defense. The loss must be more than just lost profit – it must go to the heart of the contractor's ability to produce. When the Government action, while not creating any liability on the Government's part, increases performance cost and results in distress or a loss to the contractor, fairness may dictate the need to make some adjustment appropriate.

A contract may be amended or modified to correct or mitigate the effect of a mistake or ambiguity. This occurs when the contract does not clearly express the agreement as both parties understood it, the contractor made a mistake that should have been apparent to the contracting officer, or the parties made a mutual mistake as to a material fact.

Unauthorized (or *informal) commitments* occur when a firm responds to a Government official's written or oral instructions and delivers supplies or services in anticipation of compensation without a formal contract. The official must have the apparent authority to issue the instruction, but lack real authority (which should be a rare occurrence, since somebody has overstepped their authority). Again, fairness would dictate that the firm be paid a reasonable amount for expended effort. Only the head of the contracting activity can ratify an unauthorized commitment. The resulting contract must fulfill all requirements for properness as any other contract, including a fair and reasonable price and available funding at the time of the occurrence.

The contracting officer or other agency official will request the contractor to support any request to definitize an informal commitment with any of the following information:

- amounts withheld by the Government;
- analysis of the request's monetary elements, including how the actual or estimated dollar amount was determined and the effect of approval or denial on contractor profits before Federal income taxes;
- any obligations of the Government yet to be performed;
- contemporaneous affidavits, correspondence and memorandums;
- description of the contracts involved, dates of execution and amendments, items being acquired, price or prices, delivery schedules, and any relevant contract provisions;
- financial statements or cost analyses, preferably certified by a certified public accountant, to support the request's monetary elements;
- payments received, due and to become due, including advance and progress payments;
- persons connected with the contracts who have factual knowledge of the subject matter, including their names, offices or titles, addresses, and telephone numbers;

- steps taken to reduce losses and claims to a minimum;
- when work under the contracts or commitments began, progress made to date, and the contractor's remaining obligations and expectations for completion; and
- why the subject matter cannot now, and could not at the time it arose, be addressed under the contract.

If the request involves possible amendment without consideration, and essentiality to the national defense is a factor, additional contractor information may be requested:

- any claims known or contemplated by the contractor against the Government involving the contracts;
- any tax refunds to date, and an estimate of those anticipated, for the period from the date of the first contract involved to the estimated completion date of the last contract involved;
- balance sheets, preferably certified by a certified public accountant:
  - for the contractor's fiscal year immediately preceding the date of the first contract,
  - for each subsequent fiscal year,
  - as of the request date, and
  - projected as of the completion date of all the contracts involved;
- course of events anticipated if the request is denied;
- efforts made to obtain funds from commercial sources to enable contract completion;
- estimate of the final price of the contracts, including changes, escalation and extras;
- estimated time required to complete each contract if the request is granted;
- estimated total profit or loss from other Government business and all other sources, from the date of the first contract involved to the estimated completion date of the last contract involved;
- estimated total profit or loss under the contracts at the estimated final contract price, broken down between profit or loss (both to date and at completion);
- factors causing the loss under the contracts involved;
- minimum amount the contractor needs as an amendment without consideration to enable contract completion, and the detailed basis for that amount;
- original breakdown of estimated costs (including contingency allowances) and profit;
- present estimate of total costs under the contracts involved, broken down between costs accrued to date and completion costs, and between costs paid and those owed; and

- salaries, bonuses, and other compensation paid or furnished to the principal officers or partners, and of all dividends and payments to stockholders in any form since the date of the first contract involved.

If the request involves possible amendment without consideration because of Government action, and essentiality to the national defense is not a factor, the Government may request, instead of the above, the precise Government action that the contractor considers to have caused a loss under the contract, with supporting evidence. The contractor will also be requested to furnish its original breakdown of estimated costs (including contingency allowances) and profit, and its estimated total loss under the contract, including that resulting specifically from the Government action.

The contractor must also include income statements for annual periods subsequent to the date of the first balance sheet. All statements must be consolidated and then broken down by affiliates. They show all transactions between the contractor and its affiliates, partners and stockholders, including loans to the contractor guaranteed by any stockholder or partner.

Contract Clauses

FAR 52.250-1, Indemnification Under Public Law 85-804, whenever the approving official determines that the contractor shall be indemnified against unusually hazardous or nuclear risks. Use the clause with its Alternate I in cost-reimbursement contracts.

5.18 DISPUTES

FAR 33.202

The Contract Disputes Act of 1978, as amended (41 U.S.C. 601-613), establishes procedures and requirements to assert and resolve claims. It does not apply to a foreign agency or government, or an international organization, if the agency head determines that application of the Act to the contract would not be in the public interest.

5.18.1 Claims

FAR 33.202

A contractor's allegation that it is entitled to rescission or reformation of its contract in order to correct or mitigate the effect of a mistake is treated as a claim under the Act. A contract may be reformed or rescinded by the contracting officer if the contractor would be entitled to such remedy or relief under the law of Federal contracts. The claim must be certified if it exceeds $50,000 ($150,000 for small businesses).

All issues are initially handled by the contracting officer until his/her final written decision is rendered. After that, the contractor can file suit in the Court of Claims. Defense contractors could also go to the Armed Services Board of Contract Appeals after the contracting officer's decision, and then go to the U.S. Claims Court if the Board does not concur with its claim. The parties may agree to an accelerated procedure which requires a hearing within six months of filing the claim. The contracting officer will compile a *Rule 4 File* of the contract, correspondence, affidavits, and final decision.

Contractor claims are submitted in writing to the contracting officer for a decision within six years after accrual of a claim, unless the contracting parties agreed to a shorter time period.

When submitting any claim exceeding $100,000, contractors must certify to the following:

> I certify that the claim is made in good faith; that the supporting data are accurate and complete to the best of my knowledge and belief; that the amount requested accurately reflects the contract adjustment for which the contractor believes the Government is liable; and that I am duly authorized to certify the claim on behalf of the contractor.

This discourages submission of frivolous claims and encourages settlement. Certification is not required if the contracting officer renders a final decision without it – otherwise, a failure to certify precludes contractor recovery and judicial review. The Government pays interest at the rate fixed by the Treasury on a contractor's claim for the amount due from the date that the contracting officer receives the claim or payment otherwise would be due, whichever is later, until the date of payment.

The contracting officer issues the decision within 60 days after receiving a certified claim (if over $100,000) or written request for a decision (if not over $100,000). Any failure of the contracting officer to issue a decision within the required time periods is deemed a denial of the claim, and the contractor may appeal or file suit.

The contracting officer must respond to any claim with a final decision. An appeal must be submitted within 90 days from the date of receipt to the agency board of contract appeals, with a copy to the Contracting Officer. The offeror may also bring action directly in the United States Court of Federal Claims within 12 months after date of receipt.

Any amount determined payable under the decision, less any portion already paid, is paid without awaiting contractor action as to appeal, without prejudice to the rights of either party.

Agencies may require a contractor to continue contract performance in accordance with the contracting officer's decision pending a final resolution of any claim arising under (or relating to) a contract clause, other than the Disputes clause.

Claims over $50,000 in value are entitled to interest payments from the Government. Similarly, fraudulent claims or those based on misrepresenting facts are subject to civil penalties.

Solicitation Provisions and Contract Clauses

FAR 52.233-1, Disputes, unless with a foreign government or international organization. Use the clause with its Alternate I if continued performance is necessary pending resolution of any claim arising under or relating to the contract.

FAR 52.233-4, Applicable Law For Breach Of Contract Claim.

5.18.2 Alternative Dispute Resolution

FAR 33.214

Alternative dispute resolution (ADR) is a procedure voluntarily used to resolve controversies by mutual consent (e.g., arbitration, conciliation, facilitation, fact-finding, mediation, mini-trials, and ombudsmen). This increases the opportunity for inexpensive and expeditious resolution. Essential elements include all of the following:

- agreement on alternative procedures and terms used in lieu of formal litigation;
- existence of an issue in controversy;
- participation by officials of both parties with the authority to resolve the issue; and
- voluntary election by both parties to participate in the ADR process.

If either party rejects a request for ADR proceedings, it provides to the other party a written explanation citing specific reasons that ADR procedures are inappropriate for the resolution of the dispute. ADR procedures may be used whenever the contracting officer has authority to resolve the issue. If a claim has been submitted, ADR procedures may be applied to all or a portion of the claim. The claim must be certified if it exceeds $100,000. Then the contracting officer's decision is required within 60 days, however if above that dollar threshold the contracting officer can take longer upon notifying the contractor of the anticipated decision date. When ADR procedures are used after the contracting officer's final decision, the time limitations or procedural requirements to file an appeal of the contracting officer's final decision continue in effect and do not result in a reconsideration of the final decision.

Several possible procedures can be utilized to resolve disputes. A third party may become involved to facilitate a negotiated settlement. A mediator could be used to go one step farther and recommend a solution without imposing it. Attorneys could represent each party to derive a collaborative law settlement. Finally, voluntary arbitration can be invoked for a third party to impose a solution.

Unless required by law and specified in agency guidelines, a solicitation does not require arbitration as a condition of award. Contracting officers have flexibility to select the appropriate ADR procedure to resolve the issues in controversy as they arise. Any written agreement to use arbitration specifies a maximum award that may be issued by the arbitrator.

5.19 CONTRACT TERMINATION

5.19.1 Notification and Response

FAR 49.1

The contracting officer terminates contracts for default or convenience only in the Government's interest.[30] The contracting officer issues a no-cost settlement instead of a termination notice when the contractor will accept it, no GFP was furnished, and no outstanding payments or debts are due to the Government. When the price of the undelivered balance of the contract is less than $5,000, the contract is not normally terminated for convenience, but rather allowed to run to completion.

The contracting officer issues a notice of termination by a written notice to the contractor via certified mail and return receipt, which cites the effective date and extent of termination, along with steps the contractor must take to minimize the impact on personnel. The Government will assign a termination contracting officer (TCO) to negotiate any settlement with the contractor, including a no-cost settlement if appropriate. The TCO may be the procuring or administrative contracting officer, or may be a specially designated individual. The procuring contracting officer will release excess funds resulting from the termination unless this responsibility is specifically delegated to the TCO.

If the same item is under contract with both large and small business concerns and a partial termination for convenience is necessary with the balance of the effort still required, preference is given to the continuing performance of small business contracts over large business contracts, unless the chief of the contracting office determines that this is not in the Government's interest.

If in the best interest of the Government, and with the contractor's written consent, the contracting office may reinstate the terminated portion of a contract in whole or in part by amending the termination notice. Sometimes, in lieu of a termination, the Government will issue a stop-work order to direct the contractor to suspend work on the affected portion of the contract and take steps to mitigate risk and liability of the parties. Such an order may cover all or only part of the work, which may be reinstated only by mutual agreement of the parties. It is good for 90 days unless the parties agree to a different time frame. The contractor must stop the designated work to minimize cost incurrence, and could negotiate an equitable adjustment to address any cost or schedule impact.

The notice and Termination for Convenience clause generally require that the contractor:

- advise the TCO of any special circumstances precluding the stoppage of work; otherwise stop work immediately on the terminated portion of the contract;
- continue performing any continued portion of the contract;
- dispose of termination inventory per TCO direction;
- notify the TCO in writing of any legal proceedings growing out of any subcontract or other commitment;
- protect and deliver property in which the Government has or may acquire an interest;
- settle outstanding liabilities and proposals;
- submit a complete settlement proposal and any request for an equitable adjustment for the continued portion, supported by evidence of any cost increase; and
- terminate all subcontracts thereunder.

The TCO will hold a conference with the contractor and plan to examine the settlement proposal of the prime contractor and subcontractors, referring each subcontractor settlement proposal of at least $100,000 to the audit agency for review and recommendations. The TCO will negotiate settlement with the contractor, and determine any elements that cannot be agreed on.

Within 30 days, the TCO shall recommend release of excess funds to the contracting officer (generally, no action is taken if this amount is below $1,000). When the contracting officer terminates a contract for commercial items for the Government's convenience, the contractor is paid a settlement calculated by either the percentage of the contract price reflecting the percentage of the work already performed, or else by multiplying the number of direct labor hours expended before the effective date of termination by the hourly rates(s). Such a contractor is not required to comply with the cost accounting standards or contract cost principles, nor is the Government allowed to audit the contractor's records solely because of the termination.

5.19.2 Settlement of Subcontracts

FAR 49.108

A subcontractor has no rights against the Government upon the termination of a prime contract, but may have rights against the prime contractor or its customer subcontractor. The prime contractor and each subcontractor must submit a *settlement proposal* to determine final pricing of their subcontract. A settlement proposal is considered a claim under the False Claims Act and is deducted from the gross settlement amounts payable for completed articles or work at the contract price. Deductions are not made to retain or dispose of termination inventory, nor for advance or partial payments. *Partial payments* are authorized to be made upon completion of a specified unit(s) being delivered and accepted under the contract.[31]

Contractors settle with subcontractors following the same policies and principles as settling prime contracts. However, the basis and form of the subcontractor's settlement proposal need only be acceptable to the prime contractor or the next higher-tier subcontractor. Each settlement requires accounting and other data sufficient for adequate review by the Government. Absent a court order, the Government will not pay the prime contractor for loss of anticipatory profits or consequential damages due to termination of a subcontract.

The TCO examines each subcontract settlement to determine its good faith, need and reasonableness, as well as allocability to the terminated portion of the contract. The TCO may, upon written request, give written authorization to the prime contractor to settle subcontracts in whole or in part without approval when the amount of settlement is $100,000 or less, if satisfied with the adequacy of the procedures used by the contractor to settle settlement proposals. Any termination inventory included in the settlement is disposed of as directed by the prime contractor, without TCO review or screening requirements. The TCO does not authorize subcontractors to settle with lower-tier subcontractors, but may authorize a prime contractor to approve such a request.

The TCO treats any subcontractor judgment against a prime contractor as a cost of settling with the prime contractor, provided the subcontract contained a termination clause excluding payment of anticipatory profits or consequential damages. The prime contractor must have made reasonable efforts to settle with the subcontractor, and cooperated with the Government in defense of the court action.

The TCO may direct the prime contractor to assign to the Government all interests, rights and titles under any subcontract terminated because the prime contract was terminated. The Government also has the option to settle and pay any settlement proposal arising out of the termination of subcontracts when it is in the Government's interest. This could occur if a sole-source subcontractor faces a delay by the prime contractor in settlement or payment of the subcontractor's proposal that will jeopardize its financial position.

5.19.3 Settlement Agreements

FAR 49.109 and .112

A *settlement agreement* is a contract modification settling all or a severable portion of a settlement proposal. The TCO executes a no-cost settlement agreement if the contractor has not incurred (or agrees to waive) costs for the terminated portion of the contract and no amounts are due the Government.

The TCO attempts to settle in one agreement all rights and liabilities of the parties under the contract or its terminated portion, rather than partial settlements for particular items of the prime contractor's settlement proposal. A partial settlement may be executed if the issues are clearly severable from other issues and partial settlement will not prejudice either party's interests in disposing of the unsettled part of the settlement proposal.

The TCO may negotiate jointly two or more termination settlement proposals of the same contractor under different contracts, even if with different contracting offices or agencies. The resulting settlement may lead to one agreement covering all contracts involved, or a separate agreement for each contract involved.

If the contractor and TCO cannot agree on a termination settlement, or if a settlement proposal is not submitted within the period required by the termination clause, the TCO gives the contractor at least 15 days notice by certified mail to submit written evidence substantiating the amount previously proposed. The contractor has the burden of establishing proof satisfactory to the TCO of the amount proposed (e.g., affidavits, audit reports, vouchers, verified transcripts of books of account, etc.). The TCO may request the contractor to submit additional documents and data. After reviewing the information available, the TCO determines the amount due and transmits a copy by certified mail (return receipt requested) to the contractor. The contractor may appeal, under the Disputes clause, any settlement by determination, except if it failed to both submit the settlement proposal in the required time frame and failed to request an extension of time.

Before approving any partial payment, the TCO obtains accounting or engineering reviews of the data submitted in the settlement proposal. If review of the data indicates that the requested partial payment is proper, reasonable payments may be authorized in the discretion of the TCO up to:

- 100% of the contract price, adjusted for undelivered acceptable items completed before the termination date, or later completed with the approval of the TCO;
- 100% of the amount of any subcontract settlement paid by the prime contractor if the settlement was approved or ratified by the TCO;
- 90% of the direct cost of termination inventory, including costs of direct labor, purchased parts, raw materials, and supplies;
- 90% of other allowable costs (including indirect costs and settlement expense) allocable to the terminated portion of the contract; and
- 100% of partial payments made to subcontractors.

When an assignment of claims has been made under the contract, the Government shall not make partial payments to other than the assignee unless the parties to the assignment consent in writing.

If any partial payment is made for completed end items or for costs of termination inventory, the TCO must protect the Government's interest in the inventory. This is done by either obtaining title to the completed end items or termination inventory, or else creating a lien in favor of the Government, paramount to all other liens, on the completed end items or termination inventory.

The TCO deducts from the gross amount of a partial payment all unliquidated balances of progress and advance payments (including interest) allocable to the terminated portion of the contract. (S)he also deducts all credits arising from the purchase, retention or sale of property included in the payment request.

The total amount of all partial payments should not exceed the amount that will become due to the contractor because of the termination. If the total of partial payments exceeds the final settlement amount, the contractor must repay the excess to the Government on demand, together with interest computed at the rate established by the Secretary of the Treasury from the date the excess payment was received by the contractor to the date of repayment. However, interest will not be charged for any excess payment caused by a reduction in the settlement proposal due to disposition or retention of termination inventory, as determined by the TCO. Nor is interest charged on overpayment under cost-reimbursement research and development contracts without profit or fee if the overpayments are repaid to the Government within 30 days of demand.

If the contract authorizes partial payments on settlement proposals before final settlement, a prime contractor may request them after submission of interim or final settlement proposals. A subcontractor submits its application through the prime contractor, which attaches its own invoice and recommendations to the subcontractor's application. Partial payments to a subcontractor are made only through the prime contractor after it submits its settlement proposal.

5.19.4 Additional Principles for Fixed-Price Contracts Terminated for Convenience

FAR 49.2

The TCO allows profit on preparations made and work done on the terminated portion of the contract, but not on the settlement expenses. Anticipatory profits and consequential damages are not allowed. The contractor's efforts in settling subcontractor proposals are considered in determining the final profit rate. Profit is not allowed for subcontracted material or services that, as of the effective date of termination, have not been delivered. Nor is profit allowed if the contractor would have incurred a loss had the entire contract been completed. For a construction contract, profit is allowed on the prime contractor's settlements with subcontractors for actual work in place at the job site, but not on settlements for materials on hand or for preparations made to complete the work.

From the settlement amount, the TCO deducts the agreed price for any part of the termination inventory purchased or retained by the contractor for the terminated contract, and the proceeds from any materials sold but not paid or credited to the Government. The TCO also deducts the fair value of any of the termination inventory that (before transfer of title to the Government or buyer) is undeliverable due to damage, destruction, loss, or theft. Normal spoilage and inventory for which the Government assumed the risk of loss are not deducted.

Promptly after the effective date of termination, the TCO arranges for all completed but undelivered end items to be inspected and accepted, and determines which ones should be delivered under the contract. The contractor invoices any accepted and delivered end items at the contract price and excludes them from the settlement proposal. However, accepted end items which are not to be delivered under the contract are included in the settlement proposal at the contract price, adjusted for any saving of freight charges and any purchase, retention or sale credits. For construction contracts, work in place accepted by the Government is not considered a completed item even though the work may have been paid for.

5.19.5 Settlement Proposals

FAR 49.206

The final settlement proposal must be submitted within one year from the effective date of the termination, unless the period is extended by the TCO.

With the consent of the TCO, proposals may be filed in successive steps covering separate portions of the contractor's costs. The contractor prices out its proposal using either the inventory or total-cost basis.

Use of the *inventory basis* for settlement proposals is preferred. The contractor may propose only costs allocable to the terminated portion of the contract, and must itemize:

- components, dies, fixtures, jigs, and tooling;
- engineering costs;
- general and administrative costs;
- initial costs;
- metals, purchased parts and raw materials at purchase cost;
- other proper charges;
- profit or adjustment for loss, less unliquidated advance and progress payments and other credits;
- settlement costs with subcontractors;
- settlement expenses; and
- work-in-process and finished parts at manufacturing cost.

The inventory basis is also appropriate for partial termination of a construction or related professional services contract, partial or complete termination of supply orders under any terminated construction contract, and complete termination of a unit-price professional services contract.

When use of the inventory basis is not practicable or will unduly delay settlement, the *total-cost basis* may be used if approved in advance by the TCO and if:

- production has not begun and accumulated costs represent planning and preproduction expenses only;
- termination is complete and involves a letter contract;
- the contract does not specify unit prices; or
- unit costs for work-in-process and finished products cannot readily be established.

A total-cost proposal is priced at the difference between original contract price and actual cost of performing the contract as changed.

For a complete termination, the contractor itemizes costs incurred under the contract up to the effective date of termination, including the costs of settlements with subcontractors and an allowance for profit or adjustment for loss. The settlement price includes deductions for all end items delivered (or to be delivered) and accepted, and all unliquidated advance and progress payments and disposal and other credits. Consideration for allowable profit includes avoiding anticipatory profits or consequential damages, and calculating loss.

When the total-cost basis is used under a partial termination, the settlement proposal is not submitted until the continued portion of the contract is completed. The same pricing rules apply, but include all costs incurred to the date of completing the rest of the contract. Within 120 days from the effective date of termination, the contractor submits to the TCO complete disposal schedules reflecting inventory allocable to the terminated portion of the contract.

The total amount payable to the contractor for a settlement, before deducting disposal or other credits and exclusive of settlement costs, must not exceed the contract price less payments otherwise made or due under the contract.

After partial termination, a contractor may request an equitable adjustment in the price(s) of the continued portion of a fixed-price contract. The TCO forwards the proposal to the contracting officer, except when negotiation authority is delegated to the TCO.

The TCO determines any adjusted fee based on a percentage of contract completion or terminated portion thereof. This amount is a function of the extent and difficulty of the contractor's:

- effort to stop performance;
- planning and scheduling;
- production;
- settlement of terminated subcontracts;
- supervision;
- technical and engineering effort; and
- termination inventory disposal.

The completed effort is compared with the total work required by the contract. The ratio of costs incurred to the total estimated cost of performance or the terminated portion is only one factor in computing the percentage of completion. The contractor's adjusted fee excludes any fee for subcontract effort included in subcontractors' settlement proposals.

5.19.6 Termination for Default

FAR 49.4

Termination for default occurs because of the contractor's actual or anticipated failure to perform its contractual obligations. This means that the contractor has failed to deliver the supplies or perform the services within the time specified in the contract, or failed to make progress to the point of endangering contract performance. It also could entail failure to comply with a contract provision, or perhaps the contractor has notified the Government that it does not intend to perform (known as *anticipatory repudiation*). However, if the contractor can establish that it was not in default or that the failure to perform is excusable (i.e., arose out of causes beyond the control and without the fault or negligence of the contractor), a termination for default will convert into a termination for the convenience of the Government.

The Government's rights after a termination for cause include all the remedies available to any buyer in the marketplace. The Government's preferred remedy is to acquire similar items from another contractor and to charge the defaulted contractor with any excess reprocurement costs, along with any incidental or consequential damages incurred due to termination.

The Government is not liable for the defaulted contractor's costs on undelivered work and is entitled to repayment of advance and progress payments. The Government may elect to require the contractor to transfer title and deliver to the Government any completed supplies and manufacturing materials. However, the Government may not acquire any completed supplies or manufacturing materials unless it does not already have title under another provision of the contract. The contracting officer may acquire manufacturing materials to furnish to another contractor only after considering any difficulties that the other contractor may have in using the materials. The Government pays the contract price for any completed supplies and manufacturing materials.

After the Government has paid the contractor, it protects itself from overpayment due to potential liability to laborers and material suppliers for lien rights against the completed supplies or materials. Hence, before paying for supplies or materials, the contracting officer must:

- ascertain whether the payment bonds are adequate to satisfy all claims, or if similar bonds should be obtained;
- obtain agreement from the contractor and lienors to ensure release of the Government from any potential liability to the contractor or lienors;
- require the contractor to furnish appropriate statements from laborers and material suppliers disclaiming any lien rights they may have to the materials and supplies; and
- withhold from the amount due for the materials or supplies any amount the contracting officer determines necessary to protect the Government's interest.

The contractor is liable to the Government for any damages or excess costs to acquire supplies and services similar to those terminated for default.

If the contractor has failed to perform or deliver, no notice of failure or possibility of termination for default need be sent to the contractor before the actual notice of termination. However, if the Government has taken any action that might be construed as a waiver of the contract delivery or performance date, the contracting officer sends a notice to the contractor setting a new date to make delivery or complete performance, and reserving the Government's rights under the Default clause.

If the contractor merely fails to perform some other contract provision (e.g., not furnishing a required performance bond), or so fails to make progress as to endanger performance of the contract, the contracting officer gives the contractor a written *cure notice* specifying the failure and providing 10 days (or longer period as necessary) to cure the failure. Upon expiration of this time period, the contracting officer may issue a notice of termination for default unless the failure to perform has been cured.

If termination for default appears appropriate, the contracting officer may issue a *show cause notice* to notify the contractor in writing of the possibility of the termination, repeats the contractual liabilities if the contract is so terminated, and requests the contractor to show cause as to why the contract should not be terminated for default. The notice may state that failure of the contractor to present an explanation may be taken as an admission that no valid explanation exists.

Any such notice or termination document is copied to the surety. If requested by the surety and agreed to by the contractor and any assignees, future checks may be mailed to the contractor in care of the surety. The contractor forwards a written request to the disbursing officer to direct the change in address.

If the contractor is a small business, the contracting officer provides a copy of any cure notice or show cause notice to the contracting office's small business specialist and the contractor's SBA Regional Office.

The contracting officer considers several factors to determine whether to terminate a contract for default:

- applicable laws and regulations;
- availability of the supplies or services from other sources;
- best interest of the Government;
- contract terms;
- cost of reprocurement;
- effect of a termination for default on the ability of the contractor to liquidate guaranteed loans, progress payments or advance payments;
- essentiality of the contractor and the effect of a termination for default upon the contractor's capability as a supplier under other contracts;
- impact of default on other contractor obligations;

- the specific failure and reasons for it; and
- urgency of the need and the time period required to obtain them from other sources, compared with the time delivery could be obtained from the delinquent contractor.

If the contracting officer determines before issuing the termination notice that the failure to perform is excusable, the contract is not terminated for default, but may be terminated for convenience. In lieu of termination for default, the contracting officer may permit the contractor, surety or guarantor to continue performance of the contract under a revised delivery schedule, or permit the contractor to continue performance by means of a subcontract or other business arrangement with an acceptable third party. If the requirement for the supplies and services no longer exists, and the contractor is not liable to the Government for damages, then the parties may execute a no-cost termination settlement.

The termination for default notice must state:

- contract number and date;
- acts or omissions constituting the default;
- the contractor's right to proceed further under the contract (or a specified portion of the contract) is terminated;
- the supplies or services terminated may be purchased against the contractor's account, and that the contractor will be held liable for any excess costs;
- if the contracting officer has determined that the failure to perform is not excusable, that the notice of termination constitutes such decision;
- the Government reserves all rights and remedies provided by law or under the contract, in addition to charging excess costs; and
- the notice constitutes a decision that the contractor is in default as specified and that the contractor has the right to appeal under the Disputes clause.

When the supplies or services are still required after termination, the contracting officer repurchases them against the contractor's account as soon as possible. The contracting officer may repurchase a quantity in excess of the undelivered quantity terminated for default if necessary, but cannot charge excess costs against the defaulting contractor for more than the undelivered quantity terminated for default (including variations in quantity permitted by the terminated contract). Generally, the contracting officer decides whether or not to repurchase before issuing the termination notice. If repurchase is made at a higher price than in the terminated contract, the contracting officer makes written demand on the contractor for the total amount of the excess. In addition to excess repurchase costs, the contracting officer promptly assesses and demands any liquidated damages to which the Government is entitled under the contract.

FAR 49.403

Settlement principles for a cost-reimbursement default are the same as when a contract is terminated for convenience, except that:

- a 10-day notice to the contractor before termination for default is required;
- costs of preparing the contractor's settlement proposal are not allowable;
- the contractor is reimbursed all allowable costs, and an appropriate reduction is made in the total fee; and
- excess repurchase costs cannot be recovered.

FAR 42.9

When notified of bankruptcy proceedings, agencies:

- determine the amount of the Government's potential claim against the contractor for unclosed-out contracts;
- furnish notice of bankruptcy to contract, financial, legal, and property offices; and
- take action to protect the Government's financial interests and property.

Solicitation Provision and Contract Clause

FAR 52.242-13, Bankruptcy, if exceeding the simplified acquisition threshold.

5.19.7 Surety-Takeover Agreements

FAR 49.404

Because the surety is liable for damages resulting from contractor default, the surety has rights and interests to complete the contract work and apply any undisbursed funds. Therefore, the contracting officer must consider any surety proposals for completing the contract. Hence, the contracting officer permits surety offers to complete the contract, unless the contracting officer believes that the firms or persons proposed by the surety to complete the work are not competent and qualified, or the proposal is not in the best interest of the Government.

The surety may include a takeover agreement in its proposal, fixing its rights to payment from retained percentages and unpaid progress estimates. After the effective date of termination, the contracting officer may enter into a written agreement with the surety (or a tripartite agreement including the defaulting contractor) to resolve the contractor's residual rights and assertions to unpaid prior earnings.

Any takeover agreement requires the surety to complete the contract and the Government to pay the surety's cost and expenses up to the balance of the contract price unpaid at the time of default. The contracting officer does not pay the surety more than the amount spent to complete the work and discharge its liabilities under the defaulting contractor's payment bond. Such payments must be only on authority of a tripartite agreement, GAO or court. If contract proceeds have been assigned to a financing institution, the surety is not paid from unpaid earnings without the institution's written consent.

The defaulting contractor's unpaid earnings, retained percentages, and progress estimates for work accomplished before termination are subject to debts due the Government. However, these earnings can be used to pay the surety its actual costs and expenses incurred in the completion of the work, but excluding its payments and obligations under the payment bond. The surety is bound by contract terms governing liquidated damages for unexcused delays in completion of the work. If the surety does not arrange for completion of the contract, the contracting officer awards a new contract based on the same plans and specifications.

FAR does not prescribe a clause to terminate orders under communication service contracts with common carriers because special agency requirements and clauses apply to these services. FAR 49.6 contains sample letters for all termination scenarios.

Solicitation Provisions and Contract Clauses

FAR 52.213-4, Terms and Conditions—Simplified Acquisitions (Other Than Commercial Items).

FAR 52.249-1, Termination for Convenience of the Government (Fixed-Price) (Short Form), if fixed-price and not expected to exceed the simplified acquisition threshold, except for architect-engineer services or research and development work with an educational or nonprofit institution on a nonprofit basis. Do not use this clause if the contract contains FAR 52.249-4, -12 or -14. Use the clause with its Alternate I if the contract is for demolition, dismantling or removal of improvements.

FAR 52.249-2, Termination for Convenience of the Government (Fixed-Price), if fixed-price and expected to exceed the simplified acquisition threshold. Do not use for dismantling and demolition contracts, or any exception cited under FAR 52.249-1. Use the clause with its Alternate I if the contract is for construction. Use the clause with its Alternate II if the contract is with a Government agency, foreign or domestic, and it is inappropriate to pay interest on excess partial payments. Use the clause with its Alternate III in contracts for construction, if desired.

FAR 52.249-3, Termination for Convenience of the Government (Dismantling, Demolition, or Removal of Improvements), if fixed-price to dismantle, demolish or remove improvements, and exceeding the simplified acquisition threshold. Use the clause with its Alternate I to contract with a Government agency, foreign or domestic, and it is not appropriate to pay interest on excess partial payments.

FAR 52.249-4, Termination for Convenience of the Government (Services) (Short Form), in fixed-price contracts for services where the successful offeror will not incur substantial charges to prepare for and execute the contract, without additional termination settlement charges.

FAR 52.249-5, Termination for the Convenience of the Government (Educational and Other Nonprofit Institutions), for research and development work with an educational or nonprofit institution without a fee or profit payment.

FAR 52.249-6, Termination (Cost Reimbursement), if cost-reimbursement, except for research and development with an educational or nonprofit institution on a no-fee basis. Use the clause with its Alternate I in construction contracts. Use the clause with its Alternates II and V in a contract with a Government agency, foreign or domestic, and the requirement to pay interest on excess partial payments is inappropriate, and then add Alternate III if the contact is for construction. Use the clause with its Alternate IV for a time-and-material or labor-hour contract.

FAR 52.249-7, Termination (Fixed-Price Architect-Engineer), for fixed-price architect-engineer services.

FAR 52.249-8, Default (Fixed-Price Supply and Service), if fixed-price and exceeding the simplified acquisition threshold. Use the clause with its Alternate I for transportation or related services.

FAR 52.249-9, Default (Fixed-Price Research and Development), for fixed-price research and development exceeding the simplified acquisition threshold, except those with educational or nonprofit institutions on a nonprofit basis.

FAR 52.249-10, Default (Fixed-Price Construction), if fixed-price exceeding the simplified acquisition threshold. Use the clause with its Alternate I if the contract is for demolition, dismantling or removal of improvements.

Use the clause with its Alternate II for a fixed-price contract for construction if the contract is to be awarded during a period of national emergency. Use the clause with its Alternate III for demolition, dismantling or removal of improvements during a period of national emergency.

FAR 52.249-12, Termination (Personal Services).

FAR 52.249-14, Excusable Delays, if cost-reimbursable for supplies, services, construction, and research and development, and in time-and-material and labor-hour contracts.

5.20 SOME FINAL THOUGHTS

Over the past 50 years, risk in Government contracting has shifted considerably through changes in Government policy. Contract type for research and development has shifted away from firm-fixed-price to more flexible forms of contracting. Repeated cost overruns on design issues have led to a "fly-before-you-buy" approach. Total Package Procurement was a fad in the 1970s but has now fallen into disuse. Market instability has fallen due to greater spending and longer lead times. Some firms are dismayed by the exculpatory clauses that excuse the Government from responsibility for inadequate performance. And so forth.

The Federal Government strives to maintain and expand the industrial base. Nevertheless, many factors preclude companies from entering Federal contracting and thereby constrict the industrial base. Contractors must address a number of issues that bear on Federal sales and national security:

- accounting practices;
- complexity and paperwork due to legislation and regulation;
- computer-aided design and manufacturing;
- contract disputes and remedies;
- cost of environmental compliance;
- critical material sources;
- facilities and processes;
- foreign competition and sources of supply;
- idle capacity;
- intellectual property rights;
- lead times for critical parts and components;
- limited potential growth;
- make-or-buy;
- manpower skills;
- need for new manufacturing technologies;

- need to increase competition;
- productivity;
- profit policy;
- socioeconomic concerns;
- source selection procedures;
- stability of requirements and funding;
- strategic resource base planning;
- subcontractors;
- surge capacity and surge planning;
- technology transfer; and
- vertical integration to ensure resource base.

The Government also faces challenges in today's market. Contract spending is squeezed due to contemporary budget woes. Less flexible contract types are advocated to curb cost overruns. Thousands of contractor positions are being brought back in-house to civil service positions, although the slow Federal hiring process challenges the success of this initiative. Also, Federal managers have seen reforms proposed many time in the past, usually with little or no effect. Proper management and implementation of such issues will impact the future of Federal Contract management for all affected parties.

NOTES

1. Subsequent extensions are authorized only upon concurrence of the contracting office.

2. *Provisioning* is a process to determine the items required to maintain and support equipment for a set time period. Firm requirements for quantity or type are not known at time of award, so a generic line item is used to order items later after requisition. Provisioning is best known to procure spare and repair parts, but can also be used for data, engineering support, equipment, and GFP repair.

3. CORs may not be assigned for contracts that do not require frequent interaction with the contractor; a contract specialist or program management analyst may fulfill these duties in such cases. This certainly saves money and effort, however these individuals may not have in-depth program knowledge to address any programmatic issues that might arise.

4. See Executive Order 11755, Relating to prison labor, December 29, 1973 (as amended by Executive Order 12608, Elimination of unnecessary Executive orders and technical amendments to others, September 9, 1987), and Executive Order 12943, Further amendment to Executive Order No. 11755, December 13, 1994.

5. This definition specifically excludes executives, supervisors, administrators, and clerks.

6. *Fulilove v. Klutznick*, 448 U.S. 448 (1980).

7. These include the Vietnam Era Veterans' Readjustment Assistance Act of 1972 (38 U.S.C. 4212), Executive Order 11701, Employment of veterans by Federal agencies and Government contractors and subcontractors (1973), and the Veterans Employment Opportunities Act of 1998 (5 U.S.C. 2108).

8. However, since the SAM update is only semiannual, any negative decision within the past six months may not be reported yet, so the contracting officer cannot rely solely on these databases for updated information.

9. Subcontracts for commercial off-the-shelf items are exempt from both the pay stub and sexual harassment requirements.

10. As of the date this book was written, most of the implementation of this Executive Order has been enjoined by Federal court order. However, the sentence discussing wage statement transparency is in force. Of the five FAR clauses, only FAR 52.222-60 is currently in effect due to the court injunction.

11. Federal Funding Accountability and Transparency Act Subaward Reporting System is managed by GSA.

12. This differs from *quality control*, which is a quantitative approach to measure performance, compare it to a standard, and then act on the difference. It is an axiom of Federal procurement that the contractor is responsible for quality control, but the Government is responsible for quality assurance.

13. Kaizen is a well-know example of a manufacturer's quality program. Designed to humanize the workplace and eliminate unnecessary hard work and waste in processes, kaizen requires all employees to participate, including external stakeholders. The format for kaizen can be individual, a suggestion system or a working group chaired by a supervisor. Kaizen's approach focuses on making small changes and monitoring results, then adjusting the process for continual improvement. At Toyota, where kaizen began, the culture of continual small improvements and standardization tended to compound productivity improvement.

14. For those who enjoy demystifying acronyms: ANSI – American National Standards Institute, ASME – American Society of Mechanical Engineers, NQA – National Quality Assurance, and ASQC – American Society for Quality Control. These are standards-issuing bodies accepted by various industries.

15. Alternate I was deleted and is no longer in use.

16. Contracts for architect-engineer services require a mandatory value engineering program to reduce total ownership cost, but no sharing of value engineering savings.

17. Lease-or-buy decisions are made in a similar manner, except the option is to possess the item or equipment for a short term rather than permanently. The evaluation methods and constraints are identical.

18. The Government donates surplus property to eligible donees in lieu of abandonment only if it will not bear any costs incident to donation.

19. This includes a vessel based principally in the United States on which U.S. income tax is paid and whose insurance coverage is subject to regulation in the United States.

20. This policy is reflected in Executive Order 12873, Federal Acquisition, Recycling, and Waste Prevention, October 20, 1993.

21. This policy is encapsulated in Executive Order 12843, Procurement Requirements and Policies for Federal Agencies for Ozone Depleting Substances, April 21, 1993.

22. Of course, the contractor should have included these transportation costs in the proposal.

23. The Government is also not liable for *constructive placement* as defined in carrier tariffs, where the shipping container cannot be unloaded at the planned location, but must unload elsewhere.

24. Progress payments will be discussed in detail later.

25. Similarly, a financial accounting data addendum sheet is attached to the procurement request. It includes the budgetary data, but of course lacks any obligated amount. Note that when bulk funding is used, the contracting officer receives a block of funds to assign against several awards for a specified purpose and period of time, but must still track all awards to ensure that the total amount of obligations does not exceed the total amount funded.

26. DoD contracts have different, unique thresholds.

27. A not-to-exceed clause can also be used in a cost-reimbursement contract to limit a particular cost element, such as material or travel.

28. *United States v. Wunderlich*, 342 U.S. 98 (1951).

29. The very lengthy title of E.O. 10789 is "Authorizing agencies of the Government to exercise certain contracting authority in connection with national-defense functions and prescribing regulations governing the exercise of such authority" and is dated July 22, 1971.

30. The Government cannot terminate a contract merely to avoid anticipatory profits without a change in circumstances after award. This is known as the Torncello Rule, after the case where it was raised by the court (*Torncello v. United States*, 231 Ct.Cl. 20, 1982).

31. The term *partial payment* also applies to an approved termination claim prior to final settlement of the total termination claim.

Bibliography

RECURRING REFERENCES

Federal Acquisition Regulatory Council (2005). *Federal Acquisition Regulation.* Washington, D.C.: Government Printing Office, 2005. FAR is also printed in the Code of Federal Regulations, Title 48, Chapter 1, and available online at www .acquisition.gov/far/loadmainre.html. This is the bible of Federal contracting and a necessary reference book for all practitioners.

Government Printing Office (2016). *United States Reports.* Washington, D.C.: Government Printing Office. This is where Supreme Court decisions are published.

National Archives and Records Administration (2007). *Code of Federal Regulations.* Washington, D.C., National Archives and Records Administration. This is the repository for all Federal regulations.

Office of the Law Revision Council, House of Representatives (2012). *United States Code.* Washington, D.C.: Government Printing Office. This is the official record of all Federal statutes.

The American Law Institute and the National Conference of Commissioners on Uniform State Laws (2014). *Uniform Commercial Code.* Eagan, MN: Thomson West. This is the code that governs commercial transactions and provides a baseline for understanding the concepts of contract law. A readily available location to access the UCC is https://www.law.cornell.edu/ucc.

OTHER SOURCES

Air Force Institute of Technology. *Contract Pricing Reference Guide.* Retrieved December 29, 2016 from http://www.acq.osd.mil/dpap/cpf/contract_pricing_reference_ guides.html.

American National Standards Institute/American Society of Mechanical Engineers *National Quality Assurance – 1*. Washington, D.C.: American National Standards Institute 2015.

American National Standards Institute. *E4 – A Quality System Standard for Environmental Data Collection and Technology*. Washington, D.C.: American National Standards Institute, 1994.

―――. *Q9001, Quality Management Systems – Requ2008irements*. 2008.

―――. *Q9002, Quality Systems – Model for Quality Assurance in Production, Installation, and Servicing*. 1994.

―――. *Q9003 Quality Systems – Model for Quality Assurance in Final Inspection and Test*. 1994.

―――. *QS-9000 Handbook – A Guide to Registration and Audit*. October 1998.

―――. *Standard 748 – Earned Value Management Systems*. June 1998.

APICS, *The Most Recognized Supply Chain Framework*. Retrieved December 12, 2016 from http://www.apics.org/sites/apics-supply-chain-council/frameworks/scor.

Defense Contract Management Agency. *Federal Directory of Contract Administration Services Components*. Retrieved December 2, 2016 from https://pubapp.dcma.mil/CASD/main.jsp.

Defense Logistics Agency. *DoD Acquisition Streamlining and Standardization Information System (ASSIST)*. Retrieved December 14, 2016 at http://assist.daps.dla.mil.

―――. "Welcome to the Assist." Retrieved December 29, 2016 from https://assist.dla.mil/online/start.

Defense Logistics Management Standards Office (2016). *Military Standard Requisitioning and Issue Procedures*. Alexandria, Va.: Defense Logistics Agency.

Defense Procurement and Acquisition Policy, Department of Defense. *Contractor Performance Assessment Reporting System*. Retrieved November 28, 2016 from www.cpars.gov.

Department of Agriculture. *BioPreferred*. Retrieved December 29, 2016 from https://www.biopreferred.gov/BioPreferred/.

Department of Commerce (2016). *The Export Administration Regulations (15 CFR 730-774)*. Washington, D.C.: Department of Commerce.

―――. *North American Industry Classification System*. Retrieved December 19, 2016 from www.census.gov/eosd/www/naics.

―――. *National Technical Information Service*. Retrieved December 8, 2016 from https://www.ntis.gov.

Department of Defense (2012). *DoD Index of Specifications and Standards* (41 CFR 101-29.216). Washington, D.C.: Department of Defense.

―――. (2002). *DoD Instruction 4200-15, Manufacturing Technology (Mantech) Program*. Washington, D.C.: Department of Defense.

―――. *MIL-STD-129, Military Standard Marking for Shipment and Storage*. October 29, 2004.

―――. The Per Diem, Travel and Transportation Allowance Committee (October 1, 2014). *Joint Travel Regulations*. Washington, D.C.: Defense Travel Management Office. Also available at http://www.defensetravel.dod.mil/site/travelreg.cfm.

————. Federal Standard 123H, Marking for Shipment (Civil Agencies), June 6, 1997.

Department of Energy (June 2005). *Architectural and Transportation Barriers Compliance Board Electronic and Information Technology (EIT) Accessibility Standards* (36 CFR 1194). Washington, D.C.: Department of Energy.

————. Office of Energy Efficiency and Renewable Energy. Retrieved December 19, 2016 from www.eren.doe.gov/femp/resources/legislation.html.

Department of Labor. *Wage Determinations Online.gov.* Retrieved December 4, 2016 from http://www.wdol.gov/sca.aspx.

————. *VETS-4212 Veterans Contract Reporting.* Retrieved December 8, 2016 from https://www.dol.gov/vets/vets4212.htm.

————. *List of Products Requiring Contractor Certification as to Forced or Indentured Child Labor.* Retrieved December 2, 2016 from at https://www.dol.gov/ilab/reports/child-labor/list-of-products/.

Department of State (2016). *The International Traffic in Arms Regulations* (22 CFR 120–130). Washington, D.C.: Department of State.

————. *Department of State Standardized Regulations.* Retrieved December 29, 2016 from https://aoprals.state.gov/content.asp?content_id=231&menu_id=81.

Department of the Treasury (July 2016). *Circular 570, Surety Companies Acceptable on Federal Bonds.* Washington, D.C.: Department of the Treasury.

————. (2014). *Federal Financial Management System Requirements*, in the *Treasury Financial Manual.* Washington, D.C.: Department of the Treasury. See also http://tfm.fiscal.treasury.gov/v1/p6/c950.pdf.

————. (2016). *Office of Foreign Asset Controls.* Retrieved December 2016 from http://www.treas.gov/offices/enforcement/ofac.

————. *USASpending.gov.* Retrieved December 4, 2016 from www.usaspending.gov.

Environmental Protection Agency, Office of Solid Waste, November 9, 2016. *Consolidated Recovered Materials Advisory Notice (RMAN) for the Comprehensive Procurement Guideline (CPG).* Washington, D.C.: Environmental Protection Agency.

————. *Significant New Alternatives Policy (SNAP) program.* Retrieved December 5, 2016 from www.epa.gov/snap.

Federal Emergency Management Agency. *Federal Continuity Directive 1, Federal Executive Branch National Continuity Program and Requirements.* Washington, D.C.: Federal Emergency Management Agency, July 14, 2014.

————. *Federal Continuity Directive 2, Federal Executive Branch Mission Essential Functions and Candidate Primary Mission Essential Functions Identification and Submission Process.* Washington, D.C.: Federal Emergency Management Agency, December 9, 2013.

————. *Federal Preparedness Circular 65, Federal Executive Branch Continuity of Operations.* Washington, D.C.: Federal Emergency Management Agency, June 15, 2004.

————. *Homeland Security Presidential Directive 20, National Continuity Policy.* Washington, D.C.: Federal Emergency Management Agency, May 4, 2007.

————. *National Response Framework.* Washington, D.C.: Federal Emergency Management Agency, June 16, 2016.

General Services Administration. *Acquisition.gov.* Retrieved December 30, 2016 from https://www.acquisition.gov.

————. *FedBizOpps.* Retrieved December 19, 2016 from www.fedbizopps.gov.

————. *Federal Funding Accountability and Transparency Act Subaward Reporting System.* Retrieved December 5, 2016 from https://www.fsrs.gov/.

————. *Federal Management Property Regulation.* Washington, D.C.: General Services Administration, 1992.

————. *Federal Standard 123H, Marking for Shipment (Civil Agencies).* Washington, D.C.: General Services Administration, June 6, 1997.

————. *Federal Standard No. 313E, Material Safety Data Sheet, Preparation and Submission of.* Washington, D.C.: General Services Administration, July, 2014.

————. *Federal Travel Regulation.* Washington, D.C.: General Services Administration, September 14, 2016. This document is also accessible from https://www.gsa.gov/portal/content/102886.

————. *Index of Federal Specifications, Standards and Commercial Item Descriptions.* Accessed December 9, 2016 at https://www.gsa.gov/portal/content/100847.

Government Printing Office. *Court of Claims.* Washington, D.C.: Government Printing Office, 1981.

————. *United States Statutes at Large.* Washington, D.C.: Government Printing Office, 2016.

Green Electronics Council. *epeat.* Retrieved December 28, 2016 from www.epeat.net.

International Standards Organization. *ISO 1680. IEEE Standard for Environmental Assessment of Electronic Components.* Geneva, Switzerland: International Standards Organization, 2009.

————. *ISO 9001, Quality management systems.* 2015.

————. *ISO 31000, Risk management – Principles and guidelines on implementation.* Geneva, Switzerland: International Standards Organization. 2009.

————. *ISO 14001 Environmental management systems – Requirements with guidance for use.* 2015.

National Conference of Commissioners on Uniform State Laws. *Uniform Computer Information Transactions Act.* Retrieved December 8, 2016 from www.ucitaonline.com.

National Institute of Building Sciences. Guiding Principles for Federal Leadership in High-Performance and Sustainable Buildings. Retrieved December 28, 2016 from www.wbdg.org/pdfs/hpsb_guidance.pdf.

National Institute of Standards and Technology. *Federal Information Processing Standards Publication Number 201, Personal Identity Verification of Federal Employees and Contractors.* Gaithersburg, Md.: National Institute of Standards and Technology, 2013.

————. *Special Publication 500-267: A Profile for IPV6 in the U.S. Government.* Gaithersburg, Md.: National Institute of Standards and Technology, 2008.

National Science Foundation. *Master Government List of Federally Funded R&D Centers.* Retrieved December 8, 2016 from www.nsf.gov/statistics/ffrdclist.

National Security Council (September 21, 1985). *National Security Decision Directive 189, National Policy on the Transfer of Scientific, Technical and Engineering Information.* Washington, D.C.: National Archives and Records Administration.

Office of Federal Procurement Policy. *Interagency Acquisitions.* Retrieved December 20, 2016 from http://www.whitehouse.gov/omb/assets/procurement/iac_revised.pdf.

————. *OMB Circular A-11, Preparation and Submission of Budget Estimates.* Washington, D.C.: Office of Management and Budget, July 1, 2016.

————. National Preaward Registry. Retrieved December 4, 2016 from https://ofccp.dol-esa.gov/preaward/pa_reg.html. Washington, D.C.: Office of Management and Budget.

Office of Management and Budget. *OMB Circular A-11, Preparation, Submission and Execution of the Budget.* Washington, D.C.: Office of Management and Budget, 2015.

————. *OMB Circular No. A-21, Cost Principles for Educational Institutions.* 2012.

————. *OMB Circular No. A-87, Cost Principles for State and Local Governments.* 2012.

————. *OMB Circular A-94, Guidelines and Discount Rates for Benefit-Cost Analysis of Federal Programs.* 2004.

————. *OMB Circular A-119, Federal Participation in the Development and Use of Voluntary Consensus Standards and in Conformity Assessment Activities.* 2016.

————. *OMB Circular No. A-122, Cost Principles for Nonprofit Organizations.* 2009.

————. *Executive Order 10789, Authorizing agencies of the Government to exercise certain contracting authority in connection with national-defense functions and prescribing regulations governing the exercise of such authority.* July 22, 1971.

————. *Executive Order 11141, Declaring a public policy against discrimination based on age.* February 12, 1964.

————. *Executive Orders 11246, Equal employment opportunity.* October 5, 1978.

————. *Executive Order 11701, Employment of veterans by Federal agencies and Government contractors and subcontractors.* January 24, 1973.

————. *Executive Order 11755, Relating to prison labor.* December 29, 1973.

————. *Executive Order 11758, Delegating authority of the President under the Rehabilitation Act of 1973.* January 15, 1974.

————. *Executive Order 12549, Debarment and Suspension.* February 18, 1986.

————. *Executive Order 12608, Elimination of unnecessary Executive orders and technical amendments to others.* September 9, 1987.

————. *Executive Order 12943, Further amendment to Executive Order No. 11755.* December 13, 1994.

————. *Executive Order 13005, Empowerment Contracting.* May 24, 1996.

————. *Executive Order 13101: Greening the Government through Waste Prevention, Recycling, and Federal Acquisition.* September 14, 1998.

————. *Executive Order 13496, Notification of Employee Right Under Federal Labor Laws.* January 30, 2009.

————. *Executive Order 13502, Use of Project Labor Agreements for Federal Construction Projects.* August 2, 2005.

————. *Executive Order 13658, Establishing a minimum wage for contractors.* February 12, 2014.

————. *Executive Order 13672, Prohibiting discrimination based on sexual orientation and gender identity.* July 21, 2014.

————. *Executive Order 13673, Fair pay and safe workspaces.* February 12, 2014.

————. *Executive Order 13693, Planning for Sustainability in the Next Decade.* March 19, 2015.

————. *Memorandum M-05-22, Transition Planning for Internet Protocol Version 6.* August 2, 2005.

————. *Guidance M-05-24, Implementation of Homeland Security Presidential Directive (HSPD) 12 – Policy for a Common Identification Standard for Federal Employees and Contractors.* August 5, 2005.

————. *Nonprofit Organizations Exempted from Subpart E – Cost Principles of Part 200 (2 CFR part 200, appendix VIII).* January 1, 2004.

————. *Presidential Decision Directive 67, Enduring Constitutional Government and Continuity of Government Operations.* October 21, 1998.

————. *2014 Status of Telework in the Federal Government.* November 2015.

John Raithby, ed. (1819). *Statutes of the Realm: Volume 5, 1628–80.* South London, United Kingdom: Great Britain Record Commission Institute of Historical Research. This is the location of the Statute of Frauds. See also http://www.british-history.ac.uk/statutes-realm/vol5/pp839-842. London: Institute of Historical Research.

Small Business Administration, Office of Advocacy (2012). *Frequently Asked Questions About Small Businesses.* Washington, D.C.: Small Business Administration.

Software Assurance Acquisition Working Group. *Software Assurance in Acquisition: Mitigating Risks to the Enterprise.* Retrieved December 14, 2016 from https://acc.dau.mil/CommunityBrowser.aspx?id=150410&lang=en-US as download SwA_in_Acquisition_102208.pdf. This document is now managed by United States Computer Emergency Readiness Team, Department of Homeland Security.

Under Secretary of Defense (Comptroller) (December 15, 2013). *DoD Financial Management Regulation 7000.14-R, Volume 15.* Washington, D.C.: Department of Defense.

U.S. International Trade Commission (October 1, 2015). *Harmonized Tariff Schedule of the United States.* Washington, D.C.: U.S. International Trade Commission.

Index

advance agreements, in cost
principles, 380
advance payment bonds, 467
advance payments, 87n18, 523; interest-
free, 530; for non-commercial
items, 529–31; Progress Payments
clause on, 533–34; sealed bidders
and, 530
advertising and public relations costs,
382–83
advisory and assistance services, in
service contracts, 172–73
agencies, 88n32; acquisition strategy
of, 113–14; annual ethics training
plans of, 51; authority in, 13;
for blind or disabled, 107–10;
delegation of procurement
authority issued by, 42; as
fiduciary relationship, 12; march-
in-rights, 72–73; protests to,
337–38
agency, in commercial contracting,
12–14
agency needs description, in placement,
240–45; delivery or performance
schedules for, 244–45; general
specifications for, 241–44
agent, commercial contracting duties
of, 13
agreements: bilateral, of Federal
Government express, 4; breach
of, 2; click-wrap, 211; collective
bargaining, 167–68; grants and
cooperative, in R&D, 158–59;
international, 102, 225–26, 228–
29; non-disclosure, 53; novation,
550–51; reciprocal purchase and
tying, 27; service level, 163;
settlement, 561–63; supplemental,
433, 545; surety-takeover, 569–72
agreements, in placement, ix; basic,
277–78; basic ordering, 278–79;
master, 278
Alaskan Native Corporation (ANC),
147; subcontractors and, 139, 144

alcoholic beverages costs, 406
allocable costs, 381
allotments, in federal budget, 63–64
alpha contracting, 205–6
alternative dispute resolution (ADR),
557–58
American Law Institute, 2
American National Standards Institute/
Electronics Industries Alliance
(ANSI/EIA), 514
American Productivity & Quality Center
(APQC), Process Classification
Framework, 214
American Recovery and Reinvestment
Act (Recovery Act), of 2009, 67,
229–30, 232
American Standard Code for
Information Interchange, 211
Americans with Disabilities Act,
127, 152
analog communication signals, 184
analogy, in offers evaluation
process, 325
ANC. *See* Alaskan Native Corporation
annual bid bonds, 467
annual performance bond, 467
ANSI/EIA. *See* American National
Standards Institute/Electronics
Industries Alliance
anticipatory repudiation, in breach of
contract, 20
Anti-Deficiency Act, 63, 538, 539
Anti-Kickback Act (Copeland Act), of
1986, 25–26, 56–57, 438
anti-trust actions: Clayton Anti-Trust
Act and, 27; reciprocal purchase
agreement and, 27; Robinson-
Patman Act and, 27; Sherman
Anti-Trust Act and, 27; tying
agreement as, 27
apparent authority, 13
applied research, 153
apportionment, of federal budget, 63
appropriation process, in federal budget,
62–63

Defense Acquisition Workforce
Improvement Act (DAWIA),
89n38
Defense Base Act, 474, 475
Defense Contract Audit Agency
(DCAA), 408, 419–20
Defense Logistics Agency, 487; CAGE
codes assigned by, 43, 89n39
Defense Priorities and Allocations
System (DPAS), quality and,
461–62
Defense Production Act, of 1950, 128,
461, 527
defense production loan guarantees,
527–29
definite quantity contract, 275–76
delays and suspensions, 549
delegation, assignment of title
through, 15
delegation of authority: legal
considerations for, 65–66; Public
Law 85-804 and, 65; unauthorized
(or informed) commitments for,
66, 553
delegation of procurement authority,
agencies issuing of, 42
delivery: in commercial contracting, 16;
Federal Government clauses for,
16; leases and, 30; order contract,
272–74; tender in, 16
demilitarization, inventory disposal
schedules and, 491
Department of Commerce, 130, 236n25
Department of Defense (DoD), 88n30;
contract payment authority for
fraud by, 58; DAR Council
created by, x, 37, 38, 89n36;
Government Purpose License
Rights of, 90n61; Industrial
Modernization Improvement
Program of, 124; Mantech
program of, 124, 235n13;
procurement policies of, 89n37;
SDB price evaluation restrictions
for, 145

Department of Energy, Architectural
and Transportation Barriers
Compliance Board EIT
Accessibility Standards, 237n37
Department of Homeland Security
(DHS), 193, 237n38; block
certification by, 493; E-Verify
program under, 447; pre-
qualification designation notice
by, 493; QATT issued by, 493;
SAFETY Act and, 492, 493
Department of Labor (DOL), 35,
168–69; Notice to Employees
Working on Government
Contracts publication of, 170;
wage determinations by, 348–49
Department of Treasury, 237n36;
Financial Systems Integration
Office within, 180–81
Department of Veterans Affairs, 487
depreciable property disposition or
impairment, 392
depreciation, 373–74; book value and,
390; capital costs and, 388;
double declining balance method
of, 390; fair value accounting
and, 361–62, 390; going-concern
concept for, 388; straight-line
method of, 389; sum of the years
digits method of, 389; tangible
capital asset and, 389; unit of
production method of, 389
design-bid-build delivery method, in
construction contracts, 340–41
design-build method, 359n26
design errors or deficiencies
responsibility, in architect/
engineering services, 356–57
design-to-cost techniques, 115
design within funding limitations,
in architect/engineering
services, 356
desirable change, in costs, 379–80
destination, quality assurance at, 453
detective control measures, 191

personal services contract and,
164–65
Federal socioeconomic programs
factor, 423
Federal statutes: open-market purchases
and, 34; procurement sources of
information listings in, 34–35
Federal Supply Schedule Program, 110,
120; RFQ and, 112–13; Special
Item Number for, 111
federal supply schedules: Federal
Property and Administrative
Services Act, Title III of, 110; in
planning, 110–13
Federal Trade Commission,
monopolization investigation by,
426n1
felonies, 358n19
FEMA. *See* Federal Emergency
Management Agency
FEMP. *See* Federal Energy Management
Program
FFRDCs. *See* Federally Funded
Research and Development
Centers
fiduciary relationship, agency as, 12
FIFO. *See* First-In-First-Out
financial accounting data addendum
sheet, 575n25
Financial Accounting Standards Board,
GAAP issued by, 379
financial interest disclosure, from
contractor, 53–54
financial protections, in post-award
actions: bonds as, 466–70;
insurance as, 472–74; Miller
Act and, 466; overseas workers
compensation and war hazard
insurance as, 474–75; sureties and
bond security as, 470–72
Financial Systems Integration Office,
within Department of Treasury,
180–81
financing methods: advance payments
as, 87n18, 523; contract financing

payment as, 521–22; customary
contract financing as, 523; loan
guarantees as, 523; performance-
based payments as, 523; unusual
contract financing as, 523
fines, penalties and mischarges, 391
finished goods, in inventory, 217
FIPS. *See* Federal Information
Processing Standards
FIPS PUB. *See* Federal Information
Processing Standards Publication
firm-fixed-price contract, 324, 342,
426n11; with economic price
adjustment, 257–58; level-of-
effort term in, 258
firm target fixed-price incentive
contract, 261
first article testing and approval, for
responsible offerors, 314–15
First-In-First-Out (FIFO) value
adjustment, 223–24, 372
fiscal year: in federal budget, 61; in
indirect costs, 374
fitness for purpose: in service contracts,
163; in warranties, 14
fixed costs, in cost accounting, 364
fixed-order period tracking model, for
inventory, 221
fixed-order quantity tracking model, for
inventory, 221
fixed-price contracts, 254, 342; with
award fees, 263; with economic
price adjustment, 324; with
prospective price redetermination,
262; with retroactive price
redetermination, 262–63;
terminated for convenience, 563
fixed-price incentive (FPI) contract, 258,
324, 358n10; Constant Dollar
price change method for, 261,
266; Constant Percentage price
change method for, 261, 266;
firm target in, 261; Individual
Adjustment price change method
for, 261; PTA for, 260; Severable

on, 118–19, 235n10; in planning,
118–29; production control
for, 122–24; production design
for, 121–22; productivity in,
125–27; program manager
considerations in, 127–29;
systems engineering in, 119
make-or-buy decisions, in inventory, 224
make-or-buy program, 481–82
managed costs, 366
management and operating contracts,
202–3
management proposal, 321
managerial accounting, 363–64
Mantech. *See* Manufacturing
Technology Program
manufacturing and production
engineering costs, 396
manufacturing labor: level time
estimate for, 417–18; personal,
fatigue and delay allowance in,
418; predetermined-leveled-
time technique in, 418; in
WBS, 417–18; work sampling
technique in, 418
manufacturing resource planning,
123–24
Manufacturing Technology (Mantech)
Program, of DoD, 124, 235n13
march-in rights, of agency, 72–73
market-based pricing: differentiated
sellers in, 362; efficient price
in, 361; fair value offering in,
361–62; monopoly and, 362, 363;
monopsony and, 362; oligopoly
and, 362, 363; transaction level
in, 361
market entry, 93
marketing and research, in planning,
91–99
marketing consultant, non-disclosure
agreement for, 53
marketing domination, 91
marketing strategy, 91; customer type
consideration for, 92; market
segmentation in, 92

market research, 94; on all acquisitions,
95; techniques for conducting,
95–96
market segmentation, 92
markings, 80–81
master agreement, 278
master solicitation, in competitive
negotiations, 295
material acquisition, profit and, 422–23
material costs, 396–97, 412; in bill of
materials, 372; contra preferentum
concept for, 9–10, 372; other
direct costs and, 372–73;
purchased parts as, 372; raw
material as, 372; scrap and, 372;
subcontracted items and, 372; in
WBS, 416
material management and accounting
system, in inventory, 217
material overhead, 374
material quality management, 450
materials requirements planning,
inventory and, 217
memorandum of agreement (MOA), 312
merchantability, 14
micro-purchase threshold, actions at or
below, 302–3
Military Assistance Program, 234
military officers, ethics rules of, 51
Miller Act, 466
minor informality, in sealed bidding, 288
minor nonconformance, 452
mistake, illegal contracts and, 25–26
MOA. *See* memorandum of agreement
mobile code, 182
modifiable off-the-shelf software, 182
modified CAS coverage, 410
Modified Cost Recovery System, 388
monopolization, Federal Trade
Commission investigation
of, 426n1
monopoly, 362, 363
monopsony, 362
motor vehicles, leasing of, 109
Multiple Award Schedule Program. *See*
Federal Supply Schedule Program

Index

unauthorized (or informed)
commitments, 66, 553
unbalanced pricing, 415
unconscionable contract, 5, 11
undue influence: illegal contracts and,
26; void contract due to, 8
unenforceable contract, 4
unexpired costs, 366
UNICOR. *See* Federal Prison Industries,
Inc.
Uniform Commercial Code (UCC), 2, 5,
7, 87n4
Uniform Computer Information
Transactions Act (UCITA), 2,
87n7
Uniform Contract Format, placement
and, 251–54
Uniform Law Commission, on trade
secrets, 90n60
Uniform Trade Secrets Act, 77
unilateral contracts: acceptance act
and, 6; performance and, 3
unilateral modification, 545
United States v. Spearin, 357
United States v. Wunderlich, 548,
575n28
unit of production depreciation
method, 389
unjust enrichment, 3, 6
unlimited rights, 76
unrestricted competition, 100
unsolicited proposal, in competitive
negotiations, 297–99
unusual contract financing, 523
usage of trade, in contract
interpretation, 11
US Department of Agriculture (USDA),
on recovered materials, 496–97
USGv6 Test Program, 116
utility services, in service contracts,
173, 176, 236n33; connection
charge for, 175; franchise territory
for, 174–75; termination liability
in, 175
utilization report, of contractors, 90n58

value-added base, G&A expenses on, 376
value analysis, as cost analysis
technique, 415
value engineering, 235n11; acquisition
savings in, 477; collateral
savings in, 478; concurrent
contract savings in, 477; future
contract savings in, 477; future
unit cost reduction in, 477–78;
government/contractor share, of
net acquisition savings, 478–79;
government costs in, 478; instant
contract in, 476; instant contract
savings in, 477; instant unit
cost reduction in, 477; negative
instant contract savings in, 478;
net acquisition savings in, 478;
post-award actions and, 476–80;
sharing base in, 478, *478*; VECPs
and, 476–79
value engineering change proposals
(VECPs), 476–79
variable costs, in cost accounting,
364–65
VECPs. *See* value engineering change
proposals
vertical integration, 92
veterans affairs, 443–44
Veterans Benefit Act, of 2003, 146
Veterans' Readjustment Assistance Act,
of 1972, 574n7
virtual office, for productivity
improvement, 127
voidable contract, 4
void contract: courts rejection of, 8; due
to blackmail and duress, 7–8; due
to contract substitution, 8; due to
fraud, 4, 8; due to undue influence,
8; willful misrepresentation or
concealment in, 8

wage determinations, by DOL, 348–49
waiver: for conflict of interest,
52; retraction of, in contract
interpretation, 11

About the Author

Dan Lindner possesses more than 30 years of experience in Federal acquisition and program management for the Departments of Defense and Homeland Security. He was a long-time contracting officer for the Navy, and is well-versed in Federal acquisition policy and procurement regulations. He has chaired review panels and study teams, negotiated contracts for major weapons system components, worked daily with administrative contracting officers, established a remote buying office, and served as a Small and Disadvantaged Business Utilization Specialist. As a staff aide to the Assistant Secretary of the Navy, he conducted personal briefings on pending congressional issues affecting defense acquisition, and co-authored the Procurement Reform Act of 1986. Lindner also established and chaired the Environmental Committee for Defense Acquisition Regulatory (DAR) Council, and was a member of the Cost Principles Committee, gaining expertise with Cost Accounting Standards.

Lindner also has a lengthy career in the private sector, working closely with technical and acquisition clients to define business needs and product requirements, counseling program managers and contracting officers to develop effective strategies, and helping to develop winning proposals. He also served as Vice President for Mindcorp, Inc., a small business which furnished program management support to both Federal and commercial clients.

In academia, Lindner was an instructor for both the Navy Office of Human Services and Fairfax County (Virginia) Adult Education to develop and teach newly hired employees and acquisition professionals about procurement basics. He has developed and delivered presentations at national conventions and corporate meetings on Portfolio Management, Network Security and Contract Administration. He has written numerous monographs on Defense Acquisition, baseball, information technology, and travel.

Lindner has been cited over ten times by Marquis and International Who's Who of America, Information Technology, Science and Engineering, and the World. He earned five Navy Performance Awards and the Director of Defense Procurement Award for Innovation in Procurement. He has several professional designations, including Certified Professional Contracts Manager, Project Management Professional, Level III Certification under the Defense Acquisition Workforce Improvement Act, Certified Information Systems Manager, and Certified in Risk and Information Systems Control.

Lindner earned his Bachelor of Arts degree in Government and Economics from Lehigh University, and an M.B.A. from The George Washington University. He was cited as an Honors Graduate from both schools. He resides with his family in Virginia.

CPSIA information can be obtained
at www.ICGtesting.com
Printed in the USA
BVOW09s0900101017
497201BV00001B/1/P